LEGAL ASPECTS
OF SPORT
ENTREPRENEURSHIP

Dianne B. O'Brien, Ph.D.
Murray State University

James O. Overby, J.D.
Murray State University

Fitness Information Technology, Inc.
P.O. Box 4425, University Avenue
Morgantown, WV 26504–4425

Illustration Credit: Drawings are by Timothy T. Scarbrough

Library of Congress Card Catalog Number: 97–60219

ISBN 1–885693–08–7

Copyeditor: Sandra R. Woods
Cover Design: Pegasus
Production Editor: Craig Hines
Printed by: BookCrafters

Printed in the United States of America
10 9 8 7 6 5 4 3 2 1

Fitness Information Technology, Inc.
P.O. Box 4425, University Avenue
Morgantown, WV 26504–4425
(800) 477–4348
(304) 599–3482 (Phone/Fax)
E-mail: fit@fitinfotech.com
www.fitinfotech.com

$ 41.40

Sport Management Library

The Sport Management Library is an integrative textbook series targeted toward undergraduate students. The titles included in the library are reflective of the content areas prescribed by the NASPE/NASSM curriculum standards for the undergraduate sport management programs.

Forthcoming Titles in the Sport Management Library
Case Studies in Sport Marketing
Communication in Sport Organizations
Economics of Sport
Ethics in Sport Management (NOW AVAILABLE)
Financing Sport (NOW AVAILABLE)
Fundamentals of Sport Marketing (NOW AVAILABLE)
Sport Facility Planning and Management (NOW AVAILABLE)
Sport Governance in the Global Community (NOW AVAILABLE)
Sport Management Field Experiences (NOW AVAILABLE)

ABOUT THE AUTHORS

James O. Overby earned degrees from Columbia University (J.D.), the University of Kentucky (M.A.), and Murray State University (A.B.). He recently retired as General Counsel, and remains "Of Counsel" for Murray State University, Murray, KY, and is conducting legal research for that institution.

As a high school and college student he participated in several extra-curricular activities. In high school and college he was a varsity debater. In high school he was a member of the basketball team, and in graduate school was a member of the University of Kentucky boxing team.

In addition to practicing law, Overby has also been employed as a teacher. He has enjoyed teaching at the University of South Carolina, George Peabody (Vanderbilt University), and Murray State University. The subjects he has taught include constitutional law, administrative law, business law, the law of higher education, and international law. He also assisted in teaching courses in the "Law of Physical Education and Recreation" and "Legal Aspects of Sport and Recreation Management" at Murray State University.

These academic endeavors referred to have been supplemented by assisting young men and women in setting up business enterprises. This assistance occurred while Overby was engaged in the private practice of law. The blend of theoretical and practical aspects of law are reflected in this book. His practice in the business world has given him unique experiences in evaluating the needs, capabilities, and challenges of business entrepreneurs.

Dianne Boswell O'Brien earned degrees from Southern Illinois University at Carbondale (Ph.D.), Indiana University (M.A.), and Murray State University (B.S.). She is presently a professor in the Department of Health, Physical Education, and Recreation at Murray State University, Murray, Kentucky. She has published over 30 articles. Her national and international presentations include many topics related to sport law. Following the 1996 U.S. Olympics, she was selected to represent the U.S.A. at an international conference on "Doping and the Athlete."

Three of her graduate classes have used manuscripts she has authored or co-authored with James O. Overby. The present manuscript has been field-tested at Murray State University as a text in "Legal Aspects of Sport and Recreation Management."

Dr. O'Brien was awarded the Mabel Lee Award as "The Nation's Most Outstanding Young Professional" by the American Alliance of Health, Physical Education, Recreation, and Dance (AAHPERD). She was elected national chair of the Secondary School Physical Education Council of AAHPERD, and state president of the Kentucky AHPERD. As a high school teacher, her physical education program received an award from the President's Council on Physical Fitness as a National Demonstration Center. Her sport experiences include coaching track, basketball, soccer, and employment in recreational facilities. Today her favorite sport experiences include swimming and playing soccer and basketball with her two children, Lee and Clark. She also stays active through involvement in sport associations and consulting in the business and educational arenas.

TABLE OF CONTENTS

ABOUT THE AUTHORS v

FOREWORD ix

PREFACE xi

ACKNOWLEDGMENT xv

COMMON LEGAL TERMS xvii

I. GETTING THE BUSINESS STARTED 1
   Focus 3
   Chapter 1 - Legal Framework 7
   Chapter 2 - Contracts 15
   Chapter 3 - Deeds and Leaseholds 37
   Chapter 4 - The Form of Business Organization 47
   Perspective 59

II. INJURY AND RISK MANAGEMENT 61
   Focus 63
   Chapter 5 - Negligence 65
   Chapter 6 - Defenses to Negligence 79
   Chapter 7 - Injury and Intentional Torts 97
   Perspective 115

III. INJURY AND STRICT LIABILITY 117
   Focus 119
   Chapter 8 - Workers' Compensation 121
   Chapter 9 - Product Liability 139
   Chapter 10 - Nuisance 155
   Perspective 167

IV. DAY-TO-DAY OPERATIONS—SPECIAL PROBLEMS . . 169
   Focus 171
   Chapter 11 - Dress and Grooming 173
   Chapter 12 - Crowd Control 187
   Chapter 13 - Alcohol, Drugs, and Business 203
   Perspective 225

V.   CONSTITUTIONAL QUESTIONS 227
      Focus 229
      Chapter 14 - Constitutional Restraints and
           Statutory Interpretation 231
      Chapter 15 - Due Process 247
      Chapter 16 - The First Amendment 265
      Perspective 289

VI.   CIVIL RIGHTS: SEX DISCRIMINATION 291
      Focus 293
      Chapter 17 - Sex Discrimination Connected
           With Pregnancy 295
      Chapter 18 - Sex Discrimination: Harassment 315
      Chapter 19 - Sex Discrimination: Equal Pay Act 337
      Perspective 359

VII. CIVIL RIGHTS: RACE DISCRIMINATION,
      AMERICANS WITH DISABILITIES ACT
      OF 1990, CIVIL RIGHTS ACT OF 1991 361
      Focus 363
      Chapter 20 - Race Discrimination: Early Legislation 365
      Chapter 21 - Race Discrimination: Public
           Accommodations, Public Facilities, and Title VII 385
      Chapter 22 - Americans With Disabilities Act of 1990
           and the Civil Rights Act of 1991 401
      Perspective 411

VIII. RISK MANAGEMENT: YOUR BEST INVESTMENT . . . 415
      Chapter 23 - Risk Management 417
           A summary statement designed to provide tips on
           prevention for the various problem areas noted
           throughout the book.

GLOSSARY 427

APPENDIX 441

INDEX OF TERMS 443

INDEX OF CASES 449

FOREWORD

Sport management is an exciting area of professional pursuit. My career as a professor and administrator of sport management spans more than a quarter century. A prime interest of mine is the application of legal concepts to the business of sport. In pursuit of this interest, I have conducted research and written a variety of articles related to this area. I have also taught graduate and undergraduate courses in sport law at several universities.

Numerous sport law textbooks have been published in which the author(s) review a host of legal concepts and present situations illustrating their application to the sport enterprise. Frequently, however, the author's perspective has been restricted to his/her area of employment -- that is, coach, athletic director, public school administrator, physical education or recreation professor, lawyer, etc. Such perspectives, although valuable in and of themselves, are no longer totally appropriate to the profession of sport management as currently constituted.

Today, a significant segment of sport management students aspire to careers in the business world rather than the traditional coaching and educational venues of the past. Today's student ventures into areas such as professional sport, event management, facility management, amateur sport, health and fitness, sport merchandising, sport marketing and a sundry of other professional endeavors encumbered under the sport business umbrella. In fact, many individuals envision establishing their own sport related businesses. Thus, with respect to a legal education, what today's sport management student needs most is a course (and a textbook) that focuses on those legal concepts most frequently encountered by the sport business practitioner.

Legal Aspects of Sport Entrepreneurship is the only textbook I have read that fulfills this need. Authors Dianne B. O'Brien, Ph.D., and James O. Overby, J.D., have done a superb job of blending their respective professional expertise (sport administration and law) in a way that has resulted in the production of an outstanding sport law textbook - a text focused specifically on the needs of those contemplating sport business careers.

It is imperative that sport business professionals possess a basic understanding of legal concepts and their application. As with most things in life, to be successful, one must understand the rules of the game before entering the competitive arena. Judge Learned Hand once remarked that a society that esteemed law above justice was a truly civilized society. For most, a remark of this nature tends to cause one's neck hairs to rise. Yet, given a second reflection, it is quite reasonable for one to conclude that such a statement simply infers that justice is, on the whole, a subjective idea, judged differently according to personal points of view and passions, while law is the set of rules written to control the conduct of the enterprise, rules without which participation in the enterprise could be as shapeless and unfair as life itself. In today's business environment, professional growth, indeed professional survival, is to a large degree based on one's understanding of and adherence to the "rules of the game."

A significant difference exists between being interested in versus being committed to a specific concept or ideal. Most business managers are interested in protecting themselves, their clients, and their employees from harm that might arise because of a failure to abide by appropriate and customary legal practices. On the other hand, I am not sure of the proportion of managers fully committed to the understanding and application of those legal concepts. Nonetheless, the one thing I am sure of is that by reading *Legal Aspects of Sport Entrepreneurship* you will have taken the initial step toward becoming committed.

Peter J. Graham, Ed.D.
University of South Carolina
Columbia

PREFACE

This book affirms the ability and willingness of college students to study legal materials. More specifically, it affirms the ability of students who plan on entering the field of sport management to study legal materials. The utility of such a study is also affirmed. Clarity and simplicity are paramount in developing the style for the book. No legal terms are introduced without an explanation. The book is not designed to educate attorneys. However, it is accurate in its exposition of legal principles. The contents are designed to provide assistance to owners and managers of a business enterprise related to sports.

ORGANIZATION, PEDAGOGICAL CONCERNS, OBJECTIVES, AND SCOPE OF MATERIALS

Organization of Materials

The book is divided into seven parts, each of which is introduced by a short statement intended to focus attention on the materials covered in that part. Each part is designed to represent one aspect of the work confronting the owner or manager of a sport business. Each part of the book is composed of two or more chapters. Each part is introduced by a short statement called "Focus," which is designed to introduce the reader to the materials covered in that particular part. A hypothetical case usually follows to demonstrate the relevancy of the materials. At the end of each part (I - VII) a brief summary ("Perspective") is given that directs attention back to the materials that were covered in that particular portion of the book. A brief statement dealing with risk management follows in Part VIII.

Each chapter follows a general format including

- A brief introductory statement.
- A statement of things to be learned in the chapter.
- Key legal terms.
- This could be you! A practical example.
- At least one judicial decision.
- Questions and comments concerning the case.
- Chapter summary.
- This could be you - check your response.

Following the questions and comments and references, text materials may be introduced dealing with the general subject matter. On occasion, these text materials are supplemented by note cases (brief statements of the cases) that will state a principle or rule of law in an abbreviated form. After the text and note materials there are summaries of the chapter contents and a bibliography.

Pedagogical Concerns

The discovery method of learning is implicit in the use of this text. Like finding the solution to a mystery, the use of the case study method challenges the reader to think and solve problems. Furthermore, it builds skill in learning to read and explain cases, a skill that is important in legal analysis and application.

The text is appropriate for graduate or undergraduate courses. The materials are inclusive enough so that use of a law library should not be required. The cases in the text were chosen to illustrate certain principles of law. The chapters and cases are not intended to be all-inclusive but are representative of the litigation that challenges the field of sport management.

Readers who have learned the principles presented in this text will be aware of risk management techniques that aid in preventing injuries and litigation resulting from those injuries. Principles of law presented in the text also will be helpful in preventing litigation resulting from lack of knowledge regarding constitutional rights, faulty contracts, discriminatory actions and from unwritten policies.

Objectives
- Students should develop knowledge and appreciation of the legal system in the United States.
- Students should become aware of the legal problems that have confronted sport managers.
- Students should develop skills in examining and solving legal problems.
- Students should apply rules and principles of law to sport management situations

Scope

Students will be presented with a range of materials that is far broader in scope than that customarily presented in works of this type. Negligence that results in injury is important. Other topics, such as constitutional problems, are of equal importance.

Students will be given an opportunity to study some judicial decisions in their entirety. Discussion questions are included to aid student understanding.

The wide range of topics will necessitate the use of note cases and text materials. Accuracy and clarity will continue to be a basic concern.

Students will benefit from the experience of the authors. This experience includes classroom teaching, coaching, participation as an athlete, employment in a recreational facility, and the practice of law. These multifaceted experiences are believed to add to the practical value of the publication.

A CONSCIOUS EFFORT

In this book a conscious effort is made to present cases that have a factual situation involving sport management in some fashion. For example, if a chapter deals with an injury that results from negligence, the case selected to teach principles of negligence will involve such things as the operation of a ski lodge, a swimming pool, or a fitness center. On occasion, however, the principle of law is best expressed in a case that involves a factual situation different from the sport enterprise. In such instances, an effort is made to give examples whereby the principle illustrated can be applied to sport management. For example, the classic expression of procedural due process involves fundamental fairness. This is set forth in a United States Supreme Court decision that does not involve sports. Nevertheless, the case is relevant in discussing the law as it applies to sport management. It would be entirely possible to teach the law of sport management without involving cases that have a factual situation involving sports. Such teaching would be unfortunate from a practical standpoint.

For purposes of economy of expression, it is sometimes necessary to quote the principle, in a case without copying the entire case. When this happens, a short statement about the case is provided if the case involves the sport industry. If the principle is articulated in a case outside the sport industry, an example of the use of the principle within the sport industry is undertaken. The example may involve an actual court decision although hypothetical cases are given freely. In any event, the student seeking guidance as to legal principles applicable to sport management can find answers in established fields of law. Thus, when someone says to the reader, "This case doesn't involve sport law. I have no use for it," the reader will be able to say with confidence, "The case may not have a fact situation in sport law, but it is relevant and useful. The case has significance for the sport manager or owner." In like fashion, when confronted with a principle of law without an accompanying set of facts, the student of sport law can say with equal confidence, "This principle has value. It is applicable to the discipline."

Another point to remember is that the law is a discipline with its own vocabulary, literary style, and method of reasoning. No reader can expect "an easier, softer way." No writer need apologize for using the vocabulary of the craft. This text makes a conscious effort to soften the adjustment. When new or important words are used, attention is directed to them. Explanations of the reasoning process are offered. No student need be an attorney or be destined to attend law school. A conscious effort is made to reconcile complication with simplicity, and the theoretical with the practical. When appropriate, references to sports will be used to explain a concept. The point is that one who expects to enjoy and learn from a particular discipline must be willing to learn something about the vocabulary of that discipline.

Law is said to reconcile competing interests. The rights of management are weighed against the rights of labor. The power of government to control and regulate is balanced against the right of an individual to be left alone. Teaching and writing in sport management involve the same process. A need for completeness and accuracy must be balanced against the need for simplicity and clarity. The desire to impart advanced materials must be tempered to the academic status of the student. The result, insofar as this textbook is concerned, is an effort to minimize mistakes and significant omissions, but there is more to the story. A teacher who possesses a legal background can expand as appropriate; a teacher without a legal background can build on knowledge of the sport and proceed without discomfort.

Every case book should be up-to-date. This laudable objective sometimes results in the belief that all cases must be of recent vintage. This is not necessarily true. Many times an older case is preferable. The older case may trace the development of the principle that it expresses in a more thorough fashion. The older case will take lower court opinions and explain, reconcile, and distinguish. The rationale behind the new rule will be given. Sometimes, the more recent case will cite the rule of law with no explanation as to its origin or purpose. This case book makes a conscious effort to offer cases that are current from the standpoint of their pronouncement of law. No great premium is placed on the date in which a decision is rendered. The law has developed better ways in which to evaluate decisions.

To summarize, a book should be readable and teachable. In addition, the facts in cases should be recognizable. To the extent this is accomplished, the book will be both helpful and practical.

Names used in hypothetical situations are fictitious. The book is not intended to be legal advice. Students are encouraged to be enlightened consumers of legal services.

ACKNOWLEDGMENT

The authors have received assistance from all levels of the university community at Murray State University. The Vice President for Academic Affairs and Provost, Dr. James Booth, has been a source of constant encouragement and help in many ways too numerous to be detailed. Other employees have given support ranging from a leave of absence to advice on isolated matters, to the tedium of typing, checking of citations, proofing, and the multitude of other details necessary in the preparation of a manuscript. The secretarial work has been handled primarily by Linda Chadwick, Charlotte McDougal, and Joy Seavers, the secretarial staff of the Office of General Counsel, Murray State University, and without which the work could not have been completed.

Special mention should be made of the expert assistance in all phases of the manuscript by Dr. Janet Parks of Bowling Green State University. Valuable critiques have been made by Dr. Andy Pittman, Baylor University; Dr. Mary Hums, University of Massachusetts; Dr. Cathryn L. Claussen, Bowling Green State University; and Dr. Larry Janes, Eastern Illinois University. The finished product has been greatly improved by their suggestions. Needless to say, the authors assume full responsibility for any errors or weaknesses in the finished product.

Finally, the authors wish to express their thanks to immediate family members. These individuals have patiently endured the many months while the manuscript was being prepared. To Bill O'Brien, Clark O'Brien, Lee O'Brien, Alberta Beggs, and Dorothy E. Overby, our heartfelt gratitude.

COMMON LEGAL TERMS

The definitions that follow are working definitions and are not designed to cover each and every nuance or variance in the meaning of the terms. The terms that follow are designed to get the reader started. The terms are elementary but often repeated.

ADMINISTRATIVE BODY: One individual, or a group of individuals, entrusted with carrying out broad policy. The action of the administrative body may be judicial or legislative in nature. Sometimes referred to as "quasi-judicial" or "quasi-legislative."

ADMINISTRATIVE RULE: A regulation in the nature of legislation but emanated from the administrative branch.

ANSWER: The response of a party to a complaint.

APPELLANT: The party who disagrees with the decision at the trial level and seeks to have that decision corrected.

APPELLATE COURT: The court that reviews the action of a trial court.

APPELLEE: The party who has won on some point of law at the trial level and against whom an appeal is taken.

BILL OF ATTAINDER: A legislative act declaring someone guilty of a crime.

CHECKS AND BALANCES: A system whereby one branch of government checks on another branch. The check normally involves a part to be played by two of the branches in accomplishing an objective.

CITATION: The name of a case plus a reference as to where the case is found.

COMPLAINT: A pleading that commences a legal action.

CONCURRING OPINION: An opinion that agrees with the majority opinion but usually for different reasons.

CONSTITUTION: A basic, fundamental document that establishes broad principles of government. The United States has both a national constitution and individual state constitutions.

CONSTITUTIONAL LIMITATIONS: A principle that denies power to a governmental body for the purpose of protecting individual liberty.

CONTRACT: An agreement enforceable by law.

CRIME: An act or omission punishable by law in the form of a fine or imprisonment.

DEFENDANT: The party against whom legal relief is sought.

DICTUM: An expression of a legal rule or principle not necessary to the reasoning of the court. A legal aside.

DISSENTING OPINION: An opinion that disagrees with the majority opinion.

DIVISION OF POWERS: The allocation of power between the central unit of government and the various state governments.

EX POST FACTO LAW: A retroactive criminal law that operates to the detriment of the accused.

FACT: A fact is or is not, and is whatever it is. Usually associated with something relating to the senses. A fact may be simple or conclusionary in nature.

HEADNOTE: A reference to a principle of law asserted in a case; used in reporters published by West Publishing Company.

ISSUE: A question, something to be decided. It may deal with fact; it may deal with law.

JUDICIAL REVIEW: Generally referred to as the power of the courts to declare an act of the legislative body unconstitutional.

JURISDICTION: The power to hear a case.

LAW: A system of norms for the breach of which a penalty is prescribed. One can refer to law generally as opposed to a *law* which deals with a particular.

MAJORITY OPINION: The decision of an appellate court. The opinion may be unanimous; it must be over half.

MOTION: A method whereby some relief is sought. An application for a rule or an order.

PLAINTIFF: The party who files a legal action.

POPULAR SOVEREIGNTY: Generally defined as government by the people.

PRECEDENT: A case that has been decided based on a set of facts and that enunciates a rule or principle of law that may be applied to a similar set of facts.

SEPARATION OF POWERS: A division of power as between the executive, legislative, and judicial branches of government.

STARE DECISIS: Precedent, "Let the decision stand."

STATUTE: The product of a legislative body, either national or state law.

TORT: A civil wrong. A primary form of relief is compensation to the victim.

TRIAL COURT: The court which reviews both facts and law and makes the initial ruling.

GETTING THE BUSINESS STARTED

FOCUS

PLEASE READ
THE PREFACE
BEFORE READING
THE FOCUS.

Overview

All sport managers need to have adequate knowledge of the law. The person who manages a sport business for a public or private entity might be considered an entrepreneur. An entrepreneur is "one who organizes directs a business undertaking assuming the risk for the sake of profit, also the organizer or manager of public entertainments," *(Webster's New Universal Dictionary, 1972, p. 608)*.

Knowledge of the law will be helpful in the professional life of the sport manager as well as in personal matters. Many people who study sport management do not actually maintain occupations in that field of study. However, reading through this book will assist in many legal decisions, both professional and personal.

When sport management graduates were studied by Parks and Parra (1994), they found 29% of the alumni were working in positions not related to sport management. Seventy-one percent were employed in various fields of sport management. Approximately one-fourth of the graduates were working in positions such as resort office management, facility special events management, team scouting, team player development, sport association administration, and recreation center management. Slightly less than one-fourth were in other areas of sport management employment, such as sport journalism, sport information and marketing, wholesale or retail sporting goods sales, advertising, ticket sales, and health club membership sales. Other respondents were employed in areas such as fitness centers, hospitals, rehabilitation centers, corporate fitness centers, aquatics/health/racquet clubs, and high school or college physical education.

There are many opportunities for sport managers within small business. Just read the yellow pages in your telephone directory, and see the number of sport-related businesses. Regardless of the type of sport business, an entrepreneur needs to know about contracts, deeds, leases, and forms of business organizations. Each of these will have a practical application to the sport business. Individuals starting a business must decide upon the appropriate form of business organization. A decision to set up a corporation may be involved. On the other hand, a partnership or sole proprietorship may be preferred. The next four chapters will help you learn more about these concepts.

Sport management students do not necessarily start a small business when they graduate from college. However, it is much easier to start a small business than most people think. Leasing land or facilities is relatively easy when compared to owning the New York Yankees. In other words, having a large amount of capital is not necessary. Having a knowledgeable background is extremely helpful. Employment possibilities within small businesses in the sport industry are vast, and eventual ownership is a desirable goal. You might first work as the manager of a health club and then later own all or part of the health club.

Regardless of occupation, virtually all people in sport management will need some personal knowledge of contracts, deeds, or leases in their lifetime. Part I is designed to provide information that will enable a sport manager to proceed with a greater degree of confidence. No effort has been made to provide exhaustive information concerning these topics. However, certain information can help a sport manager be more comfortable in dealing with these topics. Contracts, for example, will probably be a recurring aspect insofar as

KNOWLEDGE OF THE LAW
WILL GIVE YOU POWER

the new business is concerned. The subject of deeds will occur far less frequently. Leases may need to be reexamined at periodic intervals, as will the form of business organization.

Practical considerations will give each of the topics in the next four chapters a special meaning. As the sport business grows and develops, a certain amount of expertise will be developed by the sport manager. This is especially true if the topics are approached with a proper attitude. Understanding the following materials will assist an owner or manager to successfully launch the business endeavor.

Practical Application - Hypothetical Case

The hypothetical case that follows is designed to focus attention on problems presented in getting a sport management business started. Attention is directed to matters that span the scope of the four chapters that are included in Part I.

John Jones has recently graduated from college with a major in sport management. John is 21 years of age. He and his wife, Maria, are expecting their first child in about two months. Maria is still a student but expects to graduate at the end of the current semester.

Mr. Jones wishes to enter into some aspect of business that will reflect his training in sport management. A quick survey of his hometown reveals a

dearth of recreational opportunities available. More specifically, there is nothing along the lines of a fitness center, which, on the surface, would appear to be a worthwhile venture. Mr. Jones' hometown has a population of 10,000 and is approximately 10 miles from other centers of population. Ms Jones has recently inherited $30,000, which she has agreed to put into the business. What questions should Mr. and Ms Jones ask? Whom should they consult? What pitfalls might they encounter? These questions will be answered in the chapters that follow.

CHAPTER 1

LEGAL FRAMEWORK

INTRODUCTION

As you read through this book, think of ways that you might make applications of the materials to sport- or fitness-related occupations. Also think of ways in which you might apply legal concepts to your personal life. Many opportunities for sport managers exist in small businesses. Legal concepts have many applications for your private life. For example, most people sign contracts, deeds, or leases. Further, you can be personally sued for negligence if someone is injured in your home. You might also be victimized in an assault, or by sexual or racial harassment.

The point is this: Read the following chapters and think about applications for your professional life and your personal life as well.

The following section will help prepare you to understand the law of the United States. It will also give you a background for reading the court cases in the book. By reading the court cases, you will be provided with examples of how specific law was applied in a sport setting.

IN THIS CHAPTER YOU WILL LEARN:
How to read and understand a court case
How to track a case through the judicial system
The meaning of democratic framework for the judicial system

KEY WORDS: *First Amendment, separation of powers, citation of a case, the facts, the questions before the court, the holding, principles of law, judicial opinions*

READING AND UNDERSTANDING COURT CASES AND THE JUDICIAL SYSTEM

The Discovery Method of Learning

One of the most interesting aspects of the field of law is that a person can learn from the judicial decisions that have been rendered. Reading court cases can be intriguing and fun. Furthermore, it is easier to remember legal principles when they are associated with real life situations. Discovery and association are good learning tools.

Court decisions are a matter of public record and can be reproduced without concern for copyright laws. Case law is formulated through appellate court decisions. Hence, most of the cases in this text are appellate decisions. Actual court cases are given in the chapters for the reader to analyze.

How to Read a Case

Citations. When first taking notes on a case, the reader should record the specific citations of the case. For example, in the reference *Shearer v. Perry Community Sch. Dist.,* 236 N.W.2d 688 (Wa. 1976), *Shearer v. Perry Community Sch. Dist.* is the name of the case, and 236 is the volume number of the North Western Reporter, second series. The number 688 is the starting page number for the case. Wa. represents the state. This information also tells you the level of the state court, Wa. in this instance, is the Supreme Court of Washington. 1976 represents the year. North Western refers to a reporter system by West Publishing Company. (West Publishing groups the states by geographic location.)

Federal cases are cited in a similar fashion. Trial court citations will be cited as ____ F. Supp. ____ (district, state and date). The federal circuit court is primarily an appellate court. These cases are cited as ____ F. ____ (____ circuit, date). There is also a second series that is cited as ____ F.2d ____ (circuit, date). A third series has been commenced. It is cited as ____ F.3d ____ (circuit, date). Remember that in each case, the first blank represents the volume number, and the second blank represents the page number.

The United States Supreme Court decisions are to be found in one of three collections of reporters. The government printing office prints the United States Reports; hence, a citation would be ____ U.S. ____ (date). West Publishing Company publishes the same decisions, but the name of the series is Supreme Court Reporter. These are cited ____ S.Ct. ____ (date). The third collection is known as United States Supreme Court Reports, Lawyers' Edition. It is now in the second series, published by Lawyers Co-op Publishing Co. This collection is valuable because it contains useful annotations. A typical citation would be ____ L.Ed 2d ____ (date). The cases in this book are mainly appellate court decisions. Lower court decisions are of lesser value in determining case law. A lower court decision may be overturned. Some sources recommend that a citation to a United States Supreme Court decision encompass all three of the sets of books described. One reader might have one set of books, and a different reader might have another set. When all three are cited, only one date is necessary.

The facts. In reading a case, the second thing the reader should do is to carefully note the facts in the case. List the plaintiff, the defendant, the purpose of the litigation, and the facts in the case.

The question. The initial problem for the reader is to determine the question before the court. One legal assumption is that a court must decide on a dispute. A second legal assumption is that the court's decision must be specific to the case before it. In other words, the objective for the court is to decide a particular dispute and only that dispute.

The holding. It is most important for the reader to remember how the court ruled on the question before it. This ruling is called the holding.

Reasoning and principles of law. In further analysis of the case, the reader should note how the court reasoned in the case. A legal assumption is that the court will decide on general rules of law that are applicable to the case. Facts of the case are considered by the court, and principles of law are applied. In reading the case, carefully note the facts, the reasoning of the court, and the principles of law that were applied.

Headnotes. Headnotes are principles of law referred to in the case. They are prepared by West Publishing Company and are the company's attempt to reference points of law in the order in which they appear in the case. Readers of cases in the West Reporter Series are encouraged to read the body of the case, not just the headnotes.

Applications. In reading a case, it is important to think of applications for future situations. The courts use previous decisions in deciding cases. Furthermore, a particular case may have professional applications or personal meaning to you as a reader.

Remember, the plaintiff is the party who is bringing the suit against the defendant. In reading the case, analyze what the plaintiff wanted. Were there general applications of this issue to society? Were there general applications for other persons or professions? Specifically, can the holding in this case be applied to other cases?

Throughout this book, actual cases will be given. The reader is encouraged to list

1. The citation
2. The facts
3. The question before the court
4. The holding
5. The reasoning of the court
6. The applications to sport management.

For further clarification, the reader is encouraged to turn to the following chapter and read and analyze the first case. As you read, there may be legal terms you will see defined in the body of the case. If you need help in defining a term, it may be helpful to refer to the glossary in the back of the book.

Judicial opinions. Each case will list the judge(s) in the case. Judges in addition to a ruling may give an opinion. The opinion includes the reasons for the holding. The opinion may be *en banc,* meaning by all the judges on that panel. A judge may want to express an agreeing or concurring opinion. Further, a specific judge may have a dissenting or disagreeing opinion. Another judge may feel strongly about a specific issue and express himself or herself on a legal issue not necessary to the holding in the case. These comments are called *dicta*. A *per curiam* opinion has no identification of the author. These judicial opinions in a case will give the reader understanding of the reasoning by the court.

Other terms. The parties in the case may ask for a summary judgment. In this event, the court issues an opinion without full judicial proceedings.

A lower court's decision may be appealed to a higher court. However, the court may remand the case and send it back to the lower court for further action. Furthermore, the higher court may decide not to even hear the case. When the issue is of special social significance, the higher court may issue a writ of *certiorari* to review the case.

SUMMARY

In order to read and understand judicial decisions, a person should be aware of the facts, the question before the court, the holding, the reasoning of the court, and the legal principles. The reader should consider applications of the legal principles to other social and personal issues.A sport management student should ask, "What can I learn from this case that would apply to my area of expertise?"

The following tables summarize the judicial system in the United States (Figure 1) and progress of a lawsuit (Figure 2). The various cases that are reproduced in this volume will indicate where and how the case started and where and how it was appealed.

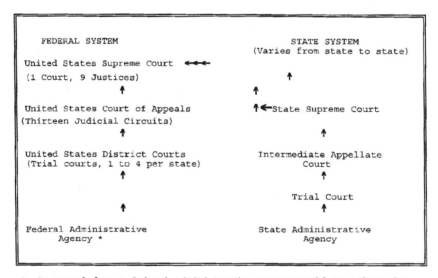

FEDERAL SYSTEM

United States Supreme Court
(1 Court, 9 Justices)

United States Court of Appeals
(Thirteen Judicial Circuits)

United States District Courts
(Trial courts, 1 to 4 per state)

Federal Administrative
       Agency *

STATE SYSTEM
(Varies from state to state)

State Supreme Court

Intermediate Appellate
        Court

Trial Court

State Administrative
        Agency

*   An appeal from a federal administrative agency could move from the agency to the United States Court of Appeals in certain situations.

FIGURE 1. JUDICIAL SYSTEMS IN THE UNITED STATES

```
  I. Deciding to Use the Court System

     Consider policies, the law, nature of the problem, time and money.

 II. Expert Advice

     Select attorney.  Discuss fee.  Keep records.

III. Pleadings

     Complaint filed by plaintiff.  Issue of law and facts presented.  Answer filed by
     defendant.

 IV. Pretrial Activities

     Depositions (sworn statements) taken.  Evidence collected.

  V. Summary Judgment (In some cases)

     Attorneys may ask for judgment based on pleadings when there are no disputed
     issues of fact.  When summary judgment is granted, there is no trial.

 VI. Trial Court

     Judge or jury hears opening statements, sees evidence produced. Attorneys make
     closing arguments.  Judge or jury makes judgment/gives verdict.

VII. Appellate Court

     Notice of appeal is filed by attorneys.  Appellate court may elect to hear the
     case.  Appellate court does not hear evidence.  Appellate court reviews briefs of
     issues, facts, and points of law.

VIII. Judgment Implemented

     If case is "remanded," it would go back to the lower court to do what the
     appellate court requested.
```

FIGURE 2. PROGRESS CHART OF A LAWSUIT

INTELLECTUAL FRAMEWORK

Philosophic Expression

Democracy in the American tradition postulates the inherent dignity of the individual. This principle reflects the rights of individuals as opposed to governmental power. Traditionally, this balancing process is referred to as liberty versus authority. Democracy prides itself on being a government of laws rather than a government of people. Such a principle mandates that all individuals be treated equally if they come to the forum under like circumstances. Such a principle proscribes arbitrary and capricious action.

Majority rule is the linchpin of the democratic process. This is sometimes known as the doctrine of popular sovereignty. As a corollary to majority rule, democracy emphasizes the right of the minority to be heard. Thus, democracy offers a forum for the unpopular cause. In addition to the right to be heard, the minority has a right to become the majority. Basic to the rights of the majority and the minority are the rights imbedded in the guarantees accorded by the First Amendment to the United States Constitution.

The First Amendment rights of free speech, press, assembly, and religion are often expressed in legal issues confronting sport managers. The political freedoms enunciated above go hand-in-hand with the concept of private property and freedom of contract. A free enterprise system postulates rugged individualism and, initially at least, de-emphasizes governmental interference.

The notion of peaceful change complements the requirement for stability and predictability within the law. This is true both in the political and economic spheres of the democratic process. No attorney can afford to be ignorant of these basic principles. It is believed that no judge can effectively function without being mindful of the democratic climate under which that judge works and functions. Likewise, the sport manager is influenced by political and economic legal applications. This is especially true when measured by historical development. Political changes have led to the expansion of legal rights of individuals. Political and legal changes influencing the business environment include the following:

- Suffrage has been broadened. Religion and property qualifications for voting have been removed.
- Discrimination based on sex, race, religion, and national origin has been the subject of legislation.
- Popular election of senators has been legislated.
- The electoral college has been reduced to a "rubber stamp" for the states because of custom and usage.

Certain economic changes influence sport businesses. Freedom of entry into the economic system has been assured by controlling large-scale concentrations of wealth. The Sherman Anti-Trust Act and the Clayton Antitrust Act speak to this development. As a corollary, a guarantee of minimum standards has come about through minimum wages and maximum hours and the rights of labor to bargain collectively. In short, democracy has taken on an economic component alongside its political mainstem. The four freedoms articulated by President Franklin D. Roosevelt in a speech to Congress on January 6, 1941, stressed freedom of speech and religion, and freedom from want and fear. The inherent dignity of the individual has both political and economic consequences.

The American Form

Separation of powers. A survey of the basic principles set forth in the United States Constitution is helpful. The first principle is known as "separation of powers." The framers of the Constitution were well aware of the principle that affirms that the possession of power tends to beget the abuse of power. There is a danger in concentrating power in one individual or a small group of individuals. Liberty is precious to free people. To accomplish the objective of protecting liberty, power was distributed among the three branches of government: the legislative branch, the executive branch, and the judicial branch. Constitutional scholars refer to the so-called "distributing clauses" in the Constitution; namely, art. I, §1; art. II, §1; art. III, §1. Figure 3 that follows illustrates separation of powers.

Division of powers. A second basic principle is known as "division of powers." Under a federal system, the national unit of government possesses

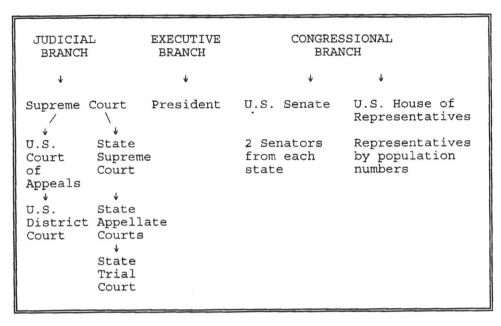

FIGURE 3. SEPARATION OF POWERS

supremacy, but the states have important residual powers. The supremacy of the national unit is accomplished in three steps:

1. The Supremacy Clause affirms in clear and certain language:
    This Constitution, and the Laws of the United States which shall be made in Pursuance thereof; and all Treaties made, or which shall be made, under the Authority of the United States, shall be the supreme Law of the Land; and the Judges in every State shall be bound thereby, any Thing in the Constitution or Laws of any State to the Contrary notwithstanding. U.S. CONST. art. VI, ¶2

2. The national unit has specific delegated powers designed to correct weaknesses in the old Articles of Confederation; that is, the power to tax, the power to regulate interstate commerce, the power to wage war, and implied powers that will supplement delegated powers. See U.S.CONST. art. I, §8. The states have residual powers as set forth in the Tenth Amendment.

3. Certain powers are also prohibited to the states. The areas in which these prohibitions operate include interstate commerce or foreign affairs. See U.S. CONST. art. I, §10.

    Checks and balances. Power is also controlled through the doctrine of checks and balances. Each branch of government, in one way or another, will check on the other branches. For example, certain powers may be divided, such as the appointing power wherein the executive branch nominates and the Senate advises and consents. Another check is to be found in the treaty-making process. The President negotiates treaties. The Senate advises and consents to the treaty. The President then ratifies the treaty. These are but two of many examples that could be cited.

The judicial branch exercises the power of judicial review. Technically, this means the power of the courts to declare an act of Congress unconstitutional. This power is not expressly stated in the United States Constitution, but it was asserted by Mr. Justice John Marshall in the case of Marbury v. Madison (1803). Judicial review is also exercised by the court when it reviews decisions of administrative agencies.

Limitations of governmental power. The rights of individuals as opposed to governmental rights were affirmed in isolated instances in the original Constitution by prohibitions against a bill of attainder or ex post facto law.[1] Later, the powers of government were limited by Amendments I through X, known as the Bill of Rights.

SUMMARY

This book does not purport to be a textbook on American government; nor does it purport to expound on constitutional law generally or American political theory. Nevertheless, a capsuled synopsis of the form and philosophy of American government is believed to be important to the sport manager who operates in the political and economic arena of a democratic society. In this chapter, you were given important information that will help you learn more about the law and sport entrepreneurship.

REFERENCES

Marbury v. Madison, 1 Cranch 137, 2 L.Ed. 60 (1803).

Parks, J. B., & Parra, L. G. (1994). Job satisfaction of sport management alumni. *Journal of Sport Management 8,* 49-56.

1. Refer to glossary for definitions.

CHAPTER 2

CONTRACTS

INTRODUCTION

Contracts are important to the sport manager. Employment contracts, insurance contracts, lease contracts, contracts for the purchase of real estate, contracts with vendors, contracts with officials, and contracts for the purchase of equipment are typical contracts that a sport manager might sign.

Anyone entering into sport management will need to be familiar with certain elemental principles of contract law. Such knowledge will continue to be useful throughout the life of the sport manager and the business enterprise. The nature of the sport business will dictate the type of contract that confronts the owner or manager of the enterprise. Types of recreational sport businesses vary considerably in the private sector. In addition to the private commercial enterprises, there are some recreational activities that are governmental in nature. Such public enterprise extends beyond public schools and colleges. For example, parks are recreational in nature and are an integral part of local, state, and federal government activity.

Obviously, a casebook that is limited in size cannot address contract matters in great detail. The multivolume treatises of Williston (1990) and Corbin (1993), dealing with the law of contracts, illustrate the complexity of the subject matter. This chapter is limited to essential aspects of contracts. An owner or manager of a small business enterprise needs to be informed as to certain basics. For example, the essential prerequisites of a valid, enforceable contract are fundamental information. Knowledge of the remedies available for the breach of a contract is always helpful. Aside from purely legal matters, dangers and pitfalls likely to be encountered are worthy of note.

IS A HANDSHAKE A
LEGAL CONTRACT?

IN THIS CHAPTER YOU WILL LEARN:

The requirements for a valid enforceable contract

The requirements for a valid offer

The ways in which an offer can be terminated

The exceptions to the requirement for consideration

The types of contracts that must be in writing

The ways in which consent can be avoided

The remedies for breaches of contract that are equitable in nature

The remedies for breaches of contract that are legal in nature

The primary advantage and disadvantage of a form contract

The occasion when rules of construction become necessary

The primary rules for interpreting a contract

The ways in which contract rights may be transferred

KEY WORDS: *offer, acceptance, offeror, offeree, undue influence, Sunday laws, specific performance, rescission, compensatory damages, mailbox rule, nominal damages, bilateral contract, firm offer, unilateral contract, punitive damages, liquidated damages, indemnify, parol evidence rule, counteroffer, fraud, consideration, competent to sign, legality, contract not to compete, equitable remedy, common law damages, third-party beneficiary, form contract, valid, enforceable contract*

This could be you!

John Jones, the student referenced in the hypothetical situation shown under the Focus for this Part, has been advised by his banker that a building is for sale just off the courthouse square and adjacent to one of the local churches. The building is of sufficient size to accommodate a fitness center. The owner of the building, Rufus "Speedy" Smith, has left a contract with the banker for the sale of the property for the sum of $80,000. The contract has been prepared by "Speedy's" attorney and consists of some five pages of single-spaced, typewritten materials. The banker advises that the property will eventually sell, in his judgment, for this sum. Should Jones sign the contract? What questions should he ask? What steps should he take to protect himself? Incidentally, Maria Jones is 20 years of age. Should her name be on the deed? How can the rights of their unborn child be protected? Does this create any problems?

PREREQUISITES, REMEDIES, MISCELLANEOUS, PITFALLS AND PRIMARY SOURCES

Prerequisites

The basic provisions of a valid, enforceable contract can be stated simply. First, there must be an agreement. An agreement involves an offer and an acceptance. Second, the consent of the parties must be real; the agreement should not be tainted by fraud, duress, undue influence, or mutual mistake. Third, the agreement should be supported by consideration. Stated differently, a contract should indicate the price paid for the promise. In some cases, the price will be another promise. In other cases, it will be an act or refraining from an act. Most contracts will involve promises as consideration. Fourth, the contract document must be in a form prescribed by law. This simply means that certain contracts must be in writing in order to be enforceable. To determine the contracts that must be in writing one turns to a "statute of frauds," which will be found in the state statutes. Fifth, the subject matter of the contract must be legal. Sixth, the parties to the contract must be competent. Competency is measured in terms of age and mental condition. Each of these prerequisites will be discussed in some detail.

As in other principles of law, the general conclusions stated in this chapter are subject to exceptions. An effort is made to describe these exceptions as departures from the general rule of law.

Offer. A valid, enforceable offer must be definite, communicated, and must evince a contractual intent. An offer that is indefinite will be too vague and general. The offeree will not know precisely what is being offered. Obviously, an offer that does not pass effectively from the offeror to the offeree cannot have legal consequences. An exaggerated example would be a written offer that remains on the desk of the offeror. Furthermore, offers made in jest, or statements made in a fit of anger, do not postulate a situation wherein the one making the offer contemplates a binding contract.

In general, an offer can be withdrawn at any time before acceptance. An offer will be terminated in the event of death or incapacity of a party. An offer will also be terminated if the subject matter of the offer becomes illegal. If there is a time limit on the offer, an expiration of the time stipulated will terminate the offer. Should the offeree purport to accept but vary the terms of the offer, such a variance constitutes a counteroffer, and this effectively terminates the original offer.

Sometimes an offer cannot be withdrawn for a stipulated period of time. For example, the offeree, for a price paid, may be given an option to accept within a certain period of time. The option paid for thus constitutes a contract that is binding. It should be added that the law of sales, which is a part of Section 2 of the Uniform Commercial Code (U.L.A §2), has developed a concept known as the firm offer. The law of sales involves a transfer of personal property. This will be explained in the paragraphs that follow.

Acceptance. An acceptance involves an expression on the part of the offeree that he or she will enter into a contract as outlined in the offer. A substantial variation of the offer in the acceptance terminates the original offer as previously indicated, and no contract results. Sometimes letters cross in the mail. In such cases, the courts have developed what is known as the mailbox rule. A letter of acceptance is effective when mailed. This rule provides guidance as to the existence or nonexistence of a contract.

Consideration. The price paid for a promise is known as *consideration*. This is a bargain concept. The law of contracts recognizes various forms of contracts. A bilateral contract is one in which the parties exchange promises. In this situation, one promise constitutes consideration for the other. For example, a sport manager wishes to have pieces of equipment installed. An engineer promises to make the installation for a certain sum of money. The sport manager promises to pay the sum stipulated in the contract. The two promises constitute a bilateral contract. One promise is the offer; the other is the acceptance. Each promise is the consideration paid for the other party's promise. A unilateral contract, on the other hand, requires an act or a forbearance from acting in exchange for a promise. The act or forbearance is said to be the price paid. In other words, doing something (the act) or not doing something (the forbearance) can be consideration.

There are other classifications of contracts. A contract is said to be either an executed or an executory contract: the former is performed; the latter is yet to be performed. Of greater significance is the distinction between public and private contracts. For example, private contracts would be used by sport managers in a privately owned racquet club. Public contracts might be made with state agencies such as a recreation facility of a state park. The subject matter of this casebook deals primarily with private contracts. To the extent that public contracts are involved, special regulations can be found in the statutory and decisional law. For example, the statute of limitations in a suit against a state agency is probably shorter than that for private contracts.

The requirement for consideration has exceptions. Historically, a contract to which a seal has been affixed does not require consideration. The seal gives the contract validity. Second, a *firm offer* under the law of sales does not require consideration. Section 2-205 of the Uniform Commercial Code states:

> An offer by a merchant to buy or sell goods in a signed writing which by its terms give assurance that it will be held open is not revocable, for lack of consideration, during the time stated or if no time is stated for a reasonable time, but in no event may such period of irrevocability exceed three months; but any such term of assurance on a form supplied by the offeree must be separately signed by the offeror.

Third, a contract may arise as a result of a court order. Such a contract is said to arise by operation of law.

The doctrine of *promissory estoppel* acts in a similar fashion as an exception for consideration. Specifically, when one individual makes a promise and another individual, justifiably, in reliance on the promise acts upon that promise, the party making the promise is barred from relying on the absence of consideration as a defense. For example, Smith, a coach at State University, promises Brown, a coach at another institution, that he will add Brown's school to his Christmas schedule. In reliance on that promise, Brown drops another school from his Christmas schedule. If Smith is sued, then Smith cannot plead lack of consideration as a defense to the suit.

A general rule has developed to the effect that the court will not weigh the adequacy of consideration. Stated differently, a court will not make a contract for the parties. Such a premise is consistent with the notion of freedom of contract. The law is concerned with the validity of a contract. It is not concerned with weighing the value of the contract for each of the parties. A general exception to the rule regarding adequacy of consideration can be found whenever consideration is so out of line as to serve as a badge of fraud or overreaching. Contract law, therefore, gives freedom to the contracting parties, but such freedom is not unlimited.

Requirements for writing. Certain types of contracts must be in writing in order to be enforceable. This rule is encompassed by the various provisions in a statute of frauds. Certain types of contracts are considered to be more important than others. For example, a contract that deals with land is unique. Thus, an agreement with respect to land must be in writing in order to be enforceable. A contract wherein one promises to answer for the debt, miscarriage, or default of another must be written. A contract for the sale of goods over a certain amount also requires a writing. This amount initially was $500.00. Individual states sometimes vary the amount. A contract whereby an executor or administrator promises to pay the debts of an estate from his own funds requires a writing. Finally, a contract in consideration of marriage must be in writing and is within the statute of frauds.

Practical considerations undergird a statute of frauds. Memories fade, witnesses move, and oral testimony tends to be self-serving. Putting a contract in writing gives certainty to the content of an agreement.

The requirement for a writing is supplemented by a rule of law known as the *parol evidence rule*. Briefly, oral testimony cannot be introduced to vary the terms of a written agreement. Exceptions to the parol evidence rule exist. One of the most important exceptions permits oral testimony to clarify ambiguity in the written document. Another exception is a pledge to a charitable institution.

Legality. The subject matter of a contract must be legal. An agreement that purports to authenticate a criminal act or a tort is not permissible. (A tort is a civil wrong.) Legality of the contract is determined by statutory and decisional law. Examples that illustrate this point are

1. A contract that is usurious involves an impermissible rate of interest because the rate is too high. This amount varies from state to state. This is not to be confused with a "legal" rate of interest. The legal rate is set by statute when interest is due but an amount of interest is not stated in the contract.

2. An agreement "not to compete" will not be legal unless it is reasonably limited as to time and place. Such a contract usually arises out of the sale of a business. For example, this might occur if a person sold a tennis club on the west side of the community but wanted to open a similar facility on the south side. A contract not to compete might be entered into for a certain period of time. The distance between businesses would also be relevant.

3. Sunday Laws, also known as Blue Laws, may also involve considerations of legality. These are laws that prohibit certain activity on the Sabbath. Most Protestant religions will consider Sunday as the Sabbath. It should be noted, however, that recreation is more likely to be tolerated than is

labor in the conventional sense. In any event, Sunday Laws are also subject to exceptions predicated on acts of necessity. These exceptions are frequently spelled out in some detail in the statute itself. Enforcement of Sunday Laws may be weak and ineffectual because of changing values by society as a whole.

4. An agreement that obstructs the legal process, such as payment for witnesses over and above a permissible sum, is subject to the charge of illegality.

Capacity of parties. With limited exceptions, a minor cannot enter into a contractual arrangement. Stated simply, this now means that a person under 18 years of age (a minor) does not have the power to enter into a contract. Like most rules, there are exceptions. One exception has to do with the purchase of necessaries such as food. Necessaries are limited in scope but will vary depending upon the economic and social condition of the minor. Conditions that may be illegal because of minority can be ratified when the minor becomes of age. Further, such a contract can be cosigned by one who has achieved majority status and who promises to pay if the minor does not. (This means the adult will indemnify in the event of a default by the minor.)

An adult cannot contract away the right of a minor to recover in tort.[1] However, the adult can promise to indemnify. Realistically, such a promise is only as valuable as the financial ability of one who signs for purposes of indemnification. A distinction should be made between void contracts and those that are voidable. As a general rule, void contracts have no legal effect. A void contract has no binding force; it is not enforceable. For example, a contract to give a coach tenure may be void if it is against public policy. Voidable contracts can have a legal effect as a result of some action taken. For example, individuals under disability may affirm the contract when the disability is removed. When a party entering a contract lacks capacity, the contract is voidable but is not void. For example, a person who has had a stroke may get better.

Remedies

Equitable remedies. The party filing suit is seeking to obtain a remedy. Remedies may be equitable or common-law in nature.

Equity is a body of law that developed to supplement the common law. Equity gives a remedy where the common law could not. Equity is said to act *in personam,* namely, on the person rather than the thing. The common law is said to be highly technical. Thus, the necessity for equitable remedies is predicated upon the harshness of the common law.

Equitable remedies in the law of contracts are threefold: first, specific performance; second, rescission and reformation; and third, the injunction. Common-law remedies for breach of contract involve damages. Many times damages are not sufficient to satisfy a plaintiff. In such cases, an order of the court directs the defendant to perform as promised. This is known as the *doctrine of specific performance.* One example is where the subject matter of the contract is one of a kind or has special sentimental value to the party who

1. A tort is a civil wrong. An adult cannot say that his or her child will not file suit when the child becomes of legal age.

seeks performance. A descendant of an athlete who has located a particular bat, ball, or memorabilia associated with a particular event, which memorabilia cannot be replaced or may have a unique value to the plaintiff, illustrates this point. Obviously, damages will not suffice if a contract to purchase the memorabilia is breached. The plaintiff seeks specific performance.

The second type of equitable remedy involves rescission or reformation. When a contract is rescinded, it seeks to put the parties back to their original position. A rescission is usually based upon fraud, mistake, duress, or some type of overreaching that mandates undoing the contract. Reforming a contract makes the agreement conform to the real intent as opposed to the situation in which the parties find themselves. Once again, considerations of fraud, mistake, and duress enter into the case.

An injunction is an order that usually restrains action. It is possible to have a mandatory injunction that directs action, but this is not as common as the injunction that prohibits action. Generally speaking, the injunction will fall into three categories: (a) A *permanent injunction* is an order of the court that directs a party to do or not to do a particular thing; (b) a *temporary injunction* is designed to hold the problem situation in manageable proportions until such time as the case can be litigated; (c) a *restraining order* directs a party not to do a certain thing and is issued without the usual precautions associated with the injunction process. In short, a restraining order can be issued without notice and a hearing. For example, a judge might issue a restraining order preventing an athlete from playing until certain contract obligations were met. This, of course, is not the case with a temporary or permanent injunction.

Common law - Damages. A contract remedy at common law involves damages. A party to a contract who suffers as a result of a breach of the contract by the other party needs to be made whole. The method devised is the awarding of damages. Damages are usually classified under four separate headings: nominal, compensatory, punitive, and liquidated.

Nominal damages, as the name implies, means damages in name only. A claimant is given a token sum, usually one dollar, and is awarded costs. The purpose of the nominal damage award is to establish a principle that can serve as a guide in the future.

Compensatory damages, on the other hand, make a party whole. Compensatory damages put the party in the position he or she would have been in had the contract been honored.

Punitive damages are normally associated with tort law rather than contract law. It is sometimes said that punitive damages are "smart money." Punitive damages punish willful or wanton misconduct. Occasionally, punitive damages are in the form of triple damages mandated by a statutory provision designed to enforce a public policy.

Liquidated damages are those damages that are agreed upon by the parties at the outset of the contract. These damages are payable in the event of breach or nonperformance. A provision for liquidated damages recognizes the difficulty in fixing an actual sum but recognizes the fact that a party will be injured as a result of breach, that is, performance by a certain date. For example, a contractor has a contract to complete building a fitness center by a specific date. The failure to open the fitness center means a loss of revenue to the owner. Therefore, liquidated damages could be agreed upon in advance. The fixing of a sum certain in advance of the breach of the contract by the building contractor obviates the necessity for proving actual damages.

Miscellaneous

Interpretation. The terms of a contract are sometimes vague and indefinite. In such situations a court finds it necessary to resort to so-called "canons of construction." The primary purpose of construction is to ascertain the intent of the contracting parties. If the intent is not clear from the language of the contract, a resort to principles of construction becomes important. Some examples of these principles of construction or interpretation follow:

1. The word *shall* is generally mandatory; the word *may* is permissive.
2. Technical words should be given a technical construction.
3. The various parts of the contract should be harmonized, or considered one part in relation to another.
4. The purpose or objective of the contract is always relevant.
5. Custom and usage may be important, that is, customs in the trade or profession, or a course of dealing as between the parties to the contract.

Third parties. The common law developed a concept of privity of contract, specifically: Remedies were accorded to the parties to the contract, but generally speaking, third parties could not avail themselves of its provisions. Later, however, it was decided that in certain instances a contract right could be transferred to a third party. This transfer is called *an assignment.* The person making the transfer is *the assignor.* The person to whom the transfer is made is known as *the assignee.* For example, Amy has a contract with Brad. Amy transfers her contract interest to Chad. The transfer process is known as an assignment. Amy is the assignor; Chad is the assignee. Any defense of the contract that would have been available to Amy as against Brad remains viable even though the contract has been transferred to Chad. Under general contract law, a transfer was made subject to any defenses available as against the assignor. In other words, assignors can only transfer what they have. Stated differently, the rights of the assignee could rise no higher than the rights of the assignor.

In other situations the law developed what is known as a *third-party beneficiary status.* Third-party beneficiaries are classified as incidental, donee, or creditor. An incidental beneficiary is one who benefits only casually as a result of a contract between the primary parties. In such a case the incidental beneficiary cannot sue on the primary contract. For example, *A* promises to build an expensive sport complex. The building of such a complex will benefit the adjoining property owner. Failure to honor the contract, however, will not give the adjoining property owner the right to recover.

Where the contract designates the beneficiary, the legal entity so designated is known as a *donee beneficiary.* An example is the life insurance contract whereby *A* contracts with the insurance company and names *X* as the beneficiary. An insurance company that refuses to honor the contract can be sued successfully by *X*. Creditor beneficiaries involve creditors who are indebted to the promisee, that is, the original holder of an indebtedness that has been assumed by the promisor.

Pitfalls

Form contracts. A contract that has been prepared by one of the parties will concentrate on protecting the party who supplies the form. Thus, an owner or manager should generally have such a contract reviewed by his or her own attorney. Not only does a form contract concentrate on protecting one party, but it also may have been designed to enable office staff to fill in the blanks. Consequently, the form may not take into consideration a particular factual situation, that is, a form developed for private entrepreneurs may not stretch to cover a situation involving a public agency as a contracting party. Form contracts are risky. Common sense needs to be employed. The nature of the contract and the amount of money involved may dictate the decision to seek legal advice. Sport managers who seek to develop their own contracts should avoid extremes in protecting their interests. Managers would be well-advised to include customary provisions designed to protect the other contracting party. Such a form contract avoids overreaching and the designation of such a document as an adhesion contract, namely, unconscionable contracts that reflect or signal the unequal bargaining power of the parties.

Preparing for contract negotiations. The owner or manager of a sports enterprise should assist the attorney. Knowledge of the purpose for which the contract is entered is crucial. The purpose will signal steps that need to be taken. A contract should be drafted to accomplish its objective. A contract should provide the assurance of fair and reasonable treatment for each party. A party should not yield to the temptation of speeding up the signing process because there is a good understanding as to a particular point. Such an understanding does not suggest omitting a contractual provision on that point. Instead, such an understanding enables one to better articulate that point in a contract provision. Failure to include such an understanding when the parties are agreed can lead to second-guessing at a later point when problems have arisen. Parties who have agreed in principle are fortunate. The drafting of the contract is easy, but it should be drafted so as to express that understanding. One should assume that each party has legitimate concerns. Consequently, a party is entitled to have those concerns recognized in the agreement.

A contract should be predicated on the assumption that each party is honest. However, it should be drafted in such a way that it will accord protection in the event that one's faith is misplaced. Exceptions trigger litigation.

Some Primary Source Materials - Decisional Law

Legality. To be valid, a contract must not be tainted with illegality. The following case deals with the legality of gambling on a golf shot.

••

LAS VEGAS HACIENDA, INC., v. GIBSON
359 P.2d 85 (Nev. 1961)

MC NAMEE, Justice.

Respondent commenced this action in the lower court to recover the sum of $5,000 based on the following transaction.

Appellant made a public offer to pay $5,000 to any person who, having paid 50¢ for the opportunity of attempting to do so, shot a hole in one on its golf course. There were certain specified conditions in connection with said offer.

The lower court found from the evidence that the respondent complied with said conditions, that he shot a hole in one, and that appellant refused to abide by its offer. It further determined that this transaction was a valid contract enforceable at law and not a gambling contract. Judgment was entered in favor of respondent in the sum of $5,000 plus interest and costs. Appeal is from said judgment.

On this appeal we are not concerned with any factual matters, the lower court properly having resolved such matters in favor of respondent.

Appellant specified the following two errors:

1. The court below erred in not holding that the alleged contract on which the action is based was a wagering contract and therefore unenforceable.

2. The court below erred in finding that the shooting of a "hole in one" is a feat of skill and not a feat of chance.

Although gambling, duly licensed, is a lawful enterprise in Nevada (Nevada Tax Commission v. Hicks, 73 Nev. 115, 310 P.2d 852), an action will not lie for the collection of money won in gambling. Weisbrod v. Fremont Hotel, 74 Nev. 227, 326 P.2d 1104. It is therefore necessary to determine whether the transaction between appellant and respondent in this case constituted a gaming contract.

It is generally held, in the absence of a prohibitory statute, that the offerer of the prize to a contestant therefor who performs a specified act is not invalid as being a gambling transaction. Porter v. Day, 71 Wis. 296, 37 N.W. 259. The offer by one party of specified compensation for the performance of a certain act as a proposition to all persons who may accept and comply with its conditions constitutes a promise by the offeror. The performance of that act is the consideration for such promise. The result is an enforceable contract. Robertson v. United States, 343 U.S. 711, 72 S.Ct. 994, 96 L.Ed. 1237. There is no statute in Nevada prohibiting such offers.

A prize or premium differs from a wager in that in the former, the person offering the same has no chance of gaining back the thing offered, but, if he abides by his offer, he must lose; whereas in the latter, each party interested therein has a chance of gain and takes a risk of loss. Toomey v. Penwell, 76 Mont. 166, 245 P. 943, 45 A.L.R. 993; Pompano Horse Club v. State, 93 Fla. 415, 111 So. 801, 52 A.L.R. 51.

Ballentine's Law Dictionary, 2d Ed., p. 1002, defines premium as "a reward or recompense for some act done. It is known who is to give before the event. It is not to be confounded with a bet or wager, for in a wager, it is not known who is to give until after the event."

Misner v. Knapp, 13 Or. 135, 9 P. 65, 66, was an action to recover the sum of $250 offered by defendants to the owner of a horse that should trot a mile in the best time, less than two minutes and twenty-five seconds at City View Park, it being alleged therein that plaintiff complied with the terms and conditions specified. The contention of defendants that the purse offered was a bet or wager and that no action would lie to enforce the payment thereof was held to be without merit, the court saying:

"Now, according to the definition of 'wager,' there must be two or more contracting parties, having mutual rights in respect to the money or other thing wagered or, as sometimes said, 'staked,' and each of the parties necessarily risks something, and has a chance to make something upon the happening or not happening of an uncertain event. But a purse or prize offered by a party, and to be awarded to the successful competitor in a contest in which such party does not engage, nor has any chance of gaining, but only, perhaps, of losing, is without the element of a chance of gain or a risk of loss which characterizes the wager agreement. The distinction has been stated thus:

> "In a wager or a bet, there must be two parties, and it is known, before the chance or uncertain event upon which it is laid or accomplished, who are the parties who must either lose or win. In a premium or reward there is but one party until the act or thing or purpose for which it is offered has been accomplished. A premium is a reward or recompense for some act done; a wager is a stake upon an uncertain event. In a premium it is known who is to give before the event; in a wager it is not known until after the event. The two need not be confounded. Alvord v. Smith, 63 Ind. 59."

The fact that each contestant is required to pay an entrance fee where the entrance fee does not specifically make up the purse or premium contested for does not convert the contest into a wager. Toomey v. Penwell, supra.

Inasmuch as the contesting for a prize offered by another, which the one offering must lose in the event of compliance with the terms and conditions of his offer is not gambling, it was not error to hold that the said contract was valid and enforceable.

Whereas we have concluded that the contract does not involve a gaming transaction, consideration of appellant's second assignment of error, that the lower court erred in finding that the shooting of a "hole in one" was a feat of skill, becomes unnecessary. We do wish to state however that the record contains sufficient evidence to sustain the court's finding in this regard. Appellant insists however that the testimony of one Capps, a golf professional, precludes such a finding. He testified that luck is a factor in all holes in one where skill is not always a factor. He further testified that "a skilled player will get it (the ball) in the area where luck will take over more often than an unskilled player."

The test of the character of a game is not whether it contains an element of chance or an element of skill, but which is the dominating element. People ex rel. Ellision v. Lavin, 179 N.Y. 164, 71 N.E. 753, 66 L.R.A. 601. It was within the province of the trial court to determine this question. Brown v. Board of Police Commissioners, 58 Cal.App.2d 473, 136 P.2d 617.

Affirmed. [Court held for the respondent, golfer.]

Questions and Comments

1. What are the facts in the case?
2. What are the questions of law?
3. What is the reasoning of the court?
4. What are the principles of law in the case?
5. What is the holding?
6. Did the facts in this case show that a gambling contract existed? Why or why not?

Remedy. The following case involves an offer, acceptance, and modification of a contract. Specific performance of the contract was sought as a remedy. Read the case and see if fraud is mentioned. See if a written contract was needed.

••

D'AGOSTINO v. BANK OF RAVENSWOOD
563 N.E.2d 886 (Ill.App.Ct.1990)

Justice McNAMARA delivered the opinion of the court:

Plaintiff, Vincenzo D'Agostino, brought this action against defendants Bank of Ravenswood, as Trustee for Steve Spanos, the original seller, and Commercial National Bank of Chicago, as Trustee for Peter Tselepatiotis, the subsequent purchaser, for specific performance of an alleged contract dated May 8, 1986 for the sale of a commercial building. Plaintiff asserted that the alleged contract between plaintiff and Spanos for the sale of the building for $230,000 was valid. At the time of trial, the property was held in trust for the subsequent purchaser, Tselepatiotis, who paid $232,500 for the property on October 16, 1986. Tselepatiotis subsequently purchased the restaurant business located in the building from the current lessee in July, 1987. Only defendant Tselepatiotis is involved in this appeal.

At the conclusion of plaintiff's case in a trial without a jury, the court held that the agreement of May 8 was valid, and awarded specific performance to plaintiff. After an evidentiary hearing, the court ordered plaintiff to pay Tselepatiotis the contract price of $230,000, and an additional $22,000 for improvements Tselepatiotis made to the restaurant. The court also ordered Spanos to pay Tselepatiotis $2,500, thereby returning to him the entire purchase price paid for the property. Additionally, the court found that Tselepatiotis held only a month-to-month tenancy in the restaurant premises.

On appeal, Tselepatiotis maintains that the court erred in awarding specific performance to plaintiff because the agreement of May 8 did not constitute a binding contract; and that it violated the Statute of Frauds. Alternatively, Tselepatiotis contends that if the contract was valid, plaintiff abandoned it when he later submitted another contract on May 29 containing substantial changes from the May 8 offer. Finally, Tselepatiotis argues that the trial court erroneously concluded that he held only a month-to-month tenancy in the restaurant premises.

The following facts were brought out at trial. Spanos owned the building located at 3928-32 N. Broadway in Chicago, and was three years behind in property tax payments. Spanos listed the property for sale with a real estate broker, William Vranas. In March 1985, plaintiff submitted an offer to buy the property for $225,000, and tendered an earnest money check for $1,000. Spanos rejected the offer, and did not accept the check. (That offer is not an issue here.)

Vranas presented Spanos with a written offer from plaintiff to purchase the property for $230,000. An earnest money check in the amount of $1,000 from the initial offer dated March 22, 1985, was submitted with the offer.

Spanos testified that when he received the offer of May 13, 1986, he drew a line through the $230,000 figure, raised the price to $235,000, initialed the price change, and signed the offer at the bottom. Later that day, Vranas informed Spanos that plaintiff would not accept the offer at $235,000.

The parties stipulated at trial that Spanos orally agreed with Vranas during a telephone conversation that he would reduce the price to the original $230,000. Plaintiff later drew a line through the $235,000 figure which Spanos had inserted in the offer, reduced the price to $230,000, and initialed the change. Spanos never initialed the document after Plaintiff changed the written price to $230,000.

On May 20, plaintiff asked his attorney, Garry Barker, to review the alleged contract. Vranas testified that he met with plaintiff and Barker on May 21, intending to pick up a new check from plaintiff for $1,000 as earnest money, thereby replacing the previous outdated check of March 22, 1985. According to Vranas, Barker stated at the meeting that the May 8 contract should be "ripped up" because it was not acceptable to plaintiff for several reasons, and that he wanted plaintiff's outdated earnest money check returned. Barker wanted to draft another contract that would meet plaintiff's objections by including mortgage and inspection contingencies, as well as certain seller's warranties.

Vranas spoke with Spanos following the meeting with plaintiff and Barker on May 21, and explained that they wanted to rip up the contract, prepare another, and that they had taken back the earnest money. Spanos indicated that he still wanted to sell the property because he was behind in his taxes, and requested Vranas to try to find another buyer.

Vranas testified further that he met with Barker and plaintiff on May 29, at which time they presented him with a new offer setting forth the proposed changes and tendered a check for $1,000. This new real estate contract drawn by Barker provided for a reduction in earnest money, mortgage and inspection contingencies, and seller's representations regarding the heating, cooling, lighting and plumbing fixtures and systems in the building. There is no reference in the new contract to the previous May 8 offer.

Spanos rejected the offer of May 29. Vranas next contacted Spanos in the middle of June, indicating that he had several offers for the property. On June 10, 1986, Spanos accepted an offer to sell the subject property to Tselepatiotis for $232,500, and closed that sale on October 6, 1986.

After plaintiff learned from Vranas that the property had been sold to Tselepatiotis, he filed this suit for specific performance of the May 8 contract. In addition, plaintiff filed a *lis pendens* covering the subject property. Spanos filed a counterclaim for damages against plaintiff and Barker which the trial court dismissed. That dismissal is not at issue in this appeal.

The trial court found that there was a meeting of the minds between the plaintiff and Spanos, and that the May 8 contract was valid. Specifically, the judge held that on May 13 when Spanos struck the original price of $230,000, raised the price to $235,000 and subsequently acquiesced to the original amount of $230,000, it had no impact on the moment in time when the parties entered into the alleged contract.

We disagree with the trial court's finding that the May 8 contract was valid, and that the subsequent negotiations between plaintiff and Spanos concerning the price were of no consequence.

An acceptance requiring any modification or change of terms constitutes a rejection of the original offer and becomes a counteroffer that must be accepted by the original offeror before a valid contract is formed. (*Ebert v. Dr. Scholl's Foot Comfort Shops* (1985), 137 Ill.All. 3d 550, 558, 92 Ill. Dec. 323, 484 N.E.2d 1178, citing *Loeb v. Gray,* 131 Ill.App.3d 793, 799, 86 Ill.Dec. 775, 475 N.E.2d 1342.) In the present case, plaintiff's original May 8 offer of $230,000 was rejected by Spanos when he drew a line through the $230,000 figure, increased the price to $235,000, initialed the price change and signed the offer at the bottom. This created not an acceptance, but a counteroffer. Spanos' oral acquiescence to the previously offered price constitutes an acceptance of a rejected offer. A rejected offer cannot be revived by later acceptance. (*Ebert v. Dr. Scholl's; Johnson v. Whitney Metal Tool Co.* (1950), 342 Ill.App. 258, 96 N.E.2d 372.) On that basis alone, we find that the trial court erred in awarding specific performance to plaintiff.

We also believe that the action is barred by the Statute of Frauds. Ill.Rev.Stat.1985, ch.59, par.2, Section 2 of that statute provides in relevant part:

> "No action shall be brought to charge any person upon any contract for the sale of lands * * * unless such contract or some note or memorandum thereof shall be in writing, and signed by the party to be charged therewith, or some other person thereunto by him lawfully authorized in writing, signed by such party."

Further, to be specifically enforceable, a contract for the sale of land must contain in writing the essential contract terms such as the names of the vendor and vendee, the price, and the terms and conditions of the sale. *Chicago*

Investment Corp. v. Dolins (1981), 93 Ill.App.3d 971, 49 Ill.Dec. 415, 418 N.E.2d 59.

Although the parties stipulated at trial that Spanos orally agreed with Vranas during a telephone conversation that he would reduce the price to the original $230,000, Spanos never initialed the document after plaintiff changed the written price to $230,000. Thus, the alleged contract fails to comply with the Statute of Frauds because one of the essential terms of the contract, the price, was never reduced to writing and signed by Spanos, the party to be charged.

We also note that this court has consistently held that specific performance may be granted only where there is a valid and enforceable contract. (*Perkins v. Garcia* (1990) 194 Ill.App.3d 590, 141 Ill. Dec. 265, 551 N.E.2d 258, citing *Chicago Investment Corp. v. Dolins.*) In addition, where a party seeks specific performance of a contract, the law requires a greater degree of specificity than is demanded for other purposes. Where the court would be left to order further negotiations and where the parties have yet to reach agreement on essential terms, specific performance is not available. *Cinman v. Reliance Fed. S. & L. Ass'n* (1987) 155 Ill.App.3d 417, 108 Ill. Dec. 78, 508 N.E.2d 239.

We conclude that a valid contract was not established. Accordingly, plaintiff is not entitled to specific performance. Having so concluded, we need not reach the issue raised by Tselepatiotis as to whether plaintiff's later actions in submitting another contract on May 29 constituted an abandonment of the previously submitted offer. The issue of Tselepatiotis' month-to-month tenancy in the restaurant premises also need not be reached, as he is now the owner of the entire building.

For the foregoing reasons, the judgment of the circuit court of Cook County granting specific performance to plaintiff and ordering Spanos to pay Tselepatiotis $2,500 is reversed.

Judgment reversed.

EGAN and RAKOWSKI,JJ., concur.

Questions and Comments

1. What are the facts in the case?
2. What are the questions of law?
3. What is the reasoning of the court?
4. Could a fitness center have a restaurant or snack bar?
5. Was a valid contract established in this case?
6. The remedy sought in this case was specific performance. How did the validity of the contract affect specific performance?
7. Was a written contract needed in this case? If so, why?

Failure to read a contract. In the case that follows, a racetrack spectator was injured. The spectator had signed a release.

In the following appellate court case, there are several issues based on a release that Dale Huber signed. The district court granted summary judgment to the defendants, the driver of the car, the lessee of the track, the fair board, the owner of the property, and the K & K insurance group responsible for the inspection of the wheel fence. Dale and Karen Huber appealed the lower court's decision.

The issues are as follows. First of all, is a contract invalid if the person has signed but has not read the contract?

Second, does Dale's release bar wife Karen's claim of lack of consortium (companionship)? Just because he signed a release, does it keep her from having a claim?

Third, does K & K insurance group have a duty of care, related to their inspection of the safety of the fencing?

Read the case and see if the appellate court reversed the lower court on issues one and two. The K & K insurance issue has been deleted from the case in order to shorten the case.

....

HUBER v. HOVEY
501 N.W. 2d 53 (Iowa, 1993)

NEUMAN, Justice.

This case stems from an accident at the Winneshiek County Fairground racetrack, when a car's detached wheel struck and injured plaintiff Dale Huber. The district court granted all defendants summary judgment based on a release Dale signed. We affirm in part, reverse in part, and remand for further proceedings.

The record viewed in the light most favorable to the Hubers reveals the following facts. On September 2, 1989, Dale went to the racetrack to watch a friend race. He had been to races before, though not at this track. Dale saw that spectators were going to the grandstand, instead of the pit area, but he followed his friend to the pit area anyway. He paid the $10 admission fee, and was told to add his signature to a printed form. The form, captioned "Release and Waiver of Liability and Indemnity Agreement," provided:

IN CONSIDERATION of being permitted to enter for any purpose any RESTRICTED AREA ... including ... pit areas ... EACH OF THE UNDERSIGNED ....

1. hereby releases, waives, discharges and covenants not to sue the promoter, participants ... track operator, track owner, officials, car owners, drivers, pit crews, any persons in any restricted area ... owners and lessees of premises used to conduct the event ... for the purposes herein referred to as "releasees", from all liability to the undersigned, his personal representatives, assigns, heirs, and next of kin for any and all loss or damage, and any claim or demands therefor on account of injury ... whether caused by the negligence of the releasees or otherwise while the undersigned is in or upon the restricted area....

EACH OF THE UNDERSIGNED expressly acknowledges and agrees that the activities of the event are very dangerous and involve the risk of serious injury....

THE UNDERSIGNED HAS READ AND VOLUNTARILY SIGNS
THE RELEASE AND WAIVER OF LIABILITY....

The words "I have read this release" were printed in red above each signature line.

Feeling pressured to keep the line behind him moving, Dale signed the form without reading it, and entered the pit area. He was standing about ten feet behind a protective "wheel fence," watching the race, when one of the cars lost a wheel and axle. The wheel tore through the fence, striking and injuring him. Dale sued for damages, and his wife Karen sued for loss of consortium.

The Hubers claimed several parties were negligent: Dennis Hovey, the car's driver; Nordic Speedway, Inc. (Nordic), the lessee of the track; and the Winneshiek County Fair Board and the Winneshiek County Agricultural Association, owner and operator of the racetrack property. The Hubers also claimed the track's insurance broker, K & K Insurance Group (K & K), was liable for negligent inspection of the wheel fence. The defendants jointly moved for summary judgment based on Dale's release. K & K also moved for summary judgment on the ground its inspection created no duty to the Hubers.

The district court granted summary judgment for all defendants, ruling that Dale's release barred both his claim for damages and Karen's claim for loss of consortium. The court declined to rule on whether K & K was entitled to summary judgment based on its affirmative defense that no duty flowed from its inspection.

The Hubers appeal, arguing preliminarily that racetracks have a nondelegable duty to insure their patrons' safety, and that the release Dale signed is ambiguous. They also contend on appeal that the release cannot bar (1) claims by spectators, (2) Karen's consortium claim, and (3) claims against K & K. K & K cross-appeals, asserting that even if the release is no bar to the Hubers' claims, it owes no duty to the Hubers as a matter of law.

I.   Our review is for correction of errors at law. Iowa R.App.P. 4. When reviewing a grant of summary judgment we ask whether the moving party has demonstrated the absence of any genuine issue of material fact and is entitled to judgment as a matter of law. *Suss v. Schammel,* 375 N.W.2d 252, 254 (Iowa 1985). The resisting party must set forth specific facts showing that a genuine factual issue exists. *Id.* Summary judgment is proper if the only issue is the legal consequences flowing from undisputed facts. *Sankey v. Richenberger,* 456 N.W. 2d 206, 207 (Iowa 1990).

II.   Dale asserts that racetracks have a nondelegable duty to ensure their patrons' safety, and that any attempt to insulate themselves from liability violates public policy. We find no merit in this argument. Although track owners and operators have a duty to provide safe premises, see *Gibson v. Shelby County Fair Ass'n,* 241 Iowa 1349, 1352, 44 N.W.2d 362, 364 (1950), we have repeatedly held that contracts exempting a party from its own negligence are enforceable, and are not contrary to public policy. See, e.g., *Bashford v. Slater,* 250 Iowa 857, 865, 96 N.W.2d 904, 909 (1959) (injured racetrack flagman's release enforceable).

Dale also seeks to avoid the effect of the release on the ground he did not read it. It is well settled that failure to read a contract before signing it will not invalidate the contract. *Small v. Ogden,* 259 Iowa 1126, 1132, 147 N.W.2d 18, 22 (1966). Absent fraud or mistake, ignorance of a written contract's contents will not negate its effect. *Id.,* 147 N.W.2d at 22.

III.   The release Dale signed is a contract, and its enforcement is governed by principles of contract law. *Stetzel v. Dickenson,* 174 N.W.2d 438, 439 (Iowa 1970). Construing a contract--determining its legal effect--is a matter of law to be resolved by the court. *Farm Bureau Mut. Ins. Co. v. Sandbulte,* 302 N.W.2d 104, 107 (Iowa 1981).

When construing contracts, courts are guided by the cardinal principle that the parties' intent controls, and except in cases of ambiguity, that intent is determined by what the contract itself says. Iowa R.App.P. 14 (f)(14).

Dale asserts the release is ambiguous. He claims it is unclear whether the parties intended to release claims by spectators, or just participants, and whether the parties contemplated the specific accident that occurred. By its terms, however, the release applies to anyone who, like Dale, enters a restricted area. It makes no distinction between spectators and participants. It clearly identifies the track's owner, operator, and lessee, as well as race participants, as releasees. The release covers personal injuries, including injury caused by the releasee's own negligence.

The court of appeals has upheld a similar release against the same attack. See *Korsmo v. Waverly Ski Club,* 435 N.W.2d 746, 747-49 (Iowa App. 1988) (release not ambiguous as to the types of injuries the parties intended to include). The district court correctly held the release is not ambiguous as to the particulars claimed by Dale.

IV.   Dale next asserts the release is unenforceable against spectators as a matter of law. He argues releases are only valid when signed by a party knowledgeable and informed about the risks. While conceding that participants are presumed knowledgeable, and do not have a reasonable expectation of safety, he argues that spectators are unaware of the risks of pit areas, and cannot sign away their reasonable expectations without being informed of such risks.

We disagree. We believe there is no valid legal distinction between a release signed by a spectator permitted entry into a restricted area, and a release signed by a participant. Courts throughout the country have upheld such releases. *[Examples are] Valley Nat'l Bank v. National Ass'n for Stock Car Auto Racing, Inc.,* 153 Ariz. 374, 378, 736 P.2d 1186, 1190 (1987) (spectators who signed release estopped from arguing release not meant to cover spectators, or that no meeting of minds occurred); *Barker v. Colorado Region-Sports Car Club of Am.,* Inc., 35 Colo.App. 73, 532 P.2d 372, 376 (1974) (spectator's release bars recovery for ordinary negligence); *Rudolph v. Santa Fe Park Enters., Inc.,* 122 Ill.App. 3d 372, 374-75, 78 Ill. Dec. 38, 40, 461 N.E.2d 622, 624 (1984) (spectator injured when car drove off track; court enforced release, noting plaintiff's knowledge of risk only relevant if fraud in contract's execution is alleged); *Lee v. Allied*

Sports Assocs., Inc., 349 Mass. 544, 550, 209 N.E.2d 329, 332 (1965) (spectator who failed to read contract and who did not claim fraud was bound by release); *Church v. Seneca County Agric. Soc'y,* 41 A.D.2d 787, 788 341 N.Y.S.2d 45, 47 (1973), *aff'd,* 34 N.Y.S.2d 571, 310 N.E.2d 541, 354 N.Y.S.2d 945 (1974) (spectator who signed release in order to enter racetrack's infield, where he was injured by an out-of-control car, cannot complain about release's effect).

Courts that have refused to enforce spectator releases rest their decision on the notion that some accidents are so unusual that a fact question is raised as to whether the plaintiff was aware of the risk. . . . .

Dale has not come forward with any proof that the risk he faced was unusual. To the contrary, the record contains evidence that several detached wheels had hit the fence in the past, although none had gone through. Absent any proof the risk was unusual or exceptional, Dale must be bound by his release.

We therefore hold the district court was correct in refusing to recognize a distinction between spectator releases and participant releases, and in granting summary judgment to Hovey, Nordic, and the fairground board and agricultural association on Dale's claims.

V.   Next, we consider whether Dale's release also bars Karen's consortium claim. . . . .

> [Loss of consortium] is comprised of [the deprived spouse's] own physical, psychological and emotional pain and anguish which results when her husband is negligently injured to the extent that he is no longer capable of providing the love, affection, companionship, comfort or sexual relations concomitant with a normal married life.... From the vantage point of the negligent defendant, [the deprived spouse] is simply a foreseeable plaintiff to whom he owes a separate duty of care.

Fuller v. Buhrow, 292 N.W.2d 672, 675 (Iowa 1980) (quoting *Lantis v. Condon,* 95 Cal.App.3d 152, 157, 157 Cal.Rptr. 22, 24 (1979)).

In *Fuller* we held that under principles of contributory fault, an injured spouse's negligence does not bar a consortium claim brought by the deprived spouse. . . . .

These same principles of autonomy apply to releases signed by only one spouse. One spouse's signature on a release is not imputed to the other spouse any more than is one spouse's negligent act. [Citation omitted.] [one spouse's release cannot bar the other, unless the other spouse also signs it]; . . . .

. . . . .

. . . . Thus, a separate tort is committed when an actor's conduct deprives a spouse of the right to consortium. We therefore reverse the district court's grant of summary judgment to all defendants on Karen's claim....

. . . . .

VIII.   *Disposition.* We affirm the district court's grant of summary judgment in favor of Hovey, Nordic, and the fairgrounds board and agricultural association on Dale's claim, but reverse summary judgment for these defendants on Karen's consortium claim. On Hubers' claim against K & K, we reverse the court's entry of summary judgment and remand for further proceedings.

AFFIRMED IN PART, REVERSED IN PART, AND REMANDED. (p. 59)

Questions and Comments

1. Is a release a contract?
2. Does a failure to read a contract invalidate it?
3. If one spouse signs a release, is it also a release for the other spouse?
4. Releases and waivers will be discussed in greater depth in the section on negligence.

SUMMARY

In order to be valid and enforceable, a contract should contain the following elements: competent parties, agreement (offer and acceptance), and consideration with legal subject matter. A contract should be in a form prescribed by law. The consent must be real. A sport manager can check the contract for these elements.

Remedies for a breach of contract may be equitable or at common law. Equity remedies include specific performance, rescission, and reformation. Common-law remedies involve damages. The damages may be nominal; they may compensate the party for the loss of a bargain, or they may punish. A sport manager should be aware of these remedies both as a plaintiff and a defendant.

A contract, like any other document, is subject to rules of interpretation. The primary thrust is to find the intent of the parties. When the intent is not clear, the canons of construction are applicable. Sport managers should read contracts for clarity and intent.

Historically, only a party to a contract could recover for its breach. However, in some cases a third party may be permitted to sue on a contract, for example, donee or creditor beneficiaries. A traditional contract is transferred by way of an assignment.

Form contracts are usually drafted to protect a particular individual or group of individuals. Sport managers may be asked to sign form contracts in various areas, for example, contracts with concessionaires or officials.

There are advantages to reducing a contract to writing even though some contracts do not have to be in writing in order to be enforceable. Time spent in the preparation of a contract is usually a wise investment. At this point parties are agreeable and are not immediately threatened with adverse consequences.

This could be you - check your response

It would be wise for John and Maria to have their attorney read the contract before signing the document. They want a clear title to the property. The next chapter discusses this concept.

Maria could protect her interest by becoming a co-owner of the property. As a co-owner she would sign any contracts. The age of majority is 18 in most states. An infant child cannot sign a legal document.

REFERENCES

Authors

Corbin, A. L.. (1993). *Corbin on contracts* (1 Vol. Ed.1952, (Revised 1993 Joseph M. Perillo). St. Paul, MN: West Publishing Co.

Williston, Samuel (1995). *Williston on contracts* (6 Vol. Ed. 1920, (Revised 1995 Richard A. Lord). Rochester, NY: Lawyers Cooperative Publishing.

Cases

D'Agostino v. Bank of Ravenswood, 563 N.E.2d 866 (Ill. App. 1 Dist. 1990).

Detroit Football Company v. Robinson, 186 F. Supp. 933 (1960).

Holmes v. Health and Fitness Corp. of America, 659 N.E.2d 812 (Oh.App. 1995).

Huber v. Hovey, 501 N.W.2d 53 (Iowa, 1993).

Las Vegas Hacienda Inc. v. Gibson, 359 P. 2d 85 (Nev. 1961).

Monson v. State, 901 P.2d 904 (Or.App. 1995).

Prince William Professional Baseball Club v. Boulton, 882 F.Supp. 1446 (D.Del. 1995).

Roskowske v. Iron Mountain Forge Corp., 897 S.W.2d 67 (Mo.App.E.D. 1995).

Thompson v. Peninsula Sch. Dist. No. 401, 892 P.2d 760 (App.Ct.Wash. 1995).

Woods v. Morgan City Lions Club, 588 So.2d 1196 (La. Ct. App. 1991).

Legal Encyclopedias

17A Am. Jur. 2d *Contracts* §§ 1-748 (1991) with current updates.

17 C.J.S. *Contracts* §§ 1-293 (1963), with current updates.

17A C.J.S. *Contracts* §§ 294-644 (1963) with current updates.

Model Codes, Restatements and Standards

Kentucky Revised Statutes Annotated, §436.160.

Uniform Commercial Code (U.L.A.) §2-205.

CHAPTER 3

DEEDS AND LEASEHOLDS

INTRODUCTION

Anyone contemplating starting a sport business or organization is well-advised to select professional assistance. These advisors will include a banker, a real estate agent, an accountant, and an attorney. Each of these advisors will play a part in the acquisition of real property. The purpose of this discussion is to explore some of the more basic steps that will need to be taken toward purchasing or leasing property for a sport business.

THE PROBLEM IS NOT SIMPLE

IN THIS CHAPTER YOU WILL LEARN:
Professional agents who can offer assistance
The various types of deeds
The meaning of terms such as grantor, grantee, granting clause, consideration, easements, source of title, notary public
The relationship between real property law and the statute of frauds
Items that a landlord would normally expect to have in a lease
Items that a tenant would normally expect to have in a lease
The purpose in obtaining a title examination to real property

---

KEY WORDS: *Deed, real estate, personal property, general warranty deed, special warranty deed, quitclaim deed, grantor, grantee, source of title, notary public, abstract, title examination, lease, consideration, lien*

This could be you!

Upon inquiry, the Joneses learn that the owner of the real estate, "Speedy" Smith, is proposing to give them a special warranty deed. Additionally, Mr. Smith demands cash when the property is transferred. The Joneses have no property, and they are limited to the $30,000 inheritance previously mentioned. Further, the Joneses have been advised that a previous owner of the property had been married for a short time to a woman his family strongly disliked. Although the couple had one child, family members never discussed the matter, and the child had not been heard from in many years. What problems are presented? (Hint: Would a child that a family does not recognize as an heir actually be an owner of the Smith property that the Joneses are considering purchasing? Could this possible ownership cloud the title to the property the Joneses are considering purchasing?)

ACQUIRING LAND
Real Estate Agent

Assuming a preliminary decision is made to acquire real property (land), certain steps will follow almost automatically. Generally speaking, services of a real estate agent will be necessary or at least helpful. It is always possible to deal with a seller directly, but one cannot count on being able to dispense with an agent's services. A real estate agent is trained to perform a service in bringing a buyer and seller together. Assuming the services of the real estate agent are obtained, one will need to be prepared to give certain information such as location, price range, zoning requirements, and ability to make satisfactory financial arrangements.

A potential buyer or seller of real estate who enlists the aid of a real estate agent will be expected to sign a listing contract. The listing contract can probably be referred to as a form contract. This means two things: First, it was prepared by the real estate agent or the real estate agent's principal association; and second, the listing contract will go to great lengths to protect the commission of the real estate agent. This is only fair. Many times potential buyers will decide to purchase property but defer closing the deal until the expiration of the listing contract because they think they will save the realtor's commission. Such a ploy will be unsuccessful in a majority of the cases. If the realtor has shown the property, the contract will generally provide that the commission is to be paid. This means that the question of intent to purchase is no longer the guiding principle, but the obligation is triggered by the fact that the realtor has shown this particular piece of property to this potential buyer. The wording will vary, but the intent is clear. The realtor will not be prevented from collecting a commission.

Many times a purchase contract will be entered into as between the buyer and the seller. When this happens, close attention should be paid to such things as the description of the land to be purchased, the purchase price, the type of deed to be used in the conveyance, and the requirement for good and merchantable title. Questions that will need to be answered include the following: Who pays for the title examination? Who pays for any corrective work that may be necessary if good title is to be conveyed? Under what circumstances can the contract be terminated? What happens in the event of fire or casualty loss? These and many other items are important in the land contract.

Governmental Agencies

A beginning sport business would need to check with state and local authorities about appropriate licenses and permits. Local agencies are especially important in providing assistance, either by having the necessary information or by directing the sport manager to the proper authority.

For example, the fire marshal will be in a position to provide assistance with that office's regulations. The local health department can advise as to any problems that fall under its jurisdiction. Other concerns might relate to employee health screenings, food service issues, sewers, safe drinking water, or swimming pool regulations and inspections. City engineers could offer suggestions as to who should be contacted at the state and federal levels. For example, there may be OSHA (Occupational Safety and Health Act) regulations that govern employee safety and patron safety. There may be EPA (Environmental Protection Agency) regulations concerning the handling and the containing of hazardous chemicals such as chlorine for swimming pools.

Finally , the city clerk should be able to advise about any business license, occupational license, or zoning requirements. Often, a sport business is confronted with special problems that have resulted in regulations. The regulation in question may be designed to protect the individuals who patronize the establishment. In some states, a fitness center cannot arbitrarily close or move and leave the customer without certain services for which they have paid (e.g., Kentucky Revised Statutes 367.900). Again, local agencies are especially important in providing assistance.

Case Example

In the case of *City of Ladue v. Zwick* (1995), the City of Ladue required the removal of a tennis court. The land owners did not have a building permit.

Furthermore, the tennis court violated Ladue's zoning requirement of a 50-foot setback.

Question: How could a sport entrepreneur avoid the kind of problems noted in this case?

Deeds

In general. When property is found that meets the buyer's requirements, arrangements are made for the title to be transferred. The instrument whereby the title is transferred is known as a deed. Deeds are classified in various ways. A *general warranty deed* is one in which the seller warrants the title against everyone. A *special warranty deed* is one in which the seller warrants that neither the seller nor the seller's heirs will disturb the buyer in possession of the land. Buyers are often misled into thinking that a special warranty deed has unusual features that inure to the buyer's benefit. This conclusion is inaccurate. A special warranty deed is not as desirable as a general warranty deed. Many times a corporate owner will transfer by special warranty deed as an abundance of precaution. Such cases require the opinion of someone trained in the examination of title to real estate in order to properly assess the quality of the title obtained.

Another type of deed is known as a *quitclaim deed*. This deed does not warrant anything. It merely says that whatever title the grantor has will be conveyed to the grantee or buyer. Frequently, quitclaim deeds are used to correct deficiencies in a title. Thus, although the quitclaim deed has its purpose, it is not the best instrument to pass title.

Finally, there is a deed known as a *commissioner's deed*. This deed is normally used when land has been litigated for one reason or another and the court directs the master commissioner, or special commissioner as the case may be, to transfer title to the buyer.

Parties. The reader will note the use of the terms *buyer* and *seller* as well as *grantor* and *grantee*. For purposes of clarification, the grantor is the seller and the grantee is the buyer. It would also be possible to use the words *transferor* and *transferee* or *vendor* and *vendee*. However, the latter classifications are used more frequently in the transfer of personal property.

Standard provisions. Deeds generally have certain distinct parts. The parts and a brief explanation are listed below.

1. Grantor and Grantee—as previously indicated, these are the buyer and seller. The spelling of the names of these parties should remain consistent throughout the instrument.

2. The words that effectuate the transfer are known as the granting clause. The grantor bargains, sells, and conveys. This is the operative language.

3. Consideration—this is the statement as to what is being paid for the property. Assuming that the purchase is not entirely for cash, then a statement as to the unpaid balance, together with due dates on the evidence of indebtedness, should be included. Such a statement will assist the clerk in the county recorder's office in determining the amount of tax that must be paid in order to effectuate the transfer.

4. In the event that the deed shows an unpaid balance, such will be secured by a vendor's lien. The vendor's lien is the same as a real estate mortgage. When the indebtedness is paid, the clerk, for a small fee, will release the lien.

5. The property will need to be described. Surveyors are frequently employed when a deed is initially drafted. This ensures adequacy of a legal description that is made with definite geographic coordinates and that can be located with reference to such things as plats or township and ranges.

6. The marital status of the grantors should be shown. Assuming that a grantor is married, his or her spouse will need to sign giving up rights as a spouse. These rights are known as *homestead, dower,* or *curtesy.*

7. Sometimes specific reservations are contained in a deed, for example, a right-of-way for the benefit of the seller. Should the land be subject to easements for utility lines, these may be shown in the deed. Restrictions on types of businesses may also be shown. On the other hand, these types of easements and restrictions may be found in separate documents found of record in the recorder's office.

8. Such items as party walls or mutual access to parking space will need to be referenced in the deed.

9. Sources of title—the deed should reference the immediate source of title. In the event the land was inherited, the deed will show either the will or the affidavit of descent (testate or intestate succession) plus the instrument whereby the deceased obtained title.

10. The sellers will sign the deed. The signatures should be the same as shown in the body of the instrument.

11. The signatures will need to be acknowledged before a notary public or witnessed. Notaries are easy to locate—witnesses are seldom used. A notary public is a public officer used primarily to authenticate signatures.

12. When a deed has been properly executed and delivered to the buyer, the buyer should have the instrument recorded. This involves taking the deed to the appropriate court office and paying the appropriate fees. Such a step prevents the trouble and inconvenience arising out of a lost, destroyed, or misplaced deed.

13. Many states now require that an instrument must show a preparation statement in order for that instrument to be recorded. The purpose of such a provision is to prevent the unauthorized practice of law.

Title examination. Before deeds are prepared, it is becoming quite common to have the title to the property checked. In addition to law firms, banks and abstract companies are businesses that can aid the sport manager in checking a title. Checking a title is far more complicated than writing a deed. Perhaps the most tedious part of this work is to trace the land back for the required number of years and determine if any of the land noted in the deed has been sold away (conveyed). If this has happened, the off conveyance will be noted, and appropriate adjustments can be made in the instrument of conveyance. Liens on the property, such as real estate mortgages, will need to be checked for the requisite number of years. If a real estate mortgage has been given on the property, this will need to be released simultaneously with the transfer of title. In short, the buyer will normally want to obtain title free and clear of the real estate lien. This may mean that an attorney checks 500 deeds to get a clear title for a sport property. Occasionally, the buyer will assume an existing lien, which means the buyer will simply pick up the payments.

Other liens that will be checked as a part of the title examination include mechanic's liens and tax liens. Some states recognize a general category known as encumbrances on real estate. Further, a state may have a set of books simply called miscellaneous, which could create some sort of lien.

In addition to the liens and off-conveyances, the title will need to be checked to determine if there are outstanding leases or options. Such instruments, if extant, will, of course, affect the title. Lawsuits that will serve as notice that the title to the real estate is affected will also need to be examined. The set of books in which such instruments are indexed is known as *lis pendens*.

The above description of a title examination is an abbreviated one. Lending institutions customarily require a title to be examined. Such institutions will vary as to the strictness of the examination required. The Federal Land Bank, for example, has historically been noted for the rigor of its examination. The Farmers' Home Administration and the Veterans' Administration, together with conventional banking institutions, also have requirements designed to ensure a good title, thus protecting the lending institution as well as the buyer. The buyer should make certain that the title opinion/title insurance protects him or her as well as the lender.

Insurance and deeds. Land law is highly technical. Each piece of land is said to be unique. A buyer will be well-advised to have his or her own attorney in matters of this type. Lending institutions will probably demand title insurance. Such a policy will protect the lending institution in the event of a defective title. Additionally, it is sometimes recommended that the buyer purchase term life insurance that can be used to pay the unpaid balance of a loan in the event the buyer dies and his or her estate is confronted with the necessity of completing payment. Insurance also may be obtained to enable one co-owner to buy out the other. Such a policy will enable a business to continue uninterrupted even though one of the owners is no longer available to assist in the operation of the business.

Leases

A lease represents an interest in real estate. A lease results in a landlord and tenant relationship. Frequently, a lease arrangement will be sufficient to get a business started. Care should be taken, however, to make certain that anyone having an interest in the property should sign the lease, either in person or through an authorized agent. In the event an agent signs, the power of attorney authorizing such a signature should be recorded. The record of the power of attorney will validate the lease insofar as a chain of title is concerned.

Contents of the lease. A lease arrangement should show the parties to the lease, the term of the lease, and the property that is subject to the lease arrangement. Additionally, a lease will set forth the rental payment both as to the amount and what happens in the event of default. Most leases will contain a provision that prohibits criminal activity. Leases will also make provision for the possible alteration of the premises. Usually a tenant can alter premises provided the alteration does not affect the structural soundness of the building. At the conclusion of the lease, the tenant may very well be obligated to restore the building to its original condition, reasonable wear and tear excepted.

Some decisions will need to be made as to the following contingencies: First, what happens in the event of fire? Second, what happens in the event the title appears to be defective? Third, what happens in the event someone is injured on the premises? Fourth, is there a duty to make repairs? If so, who pays for them? Usually tenants will be obligated to make minor repairs such as changing light bulbs, but major repairs will be the responsibility of the landlord, absent negligence on the part of the tenant that occasioned the necessity of repair.

Frequently, a lease will contain provisions for its extension or amendment and may even contain an option to buy, with rental payments being counted toward the purchase price. Real estate taxes will remain, in most instances, the responsibility of the owner with taxes on personal items in the building being the responsibility of the tenant. All in all, the drafting of a lease is perhaps more difficult than the preparation of a deed.

A tenant will wish to obtain a clause giving the right to sublease. Such a provision enables a tenant to be relieved from obligations by substituting another tenant. Landlords, as a general rule, will only grant such a right if there are appropriate limitations. A landlord may be agreeable to giving the right to sublease subject to the landlord's approval. The significance of this limitation is that it permits a landlord to pass judgment on a new tenant. The rentals could be protected by a provision that compels the original tenant to act as a surety in the event of nonpayment. However, the assurance of rental payment does not protect a landlord against the aggravation occasioned by a troublesome tenant. A tenant can provide a subtenant, but it must be someone acceptable to the landlord.

A lease should also contain a statement as to the intended use of the property. This is especially important to an owner who is seeking to prevent unnecessary competition between his tenants. It is to the landlord's interest that a tenant operate a profitable business. Consequently, it is helpful if the businesses complement each other as opposed to being competitive efforts. Aside from the reason stated herein, a landlord may simply not wish to own property that is being put to use in a particular manner. A usage that annoys one's neighbors or detracts from the appearance of the immediate surroundings should be under the landlord's control.

A landlord will also wish to have the right of inspection. Such a right should be exercised in a careful and prudent manner. This means that the inspection should be reasonable as to time and extent. A landlord who gives the impression of being nosey, as opposed to someone who is seeking to be helpful, can create a bad impression. It should be remembered that a lease is an interest in land. Therefore, certain leases must be in writing if they are to be enforced.

Practical suggestions. As a practical matter, each party should have a signed copy of the lease. Some attorneys recommend that their clients keep legal papers in a secure place such as a safe deposit box. Extra photocopies of the document are retained at home. These latter copies can be examined at a time when it would be inconvenient or impossible to gain access to the safe deposit box.

Clients are cautioned to give adequate time for the instruments to be prepared. Many times one forgets that the attorney has other work that is being carried out. This means that the work for a particular client does not continue on constantly but probably is interspersed with additional work. In any event, preparing an instrument is a task that should not be hastened.

The owner who is renting a facility may want to have the tenant promise to indemnify the landlord in case of a lawsuit. Furthermore, the owner may also want a statement in the contract that the renter will purchase liability insurance.

A precaution that most landlords will need to observe has to do with dealing with a tenant that is incorporated. A corporation may be represented by an influential citizen. However, in the event of nonpayment of rentals, it is to the corporation that the landlord will be compelled to look for his rental payments. If the corporation has no funds, it matters not that the individual with whom the landlord has dealt has assets. It is a wise move for the landlord to insist that the shareholder agree to assume individual liability along with the corporation.

Assuming that the location and physical facilities, including parking, are accompanied by a fair rental, the option to renew or extend becomes increasingly important. This right, together with a right to purchase, can ensure the business venture retaining a degree of continuity that may be essential to survival.

SUMMARY

The entrepreneur who is entering the sport management field will need to obtain a location. Assurance of a location can be in the form of a deed or a lease. The purely legal considerations include attention to such matters as title examination and type of deed. If the business is depending upon a leasehold arrangement, a fair rental, security of location (term of the lease), and rights of renewal are important.

This could be you - check your response

Smith is proposing a special warranty deed. A special warranty deed will protect the buyer from the seller or the seller's heirs. This is *not* as desirable as a general warranty deed, which protects the seller against *all* heirs. The Joneses should ask for a general warranty deed.

If the Joneses elect to borrow from a lending institution, they will be better served if a general warranty deed is provided. A lending institution will require a title examination. This title examination will protect the institution and the buyer. If someone other than the seller claims an interest in the property, the Joneses should demand that any cloud on the title be removed prior to the purchase of the property. (The cloud in the story is the child that the family did not recognize. The child would inherit a portion of the property.)

REFERENCES

Authors

Basye, Paul E. (1970). *Clearing land titles* (2nd ed). St. Paul, Minn: West Publishing Company.

Case

City of Ladue v. Zwick, S.W.2d 470 (Mo.App.E.D. 1995).

Hopkinsville-Christian v. Christian Bd. of Ed., 903 S.W.2d 531 (Ky.App. 1995).

Legal Encyclopedias

23 Am.Jur.2d *Deeds* §§1-362 (1983) with current updates.

49 Am.Jur.2d *Landlord and Tenant* §§1-1153 (1970) with current updates.

50 Am.Jur.2d *Landlord & Tenant* §§ 1154-1262 (1970) with current updates.

26 C.J.S. *Deeds* §§1-178 (1956) with current updates.

26A C.J.S. *Deeds* §§ 179-213 (1956) with current updates.

51C C.J.S. *Landlord and Tenant* §§1-416 (1968) with current updates.

52 C.J.S. *Landlord and Tenant* §§417-715 (1968) with current updates.

52A C.J.S. *Landlord and Tenant* §§716-834 (1968) with current updates.

11A Words & Phrases *Deeds* pp. 144 - 170 (1971) with current updates.

24A Words & Phrases *Lease* pp. 235-279 (1966) with current updates.

Statutes

Kentucky Revised Statute 367.900 (1993)

Form Books

7 Am.Jur. Legal Forms 2d *Deeds* §§87:1-87:271 (1972) with current updates.

11 Am.Jur. Legal Forms 2d *Leases of Real Property* §§161:1-161:410 (1991) with current updates.

11 A Am.Jur. Legal Forms 2d *Leases of Real Property* §§161:411-161:1506 (1991) with current updates.

CHAPTER 4

THE FORM OF BUSINESS ORGANIZATION

INTRODUCTION

An individual seeking to establish a sport management business will need to determine the appropriate form of business organization. Generally speaking, three forms are available: the corporation, the partnership, and the sole proprietorship. This chapter will limit itself to a statement of the more salient features of each of these forms of business organization. The purpose of this chapter is to assist sport managers in making an intelligent choice as to the form of business organization to be used. The advantages and disadvantages will be stated along with some of the more significant aspects of the corporation, the partnership, and the sole proprietorship.

IN THIS CHAPTER YOU WILL LEARN:
The advantages and disadvantages of the corporate form of business organization
The advantages and disadvantages that accrue to a general partnership as a form of business organization
The advantages and disadvantages of the sole proprietorship as a form of business organization

---

KEY WORDS: *corporation, shareholder, piercing the corporate veil, general partnership, limited partnership, sole proprietorship, articles of incorporation*

FORMS OF A BUSINESS ORGANIZATION

This could be you!

John Jones is having trouble borrowing money from the bank in order to consummate the purchase of the real estate to be used for the fitness center. Remember, John and Maria Jones decided to be co-owners of the business. As with many small businesses, they are underfunded with the $30,000 Maria inherited. "Speedy" Smith suggests that a partnership be formed between the Joneses and himself. The profits in the partnership would be divided in proportion to the value each partner contributed to the business. Mr. Jones is hesitant because Mr. Smith has a reputation that is suspect, at best. Is the hesitancy warranted? Could the Joneses and Mr. Smith use the corporate form and avoid the problem inherent in the partnership form of business organization?

FORMS OF BUSINESS ORGANIZATION

The Corporate Form

The case that follows sets forth the primary advantages generally associated with the corporate form of business organization. One advantage is known as limited liability. The case also sets forth the circumstances under which limited liability is not applicable. The fact situation involved the renting of tents. The defendant corporation, WOCT, was owned by two individuals, Schmidt and Ulven. The plaintiff, Salem Tent and Awning Co., brought suit against WOCT. The case that follows is an appellate court decision. Salem Tent is appealing a ruling by the lower court, which allowed judgment only against WOCT (the corporation), and not against its stockholders.

···

SALEM TENT & AWNING v. SCHMIDT
719 P.2d 899 (Or. Ct. App. 1986)

VAN HOOMISSEN, Judge.

This is an action for damages arising out of a contract for the rental of tents. After a trial to the court, plaintiff received judgment against the corporate defendant only. On appeal, it contends that the trial court erred in fixing the amount of damages, in finding that defendants Schmidt and Ulven were not liable for the damages and in denying its claim for attorney fees. The dispositive issue is whether plaintiff may hold Schmidt and Ulven individually and personally liable, either as agents for an undisclosed principal or by piercing the corporate veil.

Before the 1981 Christmas season, Schmidt and Ulven, dba "Western Oregon Christmas Trees," a partnership owned by Schmidt, Ulven and Hari, met with plaintiff to discuss renting tents. An agreement was reached. When the tents were returned, there was some discussion about repeating the arrangement during the 1982 Christmas season.

In 1982, unknown to plaintiff, Schmidt and Ulven formed a new partnership without Hari.[1] They continued using the name "Western Oregon Christmas Trees." During the summer of 1982, plaintiff contacted Ulven to see if the partners wanted to rent tents for the 1982 Christmas season. Before an agreement was reached, Schmidt and Ulven incorporated under the name "Western Oregon Christmas Trees, Inc." (WOCT). A certificate of incorporation was issued in August, 1982. Plaintiff was not told that the business had been incorporated.

In November, 1982, an agreement was reached for tent rental. Plaintiff prepared an invoice that indicated that the tents were being rented to "W. Oreg.Christmas Tree." Schmidt signed the invoice without indicating that he was signing as an officer, agent or employee of a corporation. The invoice stated: "Renter is Responsible for Damages" and "In case any legal action is instituted to collect the account, I agree to pay such attorneys fees as the court may deem reasonable and the costs and disbursements of said action." Schmidt gave plaintiff a $2,000 down-payment check on which was printed "Western Oregon Christmas Trees." The check, which had been printed for one of Schmidt's and Ulven's previous partnerships, did not indicate that it was a corporate check. Defendants received the tents in November, 1982. While they had them, several were destroyed and others were damaged during a storm. When defendants refused to pay for the damages, this action resulted. The trial court found that WOCT was liable for $12,364 in damages but that Schmidt and Ulven were not individually and personally liable. The court awarded no attorney fees.[2]

Plaintiff first contends that the trial court erred in fixing the amount of damages. That contention lacks merit. There is evidence in the record to support the court's findings, and we find no error. [Citing cases.]

Plaintiff next contends that the trial court erred in finding that Schmidt and Ulven were not individually and personally liable for the damages.

1. Plaintiff's evidence shows that at some time during the 1982 discussions, Schmidt told plaintiff that the three-person "Western Oregon Christmas trees" partnership had become a two person partnership, of which Schmidt and Ulven were the partners. Defendants did not deny that Schmidt had made such a statement. They assert only that the date when the statement was made was not established at trial.

2. It is not clear why the trial court denied plaintiff attorney fees.

Plaintiff pled and argued two theories of personal liability. Its first theory was that they were agents of an undisclosed principal. Defendants argue that, because the damages plaintiff claims did not result from nondisclosure and because there was no evidence that plaintiff would not have rented the tents to Schmidt and Ulven had it known that WOCT was incorporated, they cannot be held liable on the basis of nondisclosure.[3] Defendants miss the point. Plaintiff's claim is based on the contract, not on misrepresentation. Thus, plaintiff did not need to prove that the misrepresentation caused the damages.

Restatement (Second) Agency § 322 provides:

"An agent purporting to act upon his own account, but in fact making a contract on account of an undisclosed principal, is a party to the contract."

Oregon recognizes the rule that an agent who fails to disclose the existence and identity of the agent's principal at the time of entering into a contract with a third person may be held personally liable on that contract. *See William. T. & B. Co. v. Com. Dis. Corp.,* 180 Or. 657, 178 P.2d 698 (1947). Plaintiff pled that Schmidt and Ulven dealt with it as individuals or as partners and there is evidence to support those allegations. The trial court held that plaintiff had to prove that any nondisclosure caused it damage in order to hold Schmidt and Ulven personally liable on the contract. That was error.

Plaintiff's second theory is "piercing the corporate veil." *See Amfac Foods v. Int'l Systems,* 294 Or. 94, 654 P.2d 1092 (1982); Barber, "Piercing the Corporate Veil," 17 Will L J 371 (1981). Plaintiff's second amended complaint states, in part:

"XVII

"At all times material herein, defendant WESTERN OREGON CHRISTMAS TREES, INC., was and is a corporation duly organized under the laws of the State of Oregon with principal place of business in Marion County, Oregon.

"XVIII

"Defendant corporation was, and is, a mere sham and did organize and operate as the alter ego of individual defendants for their personal advantage, in that individual defendants have at all times herein mentioned exercised total dominion and control over corporate defendant. Individual defendants were the first and, plaintiff is informed and believes and thereon alleges, the only directors of the corporate defendant. Individual defendants own or control all of the stock of the corporate defendant WESTERN OREGON CHRISTMAS TREES, INC. Individual defendants and corporate defendant have so intermingled their personal and financial affairs that corporate defendant was, and is, the alter ego of individual defendants."

---

3. At trial, plaintiff's only evidence on its damages resulting from nondisclosure was that, had it known that Schmidt and Ulven were incorporated, it would have required payment in full rental fee in advance before delivering the tents. The evidence shows, however, that plaintiff eventually was paid the full rental fee.

Plaintiff's specific assignment is that the trial court erred in holding that evidentiary facts tending to prove ultimate facts in a pleading seeking to pierce a corporate veil must also be pleaded. Defendants denied the allegations contained in paragraphs XVII and XVIII, *supra*. As an affirmative defense, they alleged that those allegations failed to state a claim for relief. At trial, defendants objected on relevancy grounds to plaintiff's evidence on the question of gross corporate undercapitalization. They argued that plaintiff's pleadings only stated a piercing theory based on commingling and that, because undercapitalization had not been pled as a *separate* theory, evidence of alleged undercapitalization was inadmissible.[4] The trial court agreed and sustained defendant's objection. [Footnote omitted.] We conclude that the court was actually asked to rule on the sufficiency of plaintiff's pleadings.[6]

4. Defendants' memorandum in support of their motion for partial summary judgment states:

"Salem Tent has raised the issue of whether WOCT was undercapitalized, presumably contending that this is leading to an alleged inability to collect from WOCT. The question is one of whether there was sufficient capital to cover the expected problems that would occur in the business. As shown above, the windstorm that created the problem herein was unexpected and 'an act of God.' WOCT did have insurance to protect it from the expected problems.

"Gross undercapitalization of a corporation is required before a shareholder can be held 'liable to a creditor who is unable to collect against the corporation because it was inadequately capitalized.' (*Amfac Food v. Int'l Systems, supra*, 294 Or (sic) at 109 [654 P.2d at 1092]) (dicta) and the cases cited therein. WOCT was not grossly undercapitalized, it had adequate capital to provide for the normal risks of its business, as well as adequate funding for all its operations."

5. Omitted

6. The objection and colloquy occurred as follows:

"Q. [By plaintiffs' counsel] Now at the time of your incorporation at least the minutes suggest that each of you, you and Terry, contributed $2,500 in equipment—to the corporation. What was the anticipated magnitude of your sales effort for 1982?

"MR. THOMPSON: Your Honor, I object in that I don't see where this is relevant to the claim that plaintiff has plead (sic) in paragraph 18 * * *. It appears that what Mr. Kersh is attempting to do is pierce the corporate veil at this point by contending inadequate capitalization. That was not alleged. That is a separate theory by which one can pierce the corporate veil possibly set out in *Amfac* as one possible method in *dicta* like commingling of assets * * *.

"MR. KERSH: Your Honor, the issue is whether or not Mr. Ulven and Mr. Schmidt used Western Oregon Christmas Trees, Inc. as their *alter ego*.

"The issue that Mr. Thompson is raising is really factual issues and these factual issues are the issues that we're addressing here.

"The *Amfac* case stands for the proposition, amongst other things, that there are certain facts that should be taken into consideration when we're determining whether or not a corporation is an *alter ego* of its primary directors, officers and shareholders. Those factual elements include whether or not *** the corporation was adequately financed * *. (Sic) These are all factual determinations going to the legal question of whether or not the corporation was the *alter ego* of those individuals.

"THE COURT: * * * We are bound by that which is in our pleading. Your motion is well taken and I will sustain your objection."

Defendants also contend that plaintiff cannot raise this issue on appeal, because it failed to make an offer of proof at trial. Because we hold that the court was actually asked to make a ruling on the pleadings, and because the evidence was admitted for other purposes at other points in the trial, we hold that plaintiff is not precluded from raising this issue on appeal.

Generally, corporate shareholders enjoy limited liability—they are not responsible for the debts of a corporation beyond their capital contribution. ORS 57.131;[7] *Amfac Foods v. Int'l Systems, supra,* 294 Or. at 102, 654 P.2d at 1092. Piercing the corporate veil to hold shareholders liable beyond their capital contribution is an extraordinary remedy to be used only as a last resort when a party is unable to obtain an adequate remedy from the corporation. *Amfac Foods v. Int'l Systems, supra,* 294 Or. at 103, 654 P.2d at 1092. Under certain circumstances, however, corporate creditors may "pierce the corporate veil" and recover directly from shareholders. *Amfac Foods v. Int'l Systems, supra,* 294 Or. at 105, 654 P.2d at 1092. [Citing cases.]

Plaintiff must plead and prove three things to secure the benefit of piercing a corporate veil in order to impose liability on a shareholder under the alter-ego theory: (1) the shareholder must have actually controlled or shared in the actual control of the corporation; (2) the shareholder must have engaged in improper conduct in the exercise of control over the corporation; and (3) the shareholder's improper conduct must have caused the plaintiff's inability to obtain an adequate remedy from the corporation. *Amfac Foods v. Int'l Systems, supra,* 294 Or. at 106-12, 654 P.2d at 1092. Plaintiff pled that the corporation was under the control of shareholders Ulven and Schmidt, that they had commingled their affairs with those of the corporation, a form of improper conduct, and that as a result plaintiff was unable to collect its debt. Thus, plaintiff was entitled to present proof on the issue of piercing the corporate veil to establish the factors to be considered in determining whether to pierce. Undercapitalization is one of those factors; it is not a separate piercing theory which they must plead. 294 Or. at 109, 654 P.2d at 1092.

We conclude that plaintiff has presented a *prima facie* case for disregarding WOCT's corporate form. First, there was evidence that Schmidt and Ulven controlled the corporation. They were the corporation's only officers, they owned all of the corporate stock and they controlled its day-to-day operations. Second, there was evidence that Schmidt and Ulven engaged in improper conduct in their exercise of control over WOCT. They commingled personal and corporate assets; they failed to keep corporate records; and, despite the fact that WOCT had other creditors, they received all of its assets as compensation for their services on its dissolution.[8] They permitted WOCT to be involuntarily dissolved as a corporation and then transferred all of its personal property to their new corporation.[9]

---

7. ORS 57.131(1) provides:

"A holder of or subscriber to shares of a corporation shall be under no obligation to the corporation or its creditors with respect to such shares other than the obligation to pay to the corporation the full consideration for which such shares were issued or to be issued."

8. Plaintiff also argues that Schmidt and Ulven "milked the profits of the corporation" in order to pay off a $50,000 loan. *See Amfac Foods v. Int'l Systems, supra,* 294 Or at 109-110, 654 P.2d at 1092. However, the evidence shows that the loan was made to the corporation with Schmidt and Ulven as guarantors and not to them as individuals.

9. Schmidt and Ulven transferred all of WOCT's personal property to their new corporation,

There also was evidence that WOCT was undercapitalized. Its stated capital was represented to be $5,000. Schmidt's and Ulven's actual contributions were $1,559. WOCT needed to buy trees and rent tents. It borrowed $50,000 and then immediately spent $62,000 to buy trees. Plaintiff's tents were worth several thousand dollars. There was evidence that the tents were not insured while defendants had them.[10] There is no statutory minimum capitalization in Oregon, but a corporation must have sufficient capital, determined at the time it is formed, to cover its reasonably anticipated liabilities, measured by the nature and magnitude of its undertaking, the risks attendant to the particular enterprise and the normal operating costs associated with its business. *See Amfac Foods v. Int'l Systems, supra,* 294 Or. at 109, 654 P.2d at 1092. *Rice v. Oriental Fireworks Co., supra; Gardner v. First Escrow Corp, supra.* Third, there was evidence that Schmidt's and Ulven's misconduct caused plaintiff to have an inadequate remedy against WOCT.

Plaintiff's pleadings, although not a model of clarity, nonetheless were sufficiently specific to put defendants on notice of plaintiff's "piercing" theory. The court should have permitted it to pursue its theory by offering any competent and relevant evidence on the issue.

Last, plaintiff contends that the trial court erred in denying its claim for attorney fees. This case involves an action on a contract. The obligation to pay damages that is alleged and under which plaintiff recovered is set out in the contract, and the attorney fees provision of the contract is applicable. Having prevailed, plaintiff is entitled to a reasonable attorney fee against WOCT and against Schmidt and Ulven, if, on remand, it is successful in imposing personal liability on them.

Judgment against Western Oregon Christmas Trees, Inc. affirmed and remanded for award of attorney fees; reversed and remanded as to defendants Schmidt and Ulven.

Questions and Comments

1. Why was a judgment against the corporation insufficient?
2. What was the dispositive issue (the major issue the case turns on) before the court?
3. What is the effect of piercing the corporate veil?
4. What must a plaintiff prove in order to pierce the corporate veil?
5. What principle of agency law did the plaintiff invoke?
6. What sources of law did the court rely upon?
7. What rule of law does the court assert?

"Greenvalley Trees." The trial court's judgment provides that "[A]ny transfer of personal property from Western Oregon Christmas Trees, Inc. to Greenvalley Trees * * * is to be transferred [back] as part of the judgment."

10. At trial, Ulven testified that the insurance company would not insure property in which defendants did not have an equity.

Note Cases - Limited Liability

Recreation cases that discuss the principle of limited liability include the following:

....

CAHILL v. HAWAIIAN PARADISE PARK CORP.,
543 P.2d 1356 (Haw. 1975)

This case involved alleged defamation. The so-called defamation involved a radio broadcast labeling a private individual as a Communist. The principle of limited liability for a shareholder was set forth in the following opinion:

> Officers, directors or shareholders of a corporation are not personally liable for the tortuous conduct of the corporation or its other agents, unless there can be found some active or passive participation in such wrongful conduct by such persons.

....

MILTON v. CAVANEY,
364 P.2d 473 (Cal. 1961)

Abuse of corporate privilege was considered in this case where a girl drowned in a public swimming pool leased and operated by a Seminole Hot Springs Corporation. Her father brought suit for her wrongful death and sought to hold Cavaney personally liable.

Cavaney, the defendant, was the director and secretary of the corporation, Seminole Hot Springs Corporation. The company never issued any stock. The corporation had no assets. The lease was forfeited for failure to pay the rent. There was inadequate capitalization. Cavaney withdrew funds at will from the corporation. He was held personally liable for the debts of the corporation. These factors were considered in finding abuse of corporate privilege. Thus, Cavaney was held personally liable for the judgment against the corporation.

Authors' Note

The primary advantages that flow from corporate business organization include the following:

1. The shareholder enjoys limited liability; namely, as a general rule, a shareholder will not be liable beyond the amount of money that has been invested in the corporation as represented by shares of stock.
2. The shareholder has the ability to invest in a going concern without the accompanying headaches involved in policy-making or day-to-day management.
3. A close or family corporation can be utilized to deduct certain expenses, which may be advantageous to the shareholder.

4. The duration may be perpetual.

5. The corporation continues even though a shareholder dies or disposes of any stock owned.

The primary disadvantages in the corporate form include the following:

1. Expense is involved in setting up the corporation.

2. The corporation involves double taxation; namely, the corporation is taxed, and the shareholder is taxed when dividends are declared. If the corporation meets certain specifications, double taxation can be avoided through the use of a subchapter *S* corporation. Under Subchapter *S*, the dividends and losses pass through the stockholders as though they were general partners.

3. The corporate form is impersonal and may not receive a favorable reaction from juries in the event of litigation.

The establishment of a small corporation is not difficult. The articles of incorporation are submitted to a secretary of state. The articles usually will include such things as the name of the corporation, the purpose for which the corporation is established, the names and addresses of the incorporators, the initial board of directors, and the agent for the purpose of service of process. Additionally, the corporation's organizational framework will be set out in some detail along with the capital stock structure. Following approval of the articles of incorporation and filing with the appropriate county recorder, organizational meetings are held to approve the bylaws and issue stock certificates. These are matters of routine, and the new business can be walked through the process by corporate counsel. It may also be necessary to approve certain preincorporation contracts that have been entered into by the promoters of the corporation.

HOW CAN I REDUCE MY LIABILITY?

The General Partnership

The law that governs the general partnership in most states is the Uniform Partnership Act (1914). This act is subject to individual variations when it is adopted by a particular state. Nevertheless, the partnership form is not dependent upon acceptance by a state office in order to establish its existence. A partnership does not require state approval. The Uniform Partnership Act predicates the existence of the partnership form upon consent of the partners. A partnership need not be expressed in writing unless there are special circumstances. Obviously, when a partnership comes within the purview of the statute of frauds, then a writing will be necessary. Significant aspects of partnership law are covered by Parts 2, 3, and 4 of the Uniform Partnership Act. Portions of that act are summarized below.

Unified Partnership Act Parts 2, 3, 4
Brief Statements and Questions for Application

1. A partnership is an association of two or more persons who carry on as co-owners of a business for profit (Sect. 6).
2. The sharing of profits does not itself establish a partnership (Sect. 7).
3. Sharing ownership as tenants in common does not establish a partnership (Sect. 7).
4. Property brought into the partnership by one partner is partnership property (Sect. 8).
5. Any property purchased with partnership funds is partnership property (Sect. 8).
6. If property is owned by the partnership it can only be conveyed by the partnership (Sect. 8).
7. Every partner is an agent of the partnership — unless one partner acts where he or she has no authority to act for the partnership and the person with whom that partner is dealing has knowledge of the fact that he or she has no such authority (Sect. 9).
8. If any partner makes a representation concerning the partnership that is within his or her authority, that act is confessed to the partnership (Sect. 11).
9. The partnership is liable for the acts of the individual partners (Sect. 13).
10. Partnership may be liable for the monetary losses of the individual partners (Sect. 14).
11. If a person is admitted to a partnership, that person is liable for all the obligations of the partnership which arose before his or her admission to the partnership (Sect. 17).
12. The partnership must indemnify every partner in respect to payments made and personal liabilities incurred by each partner in conducting the business of the partnership (Sect. 17).
13. All partners have equal rights in management of the business (Sect. 17).
14. A person cannot become a member of a partnership without the consent of all the partners (Sect. 17).
15. Partners must have access to all the information on the business (Sect. 17).

Questions and Comments

1. a. If X and Y have a bank account as tenants in common, are they partners?
    b. G brought suit against M. He alleged a partnership existed with M. Property was in M's name. The books and bank account were kept by M, and G was paid in cash. Could G establish that there was a partnership? [Facts based on *Grau v. Mitchell*, 397 P.2d 488 (Colo. 1964).]

2. Partner A decided to pay the debts of the partnership by selling several of the computers owned by the partnership. Can partner A sell the computers without authorization from Partner B?

3. Partner C (in a ski rental business) ordered expensive skiing equipment from Y. Partner B found less expensive equipment to purchase. Is the ski rental partnership bound by C's contract with Y?

4. Partner R introduces S as his partner in a new sport equipment business. S then represents himself to the local racket club as a salesperson for R's sport equipment business and proceeds to collect money for custom-made rackets. Is R's partnership liable for the sales that S made even though S is not an existing partner in the business?

5. Partner D was admitted as a full partner in 1996. Is Partner D liable for the debts of the partnership before 1996?

The primary disadvantage of the partnership form is unlimited liability. This point is stated precisely in *The Law of Business Organizations* by John E. Moye (1974) in §2.06:

> Like sole proprietorships, general partnerships suffer the disadvantage of unlimited liability for each partner. If the assets of the partnership are inadequate to pay partnership creditors, the personal assets of the individual partners may be reached to satisfy these obligations. (p.18)
>
> The element of unlimited liability is a substantial disadvantage to hazardous and speculative enterprises, and it further imposes an unwelcome burden on a partner who enjoys substantially greater personal wealth than his fellow partners. . . . (p. 19)

Unlimited liability impresses upon a potential partner the necessity of extreme care in selecting those individuals with whom a partnership is shared. A partnership postulates trust and confidence, loyalty, the duty to provide information and to exercise due care. In short, principles that characterize an agency relationship undergird the partnership form.

One way of avoiding unlimited liability is through the limited partnership. Such an arrangement is not automatic, but requires certain information to be filed as a matter of law. This information is set forth in the Limited Partnership Act (1916).

Limited Partnership

Limited partnerships may have one or more general partners and one or more limited partners. They are often used to attract investors who desire tax advantages and limited liability. In a limited partnership, the limited partner's liability for debts extends only to the extent of the capital he or she has contributed.

The Sole Proprietorship

The sole proprietorship, an individually owned business, is the simplest form of a business organization. A sole proprietorship is easy to establish. Furthermore, it permits complete control where management is concerned. An individual who is confident of his or her ability to run a recreation business and who has sufficient capital with which to operate may very well prefer the sole proprietorship. A sole proprietorship will be subject to zoning and licensure laws, along with customary regulations for employees. Each of these items can be effectively anticipated by consultation with legal and financial advisors. Appropriate government officials can also lend assistance.

SUMMARY

The primary advantage of a corporation is the limited liability of the shareholder. The primary disadvantage of the corporation lies in the impersonal nature of the business entity.

The primary advantage of a general partnership arises out of the additional capacity to handle business. The primary disadvantage of a general partnership is the unlimited liability.

A sole proprietorship puts the emphasis on individualism and initiative and is especially suited to the small business enterprise.

This could be you - check your response

The question posed is whether the Joneses should enter into a partnership agreement with Mr. Smith. Smith's character was questionable. There is unlimited liability that accompanies a general partnership. Therefore, the Joneses would be ill-advised to enter into a partnership with Smith.

The corporate form of business organization would have limited liability in most incidents. However, the Joneses should probably avoid a continuing relationship with Smith if his reputation is suspect.

REFERENCES

Authors

Moye, John E. (1974). *The law of business organizations,* §2.06. St. Paul, MN: West Publishing Co.

Cases

Cahill v. Hawaiian Paradise Park Corp., 543 P.2d 1356, (Haw. 1975).

George A. Davis, Inc. v. Camp Trails Co., 447 F.Supp 1304, (E.D. Pa. 1978).

Grau v. Mitchell, 397 P.2d 488 (Colo. 1964).

Milton v. Cavaney, 364 P.2d 473 (Cal. 1961).

Paciaroni v. Crane, reported at 408 A.2d 946 (Del. Ch. 1979).

Salem Tent & Awning v. Schmidt, 719 P.2d 899 (Or. Ct. App. 1986).

Codes, Restatements, and Rules

Revised Uniform Limited Partnership Act (1993) 6 U.L.A.

Uniform Partnership Act (1914) 6 U.L.A.

GETTING THE BUSINESS STARTED

PERSPECTIVE

Part I has provided information that was designed to be practical rather than theoretical. Specifically, the reader has been exposed to the following:

A. Legal Framework
1. Reading and understanding court cases
2. The judicial system
3. Democratic society an intellectual framework
4. Separation of powers
5. Division of powers
6. Limitation of governmental power

B. Contracts
1. The requirements for a valid, enforceable contract
2. The circumstances under which contracts should be in writing
3. The advantages and disadvantages of a written contract
4. Guidelines for the interpretation of a contract
5. The various remedies available when a contract is breached
6. The ways in which a contract right can be transferred

C. Deeds
1. The types of deeds
2. The various parts of a deed
3. The necessity for title examinations

D. Leases
1. The contents of a lease
2. Practical suggestions concerning a lease

E. Forms of Business Organization

The advantages and disadvantages associated with the corporate form, the partnership, and the sole proprietorship

Hypothetical Case - Part I - Check Your Response

In beginning the business, Mr. and Ms Jones should ask questions that would assist them in avoiding legal and financial pitfalls. An attorney, a real estate agent, a banker, and state and local licensing officials would be good advisory contacts for the Joneses. They should examine closely documents related to deeds, leases, and other forms of contracts. They should also consider the advantages and disadvantages of various forms of business organization.

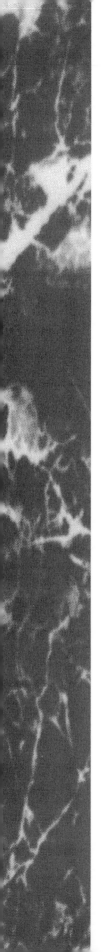

INJURY AND
STRICT LIABILITY

Focus

Overview

The owner or manager of a sport enterprise can reasonably expect to encounter injuries to his or her customers and employees. Generally speaking, these injuries will result from negligence or intentional misconduct. Another category usually discussed in the law of torts is referred to as strict liability. This part is primarily concerned with negligence and intentional torts. As a result, one chapter is devoted to negligence. This chapter concerns itself with definitions, types, and elements of negligence. In addition, attention is directed to categories of fact situations that offer the possibility for negligent conduct. Because a high percentage of injuries resulting in litigation arise out of negligent conduct, another chapter is devoted to the defenses customarily associated with law suits predicated on negligence. Contributory negligence, comparative negligence, assumption of risk, statutes of limitation, and releases will be analyzed in some detail. Other defenses, such as sovereign immunity, are discussed in relationship to the particular fact situation, namely, "state agency" status of a party litigant, which is essential to the defense. Intentional torts, together with the defenses customarily associated with each, are the subject matter of a third chapter. This chapter isolates the primary elements of such causes of action as assault, battery, and false imprisonment. Strict liability is referenced only briefly in this portion of the textbook. Space limitation mandates only a summary explanation of this body of materials.

Practical Application - Hypothetical Case

The hypothetical case that follows is designed to focus attention on representative problems presented by the risk of injury to individuals connected with the sport industry, whether occasioned by negligence or intentional misconduct.

Assuming that John and Maria Jones have established their sport business, what happens if a patron slips and falls on the floor inside the building? Assume further that the patron was visually impaired and that someone had spilled a soft drink in the area where the slip occurred. Does this affect the outcome?

What would be the effect, if any, of a sign posted that purported to caution customers and to place sole responsibility on the customer for injuries occasioned by a defective condition on the floor's surface?

As a result of the fall, the customer's companion is involved in an altercation with the manager of the business. Who is responsible and for what? Are there defenses that can be urged to a resulting injury?

Assume that the injured party was an employee of the business as opposed to a customer. Is the resulting injury compensable? Must negligence be shown? The following chapters will aid in answering these questions.

CHAPTER 5

NEGLIGENCE

INTRODUCTION

Liability is a primary concern for anyone engaged in sport management. A large area of liability exposure hinges around the concept of negligence. *Negligence*, broadly defined, refers to a duty of care owed to someone, a breach of that duty, and a resulting injury from that breach. This chapter directs attention to definitions, classifications, elements, and factual situations in which negligence is likely to occur. A chapter on negligence obviously cannot supply the detail to be found in a legal treatise that devotes major attention to negligence. The objective of the present chapter is to set forth elemental principles useful to sport managers. Actual cases that have been litigated beyond the trial level will help the reader to remember the principles of negligence illustrated in the case. The reader should also develop an appreciation of the adversary process as well as a better concept of risk management related to negligence.

IN THIS CHAPTER YOU WILL LEARN:

A definition of negligence
Classifications of negligence
Elements of negligence
Factual situations in sport management that give rise to a charge of negligence
Specific legal concepts associated with negligence, such as, *res ipsa loquitur*

KEY WORDS: *negligence, negligence per se, gross negligence, proximate cause, inherently dangerous, respondeat superior, vicarious liability*

This could be you!

The Joneses' fitness center has been highly successful. In an effort to expand the business, another downtown building is purchased, and classes for students in gymnastics are offered. One student is 12 years of age, overweight, and in poor physical condition. McKenzie, "Mac," as he is affectionately called by his classmates, is not especially interested in gymnastics. His parents are forcing him to attend class. In an effort to improve his performance, the instructor in the tumbling class, Ms Wong, tells Mac to undertake a forward somersault without spotters. Mac suffers an injury to his spinal cord and is paralyzed. What must be established in order to permit recovery of damages on Mac's behalf? Are the Joneses responsible for the injury even though an instructor has been hired to conduct the class? What duty does the instructor owe to Mac? Would Mac's recovery in court be predicated upon law or equity? Hint: What is the nature of the remedy being sought?

BASIC CONSIDERATIONS

Definitions, Classifications, and Elements

Negligence is generally defined as a failure to perform a duty owed, and that failure is the proximate cause of an injury. Thus, negligence can be said to have the following elements: a duty owed to someone (or legal entity), a breach of that duty, an injury occasioned by the breach, and a causal relation as between the breach of the duty and the resulting injury.

Negligence, generally speaking, arises out of the common law. Nevertheless, negligence is sometimes codified. In other words, there may be a statute or code that relates to negligence. When this occurs, negligence has a statutory basis.

The law refers to negligence as simple or gross. Such a classification stresses the extent of the negligence. A breach of a statutory duty is referred to as negligence *per se*. This is negligence in and of itself. Simple negligence exists when a person fails to exercise a reasonable degree of care that a normally prudent person would render. In contrast, gross negligence exists when a person fails to perform a duty of care and acts with wanton disregard that is not attributable to the normally prudent person. To be actionable in the courts, the breach of the statutory duty must be the proximate cause of the resulting injury. The sport manager has a statutory duty to provide ordinary care to protect clients.

Respondeat superior refers to the concept that the master is responsible for the acts of the servant. This is an example of vicarious liability. The employer is responsible for the negligence of the employee, within the scope of employment. (Hint: Look at *This could be you!*)

Supervision and Instruction

The case that follows involved an injury whereby the plaintiff was rendered quadriplegic. The case affirms a duty of ordinary care in instructing and supervising a permissive use of a parasail. In reading the case, note which standards of negligence that the court applies. How is failure to instruct important to the case? What is the concept of *inherently dangerous* as noted in the case?

•••

BANGERT V. SHAFFNER
848 S.W. 2d 353 (Tex. Ct. App. 1993)

ABOUSSIE, Justice.

Appellee Jeffrey M. Shaffner was injured in a parasailing accident. He sued appellant Charles Bangert, claiming Bangert had negligently failed to instruct or supervise the operation of a parasail Bangert owned and allowed Shaffner and others to use. The jury found Bangert negligent and failed to find Shaffner negligent; the trial court subsequently rendered judgment against Bangert. He appeals, bringing two points of error concerning the proper jury submission. We will affirm the judgment.

FACTUAL BACKGROUND

Bangert brought his parasail to a party for Southwest Airlines employees held at Lake Travis. Shaffner also attended this outing. Bangert instructed some partygoers about the operation of his parasail[1] and then left to return to Houston. Shaffner put on the harness, and Dick East, another partygoer, drove the boat to which the tow rope was attached. Unfortunately, the parasail had been attached upside down to Shaffner's harness in a manner which prevented it from inflating. Shaffner was dragged along the ground and hit his head on rocks near the shore. He suffered injuries rendering him a quadriplegic.

Shaffner sued Bangert after settling with East. Shaffner claimed Bangert acted negligently when he (1) failed to inform Shaffner and the other party-goers about the necessity of keeping the parasail right-side up; (2) failed to identify which side was supposed to be the "top"; and (3) left the parasail with others and abandoned personal supervision of its use. The jury found East 60% negligent and Bangert 40% negligent, but it failed to find Shaffner negligent. The trial court deducted the amount of Shaffner's settlement with East and rendered judgment against Bangert.

DISCUSSION

In the trial court, Bangert disputed that parasailing is an inherently dangerous sport. In his two points of error on appeal, Bangert now contends that because it is a recreational activity or an inherently dangerous sport, in order to recover damages Shaffner was required to show that Bangert was not

---

1. In parasailing, one wears a harness which is attached both to the sail and to a tow rope. When parasailing over water, a motor boat is used to tow the participant. The chute portion of the parasail resembles a round ice cream cone in its design. The top half is a solid piece of fabric. The bottom half has slits in it to allow air to enter and lift the sail. If the parasail is attached to the harness upside down, air will push down and collapse the chute, rather than inflating it.

merely negligent but that he acted with reckless disregard for Shaffner's well-being, a more difficult burden of proof. Bangert did not object to the charge except to request an additional instruction and inquiry concerning his reck-lessness.[2] He asserts the trial court erred when it 1) failed to submit his requested jury question on recklessness and 2) overruled his motion for judg-ment notwithstanding the verdict, arguing proof of mere negligence can never support recovery for an injury received while engaging in a recreational activ-ity or inherently dangerous sport.[3] Bangert complains that because the jury was instructed on an improper standard of care—ordinary negligence—the verdict will not support the judgment.

Traditionally, most courts have held as a matter of law that persons injured while participating in contact sports could not recover damages, on the theory that the risk of injury was inherent in the activity. One of the first cases to create an exception to this rule and allow an injured participant to pursue recovery was *Nabozny v. Barnhill*, 31 Ill. App. 3d 212, 334 N.E. 2d 258 (Ill. App. 1975). The court there allowed a plaintiff injured by an illegal kick to the head in a soccer game to pursue a cause of action. The court held that

> when *athletes* are engaged in an *athletic competition* ... a player is then charged with a legal duty to every other player on the field to refrain from conduct proscribed by a safety rule. A reckless disregard for the safety of others cannot be excused.... [A] *player* is liable for injury in a tort action if his conduct is such that it is either deliberate, willful or with a reckless disregard for the safety of the other *player* so as to cause injury to that *player.*

Id. 334 N.E. 2d at 260-61 (emphasis added). Other jurisdictions have adopt-ed this reasoning to permit recovery in limited circumstances. *See, e.g., Gauvin v. Clark*, 404 Mass. 450, 537 N.E. 2d 94 (Mass. 1989); *Dotzler v. Tuttle*, 234 Neb. 176, 449 N.W. 2d 774 (Neb. 1990).

Bangert would have us hold that the rule controls the circumstances of Shaffner's injury. He contends that one Texas court of appeals has held that a party who suffers an injury while engaging in *any* recreational activity or inherently dangerous sport cannot recover by proving that the injury was

---

2. The parties disagree whether Bangert's charge complaint was preserved. Shaffner con-tends that he failed to request the additional instruction and question in substantially correct form. Because we hold that Bangert has failed to demonstrate error in submission of the cause to the jury, we need not address this issue.

3. The term "inherently dangerous," often used interchangeably with "ultra-hazardous," more accurately describes an activity that requires a *higher* degree of care than ordinary care, or even imposes strict liability for resulting damages. These activities include owning danger-ous animals and storing combustible gases *Marshall v. Ranne*, 511 S.W. 2d 255 (Tex. 1974); *Farmers Butane Gas Co. v. Walker*, 489 S.W. 2d 949 (Tex. Civ. App. - Waco 1973, no writ)

Bangert's use of "inherently dangerous activity" confuses his argument on appeal with another disputed issue below. Shaffner pleaded that parasailing required a high degree of care on the part of Bangert because it was an inherently dangerous and ultrahazardous activity. The court did not submit this standard to the jury, but instead used the ordinary care stan-dard. Shaffner has not complained about this action by cross-point on appeal.

caused by another's negligence but instead must prove that the person caused the injury by acting recklessly or intentionally. *Connell v. Payne*, 814 S.W. 2d 486 (Tex. App.—Dallas 1991, writ denied). He acknowledges that no other Texas court has adopted such a rule. Relying on *Connell*, Bangert asserts that he owed Shaffner only this lesser duty of care and, absent proof Bangert acted not just negligently but with reckless disregard for Shaffner's safety, he cannot be held liable for the injuries he caused.

The plaintiff in *Connell* sued for injuries inflicted by an opponent in a polo match. The court noted, "All parties agree polo is a dangerous *game.*" *Id.* at 487. It then said.

> No Texas court has decided the issue of the legal duty owed by one participant to another participant in a *competitive contact sport....* By participating in a dangerous *contact sport* such as polo, a person assumes a risk of injury.... We hold that for a plaintiff to prevail in a cause of action for injuries sustained while participating in a *competitive contact sport*, the plaintiff must prove the defendant acted "recklessly" ....

Id. at 488-89 (emphasis added). *Connell* clearly addressed the legal duty participants owe one another while engaging in a competitive contact sport; Bangert concedes parasailing is not a contact sport. Despite Bangert's argument otherwise, we cannot read *Connell* as applying to noncontact activities.[4]

At least two jurisdictions have applied the "reckless disregard" standard to activities that are not ordinarily considered contact sports. *Ford v. Gouin*, 3 Cal. 4th 339, 834 P.2d 724, 11 Cal. Rptr. 2d 30, 34 (Cal. 1992) (water skiing); *Ridge v. Kladnick*, 713 P.2d 1131 (Wash. App. 1986) (ice skating). In both instances, the courts were concerned with a party who was injured by a co-participant's conduct: in *Ford*, the motor boat driver, and in *Ridge*, a fellow skater. The facts of these cases are distinguishable from the present one. Parasailing does not involve contact among any participants. Moreover, Bangert was not even present at the time of Shaffner's injury. Furthermore, both courts used an assumption of risk analysis, which has been abolished in Texas. *Farley v. MM Cattle Co.*, 529 S.W. 2d 751 (Tex. 1975).

We find it instructive to examine a case interpreting the proper scope of *Nabozny* and its reckless disregard standard. In *Novak v. Virene*, 224. Ill. App. 3d 317, 166 Ill. Dec. 620, 586 N.E. 2d 578 (Ill. App. 1991), a court in the same jurisdiction as Nabozny held that it had created a "limited contact-sports exception" to the usual standard of ordinary negligence and refused to apply the reckless disregard standard to a skiing accident where one skier collided with another. *Novak*, 166 Ill. Dec. at 628, 586 N.E. 2d at 580. The court reasoned that a skier "does not voluntarily submit to bodily contact with

---

4. Bangert contends that *Connell* applies to noncontact activities because the court noted with approval an Ohio court's holding that "a mere showing of negligence is not enough to allow recovery in sport or recreational activity." *Id.* at 488, *citing Marchetti v. Kalish*, 53 Ohio St. 3d 95, 559 N.E. 2d 699 (Ohio 1990). However, the Ohio case involved a game of kick-the-can played by teenagers, which though not a formal competitive contact sport, involves rambunctious conduct with a high risk of contact with other participants.

skiers, and such contact is not inevitable.... Many activities in life are fraught with danger, and absent a specific assumption of risk, one may obtain damages when injured by another's negligence." *Id.* *Connell* likewise rested its holding upon the consent a polo competitor gives when he enters a match anticipating the possibility of collision and injury.

We hold that Bangert has failed to demonstrate that the trial court improperly submitted the case to the jury, and we decline to adopt the reckless disregard standard for *every* recreational activity or sport that might be considered dangerous. Although Shaffner may have consented to the possibility of the usual dangers inherent in the activity he was attempting, the record contains no evidence he was aware the parasail might be negligently attached to the rope. We hold, on these facts, that Bangert owed Shaffner a duty of ordinary care and the trial court correctly submitted the issue of negligence to the jury. We overrule Bangert's points of error. [5]

Shaffner raises two cross-points on appeal. He asks us to award him an additional ten percent of his damages as a sanction against Bangert for bringing a frivolous appeal. We decline to do so. Although we find no merit in his argument, we cannot hold that Bangert's appeal was taken for delay and without sufficient cause. *See* Tex.R. App.P. 84. We overrule this cross-point.

Shaffner's second cross-point asserts the trial court erred in calculating the amount of offset to be credited for Shaffner's settlement with East. As part of the settlement, East assigned Shaffner his cause of action against his homeowner's insurance carrier, which Shaffner pursued, resulting in a $352,356.16 judgment for Shaffner. Shaffner contends this recovery was not part of his settlement with East and should not have been deducted from the damages awarded him by the jury. He suggests no legal authority for his position, either in his brief or at oral argument, and he acknowledges the "assignment from East [was] made as part of the settlement agreement." We also overrule this cross-point.

We affirm the judgment of the trial court.

Questions and Comments

1. What standard of care did the court accept? Was there an issue of failure to supervise? Was there a duty to instruct?
2. Is there a relationship between standard of care and assumption of risk? (Assumption of risk involves several elements. First, the nature of the risk must be inherent to the activity, for example, a contact sport such as football where the risk of injury is high. Second, the participant may under-

---

5. Bangert himself appears to have believed at some point that the reckless disregard standard should be directed to contact sports. His proffered jury instruction read as follows:

> You are instructed that a person acts with "reckless disregard" when he knows that an act is harmful and intends to commit the act but does not intend by the act to harm *his opponent*.

Obviously, Shaffner had no "opponent" while parasailing.

stand the risks of the activity and knowingly participate in the activity despite the risks involved.)

   Res ipsa loquitur, loosely translated, means "The thing speaks for itself." It is a form of circumstantial evidence.

3. Suppose the court had adopted a strict liability standard. Would this have affected the outcome of the case? (Strict liability refers to liability without fault. Proof of fault is not necessary. The activity is inherently dangerous. The activity is conducted with full knowledge of the people conducting the event.)

4. Was parasailing a contact sport? What concepts from this case might apply to "contact" activities?

Duty of Ordinary Care

Plaintiff golfer, Bartlett, was struck by a ball hit by defendant golfer, Chebuhar. In reading the case note the standard of care that was explored by the court.

LIABILITY FOR?

BARTLETT v. CHEBUHAR
479 N.W.2d 321 (Iowa, 1992)

PER CURIAM.

The Bartletts have appealed from a district court ruling dismissing their claims against Martin Chebuhar. The Bartletts claim that Chebuhar was negligent when he hit a golf ball that struck Larry Bartlett in the eye. We reverse and remand.

On May 15, 1987, both Larry Bartlett and Martin Chebuhar were playing golf at the Washington Golf and Country Club. Larry was playing hole number three at about the same time Martin was playing hole number nine. Martin's tee shot on hole nine fell somewhat towards the right of the fairway. Martin's second shot went sharply to the right and landed in front of the number four tee. When Martin prepared to take his third shot, he saw that there were people at an angle to his right on the number three green; he saw no individuals on his intended path to the number nine green. After hitting his third shot, Martin realized his golf ball was traveling towards the number three green and he testified that he yelled "fore" after striking the ball. Martin's ball hit an embankment in front of the third green and ricocheted up and hit Larry in the eye.

Larry, and his wife Sara, filed a petition seeking damages based on Martin's negligence in hitting the ball and failing to warn when Larry was reasonably within the range of danger of being struck by the ball. Martin answered, denying that he was negligent and alleging several affirmative defenses. The case proceeded to trial before the court.

Following trial, the district court entered its findings of fact and ruling. The court found that, "In the case before the court, plaintiff was not in defendant's line of sight or intended flight of the ball. There is no showing that defendant's actions constituted negligence." Finding no legal duty and thus no negligence, the district court dismissed the Bartletts' petition at their cost. The Bartletts have filed this appeal.

Our case law on negligence is succinctly summarized in a uniform civil jury instruction as "...failure to use ordinary care. Ordinary care is the care which a reasonably careful person would use under similar circumstances. 'Negligence' is doing something a reasonably careful person would not do under similar circumstances, or failing to do something a reasonably careful person would do under similar circumstances." 1 Iowa Civil Jury Instructions 700.2 (1987); see Christianson v. Kramer, 255 Iowa 239, 245, 122 N.W.2d 283, 287 (1963). In a situation where a person is struck by a golf ball, the general rule is that, "... a golfer is only required to exercise ordinary care for the safety of persons reasonably within the range of danger of being struck by the ball." Annotation, Liability to One Struck by Golf Ball, 53 A.L.R. 4th 282, 289 (1987). "Although a golfer about to hit a ball must, in the exercise of ordinary care, give an adequate and timely warning to those who are unaware of his intention to play and who may be endangered by the play, this duty does not extend to those persons who are not in the line of play, if danger to them is not reasonably to be anticipated." Id. In applying this general standard, courts have noted that a bad shot that causes injury to another does not of itself establish negligence. Jenks v. McGranaghan, 30 N.Y. 2d 475, 334 N.Y.S. 2d 641, 285 N.E. 2d 876 (1972). Still, a bad shot may constitute negligence in a situation where the defendant has a propensity to shank his golf shots. Cook v. Johnston, 141 Ariz. 589, 688 P.2d 215 (App. 1984).

In this case, the district court concluded that since Larry was not in the intended path of Martin's shot, Martin owed no duty to Larry as a matter of law to either warn him prior to the shot or not take the shot. In effect, the district court is equating the intended path of a shot with the reasonable zone of danger. We disagree with the district court's restrictive definition of what was reasonably within Martin's zone of danger when he took his third shot. In fact, some cases have suggested that the zone of danger might include someone standing at a point 50 degrees from the intended line of flight where it was foreseeable that the ball would go in that direction. *Boozer v. Arizona Country Club*, 102 Ariz. 544, 547, 434 P.2d 630, 633 (1967). In any event, courts agree that a golfer's duty extends beyond the intended path of the ball and encompasses a wider zone of danger based on the facts and circumstances in each individual case. *Cook*, 141 Ariz. at 591, 688 P.2d at 217.

In *Cook*, the court determined that the zone of danger was wider given the golfer's propensity to shank. In this case, however, we fail to find a similar analysis by the district court in establishing what was reasonably within Martin's zone of danger when he took the tragic shot. Since we find that the district court failed to adequately apply the proper legal standards to the facts in this case, we reverse and remand for reconsideration by the district court based on the present record consistent with this opinion.

REVERSED AND REMANDED.

Questions and Comments

1. How does this court define negligence?
2. What standard of care does the court employ?
3. Under what circumstances would a particular golf shot constitute ordinary negligence?
4. What does the court mean by a zone of danger?
5. To what extent does the court rely on precedent?
6. The court cites *American Law Reports (ALR)*. This is a secondary source of information.
7. A *per curiam* opinion is given by the whole court, not just one judge.

Slip and Fall

A patron at a race track slipped and fell on liquid allowed to accumulate on the floor. The appellants, the McCurrys, asked the court for a reversal of a lower court's directed verdict for the defendant (appellee), the Investment Corp. The appellate court held that the question of liability was one for the jury.

••

McCURRY v. INVESTMENT CORPORATION OF PALM BEACH
548 So. 2d 689 (Fla. Dist. Ct. App. 1989)

POLEN, Judge.

These are consolidated appeals from a final judgment for the defendant and a final judgment on defendant's motion to tax costs. We will address appellants' second point first, as that will be dispositive of both issues on appeal.

Appellants were attending the dog races at appellee's facility, Palm Beach Kennel Club, when Mrs. McCurry allegedly slipped and fell on a liquid allowed to accumulate on the floor. Although Mrs. McCurry could not identify the exact substance which caused her to slip, she testified as to the back of her pants being wet immediately after the fall. Mr. McCurry testified that beer and Coca-Cola were on the floor, as well as betting tickets that were allowed to pile up from race to race. Appellants do not contend that Mrs. McCurry slipped on a betting ticket, but offered that evidence to support their theory of constructive notice to appellee.

Appellants offered testimony at trial to the effect that other patrons of the kennel club, on the night of the accident, were walking back and forth across the area where Mrs. McCurry fell with their beverage cups, and were drinking their beverages in the aisles. There was no specific offer of testimony that any particular patron was seen spilling his beverage. The trial court sustained appellee's objection on grounds of relevancy.

At the close of appellants' case, the trial court granted a directed verdict in favor of appellee, relying on *Publix Super Markets, Inc. v. Schmidt*, 509 So. 2d 977 (Fla. 4th DCA 1987).

We find that this matter is most closely related to the supreme court case of *Wells v. Palm Beach Kennel Club*, 160 Fla. 502, 35 So. 2d 720 (1948), and our own opinion in *Fazio v. Dania Jai-Alai Palace, Inc.*, 473 So. 2d 1345 (Fla. 4th DCA 1985). In the *Wells* case, the court said:

> One operating a place of amusement like a race course where others are invited is charged with a continuous duty to look after the safety of his patrons. Both sanitary and physical safety of its patrons require that receptacles be provided for bottles and that they be so placed.
>
> We do not mean to imply that they are insurers of the safety of their patrons, but we do say that reasonable care as applied to a race track requires a higher degree of diligence than it does when applied to a store, bank or such like place of business.

Id. 35 So. 2d at 721. We find that it was error for the trial court to preclude appellants' offered testimony as to what the other patrons were doing with their beverages on the night of the accident. Such testimony would be clearly relevant to the issue of constructive notice of the dangerous condition to appellee, when taken together with Mr. McCurry's testimony of observing beer, Coca-Cola, and race tickets on the floor.

Upon admission of such testimony, we could not then say it would be proper for the trial court to grant a directed verdict in favor of appellee. This additional evidence, coupled with evidence in favor of appellants that was adduced at the first trial, and the permissible inferences the jury might draw therefrom, may be sufficient upon retrial so as to preclude the granting of a directed verdict.

We therefore reverse and remand for a new trial consistent with this opinion.

DOWNEY and GARRETT, JJ., concur.

ON REHEARING

In its motion for rehearing, appellee correctly identifies error in our opinion dated July 7, 1989, wherein we said:

Mr. McCurry testified that beer and Coca-Cola were on the floor as well as betting tickets that were allowed to pile up from race to race. While Mr. McCurry did refer to seeing the betting tickets on the floor, our incorrect reference to his testifying to seeing beer and Coca-Cola on the floor was inadvertently derived from the following exchange in the testimony:

Q. Now, do you know what kind of substance it was that she slipped on?
A. No, I'm not sure what it was. I always thought it was coke or beer.
Q. Why do you say that?
A. Well there was a lot of people around there drinking coke and beer. You hardly ever see anybody drinking water.

Appellants offered testimony that on the night of the accident, other patrons of the Kennel Club were drinking beverages in the aisles and carrying beverage cups while walking back and forth across the area where Mrs. McCurry fell. There was no specific offer of testimony that any particular patron was seen spilling his or her beverage. The trial court sustained appellee's objection to the testimony on grounds of relevancy.

On rehearing, we must recede from that portion of our July 7, 1989, opinion finding it was error for the trial court to exclude such testimony. Appellee having brought to our attention that Mr. McCurry never testified as to having actually seen Coke or beer on the floor, it would have been at best discretionary for the trial court to allow the proffered testimony about what the patrons were doing concerning their beverages.

Having made this correction, we are still of the view that it was error for the trial court to grant a directed verdict in favor of appellee. The testimony that there were betting tickets on the floor would still give rise to an inference that appellee's personnel were negligent as to their maintenance of the area in which Mrs. McCurry fell. We still find *Wells v. Palm Beach Kennel Club*, 160 Fla. 502, 35 So. 2d 720 (1948) and *Fazio v. Dania Jai-Alai Palace, Inc.*, 473 So. 2d 1345 (Fla. 4th DCA 1985), support our conclusion that the question of liability was one for the jury and would preclude the granting of a directed verdict.

Accordingly, the result as stated in our opinion of July 7, 1989, stands. The cause is reversed and remanded for a new trial consistent with this opinion.

Questions and Comments

1. What guidance does this decision give for the owner or manager of a place of amusement?
2. Does this case turn on defective premises or defective maintenance of the premises?
3. What safety standards could an owner or manager use to avoid liability?

Causation and Damages Issues - A Note Case

A passenger on a miniature train in a city park sued the park association for injuries when the train derailed. The park association was held negligent. Recovery was permitted. Plaintiff Morris was awarded damages. He appealed and the defendants appealed. The lower court's decision was affirmed. Notice how the court reasoned on causation and damages.

···

MORRIS v. NEW ORLEANS CITY PARK IMPROVEMENT ASS'N
586 So. 2d 629 (La. Ct. App. 1991)

ARMSTRONG, Judge.

Plaintiff, Michael Morris, appeals the quantum of the jury award in this personal injury cause of action. Defendants, New Orleans City Park Improvement Association and C.N.A. Insurance Company, appeal the trial court's refusal to grant judgment notwithstanding the verdict. We affirm.

Plaintiff, Michael Morris, and others were passengers on the miniature train located in New Orleans City Park on August 2, 1987. During the tour, one of the wheels of the train slipped from the track and Morris alleges he suffered numerous personal injuries, including back, neck and knee injuries.

Subsequently, Morris sued City Park and its insurer alleging that he sustained personal injuries caused by the negligence and strict liability of City Park. Following a jury trial the trial court granted a directed verdict in favor of City Park and its insurer on the Article 2317 strict liability issue after it was determined that City Park had no prior knowledge of any defect with respect to the train or its track.

During deliberation the jury requested information from the Court, wherein the Court entered the deliberating room in the presence of all counsel. The jury foreman requested the total amount of medical bills which were presented at trial. The court responded that the amount of medical expenses alleged was $7,110.00.

Upon return, the jury found that City Park was negligent, that the negligence was a proximate cause of the injuries to Mr. Morris and the amount of damages awarded was $7,110.00. After entry of the judgment, both parties moved for respective judgments notwithstanding the verdict. Each was denied by the trial court. Morris then took this appeal on the contention that the jury award was inadequate.

Subsequently, City Park and CNA Insurance Company answered Morris' appeal seeking reversal of the trial court's finding of liability based upon a contention that Morris failed to prove any negligence on the part of City Park . . . .

· · · · ·

We decline to reverse the jury on the liability issue. It is uncontroverted that the train derailed, that its passengers were jostled and tossed about. Morris, who was recovering from a gun shot injury, began to complain for the first time about his knee, as well as his back and his neck, after the train accident. There was conflicting testimony regarding the source of the knee injury and the extent of the knee injury. The jury reached the obvious conclusions; that City Park was at fault for the train's derailment and it was liable to Morris. We find that the jury's verdict was based on facts in evidence.

For the foregoing reasons, the trial court's judgment is affirmed.

Questions and Comments

1. Why did the court find a causal connection between the train's derailment and plaintiff's injury?
2. What evidence was proffered to show absence of causation?

SUMMARY

Negligence permits recovery for injury based on fault. Negligent conduct may be fixed by statute, or it may be determined by the common law. In any event, it operates on the theory that one who injures another, albeit without intent, is expected to compensate the victim who has suffered from the negligent act. In some instances, especially when dealing with public agencies, the law may require willful or wanton misconduct as a condition of recovery. The laws may consider noncommercial purpose of government and the intent of the actor.

The law will hold individuals or legal entities responsible for the acts of servants or employees acting within the scope of their employment. This is the doctrine of *respondeat superior*, sometimes referred to as vicarious liability. *Res ipsa loquitur*, loosely translated, means the thing speaks for itself. It is a form of circumstantial evidence.

The materials presented in this chapter are elemental. Nevertheless, when considered in connection with the chapter on defenses to negligence, the material will be both meaningful and useful to those working in the field of sport management. A sport industry that involves active participation must be mindful of defective instruction, supervision, equipment, and facilities generally. The elements of negligence are a duty owed to someone, a breach of that duty with a resulting injury caused by the breach.

This could be you - Check your response

In order to establish negligence it must be determined that Ms Wong, the instructor, had a duty to care for Mac, the student. Ms Wong did not use spotters when she asked Mac to complete a forward somersault. Mac was an overweight and out-of-shape student. Was the lack of spotters a breach of the duty to care for the overweight student? Was there a causal relation between the duty to care and the resulting spinal cord injury?

Jones employed Ms Wong as an instructor. Under the doctrine of *respondeat superior*, the employer (master) is responsible for the acts of the employee (servant) when the injury is a result of acts performed during the scope of the employee's job. It would be important to know if Jones employed Wong knowing that Wong had some kind of teaching certificate in gymnastics.

(This is not directly relevant to vicarious liability. However, this would show that the Joneses had employed someone who was professionally trained, and that credential would help to evade the issue of negligent hiring.) Did Jones have employee safety training? Did Jones have safety rules posted? Ultimately, Jones has a duty to care for the students in the gymnastics class. A failure to fulfill this duty that results in injury can justify damages. Thus the recovery is in law rather than equity.

As the owner of a business, Jones should purchase insurance. Wong should carry professional liability insurance. However, insurance would not protect them from being sued.

REFERENCES

Authors
Keeton, W. Page (1984). *Prosser and Keeton on the law of torts* (5th ed). St. Paul, MN: West Publishing Co.

Kionka, Edward J. (1977). *Torts in a nutshell: Injuries to persons and property.* St. Paul, MN: West Publishing Co.

Cases
Bangert v. Shaffner, 848 S.W.2d 353 (Tex. Ct. App. 1993).

Bartlett v. Chebuhar, 479 N.W.2d 321 (Iowa 1992).

Cope v. Scott, 45 F.3d 445 (D.C.Cir. 1995).

Hernandez v. Renville Public Sch. Dist. No. 654, 542 N.W.2d 671 (Minn.App. 1996).

Hoke v. Cullinan, 914 S.W.2d 335 (Ky. 1995).

Isley v. Capuchin Province, 880 F.Supp. 1138 (E.D.Mich. 1995).

McCurry v. Investment Corporation of Palm Beach, 548 So. 2d 689 (Fla. Dist. Ct. App. 1989).

Morris v. New Orleans City Park Improvement Ass'n., 586 So. 2d 629 (La. Ct. App. 1991).

Legal Encyclopedias
57A Am.Jur.2d *Negligence* §§ 1-1127 (1989), with current updates.

57B Am.Jur.2d *Negligence* §§ 1128-2241 (1989), with current updates.

65 C.J.S. *Negligence* §§ 1-115 (1966) with current updates.

65A C.J.S. *Negligence* §§ 116-306 (1966) with current updates.

28 Words and Phrases *Negligence* pp. 521-680 (1955) with current updates.

Model Codes, Restatements, and Standards
Restatement (Second) of Torts §§ 1-951 (1965) with current updates.

CHAPTER 6

DEFENSES TO NEGLIGENCE

INTRODUCTION

The initial and obvious defense to a suit based on negligence is a denial that negligence occurred. Indeed, one can defeat a claim for negligence by showing that any one of the elements of negligence does not exist. More specific defenses are statute of limitations, releases, assumption of risk, contributory negligence, comparative negligence, and the recreational user statute. Each of these defenses will be considered in the materials that follow.

IN THIS CHAPTER YOU WILL LEARN:
The significance of a general denial
Affirmative defenses; such as, statute of limitations, release or waiver, assumption of risk, contributory negligence, comparative negligence, recreational user statute

---

KEY WORDS: *general denial, affirmative defenses, contributory negligence, assumption of risk, comparative negligence, statute of limitations, release, waiver, recreational user statutes, sovereign immunity, complaint, plaintiff, answer, defendant*

ASSUMPTION OF RISK

This could be you!

In the hypothetical case posed in the preceding chapter, an injury to the gymnastics student, Mac, was stated. Assume that Mac waits until he is 18 years of age to file the suit. Is this too long? Assume that Mac himself requested permission to perform the stunt without spotters. Would this be a good defense? Assume that Mac's parents had signed a release for any injury to Mac as a condition to his enrolling in the course. Would this adequately protect the instructor? Would this adequately protect the Joneses, the owners of the business?

GENERAL DENIAL AND AFFIRMATIVE DEFENSES

General Denial

A suit is commenced by a pleading known as a complaint. The complaint is filed by the plaintiff. The defendant then files a pleading known as the answer. Although it may be worded in various ways, the substance of a general denial is that the defendant did not act in a negligent fashion. Rules of pleading require a defendant to admit or deny the specific allegations in a complaint. If a defendant is unable to admit or deny the allegations in the complaint, the answer the defendant files must allege insufficient information upon which to state a reply to a specific allegation. Thus, the defendant states a denial. A defendant will frequently enter a statement along the following lines, "Defendant denies each and every allegation not specifically admitted." A defendant can prevail if a plaintiff fails to allege and prove one of the elements of negligence. This substantially reduces a defendant's burden.

The excerpt that follows is from a decision in the State of Illinois. Suit was filed by a passenger on a boat against the operator of the boat and the owners. The complaint alleged that an injury was sustained when the passenger fell from the boat while it was docking. The passenger, plaintiff, filed suit against the boat owners and the operator, the defendants. The lower court ruled in favor of the defendants, boat owners and operator. The appellate court affirmed a lower court decision, holding that the evidence failed to establish that defendants' negligence proximately caused the injury. Other relevant facts and that portion of the decision dealing with proximate cause are excerpted below.

••

WILSON v. BELL FUELS, INC.
574 N.E.2d 200 (Ill.App. Ct. 1991)

Justice BUCKLEY delivered the opinion of the court.

This appeal arises from the circuit court's grant of summary judgment in favor of defendants Charlene Troch (Mrs. Troch), operator of the boat, and Bell Fuels, Inc. (Bell Fuels) and Kelly Leasing Co. (Kelly Leasing), owners of the boat in the personal injury action brought by Mr. and Mrs. Wilson. Plaintiffs, Mr. and Mrs. Wilson, filed the original complaint against defendants alleging negligence; more specifically, that Mrs. Troch was negligent both in operating the boat and failing to instruct Mr. Wilson on safety procedures for docking the boat. Plaintiffs appeal from the circuit court's ruling contending that the circuit court erred in entering summary judgment in favor of defendants by (1) ruling that plaintiffs could not establish that defendants' negligence proximately caused Mr. Wilson's injuries, (2) failing to consider whether the conduct of Mrs. Troch in failing to take appropriate measures to protect Mr. Wilson proximately caused Mr. Wilson's injuries and (3) failing to allow adequate time for discovery.

On February 8, 1987, Mrs. Troch invited the Wilsons to go for a sightseeing ride on the "Road Pilot," a fiberglass, twin engine 32-foot Carver boat. The Wilsons accepted, and Mr. Wilson changed into crepe-sole loafers in anticipation of the boat ride. Prior to this ride, both of the Wilsons had been on a boat a few times. The boating excursion began at about 2 p.m. It was a clear, sunny, calm afternoon. Mrs. Troch untied two of the lines which secured the boat to the dock while Mr. Wilson untied the third. Once on the boat, the Wilsons and Mrs. Troch proceeded to the flying bridge area. Mrs. Troch sat in front of the controls, Mr. Wilson sat on her right, and Mrs. Wilson to her left.

After smoothly pulling away from the dock, Mrs. Troch drove the boat around and pointed out various sights to the Wilsons. Throughout the ride, Mrs. Troch was consistently driving the boat at four to six miles per hour. Thereafter, Mrs. Troch approached the dock at Lot 38, the site of the Trochs' future home. As Mrs. Troch maneuvered the boat toward the dock, Mr. Wilson volunteered to tie a line to the dock. Mr. Wilson asked Mrs. Troch where her husband stands while docking the boat. Mrs. Troch replied that he stands on the bow. At that point, Mr. Wilson descended the ladder from the flying bridge, went down onto the bow and stood midway between the bow and the windshield of the cabin near the center cleat on an abrasive-coated area. A metal railing extends from the bow to midship around the perimeter of the boat which is about 25 inches high. Mr. Wilson testified that the railing came about two to three inches above his knee. Mr. Wilson stood on the deck of the boat while Mrs. Troch ran the boat at "dead slow" with no power. Mrs. Troch did not use the throttle as she was docking the boat. Mrs. Troch testified in detail how she guided the boat into the dock at a 45 degree angle and then turned the bow and the stern by putting the starboard engine in forward and the port engine in reverse to allow the boat to coast into the dock.

Mr. Wilson remained standing in the same place near the cleat. Mrs. Troch had no unusual difficulty maneuvering the boat the last 50 feet into the dock. There was no wind and the water was calm. Mrs. Wilson was still seated next to Mrs. Troch when they both turned back to make sure the stern was into the dock. When Mrs. Troch turned back to face the bow, she noticed Mr. Wilson was no longer standing on the boat.

Mr. Wilson testified that from the time he left his seat next to Mrs. Troch until his last memory of being on the boat, he did not notice any changes in speed or direction of the boat and does not recall feeling any movement that would suggest the boat hit the dock. Mr. Wilson does not remember if he attempted to climb over the rail or jump from the boat.

Mrs. Wilson testified that she thought Mrs. Troch was docking the boat in a normal fashion by bringing the boat in slowly, making sure the bow and the stern moved closer to the dock. Mrs. Wilson stated that from the "feel" of the water, the procedure was not smooth. She later clarified this statement by saying that she realized Mrs. Troch was docking the boat and that the boat would not be traveling at the normal rate of speed and that Mrs. Troch would have to eventually stop the boat.

There is no evidence that the boat ever came into contact with the dock. For example, no one heard, felt or saw anything that would suggest the boat came into contact with the dock. Likewise, there is no physical evidence from the boat that indicates it made any relevant contact with the dock.

When Mrs. Wilson discovered her husband was no longer on the boat, she descended the ladder from the flying bridge and attempted to exit the boat off the stern. The boat, however, according to Mrs. Wilson's own testimony, was parallel to the dock, but was two to three feet away from it. When Mrs. Wilson finally exited the boat, she found her husband unconscious and lying on the dock. Mr. Wilson had blood coming from his ears, mouth, and nose.

The circuit court found that there was no negligence on the part of Mrs. Troch and granted defendants' motions for summary judgment. Summary judgment should be granted when the pleadings, depositions and affidavits on file clearly show that no issue exists as to any material fact and that the moving party is entitled to judgment as a matter of law. (Ill.Rev.Stat. 1985, ch. 110, par. 2-1005(c).) In deciding whether a material fact exists, the pleadings, depositions, admissions, exhibits and affidavits on file must be construed strictly against the movant and liberally in favor of the opponent. [Citation omitted.] Where the evidence before the court in a motion for summary judgment shows that at trial a verdict would have to be directed, summary judgment is proper. [Citation omitted.] The non-movant need not prove his case at the summary judgment stage; he must, however, show a factual basis to support the elements of his claim. [Citation omitted.] Thus, facts, not conclusions, must be presented. [Citation omitted.]

The plaintiffs allege Mrs. Troch was negligent. In order to prevail on a claim of negligence, the plaintiffs must offer enough evidence to show that defendants' negligence was arguably the proximate cause of Mr. Wilson's injuries. [Citation omitted.] Negligence can be shown by circumstantial evidence, and a plaintiff can rely on reasonable inferences which can be drawn from the facts. [Citations omitted.] Inferences and liability for negligence cannot be based on mere speculation, guess, surmise or conjecture. [Citation omitted.]

The plaintiffs contend that Mrs. Troch negligently operated and maneuvered the boat in a manner which either caused the boat to change direction and/or speed or caused the boat to hit the dock, thus, resulting in Mr. Wilson being catapulted from the boat. It is clear, however, from Mrs. Troch's, Mr. Wilson's and Mrs. Wilson's deposition transcripts that none of these eyewitnesses could testify that Mr. Wilson was catapulted from the boat to the dock either as a result of the boat coming in contact with the dock or from some movement of the boat during the docking maneuver.

First, none of the witnesses saw the boat come into contact with the dock or heard anything that would suggest such contact. Mrs. Troch testified that the boat was running at a "dead slow speed" and that she did not even use the throttle. There was no wind and the water was calm. Even more telling is Mrs. Wilson's testimony that immediately after learning of her husband's absence from the boat, she descended the ladder from the flying bridge and attempted to disembark the boat at the stern. The stern of the boat, however, was two to three feet away from the dock. The only reasonable inference which can be drawn from this testimony is that the boat did not come into contact with the dock. Second, Mrs. Troch and Mrs. Wilson agree that there was no sudden movement of the boat, and Mr. Wilson has no recollection of what happened after the boat was about five feet away from the dock.

In order to prevail at summary judgment stage, plaintiffs are required to show some evidence of what caused Mr. Wilson to sustain his injuries. The grant of summary judgment, therefore, was proper because plaintiffs have failed to produce evidence of an element of their claim, specifically, that Mrs. Troch's alleged negligence proximately caused Mr. Wilson's injuries.

Plaintiffs contend that the issue of proximate cause is properly a question of fact for the jury; normally this is true. Proximate cause becomes a question of law, however, when the material facts are undisputed and there can be no difference in judgment of reasonable men as to the inferences to be drawn from them. [Citations omitted.] The material facts in this case are undisputed. The record is devoid of any evidence as to why or how Mr. Wilson sustained his injuries. There is nothing in the record from which it can be inferred that any action by Mrs. Troch in operating the boat proximately caused Mr. Wilson's injuries. The element of proximate cause is established only when defendant's conduct is shown with *reasonable certainty* to have caused plaintiff's injury. [Citation omitted.] In the case at bar, the issue of proximate cause was a question of law, properly determined by the circuit court.

Illinois courts support the conclusion reached by the circuit court. In *Koukoulomatis v. Disco Wheels, Inc.* (1984), 127 Ill.App.3d 95, 100, 82 Ill.Dec. 215, 220, 468 N.E.2d 477, 482, the court found that plaintiff's statement that the carpet "[m]ust have gone up a little bit that I tripped over it," indicated that the plaintiff did not know with certainty the cause of her fall. The plaintiff's allegations were based solely on the speculation that something must have been wrong with the carpet. Since mere conjecture or surmise is insufficient to establish a genuine issue as to negligence, the court affirmed the grant of summary judgment. [Citations omitted.] The case at bar is directly analogous to the above case. Plaintiffs assert that Mrs. Troch must have done something wrong because neither of the Wilsons knew with any certainty why or how Mr. Wilson sustained his injuries. Plaintiffs must present *bona fide* facts to withstand a motion for summary judgment; the Wilsons cannot hide behind equivocations and conjecture and expect to prevent the entry of summary judgment.

See *Wainscott v. Penikoff* (1936), 287 Ill.App. 78, 4 N.E.2d 511.

In *Snell v. Village of University Park* (1989), 185 Ill.App.3d 973, 978, 134 Ill.Dec. 49, 52, 542 N.E.2d 49, 52, the plaintiff asserted that the circumstantial evidence, including the close proximity of a defective curb to the location of the accident, the way the plaintiff fell and the position of the body after the fall, supported a reasonable inference that the defective curb caused the decedent to fall and suffer injuries. The record indicated that none of the witnesses testified that the decedent or her bicycle came into contact with the curb and in fact, three of the witnesses stated that she did not strike the curb. The court held that the evidence failed to support the conclusion that the curb caused the fall. *(Snell,* 185 Ill.App.3d at 977, 134 Ill.Dec. at 53, 542 N.E.2d at 53.) In the instant case, the testimony of the three eyewitnesses indicate that there was no contact between the boat and the dock and no noticeable change in speed, direction or sound. The evidence fails to support an inference of probability, rather than possibility, that Mrs. Troch's actions proximately caused Mr. Wilson's injuries. *Snell,* 185 Ill.App.3d at 977, 134 Ill.Dec. at 53, 542 N.E.2d at 52.

Questions and Comments

1. What was the theory upon which the operator of the boat was sued?
2. What was the theory upon which the owners of the boat were sued?
3. What elements of negligence does this case illustrate?
4. What evidence was introduced to show negligence or the lack thereof?
5. As noted in the case, summary judgment is granted when there is no issue about the material facts of the case.

Affirmative Defenses

Statute of limitations. The case that follows arose out of an injury to a skier. The injury occurred when the skier hit an unmarked tree stump on the trail. Suit was filed by the skier (a minor) and his father. The father claimed emotional distress and loss of companionship. The father's claim was barred by the statute of limitations. Read the following case and find the meaning of statute of limitations.

••

SANCHEZ v. SUNDAY RIVER SKIWAY CORP.
802 F. Supp. 539 (D. Me. 1992)

MEMORANDUM OF DECISION AND ORDER ON DEFENDANT'S MOTION TO DISMISS GENE CARTER, Chief Judge.

Defendant Sunday River Skiway Corporation has moved to dismiss all counts of Plaintiffs' Complaint arguing that they have failed to state a claim upon which relief can be granted. *See* Fed.R.Civ.P. 12(b)(6). Plaintiffs' Complaint alleges that Sunday River was negligent in failing to groom and clear the trail (Count I) and negligent in failing to mark or pad an obstruction

(Count II). The Complaint also alleges that Plaintiffs suffered emotional distress (Count III) and loss of companionship (Count IV) as a result of Sunday River's negligent conduct. Finally, Plaintiffs assert that they sustained damages as a result of Defendant's breach of contract (Count V). For the reasons that follow, the Court will grant the motion with regard to Counts III, IV, and V, and deny the motion with regard to Counts I and II.

The pertinent allegations in Plaintiffs' Complaint are as follows. On January 14, 1992, minor Plaintiff, Luis Sanchez, Jr., was seriously injured while skiing at Sunday River Ski Resort in Newry, Maine.[1] Luis Jr. was accompanied by his father, Luis Sanchez, Sr., and a family friend. Father and son were on their initial ski run of the day on a trail called "American Express" when Luis Jr. struck a patch of ice and fell, sliding downward on the slope. As he fell, his right leg hit a tree stump protruding from the snow. The stump was unmarked and at least 30 feet into the ski trail.

To resolve Sunday River's Motion to Dismiss, the Court must accept as true all factual allegations in the Complaint, construe them in favor of Plaintiffs, and decide whether, as a matter of law, Plaintiffs could prove any set of facts which would entitle them to relief. *See Roeder v. Alpha Industries, Inc.*, 814 F.2d 22, 25 (1st Cir. 1987); *Gott v. Simpson*, 745 F.Supp. 765, 768 (D.Me. 1990). Sunday River asserts a number of separate arguments in support of its Motion to Dismiss. As each argument addresses different counts, the Court will discuss each separately.

I.

Count I alleges that Sunday River was negligent in its operation and maintenance of the ski area by failing to groom and clear the ski trail of the stump.[2] Count II alleges that Sunday River was negligent in its operation and maintenance of the ski area by failing to mark or pad an obstruction in the trail.[3] Sunday River argues that these claims must fail because Maine's "Skiers' and Tramway Passengers' Responsibilities" statute, 26 M.R.S.A. § 488 (1988), does not permit recovery for injuries caused by inherent risks of skiing, such as ice and stumps.[4]

Skiing is a sport that involves certain risks. In recognition of that fact, the Maine Legislature has enacted a statute which limits the scope of liability of ski area operators. The statute provides in pertinent part that:

1. Sanchez is a resident of Massachusetts; Sunday River Skiway Corp. d/b/a Sunday River Ski Resort is a corporation organized under the laws of Maine. Thus, the basis for jurisdiction in this case is diversity of citizenship, 28 U.S.C. § 1332 (1988)

2. Count I is brought by Luis Jr.'s parents, Luis Sanchez, Sr. and Manuela P. Su, in their individual capacities, as well as on behalf of Luis Jr.

3. Count II is also brought by Luis Jr.'s parents, Luis Sanchez, Sr. and Manuela P. Su, in their individual capacities, as well as on behalf of Luis Jr.

4. Sunday River relies on a number of statutes and decisions from other jurisdictions in an attempt to show that this injury was caused by an "inherent risk" of the sport. Because the statutes vary in their wording and because the language of the Maine statute is clear on its face, it is unnecessary to discuss those other statutes and decisions in order to resolve this Motion to Dismiss.

each skier who participates in the sport of skiing shall be deemed to have assumed the risk of the dangers inherent in the sport and assumed the legal responsibility for any injury to his person or property arising out of his participation in the sport of skiing.

26 M.R.S.A. §488. But the statute then makes an important exception to this assumption of the risk: "unless the injury or death was actually caused by the negligent operation or maintenance of the ski area by the ski area operator, its agents or employees." *Id*. Thus, although ski area liability is limited, the statute does not prohibit lawsuits for "negligent operation or maintenance" of a ski area.

Count I, which alleges negligent grooming or clearing of the trail, raises the issue of negligent operation or maintenance, and such a claim is specifically permitted by statute. Count II, alleging failure to properly mark and pad the obstruction in the ski slope, also raises the issue of negligent operation or maintenance of the ski slope. Thus, Count II is similarly permitted by 26 M.R.S.A. § 488.

II.

Next, Sunday River contends that Count III, negligent infliction of emotional distress, and Count IV, loss of companionship, brought by Luis Jr.'s parents, Luis Sr. and Manuela P. Su, in their individual capacities, as well as Count V, breach of contract, asserted by Luis Sr. on his own behalf, should be dismissed because they are barred by the statute of limitations governing claims against ski areas. *See* 14 M.R.S.A. §752-B (1980). Plaintiffs' claims for emotional distress, loss of companionship, and breach of contract arise out of, and are derivative of, the bodily injury allegedly sustained by Luis Jr. *See Gillchrest v. Brown*, 532 A.2d 692, 693 (Me. 1987) (wife's loss of consortium claim derivative from husband's bodily injury); *Packard v. Central Maine Power Co.*, 477 A.2d 264, 268 (Me. 1984) ("Negligent infliction of emotional stress is not an independent tort, but is more properly to be perceived as subordinate to the principal cause of action."). As such, these claims are subject to the same statutory defenses as those which could be asserted against Luis Jr.'s primary claim. *See Box v. Walker*, 453 A.2d 1181, 1183 (Me. 1983).

The Defendant concedes that because Luis Jr. is a minor, 14 M.R.S.A. §853 (Supp. 1992) tolls the statute of limitations as applied to his claims so they are not time-barred.[5] His parents, however, cannot take advantage of that savings section. *See Stanczyk v. Keefe*, 384 F.2d 707, 708 (7th Cir. 1967). The statute of limitations applicable to the parents' claims provides that all civil actions for property damage, bodily injury or death against a ski area owner or operator arising out of participation in skiing shall be commenced within two years after the cause of action accrues. 14 M.R.S.A. § 752-B. Plaintiffs' cause of action

---

5. 14 M.R.S.A. § 853 provides:
If a person entitled to bring any of the actions under sections 752 to 754, including section 752-C, and 851, 852 and Title 24, section 2902 is a minor, mentally ill, imprisoned or without the limits of the United States when the cause of action accrues, the action may be brought within the times limited herein after the disability is removed.

accrued on January 14, 1990. The Complaint was filed with this Court on March 30, 1992, more than two years after the action accrued.[6] Plaintiffs provide no basis for extending the statute of limitations. Accordingly, Luis Sr.'s and Ms. Su's claims for emotional distress and loss of companionship, as well as Luis Sr.'s breach of contract claim, must be dismissed.

III.

Finally, Sunday River contends that Luis Jr.'s claim for breach of contract should be dismissed because the Complaint fails to allege any specific contractual terms which vary its duty from that suggested by the Maine statute. The Complaint alleges that the payment of money to Sunday River was an offer to use the facilities and that by accepting the money, Sunday River agreed to provide a "safe and acceptable [ski] area." Plaintiffs do not allege that Sunday River expressly agreed to these terms. They argue, rather, that when Sunday River accepted the money and provided a ticket, it impliedly agreed to provide a safe ski area.

"Contractual recovery is predicated in the first instance upon a consensual obligation between two or more parties." *Adams v. Buffalo Forge Co.*, 443 A.2d 932, 938 (Me. 1982). "Tort recovery on the other hand, does not rest upon a consensual relationship between the parties.... Rather, in tort, liability is grounded upon the *status* relationship between the parties." *Id.* In tort, the status relationship does not stem from an agreement between the parties; instead, it is created "when the requisite events necessary to support a cause of action in negligence merge—which occurs at 'the point at which a wrongful act produces an injury for which a potential plaintiff is entitled to seek judicial vindication.'" *Id.* (quoting *Williams v. Ford Motor Co.*, 342 A.2d 712, 714 (Me. 1975)). The Complaint in this case is entirely insufficient to transform an ordinary negligence action into an action based in contract in which Sunday River has agreed to insure the safety of its patrons.[7] Thus, Plaintiff Luis Jr.'s claim for breach of control must also be dismissed.

Accordingly, Defendant's Motion to Dismiss Counts I and II of Plaintiffs' Complaint is DENIED; Defendant's Motion to Dismiss Counts III, IV and V is GRANTED; and it is hereby SO ORDERED.

---

6. A federal court sitting in diversity looks to state law to determine when an action is commenced for purposes of the state's statute of limitations. *Walker v. Armco Steel Corp.*, 446 U.S. 740, 752-53, 100 S.Ct. 1978, 1986, 64 L.Ed.2d 659 (1980). Under Maine law an action is commenced "when the summons and complaint are served or when the complaint is filed with the court, whichever occurs first." 14 M.R.S.A. § 553 (1980).

7. The within case does not mean that there can never be an action for bodily injury based in contract against a ski area. A ski area may, by express contract, agree to provide a safe area in which to ski. In such instances, an action in contract may lie against the owner or operator. In the absence of any special warranty or contract, however, an action for bodily injury against a ski area owner or operator is an action in tort. In the instant case, Plaintiffs do not allege that they were given any special warranty by Sunday River. The Court has "no duty to 'conjure up unpled allegations', in order to bolster Plaintiffs' chances of surviving a 12(b)(6) motion to dismiss." *Fleet Credit Corp. v. Sion*, 893 F.2d 441, 444 (1st Cir. 1990) (quoting *Gooley v. Mobil Oil Corp.*, 851 F.2d 513, 514 (1st Cir. 1988)).

Questions and Comments

1. What is meant by statute of limitations? Why is it important for a sport manager to understand this term?
2. If the statute of limitations had run against the father, why had it not run against the son?
3. Tolling the statute of limitations in this case refers to temporarily suspending the statute of limitations until the son reached the age of majority.
4. What is the rationale behind tolling the statute in this case?
5. Can you think of other examples where it would be logical for the statute of limitations to be tolled?
6. When is an action commenced? Why is this important?
7. What is the basis for the court's jurisdiction?
8. What rule does the court assert concerning a motion to dismiss?
9. NOTE: The statute of limitations is usually codified under "Limitation of Actions."
10. Plaintiff's lawyers are well-advised to make certain as to the appropriate statute of limitations at the commencement of representation. Failure to file a lawsuit on time is a fertile source for malpractice.
11. Tort refers to a civil wrong. Notice the contrast of contractual recovery and tort recovery in this case.

Release or waiver. A release or waiver from the consequences of one's negligence is not favored in the law. The court will construe a release or waiver strictly because it is said to be against public policy. However, absent fraud, misrepresentation, or coercion, a release will generally be upheld if carefully drawn. Some jurisdictions require a release to expressly indicate that it protects against the consequences of negligence. The release may even say "whether negligent or not."

In the case that follows, a spectator at a stock car race was injured when struck by a race car. The injury occurred in a restricted area, admission to which was gained by signing a release. The failure to read the release was not a defense. The lower court granted summary judgment for the race-track owner.

•••

TOTH v. TOLEDO SPEEDWAY
583 N.E.2d 357 (Ohio Ct. App. 1989)

PER CURIAM.

This matter is before the court on appeal from a judgment of the Lucas County Court of Common Pleas.

Plaintiffs-appellants, brothers John and Louis Toth, were injured July 27, 1986, while observing a stock car race held on property leased by defendant-appellee, Toledo Speedway. Appellants were observing the race from the back of a pickup truck parked in the infield area, the "restricted area," when the truck was struck by a race car. Appellants gained access to the "restricted area" by signing a release form submitted to them by one of appellee's employees. The race car, operated, ironically, by John Toth's son, John, Jr., went out of control at the track's second turn, striking the truck and injuring appellants.

Appellants filed a complaint against appellee on June 5, 1987. Appellants alleged that appellee failed to maintain the premises in a reasonably safe condition, failed to erect adequate barriers and failed to provide a safe place to watch the race. Appellee filed a motion for summary judgment on October 11, 1988, alleging, *inter alia,* that appellants executed a valid waiver of liability and, accordingly, had expressly assumed the risk of personal injuries and/or damages. The trial court granted appellee's motion for summary judgment in an opinion and journal entry dated January 30, 1989. It is from that judgment that appellants have appealed, setting forth the following three assignments of error:

"A. Appellants did not execute a valid release that would allow appellee to escape liability.

"B. Appellants did not expressly assume the risk of injury.

"C. The appellee owed a duty to appellants since the doctrine of primary assumption of the risk does not apply."

In their first assignment of error, appellants argue that the release relied upon by appellee is invalid. Appellants assert that enforcement of the release violates public policy and that it was signed by appellants without knowledge of its purpose. As an alternative argument, appellants contend that, under the circumstances of this case, the essence of the substantive language of the document somehow prevents the exculpatory language from taking effect.

In setting forth the public policy considerations surrounding this release, appellants argue that at the time the release was executed, appellee possessed bargaining power superior to that of appellants. Appellants assert that a prospective admittee to the restricted area is unable to negotiate the terms of his admittance. Appellants argue that because they possessed unequal bargaining power and could not exclude the exculpatory language prior to accepting the agreement, the release is invalid and violates public policy. We disagree.

The record indicates that appellants were at the track approximately two and one-half hours prior to the time they executed the release and entered the pit area. By the very nature of auto racing in combination with the express language of the release, when appellants chose to relocate to the restricted area, they became "participants" in the race. Further, appellants each testified that they intended to offer John, Jr. assistance during the race. The assistance was to be in the form of mechanical help and/or advice with each appellant attempting to assume a fairly active role in the outcome of the race.

In *French v. Special Services, Inc.* (1958), 107 Ohio App. 435, 8 O.O.2d 421, 159 N.E.2d 785, paragraph two of the syllabus, the Ashland County Court of Appeals held:

"An agreement between a participant in and the proprietor of a stock car race, whereby the former assumes the risk of injuries resulting from his participation in such event and releases the proprietor from any claims for damages, is not invalid as against public policy."

The *French* court also held that a stock car participant and a proprietor were free to contract so as to relieve the latter from liability for damages or injuries to the former except when caused by willful or wanton misconduct. *Id.* at paragraph one of the syllabus. The Supreme Court of Ohio has mandated that such contracts of indemnity executed to relieve one from the results of his purported negligence must be strictly construed. *Kay v. Pennsylvania RR. Co.* (1952), 156 Ohio St. 503, 46 O.O. 417, 103 N.E.2d 751. Further, an intention to provide such indemnification must be set forth in clear, unequivocal terms. *Id.*

Our analysis of the agreement executed by the parties in the case *sub judice* indicates that the intention to release appellee of "all liability" was expressed clearly and unequivocally in the release. We find that, on the basis of the express language, an ordinarily prudent and knowledgeable person should have known that by signing the agreement, he was contracting away all rights to hold the other party liable for negligence. Appellants have presented no evidence tending to establish that appellee's conduct was willful or wanton nor have they alleged that their own conduct should be evaluated by a standard other than that of a reasonably prudent person.

We find that public policy did not prevent these parties from contracting liability away, if that was their intention. Accordingly, under the facts presented, we find that there was a valid waiver of liability for any damages arising from appellee's alleged negligence.

Appellants also assert that the release is invalid because they were mistaken as to its contents at the time they signed it. Arguing that a meeting of the minds must occur between the parties in order to effectuate a release, appellants assert that such a determination is a question of fact for the jury.

The record in the instant case is quite clear as it pertains to the execution of the release. At the gate leading into the restricted area, appellants were handed the release. One of appellee's employees requested that appellants sign their names at the bottom of the form. Appellants admit that they signed the release without reading it. Appellants entered the restricted area immediately after signing the agreement.

This court is cognizant of the almost daily challenges the average person faces in regard to determining when it is prudent to affix his signature to a document. Nevertheless, the only method by which to evaluate the pertinent characteristics of a document is by reading it. In this case, the large printing at the top of the page stated: "RELEASE AND WAIVER OF LIABILITY AND INDEMNITY AGREEMENT." Even if appellants had not read beyond this headline, they would, nevertheless, have been notified of the document's purpose. Appellants assert that they did not read any part of the agreement and did not think it was a release of liability.

Our analysis of well-established theories of law as well as the basics of contract liability indicates that appellants' argument is without merit. In *McAdams v. McAdams* (1909), 80 Ohio St. 232, 240-241, 88 N.E. 542, 544, the Supreme Court of Ohio stated:

"* * * A person of ordinary mind cannot be heard to say that he was misled into signing a paper which was different from what he intended, when he
could have known the truth by merely looking when he signed."

More importantly, if a person can read and is not prevented from reading
what he signs and enters a contract, it will not do if when the person is "* * *
` * * * called upon to respond to its obligations, to say that he did not read it
when he signed it, or did not know what it contained. If this were permitted,
contracts would not be worth the paper on which they are written; But such
is not the law. A contractor must stand by the words of his contract; and, if
he will not read what he signs, he alone is responsible for his omission. * * *
' " *Id.* at 241, 88 N.E. at 544. See, also, *McCuskey v. Budnick* (1956), 165 Ohio
St. 533, 60 O.O. 493, 138 N.E.2d 386.

In other words, we find that the release agreement is not invalid or unenforceable merely because appellants either neglected to read it or chose not to
read it prior to affixing their signatures to the document. In the absence of an
allegation of fraud or mistake, appellants alone are responsible for omitting to
read what they signed. *Dice v. Akron, Canton & Youngstown RR. Co.* (1951),
155 Ohio St. 185, 191, 44 O.O. 162, 165, 98 N.E.2d 301, 304, reversed on other
grounds (1952), 342 U.S. 359, 72 S.Ct. 312, 96 L.Ed. 398, 47 O.O. 53.

Appellants rely on *Mut. Life Ins. Co. v. Svonavec* (1929), 32 Ohio App.
195, 166 N.E. 905, in support of their argument that the release is invalid. In
Svonavec, the court stated:

"* * * A release, like every other contract entered into between parties, in
order to be binding must be the result of a meeting of the minds between the
parties.   * * * " *Id.* at 198, 166 N.E. at 906.

The contract in *Svonavec* was held invalid on the basis of the fact that
Barbara Svonavec was "* * * ignorant of the English language * * * . She
claims that she did not understand the nature of the transaction and that at
no time did she intend to execute such a release. * * * " *Id.* at 198, 166 N.E.
at 906.

We find that *Svonavec* is distinguishable from the case *sub judice.* If
appellants claimed to be "ignorant of the English language" or if they read the
agreement and understood it to be something other than a release, whether
there was a meeting of the minds would indeed be a question for the jury to
answer after it heard the witnesses and had the opportunity to determine the
credit to which their statements were entitled. *Id.* at 198, 166 N.E. at 906.
Such a situation, however, has not been demonstrated in the instant case.

. . . . .

. . . . appellants argue that the doctrine of primary assumption of risk is
not applicable to the instant case. . . . .

Primary assumption of risk concerns those " * * * cases where there is a
lack of duty owed by the defendant to the plaintiff. This type of assumption
of risk is typified by the baseball cases where a plaintiff is injured when a
baseball is hit into the stands. * * * " *Id.,* 6 Ohio St.3d at 114, 6 OBR at 174,
451 N.E.2d at 783. Due to the fact that we have affirmed the trial court's
determination that, by executing a release, appellants "expressly" assumed the

risk of their injuries, it is unnecessary for us to determine whether the risks were also "primarily" assumed. Accordingly, we find appellants' third assignment of error moot and, therefore, not well taken.

On consideration whereof, the court finds substantial justice has been done the parties complaining, and judgment of the Lucas County Court of Common Pleas is affirmed. It is ordered that appellants pay the court costs of this appeal.

Judgment affirmed.

.   .   .   .   .

Questions and Comments

1. What arguments could be advanced in favor of upholding a release signed by spectators at a recreational event?
2. What arguments could be advanced against the signing of a release by a spectator at a recreational event?
3. How does contract law generally impact the validity of a release signed by a spectator at a recreational event?
4. Can we relate the doctrine of assumption of risk to the signing of a release? (Note: The testimony by appellants Tooth indicated that they "may have believed the area to be unsafe." However, appellants did not leave the area or advise the track officials that the area was unsafe.)
5. Indemnity referenced in the case refers to the obligation of one person to make good the obligation of another person.
6. A *per curiam* opinion is the opinion of the whole court.
7. Releases or waivers for minor children that are signed by the parents, the child, or both parent and child are viewed differently than a release for an adult signed by that adult. The individual cases differ by state and the wording of the release. In general, a parent cannot sign away the rights of a child. This means that the release is not valid. The parent can promise to indemnify the sport manager. However, if the parents have no financial resources, indemnification is monetarily meaningless.

Contributory negligence. Historically, contributory negligence is an absolute defense. Briefly stated, if a plaintiff is negligent, then no recovery is permissible. The parties take their losses and go their own way. It is easy to see why such a principle could result in inequities and unfairness. Juries sometimes mitigate the harshness of the law. Stated differently, a jury will adjust the facts in such a way as to achieve what they consider to be an equitable result.

Because of the harshness of the doctrine of contributory negligence, the doctrine of comparative negligence has developed. Comparative negligence, as a general rule, allocates damages in proportion to comparative fault. For example, fault may be attributed 30% to the defendant and 70% to the plaintiff. The doctrine of comparative negligence for the most part has resulted from statutory enactment. On occasion, however, it has resulted from judicial decision. In any event, the trend appears to be in the direction of comparative negligence.

Comparative negligence. Comparative negligence is designed to allay the harshness of the contributory negligence rule. Comparative negligence apportions the loss by determining the percentage of fault. Thus, if each party to a lawsuit was 50% at fault, each party would pay 50% of the total damage. The trend is clearly in the direction of comparative negligence.

Assumption of risk. The doctrine of assumption of risk developed quite early. Athletics cases offer the prime example for this principle. When one voluntarily engages in an athletic contest, that individual is said to have assumed the risk of injury. This is especially evident in certain contact sports and in certain high-risk sports that have inherent dangers. Participants voluntarily consent to exposure to the risk. Knowledge and appreciation of the risks are important.

Such a doctrine of assumption of risk was also helpful when the transition was made from an agrarian economy to an industrial state. The industrial revolution progressed by the aid of doctrines such as assumption of risk. A price was paid for progress, and the price involved an acceptance of the notion that an individual could contract away his or her right to recovery for injury. This principle applied even though there was no formal contract. The employee was said to have assumed the risk of poor working conditions and thus could not recover if he or she were injured. Many states have now abolished the doctrine of assumption of risk. However, the doctrine has been preserved somewhat under the umbrella of contributory negligence.

On January 12, 1993, a New York court refused to dismiss an action based on the defense of assumption of risk. The case involved an injury to a tennis player. The player's foot became entangled in a net that divided the tennis court. The net draped on the floor by approximately a foot.

As you read the case, ask yourself, was there voluntary exposure to the risk? Did the participant have knowledge of and appreciation of the risk?

•••

RADWANER v. USTA NATIONAL TENNIS CENTER
592 N.Y.S.2d 307 (N.Y. App. Div. 1993)

Before CARRO, J.P., and ELLERIN, KUPFERMAN, KASSAL and RUBIN, JJ

MEMORANDUM DECISION.

Judgment of the Supreme Court, Bronx County (Barry Salman, J.), entered July 29, 1991, upon a jury verdict which, *inter alia,* awarded plaintiff $183,132.50 for past and future pain and suffering, unanimously affirmed, without costs.

Plaintiff seeks damages for personal injuries sustained in a fall on the USTA's tennis court. Plaintiff was engaged in a tennis game on court H of the USTA Flushing Meadows Center when his foot became entangled in a net that divided the tennis courts and draped on the floor by approximately a foot. Plaintiff suffered a dislocated right shoulder and a torn muscle tendon as a result of his fall.

Defendant contends that the court improperly instructed the jury on assumption of risk. However, defendant did not timely object to the court's instructions and therefore this issue is not preserved for our review.

Defendant further asserts that its motion to dismiss was improperly denied on the ground that assumption of risk is an issue of law which should not have been presented to the jury. We disagree. In the instant case we cannot say that a dragging divider net is a hazard to which tennis players must be normally exposed *(Henig v. Hofstra Univ.,* 160 A.D.2d 761, 762, 553 N.Y.S.2d 479). A triable issue of fact remains when engendered additional risks exist that "do not inhere in the sport" *(Owen v. R.J.S. Safety Equip.,* 79 N.Y.2d 967, 970, 582 N.Y.S.2d 998, 591 N.E.2d 1184).

Assumption of risk requires both knowledge of the defect and also an appreciation of the resultant risk. Among many factors to be considered in determining the risk involved are the particular skill and experience of a plaintiff and whether the plaintiff is a professional or amateur athlete. The assumption of risk to be implied from participation in a sport is usually a question of fact for a jury unless the facts indicate that the assumption of risk factor is a matter of law. Upon the facts in this case, we are not prepared to say that no factual issue exists for determination by a jury. The defense of assumption of risk was not clearly established *(see, Maddox v. City of New York,* 66 N.Y.2d 270, 496 N.Y.S.2d 726, 487 N.E.2d 553).

Questions and Comments

1. Did this case involve an express or an implied assumption of risk?
2. Did the court find that a draping net was a danger that was inherent in the sport?
3. What factors undergird the theory of assumption of risk? (See last paragraph in this case.)
4. A release is in the nature of an expressed assumption of risk.

Recreational user statutes. In 1990, approximately 47 states had recreational user statutes. These statutes encourage landowners to make their land available for recreational purposes without liability. In other words, a landowner who permits free recreational use of land is not held negligent. However, because such statutes are predicated upon no fee being charged, the defense will be of limited value to the owner of private recreational enterprises. Such enterprises usually charge for their services. When no charge is made, the statute may be invoked, as in Midwestern v. Northern Kentucky Community Center (1987). Knowledge of such a defense could assist a private recreational facility in obtaining permission to use land as a part of its recreational program. No charge would be made by the landowner; for example, the owner of an abandoned rock quarry might give permission for scuba diving in a pool of water if the owner was advised as to his defense under the recreational user statute.

Sovereign immunity. The defense of sovereign immunity precludes a state agency from being sued without its consent. (Originally, this referred to the concept that "the king can do no wrong.") Such consent is usually given by the state legislature in the form of tort claims acts. On rare occasions the defense of sovereign immunity is abolished by judicial decision. The use of sovereign immunity can be an effective defense in those jurisdictions that retain sovereign immunity. Obviously, sovereign immunity will not be available to the private entrepreneur. However, many students in the field of recreation go into government work. Those students may very well need to remember the possibilities that sovereign immunity offers, but caution is still urged. Sovereign immunity may have special rules as to venue (where the case may be heard), damages, and statutes of limitation. Special rules may also be applicable with respect to facilities that are publicly owned. Further, in some jurisdictions the purchase of liability insurance stands as an exception to the doctrine of sovereign immunity. In other words, if the insurance is purchased, then sovereign immunity is waived.

Authors' Note

Civil Rule 8.03 in the *Kentucky Rules of Court 1995* states: "In pleading to a preceding pleading, a party shall set forth affirmatively... assumption of risk, contributory negligence, release and statute of limitations." It is important to remember that the affirmative defenses listed above cannot be raised for the first time on appeal. Rationale: The trial judge should not be overturned on grounds that were not directed to his attention during the course of the trial. One exception to be noted is that which deals with jurisdiction. The question of jurisdiction can be raised by the court or litigant at any time. The sport manager has a duty to care for the participants. Elements to be considered include reasonableness of the case, foreseeability of the injury, and knowledge of the participant.

SUMMARY

A careful attention to legal defenses against a charge of negligence is important. Negligence is something to be avoided. Certainly no one wishes to cause injury to anyone. The fact that injury has occurred is not necessarily an earth-shaking event. Each party to a lawsuit is entitled to take advantage of any rule or principle of law that tends to advance that party's cause. The defenses to negligence will serve the owner or manager in good stead. There should be no hesitancy in setting up defenses. To defend oneself is not unethical, unprofessional, or immoral. The clash of competing ideas is designed to ensure a result that society looks upon as being fair and reasonable.

As a sport manager, would it be important to explain the risks of a sport to an individual? Could you have the client sign a document that he or she understands the risks as listed? When would you use a release or waiver?

This could be you - check your response

Mac could file suit when he is 18 years old if the statute of limitations is tolled for that particular state.

Even if Mac himself requested permission to perform the stunt without spotters, the instructor, not the student, is still the expert. The duty to instruct and supervise cannot be abolished.

Mac's parents signed a release for injury. However, this would not prohibit Mac from filing suit at the age of majority. Mac could sue the instructor. Mac could sue the owner of the business under the doctrine of *respondeat superior*. A parent cannot relieve an instructor from the consequences of negligence resulting in injury to a child. This principle applies both to the instructor and to the owners of the business.

REFERENCES

Authors

Keeton, W. Page (1984). *Prosser and Keeton on the law of torts* (5th ed). St. Paul, MN: West Publishing Co.

Kionka, Edward J. (1977). *Torts in a nutshell: Injuries to persons and property.* St. Paul, MN: West Publishing Co.

Cases

Bitterman v. Atkins, 458 S.E.2d 688 (Ga.App. 1995).

Conway v. Town of Wilton, 664 A.2d 327 (Conn.App. 1995).

Dicruttalo v. Blaise Enterprises, Inc., 621 N.Y.S.2d 199 (A.D. 3 Dept. 1995).

Kruse v. Iron Range Snowmobile Club, 890 F.Supp. 681 (W.D.Mich. 1995).

Midwestern v. Northern Kentucky Community Center, 736 S.W.2d 348 (Ky. App. 1987).

Radwaner v. USTA National Tennis Center, 592 N.Y.S. 2d 307 (N.Y. App. Div. 1993).

Sanchez v. Sunday River Skiway Corp., 802 F. Supp. 539 (D. Me. 1992).

Toth v. Toledo Speedway, 583 N.E.2d 357 (Ohio Ct. App. 1989).

Wilson v. Bell Fuels, Inc., 574 N.E.2d 200 (Ill. App. Ct. 1991).

Legal Encyclopedias

57A Am.Jur.2d *Negligence* §§ 1-1127 (1989), with current updates.

57B Am.Jur.2d *Negligence* §§ 1128-2241 (1989), with current updates.

65 C.J.S. *Negligence* §§ 1-115 (1966) with current updates.

65A C.J.S. *Negligence* §§ 116-306 (1966) with current updates.

28 Words and Phrases *Negligence* pp. 521-680 (1955).

Codes, Restatements, and Rules

Civil Rule 8.03, *Kentucky Rules of Court 1995.*

Restatement (Second) of Torts §§ 1-951 (1965) with current updates.

CHAPTER 7

INJURY AND INTENTIONAL TORTS

INTRODUCTION

As indicated in the Focus to this part of the textbook, one who is injured can expect to recover for the injury under certain circumstances. A recovery for acts of negligence that result in injury has been explained in previous chapters. One chapter presents the various defenses that can be offered to defeat a claim for damages predicated upon negligence. This chapter deals with an injury that is a result of an intentional act or, in some cases, an omission to act. Intentional torts include various subject matters, the more common of which include assault, battery, and false imprisonment. The constituent elements of each of these torts will be set forth in this chapter along with the possible defenses that are associated with each.

IN THIS CHAPTER YOU WILL LEARN:
The elements that make up an assault as contemplated by a civil action
The elements that make up a battery as contemplated by a civil action
The elements that make up false imprisonment as contemplated by a civil action
The defenses most commonly associated with each of the three causes of action listed
The factual circumstances that can give rise to a potential lawsuit for injury, whether occasioned by assault, battery, or false imprisonment

ACCIDENT?

KEY WORDS: *false imprisonment, assault, vicarious liability, battery, reckless misconduct, dictum*

This could be you!

Maria Jones has now finished school as a health and recreation major and desires to open her own business enterprise. To this end, she purchases 50 acres of land adjoining the city limits and constructs a building for the purpose of teaching martial arts. The 50 acres will allow for adequate parking and perhaps a playground for children.

Even though she has employed trained instructors, Maria is concerned about the legal liability for martial arts injuries to patrons. She has students in the class sign releases regarding negligent instruction and supervision. The waiver releases the Joneses from liability "whether negligent or not."

After class one evening, an argument between Ms White and Ms Foust, two of the patrons, started in the parking lot and continued into the adjacent street. A fight resulted that severely injured White. Ms Foust claimed that Ms White attacked her while she (Foust) was opening her car door, and further claimed that she was only defending herself and did not intend to put the attacking woman in the hospital.

Is Maria Jones liable in this incident? What factors would the court consider? Could Ms White sue Ms Foust?

JUDICIAL DECISIONS

Assault and Battery and False Imprisonment

In 1969 the Supreme Court of Rhode Island decided a case that spoke to both "assault and battery" and "false imprisonment." The case involved an action by a patron who was injured while being forcibly removed from a racetrack. The suit was filed against the racetrack and a protective association that provided security. Multiple points of law were considered and resolved.

Assault refers to the willful intent or threat to injure another person. Touching the person does not need to occur for assault to be committed. Any intentional display of force that would give the victim reason to fear or expect immediate bodily harm is an assault.

The elements of a criminal assault may be different from a tortuous assault. Assault and battery is an unlawful physical contact with another person. It is a crime as well as a tort.

False arrest is an unlawful detention of someone. False arrest or false imprisonment is a tort. If malice or ill will can be shown, the plaintiff could be awarded punitive damages as well as nominal or compensatory damages.

Read the following case and see if an assault, battery, or false arrest occurred. Could a sport manager legally restrain a person suspected of a crime?

··

WEBBIER v. THOROUGHBRED RACING PROTECTIVE BUREAU, INC.
254 A.2d 285 (R.I. 1969)

OPINION

KELLEHER, Justice.

These are two actions of trespass wherein the plaintiff seeks damages for false arrest and assault and battery. These actions were instituted prior to the effective date of the superior court's new rules of civil procedure. Thereafter they were consolidated and tried to a jury in the superior court which returned a verdict of $4,000 in each case. The trial justice denied the defendants' motions for a new trial, but granted such a motion to the plaintiff on the issue of compensatory damages[1] unless the defendants consented to an additur of $3,500 to each verdict. The case is before us on the defendants' appeals.

One defendant, Burrillville Racing Association, operates the Lincoln Downs Race Track. The other defendant, Thoroughbred Racing Protective Bureau, Inc., is a New York corporation specializing in the maintenance and supervision of police and security activities of personnel employed by various thoroughbred racetracks—in this country. Hereafter reference will be made to the racetrack and the bureau respectively.

James Webbier, the plaintiff, is a combat veteran of World War II. As an army infantryman, he participated in military operations incidental to the seizure of the Normandy beachhead. In July 1944 he was under artillery attack when a shell exploded nearby wounding him in the chest. He was evacuated to London where he was treated for physical injuries and combat fatigue. Five months later plaintiff was returned to the United States for further hospitalization followed by his severance from the military for medical reasons. Since that time, plaintiff has required periodic treatment by the veterans administration for psychoneurosis. This nervous disorder is causally related to his combat ordeal. He receives a government pension for his service-connected disability which at the time of the incidents described hereafter was a 70 per cent disability pension but had increased to 100 per cent at the time of the trial. A psychiatrist who testified for plaintiff reported that his patient, a man of more than 40 years, had the mental age of a 10-year old.

The plaintiff likes to watch horses. On September 6, 1952, he went to Lincoln Downs and purchased a ticket for the clubhouse section. He sat in the box-seat area with three other persons. One of these was a man described only as Joe. Prior to the third race, plaintiff and his friend left their seats and walked to a vending stand where hot dogs and soda were sold. There plaintiff "slipped" Joe a $5 bill, whereupon two men employed as racetrack detectives appeared and ordered both men to accompany them to the offices of the bureau.

The detectives were Raymond D. Tempest and Raymond J. Shannon. Both

---

1. In each case, plaintiff sought compensatory and punitive damages. The jury awarded compensatory damages only. The trial justice in granting plaintiff a new trial specifically limited it to the issue of compensatory damages. [additur: added damges]

are part-time employees at the racetrack. Each man holds high rank in the police departments of different cities in this state. Tempest is the chief inspector of the Woonsocket police department. He is over six feet tall and weighs in excess of 265 pounds. Shannon is a lieutenant in the detective division of the Pawtucket police department. Although these men are paid on a daily basis by the track, they work under the direction and control of the bureau.

The testimony as to occurrences after the initial confrontation at the hot-dog stand is in conflict. Webbier testified that when Tempest ordered him and his companion to go to the bureau's offices that he inquired as to the reason. To this Tempest replied "Just come with me." They were escorted to the upper grandstand where the bureau maintains its offices comprised of an outer and inner room.

The Plaintiff described the ensuing events as follows:

> Upon his arrival at the bureau's offices, he was kept in the outer office while Joe was first interrogated in the inner room by the bureau's agent-in-charge, Clifford A. Wickman. While he waited in the outer office, plaintiff was accompanied by Tempest. The plaintiff asked to leave but Tempest would not permit him to do so. When Joe's questioning was concluded, he was escorted out past Webbier and allowed to return to his seat in the clubhouse.

The plaintiff was then led into the inner office where Wickman undertook his interrogation. Present were Tempest, Shannon and a third detective. Wickman inquired as to plaintiff's source of income and was told of Webbier's pension. When Wickman sought the amount of the pension, plaintiff stated that he could not divulge this information. Wickman then ordered plaintiff to empty his pockets. The plaintiff refused asserting that their contents were none of their business. To this the agent-in-charge said "You're one of the wise-guys, I'll take care of you." Detective Tempest then audibly concurred with Wickman's remark indicating that he also would take care of Webbier. At this time Wickman said to Tempest "Take him and throw him out of the place."

Tempest seized plaintiff by the arm and pulled him from the office to a narrow stairway leading to a lower level. As plaintiff was descending the stairs, Tempest was behind him pushing him in the back. The plaintiff fell down the stairs. Recovering himself, he became unnerved and began to vomit. People gathered curious as to the cause of the commotion. Tempest then escorted plaintiff to the grandstand exit refusing to allow him to leave by the clubhouse gate which was closer to his automobile.

The plaintiff drove to the Lincoln barracks of the state police where he lodged a complaint concerning his treatment. This was on Thursday. On the following Monday, Mr. Webbier was admitted to the hospital for treatment of nervous upset.

Wickman and the two detectives testified to a contrary version of the afternoon's activities. The plaintiff, they said, was not mistreated nor was he confined in any manner. They denied that plaintiff had been touched physically saying that he did not have to come to the bureau's offices and once there, he could have left of his own volition. They conceded that they did not inform plaintiff that he could stay or go as he pleased. The defense witnesses agreed that they intended to permit Webbier to rejoin his friend in the clubhouse but that his boisterousness necessitated his ejection.

In their separate appeals, each defendant has alleged that the trial justice erred in numerous rulings he made during and after the trial. Many of their claims lack any merit whatever and they shall not be discussed herein. We have, however, for ease of understanding grouped defendants' claims which we deem worthy of consideration in this appeal. In many instances, defendants' contentions overlap each other.

I

The Liability of the Racetrack

In his charge to the jury, the trial justice ruled that Wickman, Tempest and Shannon were agents of the bureau. None of the parties before us disputes this conclusion. The racetrack, however, disclaims liability for the detectives' actions arguing that as related to it, the detectives were only agents of an independent contractor. We cannot agree.

. . . . . [Discussion omitted.]

It is readily apparent to us from a reading of the racing commission's rules and the statute vesting the racetrack with broad powers of ejection that the protection of the race-going public from the presence of bookmakers, touts, pickpockets and other undesirables is a duty which is imposed by law upon the racetrack. While nothing prevents a licensee from permitting a third party to carry out this activity, defendant racetrack cannot expect to avoid liability by so doing.

.   .   .   .   .

II

The Court's Failure to Direct a Verdict for Defendants

In reviewing defendants' contentions as to the denial by the trial court of their motions for a directed verdict, we have viewed the evidence produced by plaintiff in a light most favorable to his cause. We find no merit in defendants' arguments that the trial justice committed error in permitting the jury to consider plaintiff's counts for false imprisonment, assault and battery.

In Barth v. Flad, 99 R.I. 446, 208 A.2d 533, this court pointed out that the essence of an action for false imprisonment is the restraint of another without legal justification. The tort involves an imposition of unlawful restraint upon another's freedom of movement. This restraint need only continue for no more than a brief time. See Restatement (Second) of Torts, §35. If a person is unlawfully detained by another and is fearful that physical force will be used unless he submits to the detention, his submission thereto will not bar his cause of action. See Zayre of Virginia, Inc. v. Gowdy, 207 Va. 47, 147 S.E.2d 710.

While the racetrack admits that a false imprisonment action goes to the question of an illegal restraint, it takes solace in Webbier's statement that he had no fear of Tempest as he was being brought from the vending stand to the bureau's office. It claims that he consented to be interviewed by the bureau's agent. The defendants, however, overlook the events that took place after Webbier had reached the office. The plaintiff testified that Tempest remained in his company for the duration of his detention in the outer office. When he asked the detective if he could leave, he was told that he could not. As of that moment, plaintiff's freedom of locomotion was clearly infringed upon. It was not necessary for plaintiff, a man of slight proportions, to brave the consequence of resistance in the face of his physical disadvantage. A man in such a position need not risk bodily injury as a means of perfecting his right of recovery. The plaintiff acted with prudence in declining such a course of action.

Considering the evidence as it bears upon plaintiff's claim for assault, we do not dispute the racetrack's recitation of the familiar principle that words alone do not give rise to a cause of action. The defendants argue that the facts put forward by plaintiff show nothing more than a situation in which harsh words were directed at him by Wickman and Tempest. For this reason, they allege that the trial court erred in failing to direct a verdict upon plaintiff's count for assault. We feel that defendants' contention involves a considerable understatement.

Most simply stated, an assault is a physical act of a threatening nature which puts an individual in fear of immediate bodily harm. See Restatement (Second) of Torts, §21. It is the complainant's apprehension of injury which renders the defendant's act compensable. See Henry v. Cherry & Webb, 30 R.I. 13, 73 A. 97, 24 L.R.A., N.S., 991. Words alone are never a sufficient basis for a finding for assault. See Kaufman v. Kansas Power & Light Co., 144 Kan. 283, 58 P.2d 1055; Restatement (Second) of Torts, §31. However, words can give character to subsequent physical acts. See Hulse v. Tollman, 49 Ill.App. 490; Keep v. Quallman, 68 Wis. 451, 32 N.W. 233.

In the present case, Mr. Webbier's testimony reveals that his refusal to manifest the contents of his pockets was met with words of ominous connotation from both Wickman and Tempest. Both individuals said they would "Take care" of plaintiff. Wickman then told Tempest to take Webbier and "Throw him out of the place." Tempest took plaintiff by the arm. While no statement is found on the record confirming the fact that Webbier was put in fear as Tempest approached him to carry out the command, we feel that the testimony regarding this occurrence must be read in its entirety. When we do this, we are convinced that there was sufficient evidence to go to the jury on the count for assault.

Immediately after plaintiff indicated that Tempest had taken him by the arm, the following testimony was elicited from him by his attorney:

"Q What did Mr. Tempest do next?

"A He said, 'Come on, let's get out of here.' And he took me by the arm, and dragged me out.

"Q What did he do next?

"A As I was walking down the stairs, *I was scared* of him because I started to get nervous." (italics ours)

We feel that plaintiff's statement that he was *scared* as he was being dragged out must be read in the light of his previous testimony as to the detective's remarks and his perception of Tempest approaching him and seizing him by the arm. We feel that a jury considering this testimony as a whole could properly infer that plaintiff was also put in fear as Tempest moved toward him. In short, we have no difficulty in agreeing with the trial court that plaintiff's assault count was a matter for the jury.

In pressing its motion for a directed verdict, the bureau classifies plaintiff's testimony as being inherently improbable and incapable of belief citing the case of Gaudette v. Carter, 100 R.I. 259, 262, 214 A.2d 197, 199. However, we have carefully studied the record in this case and we cannot describe plaintiff's testimony as inherently improbable or unworthy of belief. Much of his testimony finds corroboration in the records of the state police and the veterans administration. While there is a conflict in the evidence as to the occurrences at Lincoln Downs on the day in question, this conflict exists in credible evidence adduced from both sides. The jury selected the evidence which it felt to be the most credible and we will not now disturb their finding.

III

The Defendants' Motion to Pass the Cases

. . . . . *[Discussion omitted.]*

IV

The Bureau's Objection to the Inadmissibility of the Bureau's Records

. . . . . *[Discussion omitted.]*

V

Was the Bureau's Action Privileged?

As noted before, the general assembly has authorized any licensed racetrack in this state to refuse admission to or to eject from its premises any persons who it believes is undesirable and whose presence is inconsistent with the proper conduct of a racing meet. The bureau claims that this provision immunizes it from any liability because of the action of its agent-in-charge and the two detectives. We do not subscribe to this theory.

In our opinion the statute is clear and unambiguous. It gives a duly licensed racetrack the right under certain circumstances to refuse admission to its premises and to eject therefrom various individuals. The legislature did not, however, grant the track any right to detain these people. . . . .

The ejection statute affords no protective shield for defendants' liability for the false imprisonment of Webbier.

VI

Motions for a New Trial

In considering the respective motions for a new trial, the trial justice made an extensive review and analysis of the evidence which related to the incidents which took place in the bureau's office on that September afternoon in

1962. The court categorically stated that he believed plaintiff. He characterized the testimony of the bureau's agent-in-charge as being evasive. The trial judge specifically rejected the detectives' tale that nobody touched plaintiff. He commented favorably on the testimony of the psychiatrist who declared that the episode of September 6, 1962 aggravated and rekindled Webbier's emotional difficulties.

. . . . Here evidence relating to plaintiff's loss of wages and aggravation of his pre-existing mental condition was admitted without objection.

. . . . The issues of plaintiff's earning capacity and his preexisting condition were proper matters for the jury's consideration.

The record discloses that Webbier was hospitalized after his visit to the track and it also shows that he was under the care and treatment by the veterans administration for an extended period of time. The plaintiff described to the jury in graphic fashion as to how his illness manifests itself. Since the injury involved in false imprisonment is in part a mental one, he is entitled to be compensated for mental suffering and humiliation he experienced particularly as he was being propelled down the stairs in front of the crowd that had gathered. We therefore do not agree with the track when it alleges that the jury's award was grossly excessive.

The jury's award of $4,000 against each defendant was for compensatory damages only. It expressly denied plaintiff's request that he also be given punitive damages. . . . . [Discussion omitted.] [The jury intended this to be a total of $8,000.]

The trial justice in granting the additur pointed out that had not Webbier been mistreated at the track, he could have continued to earn the modest sum of about $25 a week and that he was prevented from performing any gainful occupation for at least two years. He described plaintiff's pain and suffering as being real and substantial. He then concluded that $7,500 would have been a just verdict in these circumstances.

This court in Fitzgerald v. Rendene, 98 R.I. 239, 201 A.2d 137, declared that there is no precise formula by which an additur may be determined and we are reluctant to interfere with a trial judge's finding on that issue . . . . Nor do we find any grounds to order a new trial on both issues of liability and damages as requested by defendants. . . . .

. . . . .

In each case, the defendant's appeal is denied and dismissed and each case is remitted to the superior court for a new trial on compensatory damages only unless the defendants shall within the period to be fixed by that court consent to the additur heretofore awarded by the trial justice.

Questions and Comments

1. Why did the plaintiff not sue the individuals responsible for his injury and ejectment?
2. What is meant by the principle of vicarious liability?

3. Does the principle of vicarious liability apply to an independent contractor? Hint: Was the racetrack liable for the actions of the detectives?
4. How does this case define "assault and battery"?
5. How does this case define "false imprisonment"?
6. As a practical matter, what are the equities that seem to favor the plaintiff in this particular case?
7. What does this case teach with respect to damages?

Sporting Events and Intentional Misconduct or Reckless Misconduct

A golfer was struck in the eye by a golf ball propelled by another golfer. Although suit was predicated on negligence, the court took time to discuss liability for intentional tort. In this case the court found that there was not an intentional tort. The case is important for the rule of law espoused and for the dictum that relates to the subject matter of this chapter. *Dictum* refers to the judge's opinion that does not necessarily speak to the point of law in the case, but refers to some other point that the judge wishes to make.

....

THOMPSON v. McNEILL
559 N.E.2d 705 (Ohio 1990)

Syllabus by the Court
1. Between participants in a sporting event, only injuries caused by intentional conduct, or in some instances reckless misconduct, may give rise to a cause of action. There is no liability for injuries caused by negligent conduct, (*Marchetti v. Kalish* [1990], 53 Ohio St.3d 95, 559 N.E.2d 699, approved and followed.)
2. A player who injures another player in the course of a sporting event by conduct that is a foreseeable, customary part of the sport cannot be held liable for negligence because no duty is owed to protect the victim from that conduct.

———————

On July 22, 1986, appellee, JoAnn Thompson, was playing golf at Prestwick Country Club with appellant, Lucille McNeill, and two other women. When the foursome reached the twelfth tee, McNeill hit her ball onto the fairway. Her next shot went off to the right into a water hazard. Thompson went to search for the ball in the vicinity of the water hazard. McNeill and another member of the foursome testified in their depositions that McNeill said she (McNeill) was going to hit another ball. Thompson and the other member of the foursome could not remember hearing McNeill say that.

When McNeill hit her third shot from the fairway, Thompson remained to McNeill's right at the water hazard, at a distance Thompson estimated as twelve to fifteen yards from McNeill. Thompson, McNeill, and one other witness located Thompson at an angle approximately ninety degrees from the intended path of the ball. McNeill shanked the shot toward Thompson. McNeill testified in her deposition that once she realized the ball was going off toward the right, she and one of the other women, Carolyn Hammitt, yelled "fore" and "JoAnn." Thompson apparently did not hear such a warning before the ball hit her. Thompson saw McNeill swing her club and the ball coming toward her, but stated later that there was no time to move. The ball hit her in the right eye, causing severe injury.

On August 13, 1987, Thompson and her husband brought an action against McNeill in negligence. McNeill's answer, filed September 24, 1987, denied that McNeill was negligent and raised the defenses of assumption of the risk and comparative negligence. All the members of the foursome were deposed. McNeill moved for summary judgment on March 15, 1988. The trial court followed *Hanson v. Kynast* (1987), 38 Ohio App.3d 58, 526 N.E.2d 327, finding that Ohio does not recognize a cause of action in negligence for a claim of injury to a participant in a sporting activity by a co-participant.

Thompson appealed to the Court of Appeals for Summit County, which reversed the trial court and remanded. In its March 1, 1989 opinion the court of appeals declined to follow the principles enunciated in its own earlier decision in *McElhaney v. Monroe* (Feb. 1, 1989), Summit App. No. 13454, unreported 1989 WL 7987. *McElhaney* adopted the *Hanson* court's conclusion that a participant in a sport has no cause of action in negligence in Ohio for injuries inflicted by a co-participant. The court of appeals distinguished this case from *McElhaney* by stating that *McElhaney* applies only to sports with a high degree of physical contact, unlike golf, which is a nonphysical contact sport.

This cause is now before this court pursuant to the allowance of a motion to certify the record.

.　.　.　.

WRIGHT, Justice.

The issue before us is the degree of care owed between participants in a sport, in this instance the game of golf. For the reasons that follow, we hold that between participants in such sporting events, only injuries caused by intentional conduct, or in some instances reckless misconduct, may give rise to a cause of action. There is no liability for injuries caused by negligent conduct.

There is a dearth of Ohio case law in this area. In *Rogers v. Allis-Chalmers Mfg. Co.* (1950), 153 Ohio St. 513, 41 O.O.514, 92 N.E.2d 677, the issue was whether a company could be held liable for injuries inflicted by one of its employees playing on a company-sponsored golf team. In dictum, this court remarked that a golfer assumes the ordinary risks of the game, one of which is the risk of being hit by a golf ball. *Id.* at 522, 41 O.O. at 518, 92 N.E.2d at 681-682. However, the case was decided on the basis of the doctrine of *respondeat superior.* This court has never resolved the question of liability between participants in a sport.

It is necessary to fashion a special rule for tort liability between participants in a sporting event because playing fields, golf courses, and boxing rings are places in which behavior that would give rise to tort liability under ordinary circumstances is accepted and indeed encouraged. Paradoxically, however, amateur and professional athletes are expected to confine their behavior to that which is allowed by the rules of the game.

We say an act is negligent when "* * * the actor does not desire to bring about the consequences which follow, nor does he know that they are substantially certain to occur, or believe that they will. There is merely a risk of such consequences, sufficiently great to lead a reasonable person in his position to anticipate them, and to guard against them. * * * " Prosser & Keeton, Law of Torts (5 Ed. 1984) 169, Section 31. An act is negligent if it "* * * falls below a standard established by the law for the protection of others against unreasonable risk of harm." *Id.* at 170. The difficulty in applying these principles of negligence to sports is that risk of inadvertent harm is often built into the sport. Injuries are a regular occurrence in many sports, such as football and hockey. Moreover, one who plays baseball, tennis, volleyball, soccer, basketball, or golf is subjected to risk of harm from balls struck or thrown travelling at considerable speed.

Acts that would give rise to tort liability for negligence on a city street or in a backyard are not negligent in the context of a game where such an act is foreseeable and within the rules. For instance, a golfer who hits practice balls in his backyard and inadvertently hits a neighbor who is gardening or mowing the lawn next door must be held to a different standard than a golfer whose drive hits another golfer on a golf course. A principal difference is the golfer's duty to the one he hit. The neighbor, unlike the other golfer or spectator on the course, has not agreed to participate or watch and cannot be expected to foresee or accept the attendant risk of injury. Conversely, the spectator or participant must accept from a participant conduct associated with that sport. Thus a player who injures another player in the course of a sporting event by conduct that is a foreseeable, customary part of the sport cannot be held liable for negligence because no duty is owed to protect the victim from that conduct. Were we to find such a duty between co-participants in a sport, we might well stifle the rewards of athletic competition.

While we believe there can be no actionable negligence between participants in a sport, we do not embrace the notion that a playing field is a free-fire zone. We agree with the court in *Hanson, supra*, 38 Ohio App.3d at 60, 526 N.E.2d at 329, that " * * * an athlete is not immune from liability for an intentional tort," because " * * * the duty *not* to commit an intentional tort against another remains intact, even in the heat of battle * * *." (Emphasis *sic*.)

Our conclusion that between participants in a sport intentional or reckless misconduct gives rise to liability, as our conclusion that negligent misconduct does not, must be understood in the context of the rules of the sport. See *Marchetti v. Kalish* (1990), 53 Ohio St.3d 95, 559 N.E.2d 699. If, for example, a golfer knows another is within the line of flight of his shot and fails to offer the customary warning of "fore," liability might accrue. Such conduct could amount to reckless indifference to the rights of others.

The conduct of an athlete who intentionally injures another athlete in a way not authorized or anticipated by the customs and rules of the game violates the duty not to commit an intentional tort. A more subtle difficulty concerns the intermediate standard of recklessness: Can a player injured by another player's recklessness bring an action in tort? Taking into account the necessity for explaining the differences between recklessness as it is usually understood and recklessness in the context of a sporting event, we hold that one who is injured by the reckless[1] misconduct of a fellow participant in a sport may, under some circumstances, bring an action in tort.

The Restatement of Torts 2d defines "recklessness" as follows:

"The actor's conduct is in reckless disregard of the safety of others if he does an act or intentionally fails to do an act which it is his duty to the other to do, knowing or having reason to know of facts which would lead a reasonable man to realize, not only that his conduct creates an unreasonable risk of physical harm to another, but also that such risk is substantially greater than that which is necessary to make his conduct negligent." 2 Restatement of the Law 2d, Torts (1965), at 587, Section 500. Comment *f* to Section 500 contrasts recklessness and intentional misconduct: "While an act to be reckless must be intended by the actor, the actor does not intend to cause the harm which results from it." *Id.* at 590. Comment *a* to Section 500 adds that " * * * the risk must itself be an unreasonable one *under the circumstances*." (Emphasis added.) *Id.* at 588.

What constitutes an unreasonable risk under the circumstances of a sporting event must be delineated with reference to the way the particular game is played, *i.e.*, the rules and customs that shape the participants' ideas of foreseeable conduct in the course of a game.

If the rules of a sport allow conduct intended to harm another player, as they do in boxing or football, for example, it follows that those same rules also allow behavior that would otherwise give rise to liability for recklessness. But any conduct which is characterized by the strong probability of harm that recklessness entails, and which occurs outside the normal conduct and customs of the sport, may give rise to liability. In the context of the game of golf, a player who hurls a club into the air in a moment of pique and injures another golfer should be held accountable.

The Restatement of Torts 2d supports the view that different standards of care should apply to those who inflict injuries in the course of a game as opposed to those who inflict injuries under ordinary circumstances: "Taking part in a game manifests a willingness to submit to such bodily contacts or restrictions of liberty as are permitted by its rules or usages. Participating in such a game does not manifest consent to contacts which are prohibited by rules or usages of the game if such rules or usages are designed to protect the participants and not merely to secure the better playing of the game as a test of skill. * * * " 1 Restatement of the Law 2d. Torts (1965) 86, Section 50, Comment *b*. See *Kabella v. Bouschelle* (1983), 100 N.M. 461, 463, 672 P.2d 290, 292.

We cannot provide a single list of actions that will give rise to tort liability for recklessness or intentional misconduct in every sport. The issue can be

---

1. The term "reckless" is often used interchangeably with "willful" and "wanton." Our comments regarding recklessness apply to conduct characterized as willful and wanton as well.

resolved in each case only by recourse to the rules and customs of the game and the facts of the incident. In general, as Presiding Judge Milligan pointed out in his *Hanson* concurrence, " * * * the *quid pro quo* of an 'assumed greater risk' is a diminished duty. Thus, participants in bodily contact games such as basketball (and lacrosse) owe a lesser duty to each other than do golfers and others involved in non-physical contact sports." *Hanson, supra*, 38 Ohio App.3d at 64, 526 N.E.2d at 333.

Recognition of the inverse relationship between duty and dangerousness should enter into a court's decision-making process on a motion for summary judgment when the plaintiff alleges reckless or intentional misconduct. A court should inquire more specifically into the following factors suggested by Judge Milligan:

> " * * * the nature of the sport involved, the rules and regulations which govern the sport, the customs and practices which are generally accepted and which have evolved with the development of the sport, and the facts and circumstances of the particular case. * * * " *Id.*

The court of appeals explained its refusal to follow its own precedent in *McElhaney, supra*, by asserting that the *McElhaney* holding that negligence was not actionable applies only to sports involving a high degree of physical contact. This distinction reveals the awareness of the court below that there are different duties and risks appropriate to different sports, but the contact-non-contact distinction does not sufficiently take into account that we are dealing with a spectrum of duties and risks rather than an either-or distinction. Is golf a contact sport? Obviously, a golfer accepts the risk of coming in contact with wayward golf shots on the links, so golf is more dangerous than table tennis, for instance, but certainly not as dangerous as kickboxing. Analyzing liability for injuries inflicted in sports in terms of a continuum along which the standard of care rises as the inherent danger of the sport falls is more useful than distinguishing sports by applying a black-and-white distinction between contact and non-contact sports.

Applying the foregoing theoretical scheme to the facts of the case before us, we hold that summary judgment for McNeill was appropriate. Shanking the ball is a foreseeable and not uncommon occurrence in the game of golf. The same is true of hooking, slicing, pushing, or pulling a golf shot. We would stress that "[i]t is well known that not every shot played by a golfer goes to the point where he intends it to go. If such were the case, every player would be perfect and the whole pleasure of the sport would be lost. It is common knowledge, at least among players, that many bad shots must result although every stroke is delivered with the best possible intention and without any negligence whatsoever." *Benjamin v. Nernberg* (1931), 102 Pa.Super. 471, 475-476, 157 A.10, 11.

Thompson was off to McNeill's right at such a sharp angle that she was not in the intended path of McNeill's ball. There was no recklessness here and certainly no intentional misconduct. The rules of golf require that one call out "fore" when a shot goes awry, but in this instance the ball was traveling so rapidly that such a warning would have availed nothing.

McNeill's shot was within the rules. As Thompson concedes, one who hits a golf ball into a water hazard may play the next shot from a spot two club lengths from where the ball entered the water or from where the previous ball was hit. Therefore it was foreseeable and within the rules that McNeill's next shot would come from the fairway. It was not a prohibited or reckless shot. McNeill did not recklessly expose Thompson to more danger than any golfer faces in participating in a game of golf.[2]

For the foregoing reasons we reverse the judgment of the court of appeals and reinstate the judgment of the trial court.

Judgment reversed.

MOYER, C.J., and SWEENEY, HOLMES, DOUGLAS, HERBERT R. BROWN and RESNICK, JJ., concur.

Questions and Comments

1. What was the question to be decided in this case?
2. What was the rule of law that covered the outcome of the case?
3. Why, in your opinion, did this court mention intentional torts?
4. What sources of law did the court rely upon in fashioning its opinion?
5. Was golf given the same considerations as contact sports? Explain your answer.

Note Cases - Respondeat Superior

An individual who injures someone intentionally is obviously responsible for the injury. This is true whether one is speaking of an assault, a battery, or a false imprisonment. Interestingly enough, however, much of the litigation in the field of intentional torts involves a third party (master) for whom the tort-feasor (servant) is working. The master is responsible for the acts of a servant, namely, for injuries intentionally brought about by the servant while acting within the scope of employment. This is sometimes referred to as vicarious liability. The principle is also referred to as *respondeat superior*. This is important for sports managers to remember. Managers are responsible for the action of their employees if the action is within the scope of employment.

A simple restatement of the general law is to be found in the case of *Freeman v. Bell* (1978). In this case, a patron was shot by the doorman at a discotheque. Damages were awarded in the sum of $250,000. The court found both the owner and general manager liable as well as the doorman who did the

---

2. Even were we to impose a negligence standard in this case, McNeill would not be liable for Thompson's injury because Thompson's position relative to McNeill placed Thompson outside the zone of danger. Thompson did not believe herself to be in danger, and said McNeill had hit a "freak" shot.

In a case decided on uncannily similar facts, *Walsh v. Machlin* (1941), 128 Conn. 412, 23 A.2d 156, the court held that there was no negligence as a matter of law when a golfer was injured by a shot hit from about forty yards away and at an angle of approximately ninety degrees from its intended line of flight.

actual shooting. The court reasoned that the owner of a public place owed patrons a duty to exercise reasonable care to protect them. Further, the general manager of the establishment had knowledge of the doorman's propensity for violence; hence, the manager and the perpetrator were each liable.

An interesting variation of the rule of *respondeat superior* is offered by *Townsend v. State* (1987). In *Townsend*, a basketball player was struck by another player and injured. The injured player sued the person who inflicted the blow, as well as other defendants, including the state university for whom the aggressor was playing. The court ruled that the basketball player was not an employee of the state, and consequently, the doctrine of *respondeat superior* was not applicable. In brief, the offending basketball player was neither the agent nor the servant of the state university.

Another variation of the factual situation is offered by the case of *Bencivenga v. J.J.A.M.M., Inc.* (1992). In this case, the dance club was held negligent. The person who struck the blow was unknown. In the application of the doctrine of comparative negligence, an effort was made to apportion that unknown person's fault. The court refused to consider the fault of the unknown person. That individual was not named in the suit and, therefore, was not a party to the action and thus should not be factored into the equation when determining fault. The end result of the decision was that the plaintiff who was struck in the face while dancing at a night club was able to hold the dance club completely responsible under the doctrine of comparative negligence. This application of comparative negligence illustrates that damages were not applied to the unknown tort-feasor who had, in fact, struck the patron. Thus, the court permitted the injured party to recover full damages without suffering any loss. Imagine the applications here to a sport business.

Another assault and *respondeat superior* relationship was presented in the case of *In re: Stow [Ohio] City School Dist. Bd. of Education* (1992). The court held in this case that a school board should grant a leave to an employee injured as a result of a practical joke played on the injured party by a 15-year-old student. The student had pulled a chair out from under the employee, an action that caused a fall and subsequent injury. The arbitrator of the case decided that the injury was not occasioned by an accident but was caused by an intentional act as commonly used with reference to the term "assault." Thus, the student acted knowingly and recklessly and caused the harm for which the school was responsible. Hence, a leave of absence was justified under the school policy.

Note Cases - Assault the Fault of Coaches or Players

Many sport leagues now exist outside the realm of the school walls. The sport manager might be in charge of city recreational leagues, church leagues, franchised leagues, or teams with other agencies such as YMCA, JCCA, YWCA. Volunteer coaches are often zealous in their approach to coaching. The win-at-all costs philosophy may be prevalent. If these coaches inspire assault and battery on the part of players, can they be held liable if they promote willful and wanton endangerment of sport participants?

In the case of *Nydegger v. Don Bosco Preparatory High School* (1985), an injured player filed suit against the opposing coach for teaching an "aggressive and intensive manner." Although the player did not prevail, this and other suits (*Nabozny v. Barnhill*, 1975) make it clear that players and coaches may be sued for willful and reckless assault.

A reckless disregard for the safety of others cannot be excused.

> [A] player is liable for injury in a tort action if his conduct is such that it is either deliberate, willful or with a reckless disregard for the safety of the other player so as to cause injury to that player (*Nabozney*, 1975, pp. 260-261).

In cases of self-defense, when the sport participant is assaulted by another player or a spectator, the court may consider the preceding events, the nature of the retaliation, and the mental attitude of the participants. Some sports, such as hockey or soccer, have more propensity for promoting assaults.

The sport manager is responsible for the foreseeability of problems of assault. Crowd control is addressed in a later chapter.

Defenses

When there is an issue of intentional tort, defenses generally advanced to a civil action are consent, self-defense, and privilege. The court is always reluctant to permit recovery by a plaintiff who has consented to the act that is the basis of the complaint. Assumption of risk illustrates this particular point. In some sports it may be difficult to distinguish assault from aggressive behavior germane to the sport. The reader will recall from the preceding chapter that in a hazardous sport such as football the participant assumes some of the risk of that sport. As noted previously, some jurisdictions have abandoned the doctrine of assumption of risk.

Self-defense is also a standard to which defendants frequently turn. Self-defense, however, is limited to that degree of force or action that is reasonable under the circumstances. In some jurisdictions an individual is obligated to retreat. Such an obligation, however, does not extend to the abandonment of one's home. In like fashion, self-defense can apply to others. This is especially persuasive when based upon such factors as family, or when motivated by universally approved values that dictate protection for children and aged individuals who are unable to protect themselves.

The final defense to intentional tort is privilege. A teacher may be privileged to discipline a pupil. A police officer may be privileged to arrest a suspect. Good faith, restraint, and the authority of law are always relevant to the concept of privilege.

SUMMARY

An assault is predicated upon an intentional act that places someone in apprehension of harm.

A battery involves an unlawful touching of another. It is obvious that the contact can be slight or severe. The contact can also be characterized as permissible or offensive.

The gist of false imprisonment—sometimes characterized as false arrest—is the unlawful detention of someone against his or her will.

False imprisonment situations are frequently subject to legislative action designed to correct specific problems, for example, shoplifting. Shoplifting was not included in this chapter, but it is an issue that a sport manager, especially one in a sporting goods business, might address. A shoplifting statute would seek to balance the need to protect the sport business as opposed to the need to protect the liberty of an individual who might be unjustly accused.

Intentional torts are civil actions but may also be prosecuted as criminal actions. Defenses usually available to a charge of intentional torts include consent, self-defense, and privilege. Intentional torts is one of a tripartite classification of injuries that are compensable. The other two are torts predicated upon negligence and on strict liability. Damages can be classified as nominal, compensatory, and punitive.

This could be you - check your response

Under normal circumstances, Maria Jones was obligated to provide adequate instruction and supervision. The release was designed to protect Maria in the event of a failure to properly instruct and supervise. Maria would not be liable for two reasons. The duty to supervise did not extend outside the area of instruction; if the duty had extended, she would probably be protected by the release.

Ms White could sue Ms Foust for assault. However, self-defense would be considered carefully.

The sport manager is reminded that knowledge of a feud among patrons on the premises of a facility might keep a fight from developing beyond the premises. Sport managers should diplomatically include law enforcement officials early in the prevention process. In such scenarios, the sport manager should ask the patrons to leave before a fight erupts and before assault and battery take place.

REFERENCES

Authors

W. Page Keeton et al. (1984). *Prosser and Keeton on the law of torts.* (3rd ed.) St. Paul, MN: West Publishing Co. (Chaps. 2,3 and 4, pp.33-107 deal with intentional torts and defenses thereto.)

Cases

Bencivenga v. J.J.A.M.M., Inc., 609 A.2d 1299 (N.J. Super. Ct. App. Div. 1992).

Chudasama v. Metro. Govt. of Nashville, 914 S.W.2d 922 (Tenn.App. 1995).

Freeman v. Bell, 366 So. 2d 197 (La. Ct. App. 1978).

Geimer v. Chicago Park Dist., 650 N.E.2d 585 (Ill.App. 1 Dist. 1995).

Glucksman v. Walters, 659 A.2d 1217 (Conn.App. 1995).

In re: Stow [Ohio] City School Dist. Bd. of Education, 99 LA 871 rendered August 10, 1992.

Nabozny v. Barnhill, 334 N.E.2d 258 (Ill.App. 1975).

Nydegger v. Don Bosco Preparatory High School, 495 A.2d 485 (N.J. 1985).

Savino v. Robertson, 652 N.E.2d 1240 (Ill.App. 2 Div. 1995).

Thompson v. McNeill, 559 N.E.2d 705 (Ohio 1990).

Townsend v. State, 237 Cal. Rptr. 146 (Cal. Ct. App. 1987).

Webbier v. Thoroughbred Racing Protective Bureau, 254 A.2d 285 (R.I. 1969).

Legal Encyclopedias

6 Am. Jur. 2d *Assault and Battery* (1963) §§ 1-229, with current updates.

32 Am. Jur. 2d *False Imprisonment* (1982) §§ 1-154, with current updates.

57A Am. Jur. 2d *Negligence* (1989) §§ 1-1127, with current updates.

57B Am. Jur. 2d, *Negligence* (1989) §§ 1128-2241, with current updates.

74 Am. Jur. 2d, *Torts* (1974) §§ 1-88, with current updates.

6A C.J.S. *Assault and Battery* (1975) §§ 1-130, with current updates

35 C.J.S. *False Imprisonment* (1960) §§ 1-72, with current updates.

65 C.J.S. *Negligence* (1966) §§ 1-115, with current updates.

65A C.J.S. *Negligence* (1966) §§116-306, with current updates.

INJURY AND RISK MANAGEMENT

PERSPECTIVE

Part II has endeavored to set forth principles of law relevant to negligence, defenses to negligence, and injury and intentional torts. Specifically, the reader has been introduced to

A. Negligence
    1. Definition of negligence
    2. Types of negligence
    3. Elements of negligence
    4. Factual situations that may give rise to negligence

B. Defenses to Negligence
    1. General denial
    2. Affirmative defenses, i.e., contributory negligence, assumption of risk, comparative negligence, statute of limitations, release, recreational use statute (sometimes referred to as recreational users statute), and sovereign immunity.

C. Injury and Intentional Tort
    1. Assault, assault and battery, false imprisonment
    2. Intentional or reckless misconduct, relationship to negligence

The above topics should be considered in relationship to risk management. The sport management industry may be exposed to risks other than tort. Such risks outside of tort will be considered as appropriate.

Hypothetical Case - Part II - Check Your Response

Negligence involves a duty to care where a breach of that duty is the proximate cause of the injury. If the Joneses were aware of the slick floor, and they failed to remedy the situation, then they failed to keep the premises reasonably safe for patrons. Therefore, they might be negligent.

The ability of the patron to see is relevant, as are the time and manner of the spill. The presence of a sign would certainly be useful as a defensive tactic.

INJURY AND
STRICT LIABILITY

FOCUS

Overview

The business has been started and the owner and manager enlightened as to liability for negligence and intentional misconduct. Part III deals with three topics generally related to strict liability. This part of the textbook, like the preceding parts, is composed of three chapters.

One of the chapters, Workers' Compensation, sets forth rules and regulations that enable an employee to recover from injury that occurs while working in the course of employment. The liability in workers' compensation arises out of a tort concept but is not conditioned upon a finding of fault. In other words, workers' compensation allows the worker to recover without a finding of fault.

One chapter deals with Product Liability. Product liability has two theoretical bases: liability related to negligence and liability related to contracts. Discussions of liability stem from the law of contracts generally and the law of sales in particular. Sport managers need to know how the law may help them deal with defective sport products.

> To recover in action for strict products liability, plaintiff must prove injury resulting from condition of product, that condition was unreasonably dangerous, and that condition existed at the time product left manufacturer's control. (Cozzi v. North Palos Elementary Sch. Dist. No. 117, 1992, p. 683.)

These concepts are explained in the body of the chapters.

The final chapter in this part deals with principles connected with the concept of nuisance. Nuisance is well known to the common law and is influenced by principles of property law as well as tort law. A sport manager needs to be able to protect a business against a nuisance. The sport manager also needs to know how to avoid having his or her own business viewed as a nuisance.

Practical Application - Hypothetical Case

The Joneses introduced additional fitness equipment in the upstairs portion of the building. One of the machines, which was designed to strengthen muscular systems, became disengaged and struck a young fitness instructor in the mouth causing extensive dental injury. What type of action is available to the employee? Is this remedy exclusive? Assuming that the employee has a choice of more than one action, what choices would be available and what would influence the decision to select the theory upon which the suit would be based? Read the following chapter for solutions to the problems in this case.

PRODUCT LIABILITY?

CHAPTER 8

WORKERS' COMPENSATION

INTRODUCTION

Sport owners and managers are often confronted with claims arising out of the workers' compensation statute. An employee in a sport business may be injured while working without the injury being caused by the employer's intentional or negligent misconduct. Such an employee needs help. To remedy this situation the law has developed a solution whereby the worker is compensated. This method is known as *workers' compensation*. This is a statutory development and is not predicated upon wrongdoing. To reiterate, workers' compensation is a remedy provided regardless of fault. Ideally, the remedy is swift, certain, and avoids the problems associated with the legal process. Workers' compensation is a form of strict liability. The terms of the statute upon which workers' compensation is based vary from state to state. However, in each state the goal is to achieve the objectives as stated above and shift the risk of loss to the consumer. (In other words, the consumer pays the costs of increased prices or services, etc.)

IN THIS CHAPTER YOU WILL LEARN:

The purpose behind the Workers' Compensation Act

The relationship between negligence and recovery under the workers' compensation law

The defenses available to the employer under this statute

The extent to which the remedy under the Workers' Compensation Act is exclusive

The circumstances under which the Act may fall short of its objectives

Factors that determine if an injury arises out of and in the course of employment

The extent to which custom and usage can bring an employer under the Act

---

THEORY OF RECOVERY?

In workers' compensation, the following questions are always relevant: First, is the employer covered by the Act? Second, did the injury arise out of and during the course of the employment? Third, what is the extent of the injury?

A state, under the Tenth Amendment to the United States Constitution, has the power to restrict the liberty or property of an individual for the purpose of protecting the public health, safety, welfare, and morals. The constitutional base for workers' compensation statutes comes under this amendment.

KEY WORDS: *minor, tort, workers' compensation carrier, exclusive remedy, in the course of employment, arising out of employment, Tenth Amendment*

This could be you!

The Joneses' fitness center employs 10 workers. One slips on a wet spot in the floor, causing a back injury. The wet spot was caused by a soft drink that had been spilled by a patron. The injured employee filed suit in the local court, alleging negligence on the part of the employer in failing to maintain the premises in a safe condition. The amount sought by way of damages far exceeds the amount that would be recoverable under the workers' compensation law of the state.

1. Can the employee maintain the suit? In the event the employee cannot maintain a suit at common law, can he try the factual situation in a court of law when proceeding under the workers' compensation statute? Why or why not?
2. Assuming that the accident occurred after working hours and while the employee was attending a party given by the employer, would the injury be compensable under the workers' compensation statute? Why or why not?

LEGAL PRINCIPLES

Exclusive Remedy With Possible Exceptions

The case that follows involves an employee who lost a finger while working on the pinsetting machine in the bowling alley. The employee sued in the regular court system. The court held that the exclusive remedy was with the workers' compensation statute. An exception to the exclusive feature of the workers' compensation statute did exist, namely, an intentional tort; however, the court held that the action of the employer did not fall within the exception. (A tort is a civil wrong.) The action was not an intentional tort. Therefore, the worker had to use workers' compensation as the remedy.

••

JENSEN v. SPORT BOWL, INC.
469 N.W.2d 370 (S.D. 1991)

SABERS, Justice.

An employed minor was injured while working at a bowling alley. Summary judgment was granted dismissing his tort action against employer on the basis of workers' compensation exclusivity. He appeals.

Facts

Robert Jensen was 14 years old when he went to work as a pinchaser for Sport Bowl (employer) in the fall of 1986. Part of Jensen's job was to wipe oil from automatic pinsetting machines. On November 23, 1986, between 9:30 and 10:00 p.m., Jensen lost his right index finger when the rag he was using to wipe oil from a pinsetting machine became entangled in a moving pulley.

Employer's workers' compensation carrier paid all Jensen's medical bills directly to his health care providers and sent Jensen several checks for disability benefits under SDCL Title 62. Jensen's mother, as guardian ad litem, did not cash any of the checks received from employer's insurer.

On March 25, 1988, Jensen sued employer in tort for $250,000 in compensatory damages and $500,000 in punitive damages. Two years later the circuit court granted summary judgment for employer dismissing Jensen's action and holding as a matter of law that workers' compensation was Jensen's exclusive remedy against employer.

On appeal, Jensen argues that employer's conduct comes within the "intentional tort" exception to the workers' compensation exclusive remedy rule, and, in the alternative, even if employer's conduct was merely negligent, the illegal employment of a minor gives the minor, if injured, a cause of action at common law. Employer claims the facts pled by Jensen do not constitute an intentional tort, that the employment of a minor is insufficient to defeat workers' compensation exclusivity, and, on cross-appeal, that Jensen's action is barred by his acceptance of workers' compensation benefits.

1. *Intentional Tort*

Workers' compensation is the exclusive remedy for all on-the-job injuries to workers except those injuries intentionally inflicted by the employer. SDCL 62-3-2.[1] Under the intentional tort exception, workers may bring suit

---

1. SDCL 62-3-2 provides:

The rights and remedies herein granted to an employee subject to this title, on account of personal injury or death arising out of and in the course of employment, shall exclude all

against their employers at common law only "when an ordinary, reasonable, prudent person would believe an injury was *substantially certain* to result from [the employer's] conduct." [Citation omitted.] (Emphasis original).

South Dakota courts may grant summary judgment when, viewing the evidence in the light most favorable to the nonmoving party, the moving party clearly shows that there is no issue of material fact. . . . .[S]ummary judgment . . . is generally not appropriate where "the standard of the reasonable [person] must be applied to conflicting testimony." 83 S.D. at 212, 213, 157 N.W. 2d at 21, 22. Jensen argues that since the scope of workers' compensation preemption depends on whether an ordinary, reasonable and prudent person would believe the injury was substantially certain to result from the employer's conduct, and since this is generally a question for the trier of fact, the circuit court erred in disposing of it summarily.

Workers' compensation was designed by the legislature to be the exclusive method for compensating workers injured on the job in all but extraordinary circumstances. [Citation omitted.] Consequently, this court construes workers' compensation statutes liberally to provide coverage even when the worker would prefer to avoid it. [Citation omitted.]

An extraordinary circumstance where workers' compensation is not the exclusive remedy is where the employer intends to cause the injury suffered by the worker. However, it is "almost unanimous" among state and federal courts interpreting this exception that intent really means intent. 2A Larson, *The Law of Workmen's Compensation* § 68.13 (1990). . . . .

. . . . "To establish intentional conduct, *more than the knowledge and appreciation of risk is necessary*; the known danger must ... become a *substantial certainty*." *Id.* (emphasis original).

Jensen's complaint alleges that an ordinary, reasonable and prudent person would believe that his injury was "substantially certain" to result from employer's conduct. However, it is not enough simply to use the right terminology invoking the intentional tort exception. The worker must also allege *facts* that plausibly demonstrate an actual intent by the employer to injure or a substantial certainty that injury will be the inevitable outcome of employer's conduct. 2A Larson, *supra,* § 68.14 (*citing Joyce v. A.C. & S., Inc.,* 785 F.2d 1200 (4th Cir. 1986); *Keating v. Shell Chemical Co.,* 610 F.2d 338 (5th Cir. 1980)). "[S]ubstantial certainty should not be equated with substantial likelihood." *Beauchamp v. Dow Chemical Co.,* 427 Mich. 1, 398 N.W. 2d 882, 893 (1986).

Viewing the evidence and the pleadings in a light most favorable to Jensen's case, Jensen was an inexperienced, inadequately trained, 14-year-old boy ordered by his employer, without any warning of the danger, to perform a maintenance task which the employer knew from personal experience to be risky. Even so, this does not allege the elements necessary to an intentional

other rights and remedies of such employee, his personal representatives, dependents, or next of kin, on account of such injury or death against his employer or any employee, partner, officer or director of such employer, *except rights and remedies arising from intentional tort.* [Emphasis added.]

tort cause of action. Therefore, these facts do not come within the intentional tort exception to workers' compensation coverage as a matter of law. We affirm summary judgment in favor of employer on this issue.

2. *Illegally Employed Minor*

Jensen next argues that even if employer's conduct did not amount to an intentional tort but was merely negligent, Jensen has a cause of action at common law because he was not under a "contract of employment" within the meaning of SDCL 62-1-3.

SDCL 62-1-3 defines employees covered by workers' compensation as "every person, including a minor, in the services of another *under any contract* of employment, express or implied[.]" (Emphasis added.) However, under South Dakota law, any contract is "void" insofar as its object is unlawful. SDCL 53-5-3,-4. *See also* 53-9-1 and 20-2-2.

Jensen claims that he had no contract of employment with employer under SDCL 62-1-3 because the object of the purported contract violated federal and state child labor laws. Specifically, federal regulations implementing the Fair Labor Standards Act at 29 CFR §§ 570.33(b) and 570.35(6) (1990) prohibit minors between the ages of 14 and 16 from "tending ... any power-driven machinery other than office machines" and from working later than 7:00 p.m. Moreover, SDCL 60-12-3 prohibits children under sixteen years of age from working "in any occupation dangerous to life, health, or morals[.]" This court has held that "to employ a minor under 16 to adjust a belt upon a moving piece of machinery ... and to oil and grease said machinery while in motion might well be held, as a matter of law, to amount to the employment of such child in an occupation dangerous to life within the contemplation of [SDCL 60-12-3,]" and that "employment contrary to the terms of a child labor statute is sufficient, standing alone, to establish negligence on the part of the employer in the event of an injury to the minor." *Koenekamp v. Picasso,* 64 S.D. 567, 570, 571, 269 N.W. 74, 76, 77 (S.D. 1936).

Reading federal and state law together, Jensen claims that (1) his contract for employment with employer, if illegal, is outside the scope of workers' compensation coverage, and therefore, (2) whether his job with employer was illegal under state and federal child labor laws was a material issue of fact for which summary judgment was inappropriate.

First, this is primarily a question of construing South Dakota's workers' compensation law because the federal Fair Labor Standards Act, 29 U.S.C. at §§ 203(*l*) and 212 (1988), provides no private federal cause of action for its violation which would preempt the workers' compensation laws of South Dakota. [Citations omitted.]

Secondly, whether illegally employed minors are in or out of workers' compensation's exclusive coverage has been answered differently by different jurisdictions, and even differently within the same jurisdiction at different periods in history or in different factual contexts. 1C Larson, *supra,* § 47.52(a); 81 Am.Jur.2d *Workmen's Compensation* § 165 (1976); 99 C.J.S. *Workmen's Compensation* § 113, 101 C.J.S., *supra,* §930 (1958). While at one time case law in most jurisdictions tended to exclude illegally employed minors from workers' compensation coverage, 81 Am. Jur. 2d, *supra,* § 165, most states have now statutorily included illegally employed minors in workers' compensation—and many award damages to them at double or treble the usual rate. 1C Larson, *supra,* § 47.52(a) n. 86.

In general, the ambivalent state of the law reflects the ambivalent goals of legislatures and courts in this area. On the one hand, they don't want the workers' compensation remedy used as a damages-limiting shield by businesses illegally employing children. On the other hand, they want the workers' compensation remedy available as a sword to working minors whether legally employed or not.

This is a question of first impression in South Dakota. SDCL 62-1-3 brings minors within the exclusive coverage of workers' compensation, but is silent whether this includes *illegally* employed minors. There is no case law on point, except for the general rule that workers' compensation law is to be liberally construed to provide coverage, even when the worker doesn't want it. *S.D. Med. Service v. Minn. Mut. Fire & Cas. Co.,* 303 N.W.2d at 361. Given the vagueness of South Dakota law on this point and the mixed signals from jurisdictions which have addressed the issue, we appreciate the well-reasoned approach of the Connecticut and Alaska Supreme Courts in *Blancato v. Feldspar Corp.,* 203 Conn. 34, 522 A.2d 1235 (1987) and *Whitney-Fidalgo Seafoods, Inc. v. Beukers,* 554 P.2d 250 (Alaska 1976). *See also Ewert v. Georgia Cas. & Sur. Co. (Ewert II),* 548 So.2d 358 (La.App.3rd Cir.), *writ denied,* 551 So.2d 1339 (La.1989). The rule emerging from these cases can be summarized as follows:

(1) All minors under a contract for employment, whether legal or illegal, may be within the scope of workers' compensation coverage.

(2) Workers' compensation is the exclusive remedy for legally employed minors injured on the job.

(3) In the case of minors illegally employed, the employment contract is not void but *voidable.* Therefore, upon injury, illegally employed minors may pursue remedies under workers' compensation or at common law, but not both.

Although the above rule appears to be the clearest and most equitable approach to this uncertain area of the law and is the statutory rule in at least four other states (Illinois, Kentucky, New Jersey and North Dakota; 1C Larson, *supra,* § 47.52(a) n. 87), we hesitate to adopt it at this time for several reasons:

(1) Workers' compensation law is a comprehensive statutory scheme designed by and best modified by the legislature.

(2) Upon review, the legislature may wish to provide illegally employed minors additional statutory remedies, such as double or treble workers' compensation benefits as many other states have done. *See* 1C Larson *supra,* § 47.52(a) n. 86.

(3) Until such time as the legislature acts, this court must be guided by the "long-standing policy to interpret work[er's] compensation

statutes liberally [to provide coverage even if] the worker is attempting to avoid coverage." *S.D. Med. Service v. Minn. Mut. Fire & Cas. Co.,* 303 N.W.2d at 361.

Accordingly, we affirm the trial court on this issue also and need not reach the notice of review issue concerning election of remedies by acceptance of benefits.

Affirmed.

Questions and Comments

1. State the rule of exclusiveness as it applies to workers' compensation. Are there exceptions to the rule?
2. List three sources of law as set forth in this case.
3. What principle of statutory construction does this case rely upon? Remember, a statute is a law. Answer: The law is liberally construed. Workers' compensation provides coverage even when the workers do not want coverage. As noted earlier, workers' compensation provides a remedy without the need to prove fault.
4. How was summary judgment defined in the case?
5. Under South Dakota law, a contract was void if its object was unlawful. How was the principle of contract law covered in this case?

Remedies Arising Out of and in the Course of Employment

The owner of a sportswear manufacturing company gave a New Year's party for his employees. The employees were Korean nationals and were accustomed to supporting their employer. Gifts were exchanged and attendance was high. This was an annual event. One employee was struck by a car when leaving the party. The party was held on the company premises.

The court held the accident arose out of and in the course of the employment.

••

KIM v. SPORTSWEAR
393 S.E.2d 418 (Va.Ct.App. 1990)

COLEMAN, Judge.

We consider for the first time whether an injury sustained while attending an employer sponsored social or recreational event arises out of and in the course of employment. Code § 65.1-7.

Soon Deuk Lee was fatally injured on December 28, 1988, while attending a company sponsored Korean New Year's party,[1] when a fellow employee accidentally struck her with his automobile as she exited the door of the garment factory where she worked. Kum Ja Kim, her first cousin and closest

---

1. The Korean New Year falls on December 28.

relative in the United States, filed a claim with the Industrial Commission on behalf of the decedent's parents, Joe Hee Lee and Won Ja Lee, who reside in Korea, on the basis that they were destitute, Code § 65.1-66(4), or financially dependent upon their daughter, Code § 65.1-67. The commission denied the claim on the grounds that Lee's death did not arise out of and occur during the course of her employment and that the claimant failed to prove that Lee's parents were destitute or financially dependent upon her. We hold that the commission misapplied the law in ruling that Lee's injury did not arise out of and occur during the course of her employment. Also, contrary to the commission's finding, the record does contain sufficient evidence to establish that Lee's parents were destitute and dependent upon her for support. We reverse the decision of the commission and direct that an award be entered in accord with this opinion. However, because the record fails to reflect whether the award should enter against other employers, in addition to Vienna Enterprises, Inc., we remand the case for entry of the award and for the commission to reconsider who were Lee's employer or employers.

Soon Deuk Lee and approximately twenty other Korean immigrants were employed as seamstresses by both Vienna Enterprises, Inc. and its apparent affiliate, Sportswear. Vienna Enterprises and Sportswear were operated by Walter I. Park. Whether Vienna Enterprises was a sole proprietorship owned by Park or whether it was incorporated with Park being the sole or major stockholder is unclear from the record; it also is unclear whether Vienna Enterprises and Sportswear are the same firm using different names. Regardless of the legal relationship between the businesses and Park, he, with the assistance of Myung Sung Kim, the plant manager, oversaw the daily operations of the garment factory. The employees considered Park to be the owner of the factory.

The New Year's Eve party was a traditional annual function at the factory. On December 28, 1985, Mr. Park coordinated the work schedule of the employees to facilitate their attendance at the year-end party, which was being sponsored and hosted by the company. At Mr. Park's direction, employees were allowed, beginning at mid-afternoon, to leave work early to make preparation to attend the party that evening. The employees' family members and their close associates were welcome to attend the party. Park did not tell the employees that attendance was mandatory, but several employees testified that Mr. Park strongly encouraged all employees to attend, which fact Park did not deny. Mr. Park testified to the Korean custom of young and old in the family joining together in support of the employer as part of the Korean work ethic. He acknowledged that, although attendance was not mandatory, the dedication of the employees assured that attendance would be extremely high. Attendance at the event was virtually unanimous; Park surmised that a few of the older employees may not have been present.

The deputy commissioner found that Lee's attendance at the party was mandatory as an employee, and therefore her injury occurred during the course of her employment. "An accident occurs 'in the course of employment' when it takes place within the period of employment, at a place where the employee may reasonably be, and while he is reasonably fulfilling duties of his employment or engaged in doing something incidental thereto." *Bradshaw v. Aronovitch*, 170 Va. 329, 335, 196 S.E. 684, 686 (1938) (emphasis added). Clearly, an employer can enlarge the "course of employment" by extending the scope of employment to embrace recreational and social events.   1A A. Larson, *Workmen's Compensation Law* § 22.20 (1985).   When a worker is injured at a place where his employment requires him to be while engaged in an activity reasonably connected with or incidental to his or her employment, compensation is allowable, *Cohen v. Cohen's Dep't. Store, Inc.*, 171 Va. 106, 110, 198 S.E. 476, 477 (1938), even if the injury occurs after the employee's actual employment labors are completed.   *Id.; Lucas v. Lucas*, 212 Va. 561, 563-64, 186 S.E.2d 63, 65 (1972) (the employment relationship must expose the employee to the risk from which injury occurs, even though the accident results from activity not required by an employee's job or during regular working hours).   The deputy commissioner determined that, because the employees felt compelled to attend, the employer had brought attendance at the party within the course of employment. *See Jackson v. American Ins. Co.*, 404 S.2d 218, 220 (La.1981) (suggestion to attend can take on an air of compulsion in light of social norms, e.g., deference to age and seniority, which influence the employment relationship).   "[C]ompulsion need not take the form of a direct order, if employee is made to understand that he is to take part in the affair." 1A A. Larson, *supra* at § 22.22.

The full commission, on review, determined that attendance by the employees was not mandatory.   The commission ruled that because attendance was not required, the employees were at liberty to attend, and therefore, the accident did not occur during the course of employment.   The commission reasoned that, because attendance was not mandatory, the event was not so closely related to the employment that it could be considered within the course of employment.

Matters of weight and preponderance of the evidence, and the resolution of conflicting inferences fairly deducible from the evidence, are within the prerogative of the commission, *Board of Supervisors v. Taylor*, 1 Va.App. 425, 431, 339 S.E. 2d 565, 568 (1986), and are conclusive and binding on the Court of Appeals.   Code § 65.1-98.   "If there is evidence ... to support the Commission's findings, they will not be disturbed by this Court on appeal, even though there is evidence in the record to support contrary finding[s] of fact."   *Boyd's Roofing Co. v. Lewis*, 1 Va.App.93, 95, 335 S.E.2d 281, 283 (1985).   However, when the facts and inferences have been considered in the light most favorable to the prevailing party, whether those facts are sufficient to establish that an injury occurred during the course of employment is a question of law.   *Cheatham v. Gregory*, 227 Va. 1, 4, 313 S.E.2d 368, 370 (1984); *Payne v. Master Roofing & Siding, Inc.*, 1 Va.App. 413, 414, 339 S.E.2d 559, 560 (1986).

The extent to which the employer expects or requires the employees to attend a social function is but one of several factors that the commission must consider in deciding whether an event is so closely related to the employment to come within the course of employment. The dispositive question is whether the social or recreational function is so closely associated with the employment to be considered an incident of it. Among the other factors which bear upon that determination, which the commission failed to consider, are the degree to which the employer derives a benefit from the activity, the degree of sponsorship and participation by the employer, whether the activity occurs on premises associated with the employment, when the activity occurs in relation to work, and the frequency or period over which the activity has been conducted. While attendance at the New Year's eve party may not have been required of the employees, as the commission determined, that finding standing alone does not control. Had attendance been required, this factor alone may have been sufficient to bring the decedent's injury within the course of employment. *See Aronovitch*, 170 Va. at 335, 196 S.E. at 686. Although attendance was not mandatory, the degree of expectation from the employer that all employees would attend was so high, when considered in relation to the cultural and ethnic pressures that existed, the close correlation between the social event and the employment are apparent. Although attendance may not have been mandatory, it was expected of all employees. The situation was not one where the employer was sponsoring a social event and attendance was optional or not expected. Where employees are strongly urged to attend, factors other than mandatory attendance must be considered in determining whether under the circumstances the event was within the course of employment. 1A A. Larson, *supra* at § 22.23. Here, attendance was highly encouraged. Thus, it was error for the commission, based solely on a lack of compulsion, not to consider other circumstances which bear upon the relationship between the employment and the social event. The purpose, sponsorship, and organization of the event are among additional factors which reflect whether it is so closely connected to the employment to be considered an incident thereof.

Mr. Park directed the preparations for the party, which had been held at year's end in some previous years, including the prior year. The costs of the party were underwritten entirely by the employer. The employer purchased gifts for distribution to the employees. The party was held on the work premises at the end of the workday, beginning at approximately 6:30 p.m.

Mr. Park coordinated the schedule of events leading up to and at the party. He acknowledged that one purpose of the party was to foster unity among the work force. At the party, Mr. Park addressed the employees, acknowledging his appreciation for a gift which he received from them. He could not recall to what extent he made congratulatory or encouraging comments to the employees relating to their work, but did not deny making such statements. An employee testified that it appeared that Park distributed the gifts on the basis of merit, the harder working employees receiving the more expensive gifts, but Park denied that suggestion.

The plant manager testified that the portion of the party consisting of

Park's remarks and his distributing the gifts lasted from about 6:30 until approximately 9:30 p.m. Following the planned program, the employees socialized among themselves. About one-half of the employees were still in attendance when the accident occurred, at approximately 10:45 p.m. When Soon Deuk Lee exited the door of the garment factory into the parking lot, a fellow employee accidentally depressed the accelerator of his car instead of the brake while backing out of a parking space. The vehicle struck Lee and hurled her against the building. She died two days later of the injuries which she sustained.

The employer does not contest that, if the accident occurred while Lee was attending a party which was in the course of her employment, the fact that it occurred while she was going to the parking lot on the premises would not constitute grounds to deny compensation. *Brown v. Reed*, 209 Va. 562, 567, 165 S.E.2d 394, 398 (1969) (citing cases in support of the holding "that injuries sustained in automobile mishaps in company parking lots arise out of employment"); *Lucas*, 212 Va. at 563, 186 S.E.2d at 65 (injury "arises out of" where the employment in fact exposes worker to the particular danger).

The injury occurred on the employer's premises, while the decedent was coming from an event which she was reasonably expected to attend. *Cf. Norfolk & Washington Steamboat Co. v. Holladay*, 174 Va. 152, 159-60, 5 S.E.2d 486, 489 (1939). The employer sponsored and funded the function, *Martin v. Mars Mfg. Co.*, 58 N.C.App. 577, 293 S.E.2d 816, 818 (1982), and the employer supervised the conduct of the event. *Moore's Case*, 330 Mass. 1, 4-5, 110 N.E.2d 764, 767 (1953). Importantly, the employer utilized the event to its benefit, by making remarks to the employees and distributing gifts to them, which were to obtain the good will of the employees. *Martin*, 58 N.C.App. at 579, 293 S.E.2d at 818; *Feaster v. S.K. Kelso & Sons*, 22 Pa.Cmwlth. 20, 23-24, 347 A.2d 521, 523 (1975). Where the employer sponsors a social or recreational event "for the purpose of maintaining or improving relations with and among employees, the employees gratify the employer's wish by attending and thus serve the employer's business aim." *Ricciardi v. Damar Products Co.*, 45 N.J. 54, 60, 211 A.2d 347, 349 (1965). While each factor is relevant, no one is essential to a determination that the event was or was not within the course of employment. *Feaster*, 22 Pa.Cmwlth. at 24, 347 A.2d at 523. The dispositive question is whether the event is sufficiently work related, under the particular circumstances of the case, to bring an injury sustained by an employee while attending within the ambit of Code § 65.1-7. *See Ricciardi*, 45 N.J. at 59-60, 211 A.2d at 349. The commission, which made its decision solely on the basis of whether attendance was mandatory, erroneously failed to consider all of the factors material to this determination. We hold, on the facts of this case, that the employer sponsored party was so closely connected and associated with the employment in purpose, time, location, and function that the injury sustained by Soon Deuk Lee arose out of and in the course of her employment. Code § 65.1-7....

Questions and Comments

1. What factors are relevant in determining if an injury arose out of and in the course of employment?
2. Suppose the injury had occurred on an adjacent street as opposed to the parking lot. Would this have made a difference?

Accident

Some injuries do not constitute an accident within the intendment of the act. The case that follows involves a masseur in a local YMCA who aggravated a varicose vein problem while working as a masseur. The South Carolina court held that this injury was not compensable as an accident under the Workers' Compensation Law.

....

HAVIRD v. COLUMBIA YMCA
418 S.E.2d 329 (S.C.Ct.App. 1992)

BELL, Judge:

This is a workers' compensation case. Lodd Z. Havird filed a claim seeking total and permanent disability benefits for accidental injury to the vascular system of his legs. The single commissioner denied benefits and a reviewing panel of the full commission affirmed the order of the single commissioner. Havird appealed to the circuit court, which affirmed the commission's decision. Havird appeals. We affirm.

Havird suffers from varicose veins, a vascular condition in which the valves in his outer leg veins do not function properly. The valves serve to maintain constant fluid pressure throughout the venous system. When they malfunction, pressure in the outer veins of the legs increases and exceeds that in other areas of the venous system. The increased pressure in the legs causes swelling, pain, and damage to the veins and other tissues.

From 1954 until 1987, Havird worked at the Columbia YMCA as a masseur. His employment required him to stand during eighty-five per cent of his work day or about seven hours a day. In 1982, he began experiencing painful swelling in his feet and legs. In September, 1984, he went to Dr. Dan Davis, a vascular surgeon, for treatment of the problem. Dr. Davis testified that Havird's condition was so longstanding at that time and there was already so much permanent damage to his legs that the problem could not be cured. However, Davis did perform surgery to strip the damaged veins in an effort to ameliorate Havird's symptoms and decrease the ongoing damage to his legs. He explained to Havird that long periods of standing in one place without much movement are bad for people with varicose veins and that he needed to stay off his feet as much as possible and prop his legs in an elevated position as much as he could. After recovering from the surgery, Havird returned to his normal work routine at the YMCA. He continued to suffer from pain, swelling, and periodic infection in his legs. In September, 1987, these problems led him to retire from his employment.

In his testimony, Dr. Davis stated prolonged standing is not the cause of varicose veins. They are a natural condition occurring in the general population. They are found in people who do not engage in prolonged standing as part of their primary occupation. Moreover, Dr. Davis stated that standing did not cause Havird's varicose vein problem. On the other hand, he testified that prolonged standing in a limited area without much moving around is bad for people with varicose veins. He also testified that Havird's job was about as bad for his condition as anything could be.

> The nature of his job aggravated his condition and made it worse and made it progress faster than it would if he'd had a job that did not require standing for long periods in a limited area.

Dr. Davis also testified that when he examined Havird in September, 1987, his legs looked about as good as they had ever looked.

The commission found that Havird's varicose veins and their complications were not caused by his employment or by standing for long periods, but that standing with limited physical activity did make his problem worse. It also found that as of October, 1984, Havird knew that standing in his job aggravated his condition. Citing *Richardson v. Wellman Combing Company*, 233 S.C. 454, 105 S.E.2d 602 (1958), the commission concluded Havird had not proved "injury by accident."

The sole question presented for our review is whether Havird sustained "injury by accident" within the meaning of the South Carolina Workers' Compensation Act.[1] This is a question of law. [Citation omitted.]

. . . . .

We have deep sympathy for all persons who after years of work find it difficult or impossible to continue their accustomed level of physical activity at their jobs because of progressive health problems. . . . . The Workers' Compensation Law was not intended to remedy this problem. . . . . We recognize the hardship of Havird's circumstances; however, we are constrained by law to uphold the decision of the commission.

AFFIRMED.

GARDNER AND CURETON, JJ., concur.

Questions and Comments

1. What was the holding in this case?
2. What was the court's reasoning?

Custom and Usage

The case that follows involves an exercise instructor at a health spa who participated in karate practice. This was not a part of his job responsibilities. The case discusses liability arising out of custom and usage.

---

1. S.C. Code Ann. § 42-1-10 *et seq.* (1985).

••

McCRACKEN COUNTY HEALTH SPA v. HENSON
568 S.W.2d 240 (Ky.Ct.App. 1977)

Before COOPER, HAYES and HOWERTON, JJ.

HAYES, Judge.

This is an appeal from a summary judgment entered by the McCracken Circuit Court affirming an opinion and award of the Workmen's Compensation Board.

Appellee, Michael Glenn Henson, began his employment as an instructor with the appellant, McCracken County Health Spa, on July 24, 1974. Appellant is in the business of establishing exercise programs in order to promote the physical fitness of its members. On August 6, 1974, appellee, another instructor, and a club member began to discuss karate, and the different holds that might be employed. Appellee began to demonstrate a break-away hold on a club member, when both of them slipped and fell. Appellee sustained an injury to his right knee as a result of the accident. Appellant did not offer any course or program in karate or self-defense.

The Workmen's Compensation Board found that the appellee sustained a work-related harmful change to his body which entitled him to Workmen's Compensation benefits. The McCracken Circuit Court affirmed the decision of the board.

Appellant contends that appellee was not entitled to the award since his injury was sustained through "horseplay", and therefore his injury was not "workrelated" as required under the Workmen's Compensation Law.

The question presented in this case is whether or not the claimant sustained a "work-related" injury within the meaning of KRS 342.620(1).

KRS 342.620(1) provides: "(1) 'Injury' means any work related harmful change in the human organism . . ." The term "work-related" in this statute means that the injury must have arisen out of and in the course of employment, *Seventh St. Road Tobacco Warehouse v. Stillwell*, Ky., 550 S.W.2d 469 (1976).

In order for an injury to arise out of employment, there must be a causal relationship between the employment and the injury. If the injury was brought about by reason of some other cause having no relation to the claimant's employment it cannot be said to have arisen out of employment, *Hayes Freight Lines v. Burns*, Ky., 290 S.W.2d 836 (1956).

If the karate practice which resulted in appellee's injury had been shown to be one of a series of similar incidents generally participated in, to the employer's knowledge, by his employees, the Workmen's Compensation Board could find that it had become a custom of the claimant's employment. This would have made the injury arise out of employment and thus is would be work-related, *Hayes Freight Lines v. Burns, supra*.

However, the Workmen's Compensation Board failed to make a specific finding of fact on the issue of "work-relatedness." The Board's Findings of Fact stated that the claimant, "received a work related injury to his right leg while working for defendant."

This statement by the Board is a conclusion of law and not a finding of fact. The Board made no specific findings of fact to sustain this conclusion of law. "There is nothing in the Board's opinion and award concerning this conclusion of law which can serve as the basis for meaningful appellate review of the Board's conclusion." *Harry M. Stevens Company Inc. v. Workmen's Compensation Board*, Ky. App., 553 S.W.2d 852 (1977).

Further, it was clearly erroneous for the Circuit Court, upon review of the Board's opinion and award, to make its own specific findings of fact and thereby substitute itself for the Board as the finder of fact.

"The board is the sole fact finder in compensation proceedings and the circuit court may not substitute its opinion for that of the board on the weight of the evidence." *Armco Steel Corporation v. Mullins*, Ky., 501 S.W.2d 261 (1973).

Therefore, this case is reversed with directions to the Circuit Court that it remand the case to the Workmen's Compensation Board for a finding of fact sufficient to make a determination as to whether or not the claimant sustained a work-related injury within the meaning of KRS 342.610(1) and KRS 342.620(1).

All concur.

Questions and Comments

Was the injury sustained during karate practice work related? Explain your answer.

SUMMARY AND ADDITIONAL REMARKS

Workers' compensation knowledge is important to the sport manager. The workers' compensation statute seeks to compensate workers as opposed to awarding damages for wrongdoing. Consequently, relief should be prompt and certain. The presence of legal counsel often enhances the workers' compensation award. This enhancement results from many things. First, the statute may give compensation for disability to the body as a whole as well as compensation for injury to or loss of a part of the body. Further, compensation measured in terms of a company doctor will have a tendency to be less than that which results from additional medical opinion that purports to represent the patient directly.

The constitutional basis for a workers' compensation statute is to be found under the police power. This power is said to be the greatest power possessed by a state under the Tenth Amendment to the United States Constitution. Occasionally, a state constitution may need to be amended in order to validate a workers' compensation law. Because of the nature of the workers' compensation statutes, the traditional defenses to negligence are not appropriate. This is true because relief is not contingent upon the finding of negligence or intentional misconduct on the part of the employer. However, it is a defense in many jurisdictions if an employee has openly and purposely ignored certain safety regulations.

Additionally, the workers' compensation statute may contain a specific provision that excludes recreational activity either on or off the premises. Absent such a statutory provision, the court will examine various factors to determine if the injury arose out of and in the course of employment. Does the employer benefit from the recreational activity? Does the worker engage in the activity because of encouragement from management? Does management participate by providing uniforms, expenses, recreational equipment, and other amenities directly connected with and designed to encourage such activities?

Horseplay that results in injury, generally speaking, is not compensable as arising out of and in the course of the employment. Workers' compensation statutes are designed to give an exclusive remedy. There may be exceptions, but such exceptions will probably not be recognized as compensable.

The workers' compensation statutes are usually built around a set of administrative procedures designed to enhance the fact-finding process through the use of nonjudicial hearing officers or bodies. Consequently, the standard of judicial review is normally limited by the substantial evidence test. In other words, if there is substantial evidence to support the findings of the administrative commission upon judicial review, then the court will not feel free to go beyond such a finding.

It is elementary that workers' compensation statutes are interpreted in such a way as to give credence to the customary standards set forth in the canons of statutory interpretation. The intent and purpose of the statute, the history of the statute, construction of the various parts for purpose of traditional interpretation of words such as *shall* and *may*, and a liberal interpretation that carries with it a presumption of compensability are all useful when the language of a statute is other than clear and precise.

To the extent that a statute must be interpreted, then the common-law technique of *stare decisis* is useful as a quick perusal of the cases contained in this chapter will indicate. (*Stare decisis* refers to precedent: Let the decision stand.) Judges will look to previous decisions as precedent.

Monetary relief for the worker who is accidentally injured while employed is a matter of social policy. In many respects, providing such relief without the necessity of proving fault is aptly described as strict liability. The strict liability of the workers' compensation laws, however, is not contingent upon a finding of extra hazardous activity but flows from a conscious desire to shift the risk of loss to the ultimate consumer.

The cases reproduced in this chapter involve factual situations whereby the business itself is sports or recreational related. The reader should not forget that often the business will not be sports related in and of itself, but will have a component, whether as a conscious design or not, that is recreational in nature. In short, a recreation director or a wellness instructor may be employed by a business that is not directly involved in sports activity. These cases are also relevant to the student and practitioner in the field of recreation.

This could be you - check your response

1. The employee was injured during the course of her employment; hence, workers' compensation would apply. If the state statute says that workers' compensation is the exclusive remedy, then a remedy outside the statute would be disallowed. Intentional torts or gross negligence may constitute exceptions to the exclusive remedy provision of workers' compensation.

2. If injured at a company party, the worker would be eligible for workers' compensation if the injury resulted from a party at which attendance was expected. As noted above, the expression used by the courts is "arising out of" or "during the course of" employment.

REFERENCES

Authors

Larson, Arthur. (1952). *The law of workmen's compensation*, Vols. 1-4 (Updated through 1993). Matthew Bender & Company, Incorporated.

Cases

Ankrom v. Dallas Cowboys Football Club, 900 S.W.2d 75 (Tex.App.-Dallas 1995).

Beneficiaries of McBroom v. Chamber of Commerce, 713 P.2d 1095 (Or. Ct. App. 1986).

Billish v. City of Chicago, 962 F.2d 1269 (7th Cir. 1992).

Burnett v. Ina, 810 S.W.2d 833 (Tex. Ct. App. 1991).

Cary Fire Protection Dist. v. Industrial Comm'n, 569 N.E.2d 1338 (Ill. App. Ct. 1991).

Champion v. Beale, 833 S.W.2d 799 (Ky. Ct. App. 1992).

Elizabethtown Sportswear v. Stice, 720 S.W.2d 732 (Ky. Ct. App. 1986).

Havird v. Columbia YMCA, 418 S.E.2d 329 (S.C. Ct. App. 1992).

Hemmler v. Workmen's Compensation Appeal Bd., 569 A.2d 395 (Pa. Commw. Ct. 1990).

Jensen v. Sport Bowl, Inc., 469 N.W.2d 370 (S.D. 1991).

Kim v. Sportswear, 393 S.E.2d 418 (Va. Ct. App. 1990).

Kozak v. Industrial Comm'n, 579 N.E.2d 921 (Ill. App. Ct. 1991).

McCracken County Health Spa v. Henson, 568 S.W.2d 240 (Ky. Ct. App. 1977).

Mintiks v. Metropolitan Opera Ass'n, 550 N.Y.S.2d 143 (N.Y. App. Div. 1990).

Mullins v. Westmoreland Coal Co., 391 S.E.2d 609 (Va. Ct. App. 1990).

PSFS/Meritor Financial v. Workmen's Compensation Appeal Bd., 603 A.2d 692 (Pa. Commw. Ct. 1992).

Seiber v. Moog Automotive, Inc., 773 S.W.2d 161 (Mo. Ct. App. 1989).

State Accident Ins. Fund Corp. v. McCabe, 702 P.2d 436 (Or. Ct. App. 1985).

Sterling v. Mike Brown, Inc., 580 So. 2d 832 (Fla. Dist. Ct. App. 1991).

Stovall v. Dal-Camp, Inc., 669 S.W.2d 531 (Ky. 1984).

Town & Country Chrysler v. Mitchell, 833 P.2d 314 (Or. Ct. App. 1992).

Ward v. Mid-South Home Service, 769 S.W.2d 486 (Tenn. 1989).

Legal Encyclopedias

82 Am.Jur.2d *Workers' Compensation* §§ 1-731 (1992), with current updates.

99 C.J.S. *Workmens' Compensation* §§ 1-352 (1958), with current updates.

100 C.J.S. *Workmens' Compensation* §§ 353-781 (1958), with current updates.

101 C.J.S. *Workmens' Compensation* §§ 782-1045 (1958), with current updates.

CHAPTER 9

PRODUCT LIABILITY

INTRODUCTION

Product liability refers to a body of law that enables an individual who is injured while using equipment to recover from a manufacturer. Under normal circumstances a product is made by a manufacturer, then turned over to the retailer who sells it to the buyer. Suppose the buyer is injured by the product. Who is liable? Sport managers need to be familiar with the concepts of product liability. For example, a fitness club manager purchased a wall-hung weight machine. The machine was defective. During its use by a customer, the weight machine detached from the wall, struck the manager in the mouth, and knocked out her front teeth. The sport manager would want to have some knowledge of product liability. Consideration should be given to bringing suit against the manufacturer or seller of the equipment.

For many years consumers had two options. First, they could sue the retailer for negligence. Second, they could sue the manufacturer for negligence. Obviously, the manufacturers were in a superior position because they possessed extensive resources and because they could bring to the forum a chain of inspections that were under their total control. The consumer for all practical purposes was left to find something wrong with the conduct of the retailer, such as failure to properly install. However, the product may simply have been defective, with no fault attributable to the retailer.

Social policy demanded the law provide a more effective remedy for the injured consumer. This trend was predicated on the notion that the manufacturers could pass the cost of the remedy on to the consumers as a whole. This cost-shifting would be in the form of increased prices, or the purchase of liability insurance. Thus product liability was a result of the demand for more effective consumer protection.

Statutes relating to product liability have evolved around two remedies, one related to contracts and the other related to torts. Initially, the manufacturer could not be sued because there was no contract with the consumer (privity of contract). Later, the law of sales removed the requirement for privity of contract. Sales is a specialized form of contract. The sales slip is the contract. The manufacturer can be sued for breach of implied warranty of merchantability or for breach of implied warranty of fitness for a particular purpose. The product should be fit for the purpose the manufacturer intended. These legal developments removed the requirement of privity of contract and also freed the consumer from an obligation to prove negligence.

The next development involved the utilization of strict liability—specifically, liability without fault. Public policy demanded that an injured consumer be permitted to recover damages without the necessity of proving fault. This is the concept of strict liability.

These two developments supplemented the traditional suit based on negligence. The end result was a body of law known as product liability. Such concepts include negligence, breach of warranty, and strict liability. Product liability enabled a purchaser to go back to the manufacturer who was perceived as the one capable of spreading the loss to the consumer. The law now stated that there was a direct causal relationship between the manufacturer of a product and an injury to person or property.

In summary, the manufacturer is responsible for safety of design, for products that are not defective and for any warnings as to use. Two theories on which a plaintiff may recover are the theory of breach of warranty or the theory of negligence.

Owners and managers of a sport enterprise should remember that an attorney representing a plaintiff will be well versed in three basic strategies. First, all parties having liability exposure should be joined as party defendants. The plaintiff is not as concerned with who pays as with being paid. Second, all theories of liability should be explored and, to the extent permissible under local rules of procedure, should be pleaded. A plaintiff wishes to recover. The theory under which recovery is effectuated is of secondary importance. Third,

PRODUCT LIABILITY?

reference is sometimes made to the "deep pocket theory." Specifically, it is important to be able to collect a judgment that has been rendered. Consequently, a defendant's finances must be sufficient to meet the demands of a judgment, or insurance should be available to satisfy the judgment. The plaintiff makes certain to sue the "deep pocket"—the defendant with large amounts of money.

IN THIS CHAPTER YOU WILL LEARN:

The requirements to state a cause of action in negligence against the manufacturer

The requirements to state a cause of action in strict liability against the manufacturer

The requirements to state a cause of action as against the manufacturer based upon contract

The possibility that the three concepts that undergird product liability, namely, negligence, strict liability, and warranty, are subject to being pleaded in the alternative as a theoretical bases for a cause of action

The defenses that can be effectively set forth for each of the above causes of action

---

KEY WORDS: *warranty, implied warranty of merchantability, implied warranty, fitness for particular purpose, Restatement of Torts, strict liability, deep pocket*

This could be you!

Shortly after the Joneses began their businesses, each decided on the purchase of chairs and other furniture for the benefit of patrons and employees. Because money was scarce, the Joneses decided to patronize a small business that had recently started manufacturing chairs and tables suitable for use in the respective businesses. The company was owned by Maria Jones's cousin and was doing business as a corporation. The chairs that the Joneses selected were deemed to be adequate but not outstanding. It was later determined that the company had utilized nails rather than screws in putting the chairs together. A patron of the fitness center sat in one of the chairs, which caused it to collapse. The patron was injured and contemplated legal action. Who would be defendants? Could the cause of action be stated in the alternative? Assuming that the corporation that manufactured the chairs had not accumulated financial reserves, were there other means whereby a judgment could be effectuated as against the corporation?

LEGAL PRINCIPLES

Negligence

In the following case a child fell from a jungle gym. An effort to recover for injury was unsuccessful under both a negligence and strict liability claim.

The plaintiff sought to recover from both the school district and the manufacturer of the jungle gym. In reading the case, look for what the court says about negligence, strict liability, and warranty.

••

COZZI v. NORTH PALOS ELEMENTARY SCH.
DIST. NO. 117
597 N.E.2d 683 (Ill. App. Ct. 1992)

Justice McCORMICK delivered the opinion of the court:

Robert Cozzi, Jr., by his father and next friend, Robert Cozzi, Sr., sued North Palos Elementary School District No. 117, (North Palos), and Northwest Design Products, Inc., (Northwest Design), for personal injuries sustained in an accident on a school playground. The trial court granted defendants' motions for summary judgment and plaintiff appeals.

Plaintiff's second-amended complaint alleged that North Palos was negligent in maintaining the jungle gym and in failing to warn of the danger of the jungle gym. Plaintiff also alleged that North Palos's actions amounted to wilful and wanton conduct. As against Northwest Design, plaintiff alleged that Northwest Design negligently designed the jungle gym, failed to warn of its danger and manufactured the jungle gym in an unreasonably dangerous manner.

Defendants filed motions for summary judgment based on the plaintiff's deposition. In his deposition plaintiff stated that he was injured while playing on a jungle gym manufactured by Northwest Design Products. He was 11 years old at the time of the incident which occurred after school hours on the grounds of a school in North Palos Elementary School District. Plaintiff testified that he was sitting on the second level from the top of the jungle gym when he heard someone call his name. He turned his head to look and slipped backwards, catching other bars underneath his armpits. Plaintiff kept twirling to get back to a position where he could handle himself. He tried to grab the bar, but he panicked, and fell onto the wood chips under the jungle gym. Plaintiff also testified that the jungle gym was normal, not icy or wet and that he knew that he could hurt himself if he fell off the jungle gym.

In opposition to defendants' motions for summary judgment, plaintiff did not present affidavits or other evidence to the court. Defendants' motions were granted. Plaintiff subsequently filed a motion to vacate and reconsider and attached an affidavit stating that he had fallen because of the slipperiness of the bars. The court denied the motion.

On appeal, plaintiff contends that summary judgment was improperly granted because a genuine issue of material fact exists regarding the cause of his accident.

The standards governing whether a summary judgment should be granted are set forth in 2-1005(c) of the Illinois Code of Civil Procedure which provides in relevant part:

"The judgment sought shall be rendered without delay if the pleadings, depositions, and admissions on file, together with the affidavits, if any, show that there is no genuine issue as to any material fact and that the moving party is entitled to a judgment as a matter of law." (Ill.Rev. Stat. 1987, ch. 110, par. 2-1005(c).)

Summary judgment is a remedy that must be awarded with caution in order to avoid preempting a litigant's right to trial by jury or his right to fully present the factual basis of a case where a material dispute may exist. (*Wysocki v. Bedrosian* (1984), 124 Ill.App.3d 158, 164, 79 Ill.Dec. 564, 463 N.E.2d 1339.) It is well established that on a motion for summary judgment the trial court must construe the pleadings, affidavits, depositions, and admissions on file against the moving party and in favor of the opponent of the motion. (*Wysocki*, 124 Ill.App.3d at 164, 79 Ill.Dec. 564, 463 N.E.2d 1339.) However, "while a plaintiff responding to a motion for summary judgment is not required to prove his case at the summary judgment stage, he must, nevertheless, present some evidentiary facts to support the elements of his claim." *Phillips v. United States Waco Corp.* (1987), 163 Ill.App. 3d 410, 416, 114 Ill.Dec. 515, 516 N.E.2d 670.

I. NORTH PALOS ELEMENTARY SCHOOL DISTRICT NO. 117

The general rule regarding the liability of an owner or occupier of land upon which a child is injured was articulated in *Kahn v. James Burton Co.* (1955), 5 Ill.2d 614, 126 N.E.2d 836. The court held that the ordinary principles of negligence determine a landowner's liability. (*Kahn*, 5 Ill.2d at 625, 126 N.E.2d 836.) Therefore, to survive summary judgment, plaintiff must present evidence to show that defendant had a duty to plaintiff, breached that duty, and the breach proximately caused plaintiff's injury.

Where the owner or occupier knows, or should know that young children frequent the area where a dangerous condition is present, and because of their immaturity, the children are not able to appreciate the risk involved, defendant has a duty to remedy the dangerous condition. (*Cope v. Doe* (1984), 102 Ill.2d 278, 286, 80 Ill.Dec. 40, 464 N.E.2d 1023.) There is no duty to remedy the condition if it involves risks that children would be expected to appreciate and avoid. *Alop v. Edgewood Valley Community Association* (1987), 154 Ill. App.3d 482, 485, 107 Ill.Dec 355, 507 N.E.2d 19.

In *Alop*, a six-year-old child fell off a playground slide, onto an asphalt surface, and sued the owner and manager of the playground. Summary judgment was granted for the defendants and plaintiff appealed. The appellate court affirmed the trial court, concluding that the slide on the asphalt surface did not create a dangerous condition because the risk the slide presented to children was an obvious one. Consequently, the court found that defendants did not owe a duty to plaintiff to have placed the slide on a softer surface than asphalt.

The facts of the case at bar are similar to those of *Alop*. Both cases involve appeals from summary judgments, and both plaintiffs fell off recreational equipment that was of some height. The plaintiff in the instant case was older and could appreciate the risk of playing on the eleven foot jungle gym more than the six year old in *Alop* could appreciate the risk of playing on a slide.

The court followed *Alop* in *Young v. Chicago Housing Authority* (1987), 162 Ill. App.3d 53, 113 Ill.Dec. 794, 515 N.E.2d 779, where a five-year-old child fell from monkey bars onto a concrete surface. The court applied the reasoning of *Alop*, stating that "the same commonsense principle applied to both cases: if you fall, you might get hurt. This is an obvious risk that children encounter in their daily lives when at a playground." *Young*, 162 Ill.App.3d at 57, 113 Ill.Dec. 794, 515 N.E.2d 779.

Plaintiff contends that the trial court's reliance on the holdings in *Alop* and *Young* is misplaced. According to plaintiff, North Palos owed him a duty to remedy the condition of the jungle gym, and cited to *Scarano v. Town of Ela* (1988), 166 Ill.App.3d 184, 117 Ill.Dec. 72, 520 N.E.2d 62 support. In *Scarano*, a young boy fell off of a slide. He alleged that the slide was defective because the handrails were worn, slippery and loose. The court found that the defendant had a duty to remedy the condition of the handrail. The court concluded that a slide with defective handrails was a greater risk that children would normally not appreciate. *Scarano*, 166 Ill.App.3d at 190, 117 Ill.Dec. 72, 520 N.E.2d 62.) The case at bar is distinguishable from *Scarano* in that it involves an obvious danger while *Scarano* involved a latent defect of a protective device. The bars on the jungle gym enable children to swing and move about. This is the purpose of the jungle gym. The danger involved in doing so was apparent.

In addition to allegations of negligence, plaintiff contends that defendant's conduct was wilful and wanton. Wilful and wanton conduct can be established once there is a finding of duty, breach of that duty, proximate cause and an intent to injure plaintiff or reckless disregard for his safety. (*Scarano*, 166 Ill.App.3d at 187, 117 Ill.Dec. 72, 520 N.E.2d 62.) In the case at bar, there can be no finding of wilful and wanton misconduct in the absence of a duty owed plaintiff by defendant.

II. NORTHWEST DESIGN INC.

Plaintiff brought claims for negligence and strict liability against Northwest Design. The duty and breach of that duty is the same in both negligence and strict products liability claims. (*Phillips*, 163 Ill.App.3d at 417, 114 Ill.Dec. 515, 516 N.E.2d 670.) Plaintiff contends that Northwest Design was negligent because of its failure to warn of the dangers of using the jungle gym and negligent in designing the gym at such a height.

In a product liability cause of action based on ordinary negligence, a plaintiff must show that a defendant owed him a duty of reasonable care and either failed to do something which a reasonably careful person would have done or did something which a reasonably careful person would not have done. (*Sanchez v. Bock Laundry Machine Co.* (1982), 107 Ill.App.3d 1024, 1028, 63 Ill.Dec. 638, 438 N.E.2d 569.) The determination of whether a duty to warn exists is a question of law and not of fact. (*Genaust v. Illinois Power Co.*(1976), 62 Ill.2d 456, 466, 343 N.E.2d 465.) "Generally, a duty to warn exists when there is unequal knowledge and the defendant possessed with such knows or should know that harm might occur if no warning is given." (*McColgan v.*

Environmental Control Systems (1991), 212 Ill.App.3d 696, 700, 156 Ill.Dec. 835, 571 N.E.2d 815.) However, warnings are not required if the danger involved is obvious and generally appreciated. *McColgan*, 212 Ill.App.3d 696, 156 Ill.Dec. 835, 571 N.E.2d 815.

As previously discussed, the fact that one could fall from climbing heights such as the jungle gym was obvious. Plaintiff did not produce evidence which could support a finding that Northwest Design had a duty to warn plaintiff of the danger of playing on the jungle gym.

A manufacturer can be liable for the negligent design of a product that imposes an unreasonable risk of harm upon the user. (*Sanchez*, 107 Ill.App.3d at 1028, 63 Ill.Dec. 638, 438 N.E.2d 569.) A manufacturer is under a nondelegable duty to produce a product which is reasonably safe for its intended and reasonably foreseeable uses. *Cornstubble v. Ford Motor Co.* (1988), 178 Ill.App. 3d 20, 24, 127 Ill.Dec. 55, 532 N.E.2d 884.

Plaintiff failed to provide evidence to show that defendant failed to produce a reasonably safe jungle gym, or that the jungle gym was unreasonably dangerous for its foreseeable and intended users. Plaintiff relies on the fact that he slipped to establish that the jungle gym was unreasonably dangerous. No presumption of negligence arises from the mere happening of an accident. *Rotche v. Buick Motor Co.* (1934), 358 Ill. 507, 516, 193 N.E. 529.

To recover in an action for strict liability, a plaintiff must prove (1) that an injury resulted from a condition of the product; (2) that the condition was unreasonably dangerous; and (3) that the condition existed at the time the product left the manufacturer's control. (*Hunt v. Blasius*, (1978), 74 Ill.2d 203, 210, 23 Ill.Dec. 574, 384 N.E.2d 368.) Plaintiff contends that the lack of warnings caused his injury, but his deposition contradicts this claim. In *Dunham v. Vaughan & Bushnell Mfg. Co.* (1969), 42 Ill.2d 339, 247 N.E.2d 401 the Illinois Supreme Court defined products as unreasonably dangerous if they failed to perform in the manner that was reasonably expected in light of their nature and intended function. *Dunham*, 42 Ill.2d at 342, 247 N.E.2d 401.) Jungle gyms are recreational equipment to be used as such. In this case, there was no evidence presented to show that it failed to perform its function.

Finally, plaintiff failed to present evidence that the jungle gym was unreasonably dangerous when it left Northwest Design's control. A similar proof problem arose in *Miller v. Verson Allsteel Press Co.* (1984) 126 Ill.App.3d 935, 81 Ill.Dec. 861, 467 N.E.2d 983, where the plaintiff in that case was injured while working a punch press. The plaintiff in *Miller* sued the manufacturer to recover for his injuries, but he failed to present any evidence to satisfy his burden of proving that an unreasonably dangerous condition existed when the press left the manufacturer's control. Consequently, the court affirmed summary judgment granted by the trial court.

Plaintiff relies on *Pell v. Victor J. Andrew High School* (1984), 123 Ill.App.3d 423, 78 Ill.Dec. 739, 462 N.E.2d 858, to support its contention that defendant should be held strictly liable in tort for manufacturing and selling the jungle gym without warnings and instructions. The plaintiff in *Pell* suffered injuries as a result of somersaulting off a trampoline in gym class and sued the manufacturer on the theory of strict liability. In *Pell* plaintiff alleged that an unreasonably dangerous condition existed because of the defendant's failure to adequately warn of the equipment's propensity to cause severe spinal cord injuries if it was used for somersaulting without a safety device operated by a trained instructor. In affirming the jury verdict, the court determined that there was sufficient evidence from which the jury could conclude that the manufacturer's warnings were ineffective.

The case at bar is distinguishable because the *Pell* case involved an insufficient warning of danger its users might not recognize while this case involves a danger even children recognize. In addition, unlike the plaintiff in *Pell*, the plaintiff in the instant case did not present any evidence to prove that the equipment was unreasonably dangerous.

The trial court properly found that defendants did not owe the alleged duties to plaintiff, that there were no genuine issue as to any material fact and that defendants are entitled to summary judgment as a matter of law.

For the foregoing reasons, the judgment of the circuit court is affirmed.
HARTMAN, P.J., and DiVITO, J., concur.

Questions and Comments

1. Three theories that undergird product liability are negligence, strict liability, and warranty. To recover under strict liability, the plaintiff must prove that an injury resulted from a condition of the product, that the product was unreasonably dangerous, that the condition existed at the time the product left the manufacturer (*Cozzi v. North Palos Elementary Sch. Dist. No. 117*, 1992, p. 686). Under warranty for a specific purpose, a manufacturer is obligated to produce a product that is safe for its intended purpose and is not unnecessarily dangerous. A warranty may state the quality of the raw materials and the quality of the workmanship.
2. What are the elements of negligence as set forth in this case?
3. What was the defense set forth on behalf of each of the defendants in this case?
4. What was the holding in the case?

Authors' Note

A product liability suit couched in terms of negligence is subject to the traditional defenses of assumption of risk and contributory negligence. The negligence asserted can range from a failure to warn, a failure to inspect, a failure to use appropriate materials, to such things as improper design or improper instruction in the use of the product.

The significant development to be noted involves the ability to reach the manufacturer of the goods directly. A landmark decision in 1916 signalled this development in social policy as reflected by judicial decision. The case was *MacPherson v. Buick Motor Company* (1916). For the first time a manufacturer was held responsible to the ultimate consumer for injury that resulted from a defective product. Although couched in terms of negligence, the doctrine was to receive subsequent refinements as reflected by a strict liability and a warranty analysis.

Certain states put the burden of injury on the installer. The sport business might be liable if it installed the equipment. In some businesses, part of the installation cost includes inspection by a structural engineer.

Finally, the reader will note that *Cozzi* is a public school decision. Some students in the field of recreation will find employment in the public school system. This gives the case a direct practical impact. Additionally, by this time the reader should be aware of the reasoning by analogy that is appropriate to all judicial decisions. Stated differently, a case that has a factual situation completely alien to sport management may, nevertheless, provide precedent for the owner or manager of a sport management business. Cases that fall within this factual description should not automatically be discarded as irrelevant where sport management law is concerned.

Strict Liability - Note Case

In the case of *Bouillon v. Harry Gill Company* (1973), Mark Bouillon, a 12-year-old novice pole-vaulter was injured. The pole-vaulting standards were altered by school officials. Conflicting testimony was given about the condition of the standards and the amount of alteration.

The court recognized that recovery could be had under the theory of strict liability. However, the court did not make an award under the doctrine of strict liability. The doctrine of strict liability imposes a heavy burden on a person selling a product that is unreasonably dangerous.

In this case, the defendant, the Harry Gill Company, was not held liable under the doctrine of strict liability. Furthermore, the school district was not held negligent.

Authors' Note

Section 402A of the *Restatement of Torts*, Second Edition, provides:

(1) One who sells any product in a defective condition unreasonably dangerous to the user or consumer or to his property is subject to liability for physical harm thereby caused to the ultimate user or consumer, or to his property, if
  (a) the seller is engaged in the business of selling such a product, and
  (b) it is expected to and does reach the user or consumer without substantial change in the condition in which it is sold.

(2) The rule stated in Subsection (1) applies although
  (a) the seller has exercised all possible care in the preparation and sale of his product, and
  (b) the user or consumer has not bought the product from or entered into any contractual relation with the seller.

It should be noted that strict liability does not apply to an occasional seller, nor does it apply to the sale of a stock of goods not in the usual course of business. Liability is not limited by the requirement that the parties stand in the relationship of buyer and seller. The theory of strict liability is not dependent upon negligence. However, liability can arise through faulty manufacturing, design, inadequate warnings, labelling, or instruction. If the product is altered, then the product no longer meets the manufacturer's standards. Hence, subsequent alterations in the product may constitute a defense to liability on the part of a manufacturer.

Contributory negligence is not a defense to strict liability, although assumption of risk is a defense. The reader will remember that contributory negligence refers to an act of omission or commission by the injured plaintiff that occurred with the act of negligence by the defendant. In other words, the injured party contributed to the problem, for example, by disregarding safety warnings. In several states, contributory negligence has been replaced with comparative negligence. For example, the court might find the defendant 70% at fault and the plaintiff 30% at fault.

As noted earlier, assumption of risk is a defense in some states. Some sports are known to be more dangerous than others. In these dangerous sports a wise sport manager would want to make certain that the participants are knowledgeable of the risks; they appreciate the risks; and yet participants voluntarily expose themselves to the risks.

Warranty

Warranties are both expressed and implied. Each warranty has a contractual significance. An expressed warranty is in writing; an implied warranty is not. Of the implied warranties, the more significant is fitness for a particular purpose and that which asserts an ability to accomplish the function for which it was intended. The case that follows indicates the multifaceted nature of product liability.

••

FILLER v. RAYEX CORP.
435 F.2d 336 (7th Cir. 1970)

Before DUFFY, Senior Circuit Judge, CUMMINGS and KERNER, Circuit Judges.

CUMMINGS, Circuit Judge.

In this diversity action, Michael Filler sued to recover damages for the loss of his right eye, and his mother, Barbara Mitchell, sought to recover her expenses for his hospitalization, artificial eye, and physician's services.

When his injury occurred, Michael Filler was a 16-year-old student at Oak Hill High School, near Marion, Indiana. While he was practicing for a varsity baseball game in the late afternoon of June 10, 1966, fungoes were being lofted to him by a fellow player. Filler lost a fly ball in the sun, although he was wearing flipped-down "baseball sunglasses" manufactured by defendant. After tipping the top of his baseball glove, the ball struck the right side of the sunglasses, shattering the right lens into sharp splinters which pierced his right eye, necessitating its removal nine days later.

Filler's coach was Richard Beck, an experienced ballplayer whose first baseball season at Oak Hill was in 1965. During that season, Beck would not allow his players to use sunglasses, considering them too dangerous. However, before the 1966 season, he read the following advertisement of defendant in *Sporting News*:

"PLAY BALL!
and *Flip* for Instant Eye Protection with
RAYEX
Baseball
SUNGLASSES
Professional
FLIP-SPECS"

The advertisement also stated:

"Scientific lenses protect your eyes with a flip from sun and glare any-where * * * baseball, beach, boat, driving, golfing, fishing, just perfect for Active and Spectator Sports—World's finest sunglasses."

After seeing this material, Beck decided to buy six pairs of defendant's flip-type baseball sunglasses for use by his outfielders and second basemen. Each pair of sunglasses was in a cardboard box labeled "Baseball Sunglasses—Professional Flip-Specs," stating "Simply flip * * * for instant eye protection." The guarantee inside each box provided:

"Rayex lenses are guaranteed for life against breakage. If lens break-age occurs mail glasses and 50 cents (Postage Handling Charge) for complete repair service."

"Rayex Sunglasses are guaranteed to:

1. Eliminate 96% of harmful ultraviolet and infrared rays.
2. Protect your eyes against reflected glare from smooth surfaces, roads, water, snow, etc.
3. Retain clear, undistorted vision."

Except for the flip feature and elastic tape at the rear of the frame, the glass-es resembled ordinary sunglasses. The thinness of the lenses was shielded by the frames and therefore not obvious to users.

These glasses were stored in the glove compartment of coach Beck's car, and in accordance with the custom of his teammates, Filler removed a pair of the sunglasses from the coach's car and was using them at the time of his injury. Neither Filler, nor Beck, nor indeed even defendant's president knew the lenses would shatter into sharp splinters when hit by a baseball.

After a bench trial, the district judge awarded Filler $101,000 damages and his mother $1,187.75 for her consequential damages. In an unreported memorandum opinion, the district judge supported this result on three inde-pendent grounds: implied warranty, strict liability, and negligence.[1] Under any of those theories, privity between the manufacturer and plaintiff is not required by controlling Indiana law. Posey v. Clark Equipment Company,

---

1. The court reserved judgment on an express warranty count, and we also do not con-sider that theory.

409 F.2d 560, 563 (7th Cir. 1969); Dagley v. Armstrong Rubber Company, 344 F.2d 245, 252-254 (7th Cir. 1965); Greeno v. Clark Equipment Company, 237 F.Supp. 427 (N.D. Ind. 1965).

We agree that defendant is liable for breach of an implied warranty of fitness for a particular purpose. Indiana has adopted the implied warranty provision of the Uniform Commercial Code dealing with fitness for a particular purpose:

> "*Implied Warranty—Fitness for particular purpose*—Where the seller at the time of contracting has reason to know any particular purpose for which the goods are required and that the buyer is relying on the seller's skill or judgment to select or furnish suitable goods, there is unless excluded or modified under the next section an implied warranty that the goods shall be fit for such purpose." Burns Indiana Stat.Ann.§ 19-2-315.

These sunglasses were advertised as baseball sunglasses that would give "instant eye protection." Although they were intended for use by baseball fielders, the thickness of the lenses ranged only from 1.2 mm. to 1.5 mm., so that shattering into exceedingly sharp splinters would occur on their breaking. Since they lacked the safety features of plastic or shatterproof glass, the sunglasses were in truth not fit for baseball playing, the particular purpose for which they were sold. Therefore, breach of that implied warranty was properly found.

Indiana has adopted the doctrine of strict liability of sellers of products "in a defective condition unreasonably dangerous to the user," as provided in Section 402A of the Restatement of Torts Second. Posey v. Clark Equipment Company, 409 F.2d 560, 563 (7th Cir. 1969). Here the thinness of the lenses made them unreasonably dangerous to users, so that the doctrine of strict liability is applicable. However, defendant argues against strict liability, on the ground that the sunglasses were "unavoidably unsafe products" within the exception of Comment *k* to Section 402A. Even assuming *arguendo* that the state of the art is not capable of producing a shatter-resistant or splinter-free baseball sunglass as defendant claims, Comment *k* furnishes no shelter from liability in this case. The exception applies only when the product is "accompanied by proper * * * warning," which defendant's product lacked.

Finally, we also agree that defendant was liable for negligence. Defendant knew that these glasses shattered readily, for a hundred were returned daily for lens replacements. At least it had constructive knowledge that the impact of a baseball would shatter these lenses into sharp splinters, since it must anticipate the reasonably foreseeable risks of the use of the product. See Spruill v. Boyle-Midway, Incorporated, 308 F.2d 79, 83-85 (4th Cir. 1962); 2 Harper & James, The Law of Torts, p. 1541 (1956). Moreover, despite the obviously physical stresses to which these glasses would be put, inadequate tests were made concerning their physical properties. Accordingly, even if defendant is not liable for negligence in production and sale of a poorly constructed product, it was properly held liable for its negligent failure to warn users of the danger of its product. Indiana National Bank of Indianapolis v. De Laval Separator Co., 389 F.2d 674, 676 (7th Cir. 1968).

Judgment is affirmed.

Questions and Comments

1. What is the theory of breach of warranty presented in this case?
2. Was the company negligent in its failure to warn?
3. What rule with respect to privity of contract does the State of Indiana adopt concerning product liability?
4. What treatises does the court rely upon for its statement of the law?
5. What is the test to determine if strict liability applies?

SUMMARY

A product liability action is based on negligence, strict liability, or sales warranty. An injured plaintiff might recover under the theory of (a) negligence, (b) strict liability, or (c) breach of implied warranty. Any of these theories will permit recovery. Hence, the need to argue all three. This is known as pleading in the alternative. This means that the injured plaintiff has alternative remedies. As a result, this branch of the law draws heavily on the law of torts, contracts generally, and sales.

Negligence

If an injury occurs, a suit may be filed predicated on negligence. The plaintiff must allege and prove the essential elements of negligence generally. These elements include a failure to exercise due care, a resulting injury, and a causal connection as between the two. Sometimes a statute, or law, will be violated which enables a plaintiff to allege negligence per se. Principles of tort law are applicable. Defenses to a product liability suit that allege negligence are those customarily associated with negligence and which have been discussed in a previous chapter. As noted earlier, contributory negligence and assumption of risk can be set out as affirmative defenses. As would be expected, the statute of limitations, together with releases, disclaimers, and waivers, is also relevant to the defensive position. Failure to follow safety instructions, together with other misuses of the product is a viable defense. Such a defense can perhaps be labelled one of the major traditional statements of the defense of contributory negligence or assumption of risk. A word of caution is needed here. The statute of limitations for a defense predicated upon negligence will be different from that predicated on a contract defense.

Strict Liability

When strict liability is pleaded as a cause of action, it is essential that a plaintiff allege the defective and unreasonably dangerous condition of the product. A complaint will also need to allege, and of course to prove, a causal connection between such condition and plaintiff's injury. Finally, it will be necessary to connect the defendant with the product that caused the plaintiff's injury. This action may arise out of the manufacture or the sale of a product.

Defenses to a complaint predicated on strict liability may include a change in condition insofar as the product is concerned. This change in condition can involve alterations, repairs, or tampering. Strict liability, as the name implies, posits the absence of fault. Consequently, negligence does not enter into the picture either as the basis for the complaint or as a defense. Assumption of risk, disclaimer, unforeseeable misuse, and releases may be relevant.

Warranty

A product liability suit that alleges a breach of warranty will look to the law of contracts generally and the law of sales in particular. Misuse of the product and assumption of risk will each be relevant defenses. A statute of limitation together with disclaimer, waivers, and releases may also be pleaded.

In this connection it must be noted that the statute of limitations will differ from that predicated on the law of torts. Further, the statute will commence to run at the date of the sale as opposed to the date of injury. Finally, there may be a statute of repose that sets a final closing date for the bringing of an action labelled as strict liability and that purports to finally cut off all rights to proceed.

This could be you - check your response

The defendants in this case could be the Joneses and the manufacturer of the chairs.

1. The chairs should have served the purpose for which they were purchased (implied warranty).
2. Under the concept of negligence, the Joneses were responsible for exercising due care for the safety of patrons. A chair used in the business was the cause of the injury. Under strict liability, the chair's construction with nails may have been defective, rendering it excessively dangerous.
3. The cause of action could be stated in the alternative. In other words, both claims could be stated in the pleadings of the case.
4. If the manufacturer had no financial reserves, it would still be up to the court to prescribe compensation for the injured party if a complaint was filed and if the court ruled for the plaintiff patron. The attorney for the patron might try to pierce the corporate veil and thus make the individuals who own the company responsible for compensation. Insurance might serve as compensation. Possessions of the company might be attached for compensation. The judgment for the injured patron could be enforced in the future when the company has more money.

REFERENCES

Cases

Austria v. Bike Athletic Co., 810 P.2d 1312 (Or. Ct. App. 1991).
Babine v. Gilley's Bronco Shop, Inc., 488 So.2d 176 (Fla. Dist. Ct. App. 1986).
Barker v. City of Galveston, 907 S.W.2d 879 (Tex.App. Houston [1 Dist.] 1995).
Bernick v. Jurden, 293 S.E.2d 405 (N.C. 1982).

Bouillon v. Harry Gill Company, 301 N.E.2d 627 (Ill. App. Ct. 1973).

Butz v. Werner, 438 N.W.2d 509 (N.D. 1989).

Byrns v. Riddell, Incorporated, 550 P.2d 1065 (Ariz. 1976).

Cozzi v. North Palos Elementary Sch. Dist. No. 117, 597 N.E.2d 683 (Ill. App. Ct. 1992).

Dailey v. Honda Motor Co., Ltd., 882 F.Supp. 826 (S.D. Ind. 1995).

Dudley Sports Co. v. Schmitt, 279 N.E.2d 266 (Ind. Ct. App. 1972).

Economy Engineering Co. v. Commonwealth, 604 N.E.2d 694 (Mass. 1992).

Everett v. Bucky Warren, Inc., 380 N.E.2d 653 (Mass. 1978).

Filler v. Rayex Corp., 435 F.2d 336 (7th Cir. 1970).

Garcia v. Joseph Vince Co., 148 Cal. Rptr. 843 (Cal. Ct. App. 1978).

Garcia v. Kusan, Inc., 655 N.E.2d 1290 (Mass.App. 1995).

Garrett v. Nissen Corp., 498 P.2d 1359 (N.M. 1972).

Gosewisch v. American Honda Motor Co., 737 P.2d 376 (Ariz. 1987).

Hemphill v. Sayers, 552 F.Supp. 685 (S.D. Ill. 1982).

Lamb v. B & B Amusements Corp., 869 P.2d 926 (Utah, 1993).

Lukowski v. Vecta Educ. Corp., 401 N.E.2d 781 (Ind. Ct. App. 1980).

MacPherson v. Buick Motor Company, 111 N.E. 1050 (N.Y. 1916).

Wissel v. Ohio High Sch. Athletic Ass'n, 605 N.E.2d 458 (Ohio Ct. App. 1992).

Source Books and Legal Encyclopedias

American law of products liability 3d (1987) with current updates. Lawyers Co-Operative Publishing Co. and Bancroft-Whitney Co.

63 Am. Jur. 2d *Products Liability*, §§1-908 (1984), with current updates.

63A Am. Jur. 2d *Products Liability*, §§909-977 (1984) with current updates.

72 C.J.S. Supplement *Products Liability*, §1-96 (1975) with current updates.

2 Restatement of Torts 2d § 402A (1978).

CHAPTER 10

NUISANCE

INTRODUCTION

As a general rule, a person can make free use of property that he or she owns. This freedom to use is limited, however, by the proposition that the use must not injure another person. Under common law, a use of property that unduly annoys another is an impermissible use. The annoyance can take a multitude of forms: excessive noise, dust, unsightly appearance, and smells that are offensive to the average individual. The law has not been able to measure exactly what is permissible as opposed to what is not. Industrial development postulates a certain amount of inconvenience for citizens in the vicinity. The demands of progress on the one hand must be weighed against the expectation of peace and quiet on the other. Relevant also is the time when the encroachment occurred. A homeowner who moves to an area that is already devoted to activities that might be considered as undesirable is not in as good a position as someone who has owned and occupied premises for a number of years prior to the commencement of the disturbing activity.

The field of recreation offers abundant opportunities to illustrate the principles referred to above. For example, a baseball field will be accompanied by the noise of the game and the inconvenience of balls that are hit onto adjoining property. An events center that hosts a concert may be accompanied by problems of alcohol, drugs, violence, and noise pollution. Certain types of racing, such as drag racing, are also worthy of mention in this connection. A determination of what is a nuisance and what can be done about it is the subject matter of this chapter.

> **IN THIS CHAPTER YOU WILL LEARN:**
> The application of the law of nuisance to the field of recreational management
> The remedies that are accorded to individuals injured by a nuisance
> The constitutional basis for the proscription of nuisances

KEY WORDS: *interlocutory appeal, injunction, public nuisance*

This could be you!

The fitness center was an early success. Multi-age classes were organized, and families regularly enjoyed the recreational activity. One room at the center was devoted to other community activities. Local bird-watchers met on one night; a quilting society met on another. Young musicians were encouraged to further their talent, and in general the business took on an established place in the life of the community.

NUISANCE?

Other downtown recreational centers such as the local YMCA and YWCA, a sport equipment store, and a local skating rink soon formed together in an association designed to promote recreational activities in the community. At this point, the local Apollo Theater became vacant, and the owners of an adult movie industry and adult bookstore decided to occupy and use the building. The townspeople believed that drug dealing and prostitution might accompany the adult movie traffic. The officials of the new recreational society met and discussed the problem. Assuming that the reaction of the recreational association was negative, what steps, if any, could the group take to call a halt to the operation of the adult movie theater and bookstore? What facts, if any, should be elicited in order to better effectuate a remedy?

DECISIONAL LAW

Nuisance—Characteristics

A public nuisance is described and characterized in *Orlando Sports Stadium, Inc. v. State ex rel. Powell* (1972). This case abated, or rendered harmless, a public nuisance based on the unlawful use of drugs. The case is useful in that it speaks to the question of what constitutes a nuisance and the remedies available to the public.

This is an interlocutory appeal. This means that the appeal expedites the judgment on the merits of the case.

••

ORLANDO SPORTS STADIUM, INC. v. STATE
262 So. 2d 881 (Fla. 1972)

ADKINS, Justice.

This is an interlocutory appeal from the Circuit Court of Orange County,

Florida, having been transferred to this Court from the District Court of Appeal, Second District.

The State of Florida upon the relation of Powell, the County solicitor, and Eagen, the State Attorney, filed an amended complaint seeking to abate or enjoin a public nuisance pursuant to Fla.Stat. (1970) Chapters 823 and 60, F.S.A. It was alleged that defendants Ashlock and wife were the owners of certain land on which a building known as Orlando Sports Stadium was situated. The defendant Orlando Sports Stadium, Inc., operated the Orlando Sports Stadium. The amended complaint then contained the following allegations:

"5. On June 6, 1970, and at divers times thereafter up to and including December 29, 1970, said premises were visited by narcotic and other drug users for the purpose of unlawfully using hallucinogenic drugs, barbiturates, central nervous stimulants, amphetamines, narcotic drugs, habit forming drugs as described in Chapters 398, 404 or 500, Florida Statutes 1970.

"6. The matters and things alleged in paragraph 5 above constitute a public nuisance, which public nuisance will persist in the future unless abated or enjoined by this Court."

By motion to dismiss, defendants attack the constitutionality of Chapters 823 and 60 as applied to them in this case.

Fla.Stat. § 823.05, F.S.A., provides, inter alia, that

"Whoever shall erect, establish, continue, or maintain, own or lease

. . . any place where any law of the state is violated, shall be deemed guilty of maintaining a nuisance, and the building, erection, place, tent or booth and the furniture, fixtures and contents are declared a nuisance. All such places or persons shall be abated or enjoined as provided in §§ 60.05 and 60.06."

Fla.Stat. § 823.10, F.S.A., reads as follows:

"Any store, shop, warehouse, dwelling house, building, vehicle, ship, boat, vessel, aircraft, or any place whatever, which is visited by narcotic or other drug users for the purpose of unlawfully using hallucinogenic drugs, barbiturates, central nervous stimulants, amphetamines, narcotic drugs, habit-forming drugs or any other drugs as described in chapters 398, 404 and 500, Florida Statutes, or which is used for the illegal keeping, selling, or delivering of the same, shall be deemed a public nuisance. No person shall keep or maintain such public nuisance or aid and abet another in keeping or maintaining such public nuisance."

Fla.Stat. § 60.05(1), F.S.A., reads as follows:

"When any nuisance as defined in §823.05, exists, the state attorney, county solicitor, county prosecutor, or any citizen of the county may sue in the name of the state on his relation to enjoin the nuisance, the person, or persons maintaining it and the owner or agent of the building or ground on which the nuisance exists."

Fla. Stat. §398.14, F.S.A., provides:

"Any store, shop, warehouse, dwelling house, building, vehicle, boat, aircraft, or any place whatever, which is resorted to by narcotic drug addicts for the purpose of using narcotic drugs or which is used for the illegal keeping or selling of the same, shall be deemed a public nuisance. No person shall keep or maintain such public nuisance."

Rule 1.110(b), FRCP, 30 F.S.A., requires that, to state a cause of action, a complaint must contain "a short and plain statement of the ultimate facts showing that the pleader is entitled to relief," and "a demand for judgment for the relief to which he deems himself entitled."

For the purposes of the motion to dismiss for failure to state a cause of action, allegations of the complaint are assumed to be true and all reasonable inferences are allowed in favor of the plaintiffs' case. [Citing cases.]

In the case *sub judice*, for the purposes of the motion to dismiss, it is admitted that on June 6, 1970, and at divers times thereafter up to and including December 29, 1970, the premises in question were visited by narcotic and other drug users for the purpose of unlawfully using hallucinogenic drugs, barbiturates, central nervous stimulants, amphetamines, narcotics drugs, habit forming drugs as described in Fla. Stat. Ch. 398, F.S.A., the Uniform Narcotic Drug Law; Ch. 404, the Florida Drug Abuse Law; or Ch. 500, the Food, Drug and Cosmetic Law. It is also alleged that this conduct is a public nuisance and will persist in the future unless abated by this Court.

. . . . . .

A public nuisance violates public rights, subverts public order, decency or morals, or causes inconvenience or damage to the public generally. [Emphasis added.] See 23 Fla.Jur., Nuisances, §6; 18 F.L.P., Nuisances, § 49. The Legislature has broad discretion to designate a particular activity to be a public nuisance. Pompano Horse Club v. State, 93 Fla. 415, 111 So. 801, 52 A.L.R. 51 (1927). In the exercise of its police power the State has authority to prevent or abate nuisances, ***for police power is the sovereign right of the State to enact laws for the protection of lives, health, morals, comfort and general welfare.*** [Emphasis added.] Holley v. Adams, 238 So.2d 401 (Fla. 1970).

It is not possible to define comprehensively "nuisances" as each case must turn upon its facts and be judicially determined. [Citing cases.] The statutes under attack are not so vague and indefinite as to invade the constitutional rights of the defendants in the case *sub judice*, where the plaintiffs seek an injunction. If the injunction does issue, it must be definite and certain.

It has been said that an attempt to enumerate all nuisances would be almost the equivalent as an attempt to classify the infinite variety of ways in which one may be annoyed or impeded in the enjoyment of his rights. 66 C.J.S. Nuisances § 26.

. . . . . .

Appellants' reliance upon federal cases to sustain their contention that state statutes impinging upon protected speech or religious freedom are constitutionally impermissible is material to the case *sub judice* only if the illegal use of drugs and narcotics is somehow protected by the First Amendment of the United States Constitution. The statutes under consideration do not attempt to regulate protective speech, but to control a public nuisance. The enactment of the statutes was not an exercise of unconstitutional prerogative. Instead, it was an exercise of the police power to protect public health, welfare, safety and morals. In this respect, the appellants had no constitutional grounds on which to rely in asserting grounds for their motion to dismiss.

It should be noted that appellees do not seek to enjoin the overall operation of the Orlando Sports Stadium, but only a limited use thereof. The situation sought to be enjoined is analogous to that of a tavern or night club that becomes a nuisance by virtue of raucous conduct of its patrons. . . . [such as] open drinking and a general course of disorderly conduct; [citation omitted], frequent loud and disturbing noises, vulgar language, traffic jams, and obscene conduct; [citation omitted], habitual assembly of lewd women and men drinking and dancing. . . . .

Ultimately, the questions arising from this controversy are questions of fact. There is no basis for dismissing the complaint as a matter of law and the trial court was correct in denying the motion to dismiss.

The order of the trial judge is affirmed and the cause is remanded for further proceeding.

It is so ordered.

Roberts, Carlton, Boyd, McCain and Dekle concur.

DISSENTING OPINION—JUSTICE DREW

I cannot agree with my brethren. If the complaint here states a cause of action the owner or operator of any public building in this State is at the mercy of the lawless element of our society. According to the views of the majority, proof that a law has been violated in, for instance, the Orange Bowl, the Gator Bowl, or the corner grocery store, ipso facto makes the building a public nuisance and subjects it to abatement. There is no requirement that the owners have knowledge—express or implied—that the law is being violated. I can see no way an innocent owner can defend such an action. Moreover, and for the same reasons above, I think the quoted statutes, viz.: Secs. 823.05 and 823.10 F.S.A. are palpably void and unconstitutional on their face.

I therefore dissent.

Questions and Comments

1. What does the court say about defining a nuisance?
2. What sources of law did the court use in arriving at its decision?
3. Describe the dissenting opinion.

Priority of Occupation

The case that follows, *State v. Waterloo*, reiterates and adds to the information as to the nature of nuisance previously described. Especially relevant is the rule concerning priority of occupation. The case also makes it clear that courts will weigh economic consequences as a part of the total picture. Note that the case mentions the frequency and severity of the occurrence as indication of the unreasonableness of the interference.

....

STATE v. WATERLOO STOCK CAR RACEWAY, INC.
409 N.Y.S.2d 40 (Sup.Ct., Seneca Cty. N.Y. 1978)

JOHN J. CONWAY, Justice.
STATEMENT OF FACTS

This is an action brought by the State of New York, for itself and as parens patriae on behalf of the citizens of New York, seeking to enjoin permanently the use of certain property in the Village of Waterloo for stock cars. The named defendants are the Seneca County Agricultural Society, owner of the Seneca County Fairgrounds where the races take place and Waterloo Stock Car Raceway, Inc., lessors of the Fairgrounds and promoters of the stock car races. Regular weekly stock car racing was a feature at the Fairgrounds from 1954 until 1971. From 1971 until late 1976, this use was abandoned, not to be recommended until defendant, Waterloo raceway, in September 1976, reinstated weekly racing at the grounds. The racing continued into the 1977 season with the schedule beginning in April and ending the 1st of October. The hours of operation are such that the cars begin to warm up before the scheduled 7:00 P.M. starting time and the last race does not end until approximately midnight. With the exception of one date in June when operation was enjoined by a temporary restraining order, the races continued to be held. It should be noted that some auto racing had taken place at the Fairgrounds between the years 1939-1954, but only incident to the County Fair, which lasted at most one week.

At trial the Plaintiff produced sixteen lay witnesses, residents of the Village of Waterloo, who, in general, testified to the disturbance created in the neighborhood by the stock car racing. In addition, the Plaintiff produced two expert witnesses. The first, William Burnett, Director of Engineering Research and Development for the New York State Department of Transportation, testified as to the inadequacy of the guiderail surrounding the race track. Dr. Fred G. Haag, Principal Acoustical Engineer for the Department of Environmental Conservation, followed, and testified as to the noise levels created on race night by the operation of the raceway. The Court found the technical evidence presented by Dr. Haag, as well as his opinion as to the injurious effect the loud noise can have on the populous of the community, to be highly persuasive.

The evidence introduced by Dr. Haag consisted of scientific sound level data, collected at seven residential locations in the Village of Waterloo while racing was in progress. For purposes of comparison Dr. Haag also recorded sound level readings during ambient or normal activity periods at six of these same locations. The Court was impressed by the precautions Dr. Haag took to assure himself that the readings were scientifically and fairly taken and not variant, extreme noise levels. The record reflects his effort in this regard.

What he found was, on the average, during the approximately 3 1/2 hours of racing while he tested, noise levels were from two to eight times as loud as normal. This by itself is meaningless, unless it is further noted that the noise levels during the race were of such magnitude as to exceed the EPA maximum acceptable day-night sound level by a wide margin. In fact, the intensity was so great that normal conversation at the seven locations was found to be impossible at a distance greater than four feet, and at four of those locations, beyond two feet.

The standard previously mentioned as being set by the U.S. Environmental Protection Agency is 55 DBA's. Such a level is expected to protect the public with an adequate margin of safety and to prevent annoyance and excessive community complaints. The average level of decibels that Dr. Haag arrived at for the seven locations were far in excess of an acceptable range. In his opinion, Dr. Haag testified that he would expect widespread annoyance and significant community reaction in response to the noise levels.

Dr. Haag's data represents a wide sampling of readings taken both while cars were actually racing and while there was a lull in the actual racing. As such they are a representative average of noise levels that one would hear during the duration of the racing, from four to five hours or more. Loud noises of such a long duration have a more severe impact in terms of causing annoyance than do louder outbursts of shorter duration.

The sixteen lay witnesses who testified at trial were neighbors in the vicinity of the racetrack. The majority of them live within a few hundred feet of the racetrack. Others were from 2 1/2 blocks to 3/5 mile distant from the track. The main complaint of all of these residents concerning the operation of the racetrack is the loudness of the noise and the disturbing effect it has on them. . . . . Some keep their windows closed regardless of the heat, others make it a point to absent themselves from their homesteads on race nights. . . . Conversation, whether in the homes or outside, has become exceedingly difficult due to the loud noise. A common complaint was that sleep both for the adults and their children, has been inhibited. As a consequence of this lack of rest plus the constant roar, nervous tension and wracked nerves have resulted.

. . . . They also testified to clouds of dust being produced by the races which accumulated on their property. Apparently the range of the falling dust is as great as that of the noise. . . . .

Also of concern to the residents is that there is a definite danger of safety in the vicinity of the raceway from launched projectiles. Undisputed testimony was had at trial that at one time a racing tire flew across the street and hit a witness's garage, that on other occasions steel guiderails have fallen apart upon impact from the autos and have been projected as far as the public street, and that on May 30, 1977 at one of the races a car was forced off the track and landed on three parked cars, not far from a residential property. There was also testimony as to serious accidents at the track that endangered spectators and neighboring residents in years previous to Waterloo Raceway, Inc. operation. . . . .

The Court has not ignored the testimony presented by the Defendant's witnesses. However, out of the fourteen witnesses, ten have an interest in seeing the races continue, due either to a monetary stake or because they themselves or members of their families are race enthusiasts. It is to be expected that those who frequent the races are more prone to tolerate whatever disturbance it creates. The four witnesses who have no apparent interest in seeing the races continue, yet testified that they were not bothered by the din it created are to be congratulated as being extremely tolerant. . . .

The foremost issue facing this Court is whether the cumulative effect of the noise, dust and danger to safety from the operation of the raceway constitutes a public nuisance. . . . .

As the term "public nuisance" has been employed by New York courts, it is incapable of any exact or comprehensive definition. (*Melker v. City of New York*, 190 N.Y. 481, 83 N.E. 565, see also *Prosser, Torts* 4th ed., p. 571). Judge Cardozo, in *People v. Rubenfeld,* supra, perhaps came the closest to indicating what exactly a public nuisance is. "Public is the nuisance whereby 'a public right or privilege common to every person in the community is interrupted or interfered with,'. . ... Public also is the nuisance committed in such place and in such manner that the aggregation of private injuries becomes so great and extensive as to constitute a public annoyance and inconvenience, and a wrong against the community, which may be properly the subject of a public prosecution." (Citing cases.)

It should be clear that while almost any form of amusement or recreation can constitute a nuisance, as long as it is lawfully conducted it is not a nuisance per se. (*3 N.Y. Jur., Amusements, § 27*) Therefore, it must be established by clear evidence before the preventive remedy will be granted. (*County of Sullivan v. Filippo*, 64 Misc. 2d 533, 315 N.Y.S.2d 519).

. . . . "It is a public nuisance where the location at which and the manner in which the particular operation is conducted is such that substantial annoyance and discomfort are caused indiscriminately to many and divers persons who are continually or may from time to time be in the vicinity." [Citations omitted.]

The complaints generated and the facts established in this case by the operation of the racetrack are not of a private nature; rather they expose an assault on the community as a whole. The common right involved is that of the neighborhood to its normal peace and quiet, which is one of its essential characteristics. . . . .

This is not a case where the populace is grumbling about mere trifles and slight indecencies. If it were, the Court would turn a deaf ear. (see *McCarty,* supra, and *Prosser, Torts* [4th ed.], p. 577). Instead this is a completely unreasonable use of Defendant's premises to the material injury of his neighbor's premises and his person, and need not be suffered any longer. (*McCarty,* supra, *Campbell,* supra, *Pritchard v. Edison El.Ill. Co.*, 179 N.Y. 364, 72 N.E. 243)

The community has been assailed on a weekly basis. The residents fear for their own bodily safety and for that of their property because of the danger from flying guiderails, racing tires, wood and errant cars. . . . . As conditions at the track stand now, it is only a matter of time before a resident of the neighborhood or innocent passerby is injured. . . . .

Defendants have countered that the operation of the racetrack is being lawfully conducted and is not in violation of zoning ordinances, being a prior existing use in a residentially zoned area, and therefore is not subject to attack as a nuisance. As recently as in the case of *Little Joseph Realty, Inc. v. Town of Babylon*, 41 N.Y.2d 738, 395 N.Y.S.2d 428, 363 N.E.2d 1163 (May 12, 1977) the Court of Appeals stated that the use may be in full compliance with zoning ordinances but that it may still be enjoined as a nuisance. Every business has a duty to conduct its operations in a reasonable manner such that it does not materially interfere with the general well-being, health or property rights of neighbors or of people generally. (*Town of Mt. Pleasant*, supra.)

Defendant asserts its alleged priority of occupation in the neighborhood as a defense to this action. The basis for this contention is the fact that racing took place on a regular, weekly basis between the years 1954-1971 and that most of those who moved to the area since 1954 were aware of the situation and therefore were guilty of coming to a nuisance and should not be heard to complain. Defendant's contention is not well founded because, to begin with, it is established in New York that priority of occupation is not conclusive, but is to be considered in connection with all the evidence, and the inference drawn from all the facts proved whether the controlling fact exists that the use is unreasonable. (*Charlotte Docks Co.*, supra; *McCarty*, supra; *Graceland Corp. v. Consolidated Laundries Corp.*, 7 A.D.2d 89, 180 N.Y.S.2d 644, aff'd 6 N.Y.2d 900, 190 N.Y.S.2d 708, 160 N.E.2d 926). Also, in determining whether one who "came to the nuisance" may obtain relief therefrom, it is proper to consider the nature of the area where the alleged nuisance and complainant property are located. (*McCarty*, supra.) Therefore, there is no absolute defense of priority of occupation and one cannot acquire by prescription the right to maintain a public nuisance.

The facts of the case, as they relate to priority of occupation are these: that many of the complainants moved to this area before the fairgrounds were ever used as a racetrack for autos or during the period 1971-1976 when regular use for racing had been discontinued. Furthermore, this area is unquestionably residential and has been zoned as such since 1949. Persons coming into the area and established residents had come to believe by 1976 that the days of regular, weekly stock car racing at the fairgrounds were over. The fact of the previous intermittent use, which Defendant has not shown to have generated the same disturbance as the present use, does not now operate to estop this action.

The country fair itself stands in a different position. It is the type of operation which is but a minor, passing inconvenience at most, and which people who collect in cities and towns are expected to tolerate. As Plaintiff's witnesses testified, the noise is not nearly as oppressive as that of stock car races. For those who do find it unbearable it is not too much to ask of them that they suffer silently or use the occasion to occupy themselves away from their homes.

This Court concludes that while there is nothing unlawful about the operation of a stock car raceway under proper circumstances, its use at its present location in the Village of Waterloo, under all the circumstances, constitutes a public nuisance and should be discontinued. "A nuisance may be merely a right thing in the wrong place." (*Euclid v. Amber Co.*, 272 U.S. 365, 388, 47 S.Ct. 114, 118, 71 L.Ed. 303.)

As the Court of Appeals indicated in *Boomer v. Atlantic Cement Co.*, 26 N.Y.2d 219,309 N.Y.S.2d 312, 257 N.E.2d 870, an injunction is a drastic remedy which a court must carefully consider before issuing. This Court has been most circumspect in pondering on its issuance but has concluded that it is the only appropriate remedy under the circumstances. Unlike *Boomer*, there is no vast disparity in economic consequence between the use of an injunction and the injury caused by the nuisance. In *Boomer*, the Defendant corporation had a $45 million investment in the plant and it provided jobs for three hundred people. This essentially recreational operation employs a few people and, as Defendant's own affidavit details, the capital investment at most amounts to $15,000. No sound reason mitigates against the issuance of an injunction in this instance. The injury to the public is serious and permanent and no adequate remedy exists at law.

Accordingly, it is ORDERED that Defendant Waterloo Raceway, Inc. and any successor in interest is permanently enjoined from operating a stock car racetrack or any related activity involving motorized vehicles on the premises of the Seneca County Fairgrounds in the Village of Waterloo. Defendant Seneca County Agricultural Society is likewise permanently enjoined from conducting or leasing for purposes of allowing another to conduct stock car races or any related activity involving racing motorized vehicles. The foregoing injunction is subject to the following exception, that the Defendant Society may allow or conduct such events as a motorcycle race, demolition derby or stock car race, but such exception is limited to the period during the year when it holds its annual Seneca County Fair. Such period of racing and other auto events may not exceed three separately scheduled days in total.

Questions and Comments

1. How does this court define public nuisance?
2. What is the effect of prior usage in a similar fashion?
3. How did the attorneys seek to establish a factual basis for their respective positions?
4. To what extent does this case lend itself to expert testimony?
5. How many days a year did the court allow racing at the annual Seneca County Fair? Does this speak to the issue of frequency as an indicator of a nuisance?

Note Cases

Gustafson v. Cotco Enterprises, Inc. (1974) was a case in which the court enjoined the construction and operation of a drag strip. The court predicated its decision upon the unreasonable amount of noise that ensued from the operation of a drag strip. The noise seriously interfered with the use and enjoyment of adjoining property owners. Evidence was to the effect that normal conversations were impossible. Television sets had to be turned up in order to be heard, and social activities outside the house were seriously affected. The value of residential property could only decline under these circumstances. Furthermore, church services would be interrupted. The case is important because it set forth steps designed to reduce the discomfort occasioned by the drag strip. Specifically, the use of blacktop or grass was supposed to cut down on dust. Lights were turned downward to curtail their interference with adjoining property owners. It was hoped that barrier fences would reduce sound distractions. Alcoholic beverages were to be prohibited, and traffic control was to be coordinated with the local sheriff's office. Despite these efforts on the part of the owners and managers of the drag strip, the court felt that the projected construction and operation of a drag strip should be enjoined.

The holdings in *Health Clubs, Inc. v. State ex rel. Eagan* (1976) together with *People ex rel. Hicks v. "Sarong Gals"* (1972) are also important. Each of these cases involved activity of a sexual nature that was sufficiently blatant to cause action to be instituted to enjoin. One of the businesses operated as a health club; the other was a bar featuring live entertainment. The California case held that a Red Light Abatement Law (a law that prohibits prostitution) could be used to abate continuing acts of lewdness even without evidence of prostitution. The court did say, however, that the law could not be used to prohibit free expression of opinion that was not obscene. A Florida appellate court in *Health Clubs, Inc. v. State ex rel. Eagan* (1976) distinguished between legal conduct and illegal activity. Illegal activity was subject to abatement as a nuisance. (How do these cases relate to "This could be you?")

SUMMARY AND ADDITIONAL REMARKS

The law recognizes that activity of a continuing nature that unreasonably interferes with someone's enjoyment of property is illegal. This is a private nuisance. A public nuisance affects the community as a whole. Consideration of the intensity of the interference, its longevity, and the balancing of economic interests are relevant and significant. Additionally, courts are more prone to take a position that some interference with one's enjoyment of one's property rights may be inevitable if the greater good of the community is to be fostered. There are cases in which First Amendment rights (freedom of expression, freedom of speech, etc.) must be factored into the equation. Community standards are important, but First Amendment rights recognize the importance of minority opinions that are seeking not only to be expressed but also to become majority opinions.

Remedies are usually by way of injunction. An injunction is an order of the court directing a person to do or not to do something. Factors relevant to the resolution of an injunction procedure would include strict adherence to the principle that the law of equity acts only when a common-law remedy would be inadequate. An injunction is an equitable remedy. Equity postulates fairness and gives a remedy when damages could not solve the problem. Damages, of course, are a common-law remedy. Common law customarily uses a jury; equity seldom uses a jury.

On occasion, the abatement (the injunction) may proceed summarily. When summary proceedings are resorted to, problems of due process will be encountered. Hence, the question, is a hearing necessary? The chapter on due process is relevant in this connection.

On occasion, damages may be awarded, and criminal prosecution is always possible. One final observation: If a nuisance has existed for a number of years, this does not necessarily mean that it can continue.

As noted in chapter 1, one of the fields sport managers enter is event management. This chapter should have special meaning for those occupations.

This could be you - check your response

The recreation association wanted to show that the movie house and adult bookstore were nuisances. In the case *Orlando Sports Stadium, Inc., v. State ex rel Powell (1972)*, p. 267, the court stated that a public nuisance violated public rights, subverted public order, decency or morals or caused inconvenience or damage to the public generally.

If the public observed behaviors that reflected lack of decency, these behaviors might be noted. These facts might be known drug deals, prostitution, and related street traffic. Are the theater and bookstore near a school district? Do children frequently pass the theater? Are many people affected? Are there zoning laws?

The recreation association could seek an injunction to close or abate the nuisance. In addition, criminal charges might be appropriate.

REFERENCES

Authors

Keeton, W. Page (Ed.). (1984). *Prosser and Keeton on the law of torts*, Hornbook Series (5th ed.). St. Paul: West Publishing Co., together with updates.

Cases

Carter v. Lake City Baseball Club, 62 S.E. 2d 470 (S.C. 1950).
City of Chicago v. Festival Theatre Corp., 410 N.E.2d 341 (Ill. App. Ct. 1980).
Gordon v. State, 289 P.2d 396 (Okla. Crim. App. 1955).
Gustafson v. Cotco Enterprises, Inc., 328 N.E. 2d 409 (Ohio Ct. App. 1974).
Health Clubs, Inc. v. State ex rel. Eagan, 338 So.2d 1324 (Fla. Dist. Ct. App. 1976).
Monterey Club v. Superior Court of Los Angeles, 119 P.2d 349 (Cal. Dist. Ct. App. 1941).
Orlando Sports Stadium, Inc. v. State ex rel. Powell, 262 So.2d 881 (Fla. 1972).
People ex rel. Hicks v. "Sarong Gals," 103 Cal.Rptr. 414 (Cal. Ct. App. 1972).
Rohan v. Detroit Racing Ass'n, 22 N.W.2d 433 (Mich. 1946).
State v. Waterloo Stock Car Raceway, Inc., 409 N.Y.S. 2d 40 (Supt. Ct., Seneca Cty. N.Y. 1978).
State ex rel. Wayne County Prosecuting Attorney v. Levenburg, 280 N.W.2d 810 (Mich. 1979).
Wade v. Fuller, 365 P.2d 802 (Utah, 1961).

Legal Encyclopedias

58 Am. Jur. 2d *Nuisances* §§ 1-471 (1989), with current updates.
66 C.J.S. *Nuisances* §§ 1-179 (1950), with current updates.

INJURY AND STRICT LIABILITY

PERSPECTIVE

The workers' compensation claim provides compensation to an employee without proof of fault. The workers' compensation law is a matter of public policy. Requirements for receiving benefits under this law are threefold:

First, did the injury arise out of and in the course of employment?

Second, is the employer covered by the act?

Third, what was the extent of the injury?

A product liability action involves a suit against the manufacturer or retailer of a product. Such litigation can be founded on contract. The implied warranty of merchantability or fitness for a particular purpose provides the theoretical underpinnings for such an action. (In other words, is the product suitable for its intended purpose? The sales slip is the contract.) The contract action has advantages over a negligence action in that liability follows on the placing of a defective product in the stream of commerce.

Efforts to recover based on negligence run afoul of the multiplicity of inspectors and other witnesses whom the manufacturer of the product can bring to the contest. Strict liability, that is, to fix liability without fault based on the hazardous nature of the article produced, is also a possibility. Finally, a potential litigant should be aware of the possibility of recovering for a nuisance whether public or private.

Hypothetical Case - Part III - Check Your Response

The employee could file a claim for negligence against the Joneses and against the manufacturer of the product. Assuming that there was not a defect in the product, the Joneses would be liable for the installation and upkeep of the equipment. If the accident arose out of and in the course of employment, then workers' compensation would apply.

DAY-TO-DAY OPERATIONS— SPECIAL PROBLEMS

FOCUS

Overview

The day-to-day operation of a sport management enterprise presents problems and opportunities. Three areas that have involved litigation are dress and grooming, crowd control, and drugs. These topics obviously do not exhaust the categories of problems involved in connection with day-to-day operation of the business. However, these topics are timely and economically important.

Practical Application—Hypothetical Case

The Joneses' fitness center is a success. They decide to open a bowling alley in the sport complex. Various clubs and organized groups begin talking about having a bowling tournament. With customer satisfaction in mind, the Joneses organize competitive bowling leagues that include groups from adjoining counties. Although generally peaceable, on occasion problems occur. One competitive group, in particular, has caused problems that are exemplified by the intemperate use of language, loud and boisterous conduct, and occasional threats of violence. The questionable conduct is generally connected with alcohol abuse. Signs are posted that clearly indicate that intoxicated customers may be evicted from the premises. Additionally, rules and regulations pertaining to the competition state that the management reserves the right to remove patrons from the competition if, in management's judgment, their conduct is such as to interfere with the orderly progress of the competition. Assuming that a patron is sufficiently noisy and obnoxious as to create expressions of resentment from groups, and assuming further that the Joneses are notified of this particular patron's propensity in this connection, can the Joneses bar the patron from participating in a bowling competition? The following sections will help in answering this question.

CHAPTER 11

DRESS AND GROOMING

INTRODUCTION

The owner and manager of a sport business firm can be confronted with problems of dress and grooming. The problems can be grouped in various ways. First, a problem may be presented when a female employee is required to dress in a sexually provocative manner, thus subjecting the employee to embarrassment and humiliation. This type of problem is most often confronted with female servers in restaurants and cocktail lounges. Some people have even suggested that bathing suit attire may promote more sexually explicit conversations, and sexual harassment might result. However, problems with dress and grooming can surface in the more prosaic types of business organizations, especially on ad hoc occasions. Frequently, such a problem is also noticed in connection with religion and race. Turbans and yarmulkes have religious significance but may be deemed inappropriate by certain business owners.

A manager may require a female employee to wear makeup, which, in turn, may be against the religion of that particular employee. Facial hair can take on an ethnic dimension when shaving is uncomfortable for certain members of a particular ethnic group.

The wearing of jewelry may be perceived to signify a sexual orientation. Jewelry may be frowned upon or forbidden by management. This attitude or policy is not confined to a police department or military establishment. It may become a part of the dress and grooming code of a health spa or sporting goods establishment. In any event, these problems are real

---

IN THIS CHAPTER YOU WILL LEARN:
The relationship between dress and grooming
    requirements and sexual harassment
The relationship between dress and grooming
    requirements and religion
The relationship between dress and grooming
    requirements and business necessity

and to the extent that they represent discrimination will have legal consequences.

KEY WORDS: *harassment, discrimination, bona fide occupational qualification (BFOQ)*

This could be you!

In keeping with the family atmosphere that their business sought to project, the Joneses promulgated a dress code for female employees that mandated the wearing of slacks. This particular part of the dress code was designed to effectuate freedom of movement consistent with a degree of modesty expected in a small community. One of the employees, Stephanie

IS THERE A LAW?

Samuels, protested on the grounds that her religious background prohibited the wearing of male attire. The employee in question was an excellent worker and was well liked and respected by her colleagues and the patrons of the business establishment. Can the Joneses enforce the dress code? Can they make reasonable accommodations without adversely affecting their business operations? Would a simple amendment to the code that permits reasonable exceptions based on matters of conscience be acceptable under the circumstances?

JUDICIAL DECISIONS

Dress and grooming issues may be present at sport camps for youth or at public recreational activities a sport manager might sponsor. Certain colors, certain styles of dress, and emblems may be associated with gangs. The wearing of "team jackets" has even been banned at certain sports events because of the gang loyalty and violence associated with the clothing.

The sport manager should be aware of other decorated apparel such as T-shirts that may be offensive in language. Each shirt should be considered separately in regard to the message of the shirt.

Public and private sport businesses differ in the latitude that they have to control the dress and grooming issues. Private entities have more latitude in making and enforcing policy.

The legal issues on this topic include expression, negligence, and discrimination.

1. Freedom of expression: This is a form of free speech. Should employees at a health spa be allowed to wear T-shirts that have offensive messages?
2. Negligence: The sport manager has a duty to supervise. Was there breach

of that duty? Was there injury? For example, the manager knew that the wearing of certain apparel would incite gang warfare. She failed to control the dress of sport participants, and some youth were injured in a fight. Was she negligent?
3. Discrimination: Dress codes should reflect equality of treatment of sexes, races, religions, ages, and disabilities. In reading the following case, look for the points of law that relate to discrimination.

Facial Jewelry

Lockhart v. Louisiana-Pacific Corp. (1990) involved a discharge of a man who refused to comply with a company rule barring male, but not female, employees from wearing facial jewelry. The court refused to recognize the claim.

....

LOCKHART v. LOUISIANA-PACIFIC CORP.
795 P.2d 602 (Or. Ct. App. 1990)

RICHARDSON, Presiding Judge.

Plaintiff was discharged by Louisiana-Pacific Corporation (employer), after he refused to comply with the requirement of a dress and grooming rule that male employees not wear facial jewelry while on the job. The rule allows female employees to wear jewelry that is not "unusual or overly-large." Plaintiff contends that the rule is sexually discriminatory, in violation of ORS 659.030(1)(b), and that he was discharged for "resisting" the discriminatory policy. He brought this action for wrongful discharge against employer and for interference with contractual relations against his supervisor, Montel Work (Work). The trial court dismissed the wrongful discharge claim for failure to state a claim and allowed Work's motion for summary judgment on the interference claim. Plaintiff appeals and assigns error to both rulings. We affirm.

The theory of plaintiff's wrongful discharge claim is that he was fired for pursuing a statutory right related to his role as an employee. *See Delaney v. Taco Time Int'l* ., 297 Or. 10, 681 P.2d 114 (1984). The claim fails, without more, *see* note 2, *infra*, if he is incorrect in his assertion that employer's rule can offend his right against sexual discrimination under ORS 659.030.

Notwithstanding plaintiff's attempt to characterize unrelated cases as supporting his view, the cases that the parties cite that deal with issues similar to the one in this case have held that the different treatment of male and female employees under dress and grooming rules does not, in itself, violate federal or state statutes relating to employment discrimination.[1] *See e.g.,*

1. No Oregon case is directly on point. However, the Supreme Court noted in *Holien v. Sears, Roebuck and Co.,* 298 Or. 76, 90, n. 5, 689 P.2d 1292 (1984):

"We wish to make clear that although we refer to sexual harassment on the job as an act of sexual discrimination, we do not include all forms of disparate treatment founded on gender. Some forms of disparate treatment may be legitimate. A common law or statutory cause of action for wrongful discharge emanating from sex discrimination is restricted to cases when sex is for no legitimate reason a substantial factor in the discrimination."

Albertson's v. Human Rights Comm'n, 14 Wash. App. 697, 544 P.2d 98 (1976), and cases there cited. The court explained in *Albertson's:*

"The recent federal cases hold that a private employer's promulgation and enforcement of reasonable grooming regulations that restrict the hair length of male employees only is not forbidden by the sex discrimination provisions of the federal act. [Citations Omitted] The act is interpreted as prohibiting only those classifications or discriminations which afford significant employment opportunities to one sex in favor of the other. *Fagan v. National Cash Register [Company,* 481 F2d 1115 (D.C.Cir. 1973)]; *Thomas v. Firestone Tire and Rubber [Company],* 392 F.Supp. 373 (N.D.Tex. 1975). Only those distinctions between the sexes which are based on immutable, unalterable, or constitutionally protected personal characteristics are forbidden.

"* * * The federal statute was never intended to prohibit sex-based distinctions inherent in a private employer's personal grooming code for employees which do not have a significant effect on employment and which can be changed easily by the employee. * * * The enforcement of a reasonable hair length policy is permissible since such a policy is not used to inhibit equal access to employment opportunities between males and females, is not an employer's attempt to deny employment to a particular sex, and is not a significant employment advantage to either sex. *See* Note, *Employer Dress and Appearance Codes and Title VII of the Civil Rights Act of 1964,* 46 S.Cal.L.Rev. 965-1002 (1973). It is not a purpose of the federal statute to accommodate a male employee's desire to wear his hair longer than a private employer's appearance policy allows. As said in *Fagan v. National Cash Register Co., supra* at 1124-25:

"Perhaps no facet of business life is more important than a company's place in public estimation. That the image created by its employees dealing with the public when on company assignment affects its relations is so well known that we may take judicial notice of an employer's proper desire to achieve favorable acceptance. Good grooming regulations reflect a company's policy in our highly competitive business environment. Reasonable requirements in furtherance of that policy are an aspect of managerial responsibility. Congress has said that no exercise of that responsibility may result in discriminatory deprivation of equal opportunity because of *immutable* race, national origin, color, or sex classification.

"(Footnote omitted.)" 14 Wash. App. at 700-01, 544 P.2d 98. (Emphasis in original.) The court then concluded that the same reasoning was applicable under the state statute.

It is unnecessary in this case for us to address the full sweep of the Washington court's reasoning. Plaintiff advances the argument that employer may not prohibit him from wearing an earring, if it allows female employees to wear jewelry. As his argument is cast, plaintiff cannot demonstrate impermissible discrimination unless *every* difference in dress or grooming requirements for men and women under an employer's rules is impermissibly discriminatory. We reject that argument. The trial court was correct in dismissing the wrongful discharge claim. [Footnote Omitted]

Plaintiff's assignment regarding the summary judgment on his interference claim against Work does not merit discussion.

Affirmed.

Questions and Comments

1. What test did the court use to determine if a grooming policy was permissible?
2. How did the court use federal cases as an aid in interpreting state law on the subject?

Authors' Note

The Seventh Court of Appeals in *Rathert v. Village of Peotone* (1990) upheld a written reprimand for a police officer who wore an ear stud. One should ask the question, suppose this had been an employee of a health spa, or a riding academy, or a lifeguard at a swimming pool? To what extent would First Amendment rights enter the picture? The court noted that the grooming regulation affected discipline, employee morale, and public relations. The court did not find plaintiff to be impermissibly denied a constitutional right to freely associate with like-minded individuals.

Swimsuit Required Apparel

In a case decided in 1985, the court did not find an unlawful employment practice in requiring personnel to wear swimsuits as a part of a sales promotion. The court took care, however, to note that other situations in which immodest apparel was required could be found to be the basis for a finding of harassment.

· ·

EEOC DECISION NO. 85-9
37 FEP Cases 1893, May 7, 1985
(The statute bars identification of parties to
proceedings before the Commission.)

Summary of Charges

The Charging Parties, three females, allege that the Respondent engaged in unlawful employment practices in violation of Title VII of the Civil Rights Act of 1964, as amended (the Act), 42 U.S.C. §2000e et seq., by discriminating against them on the basis of their sex. Specifically, they allege that the Respondent imposed a requirement that they wear swimwear at work and discharged them for refusing to comply with the requirement. The Charging Parties allege that the Respondent's conduct constitutes sexual harassment.

Jurisdiction

The Respondent is an employer within the meaning of Section 701(b) of the Act. Timeliness and all other jurisdictional requirements have been met.

Summary of Investigation

The Respondent is a corporation that owns and operates various retail women's clothing stores. The Charging Parties were employed in one of the Respondent's "junior operations," a store carrying clothing and accessories for young women. The store is located in a shopping mall and its clientele is predominantly female, although men come to the store as customers or accompanying women customers. At the time of the alleged violation, the store's managers and sales clerk were all female. However, the Respondent employed a male as a delivery person for the store. Prior to their discharge, Charging Parties A and C were sales clerks and Charging Party B was one of the store's co-managers.

On June 18, 1981, the Respondent's president came to the store and informed the co-managers that, as part of a swimwear promotion, they and the sales clerks were to wear swim attire at work during the week of June 22nd. The outfit required to be worn consisted of a swimsuit and a cover-up with appropriate accessories, such as sandals, sunglasses, and beach hats. The president instructed the co-managers to inform the sales employees about the requirement. The employees required to participate in the promotion were to furnish their own outfits, and the choice of attire within the stated guidelines was left to the individual employees.

The following day, Charging Party B and the store's other co-manager contacted the Respondent's city supervisor to voice their own objections to the swimsuit requirement and those they had received from the sales clerks. The supervisor advised them to wait until the following Monday, the day the promotion was to begin, to speak directly with the president. On June 22, Charging Party B came to work wearing her regular working clothes, dark blue jeans and a blazer.[1] Along with her co-manager, Charging Party B was then fired by the president after stating the employees' objections and refusing to comply with the requirement.

On June 23, Charging Parties A and C, who had not been scheduled to work the previous day, similarly reported to work wearing their regular clothing. That evening, the president called a special store meeting to, in his words, "quell the objections" of the employees concerning the swimsuit requirement. During the meeting, the president discussed the clothing to be worn and informed the employees that it was necessary for them to participate in the promotion. Before the meeting closed, the president asked the city supervisor to give him the names of all employees still refusing to participate. From the president's statements, Charging Parties A and C concluded that their continued refusal meant that they were being discharged, which was confirmed by the city supervisor when they picked up their paychecks the following day.

The Charging Parties state that all the employees who refused to wear the required outfit—both co-managers, the assistant manager, and three sales

---

1. Charging Party B states that the dress code for the store's sales personnel called for a "total look" outfit, created by an employee's layering her clothes and wearing a blazer or a sweater around her shoulders.

clerks—were discharged and that only one or two employees complied with the requirement. There is no evidence of whether those employees were subjected to comments or conduct of a sexual nature as a result of wearing the swimsuit outfit as required by the Respondent.

The Charging Parties also state that the swimwear sale had been in progress about one week when the president imposed the swimsuit requirement, and that in no previous sale of swimwear during their employment had the employees been required to wear swimsuits. Although they had not been informed when they were hired that their jobs would entail occasionally wearing clothing being promoted by the Respondent, the Charging Parties admit that they had participated without objection in other promotions held in the store. During these, the Charging Parties had worn prom dresses, bathrobes over their clothes, and black jumpsuits. The Charging Parties claim, however, that the swimsuit outfit, unlike the outfits worn in prior promotions, was sexually revealing and that wearing the outfit would have subjected them to embarrassment and offensive remarks and conduct. They further claim that, because the store has no restroom or eating facilities, they would have had to wear the outfit outside the store to use the facilities in the shopping mall, thus exposing themselves to an even greater risk of harassment.

The Respondent states that, in imposing the swimwear requirement, it did not believe the promotion would cause any of the employees to be subjected to embarrassing or derogatory remarks. The Respondent emphasizes that an appropriate cover-up was to be worn with the swimsuit. The Respondent's president states, as Charging Parties A and C admit, that he informed the employees during the meeting on June 23 that he did not want "any girlie show," nor did he want "anyone hanging over their swimsuit."

Sexual Harassment

Sexual harassment is a violation of Section 703 of the Act. See §1604.11 of the Commission's Guidelines on Discrimination Because of Sex (Guidelines), 29 C.F.R. § 1604.11 (1984); and see Commission Decision No. 81-18, 27 FEP Cases 1793 and the court cases cited therein. Section 1604.11(a) of the Guidelines defines sexual harassment as follows:

> Unwelcome sexual advances, requests for sexual favors, and other verbal or physical conduct of a sexual nature constitute sexual harassment when: (1) submission to such conduct is made either explicitly or implicitly a term or condition of an individual's employment, (2) submission to or rejection of such conduct by an individual is used as the basis for employment decisions affecting such individual, or (3) such conduct has the purpose or effect of unreasonably interfering with an individual's work performance or creating an intimidating, hostile, or offensive working environment.

In various cases, the Commission and the courts have held an employer responsible for a violation of the Act where the employer required a female employee to wear a sexually provocative and revealing uniform or outfit and wearing the required attire resulted in the employee's being subjected to unwelcome sexual conduct.[2]   The present case does not fall within existing precedent because, by factual contrast, the Charging Parties never wore the outfit required by the Respondent, refusing from the outset to comply with the requirement, and were never subjected to unwelcome sexual conduct. Therefore, the issue presented to the Commission by these charges is whether, in the absence of evidence of compliance with the swimwear requirement and resulting subjection to unwelcome sexual conduct, the imposition of the requirement alone constitutes sexual harassment.[3]

For the Respondent's swimwear requirement to constitute sexual harassment, the three definitional elements set forth in §1604.11(a) of the Guidelines must be satisfied. These elements may be summarized as requiring evidence that the conduct complained of was unwelcome, that it was of a sexual nature, and that it resulted in one or more of the three types of harm identified in that section of the Guidelines.

Here, there is no question that the swimwear requirement was unwelcome to the Charging Parties. Similarly, it is undisputed that compliance with the requirement was explicitly made a term or condition of the Charging Parties' employment and also that their refusal to comply was the basis for their discharge. The question remaining to be decided is whether the Respondent's imposition of the swimsuit requirement was conduct of a sexual nature.

In determining whether conduct is of a sexual nature, the Commission will consider the record as a whole and the totality of the circumstances.[4] Thus, what makes conduct sexual in nature must be decided on a case-by-case basis.[5] In this particular case, it is the Commission's position that the Respondent's conduct in imposing the swimwear requirement would be sexual in nature where (i) the outfit required to be worn was sexually provocative or revealing

2. See Commission Decision Nos. 77-36, 21 FEP Cases 1811 and 81-17, 27 FEP Cases 1791 and EEOC v. Sage Realty Corp., 507 F.Supp. 599, 24 FEP Cases 1521 (S.D. N.Y. 1981). Cf. Marentette v. Michigan Host, Inc., 506 F.Supp. 909, 912, 24 FEP Cases 1665 (E.D. Mich. 1980) (Title VII action dismissed as moot, but court stated that a sexually provocative dress code imposed as a condition of employment which subjects persons to sexual harassment could violate Title VII).

3. In EEOC Compliance Manual § 619, Grooming Standards, the Commission stated:
    The requirement of a uniform, especially one that is not similar to conventional clothes (e.g., short skirts for women or an outfit which may be considered provocative), may subject the employee to derogatory and sexual comments or other circumstances which create an intimidating, hostile, or offensive working environment based on sex. In some cases the mere requirement that females wear sexually provocative uniforms may be itself be evidence of sexual harassment.
    See § 619.4(a).

4. CF § 1604.11(b) of the Guidelines:
    In determining whether alleged conduct constitutes sexual harassment, the Commission will look at the record as a whole and at the totality of the circumstances, such as the nature of the sexual advances and the context in which the alleged incidents occurred. The determination of the legality of a particular action will be made from the facts, on a case by case basis.

5. Id.

and (ii) wearing the outfit would likely have resulted in the wearer's being subjected to unwelcome verbal or physical sexual activity.[6] Whether these two conditions are met depends, again, on the evidence in the record.

Although the Respondent did not provide the outfit required to be worn and the Charging Parties never complied with the requirement by wearing swim attire of their own,[7] there is no dispute that the required outfit principally consisted of a swimsuit and a cover-up. However, there is no similar unanimity concerning the type or nature of cover-up the Charging Parties were required to wear. The Respondent simply describes the cover-up as having to be "appropriate." Charging Party A's description includes a romper or robe. Charging Parties B and C both state that they were instructed to wear a lacy cover-up or an open terry cloth jacket or robe. Charging Party C adds that, at the meeting following the discharge of Charging Party B, the Respondent's president told the employees that they could wear an open short or floor-length robe.

In the Commission's view, a swimsuit is a revealing outfit. How revealing is simply a matter of degree, depending upon factors such as the particular suit and the fit. However, since the required outfit did not consist of a swimsuit alone, we must consider whether the cover-up would have concealed the revealing nature of the swimsuit. Based on the evidence, we find that the Respondent intended the swimsuit to be visible under the cover-up. Consequently, even with the cover-up, part of the employee's torso and legs not ordinarily revealed would have been exposed.[8] Thus, the cover-up would only have lessened, but not eliminated, the exposure resulting from wearing a swimsuit. Therefore, we find that the total outfit required to be worn was still revealing.

However, we further find that, in the circumstances of the Charging Parties' employment, it is not likely that their wearing the required swimsuit outfit would have resulted in their being subjected to unwelcome verbal or physical conduct of a sexual nature. In making this finding, we considered the Charging Parties' description of the past conduct of males with whom

6. Cf. EEOC v. Sage Realty Corp., 507 F.Supp. at 607-608 (court found that uniform required to be worn by female lobby attendant was revealing and sexually provocative and could reasonably be expected to, *and did*, subject her to sexual harassment).

While the two conditions set forth are dispositive in this particular case, the Commission recognizes that, in other cases, determining whether a dress requirement is conduct of a sexual nature may require consideration of different or additional factors, such as the nature of the job a charging party was hired to perform (for example, modelling intimate apparel).

7. In this particular as well, this case is distinguishable from cases cited supra note 2, where the employer provided the specific outfit and the evidence showed that the outfit as worn by the employee was sexually provocative and revealing.

8. Cf. Commission Decision No. 81-17, 27 FEP Cases 1791 (costume that female clerical employee was required to wear while acting as hostess to employer's visiting VIP's consisted of a halter-bra top and a midi-skirt with a slit in front running up to her thighs) and EEOC v. Sage Realty Corp. 507 F.Supp at 604-605 (Bicentennial uniform worn by female lobby attendant consisted of a short red-white-and blue poncho closed with only one snap at each wrist and on each side but otherwise open, revealing her thighs, the sides of her body above the waist, and her underwear).

their jobs brought them into contact, both in the store and in the area of the shopping mall directly outside the store.[9]

The Charging Parties state that male customers, unlike female customers, would compliment them on their attractiveness and comment favorably about their appearance in the clothes they wore at work. They further state that men in the shopping mall outside the glass-enclosed store, particularly janitorial employees, would pass repeatedly in front of the store and stare in at the sales clerks and that some, primarily young men and high school boys, would whistle at them and call out or knock on the glass panels to get the sales clerks' attention. While the described conduct occurred on a regular basis and that of the males outside the store was disturbing and interfered with their work, the Charging Parties state that neither the comments made to them nor the conduct directed at them was vulgar or included explicitly sexual remarks, references, or gestures. Finally, the Charging Parties state that neither the Respondent's president nor the Respondent's male delivery person ever made any sexual advances toward them or engaged in other conduct of a sexual nature.

Even though the conduct of male customers and passers-by may have been motivated by the store's sales personnel's being attractive young women, the type of past conduct described does not convince us that wearing the swimsuit outfit would have resulted in overtly sexual behavior toward the Charging Parties. Therefore, although we note that our finding on this matter involves a close judgment, we conclude that the evidence presented here is not sufficient to support a finding that the Charging Parties would likely have been subjected to unwelcome sexual conduct had they worn the required outfit.

Because the second condition set forth above has not been satisfied, the Respondent's imposition of the swimsuit requirement is not conduct of a sexual nature and so cannot support a charge of sexual harassment. However, while we conclude that the Respondent's requirement does not constitute sexual harassment in this particular case, it is the Commission's position that, where both conditions are met, an employer's mere requirement that an employee wear a sexually provocative or revealing outfit can result in a violation of Title VII.

Conclusion

There is no reasonable cause to believe that the Respondent engaged in unlawful employment practices in violation of Title VII of the Civil Rights Act of 1964, as amended, by discriminating against the Charging Parties because of their sex.

---

9. While there is no evidence that the Respondent made provision for its employees to change into regular clothes before using facilities located only in the shopping mall, neither is there evidence that the Respondent required the employees to go outside of the store wearing the swimsuit outfit. Therefore, we confine our analysis to behavior to which the Charging Parties were subjected while working in the store.

Questions and Comments

1. What factors did the court consider to be important in determining if harassment existed?
2. How was this case different from *EEOC v. Sage Realty Corp.* (1981)?

Note Case - Makeup

The *Tamimi v. Howard Johnson Co.* (1987) case rejected a finding of religious discrimination based on the requirement that an employee wear makeup. The case apparently was heavily influenced by other considerations. The court found that Sondra Tamimi failed to make out a case of religious discrimination because she had not communicated to her employer that the reason she refused to wear makeup was her religious beliefs.

When she was hired to work behind the front desk at Howard Johnson, she wore no makeup. She was told that she would be required to work in the standard uniform for women. However, nothing was said about a company policy requiring women to wear makeup or lipstick. At that time there was no policy. Later, after she became pregnant and her complexion was broken out, she was fired for not wearing makeup. Concluding remarks by the appellate court judge are as follows:

. . . . . .

. . . Gallof's [the manager] discontent about the plaintiff's looks commenced the day plaintiff told him she was pregnant. The district court concluded that plaintiff established a prima facie case of sexual discrimination and that the employer did not prove any legitimate reasons for discharging the plaintiff. . . . Here the dress code was adopted to furnish a basis for discharging the plaintiff. Gallof knew the plaintiff would not wear makeup and chose that course of action as a means of effecting the discharge.

. . . The experienced trial judge saw the witnesses and evaluated their testimony and sincerity and concluded that this discharge was more than likely based upon sex discrimination. We leave it at that. (p. 1559) [In this case it was clear dress code was used to discriminate against a female employee.]

Questions and Comments

1. Did this court find the new dress code to be a pretext?
2. Does this court consider the issue of pregnancy to be significant?

Note Case - Facial Hair

The United States District Court for the Northern District of Georgia, Atlantic Division, decided in *EEOC v. Sambo's of Georgia, Inc.* (1981) that an employment policy that insisted on cleanshaven restaurant personnel did not constitute discrimination on the basis of religion. The complainant in that case was a member of the Sikh religion. This faith forbade the shaving of facial hair. Although the religious standard was clear, the court, nevertheless, reasoned that the requirement to be cleanshaven was a bona fide occupational qualification and that an accommodation of religious practices in this case would constitute undue hardship. In short, the policy was one of business necessity based on years of experience. The policy was perceived as being related to sanitation and was necessary for the safe and efficient operation of the restaurant. Quotations from the case are specific and to the point:

> The requirement that Sambo's restaurant managers be clean-shaven is tailored to actual business needs, has a manifest and demonstrable relation to job performance, and is necessary to the safe and efficient operation of Sambo's Restaurants. [Note: Sambo's had a name change after this case was litigated.]

* * * * *

Under the decision of the Supreme Court in *TWA v. Hardison*, 432 U.S. 63, 97 S.Ct. 2264, 53 L.Ed.2d 113 (1977), undue hardship is present when the employer cannot make an accommodation without incurring a more than *de minimis* cost. As outlined in the Findings of Fact, the exemption of Mr. Tucker from the defendants' no-beard rule would involve significant costs to Sambo's Restaurants, Inc. that are certainly more than *de minimis*. *See, e.g., Cummins v. Parker Seal Co.*, 561 F.2d 658 (6th Cir. 1977) (reversing district court decision for the plaintiff and holding that undue hardship shown as to accommodation of plaintiff ex-employee who could not, for religious reasons, work from Friday sundown to Saturday sundown, where fellow employees forced to substitute for plaintiff complained about having to do so); *TWA v. Hardison, supra* (undue hardship found where employer would have incurred a cost of $150.00 in premium wages for a period of three months to arrange substitutes for employee who could not work on Saturday because of his religion).

     * * * In the case of *Woods v. Safeway Stores, Inc.*, 420 F.Supp. 35 (E.D. Va.1976), *aff'd* 579 F.2d 43 (4th Cir. 1978), *cert. denied*, 440 U.S. 930, 99 S.Ct. 1267, 59 L.Ed.2d 486 (1978), the court ruled that customer preference for overall store hygiene and an appearance of cleanliness in the retail food industry makes employee grooming standards that forbid facial hair a business necessity. *Id.* at 43. The *Diaz* decision is not to the contrary. The *Diaz* case involved the defense of a bona fide occupational qualification, or B.F.O.Q., which is a defense to a claim of discrimination in the form of facially discriminatory job classification, such as the requirement that employees in a certain job be female or, conversely, male. This case involves no such facially discriminatory classification, such as in *Diaz* and, therefore, *Diaz* is not applicable. (At pages 90-91)

Note Case - Length of a Man's Hair

A case that affirms the right of a business establishment to require certain standards with reference to hair length is that of *Fagan v. National Cash Register Company* (1973). In this case the length of a man's hair was at issue. The court in upholding the right of an employer to enforce such a regulation refused to recognize any constitutional violation. Thus, there was no deprivation of rights pursuant to a 1983 action. Significant language in the court's opinion includes the following:

We may fairly assume this much, it would appear, the Supreme Court sees no federal question in this area. We are persuaded that the only basis upon which Fagan might predicate a claim must stem from 42 U.S.C.§ 2000e-2(a)(1) and (2) [42 USCS § 2000e-2(a) (1) & (2)] to which we now turn. . . (At 27 ALR Fed, page 262)

It would seem inescapable that Congress was saying that job opportunities must be opened, remain open, and not be denied or terminated because of race, color, religion, sex or national origin. The language is plain, and as here considered means that men and women so far as jobs are concerned must receive equal treatment and not be the objects of discrimination on the ground of sex. Thus speaks the Act and so spoke Judge Hamley in Rosenfeld v. Southern Pacific Company, note 12, supra, at 1223: (At 27 ALR Fed, page 264)

. . .

We have then a situation where a male was indeed employed, and with full knowledge of the company's policy, insisted upon performing his work on his own terms and upon requiring the company to accommodate to his projection of his own image.... (At 27 ALR Fed, pages 265-266) [The court affirmed the right of the business to require certain standards. Note the court spoke of the equal treatment of men and women.]

SUMMARY

As a learning experience the reader is encouraged to prepare his or her own summary of the materials contained in this chapter. Specific attention should be directed to the following:

1. Should there be any differences in dress and grooming standards for employees of state agencies such as universities and standards for employees of private entrepreneurial establishments, such as health spas? In many of the cases in this chapter, dress codes were upheld by the courts. The reader should remember that men and women should be treated equally and should not be the objects of discrimination.
2. Assuming the absence of constitutional issues such as freedom of religion, what factors determine the enforceability of a dress and grooming regulation?
3. Assuming a nongovernmental sport business enterprise, what preventative measures can the owner or manager of the establishment take to ensure that dress and grooming standards are enforceable?

The summary that you prepare should be based on the materials presented in this chapter together with any legitimate inferences that can be drawn from the materials.

This could be you - check your response

The Joneses can design a dress code appropriate to their business. The code should not be discriminatory between men and women. The code could have some flexibility. For example, there could be clauses that indicate accommodation for religious beliefs. There could also be amendments to the code.

REFERENCES

EEOC Decision No. 85-9, 37 FEP Cases 1893, May 7, 1985.

EEOC Decision No. 81-17, 27 FEP Cases 1791, February 6, 1981.

EEOC v. Sage Realty Corp., 507 F. Supp. 599 (S.D. N.Y. 1981).

EEOC v. Sambo's of Georgia, Inc., 530 F. Supp 86 (N.D. Ga., 1981).

Fagan v. National Cash Register Co., 481 F.2d 1115, 27 ALR Fed 257 (D.C. Cir. 1973).

Lockhart v. Louisiana-Pacific Corp., 795 P.2d 602 (Or. Ct. App. 1990).

Marentette v. Michigan Host, Inc., 506 F. Supp. 909 (E.D. Mich. 1980).

Rathert v. Village of Peotone, 903 F.2d 510 (7th Cir. 1990).

Roberts v. General Mills, Inc., 337 F. Supp. 1055 (N.D. Ohio 1971).

Tamimi v. Howard Johnson Co., 807 F.2d 1550 (11th Cir. 1987).

CHAPTER 12

CROWD CONTROL

INTRODUCTION

Any athletic contest can involve situations in which feelings run high and control of the crowd becomes important. School athletic contests may also occasion a reaction ranging from symbolic protests to violence. Special events as well as concerts can also create difficulties in crowd control. Various factors contribute to the problem: the size of the crowd, the presence of alcohol and drugs, and the intensity of a rivalry.

In today's increasingly violent society, the sport manager needs to be prepared to handle difficult situations. Failure to act properly and decisively can lead to injury and perhaps liability.

This chapter isolates applicable rules pertaining to crowd control and also directs attention to factors that make crowd control more difficult.

IN THIS CHAPTER YOU WILL LEARN:

Potential defendants in an action to recover for injury based on the failure to take appropriate steps toward crowd control

Some appropriate considerations to be studied in determining possible evidentiary bases for liability based on inappropriate crowd control

Some rules of law that are designed to provide guidance in determining liability on the subject of crowd control

Different factual situations that may arise in a recreational setting among public and private entities

---

KEY WORDS: *invitee, security, proximate cause, forseeability, directed verdict*

This could be you!

A sign is posted near the entrance to the fitness center that states that smoking is prohibited in the fitness center. A customer is observed lighting a cigarette. The customer is asked to go outside of the fitness center to smoke. A loud argument between the customer and the manager results. Can the Joneses enforce this regulation? There is no statute that prohibits smoking in this state.

TABLE 1. FACTORS RELEVANT TO CROWD CONTROL

the presence of alcohol	the presence of drugs
size of the crowd	seating arrangements
number of security	placement of security
posting of signs	condition of premises
auxiliary police	auxiliary security
education of ushers	education of security
disabled individuals	number and location of exits
medical technicians	doctors and nurses
fire marshall regs.	safety regulations generally
notice of past problems	notice of present threats

The factors listed in Table 1 are relevant to crowd control. Which of these factors can a sport manager control? Which of these factors are included in the following case?

DECISIONAL LAW

Invitee

The case that follows involves an injury to an individual who had attended a football game at the University of Notre Dame. The injury occurred in the parking lot when a drunk knocked a woman to the ground. The woman's leg was broken. The question presented to the court involved the alleged negligence of the University in controlling the spectators at the game.

•••

BEARMAN v. UNIVERSITY OF NOTRE DAME
453 N.E.2d 1196 (Ind. Ct. App. 1983)

STATON, Judge

Christenna Bearman suffered a broken leg when she was knocked down by a drunk as she was returning to her car after a Notre Dame football game. Bearman and her husband sued the University of Notre Dame for damages resulting from that injury. After the close of all evidence, the trial court granted Notre Dame's motion for judgment on the evidence. Bearman appeals, raising one issue:

Whether Notre Dame had a duty to protect Mrs. Bearman from injury caused by the acts of third persons.

Reversed and remanded.

The evidence and inferences most favorable to Bearman shows that on October 27, 1979, Mr. and Mrs. Bearman attended a football game at the University of Notre Dame. The Bearmans left the game shortly before it ended. As they were walking through a parking lot toward their car, they observed two men who appeared to be drunk. The men were fighting, one of them fell down, and then they walked away from each other. One of the men walked past the Bearmans. A few moments later, the man fell into Mrs. Bearman from behind, knocking her to the ground. Mrs. Bearman suffered a broken leg from the fall. There were no ushers or security people in the area when the incident occurred.

When the trial court considers a motion for judgment on the evidence, it must consider only the evidence most favorable to the non-moving party. The motion may be granted only if there is no substantial evidence, or reasonable inference to be drawn therefrom, which supports an essential element of the claim. If reasonable persons might differ as to the inferences to be drawn from the evidence, then judgment on the evidence is not proper. *Keck v. Kerbs* (1979), Ind. App., 395 N.E.2d 845, 846.

Bearman argues that she was a business invitee of the University of Notre Dame; therefore, Notre Dame owed to her a duty to protect her from injury caused by the acts of other persons on the premises. On the other hand, Notre Dame argues that absent notice or knowledge of any particular danger to a patron, the University cannot be held liable for the acts of third persons.

It is axiomatic that the conduct of a person will give rise to an action for negligence only if that person owed a duty to the plaintiff to conform his actions to the standard of care. The existence of such a duty is a question of law. *Koroniotis v. LaPorte Transit, Inc.* (1979), Ind. App., 397 N.E.2d 656.

Generally, the operator of a place of public entertainment owes a duty to keep the premises safe for its invitees. *Cory v. Ray* (1944), 115 Ind.App. 50, 55 N.E.2d 117. This duty includes a duty to provide a safe and suitable means of ingress and egress, *Verplank v. Commercial Bank of Crown Point* (1969), 145 Ind.App. 324, 251 N.E.2d 52, and a duty to exercise ordinary and reasonable care to protect a patron from injury caused by third persons. 86 C.J.S., *Theatres and Shows* § 41c. However, the invitor is not the insuror of the invitee's safety. *Hammond v. Allegretti* (1974), 262 Ind. 82, 311 N.E.2d 821. Before liability may be imposed on the invitor, it must have actual or constructive knowledge of the danger. *Id.*

The Restatement of Torts (Second) § 344 (1965) sets forth the applicable rule:

"A possessor of land who holds it open to the public for entry for his business purposes is subject to liability to members of the public while they are upon the land for such a purpose, for physical harm caused by the accidental, negligent, or intentionally harmful acts of third persons or animals, and by the failure of the possessor to exercise reasonable care to

"(a) discover that such acts are being done or are likely to be done, or
"(b) give a warning adequate to enable the visitors to avoid the harm, or otherwise to protect them against it."

Comment (f) of this section is particularly pertinent to this case:

"f. *Duty to police premises.* Since the possessor is not an insurer of the visitor's safety, he is ordinarily under no duty to exercise any care until he knows or has reason to know that the acts of the third person are occurring, or are about to occur. He may, however, know or have reason to know, from past experience, that there is a likelihood of conduct on the part of third persons in general which is likely to endanger the safety of the visitor, even though he has no reason to expect it on the part of any particular individual. If the place or character of his business, or his past experience, is such that he should reasonably anticipate careless or criminal conduct on the part of third persons, either generally or at some particular time, he may be under a duty to take precautions against it, and to provide a reasonably sufficient number of servants to afford a reasonable protection."

The University is aware that alcoholic beverages are consumed on the premises before and during football games. The University is also aware that "tailgate" parties are held in the parking areas around the stadium. Thus, even though there was no showing that the University had reason to know of the particular danger posed by the drunk who injured Mrs. Bearman, it had reason to know that some people will become intoxicated and pose a general threat to the safety of other patrons. Therefore, Notre Dame is under a duty to take reasonable precautions to protect those who attend its football games from injury caused by the acts of third persons.

The questions whether the protective measures employed by Notre Dame were inadequate and, if so, whether such inadequacy contributed to Mrs. Bearman's injury are questions for the jury. *Petroski v. Northern Indiana Pub. Service Co.* (1976), 171 Ind.App. 14, 354 N.E.2d 736. Therefore, we reverse the judgment of the trial court and remand this case for proceedings consistent with this opinion.

Reversed and remanded.

HOFFMAN, P.J., and CONOVER, P.J. (by designation), concur.

Questions and Comments

1. What was the legal status of the plaintiff who was injured?
2. What duty did the University owe to invitee who attended the game?
3. What knowledge can an invitor possess that will trigger a duty to protect?
4. In this case, what knowledge did the University have that created a duty to protect from injury caused by the acts of third persons?
5. What sources of law were cited in this case? Be specific.

Adequate Security

The case cited below involved the duty to provide adequate security for spectators at a rock concert. A patron at the concert was struck by a glass bottle thrown from a balcony. A directed verdict, referred to in this case, might be given if the evidence was so clear-cut that a trial need not progress further. A party bringing suit has failed to present sufficient evidence to stay in court.

....

GREENVILLE MEMORIAL AUDITORIUM v. MARTIN
391 S.E.2d 546 (S.C. 1990)

HARWELL, Justice:

Respondent Thomas Martin filed an action against appellant Greenville Memorial Auditorium under the South Carolina Tort Claims Act. Respondent sought damages for injuries received as a result of his being struck by a glass bottle which was thrown by an unknown third party from appellant's balcony during a rock concert. Respondent's complaint alleged that appellant's negligence in securing the premises during the concert created an unreasonable risk of harm and proximately caused respondent's injury. Despite appellant's defense which was based on the Tort Claims Act and its allegation that respondent's injury was caused by the conduct of a third party, the jury returned a $12,000 verdict for respondent. This appeal follows.

DISCUSSION

1. REFUSAL OF TRIAL JUDGE TO PERMIT TESTIMONY

REGARDING REQUIREMENT OF PROBABLE CAUSE BEFORE SEARCHING PATRONS

Appellant asserts the trial judge erred in refusing to allow the director of security to testify that security personnel could not search patrons as they entered the auditorium without probable cause. Appellant argues this testimony was crucial to its defense: that respondent's injuries were caused by a third party bringing a concealed bottle of alcohol into the auditorium rather than by appellant's failure to search all patrons as they entered the auditorium. Appellant submits that because it is a public subdivision under S.C.Code Ann. § 15-78-30(h) (1986) of the Torts Claim Act, it is subject to constitutional limitations and the jury was entitled to know appellant's security personnel could not search patrons without probable cause.

An alleged erroneous exclusion of evidence is not a basis for establishing prejudice on appeal in absence of an adequate proffer of evidence in the court below. [Citing cases.] Because appellant's trial counsel failed to make an offer of proof in order to preserve the question for appeal, we do not need to address whether the trial judge erred in excluding such testimony. *Honea v. Prior*, 295 S.C. 526, 369 S.E.2d 846 (Ct.App.1988).

2. REFUSAL OF TRIAL JUDGE TO DIRECT A VERDICT

At the close of his case, counsel for the appellant made a motion for a directed verdict which was denied by the trial judge. Appellant asserts this was error because the evidence did not establish its liability. Appellant states the evidence was uncontroverted that this was the first instance of bottle throwing at a concert that the director of security had witnessed in twenty-nine years and therefore, the resulting injury was unforeseeable.

In reviewing whether the trial judge erred in denying a party's motion for a directed verdict, we review the evidence and all reasonable inferences therefrom in the light most favorable to the party opposing such motion. *Kennedy v. Custom Ice Equipment Co.*, 271 S.C. 171, 246 S.E.2d 176(1978). Our task is to determine if the evidence warranted the submission of the case to the jury. *Id.* Contrary to appellant's assertion, in order to establish liability, it is not necessary the person charged with negligence should have contemplated the particular event which occurred. *Young v. Tide Craft*, 270 S.C. 453, 242 S.E.2d 671 (1978). It is sufficient that he should have foreseen his negligence would probably cause injury to someone. *Childers v. Gas Lines, Inc.*, 248 S.C. 316, 149 S.E.2d 761 (1966). He may be held liable for anything which appears to have been a natural and probable consequence of his negligence. *Id.*

The evidence revealed that during the rock concert, only fourteen security guards were provided to control a crowd of six-thousand persons. Additionally, there was no reserved seating on the main floor of the auditorium; those patrons simply stood before the band. Multiple witnesses testified that other patrons of the concert were openly drinking out of liquor bottles. Respondent testified there were liquor bottles and pieces of glass on the floor of the auditorium during the concert. There was testimony indicating that other patrons were smoking marijuana during the concert. The crowd was unruly as patrons were pushing and shoving each other. Respondent testified that he did not see any apparent effort by appellant's security personnel to stop the drinking, smoking, pushing, or shoving.

On the night respondent's injury occurred, *Loverboy*, a rock group, was playing in the auditorium. Appellant's security director indicated that when a rock group like *Loverboy* was in concert, whose songs invite the use of illegal drugs and alcohol, there would be the potential for greater security problems. He also acknowledged it was easier for security personnel to see into the crowds when there was reserved seating. Although appellant's security director testified this was the first instance of bottle throwing he had ever been aware of, his testimony demonstrated he was on notice that patrons of the auditorium consumed alcohol during various events.

Viewing this evidence in the most favorable light to the respondent, we find there was ample evidence from which a jury could find that respondent's injuries were foreseeable and that appellant was liable. The trial judge did not err in submitting the case to the jury.

.   .   .   .   .

Here, respondent's complaint alleged appellant and its employees were negligent in adequately securing and maintaining the premises during the concert and this negligence created a reasonably foreseeable risk of such third party conduct. Respondent's complaint did not allege appellant was liable because of the criminal act of a third party. Consequently, Section 15-78-60(20) would not operate to exonerate appellant of liability for its own conduct.

Appellant cannot successfully defend that respondent's injuries were caused by the wrongful criminal act of a third party, where the very basis upon which appellant is claimed to be negligent is that appellant created a reasonably foreseeable risk of such third party conduct. Consequently, the trial judge did not err in refusing to dismiss the action.

AFFIRMED.

Questions and Comments

1. What were the evidences of crowd control in this case?
2. What were the evidences of a lack of crowd control?
3. Why couldn't the security guards search the patrons for hidden bottles? (See Section I.)
4. What was the issue to be decided in this case?
5. What steps must a party take to preserve an issue for appeal?

Third-Party Injury

In the following case, a spectator was injured when struck by another spectator. The event was a wrestling match. This case explores the duty of the promoter to protect an invitee. In reading the case, note the appropriate steps that were taken in crowd control. Review the concepts from negligence, and note the court's reference to "proximate cause" in this case.

••

JOHNSON v. MID-SOUTH SPORTS, INC.
806 P.2d 1107 (Okl. 1991)

SIMMS, Justice:

Russell Johnson, plaintiff below, appeals from summary judgment entered in favor of defendant, Mid-South Sports, Inc. (Mid-South), in a negligence action based upon injuries Johnson received while attending wrestling matches sponsored by Mid-South.

The Court of Appeals reversed the cause and remanded it for trial, holding that Johnson's injuries were the result of the combined effects of being hit by the unknown spectator and sliding down the slippery ramp. We grant certiorari, vacate the opinion of the Court of Appeals and affirm the trial court.

We need only determine whether the evidentiary materials submitted to the trial court indicated a substantial controversy exists as to a material fact. *Ross v. City of Shawnee*, Okl., 683 P.2d 535, 536 (1984). In making this determination, we are to examine the pleadings and evidentiary material submitted to the trial court and view all inferences and conclusions that can be drawn therefrom in the light most favorable to the party opposing the motion, namely Johnson.

All of the evidence contained in the record comes from Johnson's deposition, and the parties do not dispute the facts.

Because we find no substantial controversy as to any material fact, we hold that Mid-South was entitled to judgment as a matter of law.

Johnson, a 295-pound man, purchased a ticket to a wrestling event sponsored and promoted by Mid-South in which several wrestling matches were held. He has attended such events in the past, and because of his weight and his handicapped right arm which is cut off between the elbow and wrist, he always sits in the handicapped section so that he will not have to stand up to see the action in the ring as he says is often necessary at such events and which he has difficulty doing.

On this occasion, the handicapped section was full, so the ushers at the event had Johnson sit at the end of a row next to the handicapped access ramp. Throughout the preliminary matches, a group of "rowdy" spectators sitting on the same row as Johnson made several trips to the concession stands for beer. On their return trip, they spilled beer not only on the handicapped ramp, but on Johnson's boots as well. Another patron sitting near Johnson voiced his annoyance with the "rowdy" group, and the group left the area before the final wrestling match began. After the main event concluded, Johnson remained in his seat, as was his custom, and waited for the other fans to leave so that it would be easier for him to get up from his seat and negotiate the stairs. While sitting in the seat, he noticed someone coming at him from the other end of the row so he moved his legs to let them through. However, the person came at Johnson "like a freight train," hit him in the leg, and knocked him six feet into the air. Johnson testified on deposition that although he did not see who hit him, he thought that the person was one of the rowdy fans who was probably mad at him because they had to leave the area.

Johnson further testified that after being knocked into the air, he landed on the beer-soaked handicapped access ramp which had become slippery as a result of the beer. He then slid down the ramp and struck his handicapped arm against the floor fracturing the stub in several places. He brought this action claiming Mid-South was negligent in maintenance of the handicapped access ramp and in control of the crowd, particularly the rowdy group.

In their summary judgment pleadings the parties agreed that Johnson was a business invitee, and Mid-South argued below, as it does on appeal, that Johnson's testimony failed to show that Mid-South breached its duty of ordinary care to keep the premises in reasonably safe condition for use by invitees. *C.R. Anthony Co. v. Million*, Okl., 435 P.2d 116 (1967).

Johnson testified that when one of the rowdy fans repeatedly spilled beer, another patron told the rowdy fan to sit down and stop spilling beer. An usher apparently saw what was going on, and summoned a police officer to come to the area. Johnson never testified that he said anything to the rowdy fan, the bothered patron, the usher, or the officer, nor did he claim that he was threatened by anyone at the match. In fact, Johnson testified that the man who he thought hit him was not causing any trouble himself even though he was with the group of rowdy fans. There is no evidence that any complaint was made by anyone to Mid-South or its employees concerning the rowdy fans sitting near Johnson. Eventually, this group left the area prior to the start of the final match, even though no testimony indicated that the usher or the officer asked or directed the group to leave.

From our review of the evidence, it appears that the usher, an employee or agent of Mid-South, recognized that an argument between fans might erupt, and thus exercised ordinary care in calling over an officer to assist if any of the fans got out of hand. The group left without incident, and it appears that everyone just went back to watching the wrestling matches. The evidence is void of any indication that the rowdy fans intended to return in order to hurt Johnson, or that Mid-South knew or should have known that Johnson would be singled out to be attacked as he claims he was. The undisputed facts give no indication that Mid-South should have foreseen the post-match assault. Thus, Mid-South did all that, in our view, was necessary to protect Johnson since they were unaware of any potential attacks directed at him. Mid-South exercised ordinary and reasonable care in providing not only ushers, but also police officers to control the crowd.

Moreover, we find that the proximate cause of the injury was the unknown person hitting Johnson in the leg with enough force to knock him into the air and onto the ramp.

It is well settled that proximate cause is an essential element of an action in negligence. *Loper v. Austin*, Okl., 596 P.2d 544, 546 (1979); *Rush v. Mullins*, Okl., 370 P.2d 557, 559 (1962). Furthermore, where the facts are undisputed as they are here, proximate cause is a question for the court. *Pepsi-Cola Bottling Company of Tulsa v. Von Brady*, Okl., 386 P.2d 993, 996 (1964).

The proximate cause of an event is that "which in a natural and continuous sequence, unbroken by an independent cause, produces the event and without which the event would not have occurred." *Gaines v. Providence Apartments*, Okl., 750 P.2d 125, 126-27 (1988). Were it not for the actions of the unknown spectator, the injuries would not have occurred. Thus, the unknown spectator's actions were the proximate cause of the injuries.

In coming to this conclusion, we note that negligence, if any, by Mid-South in allowing the ramp to become slippery merely furnished a condition which reacted with the independent act of the spectator to cause Johnson's injury. As such, it was a remote cause and not a proximate cause of the injuries. *See generally, Gaines, supra; Thompson v. Presbyterian Hospital, Inc.*, Okl., 652 P.2d 260, 264 (1982); *Hunt v. Firestone Tire & Rubber Co.*, Okl., 448 P.2d 1018, 1023 (1968); *Pepsi-Cola Bottling Company of Tulsa v. Von Brady*,Okl., 386 P.2d 993, 996-97 (1964); and *City of Altus v. Wise*, 193 Okl. 288, 143 P.2d 128, 131 (1943).

Johnson's injury resulted from the unforeseeable act of the unknown patron, and under the facts stated, Mid-South did not violate any duty owed to Johnson, nor was there any showing that Johnson's injury was proximately caused by an negligent act of Mid-South.

Finding no substantial controversy as to any material fact, we hold that Mid-South is entitled to judgment as a matter of law.

The judgment of the trial court is AFFIRMED.

OPALA, C.J., HODGES, V.C.J., and LAVENDER, HARGRAVE and SUMMERS, JJ., concur.

DOOLIN, ALMA WILSON and KAUGER, JJ., dissent.

Questions and Comments

1. What are the evidences of negligence by the promoter in controlling the crowd?
2. What are the evidences of appropriate steps taken to control the crowd?

Protection Away From the Premises

This case involves the duty of a producer of a concert to protect patrons after they have exited the concert premises. The case also sets forth legal rules that govern crowd control.

In reading the case one should review the elements of negligence. It is also important to note how foreseeability plays a role in the holding by the court.

••

BAREFIELD v. CITY OF HOUSTON
846 S.W.2d 399 (Tex. Ct. App. 1992)

JUNELL, Justice.

Appellants appeal from summary judgments granted in favor of appellees. Appellants brought suit against the City of Houston, Pace Concerts, and AAA Searchlight Systems, Inc., d/b/a Southwest Concert

Security to recover damages for personal injuries sustained by appellants following a rock concert. We affirm.

Appellants and their friend, Nathan Marek, attended a rock concert at the Sam Houston Coliseum (Coliseum), on February 26, 1989. Appellants parked across the street from the Coliseum in an underground parking garage owned and operated by the City of Houston. When the concert was over around 11:00 or 11:30 p.m., appellants and Marek left the Coliseum and began walking toward the parking garage. About 20 to 30 feet outside the Coliseum doors the three men were approached by a group of seven to ten youths. The youths demanded the concert t-shirt Marek was wearing. Marek refused and was attacked, beaten and robbed.

Barefield went to Marek's aid. The youths clustered around Barefield and Marek. One youth pulled a knife. Barefield told the group he had a knife and to leave him alone. After Barefield said this, four or five members of the attack group pulled their knives. Upon seeing the knives, Marek and Zacharias began running back across the street toward the Coliseum. When Barefield saw Marek and Zacharias running, he, too, began running across the street. As Barefield attempted to run across the street, he was hit by a car, resulting in a compound fracture to his leg. The driver of the car did not stop to render assistance. Barefield called to his friends for help. Marek and Zacharias returned back across the street and moved Barefield onto the sidewalk.

Marek attempted to return to the Coliseum to get help, but the group of youths stood between him and the building. A bystander saw the extent of Barefield's injury and suggested Marek and Zacharias carry Barefield to their car and take him to a hospital. Marek, Zacharias and the bystander picked up Barefield and began carrying him toward the car. They were confronted again by the youths. By this time there were 15 or 20 youths in the group. The group demanded Zacharias's t-shirt and jewelry. When he refused, the group assaulted him, breaking one rib and stabbing him in the back. The attackers began throwing rocks and bottles. Marek ran back to the Coliseum and informed a police officer inside the Coliseum about the attack.

The officer said he would call an ambulance. When Marek returned to the scene, Barefield and Zacharias were lying on the ground. Barefield was yelling he thought he was going to die. A taxi drove by and the driver offered appellants a ride to the hospital. The taxi driver took Barefield and Zacharias to the emergency room at Ben Taub Hospital. Marek drove his own vehicle to the hospital.

Barefield had surgery on his leg, was hospitalized for one week and has had four subsequent surgeries. Barefield was not injured in the confrontations with the youths; his only injury was caused by being struck by a car when he ran into the street. Zacharias was not treated at Ben Taub Hospital. He left the hospital around 2:00 a.m. and arrived at his home in Port Lavaca, Texas around 5:00 a.m. The following day, Zacharias was treated by a physician in Port Lavaca. Zacharias wore a body wrap for eight weeks. His stab wound did not require sutures.

Pace Concerts (Pace) produced the rock concert. Pace leased the Sam

Houston Coliseum from the City of Houston (City). Pace hired AAA Searchlight Systems, Inc., d/b/a Southwest Concert Security (AAA) and off-duty Houston Police officers to provide security for the concert premises. The security guards and officers were stationed inside the Coliseum; none were stationed outside the Coliseum doors.

Barefield and Zacharias brought suit against appellees for negligence in failing to provide adequate security for the premises. Marek was not a party to the suit. Appellants also alleged appellees were negligent because appellees knew or should have known of the unreasonably dangerous condition, i.e., the potential for criminal activity, and failed to correct the condition or warn appellants. Appellants further alleged their injuries were caused by a condition or use of tangible personal or real property owned and operated by the City of Houston.

Pace, AAA and The City of Houston filed motions for summary judgment, which the trial court granted. In eight points of error, appellants argue the trial court erred in granting appellees' motions for summary judgment.

A summary judgment will be upheld on appeal only if the movant has conclusively established there is no genuine issue as to any material fact, and the movant is entitled to judgment as a matter of law. *Davis v. Houston Independent School District*, 654 S.W.2d 818, 820 (Tex.App.—Houston [14th Dist.] 1983, no writ).

The summary judgment evidence is considered in the light most favorable to the party opposing the motion. *Gonzales v. Global Truck & Equipment, Inc.*, 625 S.W.2d 348, 350 (Tex.Civ.App.—Houston [1st Dist.] 1981, no writ). All doubts concerning the existence of a genuine issue of material fact should be resolved against the movant. *Id.* All conflicts in the evidence must be disregarded and the evidence that tends to support the position of the non-movant is accepted as true. *Id.*

The question to be determined on appeal is whether the summary judgment proof establishes as a matter of law that there is no genuine issue of fact as to one or more of the essential elements of plaintiff's cause of action. *Gibbs v. General Motors*, 450 S.W.2d 827, 828 (Tex.1970).

The essential elements of a cause of action based on negligence are a legal duty owed by defendants to plaintiffs, a breach of that duty, and damages proximately resulting from that breach. *El Chico Corp. v. Poole*, 732 S.W.2d 306, 311 (Tex.1987). Duty is the threshold inquiry. To establish tort liability, a plaintiff must prove the existence and violation of a duty owed to him by a defendant. *Id.*

PACE'S DUTY

In points of error one, four and seven, appellants assert the summary judgment granted in favor of Pace was granted in error because genuine issues of material fact exist as to whether Pace owed a duty of care to appellants and as to whether appellants were contributorily negligent.

Pace, producer of the concert, leased the Coliseum from the City of Houston. The terms of the lease dictated the extent of Pace's control over the

Coliseum. Appellants argue the sidewalk where the first attack took place is part of the premises under Pace's control. Pace leased only the building and not the outer premises, such as the sidewalks or the common area outside the Coliseum's entrance. The lease agreement required Pace to provide security only within the Coliseum.

As a general rule, a defendant has no duty to prevent the criminal acts of a third party who does not act under the defendant's supervision or control. *LaFleur v. Astrodome-Astrohall Stadium Corp.*, 751 S.W.2d 563, 564 (Tex.App.—Houston [1st Dist.] 1988, no writ). A defendant, however, may be subject to tort liability for another's criminal act if the criminal act occurs on the defendant's premises. *Id.* at 565. The defendant's duty to provide protection arises from his occupation of the premises. By occupying the premises the defendant has the power of control and expulsion over the third party. *Id.* If a defendant does not occupy the premises, then he has no potential control or ability to oust a third party. The defendant therefore, is not liable for his failure to provide security when he does not control the premises upon which a third party assaults a plaintiff. *Id.* The attacks took place on the sidewalks and public streets. Pace had no control over these areas.

Under the lease agreement entered into by Pace and the City, Pace did not have control over the areas outside the leased premises. Pace had no control over the area beyond the Coliseum doors. Pace, therefore, had neither a duty to make the area beyond the Coliseum's doors safe for appellants, nor a duty to warn appellants, who were invitees, of dangerous conditions on such areas. Liability follows control. *Howe v. Kroger Co.*, 598 S.W.2d 929, 930 (Tex.Civ.App.—Dallas 1980, no writ). The defendant's duty does not extend beyond the limits of the defendant's control. *LaFleur*, 751 S.W.2d at 565. Pace's duty was limited to the premises it controlled under the lease.

Appellants argue Pace owed them a duty of care because the confrontation between appellants and the group of youths was foreseeable. An exception exists to the general rule that a defendant has no duty to prevent criminal acts of a third party unless the defendant controls the premises. A defendant's negligence is not superseded when the criminal conduct of a third party is a foreseeable result of the defendant's negligence. *LaFleur*, 751 S.W.2d at 564. The defendant has a duty to prevent injuries to others if it reasonably appears or should appear to the defendant that others may be injured. *Id.*

Appellants claim Pace had a duty to warn or protect appellants from the attackers because Pace had knowledge of criminal assaults occurring at other concerts held at the Coliseum. There was no summary judgment proof that any alleged prior incidents occurred at Pace concerts. There was no summary judgment proof that Pace knew or should have known of potential criminal attacks occurring outside the Coliseum. The general knowledge of criminal activity in the Houston downtown area is not enough to raise a fact issue that the confrontation between appellants and the group of attackers was foreseeable. Although criminal acts do occur and thus may be foreseeable in the broad sense, the occupier of the premises has no duty to guard against dangers he cannot reasonably foresee in light of ordinary or common experience. *Hendricks v. Todora*, 722 S.W.2d 458, 461 (Tex.App.—Dallas 1986, writ ref'd n.r.e.).

Before appellants can hold Pace to a duty requiring protection from the criminal acts of third parties, Pace must have the power of control over the places where the criminal acts were committed, or Pace must reasonably foresee the criminal conduct. Under this criteria, Pace owed no duty to appellants.

Appellants also argue Pace owed them a duty of care because Pace caused or created a dangerous condition outside the Coliseum premises. Appellants rely on *El Chico Corp. v. Poole*, 732 S.W.2d 306 (Tex.1987), to support their argument. Employees at an El Chico restaurant served alcoholic beverages to an intoxicated person. Upon leaving the restaurant, the intoxicated person while driving his automobile, collided with another vehicle killing Larry Poole. Mr. Poole's survivors brought a wrongful death and survival action against El Chico Corp., a liquor licensee, for negligently selling alcohol to an intoxicated person. *Id.*

A liquor licensee owes a duty to the general public not to serve alcoholic beverages to a person when the licensee knows or should know the patron is intoxicated. A licensee who serves alcoholic beverages to an intoxicated person is negligent as a matter of law. *Id*, at 314. Recognition of this cause of action requires more than merely furnishing alcohol to a patron. To be liable, the licensee must know or should know the patron is intoxicated. *Id*, at 315.

Appellants argue that although the patron's intoxication in *El Chico* was created on the premises of the restaurant, the dangerousness of the act did not occur until after the patron left the premises and began driving.

Appellants maintain Pace created a dangerous condition by having a rock concert at which a crowd known to consume alcohol and drugs, would be leaving the Coliseum en masse at night in downtown Houston. Appellants argue that by negligently creating a foreseeable and dangerous condition, Pace's duty to appellants extended beyond the actual premises where the concert was held.

Foreseeability requires the actor as a person of ordinary intelligence to anticipate the dangers his negligent act creates for others. *Id*, at 313. There is no summary judgment proof that the attackers were intoxicated, were in attendance at the concert, or that appellees provided any alcohol or drugs to them. We find Pace did not create or cause a dangerous condition and therefore owed no duty to appellants.

Appellants also assert the trial court erred in granting summary judgment in favor of Pace because a fact issue exists as to whether appellants were contributorily negligent by engaging voluntarily in the confrontations. Because Pace owed no duty to appellants, any contributory negligence of appellants is immaterial. Pace has established as a matter of law its entitlement to summary judgment by negating a primary element of appellants' cause of action for negligence. We overrule appellants' points of errors one, four and seven.

AAA'S DUTY

. . . .

Pace hired AAA, a security contractor, to perform security services for the concert. AAA and Pace had an oral contract in which AAA would provide security services only inside the Coliseum. There was no agreement between the parties that AAA would provide security services outside the Coliseum, where appellants were injured.

.   .   .   .   .

AAA does not owe appellants a duty of care for the same reasons Pace does not owe appellants a duty. Appellants' injuries, caused by the criminal acts of third parties, did not occur on premises occupied or controlled by AAA and the injuries were not foreseeable by AAA. . . . . .

CITY OF HOUSTON'S DUTY

. . . . In point of error eight, appellants argue sovereign immunity does not apply to the City in this case.

Appellants claim the City was negligent because it failed to provide adequate security or failed to warn appellants of an unreasonably dangerous condition, the potential criminal activity. . . . . Appellants also assert the City contributed to their injuries by failing to provide police protection in downtown Houston where previous crimes had occurred. Appellants argue the City owes them a duty because the criminal activity was foreseeable. The City contends it is immune from liability under the Texas Tort Claims Act. TEX.CIV. PRAC. & REM. CODE ANN. § 101.001 *et seq.*

.   .   .   .   .

Pace hired off-duty police officers to provide security inside the Coliseum. Off-duty police officers are not acting within the course and scope of their employment with the City of Houston. . . . .

The Houston Police Department determines the policy for policing the downtown area. The policy, once implemented, is a method of providing police protection. The City is exempt from any liability arising from the method of providing police protection and is also immune for its failure to provide police protection. . . . .

The injuries appellants suffered were the result of criminal acts of third parties. The City is immune from liability for intentional torts committed by third parties. A municipality is exempt from liability for intentional torts "arising out of assault, battery, false imprisonment or any other intentional tort...." TEX.CIV. PRAC. & REM. CODE ANN § 101.057 (Vernon 1986).

.   .   .   .   .

Accordingly, we affirm the judgment of the trial court.

DRAUGHN, Justice, concurring.

I concur in the opinion but write separately to clarify one aspect of the case I consider important for future reference.

In my opinion, had the appellant offered specific evidence of prior acts of violence against patrons on the sidewalks immediately adjacent to the Sam Houston Coliseum during prior rock-type concerts sponsored by Pace, or of which Pace, being in the business, should have been aware, I would have held them subject to liability. But I also attach a caveat for future reference that Pace and other such sponsors are now on notice because of this tragic occurrence, that if they expect to profit from such concerts by attracting large numbers of young people, they should be prepared to assume responsibility for a modicum of security in the immediate area outside the building, which would at least allow patrons to get on and off the premises without being assaulted or robbed.

It would also seem appropriate for the Houston Police Department to re-evaluate its policy decision about patrolling the area prior to and after such concerts. . . . .

Questions and Comments

1. What are the elements of negligence as set forth in this case?
2. When does a duty to protect arise?
3. How does one establish proof on a motion for summary judgment?
4. How is foreseeability determined?
5. How does a plaintiff select the party to sue?
6. How does the question of control affect the issue of crowd control?

SUMMARY

Case law suggests the following:

1. Possible defendants are owners, lessors, lessees, promoters, security companies, officers and employees, and public agencies.
2. Appropriate rules of law are as follows:
    a. No potential defendant is an insurer of the safety of a patron (spectator).
    b. Owners and promoters together with appropriate officers and employees have a duty to exercise reasonable care to insure the safety of patrons, spectators, and business invitees.
    c. Liability is dependent upon control. If a defendant does not have control over a factual situation, it is difficult to expect liability for damages to attach.
    d. In general, for liability to attach the risk must be foreseeable.
    e. There may be legal consequences attached to entity status. There is limited liability of shareholders. There is unlimited liability of general partners. State agencies may have sovereign immunity. There is qualified immunity for state officers.

This could be you - check your response

As the owners of a private establishment, the Joneses could have a regulation prohibiting smoking. The fact that a loud argument ensued brings crowd control policy into play. It would be important for invitees to see rules posted and to be adequately informed of the rules. Additionally, appropriately trained security and fire marshall regulations could be factors.

REFERENCES

Cases

Barefield v. City of Houston, 846 S.W.2d 399 (Tex. Ct. App. 1992).
Bearman v. University of Notre Dame, 453 N.E.2d 1196 (Ind. Ct. App. 1983).
Greenville Memorial Auditorium v. Martin, 391 S.E.2d 546 (S.C. 1990).
Johnson v. Mid-South Sports, Inc., 806 P.2d 1107 (Okl. 1991).

CHAPTER 13

ALCOHOL, DRUGS, AND BUSINESS

INTRODUCTION

Substance abuse is a topic of enduring interest. The subject matter touches on many segments of the sport industry. Of necessity, the following chapter is selective as opposed to all-inclusive. The chapter only discusses the general nature of the alcohol and drug problem. The primary topic involves the duty to protect patrons and employees.

Does a sport manager have a duty to protect a customer from drunkenness and not serve alcoholic beverages to that customer who is intoxicated? Are incidents on the parking lot that involve alcohol the responsibility of the sport manager? Is the sport manager responsible for the employee who drinks on the job? This chapter will aid in answering these questions.

IN THIS CHAPTER YOU WILL LEARN:

The nature and extent of the legal problems of alcohol and business

The relationship between alcohol and drug consumption and security

The development and implementation of a company policy with reference to alcohol and drug abuse

The connection between alcohol and drug use and the duty to protect

---

KEY WORDS: *drug policy, drug testing, negligence, proximate cause, foreseeable, "dramshop" law, violent incidents, in the course of employment, duty to protect, involuntary manslaughter*

This could be you!

Maria Jones is disturbed because of what is considered to be excessive absences on the part of her employees. There is evidence to indicate that some of the absences are occasioned by the use of alcohol. Ms Jones decides to adopt a company policy for the purpose of educating the employees.

The company policy was articulated in a five-page document, three pages of which elaborated on the deterioration of moral fiber of individuals who consumed alcohol. This postulate was followed by a listing of the various dangers that are generally associated with excessive use of alcohol, specifically, the breakup of marriages, an increase in crime, the loss of employment, together with physical and moral deterioration. What effect, if any, would such a document have on Ms Jones's work force? What suggestions would you make to improve and strengthen its effectiveness as a legally sound policy?

ALCOHOL USE AND ABUSE—DUTY TO PROTECT

The Nature and Extent of the Problem

Brett's story. "Before I went to work my shift I would sit out under the oak tree and down a pint of Jack Daniels. I'd sit there and remember what it was like when I used to play baseball in the minors, when I had fun playin' ball and drinking with the guys. Now I just enjoy drinkin'. I drink before I go into my job - - - Sometimes, I can even sneak a few (drinks) from my thermos." (Brett, before he lost his job.)

Brett, a tall, strong, handsome, baseball pitcher, was a star athlete in high school. He played for a few years in the minor leagues. Later, because of his love of sports, he worked in the manufacturing plant making baseball bats. Now, he doesn't work at all. His company tried to help him with their employee assistance program (EAP), and he went to a few AA meetings. Yet, sometimes he was too drunk to report to work. Eventually, his company fired him.

Statistics. Unfortunately, there may be many Bretts out in the sport world. The sport manager should be aware of the individuals that constitute the following statistics. According to the National Council on Alcoholism and Drug Dependence (1992), up to 40% of industrial fatalities and 47% of industrial injuries can be linked to alcohol consumption and alcoholism. Alcoholism costs employers an estimated $33 billion in reduced productivity. Other drug use costs an additional $7.2 billion in reduced productivity. Absenteeism among alcoholics or problem drinkers is 3.8 to 8.3 times greater than normal and up to 16 times greater among all employees with alcohol and other drug-related problems. In the United States, alcohol is the most prevalent drug.

Substance abuse in the work place is a safety hazard. It reduces productivity and impairs the quality of work. Especially in the sport world where physical performance is important, drugs that impair performance are hazardous.

There are approximately 90 to 100 million regular users of alcohol, and 9 to 12 million classified as alcoholics. Alcohol leads to more problems for individuals, families, and society as a whole than any other drug in the United States. (Schlaadt & Shannon, 1990, p. 169.)

Historically, the public at large has treated alcoholism as a character defect that accompanies a lack of willpower. These premises have not been too helpful in rehabilitating the alcoholic worker. Unfortunately, management usually adheres to the popular conception as to the nature of alcoholism. It is generally agreed that a policy that purports to be helpful and nonjudgmental—one that avoids the moral fiber notion—should be adopted with full support from top management.

The problems of alcohol use may be isolated or may be of a continuing nature. A company policy that deals with alcohol abuse should recognize this distinction. The isolated, occasional abuse of alcohol presents problems in connection with production and employee morale. The possibility of injury and defective work products is always present. However, this is small in comparison to the employee who has developed an alcohol problem that is of a continuing nature. The American Medical Association and the American Psychiatric Association have recognized alcoholism as an illness. Alcoholism has been described as a hidden illness that is progressive and that can be arrested but not cured in the sense that an individual can return to normal or social drinking. Alcoholic employees may drink every day, or they may confine themselves to "binge" drinking. In any event, the loss to the employer in terms of productivity is great.

Drugs and Society

O'Brien and Overby (1992) noted that drug use in sports is a social phenomenon. Drug use in sports mirrors drug use in society. Often advertisements show sports events and alcohol consumption together. The mental connection of sports and alcohol is often made.

The problem of drugs in society is vast. One out of four students in a classroom has an immediate family member who is an alcoholic. Over 90% of high school seniors have consumed alcohol. Highway deaths due to alcohol-related accidents are the nation's largest cause of teenage fatalities. One out of 10 people who drink will become an alcoholic.

The problem of substance abuse encompasses both alcohol and other mind-altering drugs. Unfortunately, alcohol and marijuana are considered gateway drugs for other addictive drugs. Marijuana use among high school students has declined from 1980 to 1992. In 1993, about one out of four graduating seniors had tried marijuana. From 1992 to 1993, the University of Michigan survey indicated a slight increase in marijuana use (Levinthal, 1996).

Steroid use in sports is also increasing. The famed 1988 Olympic sprinter, Ben Johnson, lost millions in terms of endorsements when he tested positive for steroid use. Do athletes like Johnson serve as a role model for inspiring young athletes?

In a report to the Office of the Inspector General, Kusserow (1990) indicates 5 to 11% of the high school boys have experimented with steroids. In the 1985 NCAA bowl games, steroid testing revealed at least eight major universities had athletes who tested positive for steroids (Everson, 1987). Goldman, Bush, and Klatz (1984) document the demise of five steroid users in *Death in the Locker Room*. In Kusserow's research with steroid users, 42% said that they had been influenced to use steroids by adult and famous role models. He believes steroid use is motivated by socially acceptable values and life stage concerns with appearance and peer approval. What is needed are good role models, clear standards, and enforceable laws.

The Law and the Duty to Protect

The sport manager should be alert to the illegal sale of steroids on the premises. The possession of large amounts of steroids without a prescription is illegal in several states.

The sport manager or owner may be confronted with the duty to protect under various factual situations. A sport business might sell alcoholic beverages to customers who are intoxicated; sport managers might permit altercations that result in injury; managers might need to eject a patron from the premises. Each of these examples will be discussed in the following paragraphs.

Tolerating altercations. The case that follows involved an altercation between two groups that resulted in serious injury. Loud talk and verbal threats that lasted several minutes put management on notice of danger. One group was obviously intoxicated but management continued to serve the group alcoholic beverages as the possibility of an altercation grew. The actual fight took place in the parking lot. The injured party sued the bowling alley for failure to take reasonable steps to control its clientele.

••

BISHOP v. FAIR LANES GEORGIA BOWLING, INC.
803 F.2d 1548 (11th Cir. 1986)

CORRECTED OPINION

Before HILL and FAY, Circuit Judges, and MORGAN, Senior Circuit Judge.

PER CURIAM:

The United States District Court for the Northern District of Georgia granted defendant-appellee Fair Lanes Georgia Bowling, Inc.'s (Fair Lanes) motion for summary judgment in this commercial premises liability case, 623 F.Supp. 1195. While we agree with much contained in the district court's order, we reverse the grant of summary judgment and remand the case to the district court for trial.

Appeal arises from a violent altercation that occurred in the parking lot of Fair Lanes' bowling alley located in Norcross, Georgia. Plaintiffs-appellants Stephen Bishop and Deborah A. Smith were beaten severely in the brouhaha, with Bishop suffering especially egregious injuries. The Bishop group[1] sued Fair Lanes, alleging that it was liable for failing to exercise ordinary care in keeping the premises and approaches of the bowling alley safe for

---

1. Although not present on the evening of the attack, plaintiff-appellee Randy L. Smith joined in the suit seeking compensation for loss of consortium rights. For ease of citation the three plaintiffs-appellants will be referred to as "the Bishop group."

Bishop, an invitee, when Fair Lanes had actual or constructive knowledge of a dangerous condition and for continuing to serve alcoholic beverages to noticeably intoxicated patrons when the subsequent violent attack on Bishop was reasonably foreseeable.

The Bishop group attended a Fair Lanes "Midnight Madness" bowling extravaganza on the evening in question, arriving at approximately 1:00 A.M. After bowling for a period of time, the group noticed that its pitcher of beer was missing. One of the Bishop group then approached three bowlers on the adjoining lane and questioned them as to the whereabouts of the missing beer. This trio—Janet Eldridge, Randall Eldridge and Steven Burke[2] — took umbrage with the query and came over to the Bishop group's lane and began a loud conversation. The conversation clearly was heated and hostile; it lasted for somewhere between several minutes to half an hour. Although at least one of the Burke group suggested that they "go outside" and resolve the matter, no blows were struck or fists raised.

At the end of this repartee two separate members of the Bishop group went to the front counter to tell the manager on duty what had happened. They specifically told the manager that the Burke group was drunk, "loud," "unruly," "making a lot of commotion," and had acted in an *"aggressive"* manner toward the Bishop group. Furthermore, Deborah Smith told the manager that the Burke group made her "uneasy" and "uncomfortable." Both requested that the manager keep an eye on the Burke group for the balance of the evening.

The Burke group thereafter proceeded to "harass," "taunt" and "cause a difficult time" for the Bishop group until the alley closed at around 2:30 A.M. This harassment was verbal in nature, although the Burke group came over to the Bishop lane "on several occasions" to ask what had happened to the now infamous pitcher of beer.

As the bowling alley closed, Steve Burke approached Smith and Bishop and another caustic exchange ensued. Burke stated that he did not take the beer, but that if someone took *his* beer he would "beat ass." He also explained that if someone tried to harm his friends he would "beat ass" as a way of helping out a buddy. This was taken, not as a threat, but as a warning to stay away from Burke.

The Burke group then left the building while the Bishop group elected to wait a few minutes in hopes of avoiding additional unpleasantness or confrontation in the parking lot outside. A Fair Lanes employee locked the doors behind the Bishop group as they exited since they were the last patrons to leave. A violent melee occurred in the parking lot when the Burke group accosted Bishop and Deborah Smith at their car, Burke beating Bishop into unconsciousness.[3] Deborah Smith managed to flee and alert a Fair Lanes employee who called the police.

2. For ease of citation this trio will be referred to as "the Burke group."

3. It is undisputed that there had been no prior physical altercations of this type in the Norcross parking lot.

So far as Fair Lanes is concerned, the manager on duty and his assistant took little if any action. They watched the Burke group for about five minutes after the Bishop group complained about the first incident. The manager and assistant manager, however, did not separate the two groups by placing them on nonadjoining lanes, speak to the Burke group about their behavior, or tell the refreshment stand to stop selling beer to the Burke group, even though they were visibly intoxicated. The manager also stated in a deposition that he was unaware of the original confrontation until it was reported to him by members of the Bishop group, even though the argument took place in plain view of the front counter, was quite obstreperous, lasted anywhere from several minutes to a half hour, and caused all bowling to cease on the two lanes for the duration of the argument.

The district court found that there was evidence from which one could conclude that the Burke group had been drinking extensively prior to its arrival at the bowling lanes. It took note of evidence indicating that the members of the Burke group "were visibly intoxicated when they purchased beer by the pitcher at Fair Lanes." Additionally, the district court noted that the suggestion to "go outside" was made in a "threatening" manner.[4]

Georgia law specifically provides that an owner or occupier of land may be held liable if he fails to exercise ordinary care in keeping his premises safe. O.C.G.A. § 51-3-1.[5] Furthermore,

> it is the duty of a proprietor to protect an invitee or guest from injury by a third person if the host is reasonably aware of the probability or likely possibility of such an act by a third party and such injury could be avoided through the exercise of ordinary care and diligence....In order to affix liability in the case of an illegal act, the host must have had reasonable grounds to believe that a particular criminal act is likely to occur.

Donaldson v. Olympic Health Spa, 175 Ga.App. 258, 333 S.E.2d 98, 100-01 (1985); *see Great Atlantic & Pacific Tea Co. v. Cox*, 51 Ga.App. 880, 181 S.E. 788 (1935); *Moone v. Smith*, 6 Ga.App. 649, 65 S.E. 712, 713 (1909).

The danger must be apparent or foreseeable, and not the result of sudden unexpected actions, before the proprietor's duty of care attaches. . . . .

In short, if the potentially violent acts of the Burke group were reasonably foreseeable from the information about which Fair Lanes was or should have been aware, Fair Lanes is liable if it took no action to avoid the potential physical clash. The linchpins of the Bishop group's cause of action thus are foreseeability, aggression, and the actual or constructive knowledge of Fair Lanes. It will be for the jury to decide if the physical assault in this case was a sudden

---

4. The Burke group's request to "go outside" apparently was not communicated to the manager.

5. O.C.G.A. § 51-3-1 provides:

Where an owner or occupier of land, by express or implied invitation, induces or leads others to come upon his premises for any lawful purpose, he is liable to exercise ordinary care in keeping the premises and approaches safe.

act taken without warning to Fair Lanes or the culmination of an evening's worth of confrontation, taunting and harassment and that Fair Lanes was made aware of the conflict well before it erupted into physical violence.

It is uncontroverted that the individual members of the Burke group were noticeably intoxicated; that the two groups engaged in a heated and hostile disagreement; that the Bishop group twice notified the Fair Lanes manager that the Burke group was loud, obnoxious, drunk, and acting in an aggressive manner that made at least one member of the Bishop group uneasy and uncomfortable. It also is uncontroverted that Fair Lanes took virtually no steps to observe the two groups but for a few minutes. Additionally, Fair Lanes continued to serve beer to the Burke group even though that trio was unquestionably intoxicated to a noticeable degree. *See* O.C.G.A. § 3-3-22.[6]

Whatever our view may be, we believe a jury could reasonably find that it is not a "rare event" in human experience for loud and aggressive talking drunks to get into fights at 2:00 A.M on a Saturday morning. *See generally Razdan v. Parzen*, 157 Ga.App. 848, 278 S.E.2d 687 (1981) (An event is not foreseeable if it is a "rare event in experience"). Additionally, in our view, a jury reasonably could find, under the facts, that Fair Lanes should have been aware of a potential physical altercation before it actually occurred and was, therefore, negligent in taking no action to avoid the potentiality and thereby make its premises safe for its invitees. This case presents a classic factual question: was the aggression of which Fair Lanes was aware (or should have been aware) sufficient to make it reasonably foreseeable to Fair Lanes that the Burke group would take violent action against the Bishop group. As such, it was improper to grant summary judgment because the Bishop group raised a genuine issue of material fact.

Although the parties have spent considerable effort discussing whether or not Georgia law recognizes a cause of action based upon a violation of O.C.G.A. § 3-3-22, we find it unnecessary to resolve that narrow question. The claim being made here is that Fair Lanes was guilty of negligence in failing to keep its premises safe for business invitees. Part of the factual scenerio (sic) is that the members of the Burke group were drunk and that knowing that, Fair Lanes continued to serve them beer. Whether coupled with the other surrounding circumstances this amounted to negligence will be for the jury. We are totally satisfied that it is no defense for Fair Lanes to argue that by serving the beer it is somehow immune from liability.

The record contains evidence sufficient to raise questions which must be submitted to a jury under appropriate instructions. We make no effort to predict the outcome but hold it was improper to resolve the matter by way of summary judgment.

The judgment is REVERSED and the matter REMANDED to the district court for trial.

---

6. O.C.G.A. § 3-3-22 provides that "no alcoholic beverage shall be sold, bartered, exchanged, given, provided, or furnished to any person who is in a state of noticeable intoxication."

Questions and Comments

1. What was the factual evidence concerning the disorderly conduct of the aggressor in this case?
2. Was there any doubt that management was placed on notice as to the danger of physical conflict?
3. What was the evidence of intoxication?
4. Did the court find that management owed a duty to   protect in this case?

Selling to intoxicated individuals. In *Sport Facility Planning and Management,* by Farmer, Mulrooney, and Ammon (1996), the authors stated that, "beer and alcohol account for the highest percentage of concession profits . . . . "(p. 191) In fact, if a facility desires to operate with a profit a comprehensive food service is a necessity . . . . (p. 191) Of course, alcohol is only a part of food service, and the authors, Farmer, Mulrooney, and Ammon, are not promoting alcohol. However, it is abundantly clear from reading the following case that a business selling alcohol may reap more than profits. Read the case for applications to sport managers.

In the following case, a local restaurant permitted an admitted alcoholic to drink to the point of intoxication. Upon leaving the restaurant, the intoxicated individual ran a red light, an action which resulted in a fatal accident. The estate of the deceased filed suit. *El Chico Corp. v. Poole* (1987). This case is important because it discusses both the common law and statutory law connected with the liability of an individual who sells to an intoxicated person. The case is also important because it shows the capacity of the common law for change. Find the meaning of the term "dramshop" act as it is referred to in the body of the case. Portions of the case that discuss these issues are included.

· ·

EL CHICO CORP. v. POOLE
732 S.W.2d 306 (Tex. 1987)

SPEARS, Justice.

These two wrongful death and survival actions were submitted together to determine whether a person injured by an intoxicated driver may recover from the alcoholic beverage licensee who allegedly sold intoxicants to that intoxicated driver in violation of the Texas Alcoholic Beverage Code. In *El Chico v. Poole*, Mr. and Mrs. Bryan Poole sued El Chico Corporation and Rene Saenz for the death of their son, Larry, alleging that El Chico negligently served alcohol to an intoxicated Saenz who later collided with Larry's car. The trial court severed the action against Saenz and granted summary judgment for El Chico. The court of appeals reversed the trial court's summary judgment and remanded the cause for trial. 713 S.W.2d 955. We affirm.... (p. 308)

The *El Chico* summary judgment evidence established the following facts: On Friday, January 21, 1984, Rene Saenz, an admitted alcoholic, left work and proceeded with a friend to the El Chico restaurant in Northwest

Mall in Houston. Saenz arrived at El Chico shortly after 5:00 p.m. Saenz remembered ordering his first drink, but remembered nothing else until the accident which occurred around 8:00 p.m., three to five blocks from El Chico. In his deposition, Saenz stated that he did not pass out, but rather "blacked out"—forgot or erased from memory—the incidents leading to the accident. Saenz attributed his "black-out" to his inebriation and desire to "put the accident behind him." Saenz did not recall the number of beverages he drank, but he believed the quantity was sufficient to cause his black-out. Saenz did not remember his condition in El Chico nor could he recall whether his conduct would have alerted any El Chico employees to his intoxicated condition.

Saenz left El Chico around 7:45 p.m. The collision resulting in Larry Poole's death occurred a few minutes later as Saenz was speeding north on Mangum Road and ran a red light at the intersection of Mangum and the Northwest Freeway service road. His truck struck Larry's car as Larry was turning left onto the service road. Larry Poole was dead on arrival at Hermann Hospital. The police officer who investigated the accident observed Saenz was wobbly and swaying in his movements, had a strong smell of alcohol on his breath, was talkative although mumbling, and appeared to be intoxicated. A breath alcohol test administered at the scene resulted in a .18 reading. Saenz was arrested for driving while intoxicated and later convicted of involuntary manslaughter....

The courts of appeals in *Joleemo [Joleemo v. Evans*, 714 S.W.2d 394] and in *El Chico* reversed the respective trial courts' judgments. The *El Chico* court of appeals held:

> ...[A] bar owner owes a duty to the motoring public not to knowingly
> sell an alcoholic beverage to an already intoxicated person.

713 S.W.2d at 958. The court determined that whether El Chico breached its duty and whether the breach was a proximate cause of the Pooles' damages were issues for a jury to decide when the evidence raises those issues. *Id*....

On appeal here, both El Chico and Joleemo argue that in the absence of a legislative dramshop act specifically creating a civil remedy and civil cause of action against alcoholic beverage licensees, no cause of action may be maintained against them. The Pooles and Evanses contend that liability may be imposed upon an alcoholic beverage licensee based upon the common law principles of negligence and negligence *per se*. An alcoholic beverage licensee refers to the holder of an Alcoholic Beverage Commission permit or license who may sell or serve alcoholic beverages. *See generally* TEX. ALCO. BEV. CODE ANN. tit. 3 (Vernon 1978 & Supp. 1987)....(p. 309)

In recent years, modern analyses have discarded the absolute rule of no liability in favor of an approach incorporating current legal understanding as dictated by conditions and circumstances of modern society. An intoxicated person is by definition not an able-bodied nor able-minded person. Of fifty American jurisdictions (including the District of Columbia and excluding Texas), twenty-nine recognize a common law cause of action against an alcoholic beverage purveyor for injuries caused by an intoxicated customer.

Additionally, nineteen state legislatures have enacted civil dramshop liability, seven of which also have recognized a complementary and supplemental common law cause of action. In total, a civil cause of action exists in forty-one jurisdictions with a substantial majority basing the cause of action upon the common law principles of negligence, negligence *per se*, or both. Focusing on the carnage inflicted upon innocent victims by drunk drivers, courts have rejected the rationale supporting no liability as outdated and unrealistic and thus invalid. Injury to a third person is no longer unforeseeable in an age when death and destruction occasioned by drunk driving is so tragically frequent. *Alegria v. Payonk*, 101 Idaho 617, 619 P.2d 135, 137 (1980)....
[Footnotes deleted]

As demonstrated by the actions of the majority of states, the common law is not frozen or stagnant, but evolving, and it is the duty of this court to recognize the evolution. *See Otis Engineering Corp. v. Clark*, 668 S.W.2d 307, 310 (Tex. 1983). Indeed, it is well established that the adoption of the common law of England was intended "to make effective the provisions of the common law, so far as they are not inconsistent with the conditions and circumstances of our people." *Grigsby v. Reib*, 105 Tex. 597, 153 S.W. 1124, 1125 (1913). Our courts have consistently made changes in the common law of torts as the need arose in a changing society.....(pp. 310-311)

> Negligence, a common law doctrine, consists of three essential elements—a legal duty owed by one person to another, a breach of that duty, and damages proximately resulting from the breach. . . . .

In addressing foreseeability, we know by common knowledge that alcohol distorts perception, slows reaction, and impairs motor skills, while operation of an automobile requires clear perception, quick reaction, and adept motor skills. Our everyday use and reliance on the automobile is unquestionable. Also unquestionable is the tragic relationship between intoxicated drivers and fatal or injury-producing accidents. The most recent available statistics show that in 1985, there were 30,794 total motor vehicle traffic accidents in Texas involving intoxicated drivers. *See* TEX. DEP'T OF PUBLIC SAFETY, A LOOK AT DWI ... ACCIDENTS, VICTIMS, ARRESTS 1-4 (1985 ed.). In those accidents, 989 persons were killed and 25,461 were injured. The 1985 figures represent a 6% decrease over 1984, due in part to society's increased awareness of the danger of drunk driving and an increase in "driving while intoxicated" arrests. *Id.* The risk and likelihood of injury from serving alcohol to an intoxicated person whom the licensee knows will probably drive a car is as readily foreseen as injury resulting from setting loose a live rattlesnake in a shopping mall. [References deleted]

....One hundred years ago, this court recognized the risk of serving alcohol to an intoxicated person and the duty to refrain from such conduct. *See McCue v. Klein*, 60 Tex. 168, 169-70 (1883). The duty is the same whether the foreseeable injury involves the drunkard himself or a third party who may be placed in peril because of the drunkard's condition. Moreover, the common law recognizes the duty to take affirmative action to control or avoid increasing the danger from another's conduct which the actor has at least partially created....

Separate and apart from our recognition here of a common law duty of reasonable care based on the principle of foreseeability, the attendant standard of conduct may in addition be determined by a penal statute. *Nixon v. Mr. M Property Management Co.*, 690 S.W.2d 546, 549 (Tex. 1985); *Missouri Pacific Railroad v. American Statesman*, 552 S.W.2d 99, 102-03 (Tex. 1977). The unexcused violation of a statute setting an applicable standard of care constitutes negligence as a matter of law if the statute is designed to prevent an injury to that class of persons to which the injured party belongs. *Nixon*, 690 S.W.2d at 549; *see also Murray v. O & A Express, Inc.*, 630 S.W.2d 633, 636 & n.4 (Tex. 1982) (categories when statutory violation is excused). "A person commits an offense if he knowingly sells an alcoholic beverage to an habitual drunkard or an intoxicated person or an insane person." TEX. ALCO. BEV. CODE ANN. § 101.63(a) (Vernon 1978) (hereafter "Code").

The expressed public policy of the Alcoholic Beverage Code is the protection of the welfare, health, peace, temperance, and *safety* of the people of the state. Code § 101.03 (Vernon 1978). The express purpose of a statute, stated in the preamble, may evidence which persons are included within a protected class. *See Largo Corp. v. Crespin*, 727 P.2d 1098, 1108 (Colo. 1986). The safety and well being of persons like the dead Larry Poole and Patrick Evans, as members of the general public, is one of the express policies of the Alcoholic Beverage Code and extends to and encompasses § 101.63(a)....

By interpreting the general purposes of § 101.63(a) to protect the safety and welfare of the general public in addition to those named, Texas joins the modern trend in tort law and the majority of other jurisdictions with statutes similar to § 101.63(a). (Citations deleted) In the absence of a valid excuse, a liquor licensee is negligent as a matter of law under the statute when he knowingly sells an alcoholic beverage to an intoxicated person.

In order to complete a cause of action in negligence, a plaintiff must establish that the liquor licensee's negligent conduct proximately caused his injuries. Proximate cause consists of cause in fact and foreseeability....

Foreseeability, the second element of proximate cause, means the actor as a person of ordinary intelligence should have anticipated the dangers his negligent act creates for others. *Nixon*, 690 S.W.2d at 550; *American-Statesman*, 552 S.W.2d at 103. Foreseeability does not require the actor anticipate the particular accident, but only that he reasonably anticipate the general character of the injury....

Based on both common law negligence principles and a violation of § 101.63(a), we hold an alcoholic beverage licensee owes a duty to the general public not to serve alcoholic beverages to a person when the licensee knows or should know the patron is intoxicated. A licensee who violates that duty by serving alcoholic beverages to an intoxicated person is negligent as a matter of law. Whether a licensee breached his duty and whether that breach proximately caused a plaintiff's injuries are issues of fact for a jury to resolve....

In reviewing the summary judgment granted to El Chico we accept as true evidence in favor of the Pooles, indulge in every reasonable inference, and resolve any doubts in their favor. *See Montgomery v. Kennedy*, 669 S.W.2d 309, 310-11 (Tex. 1984). Although Saenz does not recall his conduct in El Chico, his apparent intoxication at the accident scene shortly after leaving El Chico raises a fact issue whether El Chico's employees sold alcohol to Saenz when they knew or should have known of his intoxication. This evidence raises issues of material fact concerning El Chico's negligence. Whether El Chico was in fact negligent and whether that negligence was a proximate cause of the Pooles' damages are fact questions for a jury. We only determine that the Pooles have stated a cause of action and that the summary judgment was improper....

Accordingly, the court of appeals' judgment in *El Chico v. Poole* is affirmed, and the cause is remanded to the trial court....

Questions and Comments

1. Did the common law permit recovery against the seller of alcoholic beverages to one who becomes intoxicated and later causes an injury?
2. Has the common law changed its position? If so, what is the reason behind the change?
3. What is meant by a "dramshop" statute?
4. What is the extent of such legislation?
5. As a practical matter, is it possible to obtain criminal convictions against intoxicated individuals who cause death through the use of an automobile?
6. What does this case teach with respect to the elements and types of negligence? How would these teachings benefit the sport manager's risk-management plan?

Company parties. In *Arrow Uniform Rental, Inc. v. Suter* (1989), a company was hosting a party during work hours, on the business premises. Alcohol was served, and the alleged assault occurred on the premises. The court ruled that the injuries occurred in the course of, and arising out of, employment.

Violence, drugs, and alcohol. In September 1994, President Clinton signed the 1994 Violent Crime Control and Law Enforcement Act, which instructed the government to appoint a commission to evaluate American crime and drug policies and to recommend changes.

Nearly 60% of federal prisoners are jailed because of drug offenses. (Kammer, cited in Langston, 1996) Alcohol is related to the increase in violent crime. (Engs & Hanson, 1994)

Of all reported assaults, 40% involve alcohol. Alcohol is associated with over three fifths of all murders. (Ray & Ksir 1993)

Some sport activities have begun to stop serving alcoholic beverages before the end of the game. It is this connection between alcohol, drugs, and violent behavior that alerts the sport manager to potential risk-management situations.

Ejecting patron from premises. In the following case, a patron was drunk and was ejected from the Kansas City Royals baseball stadium. Because of her drunken condition, she was unable to protect herself. An abduction and sexual abuse resulted. Suit was filed against the baseball corporation and security personnel. In reading the edited case, look for extent of intoxication, duty to care, and hearsay evidence.

··

KEESEE v. FREEMAN
772 S.W.2d 663 (Mo.Ct.App. 1989)

CLARK, Judge.

Rhonda Keesee sued the Kansas City Royals Baseball Corporation and two police officers, Ray Freeman and William Stupps, for injuries Keesee sustained when she was abducted after being ejected from the ballpark. The cause was submitted to a jury on the theory that defendants were negligent in abandoning Keesee in the public parking lot when she was not reasonably able to protect herself because of the state of her intoxication. The jury returned a verdict for defendants and Keesee has appealed.

A brief statement of the facts will suffice to put the points on appeal in proper context. On May 19, 1984, Keesee and other employees of a nursing home attended a company picnic and after that concluded, the group went to a night baseball game at Royals Stadium. Keesee consumed intoxicating beverages at the picnic and continued drinking beer at the ballpark. The group had been told they were not permitted to bring beer into the ballpark but several, including Keesee, did so. At some point during the game, Keesee was ascending an aisle on her way to the bathroom when she was confronted by two officers, Freeman and Stupps. Keesee was carrying a can of beer in her pocket. The officers ejected Keesee for this infraction. When last seen, Keesee was outside a fence which separates the seating area and playing field from the parking lot.

At some point after Keesee had been escorted from the Royals Stadium, the location of which was disputed by the evidence, Keesee was abducted by several men and was sexually abused. In the course of the encounter, she passed out and was later found in a public park at about 10:00 p.m., some two hours after she had been ejected from the ballpark. She was later treated at a hospital for her injuries.

On this appeal, Keesee presents seven points of alleged trial error. The first two arise because of the procedure adopted by the trial court to resolve the question of whether Freeman and Stupps as police officers employed for security purposes at the Royals Stadium were protected against liability to Keesee by official immunity.

[A discussion of procedural matters pertaining to the conduct of the trial is deleted.]

· · · · · · ·

[Extent of Intoxication]
[1]

One of the contested issues in the case was the extent of Keesee's intoxication. According to Keesee, she was highly intoxicated, stumbling and falling down. Other witnesses testified that although Keesee had been drinking, she appeared to have her faculties about her and was able to take care of herself. Under the instructions, the jury could not return a verdict for Keesee unless it found that she was intoxicated to the extent that she could not protect herself from an attack and that Keesee's appearance was such that the officers knew or should have known of that condition. On evidence consistent with the verdict and the instructions, the jury could well have found, that Freeman and Stupps were under no duty to safeguard Keesee in the process of ejecting her from the stadium because Keesee was, or appeared to be, able to take care of herself.

[Location of Abduction]
[2]

A second issue in the case was the location where Keesee's abduction occurred. According to Keesee, she was taken by men in the Royal's [sic] parking lot. Other evidence, including statements Keesee herself gave the night of the event to a police officer and to the physician who treated her at the hospital, was that she was hitchhiking on a highway outside the ballpark and was assaulted by men who stopped to give her a ride. On this evidence, the jury could have decided in conformity with the instructions that the officers and the Royals were not liable because Keesee was not abducted or attacked on premises the Royals controlled.

As the foregoing analysis demonstrates, the verdict in this case was consistent with the jury instructions and the evidence supportive of that verdict. Prejudice may not be shown on the unsubstantiated claim that the jury ignored the court's instructions and decided the case on issues not submitted. The claim is denied. [A second procedural point is discussed here.]

.   .   .   .   .   .

[Interference with One Attempting to Give Aid]
[4]

In a fourth point, appellant contends it was error for the court to direct a verdict for the defendants on her petition Count V. That count alleged an intentional tort recognized by § 326 of the Restatement (Second) of Torts (1964) as the interference with one attempting to give aid to a person in imminent danger of harm. The theory of the count, according to appellant, was that a member of the nursing home group, one Denny Barnett, was with appellant and the officers at the time appellant was in the process of being removed from the stadium. Barnett sought the permission of the officers to call a cab for appellant, but that was refused because the officers told Barnett that appellant was under arrest. By this sequence of events, appellant claims the officers committed the intentional tort of preventing Barnett from giving aid to appellant who was then in need of that assistance to avoid the threat of physical harm.

. . . . .

In the present case, Keesee was in no imminent or impending peril as she was escorted from the ballpark, the actual attack upon her coming at a later time and at another location. Although Keesee argued that Freeman and Stupps should have anticipated some potential danger because of the degree of Keesee's intoxication, that premise makes no case for intentional tort under the petition Count V. The cause of action which the Restatement postulates applies only when there is a real and immediate threat of bodily harm and active intervention by the defendant to thwart the efforts of a rescuer. Moreover, the peril must be one at hand and evident to the defendant before the intentional character of the tortious act can be demonstrated.

The trial court properly entered judgment for the defendants on Count V of appellant's petition because the petition did not state a cause of action recognized in Missouri and because appellant's proof failed to support the petition claim.

[Exclusion of Evidence?]
[5]

In her next point, appellant complains of the court's exclusion from evidence of reports of non-violent crimes and incidents at Royals stadium during a period of two years prior to May 19, 1984, the date appellant was ejected from the stadium. Reports and records of violent occurrences were admitted. The issue is whether the excluded reports of non-violent incidents should have been received as proof of the duty of care owed by the Royals to appellant.

. . . . .

In the present case, appellant's suit was based on the violent incident of abduction and assault. She was permitted to show to the jury the records of all other violent crimes and incidents which had occurred at Royals Stadium the previous two years. Records of disorderly conduct by Royals patrons and other non-violent events at the stadium were properly excluded because they did not tend to show notice to the Royals of a danger to customers from acts of violence such as kidnapping and assault.

. . . . .

[Evidence Reports]
[6]

In the sixth point, appellant contends the court erred when it gave certain admonitions to the jury regarding the reported incidents of violence at Royals Stadium during the two years prior to appellant's assault and injury. The evidence in question consisted of reports made to police officers, reports made to the Royals and admissions by the defendants that certain violent incidents had been reported. The defendants had objected to the use of the incident reports, being records from the police department and from the files of the Royals, as hearsay, but the court ruled the evidence admissible for the limited purpose of showing notice to the Royals that such occurrences had been reported.

[A discussion of instruction to the jury is deleted. The Court rules that incident reports were "hearsay".]

. . . . .

To establish the duty of care owed patrons at the stadium by the Royals, it was merely necessary for appellant to prove notice to respondents that numerous acts of violence on the premises were being reported. . . . .

[Evidence Denied]
[7]

In a final and related point to the complaint about the court's instruction described in the preceding point, appellant contends the court erred when it denied admission in evidence of certain computer print-outs. This material consisted of listings prepared by the police department and by the Royals showing all of the violent and non-violent incidents which appeared in the underlying reports. Appellant suggests the order barring the computer print-outs from introduction in evidence was erroneous for several reasons. No extended discussion of the point is needed. The summary of non-violent incidents was excludable on grounds already discussed and those incidents comprised a substantial number of the print-out items. In addition, the print-outs were compounded hearsay being drawn themselves from other hearsay.

.   .   .   .   .

[The judgment for the defendants was affirmed.]

Questions and Comments

1. What reason did the court give for finding for the defendant?
2. What practical considerations may have influenced the court's opinion?
3. How could management have avoided this lawsuit?
4. Why was some of the evidence excluded?

Hazing

One of the most recent developments in the law has been the prohibition against hazing. Hazing may occur on sport teams, in high schools, and on university campuses. Most states now have statutes prohibiting hazing. The prohibition may also be in the form of team, school, or university regulation. Judicial decisions sometimes give the appearance of lagging behind the public policy as expressed in these statutes and regulations. *People v. Anderson* (1992) shows the relationship between alcohol consumption and hazing. The defendant claimed that the statute was overbroad and did not give adequate notice. The court upheld the statute. However, the court limited its application to occasions where physical injury resulted. Hazing was not an absolute liability offense according to this court. In addition, knowledge, intent, or recklessness had to be shown by the state.

Hazing can kill. Nicholas Haben, 18 years old, died after ingesting alcohol as part of an initiation ceremony into the Lacross Club at Western Illinois

University (*Haben v. Anderson*, 1992). His father brought suit against the club members. One club member, Kolovitz, said that he would check on Haben after he was placed drunk on Kolovitz's floor. However, when Kolovitz heard him gurgling during the night, Kolovitz failed to act. The court ruled that club member Kolovitz had a duty to care and he did not act reasonably to prevent harm to Haben. In ruling in favor of the father and finding the club member negligent, the appellate court stated that "[t]he Hazing Act does not distinguish between individual members of the organization and the organization itself." What are implications here for sport managers and sport club members?

Safety Concerns

Safety of sports participants is a major consideration of the sport manager. Certain drugs such as steroids increase aggression and irritability (Kusserow, 1990). Overly aggressive participants are potentially dangerous. Marijuana and alcohol impede judgment, turning a usually good participant into a reckless participant. Many drugs hamper motor control and make a harmless sport event potentially injurious or life threatening.

In the case of *Roten v. U.S.* (1994), a hiker died from a fall in a recreation area in the Ozark National Forest. The decedent's blood alcohol level was 0.04 at the time of his death from a fall off a cliff. The court held that the National Park Service did not maliciously fail to warn against any ultrahazardous condition or structure. The 18- year-old hikers had been celebrating a birthday with several different kinds of alcohol.

Alcohol was also in evidence in a ski-boating collision in *Wade v. Grace,* (1995). Although there was not proof that the boat driver was intoxicated, six beer cans were found in the water next to the boat.

A sport manager should make decisions based on the safety of participants. Alcohol impairs coordination and judgment. Allowing customers to participant in a sport while drinking could be fatal to the customer.

Drug Policy

A drug policy may be written for customers or for employees, and should be predicated on safety of the sport management environment. O'Brien and Overby (1992) provided recommendations for a drug policy.

In constructing a drug policy, a dialogue should be established with the people who will be affected by that policy. The purpose of the policy should be carefully written. The policy should be concise and unambiguous. It should indicate who will be affected by the policy. People should be treated equally.

Prescription and over-the-counter drugs should be considered in the policy. Some people abuse these drugs. Also, some of these drugs have synergistic effects. For example, alcohol mixed with barbiturates may be fatal.

If the drug is a prescription drug, permission should be obtained to call the doctor concerning the drug. Some drugs may affect work or sport performance. (*Kruger v. San Francisco 49ers*, 1987)

Drugs that are prohibited should be indicated in the policy. Drugs that will be tested should be indicated. (The NCAA lists over 34 pages of substances that are regulated for the college athlete.) Standards of influence or impairment should be noted. For example, in most states, a .10 blood alcohol content (BAC) is considered under the influence; yet, most individuals are impaired at a .06 BAC.

Drug Testing

According to various surveys, about 85 percent of large companies use some kind of drug testing. . . . . Each year about 15 million Americans are required to take a small jar into a small room and aim carefully. One company alone, Smith Kline Beecham, conducted 3.6 million tests in 1994. They found an overall positive rate of 7.5 percent, down from 8.4 percent in 1993. (Alvics, 1996, p. 255)

Langston (1996) and Willette and Kadahajiar (1992) note that workers support drug testing:

Eighty-two percent of the workers in a Gallup Poll (1989) supported company antidrug policies, including disciplinary actions.

Ninety-two percent found testing appropriate.

Thirty-two percent knew illegal drugs were being sold at their work place.

From 1987 through 1990, federal courts handed down 39 decisions on the topic of drug testing (Thompson, Riccuci, & Bon, 1991). The courts' analyses center on the right to privacy, due process, and search and seizure. Although a full review of drug testing is beyond the scope of this book, an analysis of case law allows for insight into policy development and application.

In a drug policy, these questions should be answered related to drug testing. If drug testing is to be used who is to conduct the test? What sampling procedures will be followed? What will be the analysis procedures? How will false positive or false negative results be handled?

In addition, if blood or urine samples are to be obtained, one should establish a secure chain of custody and put it in writing. The policy should be designed to ensure that samples are not mixed or mislabeled.

When positive results are found, confidentiality is important. Discussions of false positives might be considered libelous or slanderous.

The policy should also provide procedures to handle people who refuse to take the drug test. Some state constitutions are more strictly interpreted than others. Also, some states have state statutes regarding the right to privacy. For example, in the Colorado case, *Derdeyn v. U. of Colo.* (1991), drug testing of college athletes was considered an unlawful search.

Drug testing in the work place may differ from drug testing in a school environment. In schools, drug testing of an entire student body might not be upheld by the courts (*Odenheim v. Carlstadt-East Rutherford Regional School District*, 1985). However, a university's random testing of athletes has been upheld in some court cases (*Bally v. Northeastern*, 1989), but not in others (*Derdeyn v. University of Colorado* 1991). In the latest pronouncement of the United States Supreme Court, *Vernonia School Dist. 47J v. Acton for Acton* (1995), drug testing of high school athletes was upheld. In schools and universities, athletes are treated differently from regular students on this issue because participation in athletics is not mandatory and they consent to a drug test (*Hill v. NCAA*, 1994).

The courts in *Vernonia* (1995) and in the *Schaill by Kross v. Tippicanoe* (1988) also note that athletes have a different expection of privacy . . . . They are used to locker room showers. . . . . (The right to privacy is discussed in Chapter 16.)

* * * * *

Authors' Note

This book does not address the specific problems associated with the various issues of drug testing high school athletes (e.g., *Vernonia v. Acton,* 1995), of college athletes (e.g., *Hill v. NCAA*, 1994), or of professional athletes (e.g., *Long v. National Football League*, 1994), or of Olympic Athletes (Skolnick, 1996). For more indepth discussion on this topic, listen to audio tapes O'Brien and Exum, AAHPERD National Convention, 1996, and O'Brien, AAHPERD National Convention, 1993.

The courts' analyses of these issues center on (a) the right to privacy (chapter 16), (b) due process (chapter 15), and (c) search and seizure (discussed here and in chapter 16). (*National Treasury Employees v. Von Rabb*, 1989); *Skinner v. Railway Labor Executives' Association,* 1989).

* * * * *

If searches for drugs are to be used, they must be reasonable (*New Jersey v. T.L.O.,* 1985). The policy should indicate who will conduct the searches and under what circumstances. Searches of property are best conducted by employees, not law enforcement officials. In most cases, business and school officials do not need search warrants to search their own property. For example, lockers would be considered property of the business or school. As the Fourth Amendment protects citizens from undue searches by government officials, a need exists for "probable cause" and a search warrant in the case of police officer searches. However, if it is a privately owned sport business and one has placed clients on notice that searches will be held and certain items are prohibited (e.g., guns, drugs), then a search warrant is not necessary for the search if it is conducted by the employees of the business.

The local police department should be contacted in all cases where drugs are found. There needs to be a procedure for handling stolen property that is discovered in the search.

Due process is a variable concept depending on the facts before the court. To address due process, a drug policy should consider the following:

1. giving written notice when the policy is alleged to have been violated;
2. providing a hearing so that the accused person may confront his or her accusers;
3. allowing the person adequate time to prepare for the hearing;
4. giving the person an opportunity to be represented by counsel.

Related issues. Persons who will implement the policy should be trained in recognition and documentation of drug-taking behavior. For example, disruptive conduct that interferes with the work environment might be considered "reasonable cause" for a search. Personnel should know there are personal signs and symptoms of drug abuse that, if recognized early, might help in treating an individual. A record should be kept which documents and dates suspected drug-taking behaviors.

The policy should have provisions for follow-up. If a person has been a drug user, what kinds of treatment or referral will be recommended? Community agencies, counselors, assistance programs, and court-ordered treatment may be considered.

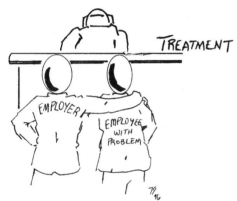

Confronting the problem is difficult for the user as well as for the people who may have been enabling the user. The policy might also cover follow-up procedures to help educate those persons who will be involved with rehabilitation. A good drug policy will give ways of monitoring follow-up activities.

As a follow-up for the treatment of the user, the person should make a written commitment to improve and should have some form of assistance program. Steps to monitor progress of the individual are vital. The written commitment may help the user overcome the denial process. The steps to monitor progress may be physiological, psychological, or both. Periodic testing to show that the person is drug free may be required. The sport manager should have scheduled discussions with the person and treatment center personnel.

Knowledge of the policy is important to all individuals affected. The policy should be made known to individuals early enough for them to rid themselves of drugs. A 45-to 90-day grace period is recommended.

SUMMARY

Sport managers should be keenly aware of the problems arising out of the use of alcohol and the duty to protect sport invitees or employees. Factual situations may involve company parties, both on and off company premises. Other situations involve the ejecting of patrons under the influence from places of entertainment such as concerts and ball games. Finally, the seller of alcoholic beverages is charged with the duty both at common law and under the statutory law of various states to refrain from selling alcohol to an individual who is intoxicated. A failure to so restrict sales may result in liability to a third party who is injured as a result of the negligence of the intoxicated party. Laws restricting the sale or service of beverages to intoxicated persons are called dramshop laws. Dramshop laws in various states cover this aspect of liability.

Many times it may appear that courts are lenient when faced with a general duty to protect. Such leniency—if, in fact, it does exist—can be the result of a belief that the primary actor is the intoxicated person as opposed to the manager of a sports enterprise or the seller of alcoholic beverages. Regardless of the outcome of such cases, a sport manager would want to avoid the time and expenditure involved in litigation. Caution has merit!

This could be you - check your response

The Joneses' policy would probably be ineffective in its present form. A policy related to alcohol and drug use on the job that did not "moralize" would be more effective. The policy would want to include (a) a statement of zero tolerance to alcohol and drugs on the job, (b) a statement of drug testing if accidents occurred, (c) a statement about rehabilitation and follow-up, (d) a statement about hiring and firing policy, and (e) a statement about pre-employment screening.

REFERENCES

Authors

Alvics, H. (1996). *Drugs and life.* Madison, WI: Brown & Benchmark.

Buckley, W. E. et al: (1988). Estimated prevalence of anabolic steroid use among male high school seniors. *Journal American Medical Association, 260 23,* 3441-3445.

Engs, R. C., & Hanson, D. J. (1994). Boozing and brawling on campus: A national study of violent problems associated with drinking over the past decade. *Journal of Criminal Justice, 22*(2), 177-180.

Everson, J. (1987, December). The steroid crunch. *Muscle & Fitness. 12,* 324.

Farmer, P. C., Mulrooney, A. L., & Ammon, R. (1996). *Sport facility, planning, and management.* Morgantown, WV: Fitness Information Technology, Inc.

Goldman, B., Bush, P., & Klatz, R. (1984). *Death in the locker room.* South Bend, IN: Icarus Press.

Kusserow, R. P. (1990). *Adolescent steroid use* (Office of the Inspector General, Office of Evaluations and Inspections, OEI-06-90-0180). Washington, DC.

Langston, P. A. (1996). *The social world of drugs.* St. Paul, MN: West Publishing Company.

Levinthal, C.F. (1996). *Drugs, behavior and modern society.* Needham Heights, MA: Allyn & Bacon.

National Council on Alcoholism and Drug Dependence. (1992). *NCAAD fact sheet alcohol and other drugs in the workplace.* Washington, DC.

O'Brien, D. B. (Speaker). (1993). *Drugs in physical education and sport, legal issues* (Cassette recording of presentation at the National Convention, American Alliance for Health, Physical Education, Recreation, and Dance [AAHPERD]). Millersville, MD: Recorded Resources Corporation.

O'Brien, D. B., & Exum, W. (U.S.O.C. Speakers, 1996) *Anupdate on legal issues, drugs and alcohol, used in physical education and sport* (Cassette recording of presentation at the National Convention AAHPERD). Millersville, MD: Recorded Resources Corporation.

O'Brien, D. B., & Overby, J. O. (1992) Drugs and sports—developing a drug policy. *Journal of Legal Aspects of Sport, 2*(1), pp.

Ray, O., and Ksir, C. (1993). *Drugs, society & human behavior* (7th ed.). St. Louis, MO: Mosby Year Book, Inc.

Schlaadt, R.G., & Shannon, P.T. (1990). *Drugs* (3rd ed.). Englewood Cliffs, NJ: Prentice Hall.

Skolnick, A. A. (1996). Tougher drug tests for Centennial Olympic Games. *Journal American Medical Association, 275,* 5, 345-350.

Thompson, F., Riccuci N., & Bon C. (1991). Drug testing in the federal workplace: An instrumental and symbolic assessment. *Public Administration Review, 51,* 515-525.

Willette, R., & Kadehajiar L. (1992). *Drug testing in the workplace* R. Swotinsky. (Ed.), *In the medical review officer's guide to drug testing* (pp. 12). New York: Van Nostrand Reinhold.

Yesalis, C. E., Kennedy, N.J., Kopstein, A.N., & Bahirke, M.S. (1993). Anabolic androgenic steroid use in the United States. *Journal American Medical Association* 270, 10, 1217-1221.

Cases

Arrow Uniform Rental, Inc. v. Suter, 545 N.E.2d 832 (Ind. Ct. App. 1989).

Ballou v. Sigma Nu General Fraternity, 352 S.E. 2d 488
(S. C. App. 1986)

Bally v. Northeastern University, 532 N.E.2d 49 (Mass. 1989)

Barefield v. City of Houston, 846 S.W.2d 399 (Tex. Ct. App. 1992).

Bishop v. Fair Lanes Georgia Bowling, Inc., 803 F.2d 1548 (11th Cir. 1986).

Board of Zoning Adj. v. Mill Bakery, 587 So.2d 390 (Ala. Civ. App. 1991).

Brigance v. Velvet Dove Restaurant, 756 P.2d 1232 (Okla. 1988).

Clark County Bd. of Education v. Jones, 625 S.W. 2d 586 (Ky. 1981)

Derdeyn v. University of Colorado, 832 P.2d 1031 (Col. App. 1991).

El Chico Corp. v. Poole, 732 S.W.2d 306 (Tex. 1987).

French v. Cornwell, 276 N.W. 2d 216 (Neb. 1979).

Gathers v. Loyola Marymount University, No. C 759,027 (Super. Ct. Cal. filed April 20, 1990)

Gordon v. State, 289 P.2d 396 (Okla. Crim. App. 1955).

Gravely v. Bacon, 429 S.E.2d 663 (Ga. 1993).

Haben v. Anderson, 597 N.E. 2d 655 (Ill. App. 3 Dist. 1992).

Hill v. NCAA, 273 Cal.Rptr. 402 Petition for review granted. See 276 Cal. Rptr. 319 (1990).

Hill v. NCAA, 884 P.2d 649 (Cal. 1994).

Keesee v. Freeman, 772 S.W.2d 663 (Mo. Ct. App. 1989).

Kruger v. San Francisco 49ers, 189 Cal. App. 3rd 823, 234 Cal. Rep. 579, 1987.

Long v. National Football League, 870 F.Supp. 101 (W.D.Pa. 1994).

Maddox v. University of Tennessee, 62 F.3d 843 (6th Cir. 1995).

National Treasury Employees v. Von Raab, 489 U.S. 656, 103 L.Ed.2d 685, 109 S.Ct. 1384 (1989).

New Jersey v. T.L.O., 469 U.S. 325 (1985), 83 L.Ed.2d 720, 105 S.Ct. 733 (1985).

Oldenheim v. Carlstadt - East Rutherford Regional School District, 510 A.2d 709 (N.J. Super.Ct. 1985).

Palmer v. Merluzzi, 689 F.Supp. 400 (N.J. 1988).

People v. Anderson, 148 Ill.2d 15, 169 Ill.Dec. 288, 591 N.E.2d 461 (Ill. 1992).

People v. Williams, 192 Colo. 249, 557 P.2d 399 (1976).

Phillips v. Wild Mountain Sports, Inc., 439 N.W.2d 58 (Minn. Ct. App. 1989).

Primages Int'l of Mich. v. Liquor Control Com'n, 501 N.W.2d 268 (Mich. Ct. App. 1993).

Roten v. U.S., 850 F.Supp. 786 (W.D. Ark. 1994).

7250 Corp. v. Bd. of County Com'rs, 799 P.2d 917 (Colo. 1990).

Schaill by Kross v. Tippicanoe County School Corp., 864 F.2d 1309 (7th Cir. 1988).

Skinner v. Railway Labor Executives' Association, 489 U.S. 602, 103 L.Ed.2d 639, 109 S.Ct. 1402 (1989).

Vernonia School Dist. 47J v. Acton for Acton, 515 U.S.
_____, 132 L.Ed. 2d 564, 115 S.Ct. 2386 (1995).

Wade v. Grace, 902 S.W.2d 785 (Ark. 1995).

Statute

Illinois Hazing Act. Ill. Rev. Stat. 1990 Supp. Ch. 144, par. 220. 9 et seq.

DAY-TO-DAY OPERATIONS—
SPECIAL PROBLEMS

PERSPECTIVE

Part IV has endeavored to set forth principles of law relative to dress and grooming, crowd control, alcohol, drugs and business. Specifically, the reader has been introduced to

A. Dress and Grooming
  1. Facial jewelry
  2. Swimsuits as required apparel
  3. Makeup
  4. Hair style
B. Crowd Control
  1. Parking lot injury
  2. Spectator injury at concert
  3. Patron injury following exit
C. Alcohol, Drugs, and Business
  1. The nature and extent of the problem
  2. Duty to protect
     a. Tolerating altercations
     b. Selling to intoxicated persons
     c. Company parties
     d. Ejecting patrons
     e. Hazing

The materials presented in the chapter on dress and grooming deal primarily with employees. The materials presented in the chapter on crowd control deal primarily with patrons of the establishment. The materials covered in the chapter on alcohol, drugs, and business deal with both employees and patrons.

This section has discussed dress and grooming, crowd control, and alcohol and drug use. These are day-to-day operational problems a sport manager might encounter. These topics are very timely. As this text is being written, the Supreme Court, as well as Congress, are discussing many of these issues. The sport manager is encouraged to continue to be aware of these very contemporary topics.

Hypothetical Case - Part IV - Check Your Response

The Joneses can post signs in the bowling alley regarding the conduct of patrons. This puts patrons on notice. The Joneses have the right to eject patrons whose conduct is disruptive.

Constitutional Questions

FOCUS

Overview

This part of the text discusses constitutional issues most often encountered by the owner or manager of a sport management enterprise. The initial chapter deals with situations where the constitutional issues can be avoided. Stated differently, under certain circumstances, it is not necessary to litigate a constitutional question. Avoiding a lawsuit can save money. Following the initial chapter, "Constitutional Restraints," chapters are devoted to due process and the First Amendment. The due process chapter is concerned with both the Fifth and Fourteenth Amendments to the United States Constitution. Efforts are made to isolate the pragmatic aspects of these constitutional questions.

Practical Application—Hypothetical Case

Toby Jones, the daughter of John and Maria Jones, has entered high school. Toby is studying civics, among other things. One assignment is to write a paper on constitutional issues as they apply to small town life. How can the Joneses assist their daughter in making a practical application of the United States Constitution to business in a small community? Be specific.

CHAPTER 14

CONSTITUTIONAL RESTRAINTS AND STATUTORY INTERPRETATION

INTRODUCTION

A young girl wanted to participate in a baseball program reserved for boys. What constitutional issue was raised to help her make her case? Did she prevail?

A skater was injured by another skater at a skating rink. There was a recreational users statute concerning skating rinks in that state. Can she collect damages from the rink owner? How does statutory interpretation play a role in this case? Read the following chapter for answers to these questions. Note the principles of constitutional restraint and statutory interpretation that apply to these cases.

TRYOUTS TODAY

There are some basic premises in considering constitutional restraints. Remember, the United States Constitution is the primary document that established the judiciary system.

For the federal courts to consider a case the controversy must be real, not hypothetical. The federal courts will not hand down an advisory opinion on a case. As a general rule, the courts will not decide the constitutional issues if the case can be decided on other grounds. The constitutional issue must also be timely pleaded.

Furthermore, the courts will presume the constitutionality of a statute. Some courts even go so far as to say that unconstitutionality must be established beyond a reasonable doubt. Courts also say that it is not their province to question the wisdom of legislation, but that courts should confine themselves to an interpretation of the law. These and other restraints mark the boundaries of constitutional issues and strengthen the Constitution as a primary source of law.

There are also basic principles concerning statutory interpretation. These principles are well articulated in decisional law. These principles are also relevant in interpreting the Constitution, administrative regulations, and contracts. The reader should remember that the basic purpose is to determine the intent of those who drafted the document. If the intent is plain and does not lead to absurd results, then the court will need to look no further. However, if the meaning is not clear, it will be necessary to resort to principles of construction. Some of these principles involve such things as definitions, ascertainment of the purpose of the statute, the need to harmonize all parts of the statute, and a recognition that a specific statute will govern a general statute. Other principles will be noted in the relevant authors' note later in the chapter.

The sport manager who has a basic understanding of constitutional restraints and statutory interpretation can do two things. First, this individual can contribute to the drafting of documents such as contracts and administrative rules and regulations. Careful drafting will promote clarity and remove the necessity of interpretation. Second, assuming that litigation is commenced, this same knowledge will enable sport managers to better cooperate with their attorneys in defending the lawsuit. Winning is important in sport and legal areas. Read this chapter and discover how knowledge of constitutional restraints and statutory interpretation may help the sport manager to prevent and win a lawsuit.

IN THIS CHAPTER YOU WILL LEARN:

The meaning of the doctrine of mootness

The relationship between the requirement for a case or controversy and the advisory opinion

The rationale behind the rule that argues for resolution of a case on other than constitutional grounds if at all possible

The Supreme Court decision that first directed attention to the doctrine of judicial restraint in summary form

The occasion for utilizing rules of statutory interpretation in sport cases

---

KEY WORDS: *mootness, presumption of constitutionality, clear and unambiguous statute, plain meaning of the statute, intent of the statute, judicial restraints*

This could be you!

John Jones is having a beer at a local tavern where he overhears a conversation at the next table. The conversation in question involves Ms Street, a visitor in town. Street is bragging that she fired a young Hebrew divinity student because the student's religion was offensive to some of her clientele. The substance of the conversation is later repeated at a meeting of a local civic group. Jones is offended by the anti-Semitic sentiments expressed and files suit in a local court to vindicate the principle of freedom of religion. The friends and neighbors of Jones approve his stand on the issue and applaud his action in filing suit. Street makes a motion to dismiss. What results? What would be the grounds for such a motion?

JUDICIAL RESTRAINTS
Mootness

The case that follows involved litigation concerning the exclusion of girls from participating in Little League Baseball. After the Little League changed their rules to allow girls to participate the defendants moved to dismiss on the grounds of mootness. In reading the case, look for the constitutional underpinnings of the doctrine of mootness. Also, identify the civil rights statutes that are invoked by the plaintiffs in the case. The civil rights issues will be discussed later in this book.

••

RAPPAPORT v. LITTLE LEAGUE BASEBALL, INC.
65 F.R.D. 545 (U.S.D.C., D.Del. 1975)

LATCHUM, Chief Judge.

The plaintiffs, young girls and their parents, filed suit on March 13, 1974 against the defendants, Little League Baseball, Inc. ("League") and selected local charter members of the League, seeking to have the defendants' policy of excluding girls from Little League baseball teams declared unconstitutional. The plaintiffs further sought to enjoin the League from revoking the charters of the local members for including female participants in their individual programs and in addition sought a mandatory injunction commanding the defendants to permit girls to play on the defendants' Little League teams. Finally, the plaintiffs asked for attorneys' fees, litigation expenses and punitive damages.

The suit was brought under 42 U.S.C. §§ 1983 and 1985 (3) and jurisdiction was based on 28 U.S.C. §§ 1343(3) and (4).

On June 12, 1974 the League issued a public statement that it would, as of that date, permit girls to register in the League's program on an equal basis with boys. The defendants thereafter moved to dismiss the suit on the ground that all the issues had become moot.[1]

Oral argument was heard by the Court and an order was issued denying defendants' motion, but granting the defendants leave to renew their motion upon submission of a more substantial and complete record.[2] In response to that order defendants have now submitted additional affidavits and have renewed their original motion to dismiss for mootness.[3]

1. Docket Item 15.
2. Docket Item 19.
3. Letter to Court dated October 8, 1974.

The plaintiffs also filed a motion for summary judgment apparently based on the argument that since the League has changed its policy with respect to girls, no material fact remains in issue.[4]

I.   Plaintiffs' Motion For Summary Judgment.

Plaintiffs' summary judgment motion is totally unfounded. The defendants' change in policy with respect to the participation of girls in their programs can not be construed as an admission that their previous policy was unlawful or injurious to the plaintiffs or even that there was a valid cause of action asserted under 42 U.S.C. §§ 1983 and 1985(3). Hence, no grounds exist for granting the plaintiffs' motion.

II.   Defendants' Motion To Dismiss.

This Court has the duty to dismiss an action as moot if changing conditions transform the question presented by the action from a concrete legal issue into an abstraction since the resolution of such a question would in effect require an advisory opinion that is beyond the constitutional function of this Court to render. Golden v. Zwickler, 394 U.S. 103, 108, 89 S.Ct. 959, 22 L.Ed.2d 113 (1969).

In the present case, the plaintiffs' request for declaratory and injunctive relief was for the purpose of prospectively assuring that girls would be allowed to participate in the defendants' Little League programs on an equal basis with boys. As stated above, girls are no longer excluded from the defendants' programs. While the mere cessation of allegedly illegal conduct does not require that a case seeking equitable or declaratory relief with respect to that conduct be dismissed, it may be dismissed if the defendants can demonstrate that there is no reasonable expectation that the conduct will be resumed. United States v. W. T. Grant Co., 345 U.S. 629, 632-633, 73 S.Ct. 894, 97 L.Ed. 1303 (1953). Thus, the equity and declaratory aspects of the present action will be dismissed if the Court finds that the defendants have in good faith permanently ceased pursuing a policy of excluding girls from their Little League programs.

Turning first to the defendant League, the Court is satisfied that there is little probability that the League will return to a policy of excluding girls from its program. A resolution of the Board of Directors of the League,[5] a press release by the League,[6] national press coverage of the League's decision,[7] notification of all members of the League of the change in policy,[8] amendment of the League's regulations[9] and the sworn assurance from the president of the League[10] convince the Court that the League is sincere in its intent to admit girls into its program on an equal basis with boys.

---

4. Docket Item 25.
5. Docket Item 15, Ex.A.
6. Docket Item 15, Ex. B.
7. Docket Item 15, par. 9.
8. Docket Item 26, par. 27.
9. Docket Item 26, par. 3.
10. Docket Item 17.

The other defendants, who are local charter members of the League, have each submitted affidavits by their presidents indicating that girls are now allowed to participate in all aspects of their Little League programs on an absolute equal basis with boys and that appropriate public notices will be distributed expressly stating that girls are now eligible to participate in these programs.[11] As a result the Court is convinced that these defendants are also sincere in their intent to admit girls into their programs on an equal basis with boys.

Since all the defendants have given public assurance that girls will be allowed to participate in their Little League programs on an equal basis with boys, the question of the constitutionality of their previous policy is rendered moot and will be dismissed from this action.

· · · · · ·

ORDER

For the foregoing reasons, it is ordered

1) that plaintiffs' motion for summary judgment is hereby denied,
2) that defendants' motion to dismiss for mootness is hereby granted, and
3) that plaintiffs' request for punitive damages, litigation expenses, attorneys' fees and court costs is hereby denied.

Questions and Comments

1. What relief did the plaintiff seek in *Rappaport*?
2. What civil rights statutes did the plaintiff invoke on her behalf?
3. What was the constitutional underpinnings for connecting the doctrine of mootness with an advisory opinion?

Presumption of Constitutionality

The following cases illustrate the presumption of constitutionality.

A. **Lewis v. Canaan Valley Resorts, Inc.**, 408 S.E.2d 634, 640-641 (W. Va. 1991)

A skier was injured while leaving a ski lift. At issue was the constitutionality of the Skiing Responsibility Act. The court, speaking to the significance of a presumption of constitutionality, stated as follows:

The generally applicable fundamental principle is that the powers of the legislature are almost plenary: "The Constitution of West Virginia being a restriction of power rather than a grant thereof, the legislature has the authority to enact any measure not inhibited thereby." Syl. pt. 1, *Foster v. Cooper*, 155 W.Va. 619, 186 S.E.2d 837 (1972). [Footnote omitted] Moreover, in light of the constitutionally required principle of the separation of powers among the judicial, legislative and executive branches of state government, *W.Va. Const.* art. V, §1, courts ordinarily presume that legislation is constitutional, and the negation of legislative power must be shown clearly . . . . (p. 635)

11. Docket Items 21, 22, 23 & 24.

B. *City of Billings v. Laedeke*, 805 P.2d 1348, 1349 (Mont. 1991)

A Montana court in 1991 stated the general rule with respect to presumption of constitutionality in simple terms. The court stated:

> A "legislative enactment" is presumed to be constitutional and will be upheld on review except when proven to be unconstitutional beyond a reasonable doubt. *Fallon County v. State* (1988), 231 Mont. 443, 445-46, 753 P.2d 338, 339-40 [citations omitted].

C. *Sedlacek v. South Dakota Teener Baseball Program*, 437 N.W. 2d 866 (S.D. 1989)

This case involved a charge of sexual discrimination. A young girl was seeking to participate in a baseball program previously reserved for boys. The court, in resolving the issue, relied heavily on the presumption of constitutionality. Specifically, the Human Rights Act, which exempted certain educational, social, or recreational programs, was presumed to be constitutional and was not a violation of the Equal Protection Clause, the United States Constitution, or the state constitutional provision against special legislation. The following language adequately expresses this rule:

> There is a strong presumption that the laws enacted by the legislature are constitutional and that presumption is rebutted only when it clearly, palpably and plainly appears that the statute violates a provision of the constitution.

Advisory Opinions

The relationship between the doctrine of mootness and advisory opinions is set forth in *Balmoral Racing Club v. Illinois Racing Bd.* (1992). The case explained the matter succinctly when considering whether to grant a race track certain racing dates, specifically:

> A case becomes moot where the issues raised in and decided by the trial court no longer exist because events have occurred since filing of the appeal which make it impossible for the reviewing court to render effectual relief. (*In re A Minor* (1989), 127 Ill.2d 247, 255, 130 Ill.Dec. 225, 537 N.E.2d 292.) Where a decision reached on the merits cannot result in appropriate relief to the prevailing party, the court has, in effect, rendered an advisory opinion. (*George W. Kennedy Construction Co. v. City of Chicago* (1986), 112 Ill.2d 70, 76, 96 Ill.Dec. 700, 491 N.E.2d 1160.) We do not review cases merely to guide future litigation or to set precedent. *Madison Park Bank v. Zagel* (1982), 91 Ill.2d 231, 235, 62 Ill.Dec. 950, 437 N.E.2d 638. (p. 496)

Judicial Restraint—the Seminal Statement

The Tennessee Valley Association involved a long-range project that looked toward national defense, the regulation of commerce, and the promotion of recreation on a scale seldom envisaged. This was important recreational legislation passed by the United States Congress. The case that upheld the constitutionality of this legislation contained a brief summary of the doctrine of judicial restraint.

The case challenged the constitutionality of the TVA statute. The Brandeis opinion in clear language states the rules that the court has developed for consideration of constitutional issues. The following summary was contained in the concurring opinion of Mr. Justice Brandeis.

· ·

ASHWANDER v. TENNESSEE VALLEY AUTH.
297 U.S. 288, 345-348, 56 S.Ct. 466, 80 L.Ed. 688 (1936)

· · · · ·

The Court developed, for its own governance in the cases confessedly within its jurisdiction, a series of rules under which it has avoided passing upon a large part of all the constitutional questions pressed upon it for decision. They are:

1. The Court will not pass upon the constitutionality of legislation in a friendly, non-adversary, proceeding, . . .
2. The Court will not "anticipate a question of constitutional law in advance of the necessity of deciding it." . . .
3. The Court will not "formulate a rule of constitutional law broader than is required by the precise facts to which it is to be applied." . . .
4. The Court will not pass upon a constitutional question although properly presented by the record, if there is also present some other ground upon which the case may be disposed of. . . .
5. The Court will not pass upon the validity of a statute upon complaint of one who fails to show that he is injured by its operation. [Footnote Omitted]
6. The Court will not pass upon the constitutionality of a statute at the instance of one who has availed himself of its benefits. [Footnote omitted]
7. "When the validity of an act of the Congress is drawn in question, and even if a serious doubt of constitutionality is raised, it is a cardinal principle that this Court will first ascertain whether a construction of the statute is fairly possible by which the question may be avoided." *Crowell v. Benson*, 285 U.S. 22, 62. [Footnote omitted] (pp. 345-348).

STATUTORY INTERPRETATION

Guidelines

In the following case, a roller skater sued the rink operator after she was injured in a collision with another skater. There were no disagreements about the facts in the case. At issue was whether the sport manager was liable for damages under the Roller Skating Act.

In reading the case, note what the court says concerning principles of statutory interpretation.

• •

SKENE v. FILECCIA
539 N.W.2d 531 (Mich.App. 1995)

WAHLS, J.

Plaintiff appeals as of right from the trial court's grant of summary disposition in this negligence action that requires interpretation of the Roller Skating Safety Act (the act), M.C.L. § 445.1721 *et seq.*; M.S.A. § 18.485(1) *et seq.* Plaintiff fractured her wrist after defendant Fileccia ran into her while skating on the rink of defendant Bonaventure Skating Center. The trial court granted defendants' motion for summary disposition pursuant to MCR 2.116(C)(10) on the basis that plaintiff assumed the risk of the dangers inherent in the sport of roller-skating. We affirm.

Plaintiff argues that because there were genuine issues of material fact regarding defendants' compliance with the act, summary disposition was inappropriate. We disagree. A motion for summary disposition pursuant to MCR 2.116(C)(10) tests the factual basis underlying a plaintiff's claim. *Radtke v. Everett*, 442 Mich. 368, 374, 501 N.W.2d 155 (1993). MCR 2.116(C)(10) permits summary disposition when, except with regard to damages, there is no genuine issue regarding any material fact and the moving party is entitled to judgment as a matter of law. *Id.* A court reviewing such a motion, therefore, must consider the pleadings, affidavits, depositions, admissions, and any other evidence in favor of the party opposing the motion and grant the benefit of any reasonable doubt to the opposing party. *Id.* This Court reviews the trial court's grant or denial of a motion for summary disposition de novo as a matter of law. *Garvelink v. Detroit News*, 206 Mich.App. 604, 607, 522 N.W.2d 883 (1994).

The Roller Skating Safety Act provides in pertinent part:

Each roller skating center operator shall do all of the following:

*   *   *   *   *

(b) Comply with the safety standards specified in the roller skating rink safety standards published by the roller skating rink operators association, (1980). [M.C.L. § 445.1723; M.S.A. § 18.485(3).]

While in a roller skating area, each roller skater shall do all of the following:

(a) Maintain reasonable control of his or her speed and course at all times.
(b) Read all posted signs and warnings.
(c) Maintain a proper lookout to avoid other roller skaters and objects.
(d) Accept the responsibility for knowing the range of his or her own ability to negotiate the intended direction of travel while on roller skates and to skate within the limits of that ability.
(e) Refrain from acting in a manner which may cause injury to others. [M.C.L. § 445.1724; M.S.A. § 18.485(4).]

Each person who participates in roller skating accepts the danger that inheres in that activity insofar as the dangers are obvious and necessary. Those dangers include, but are not limited to, injuries that result from collisions with other roller skaters or other spectators.... [M.C.L. § 445.1725; M.S.A. § 18.485(5).]

A roller skater, spectator, or operator who violates this act shall be liable in a civil action for damages for that portion of the loss or damage resulting from the violation. [M.C.L. § 445.1726; M.S.A. § 18.485(6).]

Michigan courts have held that a fundamental rule of statutory construction is to ascertain the purpose and intent of the Legislature in enacting a provision. *Farrington v. Total Petroleum, Inc.,* 442 Mich. 201, 212, 501 N.W.2d 76 (1993). Statutory language should be construed reasonably in the purpose of the statute and its objective should be kept in mind. *Grieb v. Alpine Valley Ski Area, Inc.,* 155 Mich.App. 484, 486, 400 N.W.2d 653 (1986). The first criterion in determining intent is the specific language of the statute. *House Speaker v. State Administrative Bd.,* 441 Mich. 547, 567, 495 N.W.2d 539 (1993). If the statutory language is clear and unambiguous, judicial construction is neither required nor permitted, and courts must apply the statute as written. *Turner v. Auto Club Ins. Ass'n.,* 448 Mich. 22, 27, 528 N.W.2d 681 (1995).

Here, the statute is clear and unambiguous. By participating in the sport of roller-skating, plaintiff accepted the dangers that inhere in the sport insofar as they are obvious and necessary. M.C.L. § 445.1725; M.S.A. § 18.485(5). Specifically included within such dangers are "injuries that result from collisions with other roller skaters." *Id.* Because the act is clear and unambiguous, this Court must apply the act as written. *Turner, supra,* at p. 27, 528 N.W.2d 681. Here, plaintiff was injured from an obvious and necessary danger of roller-skating and may not recover damages. M.C.L. § 445.1725; M.S.A. § 18.485(5).

Plaintiff argues that there were genuine issues of material fact whether defendants breached their respective duties under the act and are liable. However, in construing a statute, the court should presume that every word has some meaning and should avoid any construction that would render a statute, or any part of it, surplusage or nugatory. *Frank v. William A Kibbe & Associates, Inc.,* 208 Mich.App. 346, 350-351, 527 N.W.2d 82 (1995). Plaintiff's construction of the act would render § 5, the assumption of risk clause, surplusage and nugatory.

In addition, plaintiff's construction is inconsistent with the legislative intent of the act. The act's legislative history suggests that its purpose is to prescribe the duties and liabilities of roller-skating center operators and persons who patronize the skating centers. See House Legislative Analysis, SB 134, November 29, 1988, p 1. Roller-skating rink operators claimed that many injuries were caused by the skaters' own inability or carelessness and not by the owners' negligence. See *id.* Because these types of cases resulted in lawsuits that were expensive to defend, insurance rates increased significantly and some owners were having trouble obtaining insurance. See *id.*

This legislative history suggests a harmony with the Ski Area Safety Act,

M.C.L. § 408.321 *et seq.*; M.S.A. § 18.483(1) *et seq.* The object of the in pari materia rule of statutory construction is to carry into effect the purpose of the Legislature as found in harmonious statutes regarding a subject. *Jennings v. Southwood,* 446 Mich. 125, 136, 521 N.W.2d 230 (1994). Statutes should be read in pari materia when they relate to the same person or thing, to the same class of persons or things, or have the same purpose or object. *Richardson v. Jackson Co.,* 432 Mich. 377, 384, 443 N.W.2d 105 (1989).

Here, the language and legislative history of the roller-skating act suggest that it is patterned after the Ski Area Safety Act. Indeed, the relevant clause outlining the assumption of risk that roller-skaters agree to accept when they participate in roller-skating, M.C.L. § 445.1725; M.S.A. § 18.485(5), is virtually identical to that found in the Ski Area Safety Act, M.C.L. § 408.342(2); M.S.A. § 18.483(22)(2). Here, both the Roller Skating Safety Act and the Ski Area Safety Act were designed to cut down on the liability of owners and operators for injuries that result from the inherent dangers of the sports as opposed to the negligence of area operators. Accordingly, the two statutes should be read in pari materia. *Richardson, supra,* at p. 384, 443 N.W.2d 105.

In *Grieb, supra,* at p. 485, 400 N.W.2d 653, the plaintiff brought suit seeking damages for injuries she sustained after being struck from behind by an unknown skier while skiing on a slope at the defendant Alpine Valley Ski Resort. This Court held that a skier accepts the obvious and necessary dangers of the sport and that those dangers include collisions with other skiers. *Id.,* at p. 486, 400 N.W.2d 653. This Court found the Ski Area Safety Act to be unambiguous and that the statute provides that an injury resulting from a collision with another skier is an obvious and necessary danger assumed by skiers. *Id.*

Similarly, in *Schmitz v. Cannonsburg Skiing Corp.,* 170 Mich.App. 692, 693, 428 N.W.2d 742 (1988), the plaintiff's decedent died as the result of injuries incurred when he struck, while downhill skiing, the lone tree growing on a ski slope operated by the defendant. This Court found that it was the purpose of the Ski Area Safety Act to make the skier, rather than the ski area operator, bear the burden of damages from injuries. *Id.,* at p. 695, 428 N.W.2d 742. The assumption of risk clause renders the reasonableness of the skier's or the ski area operator's behavior irrelevant. *Id.,* at p. 696, 428 N.W.2d 742. By the mere act of skiing, the skier accepts the risk that he may be injured in a manner described by the statute. *Id.* The skier must accept these dangers as a matter of law. *Id.*

Here, because the roller-skating act should be read in pari materia with the Ski Area Safety Act, the assumption of risk clause of the roller-skating act renders the reasonableness of the roller-skaters' or the roller-skating rink operator's behavior irrelevant. *Schmitz, supra,* at p. 696, 428 N.W.2d 742. The statutory language is clear and unambiguous and provides that an injury resulting from a collision with another roller-skater is an obvious and necessary danger of roller-skating. *Grieb, supra,* at p. 486, 400 N.W.2d 653. Plaintiff, not the roller-skating rink, must bear the burden of the damages of plaintiff's injuries. *Schmitz, supra,* at p. 695, 428 N.W.2d 742. There is no genuine issue of material fact and defendants are entitled to summary disposition as a matter of law. M.C.L. § 445.1725; M.S.A. § 18.485(5).

Affirmed.

Questions and Comments

1. What language did the court use in describing
   a. the intent of the statute?
   b. the history of the statute?
   c. clarity of language?
   d. references to harmonize other statutes?
2. Are there similarities in managing a skating rink and managing a skiing resort?
3. In the Ski Area Safety Act referred to in this case, if a skier is injured, who is responsible, the skier or the ski area operator? (This kind of statute is often referred to as a recreational user statute.)
4. Does the court allude to a presumption in favor of constitutionality?

Authors' Note:

The following cases give more information on statutory interpretation.

A. ***Halpern v. Wheeldon***, 890 P.2d 562 (Wyo. 1995)

This case involved a suit by a horseback rider who was injured by being thrown from a horse. The defendants in the case were the owners of a riding academy. In the course of its opinion, the court noted the necessity for determining the intent of the legislature and added that if the intent was clear, there was no need to invoke rules of statutory construction.

B. ***Carpenteri-Waddington v. Com'r of Rev.***, 650 A.2d 147 (Conn. 1994)

The court in this case was presented with a question as to the regulation of a cabaret tax. In the course of its opinion, the court iterated the following with reference to finding the intent of the legislature:

> We begin our analysis by noting that it is fundamental that statutory construction requires us to ascertain the intent of the legislature and to construe the statute in a manner that effectuates that intent. *Lauer v. Zoning Commission*, 220 Conn. 455, 459-60, 600 A.2d 310 (1991). In seeking to ascertain the legislature's intent when it crafted chapter 225 of the General Statutes, the admissions, cabaret and dues tax statutes, we follow well established principles of statutory construction and "look to the words of the statute itself, to the legislative history and circumstances surrounding its enactment, to the legislative policy it was designed to implement, and to its relationship to existing legislation and common law principles governing the same general subject matter." *Id.*, at 460, 600 A.2d 310. No one invariable rule of statutory construction is controlling. (p. 151)

C. ***Graven v. Vail Associates, Inc.***, 888 P.2d 310 (Colo.App. 1994)

This case involved a negligence action by a skier who was injured while patronizing a ski resort. In the course of its opinion, the court ruled the significance of determining the overall legislative purpose of the statute in ascertaining the legislative intent:

> Our goal in interpreting any statute is to determine and give effect to the intent of the General Assembly. *United Blood Services v. Quintana*, 827 P.2d 509 (Colo.1992; *First Bank v. Department of Regulatory Agencies*, 852 P.2d 1345 (Colo.App.1993)
>
> A statute should not be interpreted in a piecemeal fashion. Rather, it should be "construed as a whole so as to give consistent, harmonious, and sensible effect to all of its parts." *Massey v. District Court*, 180 Colo. 359, 506 P.2d 128, 130 (1973); *see also Martinez v. Badis*, 842 P.2d 245 (Colo.1992). Thus, the meaning of any one section of a statute must be gleaned from a consideration of the overall legislative purpose. *People v. Alpert Corp.*, 660 P.2d 1295 (Colo.App.1982). (p. 313)

D. ***Orange Park Kennel Club v. State***, 644 So.2d 574 (Fla.App. 1 Dist. 1994)

This was a case that involved the interpretation of a statute that authorized a tax exemption as applied to the factual situation involved in the case. During the course of its opinion, the court announced the appropriate law with respect to an agency's construction of a statute. Namely,

> An agency's construction of a statute which it administers is entitled to great weight and will not be overturned unless the agency's interpretation is clearly erroneous; the agency's interpretation need not be the sole possible interpretation or even the most desirable one; it need only be within the range of possible interpretations. *Pan Am. World Airways, Inc., v. Florida Pub. Serv. Comm'n*, 427 So.2d 716 (Fla.1983), *Department of Labor & Employment Sec. v. Bradley*, 636 So.2d 802 (Fla. 1st DCA 1994). Furthermore, a statute which creates a tax exemption must be strictly construed against those who seek the exemption. *State ex rel. Wedgworth Farms, Inc. v. Thompson*, 101 So.2d 381 (Fla.1958). Any doubt in interpreting the exemption must be resolved in favor of the state. *State ex rel. Szabo Food Servs., Inc. v. Dickinson*, 286 So.2d 529 (Fla. 1973). (p. 576)

E. ***Wilderness World v. Dept. of Revenue***, 882 P.2d 1281 (Ariz.App. Div 1 1993)

An amusement tax assessment was the issue involved in the above case. The sport business involved the providing of guided river-rafting trips. For our purposes we should note the court's statement of the rule of *ejusdem generis*. Specifically,

> Under the principle of *ejusdem generis*, "where general words follow the enumeration of particular classes of persons or things, the general words should be construed as applicable only to persons or things of the same general nature or class of those enumerated." *White v. Moore*, 46 Ariz. 48, 53-54, 46 P.2d 1077, 1079 (1935); *see also*

Alvord, 69 Ariz. at 291, 213 P.2d at 366. That is, for an activity to be taxable under a general clause that follows a list of specific items, the activity must be of the same kind, class, or character. A.R.S. section 42-1214(A)(1) lists twenty-one specific business classifications, none of which include an activity similar in nature or kind to guided river rafting trips. Wilderness World is engaged in the activity of "conducting, leading, guiding, and outfitting" a river trip. None of the activities listed remotely resemble a tour, expedition, journey, or voyage similar to the rafting trips. Thus, the amusement tax cannot be extended to the services provided by Wilderness World. (p. 1284)

F. ***Stamper v. Kanawha County Bd. of Educ.***, 445 S.E.2d, 238 (W.Va. 1994)

In general, this case stands for the proposition that the last statutory enactment should govern if statutory provisions cannot be harmonized.

G. For a case involving the statement of the "plain meaning" rule, the reader is referred to *Pelletier v. Fort Kent Golf Club*, 662 A.2d 220 (Me. 1995).

SUMMARY AND OTHER REMARKS

In *Johnson v. Rapid City Softball Ass'n*. (1994), the Supreme Court of South Dakota ruled that softball was *not* included in the list of activities named in the recreational users statute. Therefore, the statute did not provide immunity for the softball association that had leased the softball field where a player (plaintiff) was injured or for the city that owned the field. A sport manager should know about these types of statutes, how they are interpreted, and when constitutional litigation can be avoided. There is usually a good reason that courts do not consider constitutional questions at a given time. A listing of rules that the courts have found helpful include the following:

1. Generally speaking, there must be a case or a controversy. See Art. III of the United States Constitution. State constitutions tend to have the same requirement.
2. Courts do not look with favor on advisory opinions. Federal courts do not issue them; state courts are generally in accord.
3. Courts will not consider a question that has become moot. The exceptions occur when the factual situation is capable of being repeated and when matters of grave public interest are concerned.
4. The constitutional issue must be raised at the first available opportunity. Rationale: This gives the lower court an opportunity to express itself on the issue.
5. There is a presumption in favor of constitutionality of a statute. Rationale: This presumption defers to the legislative branch when the constitutionality of a statute is at issue; defers to the constitution as a basic document in other cases.
6. The courts will not generally examine the wisdom of legislation. Rationale: This offers deference to the principle of separation of powers.
7. Courts will not frame a constitutional issue broader than the demands of

a particular fact situation. Rationale: This sharpens the constitutional question.

8. The courts will not decide a constitutional issue in advance of the necessity of deciding it. Rationale: This is consistent with the adversary system and permits further exploration and study by the lower courts.

9. Courts will not permit one to question the constitutionality of a statute if that person has taken advantage of the benefits of the statute. Rationale: This avoids the danger that the issue will not be presented with vigor.

10. A party that raises the constitutional issue must have "standing." Rationale: The party must stand to gain or lose.

11. The courts will not decide a constitutional issue if the case can be decided on other grounds. Rationale: This reserves constitutional issues for cases that mandate the court's attention.

12. When interpreting a document (constitution, statute, administrative rule or regulation, or contract) the primary task is to determine the intent of the drafters of the instrument.

13. The intent of the framers—legislative body, administrative body, or individual—in the drafting of adocument is ascertained by the plain meaning of the words used, together with rules that have been developed when there is doubt as to the intent. Specifically,

    a. the more recent statute will govern when there is more than one statute involved.

    b. various provisions in the statute need to be considered as a whole. This is known as harmonizing the statute.

    c. the statute should be interpreted so as to effectuate its purpose.

This could be you - check your response

Mr. Jones will not prevail in this case. He does not have standing to file suit. Also, there was no violation of a state statute noted in this case. He will not gain or lose on the religious question.

REFERENCES

Cases

Anthony v. Columbus Board of Education, 655 N.E.2d 406 (Oh. 1995).

Ashwander v. Tennessee Valley Auth., 297 U.S. 288, 56 S. Ct. 466, 80 L. Ed. 688 (1936).

Balmoral Racing Club v. Illinois Racing Bd., 603 N.E.2d 489 (Ill. 1992).

Brenden v. Independent Sch. Dist. 742, 342 F. Supp. 1224 (D. Minn. 1972).

Carpenteri-Waddington v. Com'r of Rev., 650 A.2d 147 (Conn. 1994).

Caso v. New York State Public High Sch., 434 N.Y.S. 2d 60 (N.Y. 1980).

City of Billings v. Laedeke, 805 P.2d 1348 (Mont. 1991).

Florida High Sch. Activities Ass'n v. Bradshaw, 369 So. 2d 398 (Fla. App. 1979).

Graven v. Vail Associates, Inc., 888 P.2d 310 (Colo.App. 1994).

Guelker v. Evans, 602 S.W.2d 756 (Mo. 1980).

Halpern v. Wheeldon, 890 P.2d 562 (Wyo. 1995).

In Re: Sports Complex in Hackensack Meadowlands, 300 A.2d 337 (N.J. 1973).

Johnson v. Rapid City Softball Ass'n, 514 N.W.2d (S.D. 1994).

Lewis v. Canaan Valley Resorts, Inc., 408 S.E.2d 634 (W. Va. 1991).

Orange Park Kennel Club v. State, 644 So.2d 574 (Fla.App. 1 Dist. 1994).

Pelletier v. Fort Kent Golf Club, 662 A.2d 220 (Me. 1995).

Rappaport v. Little League Baseball, Inc., 65 F.R.D. 545 (U.S.D.C. Del. 1975).

Sedlacek v. South Dakota Teener Baseball Program, 437 N.W.2d 866 (S.D. 1989).

Shearer v. Perry Community Sch. Dist., 236 N.W.2d 688 (Iowa 1975).

Skene v. Fileccia, 539 N.W.2d 531 (Mich.App. 1995).

Stamper v. Kanawha County Bd. of Educ., 445 S.E.2d 238 (W.Va. 1994).

Wilderness World v. Dept. of Revenue, 882 P.2d 1281 (Ariz.App.Div. 1 1993).

Other References

Roller Skating Safety Act M.C.L. 445, 1721 et seq. M.S.A. § 18, 485 (1) et seq.

Singer, N. J. (1985) *Southerland statutory construction* (4th Ed) Callaghan & Company, Wilmette, IL.

CHAPTER 15

DUE PROCESS

INTRODUCTION

Failure to allow for due process can be expensive in terms of time and money. The *University of Nevada v. Tarkanian* (1994) case discussed in this chapter lasted 17 years and resulted in an award of over $150,000.

The concept of due process of law is one of the more basic tenets of American jurisprudence. The origin of due process goes back to the time of Magna Carta. A copy of the more salient provisions of Magna Carta is reproduced in this chapter.

The term *due process* carries with it the notion of fair play. Arbitrary and capricious actions are taken without consideration of the facts or circumstances. Such actions are not fair. Substantive due process protects against state action that is arbitrary and capricious. Procedural due process involves both a notice and a fair hearing. These concepts are explained in this chapter.

A sport manager understands fair play. A sport manager also understands the need for decisive action that is not arbitrary and capricious. Due process is relevant to employment questions and to other management decisions.

IN THIS CHAPTER YOU WILL LEARN:

The constitutional provisions that provide for due process

The types of due process

The twofold division of procedural due process

The component parts of adequate notice

The component parts of a fair hearing

The basic premise behind the requirements for substantive due process

The extent to which the due process clause of the Fourteenth Amendment to the United States Constitution has incorporated the protections set forth in the first ten amendments

The relationship between the due process clause and the police power of a state

The constitutional basis for police power

KEY WORDS: *due process, procedural due process, notice, fair hearing, substantive due process, Magna Carta, Fifth Amendment, Fourteenth Amendment, incorporation theory, police power, administrative law, Tenth Amendment*

This could be you!

The Joneses developed an interest in polo. Together with a group of their more affluent friends, they organized a polo club. In pursuing this newly found interest, the Jones Polo Club, Inc., leased an athletic field belonging to Friendly University, which was controlled and financed by the state. The lease agreement provided, among other things, that users of the college's facility shall accord due process to all individuals having claims against the user.

Reginald Fitzhugh, a participant in a polo game, was struck by a polo stick under what Reginald considered as highly suspicious circumstances. The wielder of the stick, Bo Buford, was angry because of a business deal that had gone sour. He had openly threatened Reginald at the pregame luncheon.

University due process regulations require a public hearing, participation by counsel, the right to present witnesses, and the right to a stenographic report of the proceedings. Does the lease obligation to provide due process encompass each of the rights that are described in the university's administrative procedures?

ORIGINS, SOURCES, TYPES, ELEMENTS

Origins

The historic origin of due process of law is as broad as the development of law itself. The story of political philosophy is far too complicated to be undertaken here. Two provisions of a famous document, known as the Magna Carta (England, June 1215), will be included. Specifically,

> No free man shall be seized, or imprisoned, or disseised, or outlawed, or exiled, or injured in any way, nor will we enter on him or send against him except by the lawful judgment of his peers, or by the law of the land. [Chapter 39]
>
> We will sell to no one, or deny to no one, or put off right or justice. [Chapter 40]

The common law in England was conversant with due process. It is not surprising, therefore, that due process has been influenced by the natural law, namely, a dictate of right reason.

CONSTITUTIONAL SOURCES

The United States Constitution has two provisions that guarantee due process. These provisions are found in the Fifth and Fourteenth Amendments. The appropriate language reads as follows:

Fifth Amendment:

No person shall. . . be deprived of life, liberty, or property, without due process of law; . . .

Fourteenth Amendment:

nor shall any State deprive any person of life, liberty, or property, without due process of law; . . .

State constitutions also provide for due process. The language of state constitutions vary somewhat.

Kentucky Constitution, Sec. 2.:

Absolute and arbitrary power over the lives, liberty and property of freemen exists nowhere in a republic, not even in the largest majority.

Wyoming Constitution, Art. 1, Sec. 6:

Due process of law. No person shall be deprived of life, liberty or property without due process of law.

Governments limited - Fifth Amendment. There is no language in the Fifth Amendment that specifies what government's power is limited. However, judicial decisions have made it clear that the Fifth Amendment limits the powers of the United States government only. A recent court decision in *Pitt v. Pine Valley Golf Club* (1988) reaffirms this conclusion.

The case in question involved an individual who attempted to buy a home but was forestalled in his effort by a requirement that all homeowners be members of a private golf club. The golf club owned all of the land within the club area. Following denial of membership in the golf club, the individual filed suit, alleging a denial of due process of law. In resolving the issue, the court distinguished between the Fifth and the Fourteenth Amendments to the United States Constitution and also explored the concept of state action with reference to the Fourteenth Amendment. The scope of protection accorded by the Fifth Amendment is delineated by this language in *Pitt v. Pine Valley Golf Club* (1988):

Plaintiff asserts claims under the due process and equal protection clauses of the Fifth Amendment to the United States Constitution. However, plaintiff does not allege any action by the federal government. The Fifth Amendment is a limitation on the federal government and has no reference to state actions... . (p. 781)

Governments limited — Fourteenth Amendment. The Fourteenth Amendment, by its express terms, prohibits certain state action. In some instances the prohibition will be considered as state action when the action of private individuals or groups is so closely intertwined with governmental action as to partake of the nature of governmental action. *See Pitt, supra.* Some states have Civil Rights Statutes that grant broader rights than those granted by the United States Constitution. This will be discussed further in the section under substantive due process.

DECISIONAL LAW

A. University of Nevada v. Tarkanian (1994)

When time and money are considered, due process is important. The *Tarkanian* case began in 1977 and ended in 1995, with an award of $150,725.58. Jerry Tarkanian, former basketball coach at the University of Nevada at Las Vegas, sued the university and its board of regents after he was suspended in 1977, following several NCAA rule violations.

His suits against UNLV and the NCAA alleged that his federal due process rights were violated. After years of court battles, the United States Supreme Court ruled against UNLV and reversed the lower court's judgment against NCAA. The District Court awarded Tarkanian costs and attorney fees of $150,725.58, plus interest. UNLV appealed; however, the Supreme Court of Nevada affirmed the decision (*University of Nevada v. Tarkanian*, 879 P.2d (Nev. 1994)).

Plaintiff Tarkanian, under Civil Rights Law 42 U.S.C.A. 1983, 1988, could recover attorney fees and costs. (Civil rights legislation is discussed in a later chapter of this book.) 42 U.S.C. 1983 requires a state action. UNLV is a state agency.

B. Davenport v. Casteen (1995)

In the following case, Ted Davenport was an employee of a private foundation. In this 1995 case, Davenport charged violation of due process rights in connection with his discharge. Davenport was an employee of VSAF, a charitable corporation established to provide a source of funding for athletic grants in and at the University of Virginia. VSAF also managed a private university-affiliated golf course. John Casteen was the university president. Davenport was terminated following an investigation of violation of NCAA rules.

In the following court account, the due process concepts of *notice* and a *hearing* were evident. In this case, the president, defendant Casteen, was granted summary judgment. Davenport's dismissal from a private organization did not violate his constitutionally protected rights.

Only the due process portion of the case is used here. There were other claims of defamation and tortuous interference. The Court entered summary judgment for president Casteen and athletic director Copeland. In reading the case, remember a contract of employment is Davenport's property. A public employee with a property interest in continued employment must be given notice and a fair hearing.

· ·

DAVENPORT v. CASTEEN
878 F.Supp. 871 (W.D.Va. 1995)

· · · · · · · · ·

In May of 1991, the University reported to the National Collegiate Athletic Association (NCAA) that it had discovered possible violations of NCAA rules prohibiting payment of excess benefits to student athletes by the University or an affiliated association—VSAF. Casteen named an inquiry group to investigate the allegations, and VSAF began its own investigation. Davenport retained counsel to protect his interests. In furtherance of its investigation, the inquiry group questioned Davenport orally on two occasions, both of which were transcribed by a court reporter. (Low Aff.Def.'s Ex. M at 2.) Copies of the transcript were then provided to Davenport for correction, clarification, or supplementation. (Low Aff.Def.'s Ex. M at 2.) Later, because Davenport had health concerns, the inquiry group agreed to submit written questions to him to which he was permitted to respond in kind. (Low Aff.Def.'s Ex. M at 3.) On completion of its investigation, the inquiry group, without making formal charges, compiled a report which included findings regarding "possible NCAA violations." The inquiry group provided Davenport with an advance copy of the report for comment. (Low Aff.Def.'s Ex. M at 3.) The report was then forwarded to Casteen.

From its own investigation, VSAF concluded that Davenport had breached his employment contract. By letter of April 8, 1992, VSAF notified Davenport's counsel of its conclusion, specified the conduct that it considered wrongful, and invited a response:

> [T]he VSAF would like to give Mr. Davenport an opportunity to be heard with respect to the above transactions, and any others if he so chooses.... Accordingly, Mr. Davenport is invited to appear before the VSAF Executive Committee at 12:30 PM on April 16, 1992, at the Boar's Head Inn, to address these issues.

(Letter from Daniel to Davenport's Counsel of 4/8/92, Def.'s Ex. 0 at 2-3.) Davenport declined to attend the designated April 16, 1992, hearing. On April 23, 1992, Casteen delivered a letter to Davenport informing him that he was "directing VSAF and [Services Foundation] to initiate termination proceedings" and, in a public meeting of the University Board of Visitors, Casteen disclosed the findings of the investigation. The Board of Visitors, in turn, adopted a resolution endorsing Davenport's termination, and that same day VSAF and Services Foundation terminated him.

· · · · · · · · ·

[In the suit, Davenport filed claims against university president, Casteen, and athletic director, Copeland. The following discussion concerns *res judicata*, a bar against further action on the same issue.]

....In this suit, Davenport's pleadings, as amplified by his memoranda and submissions to the court, allege, in effect, that Casteen—the

University president—discharged and defamed Davenport without affording him due process and that Copeland—the University athletic director—conspired with Casteen to that end.[5] Under the circumstances, the court agrees with those courts that have found a sufficient identity of interests among co-conspirators to find that the privity requirement has been satisfied. Having found the privity requirement satisfied, Davenport's claims against Copeland are, like Davenport's claims against Casteen, barred by res judicata.[6]

III

The court also finds that Davenport's termination implicates no property or liberty interests because he was employed and discharged by private foundations that lacked the essential purposes or nexus to satisfy the state action requirement of 42 U.S.C. § 1983, and also because Casteen and Copeland lacked the authority and the coercive power to terminate Davenport. Any defamatory statements by Casteen and Copeland made at the time of Davenport's discharge from private employment, therefore, did not infringe Davenport's liberty interest, and if actionable, were actionable under state law.

[A discussion follows which indicates that the foundation is a private entity and not a state actor. 42 U.S.C.A. 1983 applies to a state entity. Tarkanian filed under 42 U.S.C.A. 1983.]

. . . . .

. . . . VSAf is a private, non-stock corporation governed by an independent board of trustees [footnote omitted] and funded exclusively from private charitable contributions. Services Foundation is, likewise, a private, non-stock corporation with its own independent board. Although, in the words of Davenport's counsel, "the University acted as a [paying] agent for [the foundations] in paying his salary under his [employment] contract [with the foundations]," (Def.'s Ex. D at 19.), "the University never agreed to pay

5. Davenport asserts that Casteen was "never sued" in his individual capacity. (Pl.Resp. in Opp'n to Mot. to Dismiss at 20.) That assertion is, at best, an egregious construction of the facts. In *Davenport v. VSAF*, No. 5129-L. (Albemarle County Circuit Court, 1993), Davenport sought to recover $1,000,000 from Casteen and argued in response to Casteen's demurrer that Davenport's claims against Casteen "*in his personal capacity*" were proper and that Casteen was "*individually liable*" to Davenport. (Def.'s Ex. E at 7; Def.'s Ex. B at 2, (emphasis added))

6. Davenport also contends that he did not have a full and fair opportunity to litigate in state court because the Circuit Court dismissed his claims on demurrer, and there has been no judgment on the merits. Davenport confuses the rule. A state court of competent jurisdiction reviewed his allegations and found them to be legally deficient. The Virginia Supreme Court found no error in the Circuit Court's judgment. The Circuit Court's judgment is on the merits and is final. *See supra,* note 4.

[*Res judicata*: the issue has been decided; a bar against further action on the same issue.] Res judicata does not come into play only when a plaintiff survives a demurrer and subsequently suffers an adverse judgment. Presumptively, Davenport had a full and fair opportunity to litigate his claims. He simply lost. Moreover, Davenport was the master of his pleadings, as well as the selection of his forum. State courts have jurisdiction to hear actions pursuant to 42 U.S.C. § 1983. Davenport chose, however, to split his cause of action, and after having lost on the merits, he now seeks to resurrect his "cause of action" in this forum.

[Davenport] anything. All it agreed to do was to continue to be the paymaster." (Def.'s Ex. F at 33, 34.) [Footnote omitted.] In the court's view, the performance of that single administrative function does not supply the nexus or interdependence essential to transform private employment into government employment. *See generally National Collegiate Athletic Ass'n v. Tarkanian,* 488 U.S. 179, 109 S.Ct. 454, 102 L.Ed.2d 469 (1988).

Relying primarily on *Wisconsin v. Constantineau,* 400 U.S. 433, 91 S.Ct. 507, 27 L.Ed.2d 515 (1971), Davenport contends that because Casteen acted under color of law as president of the University when Casteen allegedly defamed him and because he lost employment in connection with the alleged defamation, he was deprived of a "liberty" interest. Although the court agrees that Casteen acted under color of state law when he allegedly defamed Davenport, the court rejects Davenport's conclusion that Casteen deprived him of a liberty interest.

When given the opportunity to clarify the holding of *Wisconsin v. Constantineau,* the Supreme Court unequivocally stated in *Paul v. Davis,* that it "has never held that the mere defamation of an individual ... was sufficient to invoke the guarantees of procedural due process *absent an accompanying loss of government employment.*" 424 U.S. 693, 706, 96 S.Ct. 1155, 1163, 47 L.Ed.2d 405 (1976) (emphasis added). As Davenport was not terminated from government employment, his liberty interests have not been infringed.

Moreover, even though Casteen was a "state actor" in his capacity as president of the University, and presumptuously "directed" the foundations to "initiate termination proceedings," Casteen had not even a semblance of authority to order Davenport's termination. Each of those foundations has a board with both the authority and the responsibility to make its own decisions, a fact recognized by Davenport in his earlier state proceedings:

> The Articles of Incorporation and the Bylaws of VSAF demonstrate that it is a separate, independent corporation. [Nothing] make[s] ... VSAF subservient to the will of [the University] president John Casteen. That VSAF may have jumped when Casteen snapped his fingers does not mean that it had a legal obligation to do so.... Casteen directed an independent corporation to terminate one of its long term employees. The Board of the corporation apparently lacked the intestinal fortitude to question Mr. Casteen's right to tell them what to do.

(Def.'s Ex. D at 29, 30.) Thus, Davenport has only demonstrated that Casteen had sway with the boards. But more than the practical ability to influence action is required. The state actor must possess and exercise coercive power. . . . .

IV

Even assuming that Davenport's termination implicated constitutionally protected property and liberty interests, it is clear that Davenport was afforded all the process he was due. Casteen's decision was not in haste. Davenport's termination followed a nearly year long investigation. Davenport was asked for his version of events, and he was afforded an opportunity to attend a hearing to respond to concerns raised by the investigation. Davenport chose not to attend and instead filed suit in state court on the day of his termination. Before filing his present suit, Davenport at no time asked for an additional hearing to clear his name. In fact, Davenport's refusal to attend the VSAF hearing and respond to concerns raised by the investigation and his immediately filed state court action seem to have been designed to avoid the kind of confrontation and discourse he now alleges were necessary to protect his property and liberty interests.

A. Property Interests

Ordinarily, a public employee with a property interest in continued employment must, before termination, be given "oral or written notice of the charges against him, an explanation of the employer's evidence, and an opportunity to present his side of the story." *Cleveland Bd. of Educ. v. Loudermill,* 470 U.S. 532, 546, 105 S.Ct. 1487, 1495, 84 L.Ed.2d 494 (1985). The pretermination hearing need not finally resolve the matter: "It should be an initial check against mistaken decisions—essentially, a determination of whether there are reasonable grounds to believe that the charges against the employee are true and support the proposed action." *Id.* at 545-46, 105 S.Ct. at 1495. The process afforded Davenport satisfied the minimum requirements of due process and then some.

Although the University inquiry group and VSAF provided Davenport with several opportunities to "present his side of the story," Davenport asserts that those opportunities failed to satisfy due process. Specifically, Davenport has submitted his former counsel's affidavit that he was not given a "predetermination" opportunity to be heard, but was offered a "postdetermination formality" instead.[11] (Pickford Aff.Pl.'s Ex. C at 3.) Davenport confuses the requirements of due process. A pretermination (not predetermination) hearing must be provided.[12] It was.

·   ·   ·   ·   ·   ·

B. Liberty Interests

Due process is a flexible concept grounded in notions of fundamental fairness. *Walters v. Nat'l Ass'n of Radiation Survivors,* 473 U.S. 305, 320, 105 S.Ct. 3180, 3188-89, 87 L.Ed.2d 220 (1985). When the government discharges

11. The Pickford and Rhodes affidavits challenge the fairness and objectivity of the process leading to Davenport's termination. Rule 56 of the federal Rules of Civil Procedure provides, however, that affidavits "shall set forth such facts as would be admissible in evidence, and shall show affirmatively that the affiant is competent to testify to the matters stated therein." FED.R.CIV.P. 56(e). The Pickford and Rhodes affidavits are so generously interspersed with hearsay and so lacking in foundation that they fail to satisfy even the minimal standards of Rule 56. They are, therefore, disregarded.

12. Davenport challenges the substance of the opportunity for a hearing provided to him by VSAF because, he asserts, VSAF had already decided to fire him. Davenport's perception of VSAF's intentions, without more, does not show that the opportunity presented was meaningless. Neither do vague recollections of "UVA or VSAF officials" predicting that Davenport would "have to go" show that the hearing was fatally flawed.

an employee and disseminates information that stigmatizes his good name, fairness dictates that the state afford him an opportunity to clear his name. *See Board of Regents of State Colleges v. Roth,* 408 U.S. 564, 573, 92 S.Ct. 2701, 2707, 33 L.Ed.2d 548 (1972). Davenport, however, filed suit the same day he was terminated, having failed to take advantage of the pretermination process afforded to him and without requesting a posttermination name clearing hearing. His conduct, therefore, made the very kind of process he claims he was due impractical, if not impossible.

Under most circumstances, a plaintiff's failure to request a name clearing hearing should prevent him from complaining that one was not afforded. *See Howze v. City of Austin,* 917 F.2d 208 (5th Cir.1990); *Freeman v. Mckellar,* 795 F.Supp. 733 (E.D.Pa.1992). The circumstances of this case are even more compelling. Davenport's failure to request a hearing is preceded by his deliberate bypass of a pretermination hearing and succeeded by his immediate filing of suit in state court. If it was possible for Davenport to receive a name clearing hearing prior to filing suit, it became a practical impossibility once suit was filed. Fairness has two sides. It does not permit Davenport to complain of circumstances that were of his own making.[13]

V.

For the reasons stated above, the court finds that res judicata bars this action; that Davenport's discharge from two private foundations implicates no property or liberty interests; and that, even if property or liberty interest were implicated, they were protected by the process afforded Davenport. Accordingly, the court will enter summary judgment for Casteen and Copeland.

Questions and Comments

1. What can a sport manager learn about due proceess from this case?
2. Did Davenport have notice? Did he have a fair hearing? Why or why not?
3. What were Davenport's property interest and liberty interest?
4. Was VSAF a public entity? What difference did it make?

TWO TYPES OF DUE PROCESS

Due process has been described as either procedural or substantive.

13. Although Davenport's complaint alleges defamation, no actual statements made by Casteen or Copeland are detailed. Even in his most recent filings, Davenport has refrained from specifically identifying a false statement made about him. For instance, Davenport presents evidence of defamation through broad, general statements such as "many of the allegations Casteen made ... were either flatly untrue or presented in a false and defamatory light," and "it was insinuated [by Casteen] that Ted Davenport had been caught embezzling." (Pickford Aff.Pl.'s Ex. C at 2.) Davenport further identifies the matters about which he was defamed, including taking a pay increase and receiving other funds. (Pl.'s Resp. to Mot. to Dismiss at 7.) However, Davenport provides no actual text of a statement made by Casteen or Copeland which is allegedly false. By neglecting to identify actual false statements, Davenport failed to show a deprivation of a liberty interest. [Citation omitted]

Primary attention has been given to procedural due process. Substantive due process, although well recognized, is receiving less emphasis. The characteristics of each of the two types are described below.

Procedural Due Process

Procedural due process is usually described as having two components. The first is notice; the second is a fair hearing.

Notification: Decisional law, case A. The purpose of notice as a due process component is to advise a party litigant as to what, when, and where. One example of a deficient notice is stated in the case that immediately follows.

This case involved the suspension of a trainer by a racing commission. The suspension was the result of the trainer's selling 10 electrical shocking devices. Although somewhat complicated in its reasoning, the court was clear on the subject of notice and its relationship to due process. The due process portion of the case is included here.

....

BENOIT v. LOUISIANA STATE RACING COMM'N
576 So.2d 578 (La. Ct. App. 1991)

Before SCHOTT, KLEES and CIACCIO, JJ.CIACCIO, Judge.

The Louisiana State Racing Commission appeals a trial court judgment reversing its decision suspending trainer Norris J. Benoit, Jr.

On February 24, 1989, Benoit, who worked as a trainer at Delta Downs Race Track in Vinton, Louisiana, allegedly met with an undercover state police trooper on the race track grounds and agreed to sell him ten electrical shocking devices for $200.00. Benoit advised the officer that he would have to follow him to another location off race track grounds for delivery of the devices. The trooper followed Benoit to a residence on Louisiana Highway 3063 outside Vinton City limits. There Benoit went into a garage, got the devices and then came out and gave them to the trooper, exchanging them for $200.00 in cash.

Upon receipt of a report from the Louisiana State Police regarding Benoit's alleged illegal activities, the stewards held a hearing on July 6, 1989. Following the hearing, the stewards issued a ruling charging Benoit with a violation of LAC 35:1801 B(7), finding his "conduct detrimental to the best interest of racing." The stewards referred the matter to the Louisiana Racing Commission for further consideration and Benoit appealed the ruling.

The Commission sent a notice to Benoit informing him that a hearing on the appeal would be held on October 25, 1989. The notice stated Benoit had violated LAC 35:1001B(7) rather than LAC 35:1801B(7).

At the hearing before the Commission, Benoit's attorney moved to dismiss the complaint for the Commission's failure to provide Benoit with correct and adequate notice of the alleged violation against him. Benoit's counsel also complained that the police report relied on by the stewards in issuing their ruling erroneously stated the date of the alleged illegal activity as occurring on April 18, 1989 rather than February 24, 1989. The Commission denied Benoit's motion and after conducting a full hearing it upheld the stewards' ruling. The Commission found that Benoit had violated LAC 35:1705 by selling the devices. In addition to suspending Benoit for five years, the Commission also fined him $5000.00 and denied him access to all race tracks and off-track wagering facilities under its jurisdiction during the period of his suspension. Benoit filed a petition for judicial review of the Commission's decision in Civil District Court in Orleans Parish.

In reversing the decision of the Commission the trial judge gave the following reasons for judgment:

> This matter came for trial on the Petition for Judicial Review filed by plaintiff. This Court is of the opinion that the penalties imposed by defendant are excessive due to the fact that plaintiff violated no law. There was no evidence presented that showed that electrical or mechanical devices were possessed by plaintiff *on association premises*, as prohibited by LAC 35:1.1705. Additionally, the plaintiff did not receive proper notice of hearing of a violation of LAC 35:I.1801B(4) and (7). Without proper form and notice, plaintiff's right to due process was violated by the conduct of the hearing and the decision of the Commission. (In defendant's memorandum for new trial, on page two, it admits to these errors and deficiencies. It also seems to suggest to the court that such problems are insignificant. However, this Court finds them to be of such a magnitude as to warrant reversal of the decision of the Commission). In light of these deficiencies, the decision of the Commission was clearly erroneous.

· · · · ·

The trial judge considered the notice deficient and concluded that without proper notice of the violation of LAC 35:1801B(7), the Commission had violated Benoit's right to due process by conducting the hearing relevant to and suspending him pursuant to that rule. We cannot say that this conclusion by the trial judge was clearly wrong. However, we cannot say that the evidence in the record is insufficient, as a matter of law, to have supported the charge of LAC 35:1801B(7). Under these circumstances, we conclude the trial judge was in error not to have remanded the matter to the Louisiana State Racing Commission for further proceedings. LSA-R.S.49:964G.

· · · · ·

AFFIRMED IN PART; AMENDED IN PART AND REMANDED.

Questions and Comments

1. Was the notice in the above case deficient? Why or why not?
2. Were Benoit's rights violated? Explain your answer.

Notification: Decisional law, case B. Procedural due process in general, and notice in particular, have been described in a case decided in 1993 by the United States District Court for the Eastern District of Wisconsin. *See Hartland Sportsman's Club v. Town of Delafield* (1993). This was a case whereby a property owner sought a conditional use permit to operate a gun club on his property. The suit alleged a violation of due process under a §1983 action. The court discussed procedural due process in a rather thorough fashion:

....

HARTLAND SPORTSMAN'S CLUB v. TOWN OF DELAFIELD
827 F. Supp. 562 (E.D. Wisc. 1993)

Hartland argues that it did not receive adequate notice of the procedures to be followed at the town board's December 12, 1991, administrative hearing and thus was not able to prepare adequately for the hearing. In particular, Hartland contends that it did not receive timely notice of its right to call witnesses and present evidence at the hearing. Hartland does not challenge the procedures actually employed at the hearing.

"Parties whose rights are to be affected are entitled to be heard; and in order that they may enjoy that right they must first be notified." *Fuentes v. Shevin*, 407 U.S. 67, 80, 92 S.Ct. 1983, 1994, 32 L.Ed.2d 556 (1972). The requirements of due process vary depending upon the situation. "What due process requires is merely fair treatment under the circumstances." *Karnstein v. Pewaukee School Bd.*, 557 F.Supp. 565, 567 (E.D.Wis. 1983).

The right to notice and an opportunity to be heard "must be granted at a meaningful time and in a meaningful manner." *Id.* Notice must be "reasonably calculated to apprise interested parties of the pendency of the action," *Mullane v. Central Hanover Bank & Trust Co.*, 339 U.S. 306, 314, 70 S.Ct. 652, 657, 94 L.Ed. 865 (1950), so that they can adequately prepare. *Memphis Light, Gas, Water Div. v. Craft*, 436 U.S. 1, 14, 98 S.Ct. 1554, 1563, 56 L.Ed.2d 30 (1978). Moreover, "notice must inform the person whose protected interests are threatened of an opportunity to present objections at 'some kind of hearing' preceding the final deprivation of those interests." *Birdsell v. Litchfield Bd. of Fire & Police Commissioners*, 854 F.2d 204, 207 (7th Cir.1988) (citing *Wolff v. McDonnell*, 418 U.S. 539, 577-78, 94 S.Ct. 2963, 2985, 41 L.Ed.2d 935 (1974)).

The town board notified Hartland of the December 12, 1991, hearing by certified mail approximately 30 days before the scheduled hearing and via publication. Both forms of notice specified the nature of the hearing—to review and consider alterations or changes to the 1968 conditional use permit. Also, Hartland had detailed notice as early as May 1991 of the "pendency of the action" contemplated by the town board in connection with the conditional use permit. This is so in view of the exhaustive notice and resolution issued by the town board and served upon Hartland. (Defendants' Exs. 133 and 145)

The adequacy of the defendants' efforts in providing the plaintiff with meaningful notice and an opportunity to be heard is further supported by the fact that the entire process of modifying the 1968 conditional use permit leading up to the December 12, 1991, hearing took approximately seven months (May 1991-December 1991). At the numerous hearings held at the initiation of the defendants, Hartland, through its officers and members, was able to present its position and was represented by counsel. The conduct by the defendants over this seven month period demonstrates that Hartland was fully aware that it would be provided with an opportunity to present objections at the December 12, 1991 hearing and illustrates that the defendants showed sufficient attention to Hartland's rights and concerns.

Although Hartland did not receive notice of the procedures to be followed at the December 12, 1991, hearing until the day of the scheduled hearing, the record shows that officers and members of Hartland, in fact, testified and were represented by counsel for Hartland, who also spoke. The fact that Hartland failed to request an adjournment or continuance of the December 12, 1991, hearing on the ground that it needed more time to prepare, or on any ground, suggests that the notice provided by the defendants sufficiently apprised Hartland of the nature of the hearing and its right to be heard such that Hartland could adequately prepare.

On the basis of this record, I am not persuaded that the defendants' delay in notifying Hartland of its entitlement to call witnesses and present evidence at the hearing infringed the plaintiff's constitutional rights. Hartland has the burden to establish that the right to procedural due process under the Fourteenth Amendment was violated. See Parratt v. Taylor, 451 U.S. 527, 535, 101 S.Ct. 1908, 1912-13, 68 L.Ed.2d 420 (1981) (in any action under 42 U.S.C. § 1983, the plaintiff must establish that it was deprived of rights, privileges or immunities secured by the Constitution or laws of the United States); New Burnham Prairie Homes v. Village of Burnham, 910 F.2d 1474, 1479 (7th Cir. 1990) (same). The plaintiff has failed to satisfy its burden of proof with respect to its procedural due process claim under § 1983; thus, this claim will be dismissed, with prejudice. (pp. 567-568)

Questions and Comments

1. In your opinion, was the plaintiff given adequate time to allow for procedural due process?
2. Why did the court dismiss the claim?
3. What can the sport manager learn from this case about adequate, timely notice?

Fair hearing: Basic principles. The requirements for a fair hearing vary with the individual case. This basic principle was announced in summary form by Mr. Justice Stewart in *Cafeteria Workers v. McElroy* (1961). *Cafeteria Workers* does not involve a typical sport management case. The case involved a worker in a defense plant who was denied a security clearance. The nature of the employment factored into the equation insofar as due process was concerned. Two things are worthy of note. First, the principle of law enunciated is relevant to the sport management industry. Second, the principle enunciated has received the approval of the highest court in the land; consequently, the principle is central to a fair hearing. Specifically,

> The very nature of due process negates any concept of inflexible procedures universally applicable to every imaginable situation.... "'[D]ue process,' unlike some legal rules, is not a technical conception with a fixed content unrelated to time, place and circumstances." It is "compounded of history, reason, the past course of decisions...." Joint Anti-Fascist Refugee Committee v. McGrath, 341 US 123, 162, 163, 95 L ed 817, 848, 849, 71 S Ct 624 (concurring opinion). (6 L. Ed.2d 1230, 1236)

Fair hearing: Impartial administrative tribunal. An administrative tribunal is one way a hearing may be offered. *Hadges v. Corbisiero* (1991) poses the question of impermissible bias in an administrative hearing. The federal judge articulates the general rule to the effect that a member of an administrative tribunal is not disqualified because of prior involvement in the case. Just because a person has been previously involved does not mean that person cannot be fair.

The case referred to involves a challenge based on due process to a disciplinary proceeding against a plaintiff connected with the racing industry. The challenge alleged that the hearing officer had a previous connection with the case, which constituted impermissible bias. Note the suit involves a 42 U.S.C.A. 1983 action. The challenge of the case was direct and to the point. The court's introductory and concluding remarks concerning due process are as follows:

••

HADGES v. CORBISIERO
760 F.Supp. 388 (S.D. N.Y. 1991)

·   ·   ·   ·   ·   ·

On October 9, 1986 plaintiff drove the number two horse in the eighth race at Roosevelt Raceway. While warming up his horse, plaintiff was heard to yell, "Get the seven," to an unidentified patron. The patron was never caught and the seven horse won the race. Plaintiff was charged by the New York State Racing and Wagering Board (the "Board") with violating Board rule 4119.9(a), which prohibits "conduct detrimental to the best interests of racing." Prior to his hearing before a Board hearing officer, plaintiff filed an article 78 proceeding in state court that was eventually dismissed. The hearing was then held and on November 9, 1987 the Board adopted the hearing officer's recommendation that plaintiff's license be suspended for six months. Plaintiff appealed this ruling via a second article 78 proceeding, but in December 1988 the Board's determination was upheld. Plaintiff then began serving his suspension, but before its conclusion the instant action was filed.

Plaintiff's Supplemental Complaint alleges that his due process rights were violated, in contravention of 42 U.S.C. § 1983, due to Board policies permitting Board employees to serve as investigators, prosecutors, and hearing officers in administrative proceedings. . . . .

.   .   .   .   .

.... Obviously, the Board only brings a formal proceeding after conducting an investigation. ....

In conclusion, we find that the Boards' procedures did not violate plaintiff's due process rights. In addition, plaintiff was able to present two challenges to the Board's actions via article 78 proceedings, although neither was successful, before being suspended. Notwithstanding this conclusion, however, we recognize that the procedures employed were hardly perfect. It obviously would remove any specter of impropriety if independent administrative judges or arbitrators could be appointed. Unfortunately, such a policy might strain an already overburdened state economy. ....

.... we find that defendant Corbisiero is entitled to summary judgment. The clerk will enter judgment for the defendant.

.   .   .   .   .

Questions and Comments

1. In this case, there was a hearing board that investigated and heard the case.
2. A sport manager might have many policies such as those relating to sexual harassment, discrimination, or drug use. These policies might require a hearing before an administrative body. According to this case, is an administrator disqualified from a hearing body because she or he has previous knowledge of the case? Explain.

Fair hearing: The right to counsel. Mr. Justice White, speaking for the majority in *Goss v. Lopez* (1975) addressed the right of counsel. *Goss* involved the suspension of a student and is considered a landmark case. In the course of its opinion, the court stated:

> We stop short of construing the Due Process Clause to require, countrywide, that hearings in connection with short suspensions must afford the student the opportunity to secure counsel, to confront and cross-examine witnesses supporting the charge, or to call his own witnesses to verify his version of the incident. Brief disciplinary suspensions are almost countless. To impose in each such case even truncated trial-type procedures might well overwhelm administrative facilities in many places and, by diverting resources, cost more than it would save in educational effectiveness. Moreover, further formalizing the suspension process and escalating its formality and adversary nature may not only make it too costly as a regular disciplinary tool but also destroy its effectiveness as part of the teaching process. (42 L.Ed.2d 725, 740)

The majority opinion was careful to point out, however, that this holding was limited to the factual situation before the court.

> We should also make it clear that we have addressed ourselves solely to the short suspension, not exceeding 10 days. Longer suspensions or expulsions for the remainder of the school term, or permanently, may require more formal procedures. Nor do we put aside the

possibility that in unusual situations, although involving only a short suspension, something more than the rudimentary procedures will be required. (42 L.Ed.2d 725, 740)

It is apparent, therefore, that a situation may be serious enough to require the participation of counsel in order to meet the demands of due process.

Authors' Note

Other issues frequently posed in connection with a fair hearing are (a) the right to call witnesses, (b) the right to cross-examine witnesses, (c) the right to have witnesses testify under oath, (d) the right to a public hearing, and (e) the right to a legible transcript of the hearing. Each of these so-called components of a fair hearing should be measured within the context of an administrative proceeding. An administrative law operates under the assumption that we are dealing with fair-minded individuals who possess a degree of expertise. Consequently, it is believed to be preferable to proceed without the rigid formalities of the judicial system.

Questions and Comments

1. If a sport manager suspended an employee 7 days for bringing drugs on the job, would such an action require the same due process as dismissing the employee?
2. Does it make a difference if the sport manager is director of a recreation complex at a state-owned park? Read the following sections before you answer.

Substantive Due Process

Shocking the court's conscience. In the case referenced below, the plaintiff, a director of a university sport complex, challenged a change in his job responsibilities. This was a §1983 civil rights claim. Among the charges was one that alleged a violation of substantive due process. The plaintiff in this case believed that an adverse employment decision was based on political affiliation. Various points of law concerned with substantive due process were discussed. In denying plaintiff's substantive due process claim, the court in *Cabrero v. Ruiz* (1993), p. 597-98, reasoned along the following lines:

> Muñiz Cabrero also alleges that Defendants' arbitrary and capricious actions have violated his constitutional rights to substantive due process. It is true that substantive due process protects employees from state action that is arbitrary and capricious. [Citations omitted.] However, substantive due process has been disfavored as a basis for constitutional redress. [Citations omitted.] It is a doctrine that should be applied with caution and restraint. [Citation omitted.] It does not protect an individual from all government action that infringes liberty or property interests in violation of some law. [Citation omitted.] Rather, substantive due process protects against government action that shocks the conscience. [Citations omitted.] (p. 597)

Violation of fundamental rights. Cabrero, supra, at pp. 597-98, also discussed the violation of fundamental rights in its relationship to substantive due process.

A substantive due process violation is one that transgresses a fundamental constitutional right. [Citations omitted.] In the case before the Court, Muñiz Cabrero cannot point to a fundamental right that has been transgressed. To the extent that he is alleging a lost property interest, this Court above held that he has no claim because he has lost neither his employment nor any property interest he may have therein. [Citations omitted.] To the extent that he is alleging a deprivation of his rights to free speech and association, it is coextensive with his First Amendment claim and is addressed in that context further below. [Citations omitted.] Lastly, to the extent that he is alleging a deprivation based on Defendants' defamatory statements, such defamatory statements do not reflect fundamental constitutional rights. [Citation omitted.] Accordingly, Muñiz Cabrero's claim for the violation of his substantive due process rights is also without merit. (p. 598)
(Affirmed 1994)

SUMMARY

The United States Constitution provides for due process of law in the Fifth and Fourteenth Amendments. The Fifth Amendment limits the powers of the national government; the Fourteenth Amendment limits the powers of the state government.

Neither the Fifth nor the Fourteenth Amendment accords protection against individual action.

Individual state constitutions generally provide protection for individual rights by way of a due process clause. Such a clause may be more or less restrictive than the comparable clauses in the United States Constitution.

Due process of law is divided into two component parts: procedural due process, and substantive due process.

Procedural due process is usually divided into notice and fair hearing. The notice required has to do with what the lawsuit is all about and when the response time is expected.

Substantive due process limits the powers of all three branches of government. The limits imposed protect against arbitrary, willful, and capricious action.

Due process will vary depending upon the fact situation before the court.

Due process from a procedural standpoint mandates fundamental fairness.

The due process required in administrative hearings is less than that required in judicial proceedings. Administrative proceedings tend to be more informal and take advantage of the expertise of the individuals involved.

The due process clause of the Fourteenth Amendment incorporates most of the protections as accorded in the first eight amendments of the United States Constitution. It is generally stated that the Second and Seventh Amendments have not been formally incorporated.

The police power is the greatest power reserved to the states under the Tenth Amendment to the United States Constitution. The police power is a source of power and is limited by the protection accorded to individuals under the due process clause.

The protection accorded through due process is threefold: namely, life, liberty, and property.

Due process dates back at least to Magna Carta and assures individuals of being judged according to the law of the land.

Corporate entities are assured of due process insofar as property rights are concerned.

An individual's contract of employment is considered a property right.

It is very important for sport managers to remember the basic elements of procedural due process: notice and a fair hearing.

This could be you - check your response

The polo club's lease agreement provided that the users of the college facility should have due process. In the broadest sense this means that the polo club is responsible for a hearing and adequate notice of the hearing.

This does not necessarily mean that the provisions of the university's due process regulations must be met. For example, the representation by counsel or a public hearing may not be mandatory. What is notice and what is a fair hearing will vary with each case. It also should be recalled that protections against state agencies are different from those against private agencies.

REFERENCES

Cases

Behagen v. Amateur Basketball Ass'n of U.S., 884 F.2d 524 (10th Cir. 1989).

Benoit v. Louisiana State Racing Comm'n, 576 So. 2d 578 (La. Ct. App. 1991).

Cabrero v. Ruiz, 23 F.3rd 607 (1st Cir. 1994), 826 F. Supp. 591 (D. P.R., 1993).

Cafeteria Workers v. McElroy, 367 U.S. 886, 6 L. Ed.2d 1230, 81 S. Ct. 1743 (1961).

Davenport v. Casteen, 878 F.Supp. 871 (W.D.Va. 1995).

Davis v. McCormick, 898 F.Supp. 1275 (C.D. Ill. 1995).

De Silva v. Hartack, 559 N.E.2d 51 (Ill. App. Ct. 1990).

Ersek v. Township of Springfield, Delaware County, 822 F. Supp. 218 (E.D. Pa. 1993).

Estate of Jackson v. City of Rochester, 705 F. Supp. 779 (W.D. N.Y. 1989).

Goss v. Lopez, 419 U.S. 565, 42 L. Ed.2d 725, 95 S. Ct. 729 (1975).

Hadges v. Corbisiero, 760 F. Supp. 388 (S.D. N.Y. 1991).

Hartland Sportsman's Club v. Town of Delafield, 827 F. Supp. 562 (E.D. Wisc. 1993).

Interliners Lounge Social Club v. Department of Consumer Affairs, 574 N.Y.S.2d 190 (N.Y. App. Div. 1991).

Kansas Racing Mgmt. v. Kansas Racing Comm'n, 770 P.2d 423 (Kan. 1989).

Mertik v. Blalock, 983 F.2d 1353 (6th Cir. 1993).

Moore v. Hyche, 761 F. Supp. 112 (N.D. Ala. 1991).

Mueller v. Regents of Univ. of Minn., 855 F.2d 555 (8th Cir. 1988).

Parker v. Corbisiero, 825 F. Supp. 49 (S.D. N.Y. 1993).

Pitt v. Pine Valley Golf Club, 695 F. Supp. 778, (D. N.J. 1988).

Richardson v. City of Albuquerque, 857 F.2d 727 (10th Cir. 1988).

University of Nevada v. Tarkanian, 879 P.2d (Nev. 1994).

Model Codes, Restatements, and Standards

Ky. Const. §2.

Tenn. Const. art. I, §8.

Wyo. Const. art. I, §6.

W.Va. Const. art. III, §10.

CHAPTER 16

THE FIRST AMENDMENT

INTRODUCTION

The First Amendment to the United States Constitution has long been considered to be as basic and fundamental to our conception of ordered liberty. This chapter briefly explores typical cases in sport management that involve freedom of speech, freedom of religion, the right of association, and the right of privacy. This chapter will aid the reader in appreciating the value a democratic society attaches to basic limitations on the powers of the national government.

A democratic society values the exchange of ideas. Such an exchange becomes even more valuable when approached from the standpoint of the rights of minorities. Such rights include not only the right to be heard but also the right to become the majority. One should always remember that the right to be heard is accentuated when the opinion expressed is sharply divergent from the opinion held by the majority. People have a right to disagree on trivial things and a right to disagree on matters that are of great importance.

Legal scholars have been influenced by political theorists and have frequently expressed their belief in freedom of speech, press, the right to associate, and the right to be left alone. This chapter will help the sport manager understand how these principles impact the sport management industry.

The First Amendment was a prohibition against government intrusion into the individual's rights and freedoms: "Congress shall make no law." Many sport managers, for example, public school athletic directors, facilities and special events managers, recreation managers, and state parks managers, work for governmental entities. Application of the First Amendment to these governmental entities is easily made.

In other areas of sport management, such as sport association administration, rehabilitation centers, and health clubs, the implications for governmental action are not as easily made. However, if a private entity receives a governmental grant, it may be difficult to distinguish between a wholly private sport business and a governmental agency. The courts have made recent decisions in which private clubs may be considered public entities. For example, the court's decision in *Roberts v. United States Jaycees* (1984) clearly articulated the right of association (a First Amendment right) and the amendment's impact on a private club (the Jaycees):

> In weighing the nature of the First Amendment rights asserted against a state's right to prevent gender-based discrimination against its residents, the Supreme Court ruled that the state could bar certain private clubs from discriminating. Although the First Amendment clearly protects family relationships and small groups, which the Court labeled "intimate associational freedom," "large business enterprises" like the Jaycees were considered "remote... from this constitutional protection" because they involved only "expressive" associations (p.620). The large and unselective nature of the Jaycees was held to bar its reliance on First Amendment grounds to rationalize its discrimination against women.
>
> (*The Oxford Companion to the Supreme Court of the United States of America*, 1992, p. 679)

In reading the following chapter, note the applications of the First Amendment to a variety of governmentally operated sport management enterprises as well as to privately owned sport businesses.

IN THIS CHAPTER YOU WILL LEARN:

The scope of the limitations on the powers of government as expressed by the first ten amendments

The relationship between the First Amendment and principles of a democratic society

The impact of these basic principles on the sport management industry

The rights that are said to emanate from the First Amendment although not directly expressed therein

---

KEY WORDS: *symbolic speech, restricted speech, defamation, public forum, city ordinance, freedom of religion, Fourteenth Amendment, Bill of Rights, freedom of association, freedom of the press, right to privacy*

This Could Be You!

The Joneses hired a distant cousin to run the bowling alley that they had added to the fitness center. Katherine Karnes was college educated, had a pleasant personality, and seemed to be a stable person. After several years of employment, she developed an interest in church activities. Following her new personal religious emphasis, Katherine, the managing director of the bowling alley, had numerous confrontations with the Joneses concerning religious beliefs, specifically, the policies that did not prevent drinking and did allow bowling on Friday evenings (her Sabbath). Her disagreements were reduced to writing and published in an open letter to the editor of the local newspaper prior to her resignation as managing director.

An argument and a near physical encounter preceded the managing director's resignation. Subsequently, the Joneses were faced with a lawsuit that alleged a coerced resignation that was occasioned in part by the free speech activity of the managing director.

Discuss the First Amendment issues in this situation.

JUDICIAL DECISIONS

Freedom of Speech

A classic Supreme Court decision, *United States v. O'Brien* (1968) discusses freedom of speech from a constitutional perspective. In the case, David O'Brien burned his Selective Service registration certificate to protest the armed forces and Selective Service. There was a national statute that made such an act a crime. In simple terms, the United States Congress had the power to raise an army. Therefore, Congress had the power to write statutes to support that effort.

The issue in dispute in *O'Brien* was the constitutionality of a federal statute. Did the statute making his act a crime abridge his constitutional right of free speech (freedom of expression)? The lower court ruled that the statute was unconstitutional. However, the Supreme Court ruled that the statute making it a crime to destroy the draft certificate was not in violation of O'Brien's right to free speech. O'Brien's act was symbolic speech. The statute was constitutional on its "face" and "as applied."

In the holding in this case, the Supreme Court eloquently expressed several tests that are important for the sport manager. In *O'Brien* the Court articulated a two-part test to determine whether particular conduct is sufficient to bring certain elements of communication into focus in order to trigger the First Amendment issues:

1. Was there any intent to convey a particularized message?
2. Is it likely that those who view the message will understand it?

For example, the wearing of gang identifiable clothing may have a particularized message. Gang members will probably understand the message. This clothing could be considered a form of speech.

Sport managers should be aware that there are limitations on speech:

1. "Fighting words" are not protected speech (*Chaplinski v. New Hampshire, 1942*).
2. Advocacy of imminent lawlessness, shouting "fire" in a crowded place (*Chaplinski v. New Hampshire,* 1942), is not protected speech.
3. Obscenity is not protected speech (*Bethel v. Fraser*, 1986).

The sport manager should have no problem restricting patrons'

1. fighting words

2. words that incite panic
3. obscene language.

Expressions on apparel, such as T-shirts, that might prove to be disruptive, gang related, or obscene would probably be handled by the courts on a case-by-case basis. A prudent sport manager would not personally want to engage in speech that is restricted (obscene language) or offensive to different genders, races, ages, or persons with disabilities.

A sport manager would want to be tolerant of minority opinions of others. In the *O'Brien, supra,* and *Tinker v. Des Moines (1969)* cases, there were expressions of minority opinions against the Vietnam War hostilities. Later, many citizens were against the Vietnam War. In the *Tinker* case, armbands were worn by public school students to protest the Vietnam War. The courts ruled that this was a form of constitutionally protected free speech.

The wearing of sports team clothing or logos was disallowed in a school dress code, in *Jeglin v. San Jacinto Unified School District* (1993). In this case the court found that the ban could not be justified at the junior high school level as the school district failed to demonstrate the presence of gangs and the disruption of the school's environment.

Does the *Jeglin* decision have implications for the wearing of sports apparel in a private sports club that has had acts of violence between gang members at the club? (Answer: Yes. Explain this answer.)

Other court decisions have supported school dress codes (*Oleson v. Board of Education,* 1987). The courts weigh the actual disruption and the need to keep order against the severity of the dress code and the student's constitutional rights. In the *Jeglin* case the statute was found to violate the First Amendment.

For the sport manager in a private business, the restrictions on speech may be more liberal because the sport business as a private entity is not covered under constitutional restrictions that govern a "state actor" like a public school or state park.

The case that follows examined the issue of freedom of speech as it related to a city ordinance restricting the operating hours of an entertainment establishment. This was a Massachusetts Supreme Court decision. To determine whether the statute violated the First Amendment and was unconstitutional, the Court examined whether the statute was narrowly tailored without unduly infringing on the right of free speech. This specific issue was raised in Atlanta, Georgia, just prior to the 1996 Olympics, when Atlanta passed a statute that limited "suspicious activities" in parking lots.

CITY OF BOSTON v. BACK BAY CULTURAL ASS'N.
635 N.E.2d 1175 (Mass. 1994)

LYNCH, Justice.

This case raises the issue whether Ordinances, Title 14 § 430A (1979) (ordinance) of the city of Boston (city), restricting the hours of operation of establishments holding entertainment licenses, violates the First Amendment to the United States Constitution. A Superior Court judge determined that the ordinance did not violate the First Amendment. The defendant Back Bay Cultural Association, Inc. (Back Bay), appealed. . . . We reverse.

1. **Background.** We summarize the facts from the parties' statement of agreed facts. On May 31, 1979, Loft Twenty-one Association, Inc. (The Loft) [footnote omitted] filed a complaint for declaratory and injunctive relief seeking to have the ordinance declared unconstitutional. On July 16, 1979, a Superior Court judge issued a preliminary injunction enjoining the city from enforcing the ordinance against The Loft. The ordinance provided:

"No person shall between the hours of Two O'clock, ante meridian, and Six O'Clock, ante meridian, in any club, theater, restaurant, retail store, or in any other place of business or place of public assembly, offer, provide, perform, or set-up, or suffer another to offer, provide, perform, or set-up any entertainment or music, live, recorded, or mechanical, including but not limited to entertainment or music provided by means of a radio, television, tape recorder, phonograph or projector, except that the showing of a motion picture commenced prior to Twelve-thirty O'Clock, ante meridian may continue uninterrupted until its conclusion provided that the same is concluded prior to Three O'Clock, ante meridian." [Footnote omitted.]

In granting the preliminary injunction, the judge noted that there is "a substantial question as to whether the ordinance is sufficiently narrowly tailored to advance the legitimate governmental interests involved without unduly infringing upon both the right to engage in and to be exposed to expressive activity protected by the first amendment".

.   .   .   .   .

. . . We conclude . . . . that the ordinance violates the First Amendment.

2. **First Amendment.** The Supreme Court has recognized that "in a public forum the government may impose reasonable restrictions on the time, place, or manner of protected speech, provided the restrictions 'are justified without reference to the content of the regulated speech, that they are narrowly tailored to serve a significant governmental interest, and that they leave open ample alternative channels for communication of the information.'" . . .

.   .   .   .   .

. . . The fundamental principle underlying the requirement of content neutrality is that "government may not grant the use of a forum to people whose views it finds acceptable, but deny use to those wishing to express less favored or more controversial views." . . . . . The judge [of the lower court] ruled that the ordinance was content neutral because the city's purpose in creating the ordinance, i.e., maintaining quiet streets at certain hours, was completely unrelated to the content of any form of expression. [Footnote omitted.] We agree.

.   .   .   .   .

b. *Narrowly tailored to serve a substantial governmental interest.* Government "ha[s] a substantial interest in protecting its citizens from unwelcome noise." . . .

. . . At oral argument, the city conceded that the time restriction would apply to a "piano player" in a hotel, a harpist in a function room, a "rock band" at a concert hall, as well as a television in the lobby of a hotel. . . .

. . . . . .

Thus, not all forms of entertainment affected by the ordinance, including several types conceded by the city to be affected, create the type of noise the city legitimately seeks to eliminate. Therefore, the ordinance is not narrowly tailored because it adversely affects entertainment that does not produce the unwanted secondary effects. *Renton, supra*, 475 U.S. at 52, 106 S.Ct. at 931.

. . . . . .

Judgment reversed.

Questions and Comments

1. Was the statute in this case overly broad?
2. What has been the Supreme Court's opinion or restrictions that may be placed on speech?
3. What was the principle based on the content neutrality of speech?
4. What sport businesses might have "noise" restrictions noted in this case? Would midnight basketball leagues involve city noise regulations?
5. What was the holding in this case related to free speech?

Crime, Sport, and Free Speech Issues

A *JOHPERD* article "At Risk Youth, the Phoenix Phenomenon" (McCann & Peters, 1996) discusses recreational programs that have targeted and reduced the number of juvenile crime offenders. In Phoenix a curfew of 10:00 p.m. for youngsters under 16 was established; for 16- and 17-year-olds, 12:00 midnight was set.

In August of 1993, 467 youths were picked up for violations. Telephone calls were made to 105 of these young people, and 80 of them took advantage of the recreation program provided. The program was on its way to success.

In the Phoenix program, funding was both public and private. Partnerships were established between governmental and private agencies. Some funding was local; some was state or national. Funding agencies included Mothers Against Gangs; Nestles; Arizona State University; and Phoenix Parks, Recreation, and Library. A major funding for programs, $63,000, came from the Arizona Supreme Court, a state entity. Golf courses charged 25 cents per round and generated $150,000 for the program. The overall goal was to reduce crime. Recreational activities among other programs were vehicles used to accomplish the goal. Following implementation of several activities, according to the article, there were 10% fewer juvenile crime arrests during the programming period June 1993-April 1994. Although violent crime citywide rose 6.7%, juvenile crime was up only .5%. The program was considered successful because crime was reduced (McCann & Peters, 1996). The implication for sport managers is that managed recreational sport activities might have some potential to deter crime.

There are implications here for First Amendment issues and their applications for sport management situations. The first issue, free speech, might be abridged by a curfew. In some places parents, charging violation of free speech, have filed suit against curfews.

The second issue is the recreation program funding issue. Sport may be publicly or privately funded. When state agencies fund programs, constitutional issues regarding state action may come into consideration. If a sport complex that was privately owned took government money, like the Supreme Court grant in the Phoenix situation, would the issues that present themselves in the First Amendment—free speech—be viewed differently? Would a private entity (like a sport complex) then come under the standards expected of governmental entities (like schools)? An in-depth discussion of this particular issue is beyond the scope of this book. A variety of issues includes such topics as procedural and substantive rights guaranteed by First, Fourth, Fifth, and Fourteenth Amendments, which apply only to conduct attributable to government agencies. Whether the sport program is considered legally public or private may depend on the issue and the depth and/or source of funding.

Questions and Comments

1. Are curfews for youth a trend?
2. Could the constitutionality of curfew statutes be challenged? What would be the point of law? Refer back to the *City of Boston* case.
3. Are there valid reasons for offering nighttime sport activities for youth?
4. Could a school or a private sport complex more closely regulate apparel (symbolic speech) that would be considered gang related? (Answer: A private sport complex might regulate speech more closely. A private entity [a sport business, a church school] that accepts federal funds might come under federal enactments.)

Authors' Note

A sport manager who is a public employee does not relinquish First Amendment rights to comment on matters of public interest just because he or she is a public employee.

The United States Supreme Court held in *Connick v. Meyers* (1983) that it is necessary to balance the rights of the individual citizen and the interest of the public employer in promoting the efficiency of the public services the public business provides. The key term is whether the manager's speech involves a matter of *public concern*.

Freedom of Religion

In the *City of Boston* case, reference was made to a public forum for free speech. In the following note case, the legal issues of (a) a public forum and (b) freedom to distribute religious literature at a public forum are important to the sport manager. In reading the quote ask, "Should a sport business allow the distribution of religious literature on the parking lot? Is the sport business required by constitutional law to allow such distribution?"

In this case the Krishnas, a religious group, brought suit against the New

Jersey Sports and Exhibition Authority. They challenged the policy against distribution of literature and other goods and the solicitation of money. One point of law was whether the sport complex or the adjoining parking areas were intended or used as a public forum for the distribution of the religious literature.

The Establishment Clause of the First Amendment forbids the creation of a single official religion. Also, government should not act in such a way that promotes a particular religion. Allowing one religion to "speak" or to hand out literature and not allowing another religion to do so violates this principle.

Read the following case for implications for the manager of a sport complex. In the case, members of a religious organization brought suit to challenge the New Jersey Sport and Exhibition Authority policy that prohibited the distribution of literature and the solicitation of money.

INTERNATIONAL SOCIETY FOR KRISHNA CONSCIOUSNESS v. N.J. SPORTS AND EXPOSITION AUTHORITY, 532 F.Supp. 1088 (D.N.J., 1981)

The major issue presented is whether the Sports Complex, as it was built and operated at the time of trial, was a "forum" at all.

In those cases where the point has been dealt with, the Supreme Court has not hesitated to make clear that merely because someone wants to express views, or proselytize, or colporteur, or carry signs and banners, it does not follow that they have a constitutional right to do so whenever and however and wherever they please. When that premise has been advanced, the Supreme Court has rejected it vigorously, forthrightly and repeatedly. It has emphasized that the United States Constitution does not forbid a State to control the use of its own property for its own lawful and nondiscriminatory purposes. It has said that it is a mistake to think that whenever members of the public are permitted to enter a place owned and operated by government, then that place becomes a "public forum" for purposes of the First Amendment.

The point is significant because when the government property is not a "public forum", it need only demonstrate a rational basis for the restraints imposed or, put another way, show that they are not arbitrary, capricious or invidious.... [p. 1098]

In 1977, the race track operated for 280 racing days, with net racing revenues of more than $84.4 million....

In the same year, there were 14 professional football games (i.e., Giants) and 21 professional soccer games (i.e. Cosmos) for a total of 35 events involving the two major users, plus 9 other events for a grand total of 44 days.... For that year, stadium revenues (before Stadium expenses) were $6,357,821 which averages $145,000 a day for each of the 44 days....

Certainly, it cannot be successfully maintained, as a matter of local law under the enabling Act, or as a matter of constitutional law under the First Amendment, that the Authority is obliged now and at once to provide a public forum at which plaintiff and others may engage in the activities they desire. All of the cases on the subject deal with what exists, and none the court is aware of remotely suggests that where a facility in existence is not a public forum, there is some undefined obligation either to make it one or to provide one.

The record in this case is clear that neither the race track nor the stadium is designed, built, intended or used as a public forum. The same is true of the blacktop automobile parking areas bordering them. For this reason, neither the plaintiffs nor any others desiring to carry on like solicitation for their own ends may legitimately advance the claims made here. [p. 1100]

. . . . . .

Authors' Note

The reader may wish to consult *Paulsen v. Gotbaum* (1992). A religious organization wanted to distribute their literature. This was a case in which religious freedom was subjected to a free speech analysis. Especially relevant for a sport manager is the language on pages 828-829 of that opinion. After reading the case, ask, "How should a manager of a sport complex or of a park respond to a request to distribute religious literature?"

••

PAULSEN v. GOTBAUM
982 F.2d 825, 828-29 (2d Cir., 1992)

(B)*Constitutionality of the Distribution and Solicitation Rules*

As recently as last term, the Supreme Court reiterated its position on the regulation of speech in a public forum. The Court held that:

> "[E]xpressive activity, *even in a quintessential public forum*, may interfere with other important activities for which the property is used. Accordingly, the Court has held that the government may regulate the time, place, and manner of expressive activity, so long as such restrictions are content-neutral, are narrowly tailored to serve a *significant* governmental interest, and leave open ample alternatives for communication."

. . . . . .

While a rule of this kind must be narrowly tailored to serve a significant governmental interest, it need not be the least restrictive or least intrusive means of serving that interest. Rather, it simply must promote a substantial governmental interest that would be achieved less effectively without the rule. *Ward, supra*, 491 U.S. at 798.

The rules here involved are narrowly tailored. They restrict soliciting or leafletting only during special events, when the larger crowds may cause congestion and create more litter. The rules here serve the interest of avoiding an intrusion upon the people who attend the special events and of avoiding litter during the special events.

Special events in New York City parks do draw large crowds which increase litter in the parks. In this respect, the instant case is analogous to *Heffron, supra*, 452 U.S. 640. There, the Supreme Court upheld a rule requiring groups at a state fair to solicit or distribute literature from a booth, so as to control the crowds and avoid disorder. The Court stated that the governmental interest involved "must be assessed in light of the characteristic nature and function of the particular forum involved." *Id.* at 651. The Court also observed the similarities between the fair and a public street in that both have been used historically for assembly and communication of ideas. The differences, however, were significant. The fair is a temporary event which attracts many visitors for a short period. In this context, the flow of the crowd and the safety to the public become significant government interests. It is a valid governmental interest to protect the safety and even the *convenience* of persons in public forums. *Id.* at 650-51. (p. 828-829)

Freedom of Association

In the following case the Superior Court of Massachusetts ruled that a fishing and hunting club was a place of public accommodation, resort, or amusement that was within the antidiscrimination provision of the First Amendment. The Concord Rod and Gun Club, Inc. refused to admit a female into full membership of the club. A portion of the holding in that case is in the following paragraph.

....

CONCORD ROD AND GUN CLUB v. MASSACHUSETTS COMM. AGAINST DISCRIMINATION,
524 N.E. 2d 1364, 1367 (Mass. 1988)

· · · · · ·

There is no First Amendment impediment to application to the Club of G.L. c. 272, §§92A and 98. Constitutionally protected freedom of association may be understood in two distinct senses; the right "to enter into and maintain certain intimate human relationships," and a right "to associate for the purpose of engaging in those activities protected by the First Amendment—speech, assembly, petition for the redress of grievances, and the exercise of religion." *Roberts v. United States Jaycees*, 468 U.S. 609, 617-618, 104 S.Ct. 3244, 3249-3250, 82 L.Ed.2d 462 (1984). See *New York State Club Ass'n v. City of New York*, ____ U.S. ____, 108 S.Ct. 2225, 99 L.Ed 2d ____ (1988); *Directors of Rotary Int'l v. Rotary Club of Duarte*, ___ U.S. ____, 107 S.Ct. 1940, 1945, 95 L.Ed. 2d 474 (1987). The commissioner's findings leading to the conclusion that the Club does not have a selective process for admittance to membership establish with equal force that application of the anti-discrimination statute to the Club does not impair the members' rights of intimate association. Furthermore, there is no basis to conclude that admittance of women to the Club's membership will burden the male members' rights of expressive association. The statute does not require that women be admitted simply because they are women. It only prevents their exclusion simply because they are women. See *New York State Club Ass'n v. City of New York, supra,* _____ U.S. at _____, 108 S. Ct. at 2234.

    Judgment affirmed.

Questions and Comments

1. *Concord Rod and Gun Club, Inc.* involved the refusal to admit a female to full membership in the club.
2. Freedom of association did not permit the exclusion of females from membership in the Rod and Gun Club.
3. Did this case rely on any other case referenced in this chapter?
4. Are there applications of this freedom of association concept to homosexuals? Why or why not?

Freedom of the Press

    Congress shall make no law . . . abridging freedom of speech or of the press . . ..

    Since the Constitution was adopted before the invention of the telephone, motion pictures, television, cable network, the Internet, and satellite communication, a body of law has developed around the licensing of various communications formats. In the future, statutes and case law will continue to evolve even as sports networks begin to own sports teams and to own publishing companies. The merger of the sports and communications worlds will continue. "Vertical integration is where the sport industry is going, with companies like International Management Group who represent the athletes, who conduct the events, as well as the TV production company setting the trend" (David Stotlar, personal communication, March 5, 1996). In the future, more sport managers will be employed by the megacorporations and communication networks. Their company-owned teams will make the headlines and then publish the headlines about their teams. The promotion of sport through the media will increase gate receipts for that sport. A new view of freedom of the press may be taken.

    The framers of the First Amendment envisioned freedom of the spoken and printed word. However, freedom of speech does not mean all speech in all situations. Obscenity is restricted speech as noted in many court cases. Obscenity recently has been an issue for statutes regulating the Internet (Communication Decency Act, 1996). As noted earlier, fighting words and words that incite panic in crowds are also limited.

    The limitations put on the press are often defined by court cases. The issue in the following case was defamation. The coach of a college team, the plaintiff, might be viewed as a public figure. The coach claimed that the publishers of Preview Publications defamed her by saying, ". . . coach Marian Washington usually finds a way to screw things up" (Defendant Vitale's Ex. A, p. 6). Read the *Washington v. Smith* (1995) case and follow the points of law made by the court.

The following description of defamation serves as an introduction to the case:

> Defamation is an intentional false communication either published or publicly spoken, that injures another's reputation or good name. Holding up a person to ridicule, scorn or contempt in a respectable and considerable part of the community; may be criminal as well as civil. (*Black's Law Dictionary*, 1990, p. 417)

Defamation includes both libel and slander. Libel is a written permanent form of defamation as contrasted with slander which is oral defamation.

> To recover against a public official or public figure, plaintiff must prove that the defamatory statement was published with malice. Malice as used in this context means that it was published either knowing that it was false or with a reckless disregard as to whether it was true or false. *New York Times Co. v. Sullivan*, 376 U.S. 254, 84 S.Ct. 710, 11 L.Ed. 2d 68. (*Black's Law Dictionary*, 1990, p. 417)

••

WASHINGTON v. SMITH
893 F.Supp. 60 (D.D.C. 1995)

JOHN H. PRATT, District Judge

Defendants in this action have filed several motions to dismiss or, in the alternative, for summary judgment. We treat them as motions for summary judgment because we consider material outside the pleadings. Upon consideration of the matter, the Court concludes that plaintiff's claims are not actionable. Accordingly, defendants' motions for summary judgment are granted.

I. *Background*

A well-known sports coach, and later commentator, once said "if I were smart enough to know what I'd do two weeks from now, I'd be smart enough to be a sportswriter."[1] The statements at issue here involve an even longer time frame and center around a sportswriter's preseason attempt to predict the likely contenders for the 1992-1993 women's college basketball championship. Plaintiff Marian E. Washington is the long-time coach of the Kansas Jayhawks women's team. The parties agree that plaintiff is a prominent member of the coaching community.[2] Plaintiff's claims arise from a brief

---

1. John Madden, quoted in J. Parietti, *The Greatest Sports Excuses, Alibis, and Explanations* 245 (1990).

2. At the time the instant controversy arose, plaintiff had served twenty-one years at Kansas, during which the Jayhawks had a winning percentage of .604 in conference play, and had attended five NCAA Tournaments. She is a former president of the Black Coaches Association.

paragraph in "Dick Vitale's 1993-94 College Basketball Preview" magazine (hereafter "Preview"). Defendant Vitale's Ex. A, p.1. Defendant Joseph C. Smith, president of defendant Women's Basketball News Service ("WBNS"), agreed to write the Preview's women's basketball section. Smith allegedly made the following negative statement concerning plaintiff's chances in the 1993-1994 season:

> Talk about talent, the Jayhawks are loaded with Angela Aycock and Charisse Sampson leading the way. But playing to their ability is usually sabotaged by suspect coaching. This season should prove no different.

Complaint ¶ 61. The remaining defendants[3] are accused of "maliciously and recklessly us[ing] the defamatory statements ... from Defendants Smith and [WBSN] to formulate defamatory statements that were knowingly false" that were printed in the Preview. Complaint ¶ 62. What appeared on page 137 of the Preview is the following:

KANSAS

The Jayhawks are loaded with talent, with swingman Angela Aycock and guard Charisse Sampson leading the list. But coach Marian Washington usually finds a way to screw things up. This season will be no different.

Defendant Vitale's Ex. A, p. 6.

Plaintiff claims that the allegedly defamatory statements created the misleading inference that she is an incompetent coach. She is suing defendants for defamation, invasion of privacy, and intentional infliction of emotional distress. In addition, plaintiff is suing defendant Smith on a second count of intentional infliction of emotional distress because Smith allegedly maintains a "Hit List" of women basketball coaches in an attempt to "drive women basketball coaches from the coaching profession in order that they may be replaced by male coaches." Complaint ¶¶ 95, 97. Defendants counter with various arguments favoring dismissal. The Court need address only the First Amendment issues for purposes of this motion.

II. *Analysis*

A. *Standard of Review*

Fed.R.Civ.P. 56(c) permits a court to grant summary judgment where, as is the case here, the evidence in the record indicates that "there is no genuine issue as to any material fact and that the moving party is entitled to a judgment as a matter of law." Fed.R.Civ.P. 56(c).

Whether a statement is capable of conveying a defamatory meaning is a

---

3. Defendant Dick Vitale is a commentator and former college and professional basketball coach. Defendants Ken Leiker and Raymond Levy, respectively the editor-in-chief and publisher of the Preview, contracted with Vitale for the right to use his name and, according to plaintiff, his editorial skills. Also sued were the Preview and InfoSport, Inc., dba Preview Publications.

The Court dismissed the Preview as a defendant pursuant to Local Rule 211. *See* March 23, 1995 order.

threshold question for the Court to determine as a matter of law. *Tavoulareas v. Piro*, 817 F.2d 762, 779-80 (D.C.Cir. 1987) (*en banc*), *cert. denied*, 484 U.S. 870, 108 S.Ct. 200, 98 L.Ed.2d 151 (1987). It is then for the jury to determine by a preponderance of the evidence whether the communication was in fact so understood by its recipient. *Moldea v. New York Times Co.*, 15 F.3d 1137, 1142 ("*Moldea I*"), *modified on other grounds*, 22 F.3d 310 (D.C.Cir.1994) ("*Moldea II*"), *cert denied*, — U.S. —, 115 S.Ct.202, 130 L.Ed.2d 133 (1994). We consider whether as a matter of law defendant Smith's statement[4] and the statement contained in the Preview are actionable.

B. *Defamation and Opinion*

Under District of Columbia law, a statement is defamatory "if it tends to injure plaintiff in his trade, profession, or community standing, or lower him in the estimation of the community." *Moldea I*, 15 F.3d at 1142 (citing *Vereen v. Clayborne*, 623 A.2d 1190,1195 n. 3 (D.C.1993)). The straightforwardness of this definition belies the difficulty of its application to statements which include substantial doses of opinion. Such is the instant case. It is clear from the contents of the statement that it was intended to offer an opinion both as to the Jayhawks' potential for the upcoming 1993-1994 season, and as to Coach Washington's abilities.

There is no blanket First Amendment immunization for such opinion statements. *Milkovich v. Lorain Journal Co.*, 497 U.S. 1, 18-19, 110 S.Ct. 2695, 2705-06, 111 L.Ed.2d 1 (1990). A statement of fact is not shielded from an action for defamation when prefaced with the words "in my opinion." However, a statement is not actionable if it relates to a matter of public concern and it is clear that the declarant is expressing a subjective view, an interpretation, a theory, conjecture, surmise, or hyperbole, rather than claiming to be in possession of objectively verifiable facts. *Id.* at 17-21, 110 S.Ct. at 2704-07; *Haynes v. Alfred A. Knopf, Inc.*, 8 F.3d 1222, 1227 (7th Cir.1993). Even if the opinion does rely on facts either supplied in the statement or implied therein, the statement is immunized if the parties cannot prove the statement is either true or false on the basis of objective evidence. 497 U.S. at 21, 110 S.Ct. at 2707.

Our inquiry, however, does not end there. The D.C. Circuit instructs us that the First Amendment mandates latitude for interpretation when a writer is evaluating or giving an account of inherently ambiguous materials or subject matter. [Citing cases.] In the Court of Appeal's view, *Milkovich* did not disavow the importance of context, but merely discounted it in the circumstances of that case. *Moldea II*, 22 F.3d at 314. When the context of the writing is ambiguous, the Court must apply the "supportable interpretation" standard. *Id.* To succeed under this test, plaintiff must show that the statement was "so obviously false" that "no reasonable person could find" that the state-

---

4. Plaintiff's complaint is extremely vague about the context of the first statement allegedly made by Smith. The parties do not make much of this ambiguity, and we do not believe it is relevant for purposes of this motion. Therefore, we will consider both statements under the same standard, and our discussion of the published statement will apply equally to the earlier statement.

ment's characterizations were supportable interpretations of the underlying material. *Id.* at 315, 317 (emphasis omitted). Statements are immunized even if a reasonable jury could find that the statements were mischaracterizations. *Id.* at 316.

C. *Matter of public concern*

Courts must exercise care in determining what qualifies as a public concern or controversy.

> Newsworthiness alone will not suffice, for the alleged defamation itself indicates that someone in the press believed the matter deserved media coverage.... If the issue was being debated publicly and if it had foreseeable and substantial ramifications for nonparticipants, it was a public controversy.

Waldbaum v. Fairchild Publications Inc., 627 F.2d 1287, 1296-97 (D.C.Cir.), *cert denied*, 449 U.S. 898, 101 S.Ct. 266, 66 L.Ed.2d 128 (1980). Courts have previously held that certain sporting events are matters of public concern even though these events may be of little interest to large segments of the population. *See e.g. Don King Productions, Inc. v. Douglas*, 742 F.Supp. 778, 783 (S.D.N.Y. 1990)(outcome of boxing title fight matter of public concern); *Holt v. Cox Enterprises*, 590 F.Supp. 408, 412 (N.D.Ga. 1984) (public concern in traditional rivalry between two college teams). Although women's collegiate athletics have not traditionally garnered the attention received by major men's teams, this disparity is diminishing. The Preview itself notes that the 1993 Women's "Final Four" sold out and brought large television ratings to the network which aired the championship game. Preview, p. 136. Indeed, a LEXIS search for the period at issue in this case revealed a number of stories related to plaintiff and several other newspaper stories related to the Kansas' women's team. We conclude that the success of the Jayhawks, a major Division 1 team, is a matter of public concern.

D. *Milkovich standard*

(1). *Implication of underlying facts*

Under *Milkovich*, a statement of opinion may be defamatory if the speaker implies that the statement is based on undisclosed facts.[5]

> If a speaker says, "In my opinion John Jones is a liar," he implies knowledge of facts which lead to the conclusion that Jones told an untruth.... Simply couching such statements in terms of opinion does not dispel these implications.

Id. at 18-19, 110 S.Ct. at 2705-06. In the case at bar, the statement on page 137 of the Preview stated "coach Marian Washington usually finds a way to screw things up." Plaintiff contends that this statement implies knowledge of facts relating to past basketball seasons upon which the reviewer reached his conclusion that Washington "usually finds a way to screw things up." Regardless of whether this comment is couched as opinion, plaintiff believes that the implication that she is a bad coach is as serious and potentially

---

5. To this extent at least, *Milkovich* follows section 566 of the Restatement (second) of Torts.

damaging as the statement "John Jones is a liar." We assume for purposes of this motion that plaintiff's arguments are correct and her claim meets the first requirement of *Milkovich*.[6]

(2) *Whether the opinion's falsity can be established by objective evidence*

We now consider whether objective evidence can prove the falsity of the opinions at issue. As an initial matter, we must determine whether, in context, the statement which appeared in the Preview concerned the type of ambiguous material or subject matter to which *Moldea II* requires us to apply the "supportable interpretation" standard. In *Phantom Touring*, the First Circuit concluded that a regularly run theater column is "a type of article generally known to contain more opinionated writing than the typical news report." 953 F.2d at 729. The Court noted that the structure and tone of the language used reinforced the subjective design of the article. *Id.* ("exasperated language indicated that his comments represented his personal appraisal of the factual information"). Similarly, in *Moldea II*, the D.C. Circuit concluded that in the context of a book review, a critic "must be given the constitutional 'breathing space' appropriate to the genre." 22 F.3d at 315 (citing *New York Times Co. v. Sullivan*, 376 U.S. 254, 272, 84 S.Ct. 710, 721-22, 11 L.Ed.2d 686 (1964)); *see also Partington v. Bugliosi*, 56 F.3d 1147, 1154-55 (9th Cir.1995) (tenor of made-for-television "docudrama" negates impression that statements represent false assertion of objective facts).

We conclude that readers of a sports preview magazine understand that a considerable portion of the magazine's content is subjective opinion. *C.f. Ollman v. Evans*, 750 F.2d 970, 984 (D.C.Cir.1984) ("Courts have ... considered the influence that ... well-established genres of writing will have on the average reader"). The statement contained in the Preview must be viewed in this context. A sports preview magazine deals with such inherently ambiguous material that the Court must allow wide latitude for interpretation. Plaintiff can recover only if she meets the "supportable interpretation" standard adopted by this Circuit.

Even in situations where the general tenor of the work suggests that the author is expressing personal opinion, a particular statement of opinion may fall outside the protections of the First Amendment if it implies a false assertion of objective fact. *Partington*, 56 F.3d at 1155. Plaintiff argues that the statement about her meets this description. We disagree. To succeed, plaintiff must

---

6. In fact, we have serious doubts that the statements can reasonably be interpreted as anything but hyperbole. *Milkovich* reaffirmed the principle that the First Amendment protects "rhetorical hyperbole" and other types of "imaginative expression" used to enliven prose. *Phantom Touring*, 953 F.2d at 727; *Greenbelt Cooperative Publ. Ass'n, Inc. v. Bresler*, 398 U.S. 6, 14, 90 S.Ct. 1537, 1541-42, 26 L.Ed.2d 6 (1970) (word "blackmail" not actionable in context); *Letter Carriers v. Austin*, 418 U.S. 264, 284-86, 94 S.Ct. 2770, 2781-82, 41 L.Ed.2d 745 (1984) (word "traitor" in literary definition not actionable when used in "loose figurative sense"). Indeed, a strong case can be made that the perhaps intemperate statement concerning plaintiff's ability to "screw things up" lacks the precision necessary to support a defamation claim. This is also true of the earlier comments concerning "suspect coaching." *See Phantom Touring*, 953 F.2d at 728 (terms "fake" and "phoney" are unprovable); *McCabe v. Rattiner*, 814 F.2d 839, 842 (1st Cir. 1987)(word "scam" too ambiguous to be proven true or false).

show that *no* reasonable person could find that the characterizations were supportable interpretations of the underlying facts. This plaintiff cannot do.

Some of the underlying facts are available elsewhere in the Preview. For example, it is apparent from the listing on page 158 that Kansas has not made the women's "Final Four" since before 1972 (plaintiff was named head coach in 1973), even though the Jayhawks made the Tournament five times. The statement that Kansas' team being "loaded with talent" appears born [sic] out by a separate chart listing individual and team statistics from the previous season. *See* Preview, p. 159. Kansas ranks in two "team leaders" categories and has two "individual leaders." Despite this, the 1992-93 season ended for the Jayhawks with a first round loss in the NCAA Women's Tournament. On the other hand, there is substantial evidence indicating that plaintiff is an excellent coach. The Jayhawks have won several tournaments over the years and been ranked nationally. Complaint ¶¶31-42. Plaintiff's total wins rank among the top thirty in victories for active Division I coaches. Complaint ¶38.

Reasonable minds can interpret the statistics differently. The mere fact that plaintiff's record is open to reasonable interpretation is fatal to plaintiff's case. This ambiguity indicates why the Court cannot adopt plaintiff's position. How many wins does a coach need before a writer or fan is prohibited from criticizing the coach's ability? Do commentators know the "magic number" so they can ascertain when their opinions have become actionable? Does a team have to lose a certain number of games before they can be criticized? In reality, plaintiff's winning statistics may provide a basis for disputing or supporting the writer's opinion. Equally troubling is how a jury would consider evidence of plaintiff's ability to "screw things up." Would the jury be required to watch tapes of the Jayhawks and determine whether Coach Washington's decisions led to the team's defeat? As the Court in *Moldea II* noted, "Sports columnists frequently offer intemperate denunciations of coaches' play-calling or strategy, and readers know this and presumably take such railings with a grain of salt." 22 F.3d at 313. We believe this is equally true of the statements at issue here.

E. *Additional Claims*

Plaintiff also seeks relief for invasion of privacy and two counts of intentional infliction of emotional distress. It is well settled law that a plaintiff "may not use related causes of action to avoid the constitutional requisites of a defamation claim."*Moldea II* 22 F.3d at 319-20 (citing *Cohen v. Cowles Media Co.*, 501 U.S. 663, 671, 111 S.Ct. 2513, 2519, 115 L.Ed.2d 586 (1991)); *Hustler Magazine v. Falwell*, 485 U.S. 46, 56, 108 S.Ct 876, 882, 99 L.Ed.2d 41 (1988) (claim for intentional infliction of emotional distress based on publication of a cartoon parody must meet requirements for libel action); *Brown v. Hearst Corp.*, 862 F.Supp. 622, 631 (D.Mass. 1994), *aff'd*, 54 F.3d 21 (1st Cir. 1995) (invasion of privacy claim fails when information is in public domain). Plaintiff's claim under these counts must also fail.

III. *Conclusion*

The First Amendment protects the statement at issue here and prevents plaintiff from continuing with her action. We recognize that plaintiff is deeply offended by these comments and considers them wholly inaccurate. In evaluating these matters, however, the Court must "err on the side of nonactionability." *Liberty Lobby, Inc. v. Dow Jones & Co.*, 838 F.2d 1287, 1292 (D.C.Cir.), *cert. denied*, 488 U.S. 825, 109 S.Ct. 75, 102 L.Ed.2d 51 (1988). Defendants' motions for summary judgment are granted.

Questions and Comments

1. What did the court say about defamation and opinion?
2. What was the reasoning of the court on "matters of public concern"?
3. What applications are there for a sport manager in public relations?
4. Was there a claim for invasion of privacy? What was the holding of the court?

The Right to Privacy

In this country, 98% of the graduating seniors have tried alcohol. Drug use and violent crime have become major problems. (Ray & Ksir, 1993) Of the teenagers surveyed in a Gallup poll (1989), 60% believed that drug abuse is the greatest problem facing their generation. A sport business is not immune to these problems. Although the topic of drugs and alcohol abuse was covered in chapter 13, sport businesses must be alert to drug testing as a privacy issue. Key issues in this arena include due process; protection against unreasonable searches; and the right to privacy, a First Amendment issue (the topic of the present discussion).

Two United States Supreme Court decisions confirmed that random drug testing of adult employees was permissible under the United States Constitution. *Skinner v. Railway Labor Executives Association* (1989) and *National Treasury Employees Union v. Von Rabb* (1989) affirmed the tests for railroad workers and U.S. Customs officials.

The Court in these cases recognized that urine testing is a search of body fluids and as such is protected under the Fourth Amendment of the United States Constitution. (The Fourth Amendment protects individuals against unreasonable searches and seizures.)

The language of the Court's commentaries recognized that urination is a personal, private act traditionally performed without public observation, an act that is protected by law and custom. The Court's decisions in these cases recognizes that railroad workers as well as U.S. Customs officials have special "hazardous features" in their jobs: the operation of equipment and the possession of firearms. By accepting employment in these jobs, these employees reduced their expectation of privacy according to the courts.

This is different from a school setting where students are required by law to attend school. However, the situation is similar to an athletic setting because participation in athletics is voluntary and athletes have diminished expectations of privacy. They are accustomed to group dressing and showering situations, and they consent to be tested. (*Schaill by Kross v. Tippicanoe*, 1988) In *Schaill*, a Seventh Circuit Court decision, the court upheld the school's random drug testing of athletes and cheerleaders as not violating their right to privacy.

The manner and privacy of testing in *Vernonia v. Acton* (1995) was an issue concerning the mandatory drug testing of a high school athlete. Ultimately, the United States Supreme Court weighed the right to privacy of the athlete against the danger from drugs in the school and the compelling government interest of the school's need to keep order and provide for a safe environment. The Court, in a six to three decision, held for the school's right to drug test athletes.

In cases that involve schools, the courts often weigh students' rights to privacy against the school officials' duty to maintain order in the school. In *Odenheim v. Carlstadt-East Rutherford* (1985), random drug testing of *all* students in school was *not* supported by the courts. This ruling for all high school students is in contrast with the holding in *Vernonia* and in *Schaill*, cases in which the court considered drug testing only for athletes.

The Americans With Disabilities Act (1990) considers pre-employment drug screenings as legal, if testing is required of all potential employees and if tests are given after an offer to hire. A sport manager might have (a) employees who work with heavy equipment, (b) employees who might transport children, and (c) employees who might handle hazardous chemicals (e.g., chlorine). Pre-employment drug screenings, random drug testing, and testing following an accident would all need to consider the right to privacy. Again, the right to privacy, the job description, and the governmental need (private versus public, student versus adult) are all factors to consider in drug testing.

Drugs are not the only privacy problem a sport manager might face. Twenty percent of the youngsters of high school age sometimes carry a gun or knife with the intention of using it. In 1991, of the 11,631 students surveyed, 43% had carried a weapon four or more times in the last month. In 1980, over 11,000 people were killed by high school age assailants ("20% in High Schools," 1991).

One school decided to place a camera in a bathroom to try to curtail drug traffic and to prevent violence. However, this set off a debate as to the issue of right to privacy. This issue could be tested in the courts ("Camera In School," 1992).

In *Bailey v. District of Columbia* (1995), there was a random shooting at a recreation department sponsored cheerleading competition. There was no evidence that there had been other shootings at the building or any other criminal activity at the school. The shooting was not by a participant or spectator at the event. According to the court, the recreation department or the school district did not have prior information that there had been other shootings at the school; therefore, there was not a duty to protect against the use of guns at the event.

Questions and Comments

1. Suppose you were the sport manager in charge of the cheerleading event. Could you have checked for guns? How could you balance the need for violence control with the right to privacy?
2. Is the cheerleading competition the kind of event the Joneses might sponsor

at a gymnastics clinic? What precautions should be taken?

3.   What applications are there for a sport manager in public relations?

4.   Are metal detectors at the door of a sport complex an invasion of privacy? Would the use of metal detectors be considered a search? (Operation SAFE in Chicago uses metal detectors in the schools ["How to Keep Kids Safe," 1992].)

5.   Does a sport manager need to search baggage of team members before taking a trip? What precautions would protect the manager against allegations of a team member concerning illegal searches?

6.   If a sport manager used a camera in a dressing room to catch steroid dealers at a fitness club, what legal problems would be encountered?

The Right of Privacy — A Landmark Decision

Officials in the State of Connecticut prosecuted certain individuals for violating a statute by giving information to married people as to the means of preventing conception. The United States Supreme Court reversed and held the statute to be invalid as an unconstitutional invasion of the right of privacy of married persons.

The following case is a landmark case. Read carefully the language that relates to all First Amendment issues.

••

GRISWOLD v. CONNECTICUT
381 U.S. 479, 14 L.Ed.2d 510, 85 S.Ct. 1678 (1965)

Mr. Justice Douglas delivered the opinion of the Court.

Appellant Griswold is Executive Director of the Planned Parenthood League of Connecticut. Appellant Buxton is a licensed physician and a professor at the Yale Medical School who served as Medical Director for the League at its Center in New Haven—a center open and operating from November 1 to November 10, 1961, when appellants were arrested.

They gave information, instruction, and medical advice to *married persons* as to the means of preventing conception. They examined the wife and prescribed the best contraceptive device or material for her use. Fees were usually charged, although some couples were serviced free.

The statutes whose constitutionality is involved in this appeal are §§ 53-32 and 54-196 of the General Statutes of Connecticut (1958 rev). The former provides:

"Any person who uses any drug, medicinal article or instrument for the purpose of preventing conception shall be fined not less than fifty dollars or imprisoned not less than sixty days nor more than one year or be both fined and imprisoned."

Section 54-196 provides:

"Any person who assists, abets, counsels, causes, hires or commands another to commit any offense may be prosecuted and punished as if he were the principal offender."

The appellants were found guilty as accessories and fined $100 each, against the claim that the accessory statute as so applied violated the Fourteenth Amendment. The Appellate Division of the Circuit Court affirmed. The Supreme Court of Errors affirmed that judgment. 151 Conn 544, 200 A2d 479. We noted probable jurisdiction. 379 US 926, 13 L ed 2d 339, 85 S Ct 328.

We think that appellants have standing to raise the constitutional rights of the married people with whom they had a professional relationship. . . . In other words, the State may not, consistently with the spirit of the First Amendment, contract the spectrum of available knowledge. The right of freedom of speech and press includes not only the right to utter or to print, but the right to distribute, the right to receive, the right to read (Martin v Struthers, 319 US 141, 143, 87 L ed 1313, 1316, 63 S Ct 862) and freedom of inquiry, freedom of thought, and freedom to teach (see Wieman v Updegraff, 344 US 183, 195, 97 L ed 218, 224, 73 S Ct 215)—indeed the freedom of the entire university community. (Citing cases.) Without those peripheral rights the specific rights would be less secure. . . . Various guarantees create zones of privacy. The right of association contained in the penumbra of the First Amendment is one, as we have seen. The Third Amendment in its prohibition against the quartering of soldiers "in any house" in time of peace without the consent of the owner is another facet of that privacy. The Fourth Amendment explicitly affirms the "right of the people to be secure in their persons, houses, papers, and effects, against unreasonable searches and seizures." The Fifth Amendment in its Self-Incrimination Clause enables the citizen to create a zone of privacy which government may not force him to surrender to his detriment. The Ninth Amendment provides: "The enumeration in the Constitution, of certain rights, shall not be construed to deny or disparage others retained by the people."

The Fourth and Fifth Amendments were described in Boyd v United States, 116 US 616, 630, 29 L ed 746, 751, 6 S Ct 524, as protection against all governmental invasions "of the sanctity of a man's home and the privacies of life." (Footnote omitted) We recently referred in Mapp v Ohio, 367 US 643, 656, 6 L ed 2d 1081, 1090, 81 S Ct 1684, 84 ALR2d 933, to the Fourth Amendment as creating a "right to privacy, no less important than any other right carefully and particularly reserved to the people." . . . .

The present case, then, concerns a relationship lying within the zone of privacy created by several fundamental constitutional guarantees. And it concerns a law which, in forbidding the *use* of contraceptives rather than regulating their manufacture or sale, seeks to achieve its goals by means having a maximum destructive impact upon that relationship. Such a law cannot stand in light of the familiar principle, so often applied by this Court, that a "governmental purpose to control or prevent activities constitutionally subject to state regulation may not be achieved by means which sweep unnecessarily broadly and thereby invade the area of protected freedoms." NAACP v Alabama, 377 US 288, 307, 12 L ed 2d 325, 338, 84 S Ct 1302. Would we allow the police to search the sacred precincts of marital bedrooms for telltale signs of the use of contraceptives? The very idea is repulsive to the notions of privacy surrounding the marriage relationship.

We deal with a right of privacy older than the Bill of Rights—older than our political parties, older than our school system. Marriage is a coming together for better or for worse, hopefully enduring, and intimate to the degree of being sacred. It is an association that promotes a way of life, not causes; a harmony in living, not political faiths; a bilateral loyalty, not commercial or social projects. Yet it is an association for as noble a purpose as any involved in our prior decisions.

Reversed.

Questions and Comments

1. How did Justice Douglas conclude that the appellants had standing to sue?
2. How does Justice Douglas justify a right of privacy when such a right is not articulated in the first ten amendments?
3. From what source does the right of privacy emanate? Stated differently, where was the right first articulated?
4. How does the right of privacy influence sport businesses or athletics?

SUMMARY

The first ten amendments to the United States Constitution are known as the Bill of Rights. At an early date, the United States Supreme Court decided that these rights were limitations on the national government only. Because the Bill of Rights deals with the rights of individuals in relationship to the national government, it is apparent that the Bill of Rights constitutes a basic expression essential to a democratic society. The rights in question are believed to be essential to our faith in ordered liberty and the inherent dignity of the individual. Every business enterprise in this country is affected in a positive way by the Bill of Rights. The sport industry is no exception. The cases that have been referred to in this chapter have been taken primarily from factual situations that involve sport and recreation. Included are cases that involve rights that are not directly expressed in the first ten amendments but that are said to flow from and be closely associated with the Bill of Rights. Among these cases are those involving the right of association and the right of privacy.

The sport manager should have no trouble restricting patrons' fighting words, words that incite panic, or obscene language. Some speech is symbolic in nature. Clothing might in some cases indicate symbolic speech.

Regulations may restrict speech if there is a legitimate government interest without unduly infringing upon the right to engage in activity protected by the First Amendment. City ordinances restricting the unwelcome noise of recreational businesses are in this category.

The Establishment Clause of the First Amendment forbids the creation of a single official religion. Sport managers who work for government entities should avoid establishing a public forum for a particular religion.

Managers of a place of public accommodation such as a sport club like the Rod and Gun Club should remember that the First Amendment allows for freedom of association. Excluding members of one gender, race, or religion does not allow for this freedom.

Defamation is an intentional false communication either published or spoken. Suits for defamation may be criminal or civil.

The right to privacy is a First Amendment consideration. With violence control and drug testing, sport managers should be aware of the individual's rights.

This could be you - check your response

The First Amendment issues in this case are freedom of speech and freedom of religion. Ms Karnes could comment openly on issues that were "a matter of public policy." She could comment (free speech) on the drinking policy, but local statutes that were related to alcoholic beverages would determine what the Joneses could or could not do regarding the sale or consumption of alcohol.

In regard to Ms Karnes's belief in observing the Sabbath on Friday, the Joneses would have been wise to make accommodations for her not to work on Friday evenings. This would not have been an "undue hardship" and would not have constituted religious discrimination. The opening and closing hours of the bowling alley would be governed by local statute.

REFERENCES

Cases

Anable v. Ford, 663 F. Supp. 149 (W.D. Ark. 1985).

Bailey v. District of Columbia, 839 F.Supp. 888 (D.C. App. 1995).

Bamon Corp. v. City of Dayton, 923 F.2d 470 (6th Cir. 1991).

Barnes v. Glen Theatre, Inc., 501 U.S. ___, 111 S.Ct. 2456, 115 L.Ed.2d 504 (1991).

Bethel v. Fraser, 478 U.S. 675, 706 S.Ct. 3159, 92 L.Ed.2d 549 (1986).

Brandenburg v. Ohio, 395 U.S. 444, 89 S.Ct. 1827, 23 L.Ed. 2d 430 (1969).

Briggs v. State, 599 A.2d 1221 (Md. Ct. Spec. App. 1992).

Bruns v. Pomerleau, 319 F.Supp. 58 (D. Md. 1970).

Campanelli v. Regents of Univ. of Cal., 51 Cal.Rptr.2d 891 (Cal.App. 1 Dist. 1996).

Cannon v. City and County of Denver, 998 F.2d 867 (10th Cir. 1993).

Chaplinski v. New Hampshire, 315 U.S. 568, 62 S.Ct. 766, 86 L.Ed 1031 (1942).

Christian Knights of KKK v. District of Columbia, 972 F.2d 365 (D.C. Cir. 1992).

City of Boston v. Back Bay Cultural Ass'n., 635 N.E.2d 1175 (Mass. 1994).

City of Lincoln v. ABC Books, Inc., 470 N.W.2d 760 (Neb. 1991).

City of Renton v. Playtime Theatres, Inc., 475 U.S. 41, 89 L.Ed.2d 29, 106 S. Ct. 925 (1986).

Connick v. Meyers, 461 U.S. 139, ____ L.Ed. 2d ___, 106 S. Ct. ___ (1983).

Concord Rod and Gun Club v. Massachusetts Comm. Against Discrimination, 524 N.E.2d 1364, 1367 (Mass. 1988).

Derdlyn v. University of Colorado, 832 P.2d 1031 (Cal.App. 1991).

Edge Broadcasting Co. v. U.S., 732 F.Supp. 633 (E.D. Va. 1990).

Erznoznik v. City of Jacksonville, 422 U.S. 205, 45 L.Ed.2d 125, 95 S.Ct. 2268 (1975).

Gay Activists Alliance v. Board of Regents of Univ. of Okla., 638 P.2d 1116 (Okla. 1981).

Gay and Lesbian Students Ass'n v. Gohn, 656 F.Supp. 1045 (W.D. Ark. 1987).

Gravely v. Bacon, 429 S.E.2d 663 (Ga. 1993).

Griswold v. Connecticut, 381 U.S. 479, 14 L. Ed.2d 510, 85 S.Ct. 1678 (1965).

Hill v. NCAA, 865 P.2d 633 (Cal. 1994).

International Society For Krishna Consciousness v. Lee, 925 F.2d 576 (2nd Cir. 1991).

International Society for Krishna Consciousness v. New Jersey Sports and Exposition Authority, 532 F.Supp. 1088 (D. N.J., 1981).

Iskcon of Potomac, Inc. v. Ridenour, 830 F.Supp. 1 (D. D.C. 1993).

Jeglin v. San Jacinto Unified School District, 827 F.Supp. 1459 (C.D. Cal. 1993).

Knights of KKK v. Arkansas State Hwy. & Transp. Dept., 807 F.Supp. 1427 (W.D. Ark. 1992).

Knudtson v. City of Coates, 506 N.W.2d 29 (Minn. Ct. App. 1993).

Loper v. New York City Police Dept., 999 F.2d 699 (2nd Cir. 1993).

Medlin v. Palmer, 874 F.2d 1085 (5th Cir. 1989).

Miller v. Barberton Mun. Ct., 935 F.2d 775 (6th Cir. 1991).

National Treasury Employees Union v. Von Rabb, 489 U.S. 325, 341 (1989).

Naturist Soc'y, Inc. v. Fillyaw, 958 F.2d 1515 (11th Cir. 1992).

Odenheim v. Carlstadt-East Rutherford Regional Schls., 510 A.2d 709 (N.J. Super. 1985).

Oleson v. Board of Education of Dist. No. 228, 676 F.Supp. 820 (N.D. Ill., 1987).

Paulsen v. Gotbaum, 982 F.2d 825, 828-29 (2d Cir. 1992).

Planned Parenthood v. Clark County Sch. Dist., 941 F.2d 817 (9th Cir. 1991).

Postscript Enterprises v. City of Bridgeton, 905 F.2d 223 (8th Cir. 1990).

Robson v. Klamath County Bd. of Health, 818 P.2d 990 (Or. Ct. App. 1991).

Rock Against Racism v. Ward, 636 F.Supp. 178 (S.D. N.Y. 1986).

Rubin v. City of Santa Monica, 823 F.Supp. 709 (C.D. Cal. 1993).

S.D. v. State, 650 So.2d 198 (Fla.App. 3 Dist. 1995).

Schaill by Kross v. Tippicanoe County School Corp., 846 F. 2d 1309 (7th Cir. 1988).

Skinner v. Railway Labor Executives Association, 489 U.S. 602 (1989).

State v. Lacey, 465 N.W.2d 537 (Iowa 1991).

Tinker v. Des Moines, 393 U.S. 503, 89 S.Ct. 733, 21 L.Ed. 2d 231 (1969).

U.S. v. Doe, 968 F.2d 86 (D.C. Cir. 1992).

U.S. v. McDermott, 822 F.Supp. 582 (N.D. Iowa 1993).

U.S. v. Musser, 873 F.2d 1513 (D.C. Cir. 1989).

United States v. O'Brien, 391 U.S. 367, 288 S.Ct. 1673 (1968).

Vernonia Sch. Dist., 47J v. Acton, 515 U.S. ___, 115 S.Ct. 2386, 132 L.Ed.3d 564 (1995).

Video Store, Inc. v. Holcomb, 729 F.Supp. 579 (S.D. Ohio 1990).

Warfield v. Peninsula Golf & Country Club, 42 Cal.Rptr.2d 50 (Cal. 1995).

Washington v. Smith, 893 F.Supp. 60 (D.D.C. 1995), 80 F.3d 555 (D.C.Cir. 1996).

Washington Tour Guides v. National Park Serv., 808 F.Supp. 877 (D. D.C. 1992).

Yarbrough v. City of Carrollton, 421 S.E.2d 72 (Ga. 1992).

Other Resources

Atlanta, GA, Municipal Ordinance 96-0-0401, Chapter 106, Article II, Section 106-57.

Camera in school bathroom curbs vandalism but sets off debate. (1992, March 25) *New York Times*, p. A21.

Communication Decency Act (1996), P.L. 104-104, 110 Stat. 56. (As of June 1996, the constitutionality, First Amendment, of this act was being challenged in the courts.)

Hall, K.L. (1992). *The Oxford Companion to the Supreme Court of the United States*. New Oxford: Oxford University Press.

How to keep kids safe. (1992, March 9). *Newsweek*, p. 30.

McCann, R. & Peters, C.D. (1996, February) At risk youth, the Phoenix phenomenon. *Journal of Physical Education, Recreation and Dance, 67*(2), pp. 38-40.

National Drug Control Strategy, The White House, September 1989.

New York Times, October 11, 1991.

Ray, O. and Ksir, C. (1993) *Drugs, society & human behavior* (7th ed.). St. Louis, MO: Mosby-Year Book, Inc.

20% in high schools found to carry weapons. (1991, October 11). *New York Times*, p. 12.

Model Codes, Restatements, and Standards

Americans With Disabilities Act of 1990, Pub. L. 101-366, 104 Stat. 324, July 26, 1990, and amendments, codified as 42 U.S.C. §12101, et seq.

CONSTITUTIONAL QUESTIONS

PERSPECTIVE

Part V has provided information concerning constitutional issues to the manager or owner of a business dealing with recreation. The topics covered include constitutional restraints, due process of law, and the First Amendment. A more detailed statement of the subtopics follows:

A. Constitutional Restraints and Statutory Interpretation
   1. The purpose of constitutional restraints
   2. The types of situations affecting the need to litigate constitutional issues, such as, advisory opinions, mootness, requirement for timely pleading, presumption of constitutionality, decision on other than constitutional grounds if possible, and requirement for a case or controversy

B. Due Process of Law
   1. Types of due process
   2. Elements of procedural due process, *i.e.,* notice and fair hearing
   3. Substantive due process, *i.e.,* freedom from arbitrary action, and relationship to fundamental issues

C. First Amendment
   1. Freedom of speech
   2. Freedom of religion
   3. Freedom of association
   4. Right of privacy

NOTE: Each of the above topics should be considered in relationship to the field of sport management and recreation.

Hypothetical Case - Part V - Check Your Response

Toby Jones can write her paper on some selected constitutional issues. In due process she would discuss the right to have adequate notice and a fair hearing.

If Toby wrote about First Amendment rights she would discuss freedom of speech, religion, association and the right of privacy. She might want to describe how these rights have been applied in her family's business.

CIVIL RIGHTS: SEX DISCRIMINATION

Part VI

FOCUS

Overview

The ringing declaration of the rights of men as set forth in the Declaration of Independence was precisely so limited. The Declaration applied to men only and only to some races of men. Equality for women was not seriously considered. The Declaration constituted a giant step forward but, nevertheless, the statement was only a partial resolution of the democratic ideal of equality. The questions of discrimination on the basis of sex and race were yet to be addressed. This development was to take place in America along parallel lines with one disadvantaged group receiving support from the other.

The story of women's efforts to achieve equal status under the law is a long and fascinating tale. Students could very well expend time and effort in reviewing the lives of individuals such as Susan B. Anthony, Lucy Stone, Elizabeth Cady Stanton, Lucretia Mott, Virginia Minor, and Myra Bradwell. Added to this illustrious group of pioneers are the names of Sojourner Truth, Harriet Tubman, and Mary McLeod Bethune. To trace this story, however, is not the purpose of this section.

The broad picture of women's rights encompasses the right to vote, the right to enter into professions, and the right to work under conditions of equality. The study of sport management law will address the issue primarily from the standpoint of selected topics dealing with working conditions, such as questions that arise from the right of equal pay, procreation, and freedom from harassment. These topics will illustrate the necessity of first-class citizenship for women.

Practical Application - Hypothetical Case

The Joneses are acutely aware of the necessity of avoiding problems of sex discrimination. Consequently, they have instructed the general managers of their respective organizations to draft a proposed policy on sexual harassment. What should the policy include? Be specific. Should policies be developed that cover pregnancy and equal pay? Why or why not?

CHAPTER 17

SEX DISCRIMINATION CONNECTED WITH PREGNANCY

INTRODUCTION

Legislation designed to foster equal treatment of men and women has been the subject of statutory enactment and judicial decisions. Employment is one critical area in which questions are presented. Can management decisions be predicated upon the condition of pregnancy? More specifically, can management decisions be predicated upon pregnancy outside of wedlock? Such questions are presented frequently in the area of education. The same questions are presented to the owner or manager of sport or recreational facilities. This textbook is not written primarily for the public school teacher.

However, in certain cases, a judicial decision arising out of the public school system will be presented. The justification for including such a case is threefold. First, the case may be one of first impression. Second, the case may be described as a landmark case. Landmark cases are frequently cited in subsequent litigation involving higher education or recreation in general. Third, students in the field of recreation and sport management may seek employment with the public school system. One of the cases reproduced in this chapter is a public school case. The case referred to is *Andrews v. Drew Municipal Separate Sch. Dist.* (1975).

> **IN THIS CHAPTER YOU WILL LEARN:**
> The justification for including cases involving pregnancy of single mothers in the public school system
> The significance of the role model theory in the educational system
> The significance of the role model theory in the recreational enterprise conducted as a private business
> The constitutional questions presented by pregnancies occurring outside of wedlock
> The characterization of marriage and procreation as fundamental under the Constitution
> The legislative enactments that impact sex discrimination and pregnancy

KEY WORDS: *role model, procreation, bona fide occupational qualification (BFOQ), morality*

This could be you!

A public university wishes to conduct a soccer clinic for girls ages 10 to 15. Ms Doe, a physical education major, applies for a job as assistant clinic director. Doe is currently employed on a part-time basis in the downtown recreational complex owned and operated by the Joneses. The university in question purports to hire Doe for 3 hours per day, 5 days a week. Doe is unmarried and pregnant. Can she be refused employment? Suppose the clinic was being held at the local chapter of the YWCA and Doe applied for a position as a YWCA instructor. Would this make a difference? Why or why not?

PREGNANCY AND EMPLOYMENT CONSIDERATIONS

The Field of Education

In the case that follows, the superintendent of a public school system issued a decree to the effect that teachers who were unmarried and pregnant would not be considered for employment. As a corollary, a teacher who became pregnant out of wedlock would be terminated. Teacher's aides who came under the proscribed conduct filed an action to have the policy declared unconstitutional.

· ·

ANDREWS v. DREW MUNICIPAL SEPARATE SCH. DIST.
507 F.2d 611 (5th Cir. 1975)

SIMPSON, Circuit Judge:

This suit attacking the validity of the Drew Municipal School District's rule against employing parents of illegitimate children was initiated by two such parents, both mothers, against whom the rule militated. Named as defendants were the Drew Municipal School District (the District), George Ferris Pettey, its Superintendent, and the individual members of the District's Board of Trustees (the Board).

The complaint sought declaratory and injunctive relief to "redress the deprivation of rights and privileges and immunities of the plaintiffs guaranteed by the (sic) 42 U.S.C. 1981, 1983 et seq., Title VI of the Civil Rights Act of 1964, 42 U.S.C. Section 2000d et seq.,[1] the Fifth and Fourteenth Amendments to the United States Constitution. Plaintiffs further asked for declaratory relief under 28 U.S.C. Section 2201, 2202." Jurisdiction was invoked under Title 28 U.S.C. Section 1343.

Following a series of hearings the district court decided the case on the merits, holding that the rule violated both the Equal Protection Clause and the Due Process Clause of the Fourteenth Amendment. Andrews v. Drew Municipal Separate School District, N.D. Miss. 1973, 371 F. Supp. 27. We affirm for reasons stated below.

In the spring of 1972, Superintendent Pettey learned that there were some teacher aides presently employed in the District who were parents of illegitimate children. Disturbed by this knowledge, Pettey immediately implemented an unwritten edict to the effect that parenthood of an illegitimate child would automatically disqualify an individual, whether incumbent or applicant, from employment with the school system.[2] There is no doubt that the policy is attributable solely to Pettey; there was no evidence that he sought either the prior advice or the consent of the Board.[3]

Mrs. Fred McCorkle is one of the administrators responsible for implementing the unwed parent policy. As Coordinator of Elementary Instruction

1. In paragraphs 11, 12 and 13 of the complaint, the plaintiffs detailed their claims of violations of their rights under the heading "VIOLATIONS OF LAW". The refusal by the defendants to employ plaintiff Andrews and the termination of the plaintiff Rogers was asserted to delegate the plaintiffs into an unconstitutionally created classification based upon their race, sex and unmarried parent status in violation of the constitutional and statutory provisions enumerated in the text, including Title VI of the Civil Rights Act of 1964, 42 U.S.C., Section 2000d. It was further alleged that Andrews was refused employment because of her race, sex and single parent status and that Rogers was discharged from her teachers' aide position because of her race, sex and single parent status, all in violation of the same constitutional and statutory provisions. The district court's decision, Andrews v. Drew Municipal Separate School District, N.D. Miss. 1973, 373 F.Supp. 27, contains no findings or conclusions with respect to violation of Title VI of the Civil Rights Act, Title 42, U.S.C., Sec. 2000d.

The complaint contained no assertion that Title VII of the Civil Rights Act of 1964, the Equal Employment Opportunities provision, Title 42, U.S.C. § 2000e et seq., was violated. No assertion of any violation of Title VII was made during the district court proceedings, and the district judge made no findings or conclusions as to violations of Title VII.

2. Pettey in testimony indicated confusion as to the expanse of the policy he had promulgated. He was positive that the rule should apply to all instructional personnel. Upon questioning, he expanded the list to include not only teachers and teacher aides, but also secretaries, librarians, dieticians, cafeteria operators, nurses, social workers, school principals, school volunteers and even PTA presidents. Although he was not positive, he did not think the rule should apply to bus drivers, janitors or maids.

3. The Board and its individual members were unaware of the rule until the commencement of this action. The evidence indicates, however, that the Board then ratified the policy and all actions taken under it.

for the school district, she is in charge of the teacher aide program and recommends to Pettey who shall be hired to fill teacher aide vacancies. All potential teacher aides must submit an application to Mrs. McCorkle who then interviews them and investigates their applications. The investigation consists of consultations with other administrative staff members as well as the principals of the various schools concerning their knowledge of the applicant.

Both plaintiffs-appellees, Lestine Rogers and Katie Mae Andrews, were victims of the unwed parent policy. Lestine Rogers was hired as a teacher aide in the Fall preceding the initiation of the rule, although her application stated that she was single and had a child. After the Pettey policy rule was announced, Mrs. McCorkle informed Ms. Rogers that because she was the parent of an illegitimate child, she would not be re-hired for the following year. Katie Mae Andrews, on the other hand, knew about the Pettey rule prior to applying for a teacher aide position. Although she too was the mother of an illegitimate child, she did not so indicate on her application. Mrs. McCorkle learned of Ms. Andrews' illegitimate child in the course of her investigation of the application. She made a written notation of her finding on the application,[4] and refused to consider Ms. Andrews further.

From the beginning, unwed mothers only, not unwed fathers, were adversely affected by the rule. This factor coupled with the conclusion that the policy, by its nature, could only be applied against females, led the district court to hold alternatively that "assuming a rational relation does exist between the Drew policy and legitimate educational objectives, the rule creates an inherently suspect classification based on sex, i.e. single women, which cannot survive strict scrutiny mandated by the Fourteenth Amendment." 371 F. Supp. at 35. The district court's primary holding was that the rule "has no rational relation to the objectives ostensibly sought to be achieved by the school officials and is fraught with invidious discrimination; thus it is constitutionally defective under the traditional, and most lenient, standard of equal protection and violative of due process as well." Ibid. at 31. Thus this appeal concerns a policy or rule that has not only been held to violate equal protection for alternative reasons, but has also been held to violate due process. On the basis relied upon by the district court of traditional notions of equal protection, because the policy created an irrational classification, we affirm.[5]

"Traditional" equal protection analysis requires that legislative classifications must be sustained as long as the classification itself is rationally related

4. Across the top front of Ms. Andrews' application, Mrs. McCorkle wrote, "Single with a child 3 or 4." On the back of the application, Mrs. McCorkle wrote:

"This applicant would have been hired in January 1973 if I had not received information from Mrs. Clara Robinson and others at James Elementary that she had a child. The applicant stated on her application that she was single and had no children. When she called by phone in January I informed her of the school policy and have had no contact with this applicant since then."

5. Because we affirm upon traditional equal protection grounds, we do not consider the district court's alternative finding of a sex based classification or its legal conclusion that such classifications are inherently suspect.

to a legitimate governmental interest. [Citing cases.] To find the governmental objective ostensibly served by the rule, we turn to the testimony of Superintendent Pettey, the rule's originator and explicator. Pettey's avowed objective was to create a scholastic environment which was conducive to the moral development as well as the intellectual development of the students. Certainly this objective is not without legitimacy. See Shelton v. Tucker, 1960, 364 U.S. 479, 81 S.Ct. 247, 5 L.Ed. 2d 231; Adler v. Board of Education, 1952, 342 U.S. 485, 72 S.Ct. 380, 96 L.Ed. 517. Schools have the right, if not the duty, to create a properly moral scholastic environment. See Beilan v. Board of Education, 1958, 357 U.S. 399, 78 S.Ct. 1317, 2 L.Ed. 2d 1414. But the issue is not simply whether the objective itself is legitimate, but rather whether the Pettey rule "advances that objective in a manner consistent with the Equal Protection Clause," Reed v. Reed, 1971, 404 U.S. 71, 76, 92 S.Ct. 251, 254, 30 L.Ed. 2d 225. We hold that it does not.

The District offers three possible rationales through which it asserts that its rule under attack furthers the creation of a properly moral scholastic environment: (1) unwed parenthood is prima facie proof of immorality; (2) unwed parents are improper communal role models, after whom students may pattern their lives; (3) employment of an unwed parent in a scholastic environment materially contributes to the problem of school-girl pregnancies.

The first of these postulates violates not only the Equal Protection Clause, but the Due Process Clause as well. The law is clear that due process interdicts the adoption by a state of an irrebuttable presumption, as to which the presumed fact does not necessarily follow from the proven fact. [Citing cases.] Thus, unless the presumed fact here, present immorality,[6] necessarily follows from the proven fact, unwed parenthood, the conclusiveness inherent in the Pettey rule[7] must be held to violate due process. We agree with the district court that the one does not necessarily follow the other:

6. If a state investigates the moral character of an individual upon whom it intends either to bestow a benefit or to impose a burden, due process requires that such inquiry look to *present* moral character. Thus, in Schware v. Board of Bar Examiners of New Mexico, 1957, 353 U.S. 232, 77 S.Ct. 752, 1 L.Ed.2d 796, the Supreme Court held that the New Mexico Board of Bar Examiners violated an applicant's due process rights by refusing to consider his evidence of present good moral character in disallowing him membership to the bar. The Board relied instead on negative inferences drawn from Schware's past, in that approximately fifteen years prior to entering law school, he was a member of the Communist party, made use of aliases and had an arrest record. In reversing the Board's denial of admission, the Court noted that "if (Schware) otherwise qualifies for the practice of law and is admitted to the bar, the State has ample means to discipline him for any future misconduct." 353 U.S. at 247, n. 20, 77 S.Ct. at 760, n. 20.

7. The conclusiveness of the Pettey rule was testified to by Superintendent Pettey himself:

Q.   So I take it, Mr. Pettey, that a person who supposedly has a, quote, illegitimate child, as you put it, that fact, no matter when it took place or no matter under what circumstances it took place, is prima facie evidence of a lack of morality:

A.   It would be to me, yes.

THE COURT: Mr. Pettey, you do not think the facts or circumstances under which an illegitimate birth occurred is at all relevant to the issue of good character or bad character?

(continued on next page)

By the rule, a parent, whether male or female, who has had such a child, would be forever precluded from employment. Thus no consideration would be given to the subsequent marriage of the parent or to the length of time elapsed since the illegitimate birth, or to a person's reputation for good character in the community. A person could live an impeccable life, yet be barred as unfit for employment for an event, whether the result of indiscretion or not, occurring at any time in the past. But human experience refutes the dogmatic attitude inherent in such a policy against unwed parents. Can it be said that an engaged woman, who has premarital sex, becomes pregnant, and whose fiance dies or is killed prior to their marriage, is morally depraved for bearing the posthumous child? The rule allows no compassion for the person who has been unwittingly subjected to sexual relations through force, deceptive design or while under the influence of drugs or alcohol, yet chooses to have the child rather than to abort it. The rule makes no distinction between the sexual neophyte and the libertine. In short, the rule leaves no consideration for the multitudinous circumstances under which illegitimate childbirth may occur and which may have little, if any, bearing on the parent's present moral worth. A past biological event like childbirth out of wedlock, even if relevant to the issue, may not be controlling; and that it may be considered more conventional or circumspect for the infant to be surrendered to others for upbringing rather than be reared by the natural parent is hardly determinative of the matter. Furthermore, the policy, if based on moral judgment, has inherent if unintended defects or shortcomings. While obviously aimed at discouraging premarital (sic) sex relations, the policy's effect is apt to encourage abortion, which is itself staunchly opposed by some on ethical or moral grounds. It totally ignores, as a disqualification, the occurrence of extra-marital sex activity, though thought of by many as a more serious basis for moral culpability. Indeed, the superintendent's fiat, altogether unsupported by sociological data, equates the single fact of illegitimate birth with irredeemable moral disease. Such a presumption is not only patently absurd, it is mischievous and prejudicial, requiring those who administer the policy to "investigate" the parental status of school employees and prospective applicants. Where no stigma may have existed before, such inquisitions by overzealous officialdom can rapidly create it. 371 F.Supp. at 33-34 [Footnotes deleted].

We observe also that there are reasonable alternative means through which to remove or suspend teachers engaging in immoral conduct; means

    A. No sir. That would be hard to get at. I think the fact that the birth occurred without the benefit of matrimony is, to me, proof enough of the . . .

THE COURT: Is conclusive?

    A. Yes sir.

THE COURT:. . . Suppose a woman had an illegitimate child and then later married either the father of the child or another man. When she presented herself to you she showed she was married and had a child, one child. Would you consider her for employment?

    A. No, sir. I would not.

that guarantee the teacher a public hearing on the merits and right of appeal. 5 Miss. Code Sec. 6282-26 (1971 Supp.).[8] By denying a public hearing to which all other teachers charged with immoral conduct are entitled, the policy denies unwed parents equal protection of the laws. Insofar as the rule inextricably binds unwed parental status to irredeemable immorality, it violates both due process and equal protection.

The school district urges a second rationale for its rule based upon the holding in McConnell v. Anderson, 8 Cir. 1971, 451 F.2d 193:

> "What the school board looks at is whether, moral considerations aside, proper educational growth can be furthered and respect for marriage ingrained by employing unwed parents. The question then becomes whether the open and notorious existence of the status as an unwed parent would injure the affected students." Reply Brief of Defendants/Appellants, p. 5.

McConnell, a male homosexual, had been offered a position at the University of Minnesota pending approval of the Board of Regents. While Board action was pending, McConnell and a male friend attempted to obtain a marriage license, an event which generated at least four local newspaper articles as well as local radio and television news coverage. Following this action the Board disapproved McConnell's appointment with the statement that his "personal conduct, as represented in the public and University news media, is not consistent with the best interest of the University."[9] 451 F.2d at 194. In upholding the Board of Regents' decision, the Eighth Circuit specified that McConnell was not denied employment because of his homosexual tendencies or his desire to continue homosexual conduct clandestinely, but rather because of his "activist role in implementing his unconventional ideas concerning the societal status to be accorded homosexuals," which would have the effect of forcing "tacit approval of this socially repugnant concept" upon the University. 451 F.2d at 196.

We do not consider *McConnell* supportive of the District's position. The record before us contains no evidence of proselytizing of pupils by the plaintiffs and reveals instead that each plaintiff, along with her illegitimate offspring, is

---

8. Sec. 6282-26 reads, in pertinent part:

Suspension of superintendent, principal, or teacher—notice—appeal.—For incompetence, neglect of duty, immoral conduct, intemperance, brutal treatment of a pupil or other good cause the county superintendent of education or superintendent of the municipal separate school district, as the case may be, may remove or suspend any . . . teacher in any school district, but before being so removed or suspended the . . . teacher shall be notified of the charges against him and he shall be advised that he is entitled to a public hearing upon said charges at a date to be fixed in such notice. . . . From the decision made at said hearing the. . . teacher shall be allowed an appeal to the state board of education . . . . Any party aggrieved by the said ruling of the state board of education may effect an appeal therefrom to the chancery court. . . .

9. We think it significant also that upon request, McConnell was given an opportunity to appear before the Board of Regents with counsel to present information claimed to support his application. It was only after this hearing that the Regents adopted the resolution to disapprove the appointment.

living under the same roof as her parents, brothers and sisters. It would be a wise child indeed who could infer knowledge of either plaintiff's unwed parent status based on the manner of plaintiffs' existence. As the district court observed:

"In the absence of overt, positive stimuli to which children can relate, we are convinced that the likelihood of inferred learning that unwed parenthood is necessarily good or praiseworthy, is highly improbable, if not speculative. We are not at all persuaded by defendants' suggestions, quite implausible in our view, that students are apt to seek out knowledge of the personal and private family life-styles of teachers or other adults within a school system (i. e. whether they are divorced, separated, happily married or single, etc.), and, when known, will approve of and seek to emulate them." 371 F.Supp. at 35.

In our view then, the school district's second offered justification for the unwed parent policy also falls short of equal protection requirements.

The third rationale proffered by the school district in hopes of salvaging the Pettey rule, that the presence of unwed parents in a scholastic environment materially contributes to school-girl pregnancies is without support, other than speculation and assertions of opinion, in the record before us.

Because we hold that the Board rule under attack violated traditional concepts of equal protection, we find it unnecessary to discuss numerous other issues urged on appeal by appellees or in their behalf by *amici curiae*; for example, whether the rule creates a suspect classification based upon race or sex, or whether it infringes upon some constitutionally protected interest such as the right to privacy or the right to procreation.[10]

Finally we find insufficient justification to reverse on cross-appeal the district court's denial of attorney fees.[11]

Affirmed.

---

10. Both the Equal Employment Opportunity Commission and the Center for Constitutional Rights filed *Amicus Curiae* briefs before this court urging that the basis for our decision be broadened to include some or all of these issues. Both Amici sought and were denied leave to participate in oral argument.

11. Despite his alternative ground of decision, discrimination as to sex in violation of the Fourteenth Amendment, the district judge denied the award of attorneys' fees in a separate order entered after his injunctive and declaratory decree. No reasons were assigned. Because of the strong congressional policy against unlawful discrimination in employment, Title VII of the Civil Rights Act of 1964, 42 U.S.C. § 2000e; Weeks v. Southern Bell Tel. & Tel. Co., 5 Cir. 1969, 408 F.2d 228, we would seriously consider reversal for failure to award attorneys' fees, if we could base our affirmance on that congressional policy's proper vindication. See Clark et al. v. American Marine Corporation, 5 Cir. 1971, 437 F.2d 959, affirming per curiam, Clark et al. v. American Marine Corporation, E.D.La. 1970, 320 F.Supp. 709; cf. Newman v. Piggie Park Enterprises, 1968, 390 U.S. 400, 88 S.Ct. 964, 19 L.Ed.2d 1263. But review of the finding of discrimination as to sex, especially since no Title VII violation was asserted by the pleadings or dealt with by the trial court, (Note 1, supra) presents a thicket we deem it unwise to enter. In the procedural posture which has evolved, we perceive no error in the refusal to award attorneys' fees.

Questions and Comments

1. Was the case on the appellate or trial level?
2. What were the constitutional issues litigated?
3. What part of the United States Constitution was involved?
4. What argument was advanced by the defendants to justify the school policy?
5. How did the court reason in arriving at its decision?
6. What rule of law does this case set forth?
7. What reasons did the court give for such a rule?
8. What type of relief did the plaintiff seek?
9. What civil rights statutes were invoked?

Authors' Note

The *Andrews* case has been cited with approval in *Lewis v. Delaware State College* (1978). *Lewis* was a case in which a director of residence halls for women did not have her contract renewed because she bore a child out of wedlock. Suit was filed to protest the decision. A preliminary injunction was granted. The court reasoned that the plaintiff was entitled to freedom from arbitrary action and thus was entitled to due process to vindicate a protected liberty or property interest. The reasoning was similar to that advanced by the court in *Andrews,* which was cited with approval. The court added that a governmental policy that intruded on a person's private right to bear or beget an illegitimate child must be supported by a compelling state interest. The creation of irrebuttable presumption of disqualification to teach because of having an illegitimate child did not withstand constitutional scrutiny. The court was careful to add that it expressed no opinion on the morality of bearing illegitimate children. However, the court was firm in its opinion that the public interest would be disserved if a breach of constitutional rights was tolerated for even a minimal period of time. The right to a due process hearing was affirmed in *Johnson v. San Jacinto Jr. College* (1980) under circumstances wherein a plaintiff was demoted from registrar to teaching status.

Andrews has been cited frequently in cases arising out of the public school system. These cases have uniformly supported the rule of law established in *Andrews* and have accepted its rationale. Examples are *Street v. Cobb County Sch. Dist.* (1981) and *Avery v. Homewood City Bd. of Ed.* (1982).

The Field of Recreation

A case involving recreation follows. Here a staff member of a private social club for girls was discharged for violating the club's negative role model policy. This policy was gender neutral but did mandate the termination of unmarried staff members who either became pregnant or caused pregnancy. Here the role model rule was accepted as a bona fide occupational qualification (BFOQ) and was justified by business necessity.

• •

CHAMBERS v. OMAHA GIRLS CLUB, INC.
834 F.2d 697 (8th Cir. 1987)

WOLLMAN, Circuit Judge.

Crystal Chambers appeals the district court's orders and judgment disposing of her civil rights, Title VII employment discrimination, and pendent state law claims. Chambers' claims arise from her dismissal as an employee at the Omaha Girls Club on account of her being single and pregnant in violation of the Club's "role model rule." The primary issue in this appeal is whether the Club's role model rule is an employment practice that is consistent with Title VII because it is justifiable as a business necessity or a bona fide occupational qualification.

I

The Omaha Girls Club is a private, nonprofit corporation that offers programs designed to assist young girls between the ages of eight and eighteen to maximize their life opportunities.[1] Among the Club's many activities are programs directed at pregnancy prevention. The Club serves 1,500 members, ninety percent of them black, at its North Omaha facility and 500 members, fifty to sixty percent of them black, at its South Omaha facility. A substantial number of youngsters who are not Club members also participate in its programs. The Club employs thirty to thirty-five persons at its two facilities; all of the non-administrative personnel at the North Omaha facility are black, and fifty to sixty percent of the personnel at the South Omaha facility are black.

The Club's approach to fulfilling its mission emphasizes the development of close contacts and the building of relationships between the girls and the Club's staff members. Toward this end, staff members are trained and expected to act as role models for the girls, with the intent that the girls will seek to emulate their behavior. The Club formulated its "role model rule"

---

1. The Club's objectives are to:
    1. Create a safe and stable environment that fosters trusting relationships and individual value development through interaction with peers and adults.
    2. Develop and implement programs to enable girls to build positive self esteem through skill development and application.
    3. Make available quality health programs so girls may understand and deal with their own health problems and health maintenance.
    4. Establish a climate where girls participate in and experience the decision making process and have broad opportunity to take leadership roles.
    5. Provide opportunities for girls to explore the full range of their personal options in family roles and career choices in order to take control of their lives.
    6. Encourage a knowledge and understanding of the various cultures in our society. Promote a broad view of responsibility as a citizen of a larger community through education and civic activity.
    7. Encourage both individual and group responsibility.

Record at 30.

banning single parent pregnancies among its staff members in pursuit of this role model approach.[2]

Chambers, a black single woman, was employed by the Club as an arts and crafts instructor at the Club's North Omaha facility. She became pregnant and informed her supervisor of that fact. Subsequently, she received a letter notifying her that because of her pregnancy her employment was to be terminated. Shortly after her termination, Chambers filed charges with the Nebraska Equal Opportunity Commission (NEOC) alleging discrimination on the basis of sex and marital status. The NEOC found no reasonable cause to believe that unlawful employment discrimination had occurred. Chambers[3] then brought this action in the district court seeking injunctions and damages.[4]

Chambers ultimately alleged, after a series of amendments to her complaint, that her rights under the first, fifth, ninth, and fourteenth amendments had been violated. She asserted civil rights claims under 42 U.S.C. §§ 1981, 1983, 1985, 1986, and 1988, and state law claims for bad faith discharge, defamation, invasion of privacy, intentional infliction of emotional distress, intimidation, and conspiracy to deprive her of her livelihood. She also alleged violations of Title VII. Chambers named as defendants numerous organizations and individuals associated with those organizations: the Club, its director, deputy director, and board of directors; the *Omaha World Herald* newspaper and three of its officers; the NEOC, its executive director, and its commissioners; Charles Thone, the Governor of Nebraska; and Paul Douglas, the Attorney General of Nebraska.[5]

---

2. The Club's personnel policies state the rule as follows:

MAJOR CLUB RULES.

> All persons employed by the Girls Club of Omaha are subject to the rules and regulations as established by the Board of Directors. The following are not permitted and such acts may result in immediate discharge: [Rules 1–10 deleted]
> * * * * * *
> 11.   Negative role modeling for Girls Club Members to include such things
>   as single parent pregnancies.

Record at 28.

3. As the case caption indicates, Chambers also brought this action on behalf of her daughter Ruth, the child born of the pregnancy that brought about this litigation. The district court dismissed Ruth Chambers for lack of standing. Chambers challenges the district court's conclusion on the standing issue in this appeal. *See infra* at 704-705.

4. Chambers brought this action during the pendency of her appeal to the Equal Employment Opportunity Commission's (EEOC's) District Office. The EEOC later found reasonable cause to believe that Chambers' charge of employment discrimination was true, but did not enter into a conciliation agreement with or bring a civil action against the Club. Chambers amended her complaint to add the employment discrimination claims under Title VII after receiving a right-to-sue letter from the EEOC pursuant to 42 U.S.C. § 2000e-5(f)(1) (1982).

5. Several of the defendants were named as parties to this case primarily on the basis of Chambers' allegations that they were involved in a conspiracy to deprive her of her rights in violation of section 1985(3), section 1986, and state law. Although Chambers appeals the various determinations of the district court rejecting her conspiracy claims, *see infra* at 15-16, we

On October 19, 1983, the district court[6] issued an order dismissing Chambers' section 1983 claim against the Club,[7] finding the NEOC absolutely immune from liability under section 1983, dismissing Governor Thone and Attorney General Douglas for failure to state a claim against them, and dismissing all of the state law claims except the conspiracy and intimidation claims. On November 7, 1985, the district court entered an order granting the motion of the *Omaha World Herald* for summary judgment on the section 1985(3) and state conspiracy claims against it. On January 6, 1986, the matter went to trial. The claims remaining against the Club at the time of trial included: (1) conspiracy to deprive Chambers of her rights in violation of 42 U.S.C. § 1985(3), (2) conspiracy in violation of state law, (3) intentional race discrimination in violation of 42 U.S.C. § 1981, and (4) a combination of race and sex discrimination in the course of employment in violation of 42 U.S.C. § 2000e-2(a).[8] At the close of the plaintiff's case the court directed a verdict in favor of the Club on the section 1985(3), section 1981, and state conspiracy claims. The court explained its grounds for directing the verdict and announced its judgment in favor of the Club on the Title VII claims in its order of February 11, 1986. *Chambers v. Omaha Girls Club*, 629 F.Supp. 925 (D. Neb. 1986).

II

We turn first to the district court's determination of the Title VII questions. The district court examined Chambers' allegations of employment discrimination[9] in violation of 42 U.S.C. § 2000e-2(a) under both the disparate impact and disparate treatment theories.[10] We review in turn the court's conclusions and Chambers' arguments under each of these theories.

find it unnecessary for the purposes of this opinion to recount in detail the alleged facts in support of these claims. Stated generally, Chambers alleged that the spouses of different *Omaha World Herald* officers were members of the NEOC and the Club's board of directors, that they caused the proceedings before the NEOC to be prejudiced and caused an editorial supporting the role model rule to be published in the *Omaha World Herald*, and that public officials knew of or aided the alleged conspiratorial activities.

6. The Honorable Warren K. Urbom, United States District Judge for the District of Nebraska. On December 31, 1984, Judge Urbom granted Chambers' motion for his recusal. Recusal is the action of a judge stepping down from a case. All orders entered after that date and referred to in this opinion were issued by the Honorable C. Arlen Beam, Chief Judge, United States District Court for the District of Nebraska.

7. Hereinafter we refer to the Club defendants collectively as the "Club." Similarly, we will refer to the other groups of defendants as the "*Omaha World Herald*" and the "NEOC."

8. Chambers voluntarily dismissed her claim under the free exercise clause of the first amendment. The district court did not consider Chambers' other constitutional claims. Chambers challenges the district court's failure to do so in this appeal. *See infra* at 704-705. The district court also dismissed Chambers' state claim for intimidation.

9. Neither party challenges the district court's description of Chambers' Title VII claim as based on a "combination of race and sex discrimination." *Chambers*, 629 F.Supp. at 944. The court also noted that it was concerned with race discrimination "only insofar as [the role model rule] may have an impact upon the class of black women." *Id.*

10. 42 U.S.C. § 2000e-2(a) (1982) provides:

A

A plaintiff seeking to prove discrimination under the disparate impact theory must show that a facially neutral employment practice has a significant adverse impact on members of a protected minority group. The burden then shifts to the employer to show that the practice has a manifest relationship to the employment in question and is justifiable on the ground of business necessity. Even if the employer shows that the discriminatory employment practice is justified by business necessity, the plaintiff may prevail by showing that other practices would accomplish the employer's objectives without the attendant discriminatory effects.[11] The district court found that "because of the significantly higher fertility rate among black females, the rule banning single pregnancies would impact black women more harshly." *Chambers*, 629 F.Supp. at 949.[12] Thus, Chambers established the disparate impact of the role model rule.[13] The Club then sought to justify the rule as a business necessity.

Establishing a business necessity defense presents an employer with a "heavy burden." *Hawkins v. Anheuser-Busch, Inc.*, 697 F.2d 810, 815 (8th Cir.

It shall be an unlawful employment practice for an employer—
(1) to fail or refuse to hire or to discharge any individual, or otherwise to discriminate against any individual with respect to his compensation, terms, conditions, or privileges of employment, because of such individual's race, color, religion, sex, or national origin; or
(2) to limit, segregate, or classify his employees or applicants for employment in any way which would deprive or tend to deprive any individual of employment opportunities or otherwise adversely affect his status as an employee, because of such individual's race, color, religion, sex, or national origin.

A separate provision makes it clear that Title VII prohibits discrimination on the basis of pregnancy. 42 U.S.C. § 2000e(k) (1982) provides in part:
For purposes of this subchapter—

* * * * * *

(k) The terms "because of sex" or "on the basis of sex" include, but are not limited to, because of or on the basis of pregnancy, childbirth, or related medical conditions; and women affected by pregnancy, childbirth, or related medical conditions shall be treated the same for all employment-related purposes, including receipt of benefits under fringe benefit programs, as other persons not so affected but similar in their ability or inability to work * * *.

11. [Citing cases.]

12. The court relied on statistics showing that black women generally, and black women within certain age groups in Douglas County, Nebraska, specifically, are more likely to become pregnant than white women. *Chambers*, 629 F.Supp. at 949 n. 45.

13. The district court found that Chambers had established disparate impact under the first method articulated by this court in *Green v. Missouri Pac. R.R.*, 523 F.2d 1290, 1293-94 (8th Cir. 1975). *Chambers*, 629 F.Supp. at 948-49. The Club argues in its brief that the court erred in finding disparate impact. We are unpersuaded by the Club's argument and, furthermore, we are disinclined to devote further attention to the issue because of the Club's failure to assert a cross-appeal seeking reversal of the district court's finding of disparate impact. *See Wycoff v. Menke*, 773 F.2d 983, 985 (8th Cir. 1985) (cross-appeal necessary to modify or alter lower court decision), *cert. denied*, 475 U.S. 1028, 106 S.Ct. 1230, 89 L.Ed.2d 339 (1986).

1983). Business necessity exists only if the challenged employment practice has """a manifest relationship to the employment in question.""" *Id.* (quoting *Dothard v. Rawlinson,* 433 U.S. 321, 329, 97 S.Ct. 2720, 2725, 53 L.Ed.2d 786 (1977) (quoting *Griggs v. Duke Power Co.,* 401 U.S. 424, 432, 91 S.Ct. 849, 854, 28 L.Ed.2d 158 (1971))). The employer must demonstrate that there is a "'compelling need * * * to maintain that practice,'" and the practice cannot be justified by "'routine business considerations.'" *Id.* (quoting *Kirby v. Colony Furniture Co.,* 613 F.2d 696, 706 n.6 (8th Cir. 1980)); *see also EEOC v. Rath Packing Co.,* 787 F.2d 318, 331 (8th Cir.), *cert denied,* ___ U.S. ___, 107 S.Ct. 307, 93 L.Ed.2d 282 (1986). Moreover, the employer may be required to show that the challenged employment practice is "'necessary to safe and efficient job performance,'" *McCosh v. City of Grand Forks,* 628 F.2d 1058, 1062 (8th Cir. 1980) (quoting *Dothard,* 433 U.S. at 332 n. 14, 97 S.Ct. at 2728 n. 14); *see also Rath Packing Co.,* 787 F.2d at 328; *Donnell v. General Motors Corp.,* 576 F.2d 1292, 1299 (8th Cir. 1978), or that the employer's goals are "significantly served by" the practice. [Citing cases.]

The district court found that the role model rule is justified by business necessity because there is a manifest relationship between the Club's fundamental purpose and the rule. Specifically, the court found:

> The Girls Club has established by the evidence that its only purpose is to serve young girls between the ages of eight and eighteen and to provide these women with exposure to the greatest number of available positive options in life. The Girls Club has established that teenage pregnancy is contrary to this purpose and philosophy. The Girls Club established that it honestly believed that to permit single pregnant staff members to work with the girls would convey the impression that the Girls Club condoned pregnancy for the girls in the age group it serves. The testimony of board members * * * made clear that the policy was not based upon a morality standard, but rather, on a belief that teenage pregnancies severely limit the available opportunities for teenage girls. The Girls Club also established that the policy was just one prong of a comprehensive attack on the problem of teenage pregnancy. The Court is satisfied that a manifest relationship exists between the Girls Club's fundamental purpose and its single pregnancy policy.

Chambers, 629 F.Supp. at 950. The court also relied in part on expert testimony to the effect that the role model rule could be helpful in preventing teenage pregnancy.[14] Chambers argues, however, that the district court erred

14. Chambers' expert witness testified that the only way to resolve the teenage pregnancy problem was through economic opportunities such as education and jobs. The Club's expert agreed that these factors were important, but also testified concerning the value of role modeling and concluded that the role model rule "could be (and in her opinion is) another viable way to attack the problem of teenage pregnancy." *Chambers,* 629 F.Supp. at 951.

In addition to relying on the evidence concerning the Club's purpose and approach and the expert testimony, the district court found that the rule was adopted in response to two incidents involving Club members' reactions to the pregnancies of single Club staff members. *Id.* at 945.

in finding business necessity because the role model rule is based only on speculation by the Club and has not been validated by any studies showing that it prevents pregnancy among the Club's members.

Business necessity determinations in disparate impact cases are reviewed under the clearly erroneous standard of review applied to factual findings. Fed.R.Civ.P. 52(a); *see Hawkins*, 697 F.2d at 815; *see also Reddemann v. Minnesota Higher Educ. Coordinating Bd.*, 811 F.2d 1208, 1209 (8th Cir. 1987) (per curiam). Thus, we may reverse the district court's finding of business necessity only if we are "'left with the definite and firm conviction that a mistake has been committed.'" *Anderson v. City of Bessemer City*, 470 U.S. 564, 573, 105 S.Ct. 1504, 1511, 84 L.Ed.2d 518 (1985) (quoting *United States v. United States Gypsum Co.*, 333 U.S. 364, 395, 68 S.Ct. 525, 541, 92 L.Ed. 746 (1948)).

We believe that "the district court's account of the evidence is plausible in light of the record viewed in its entirety." *Id.* 470 U.S. at 573-74, 105 S.Ct. at 1511-12. Therefore, we cannot say that the district court's finding of business necessity is clearly erroneous. The district court's conclusion on the evidence is not an impermissible one. Although validation studies can be helpful in evaluating such questions, they are not required to maintain a successful business necessity defense. *Hawkins*, 697 F.2d at 815-16; *see Davis v. City of Dallas*, 777 F.2d 205, 217-18 (5th Cir.1985), *cert. denied*, 476 U.S. 1116, 106 S. Ct. 1972, 90 L.Ed.2d 656 (1986). Indeed, we are uncertain whether the role model rule by its nature is suited to validation by an empirical study.[15] Consequently, the court's conclusion in *Hawkins* is apt in this case: "We cannot say * * * that validation studies are always required and we are not willing to hold under the facts of this case that such evidence was required here." *Id.* at 816.

Chambers argues further, however, that the district court erred in discounting alternative practices that the Club could have used to ameliorate the discriminatory effects of the role model rule. Chambers contends that the Club either could have granted her a leave of absence or transferred her to a position that did not involve contact with the Club's members. The Club responds that neither of these alternatives was available in this case. The Club has a history of granting leaves of up to six weeks, but the purposes of the role model rule would have required a five to six month leave for Chambers, given that the pregnancy would have become visually apparent probably within

---

15. Ironically, at oral argument Chambers' counsel responded in the negative to the court's question concerning whether the rule could ever be empirically proven to prevent pregnancy among the Club's members. Counsel's response must be construed to mean either that it is impossible to perform a meaningful empirical study of such matters, or that counsel believes that no such study would ever show the rule to have the effect desired by the Club. If we were to adopt the first construction it would be ludicrous for us to reverse for lack of validation studies. Moreover, the second construction presents nothing more than counsel's own belief concerning the role model rule, a belief rejected by the district court in favor of that held by the Club.

three or four months. Moreover, employing a temporary replacement to take Chamber's [sic] position would itself have required six months of on-the-job training before the replacement would have been able to interact with the girls on the level that the Club's approach requires. The use of temporary replacements would also disrupt the atmosphere of stability that the Club attempts to provide and would be inconsistent with the relationship-building and interpersonal interaction entailed in the Club's role model approach. Furthermore, transfer to a "noncontact position" apparently was impossible because there are no positions at the Club that do not involve contact with Club members. The district court found that the Club considered these alternatives and determined them to be unworkable. *Chambers*, 629 F.Supp. at 945-46. We are unable to conclude that the district court's finding that there were no satisfactory alternatives to the dismissal of Chambers pursuant to the role model rule is clearly erroneous. Accordingly, we hold that the district court's finding that the role model rule is justified by business necessity and thus does not violate Title VII under the disparate impact theory is not clearly erroneous.

B

Unlike the disparate impact theory, the disparate treatment theory requires a plaintiff seeking to prove employment discrimination to show discriminatory animus. The plaintiff must first establish a prima facie case of discrimination. The burden of production then shifts to the employer to show a legitimate, nondiscriminatory reason for the challenged employment practice. If the employer makes such a showing, then the plaintiff may show that the reasons given by the employer were pretextual.[16] No violation of Title VII exists, however, if the employer can show that the challenged employment practice is a bona fide occupational qualification (bfoq).[17]

The district court found that Chambers had succeeded in establishing a prima facie case of discrimination but concluded that the Club's role model approach is a legitimate, nondiscriminatory reason for the role model rule. *Chambers*, 629 F.Supp. at 947. The court then found that Chambers was unable to show that the Club's reason for the rule was a pretext for intentional discrimination. *Id.* at 947-48. The court also stated in passing that the role model rule "presumably" is a bfoq. *Id.* at 941 n. 51.

Chambers argues alternatively that the district court erred in failing to find a violation of Title VII under the disparate treatment theory, and that this case should not be analyzed under the disparate treatment theory because Chambers' discharge on account of her pregnancy constitutes intentional discrimination without further analysis. Chambers also argues that the role model rule cannot

16. (Citing cases)

17. The bfoq exception, unlike the business necessity defense, is statutorily based. 42 U.S.C. § 2000e-2(e) (1982) provides in part:

Notwithstanding any other provision of this subchapter, (1) it shall not be an unlawful employment practice for an employer to hire and employ employees, * * * on the basis of his religion, sex, or national origin in those certain instances where religion, sex, or national origin is a bona fide occupational qualification reasonably necessary to the normal operation of that particular business or enterprise * * *.

be justified as a bfoq. Because we are persuaded that the role model rule qualifies as a bfoq, we find it unnecessary to address Chambers' other arguments.[18]

The bfoq exception is "'an extremely narrow exception to the general prohibition of discrimination on the basis of sex.'" *Gunther v. Iowa State Men's Reformatory*, 612 F.2d 1079, 1085 (8th Cir.), *cert. denied*, 446 U.S. 966, 100 S.Ct. 2942, 64 L.Ed.2d 825 (1980), (quoting *Dothard v. Rawlinson*, 433 U.S. 321, 334, 97 S.Ct. 2720, 2729, 53 L.Ed.2d 786 (1977)). In *Dothard v. Rawlinson*, 433 U.S. at 321, 97 S.Ct. at 2720, the Supreme Court found that a rule that prohibited employment of women in contact positions in all-male Alabama prisons was a bfoq under the particular circumstances of that case, which involved a prison system rife with violence. The statutory language, *see supra* note 17, is, of course, the best guide to the content of the bfoq exception; however, the courts, including the Supreme Court in *Dothard*, have noted the existence of several formulations for evaluating whether an employment practice is a bfoq. The formulations include: whether "'the *essence* of the business operation would be undermined'" without the challenged employment practice, *Dothard*, 433 U.S. at 333, 97 S.Ct. at 2728 (quoting *Diaz v. Pan American World Airways, Inc.*, 442 F.2d 385, 388 (5th Cir.), *cert. denied*, 404 U.S. 950, 92 S.Ct. 275, 30 L.Ed.2d 267 (1971) (emphasis in original); whether safe and efficient performance of the job would be possible without the challenged employment practice, *id.* (citing *Weeks v. Southern Bell Tel. & Tel. Co.*, 408 F.2d 228, 235 (5th Cir. 1969)); and whether the challenged employment practice has "'a manifest relationship to the employment in question.'" *Gunther*, 612 F.2d at 1086 (quoting *Griggs v. Duke Power Co.*, 401 U.S. 424, 432, 91 S.Ct. 849, 854, 28 L.Ed.2d 158 (1971)).

Although the district court did not clearly conclude that the role model rule qualified as a bfoq, several of the court's other findings are persuasive on this issue. The court's findings of fact, many of which are relevant to the analysis of a potential bfoq exception, are binding on this court unless clearly erroneous. The facts relevant to establishing a bfoq are the same as those found by the district court in the course of its business necessity analysis. As already noted, *see supra* at 701-02, the district court found that the role model rule has a manifest relationship to the Club's fundamental purpose and that there were no workable alternatives to the rule. Moreover, the district court's finding of business necessity itself is persuasive as to the existence of a bfoq. This court has noted that the analysis of a bfoq "is similar to and overlaps with the judicially created 'business necessity' test." *Gunther*, 612 F.2d at 1086 n. 8. The various standards for establishing business necessity are quite similar to those for determining a bfoq. Indeed, this court has on different occasions applied

18. Even if the district court erred in finding no discrimination under the disparate treatment theory, our conclusion that the role model rule is a bfoq means that there can be no violation of Title VII. Moreover, the *per se* intentional discrimination approach advocated by Chambers simply eliminates the burden-shifting procedure described *supra* at 703, leaving the bfoq exception as the employer's only defense. Thus, our conclusion on the bfoq issue also would prevent Chambers from prevailing under her proposed *per se* intentional discrimination approach.

the same standard—"manifest relationship" — to both business necessity and bfoq. *Compare Hawkins v. Anheuser-Busch, Inc.*, 697 F.2d 810, 815 (8th Cir. 1983) (business necessity) *with Gunther v. Iowa State Men's Reformatory,* 612 F.2d 1079, 1086 (8th Cir.), *cert. denied*, 446 U.S. 966, 100 S.Ct. 2942, 64 L.Ed.2d 825 (1980) (bfoq).[19] Inasmuch as we already have affirmed the district court's finding of business necessity as not clearly erroneous, *see supra* at 703, we feel compelled to conclude that "[i]n the particular factual circumstances of this case," *Dothard*, 433 U.S. at 334, 97 S.Ct. at 2729, the role model rule is reasonably necessary to the Club's operations. Thus, we hold that the role model rule qualifies as a bona fide occupational qualification.

III

Chambers also appeals the district court's dismissal of various other claims and parties. Specifically, she challenges the court's dismissal of the section 1983 claim against the Club for lack of state action, *Chambers v. Omaha Girls Club, Inc.*, No. CV 83-L-38, slip op. at 3-4 (D.Neb. October 19, 1983); dismissal of the NEOC on the ground of absolute immunity based on *Butz v. Economou*, 438 U.S. 478, 98 S.Ct. 2894, 57 L.Ed.2d 895 (1978), *id.* at 4; dismissal of Governor Thone and Attorney General Douglas for failure to state a claim against them, *id.* at 4-6; grant of summary judgment in favor of the *Omaha World Herald* on the section 1985(3) and state conspiracy claims because of Chambers' failure to show conspiratorial agreement or other elements of the cause of action, *Chambers v. Omaha Girls Club, Inc.*, No. CV 83-L-38, slip op. at 3-6 (D. Neb. Nov. 7, 1985); dismissal of Ruth Chambers for failure to meet constitutional standing requirements, *Chambers v. Omaha Girls Club*, No. CV 83-L-38, slip op. at 3 (D.Neb. Jan. 13, 1986); dismissal of the constitutional claims for lack of state action, *Chambers v. Omaha Girls Club*, 629 F.Supp. 925, 931 n. 9 (D.Neb. 1986); grant of a directed verdict in favor of the Club on the section 1981 claim because Chambers failed to produce any evidence of intentional race discrimination, *id.* at 932-34; and grant of a directed verdict in favor of the Club on the section 1985(3) and state conspiracy claims because no evidence was presented to show that the Club was part of a conspiratorial agreement. *Id.* at 934-42. Our review of the record, the briefs, and the memorandum opinions of the district court satisfies us that Chambers' arguments on these issues are without merit.[20]

IV

In conclusion, we hold that the district court's finding that the Club's role

19. Further indication of the similarity of business necessity and bfoq is provided in *Dothard*, 433 U.S. at 321, 97 S.Ct. at 2720, where the Court referred to the "necessary to safe and efficient job performance" standard in relation to both of the defenses. *Compare Dothard*, 433 U.S. at 332 n. 14, 97 S.Ct. at 2728 n. 14 (business necessity) *with Dothard*, 433 U.S. at 333, 97 S.Ct. at 2728 (bfoq).

20. Chambers' claim that the defendants' exercise of their peremptory challenges was unconstitutionally discriminatory is unavailing inasmuch as it was not raised below and no jury verdict even exists to be challenged in this case. Chambers' argument that Judge Beam erred in refusing to recuse himself is also without merit.

model rule is justified by business necessity is not clearly erroneous, and we find further that the rule qualifies as a bona fide occupational qualification. Chambers' other allegations of error are without merit. Accordingly, the orders and judgment of the district court are affirmed.

Questions and Comments

1. How does this case differ from a public school case from a constitutional standpoint?
2. How did the Omaha Girls Club, Inc., seek to justify its role model rule? What is a BFOQ as defined in the case?
3. Disparate treatment is direct and is obvious whereas disparate impact is indirect and may not be obvious. One form is blatant and obvious; the other is subtle and devious. Find the court's definition of disparate impact in the body of the case.

Authors' Note

The Pregnancy Discrimination Act (1978), the Americans with Disabilities Act (1990), and the Family and Medical Leave Act (1993) all influence employers' decisions concerning employment, leaves, replacement, and discipline for poor work attendance.

Under the Americans With Disabilities Act (1990), pregnancy is not an impairment. However, complications that may develop from the pregnancy, such as blood clots or high blood pressure, might be a disability.

The final regulations on the Family Medical and Leave Act (1993) became effective in 1995. The Act provides for 12 weeks of unpaid leave in a 12-month period to all eligible employees for the birth, adoption, or placement of a foster child. Every employer with 50 or more employees is affected. Leaves may also extend to care for a spouse, child, parent, or for the employee's serious illness. The employer is not required to pay the employee on leave. However, the employer is required to maintain the employee's health insurance and to reinstate the employee in the same or an equivalent position.

In addition to the federal statutes stated above, some states have additional enactments. Sport managers should be aware of appropriate state laws.

For readers who are interested in cases involving marriage and procreation as a fundamental right, attention is directed to the following cases: *Lewis v. Delaware State College* (1978); *Ponton v. Newport News Sch. Bd.* (1986); *Eckmann v. Board of Educ. of Hawthorn Sch. Dist. No. 17* (1986); cases relied on in *Eckmann* included *Loving v. Virginia* (1967) and *Eisenstadt v. Baird* (1972).

SUMMARY

Marriage and procreation come under the heading of fundamental rights. Rules for establishing irrebuttable presumptions are generally unwise.

Teachers are generally considered as role models. The effect of unmarried pregnancy on role model status in the field of education has changed over the years.

Public education involves state action. Hence, due process considerations are involved.

Private recreational activities do not involve state action. Role model regulations have been upheld for private recreational facilities.

This could be you - check your response

Doe is unmarried and pregnant when she applies for the public university's teaching position. The job interviewer cannot ask if she is married because marital status is a discriminatory area and would not be part of the job description needed for a soccer instructor at a public institution. If she is refused employment at the university, it should be on grounds other than marital status. It may be that she has been artificially inseminated or her fiance died. It would be difficult for a public institution to impose morality. As the courts have noted, the right to bear children is fundamental.

If the soccer clinic is being sponsored by a private entity (YWCA), standards might be different if the private organization can make the case that the instructor is a role model for young girls and an unmarried, pregnant female is not the role model acceptable to the standards of their organization. Refer back to the cases in this chapter.

REFERENCES

Cases

Andrews v. Drew Municipal Separate Sch. Dist., 507 F.2d 611 (5th Cir. 1975).

Avery v. Homewood City Bd. of Ed., 674 F.2d 337 (5th Cir. 1982).

Board of Ed. of Long Beach Unified Sch. Dist. of Los Angeles County v. Jack M., 566 P.2d 602 (Cal. 1977).

Chambers v. Omaha Girls Club, Inc., 834 F.2d 697 (8th Cir. 1987).

Cochran v. Chidester Sch. Dist. of Ouachita County Arkansas, 456 F. Supp. 390 (W.D. Ark. 1978).

Eckmann v. Board of Educ. of Hawthorn Sch. Dist. No. 17, 636 F. Supp. 1214 (N.D. Ill. 1986).

Eisenstadt v. Baird, 405 U.S. 438, 92 S. Ct. 1029, 31 L. Ed.2d 349 (1972).

Felts v. Radio Distributing Co., 637 F. Supp. 229 (N.D. Ind. 1985).

Hargett v. Delta Automotive, Inc., 765 F. Supp. 1487 (N.D. Ala. 1991).

Harvey v. Young Women's Christian Ass'n., 533 F. Supp. 949 (W.D. N.C. 1982).

Hollenbaugh v. Carnegie Free Library, 436 F. Supp. 1328 (W.D. Pa. 1977).

Johnson v. San Jacinto Jr. College, 498 F. Supp. 555 (S.D. Tex. 1980).

Leechburg Area Sch. Dist. v. Commonwealth, Human Relations Comm'n, 339 A.2d 850 (Pa. Commw. Ct. 1975).

Lewis v. Delaware State College, 455 F. Supp. 239 (D. Del. 1978).

Loving v. Virginia, 388 U.S. 1, 87 S.Ct. 1817, 18 L.Ed. 2d 1010 (1967).

Ponton v. Newport News Sch. Bd., 632 F. Supp. 1056 (E.D. Va. 1986).

Street v. Cobb County Sch. Dist., 520 F. Supp. 1170 (N.D. Ga. 1981).

Sullivan v. Meade Independent Sch. Dist. No. 101, 530 F.2d 799 (8th Cir. 1976).

Thompson v. Southwest Sch. Dist., 483 F. Supp. 1170 (W.D. Mo. 1980).

Model Codes, Restatements, and Standards

Americans With Disabilities Act, Pub. L. 101-336, 104 Stat. 327 (1990).

Family and Medical Leave Act, Pub. L. 103-3 & A-6 (1993).

Pregnancy Discrimination Act, Pub. L. 95-555, Oct. 31, 1978, 92 Stat. 2076 (42 U.S.C.A. § 2000e(k)). See also 42 U.S.C.A. § 2000e-2(h).

CHAPTER 18

SEX DISCRIMINATION: HARASSMENT

INTRODUCTION

Sexual harassment will be discussed under two main topics: first, "What constitutes sexual harassment?" and second, "What remedies are available?" Sexual harassment is generally divided into two categories, *quid pro quo* and hostile environment. Remedies depend upon the statutory provision alleged to have been violated. Title VII of the Civil Rights Act of 1964 forms the basis of some of the remedies for sexual harassment. The remedies available under this provision have been supplemented by the Civil Rights Act of 1991. Title IX of the Educational Amendments of 1972 provides remedies for one segment of society, educational settings. In addition, most states have enacted civil rights legislation that also governs sexual harassment. Each of these topics will be discussed in some detail in the cases that follow. Statutory enactments will also be referred to for further clarification

---

IN THIS CHAPTER YOU WILL LEARN:

The specific federal legislation available to a
    victim of sexual harassment

The types of sexual harassment

The legislation and judicial decisions that
    strengthen remedies for the victim of sex-
    ual harassment

Common law remedies available to the victim
    of sexual harassment

Some practical suggestions designed to reduce
    the incidence of sexual harassment

Some considerations for drafting and imple-
    menting a sexual harassment policy

KEY WORDS: *sexual harassment, Title VII of the Civil Rights Act of 1964, quid pro quo, hostile environment, Title IX of the Educational Amendments of 1972*

This could be you!

The unmarried status of the pregnant employee Ms Doe has not gone unnoticed by other employees. Ron Clark, a fitness instructor employed by Mr. Jones in one of his efforts at diversification, commences making sexual overtures to Doe. She lets Clark know that she is not interested. Eventually, however, she becomes intimately involved with Clark. As time goes on, Doe seeks to break off the relationship, but Clark threatens her with a disclosure of their relationship, a revelation that, in a small town, might prove devastating. Clark also indicates that he is prepared to recommend Doe's termination if she does not continue their relationship. Evaluate the potential liability of Mr. and Mrs. Jones as employers who might be confronted with the charge of sexual harassment. What advice could you give to other employers who might wish to take steps to prevent such a charge from being filed?

SEXUAL HARASSMENT

At the federal level, sexual harassment has received attention by Congress. Two applicable statutes are referenced below.

Title VII of the Civil Rights Act of 1964

(a) It shall be an unlawful employment practice for an employer—

  (1) to fail or refuse to hire or to discharge any individual, or otherwise to discriminate against any individual with respect to his compensation, terms, conditions, or privileges of employment, because of such individual's race, color, religion, sex, or national origin; or

  (2) to limit, segregate, or classify his employees or applicants for employment in any way which would deprive or tend to deprive any individual of employment opportunities or otherwise adversely affect his status as an employee, because of such individual's race, color, religion, sex, or national origin.
  [42 USCA §§ 2000e-2(a)(1) and 2000e-2(a)(2)]

Authors' Note

The statute initially did not apply to educational institutions. This exemption was removed with the Equal Employment Opportunity Act of 1972 (1972). (See 42 U.S.C.A. §2000e-1.)

The case that follows (*Karibian v. Columbia University*, 1994) delineates the two types of sexual harassment, namely *quid pro quo* and harassment arising out of a hostile work environment. The case also addresses the duty of a university to take action when information has been communicated on a confidential basis. This point is important but seldom referred to in decisional law.

Sexual harassment is a type of employment discrimination that includes sexual advances, requests for sexual favors, and other verbal or physical conduct of a nature prohibited by Federal Law (Title VII of 1964 Civil Rights Act).... (BLACK'S LAW DICTIONARY, 1990, p. 1375). *Quid pro quo* sexual harassment refers to the concept of something for something, for example, a sexual favor for a promotion on the job.

Hostile-environment sexual harassment involves a display of sexual antagonism. A hostile environment in the work place occurs when the work place is permeated with discriminatory behavior that is sufficiently severe or pervasive to create an environment a reasonable person would find hostile or abusive.

A landmark case on sexual harassment is *Meritor Saving Bank, FSB v. Vinson* (1986). Note that the *Karibian* case uses the concepts of sexual harassment taken from the *Meritor Savings Bank* case. Would these concepts be applicable to a sport business? Read the following case for its applications to sport managers.

••

KARIBIAN v. COLUMBIA UNIVERSITY
14 F.3rd 773 (2d Cir. 1994)

McLAUGHLIN, Circuit Judge:

Sharon Karibian appeals from a judgment entered in the United States District Court for the Southern District of New York (Thomas P. Griesa, Chief Judge) granting summary judgment to defendants Columbia University and John Borden, and dismissing Karibian's complaint of employment discrimination. Karibian's complaint alleged that sexual harassment committed by her supervisor, defendant Mark Urban, constituted discrimination by Columbia on the basis of sex, in violation of Title VII of the Civil Rights Act of 1964, 42 U.S.C. § 2000e-2(a)(1), and section 296 of New York's Executive Law. Karibian additionally alleged various state law tort claims against Columbia, Borden and Urban.

In the district court, Karibian proceeded under both available theories of sexual harassment: *quid pro quo,* and hostile work environment. In granting summary judgment to defendants, the district court held that Columbia could not be liable under a *quid pro quo* theory because Karibian failed to prove any actual economic loss resulting from Urban's harassment. On her hostile work environment theory, the court held that Columbia was not liable to Karibian because it did not have notice of Urban's harassment and had provided a reasonable avenue for harassment complaints. *Karibian v. Columbia Univ.,* 812 F.Supp. 413 (S.D.N.Y.1993).

We conclude that the district court erred in requiring Karibian to demonstrate actual economic loss to prove *quid pro quo* sexual harassment. We also concluded that the court failed to apply the proper legal standard to determine an employer's liability for the hostile work environment created by a supervisor. Accordingly, we reverse and remand for further proceedings.

BACKGROUND

In 1987, while a student in Columbia University's General Studies Program, Sharon Karibian worked in Columbia's fundraising "Telefund" office. Telefund was administered for Columbia by an independent contractor, Philanthropy Management Company ("PMI"), and was staffed by both PMI and Columbia employees. Karibian was an employee of Columbia. The Telefund office operated under the aegis of Columbia's "University Development and Alumni Relations" office ("UDAR").

In September 1987, Columbia appointed defendant Mark Urban as Development Officer for Annual Giving at UDAR. In that capacity, Urban had supervisory authority over Telefund, and, consequently, over Karibian. Specifically, Urban had the authority to alter Karibian's work schedule and assignments, and to give her promotions and raises (subject to approval). In addition, Urban had at least the apparent authority to fire Karibian.

This case involves Urban's alleged conduct towards Karibian while the two were employees of Columbia. Urban conceded that he and Karibian had a sexual relationship while he was her supervisor; however, the nature of that relationship—*i.e.,* whether consensual or coercive—remains hotly disputed. We limit our discussion to Karibian's version of events.

While working at UDAR, Urban "pursued" Karibian by repeatedly inviting her out to bars, ostensibly to discuss work-related matters. On those occasions, Urban often asked Karibian back to his apartment. Initially, Karibian rebuffed Urban's advances; ultimately, however, she yielded to pressure from Urban. Specifically, Karibian claimed that Urban coerced her into a violent sexual relationship by telling her that she "owed him" for all he was doing for her as her supervisor. Karibian also claimed that the conditions of her employment—including her raises, hours, autonomy and flexibility—varied from time to time, depending on her responsiveness to Urban. Karibian stated that she believed she would be fired if she did not give in to Urban's demands.

At first, Karibian told no one about her relationship with Urban. After some time, however, Karibian contacted two counselors at Columbia. In September 1988, Karibian contacted Columbia's Panel on Sexual Harassment, and met with Panel member Mary Murphy. Karibian told Murphy that she was afraid her boss would retaliate against her if she stopped sleeping with him. Shortly thereafter, Karibian met with Columbia's Equal Opportunity Coordinator, Ruth Curtis. At Karibian's request, both meetings were held confidential, and neither resulted in any investigation of Urban. According to Karibian, both Murphy and Curtis discouraged her from actively pursuing a complaint against Urban.

In April 1989, Karibian came to work upset and told her immediate Telefund supervisor, Loren Spivack, of a particularly violent sexual encounter with Urban. Spivack, a PMI employee, notified PMI's president, Ron Erdos. Neither Spivack nor Erdos informed anyone at Columbia about the incident.

Around July of 1989, Karibian applied for the position of Annual Giving Development Officer at Columbia. Columbia did not immediately consider Karibian for the position because Urban delayed forwarding her resume to the personnel department. Although Columbia eventually considered Karibian's application, she did not get the job. About the same time, Karibian applied for and received a promotion to the position of Project Director, the highest position within Telefund. As Project Director, Karibian reported directly to Urban at UDAR.

In January 1990, Karibian complained to Gertrude de la Osa, the Director of Development Services at UDAR, that she was afraid of being fired by Urban and that Urban was "sabotaging" her at Telefund. De la Osa brought Karibian's complaint to the attention of UDAR's Deputy Vice President, defendant John Borden. Around the same time, Karibian met again with Ruth Curtis; this time, Karibian dropped her request for confidentiality and gave Curtis permission to speak to others at Columbia about her troubles with Urban.

At this point, Columbia took steps to resolve the problem. Borden asked Urban to write a chronology of his relationship with Karibian, and removed him from direct supervisory authority over Karibian. (According to Urban's chronology, his relationship with Karibian was entirely consensual.) Without crediting either Karibian's or Urban's characterization of their relationship, Columbia forced Urban to resign—for reasons that remain somewhat vague. In August 1990, Columbia closed the Telefund office and Karibian was laid off.

Karibian then brought this suit against Columbia, Borden and Urban, claiming that Urban's sexual harassment violated Title VII. Following discovery, the district court granted defendants' motion for summary judgment.

The court began its analysis by recognizing that Title VII encompasses two theories of sexual harassment: *quid pro quo,* and hostile work environment. 812 F.Supp. at 416. Rejecting Karibian's *quid pro quo* claim, the court ruled that this theory requires proof of "actual—rather than threatened—economic loss because of gender or because a sexual advance was made and rejected." *Id.* Because Karibian had not suffered any economic detriment during her relationship with Urban—in fact, she had been promoted and had received pay raises during the relevant time—the court ruled that Karibian had no valid claim for *quid pro quo* harassment. *Id.*

The district court also rejected Karibian's hostile work environment theory. Relying on *Kotcher v. Rosa & Sullivan Appliance Center, Inc.,* 957 F.2d 59 (2d Cir.1992), the court held that Karibian "must prove 'that the employer either provided no reasonable avenue for complaint or knew of the harassment but did nothing about it.'" 812 F.Supp. at 416 (quoting *Kotcher,* 957 F.2d at 63). Applying this standard, the court ruled that (1) Columbia provided a reasonable avenue for making complaints, and (2) once Columbia got actual notice of Urban's misconduct in 1990, it promptly took adequate curative measures. On the latter point, the court rejected Karibian's argument that her confidential disclosures to Murphy and Curtis were sufficient to put Columbia on notice of Urban's harassment. The court also rejected

Karibian's alternative argument that notice to her supervisors at PMI, an independent contractor, constituted notice to Columbia. Having disposed of Karibian's federal claim, the court went on to dismiss Karibian's pendent state law claims for lack of jurisdiction.

Karibian now appeals.[1]

DISCUSSION

By its terms, Title VII prohibits discrimination on the basis of sex with respect to the "compensation, terms, conditions, or privileges" of employment. 42 U.S.C. § 2000e-2(a)(1) (1988). Although neither the statute nor its legislative history fleshes out the meaning of this sweeping prohibition, it is now established law that sexual harassment in the workplace violates "Title VII's broad rule of workplace equality." *Harris v. Forklift Sys., Inc.,* ___U.S.,___,___ 114 S.Ct. 367, 371, 126 L.Ed.2d 295 (1993). While the law of sexual harassment continues to develop at a brisk pace, a plaintiff seeking relief for sexual harassment may presently proceed under two theories: (1) *quid pro quo,* and (2) hostile work environment. *See Meritor Sav. Bank, FSB v. Vinson,* 477 U.S. 57, 64-65, 106 S.Ct. 2399, 2404-05, 91 L.Ed.2d 49 (1986); *Kotcher,* 957 F.2d at 62. Karibian believes that Urban's harassment fits both paradigms; and we address each in turn.

I. *Karibian's Quid Pro Quo Claim*

Under the Guidelines established by the Equal Employment Opportunity Commission ("EEOC"), *quid pro quo* harassment occurs when "submission to or rejection of [unwelcome sexual] conduct by an individual is used as the basis for employment decisions affecting such individual." 29 C.F.R. § 1604.11(a)(2) (1993). *See also Carrero v. New York City Hous. Auth.,* 890 F.2d 569, 577 (2d Cir.1989). Accordingly, to establish a *prima facie* case of *quid pro quo* harassment, a plaintiff must present evidence that she was subject to unwelcome sexual conduct, and that her reaction to that conduct was then used as the basis for decisions affecting the compensation, terms, conditions or privileges of her employment. *See Lipsett v. University of Puerto Rico,* 864 F.2d 881, 898 (1st Cir.1988); *Highlander v. K.F.C. Nat'l Mgmt. Co.,* 805 F.2d 644, 648 (6th Cir.1986); *Henson v. City of Dundee,* 682 F.2d 897, 909 (11th Cir.1982).

Because the *quid pro quo* harasser, by definition, wields the employer's authority to alter the terms and conditions of employment—either actually or apparently—the law imposes strict liability on the employer for *quid pro quo*

---

1. In the district court, Karibian also alleged that Columbia closed the Telefund office in retaliation for Karibian's sexual harassment complaint. *See* 812 F.Supp. at 417. In her main brief on appeal, Karibian does not argue the point separately. Rather, Karibian simply characterizes the "premature" closing of the Telefund office as "retaliatory" in the context of her argument that Columbia's complaint procedures were inadequate.

We have no obligation to review issues that are raised, but not independently and sufficiently developed, in an appellant's main brief. *See Freeman United Coal Mining Co. v. OWCP,* 957 F.2d 302, 305 (7th Cir.1992). We conclude that for purposes of appeal, Karibian has forfeited—if not abandoned—any independent claim she may have had for retaliatory discharge by subsuming that argument within her hostile work environment argument. *See, e.g., Brown v. Trustees of Boston Univ.,* 891 F.2d 337, 362 (1st Cir.1989).

harassment. *See Kotcher,* 957 F.2d at 62 ("The supervisor is deemed to act on behalf of the employer when making decisions that affect the economic status of the employee."); *Carrero,* 890 F.2d at 579 ("[T]he harassing employee acts as and for the company, holding out the employer's benefits as an inducement to the employee for sexual favors.").

Karibian argues that the district court erred when it required her to present evidence of actual, rather than threatened, economic loss in order to state a valid claim of *quid pro quo* sexual harassment. We agree. There is nothing in the language of Title VII or the EEOC Guidelines to support such a requirement. *See Meritor,* 477 U.S. at 64, 106 S.Ct. at 2404 ("[T]he language of Title VII is not limited to 'economic' or 'tangible' discrimination.").

True, in the typical *quid pro quo* case, the employee who refuses to submit to her supervisor's advances can expect to suffer some job-related reprisal. *See, e.g., Saulpaugh v. Monroe Community Hosp.,* 4 F.3d 134, 142 (2d Cir.1993). Accordingly, in such "refusal" cases, evidence of some job-related penalty will often be available to prove *quid pro quo* harassment. But that is not to say that such evidence is always essential to the claim. In the nature of things, evidence of economic *harm* will not be available to support the claim of the employee who *submits* to the supervisor's demands. *Lipsett,* 864 F.2d at 913; *see, e.g., Showalter v. Allison Reed Group, Inc.,* 767 F.Supp. 1205, 1212 (D.R.I. 1991). The supervisor's conduct is equally unlawful under Title VII whether the employee submits or not. Under the district court's rationale, only the employee who successfully resisted the threat of sexual blackmail could state a *quid pro quo* claim. We do not read Title VII to punish the victims of sexual harassment who surrender to unwelcome sexual encounters. Such a rule would only encourage harassers to increase their persistence.

The relevant inquiry in a *quid pro quo* case is whether the supervisor has linked tangible job benefits to the acceptance or rejection of sexual advances. It is enough to show that the supervisor used the employee's acceptance or rejection of his advances as the basis for a decision affecting the compensation, terms, conditions or privileges of the employee's job. *See, e.g., Showalter,* 767 F.Supp. at 1212 ("The obvious tangible job benefit the plaintiffs received for succumbing to the harassment was the retention of their employment."). In this case, Karibian stated that her work assignments, raises and promotions depended on her continued responsiveness to Urban's sexual demands. In addition, Karibian claimed that Urban implicitly threatened to fire her and to damage her career if she did not comply. If true, Urban's conduct would constitute *quid pro quo* harassment because he made and threatened to make decisions affecting the terms and conditions of Karibian's employment based upon her submission to his sexual advances.

In support of an "actual economic loss" requirement, Columbia relies on isolated language from the *Kotcher* and *Carrero* cases, *supra*, decided by this Court. In *Kotcher,* we broadly stated that under a *quid pro quo* theory "the plaintiff-employee must establish that she was *denied an economic benefit* either because of gender or because a sexual advance was made by a supervisor and rejected by her." 957 F.2d at 62 (emphasis added). *Kotcher,* however, was a hostile work environment case, not a *quid pro quo* case; hence, the quoted language is, at best, dictum.

Carrero was a *quid pro quo* case, and there we did say: "The gravamen of a quid pro quo claim is that a tangible job benefit or privilege is conditioned on an employee's submission to sexual blackmail and that *adverse consequences* follow from the employee's refusal."   890 F.2d at 579 (emphasis added). *Carrero,* however, was a "refusal" case, not a "submission" case; accordingly, as one might expect, the job-related consequences of Carrero's refusal were both obvious and "adverse."   Consistent with the *prima facie* case outlined above, Carrero satisfied Title VII because her supervisor made decisions affecting her employment based on her response to his sexual advances. We read *Carrero's* reference to "adverse consequences," therefore, as descriptive of the facts before the Court, not as establishing a *sine qua non* that employment decisions be "adverse" in order to state a valid claim. Accordingly, there is no inconsistency between *Carrero* and our conclusion that once an employer conditions any terms of employment upon the employee's submitting to unwelcome sexual advances, a *quid pro quo* claim is made out, regardless of whether the employee (a) rejects the advances and suffers the consequences, or (b) submits to the advances in order to avoid those consequences.

Finally, we believe imposing an "actual economic loss" requirement in a *quid pro quo* case where the employee submits to the unwelcome sexual overtures of her supervisor places undue emphasis on the victim's response to the sexual harassment. The focus should be on the prohibited conduct, not the victim's reaction.   While the employee's submission to the supervisor's advances is certainly relevant, it bears only on the issue whether the sexual advances were unwelcome, not whether unwelcome sexual advances were unlawful. *See Meritor,* 477 U.S. at 68, 106 S.Ct. at 2406 ("The correct inquiry is whether respondent by her conduct indicated that the alleged sexual advances were unwelcome....").   Ultimately, the question whether Karibian submitted to Urban's advances out of a reasonable fear of some job-related reprisal is properly one for the finder of fact. Because the district court erroneously removed this central question from the factfinder by the grant of summary judgment, we reverse.

II. *Columbia's Liability for Hostile Work Environment*

Karibian also contends that the district court erred when it held that Columbia could be liable under a hostile work environment theory only if she satisfied the standard applied in *Kotcher v. Rosa & Sullivan Appliance Center, Inc.,* 957 F.2d 59 (2d Cir.1992). In *Kotcher,* we said that the plaintiff must prove that the employer "either provided no reasonable avenue for complaint or knew of the harassment but did nothing about it." 957 F.2d at 63. Karibian contends that this standard is not applicable to all claims of hostile work environment, and that a different standard obtains here. Columbia responds that the standard described in *Kotcher* governs an employer's liability in this and *every* hostile work environment case. Again, Karibian has the better argument.

A hostile work environment exists "[w]hen the workplace is permeated with 'discriminatory intimidation, ridicule, and insult,' that is 'sufficiently severe or pervasive to alter the conditions of the victim's employment.'" *Harris*, ___ U.S. at ___, 114 S.Ct. at 370 (quoting *Meritor*, 477 U.S. at 65, 67, 106 S.Ct. at 2404, 2405). Whereas liability for *quid pro quo* harassment is always imputed to the employer, a plaintiff seeking to establish harassment under a hostile environment theory must demonstrate some specific basis to hold the employer liable for the misconduct of its employees. *Kotcher*, 957 F.2d at 62. Unfortunately, the "specific basis" of employer liability for a hostile work environment remains elusive.

In *Meritor*, the Supreme Court declined to announce a definitive rule on employer liability in hostile work environment cases. *Meritor*, 477 U.S. at 72, 106 S.Ct. at 2408. *Meritor* did, however, make two things clear: employers are not always liable for the hostile work environment created by their employees. *Id.* And, lack of notice and the existence of complaint procedures do not automatically insulate an employer from liability. *Id.* Beyond these alpha and omega rules, the Court declined to offer further enlightenment. Instead, we are instructed to be guided by common law principles of agency. *Id.*

A rule of employer liability deriving from traditional agency principles cannot be reduced to a universal, pat formula. It will certainly be relevant to the analysis, for example, that the alleged harasser is the plaintiff's supervisor rather than her co-worker. *See, e.g., Kauffman v. Allied Signal, Inc., Autolite Div.*, 970 F.2d 178, 183 (6th Cir.) (contrasting standard of employer liability in cases of co-worker harassment from that applicable in cases of supervisor harassment), *cert. denied*, ___ U.S. ___ , 113 S.Ct. 831, 121 L.Ed.2d 701 (1992); *Horn v. Duke Homes, Div. of Windsor Mobile Homes, Inc.*, 755 F.2d 599, 604 (7th Cir.1985) (suggesting that a notice requirement may be necessary in cases of co-worker harassment, but not in cases of harassment by supervisors). Yet, even such a distinction will not always be dispositive. For example, we held in *Kotcher*, that the employer was not liable for the hostile work environment caused by the plaintiff's supervisor absent notice or the failure to provide a reasonable avenue for complaint. 957 F.2d at 63. We went on to caution, however, that we were not dealing in absolutes and that the *Kotcher* rule would not necessarily apply in all cases; we noted, for example, that "[a]t some point ... the actions of a supervisor at a sufficiently high level in the hierarchy would necessarily be imputed to the company." *Id.* at 64.

We have not yet had occasion to address the proper standard of employer liability where, as here, the plaintiff's supervisor created a discriminatorily abusive work environment through the use of his delegated authority. Common law principles of agency suggest that in such circumstances the employer's liability is absolute.

The Restatement of Agency notes that an employer will be liable for the torts of its employees committed "while acting in the scope of their employment," or, if not acting in the scope of employment, if the employee "purported to act or to speak on behalf of the principal and there was reliance upon apparent authority, or he was aided in accomplishing the tort by the existence of the agency relation." *Restatement (Second) of Agency* §§ 219(1) & (2)(d)

(1958). Hence, when a supervisor makes employment decisions based on an employee's response to his sexual overtures, it is fair to hold the employer responsible because "the supervisor is acting within at least the apparent scope of the authority entrusted to him by the employer." *Henson,* 682 F.2d at 910.

We hold that an employer is liable for the discriminatorily abusive work environment created by a supervisor if the supervisor uses his actual or apparent authority to further the harassment, or if he was otherwise aided in accomplishing the harassment by the existence of the agency relationship. *See Restatement (Second) of Agency* § 219; 29 C.F.R. § 1604.11(c); *see also Hirschfeld v. New Mexico Corrections Dep't,* 916 F.2d 572, 579 (10th Cir.1990); *Sparks v. Pilot Freight Carriers, Inc.,* 830 F.2d 1554, 1559-60 (11th Cir.1987); *Watts v. New York City Police Dep't,* 724 F.Supp. 99, 106 n. 6 (S.D.N.Y. 1989). In contrast, where a low-level supervisor does not rely on his supervisory authority to carry out the harassment, the situation will generally be indistinguishable from cases in which the harassment is perpetrated by the plaintiff's co-workers; consequently, the *Kotcher* standard of employer liability will generally apply, and the employer will not be liable unless "the employer either provided no reasonable avenue for complaint or knew of the harassment but did nothing about it." *Kotcher,* 957 F.2d at 63. *See* 29 C.F.R. § 1604.11(d); *see also Lopez v. S.B. Thomas, Inc.,* 831 F.2d 1184, 1189 (2d Cir.1987); *Snell v. Suffolk County,* 782 F.2d 1094, 1104 (2d Cir.1986). *Cf. Hirschfeld,* 916 F.2d at 579 (employer not liable absent evidence that supervisor "ever invoked [his] authority in order to facilitate his harassment of plaintiff").

Applying these principles, we agree with Karibian that Columbia would be liable for Urban's alleged harassment regardless of the absence of notice or the reasonableness of Columbia's complaint procedures. The essence of Karibian's hostile work environment claim is that her supervisor capitalized upon his authority over her employment to force her to endure a prolonged, violent and demeaning sexual relationship. If the factfinder accepts Karibian's allegations, Columbia is liable to Karibian because Urban abused his delegated authority to create a discriminatorily abusive work environment.

Our conclusion that Columbia would be liable on a hostile environment claim for the harassment alleged by Karibian follows naturally from our earlier conclusion that Karibian stated a valid claim for *quid pro quo* harassment. Under the latter, courts have universally held employers liable for the actions of the supervisor because "[t]he supervisor is deemed to act on behalf of the employer when making decisions that affect the economic status of the employee. From the perspective of the employee, the supervisor and the employer merge into a single entity." *Kotcher,* 957 F.2d at 62. *See also Carrero,* 890 F.2d at 579 ("in *quid pro quo* cases the harassing employee acts as and for the company, holding out the employer's benefits as an inducement to the employee for sexual favors"); *Steele v. Offshore Shipbuilding, Inc.,* 867 F.2d 1311, 1316 (11th Cir.1989) ("When a supervisor requires sexual favors as *quid pro quo* for job benefits, the supervisor, by definition, acts as the company."); *Henson,* 682 F.2d at 910 (in a *quid pro quo* case, "the supervisor uses the means furnished to him by the employer to accomplish the prohibited purpose"). It would be a jarring anomaly to hold that conduct which always renders an employer liable under a *quid pro quo* theory does not result in liability to the employer when that same conduct becomes so severe and pervasive as to create a discriminatorily abusive work environment.

Columbia argues that holding it liable for Urban's harassment is contrary to the standard of employer liability we applied in *Kotcher*. We disagree. In *Kotcher*, the gist of the plaintiff's hostile work environment claim was that her supervisor subjected her to repeated vulgar comments and gestures. 957 F.2d at 61. We held that the employer would not be liable for the supervisor's misconduct unless the employer provided no reasonable avenue for complaint, or unless it knew of the supervisor's misconduct but did nothing about it. 957 F.2d at 63. As support for this standard of liability, we relied on *Snell v. Suffolk County*, 782 F.2d 1094, 1104 (2d Cir.1986), in which the harassment was perpetrated by the plaintiff's co-workers. In both *Kotcher* and *Snell* we simply applied the law of agency to the facts before us and concluded that liability for the misconduct alleged could not be imputed to the employer. In neither *Kotcher* nor *Snell*, however, did the harasser use his actual or apparent authority to further the harassment alleged. Thus understood, our holding today is complementary to *Kotcher*, not inconsistent with it.

CONCLUSION

The judgment of the district court granting summary judgment on Karibian's Title VII claim is reversed and the matter is remanded for further proceedings consistent with this opinion. Because we reinstate Karibian's federal claim, the judgment dismissing Karibian's pendent state law claims for lack of jurisdiction is reversed as well. Finally, Columbia's request for an order directing Karibian to share the cost of the supplemental appendix is denied.

REVERSED and REMANDED.

Questions and Comments

1. How would a plaintiff establish *quid pro quo* harassment?
2. How would a plaintiff establish harassment based on a hostile work environment?
3. What obligations does a university have to provide a remedy for the victim of sexual harassment?
4. What steps had Columbia taken to provide a remedy?
5. What is the effect of a confidential communication on the university's duty to provide a remedy? What can you learn from this?

Authors' Note

The remedy available under Title VII of the Civil Rights Act of 1964 included equitable remedies in the form of injunctions plus back pay awards and possibly attorney's fees. These remedies have been supplemented following the enactment of the Civil Rights Act of 1991 (1991). The new remedies include punitive damages as well as compensatory damages. In addition, a plaintiff can recoup expert witness fees. Lower federal court decisions indicated that the act is prospective only. This conclusion appears to have been substantiated by the decisions of the United States Supreme Court in *Landgraf v. USI Film Products* (1994), and *Rivers v. Roadway Express, Inc.* (1994).

Title IX of the Education Amendments of 1972

Title IX provides:

(a) Prohibition against discrimination; exceptions

No person in the United States shall, on the basis of sex, be excluded from participation in, be denied the benefits of, or be subjected to discrimination under any education program or activity receiving Federal financial assistance, except that:....[20 U.S.C.A §1681]

Authors' Note

Certain exclusions were noted in Title IX, for example, educational institutions run by religious organizations, educational institutions which provide training for the military service, social fraternities, boy or girl conferences, and beauty pageants. The case that revolutionized Title IX from the standpoint of damages was *Franklin v. Gwinnett County Public Schools* (1992).

The United States Supreme Court permitted Christine Franklin to recover damages in a Title IX action predicated upon sexual harassment. The harassment extended over a period of time. The individual who harassed this student was a coach and teacher in plaintiff's high school. The school refused to take action to halt the harassment. The school allowed the coach to resign and took no further action. This judicial decision is a culmination of efforts, including amendatory legislation to strengthen Title IX.

In reading the case, note that the court stated that Title VII did not apply to the situation in *Gwinnett*. Then, observe that the court examines the intent of the Title IX statute in awarding damages under Title IX. The court also analyzes other cases that conclude that the federal courts have the power to grant all necessary remedial relief for violations of the Civil Rights Act of 1964, even though the enacting Congress had not specifically provided such relief. These two factors, the history and intent of the statute and past applications of The Civil Rights Act of 1964, are critical points in the holding of the court in the *Gwinnett* case that follows.

••

FRANKLIN v. GWINNETT COUNTY PUBLIC SCHOOLS
503 U.S. 60, 117 L. Ed.2d 208, 112 S. Ct. 1028 (1992).

Justice White delivered the opinion of the Court.

This case presents the question whether the implied right of action under Title IX of the Education Amendments of 1972, 20 USC §§ 1681-1688 [20 USCS §§ 1681-1688] (Title IX),[1] which this Court recognized in Cannon v

1. This statute provides in pertinent part that "No person in the United States shall, on the basis of sex, be excluded from participation in, be denied the benefits of, or be subjected to discrimination under any education program or activity receiving Federal financial assistance." 20 USC § 1681(a) [20 USCS § 1681(a)].

University of Chicago, 441 US 677, 60 L Ed 2d 560, 99 S Ct 1946 (1979), supports a claim for monetary damages.

I

Petitioner Christine Franklin was a student at North Gwinnett High School in Gwinnett County, Georgia, between September 1985 and August 1989. Respondent Gwinnett County School District operates the high school and receives federal funds. According to the complaint filed on December 29, 1988, in the United States District Court for the Northern District of Georgia, Franklin was subjected to continual sexual harassment beginning in the autumn of her tenth grade year (1986) from Andrew Hill, a sports coach and teacher employed by the district. Among other allegations, Franklin avers that Hill engaged her in sexually-oriented conversations in which he asked about her sexual experiences with her boy friend and whether she would consider having sexual intercourse with an older man, Complaint ¶ 10; First Amended Complaint, Exh A, p 3[2]; that Hill forcibly kissed her on the mouth in the school parking lot. Complaint ¶ 17; that he telephoned her at her home and asked if she would meet him socially, Complaint ¶ 21; First Amended Complaint, Exh A, pp 4-5; and that, on three occasions in her junior year, Hill interrupted a class, requested that the teacher excuse Franklin, and took her to a private office where he subjected her to coercive intercourse. Complaint ¶¶ 25, 27, 32. The complaint further alleges that though they became aware of and investigated Hill's sexual harassment of Franklin and other female students, teachers and administrators took no action to halt it and discouraged Franklin from pressing charges against Hill. Complaint ¶¶ 23, 24, 35. On April 14, 1988, Hill resigned on the condition that all matters pending against him be dropped. Complaint ¶¶ 36, 37. The school thereupon closed its investigation. Complaint ¶ 37.

In this action,[3] the District Court dismissed the complaint on the ground that Title IX does not authorize an award of damages. The Court of Appeals affirmed. Franklin v Gwinnett Cty. Public Schools, 911 F2d 617 (CA11 1990). The court noted that analysis of Title IX and Title VI of the Civil Rights Act of 1964, 42 USC § 2000d et seq. [42 USCS §§ 2000d et seq.] (Title VI), has developed along similar lines. Citing as binding precedent Drayden v Needville Independent School Dist., 642 F2d 129 (CA5 1981), a decision rendered prior to the division of the Fifth Circuit, the court concluded that Title

2. This exhibit is the report of the United States Department of Education's Office of Civil Rights based on that office's investigation of this case. Franklin incorporated this exhibit into her amended complaint.

3. Prior to bringing this lawsuit, Franklin filed a complaint with the Office of Civil Rights of the United States Department of Education (OCR) in August 1988. After investigating these charges for several months, OCR concluded that the school district had violated Franklin's rights by subjecting her to physical and verbal sexual harassment and by interfering with her right to complain about conduct proscribed by Title IX. OCR determined, however, that because of the resignations of Hill and respondent William Prescott and the implementation of a school grievance procedure, the district had come into compliance with Title IX. It then terminated its investigation. First Amended Complaint, Exh A, pp 7-9.

VI did not support a claim for monetary damages. The court then analyzed this Court's decision in Guardians Assn. v Civil Service Comm'n of New York City, 463 US 582, 77 L Ed 2d 866, 103 S Ct 3221 (1983), to determine whether it implicitly overruled Drayden. The court stated that the absence of a majority opinion left unresolved the question whether a court could award such relief upon a showing of intentional discrimination. As a second basis for its holding that monetary damages were unavailable, the court reasoned that Title IX was enacted under Congress' Spending Clause powers and that "[u]nder such statutes, relief may frequently be limited to that which is equitable in nature, with the recipient of federal funds thus retaining the option of terminating such receipt in order to rid itself of an injunction." Franklin, 911 F2d, at 621.[4] The court closed by observing it would "proceed with extreme care" to afford compensatory relief absent express provision by Congress or clear direction from this Court. Id., at 622. Accordingly, it held that an action for monetary damages could not be sustained for an alleged intentional violation of Title IX, and affirmed the District Court's ruling to that effect. Ibid.[5]

Because this opinion conflicts with a decision of the Court of Appeals for the Third Circuit, see Pfeiffer v Marion Center Area School Dist., 917 F2d 779, 787-789 (1990), we granted certiorari, 501 US ___, 115 L Ed 2d 969, 111 S Ct 2795 (1991). We reverse.

II

In Cannon v University of Chicago, 441 US 677, 60 L Ed 2d 560, 99 S Ct 1946 (1979), the Court held that Title IX is enforceable through an implied right of action. We have no occasion here to reconsider that decision. Rather, in this case we must decide what remedies are available in a suit brought pursuant to this implied right. . . . Thus, although we examine the text and history of a statute to determine whether Congress intended to create a right of action [citation omitted], we presume the availability of all appropriate remedies unless Congress has expressly indicated otherwise. [Citation omitted.] This principle has deep roots in our jurisprudence.

A

"[W]here legal rights have been invaded, and a federal statute provides for a general right to sue for such invasion, federal courts may use any avail-

---

4. The court also rejected an argument by Franklin that the terms of outright prohibition of Title VII, 42 USC §§ 2000e to 2000e-17 [42 USCS §§ 2000e to 2000e-17], apply by analogy to Title IX's antidiscrimination provision, and that the remedies available under the two statutes should also be the same. Franklin, 911 F2d, at 622. Because Franklin does not pursue this contention here, we need not address whether it has merit.

5. Judge Johnson concurred specially, writing that the result was controlled by Drayden v Needville Independent School Dist., 642 F2d 129 (CA5 1981), and that there was no need to address whether Titles VI and IX are grounded solely in the Spending Clause and whether Title VII analysis should apply to an action under Titles VI or IX. See Franklin, supra, at 622-623 (Johnson, J., concurring specially).

able remedy to make good the wrong done." Bell v Hood, 327 US 678, 684, 90 L Ed 939, 66 S Ct 773, 13 ALR2d 383 (1946). The Court explained this longstanding rule as jurisdictional, and upheld the exercise of the federal courts' power to award appropriate relief so long as a cause of action existed under the Constitution or laws of the United States. Ibid.

The Bell Court's reliance on this rule was hardly revolutionary. From the earliest years of the Republic the Court has recognized the power of the judiciary to award appropriate remedies to redress injuries actionable in federal court, although it did not always distinguish clearly between a right to bring suit and a remedy available under such a right. In Marbury v Madison, 1 Cranch 137, 163, 2 L Ed 60 (1803), for example, Chief Justice Marshall observed that our government "has been emphatically termed a government of laws, and not of men. It will certainly cease to deserve this high appellation, if the laws furnish no remedy for the violation of a vested legal right." This principle originated in the English common law, and Blackstone described "it is a general and indisputable rule, that where there is a legal right, there is also a legal remedy, by suit or action at law, whenever that right is invaded." 3 W. Blackstone, Commentaries 23 (1783). . . .

In Kendall v United States, 12 Pet 524, 9 L Ed 1181 (1838), the Court applied these principles to an act of Congress that accorded a right of action in mail carriers to sue for adjustment and settlement of certain claims for extra services but which did not specify the precise remedy available to the carriers. After surveying possible remedies, which included an action against the postmaster general for monetary damages, the Court held that the carriers were entitled to a writ of mandamus compelling payment under the terms of the statute. . . . .Dooley v United States, 182 US 222, 229, 45 L Ed 1074, 21 S Ct 762 (1901), also restated "the principle that a liability created by statute without a remedy may be enforced by a common-law action."

The Court relied upon this traditional presumption again after passage of the Federal Safety Appliance Act of 1893, ch 196, 27 Stat 531. In Texas & Pacific R. Co. v Rigsby, 241 US 33, 60 L Ed 874, 36 S Ct 482 (1916), the Court first had to determine whether the Act supported an implied right of action. After answering that question in the affirmative, the Court then upheld a claim for monetary damages: "A disregard of the command of the statute is a wrongful act, and where it results in damage to one of the class for whose especial benefit the statute was enacted, the right to recover the damages from the party in default is implied, according to a doctrine of the common law ...." Id., at 39, 60 L Ed 874, 36 S Ct 482. . . .

B

Respondents and the United States as amicus curiae, however, maintain that whatever the traditional presumption may have been when the Court decided Bell v Hood, it has disappeared in succeeding decades. We do not agree. . . . (Discussion omitted.)

"'The power *to enforce* implies the power to make effective the right of recovery afforded by the Act. And the power to make the right of recovery effective implies the power to utilize any of the procedures or actions normally available to the litigant according to the exigencies of the particular case.'" Id., at 433-434, 12 L Ed 2d 423, 84 S Ct 1555 (quoting Deckert v Independence Shares Corp., 311 US 282, 288, 85 L Ed 189, 61 S Ct 229 (1940)).

. . . . Subsequent cases have been true to this position. See, e.g., Sullivan v Little Hunting Park, Inc., 396 US 229, 239, 24 L Ed 2d 386, 90 S Ct 400 (1969), stating that the "existence of a statutory right implies the existence of all necessary and appropriate remedies"; Carey v Piphus, 435 US 247, 255, 55 L Ed 2d 252, 98 S Ct 1042 (1978), upholding damages remedy under 42 USC § 1983 [42 USCS § 1983] even though the enacting Congress had not specifically provided such relief.

The United States contends that the traditional presumption in favor of all appropriate relief was abandoned by the Court in Davis v Passman, 442 US 228, 60 L Ed 2d 846, 99 S Ct 2264 (1979), and that the Bell v Hood rule was limited to actions claiming constitutional violations. . . . [Discussion of who may enforce a statute is omitted.] Whether Congress may limit the class of persons who have a right of action under Title IX is irrelevant to the issue in this lawsuit. To reiterate, "the question whether a litigant has a 'cause of action' is analytically distinct and prior to the question of what relief, if any, a litigant may be entitled to receive." Id., at 239, 60 L Ed 2d 846, 99 S Ct 2264. Davis, therefore, did nothing to interrupt the long line of cases in which the Court has held that if a right of action exists to enforce a federal right and Congress is silent on the question of remedies, a federal court may order any appropriate relief. . . . [Citations and footnote omitted.]

Contrary to arguments by respondents and the United States that Guardians Assn. v Civil Service Comm'n of New York City, 463 US 582, 77 L Ed 2d 866, 103 S Ct 3221 (1983), and Consolidated Rail Corp. v Darrone, 465 US 624, 79 L Ed 2d 568, 104 S Ct 1248 (1984), eroded this traditional presumption, those cases in fact support it. Though the multiple opinions in Guardians suggest the difficulty of inferring the common ground among the Justices in that case, a clear majority expressed the view that damages were available under Title VI in an action seeking remedies for an intentional violation, and no Justice challenged the traditional presumption in favor of a federal court's power to award appropriate relief in a cognizable cause of action. . . . [Citations omitted.] The correctness of this inference was made clear the following Term when the Court unanimously held that the 1978 amendment to § 504 of the Rehabilitation Act of 1973—which had expressly incorporated the "remedies, procedures, and rights set forth in title VI" (29 USC § 794a(a)(2) [29 USCS § 794a(a)(2)])—authorizes an award of backpay. In Darrone, the Court observed that a majority in Guardians had "agreed that retroactive relief is available to private plaintiffs for all discrimination...that is actionable under Title VI." 465 US at 630, n 9, 79 L Ed 2d 568, 104 S Ct 1248. The general rule, therefore, is that absent clear direction to the contrary by Congress, the federal courts have the power to award any appropriate relief in a cognizable cause of action brought pursuant to a federal statute.

III

We now address whether Congress intended to limit application of this general principle in the enforcement of Title IX. . . . [Omitted a discussion of other reasoning which the court said does not apply. The court then examines the history and intent of Title IX.] Rather, in determining Congress's intent to limit application of the traditional presumption in favor of all appropriate relief, we evaluate the state of the law when the legislature passed Title IX. Cf. Merrill Lynch, Pierce, Fenner & Smith, Inc. v Curran, 456 US 353, 378, 72 L Ed 2d 182, 102 S Ct 1825 (1982). In the years before and after Congress enacted this statute, the Court "follow[ed] a common-law tradition [and] regarded the denial of a remedy as the exception rather than the rule." Id., at 375, 72 L Ed 2d 182, 102 S Ct 1825 [footnote omitted]. As we outlined in Part II, this has been the prevailing presumption in our federal courts since at least the early nineteenth century. In Cannon, the majority upheld an implied right of action in part because in the decade immediately preceding enactment of Title IX in 1972, this Court had found implied rights of action in six cases.[6] In three of those cases, the Court had approved a damages remedy. See, e.g., J.I. Case Co., 377 US, at 433, 12 L Ed 2d 423, 84 S Ct 1555, Wyandotte Transp. Co., supra, at 207, 19 L Ed 2d 407, 88 S Ct 379; Sullivan v Little Hunting Park, Inc., 396 US 229, 24 L Ed 2d 386, 90 S Ct 400 (1969). Wholly apart from the wisdom of the Cannon holding, therefore, the same contextual approach used to justify an implied right of action more than amply demonstrates the lack of any legislative intent to abandon the traditional presumption in favor of all available remedies.

In the years *after* the announcement of Cannon, on the other hand, a more traditional method of statutory analysis is possible, because Congress was legislating with full cognizance of that decision. Our reading of the two amendments to Title IX enacted after Cannon leads us to conclude that Congress did not intend to limit the remedies available in a suit brought under Title IX. In the Civil Rights Remedies Equalization Amendment of 1986, 42 USC § 2000d-7 [42 USCS § 2000d-7], Congress abrogated the States' Eleventh Amendment immunity under Title IX, Title VI, § 504 of the Rehabilitation Act of 1973, and the Age Discrimination Act of 1975. This statute cannot be read except as a validation of Cannon's holding. A subsection of the 1986 law provides that in a suit against a State, "remedies (including remedies both at law and in equity) are available for such a violation to the same extent as such remedies are available for such a violation in the suit against any public or private entity other than a State." 42 USC § 2000d-7(a)(2) [42 USCS § 2000d-7(a)(2)]. While it is true that this savings clause says nothing about the nature of those other available remedies, cf. Milwaukee v Illinois, 451 US 304, 329, n22, 68 L Ed 2d 114, 101 S Ct 1784 (1981), absent any contrary indication in the text or history

6. J.I. Case Co. v Borak, 377 US 426, 12 L Ed 2d 423, 84 S Ct 1555 (1964); Wyandotte Transp. Co. v United States, 389 US 191, 19 L Ed 2d 407, 88 S Ct 379 (1967); Jones v Alfred H. Mayer Co., 392 US 409, 20 L Ed 2d 1189, 88 S Ct 2186 (1968); Allen v State Bd. of Elections, 393 US 544, 22 L Ed 2d 1, 89 S Ct 817 (1969); Sullivan v Little Hunting Park, Inc., 396 US 229, 24 L Ed 2d 386, 90 S Ct 400 (1969); and Superintendent of Ins. of New York v Bankers Life & Casualty Co., 404 US 6, 30 L Ed 2d 128, 92 S Ct 165 (1971).

of the statute, we presume Congress enacted this statute with the prevailing traditional rule in mind.

In addition to the Civil Rights Remedies Equalization Amendment of 1986, Congress also enacted the Civil Rights Restoration Act of 1987, Pub L 100-259, 102 Stat 28 (1988). Without in any way altering the existing rights of action and the corresponding remedies permissible under Title IX, Title VI, § 504 of the Rehabilitation Act, and the Age Discrimination Act, Congress broadened the coverage of these antidiscrimination provisions in this legislation. In seeking to correct what it considered to be an unacceptable decision on our part in Grove City College v Bell, 465 US 555, 79 L Ed 2d 516, 104 S Ct 1211 (1984), Congress made no effort to restrict the right of action recognized in Cannon and ratified in the 1986 Act or to alter the traditional presumption in favor of any appropriate relief for violation of a federal right. We cannot say, therefore, that Congress has limited the remedies available to a complainant in a suit brought under Title IX.

IV

Respondents and the United States nevertheless suggest three reasons why we should not apply the traditional presumption in favor of appropriate relief in this case.

A

First, respondents argue that an award of damages violates separation of powers principles because it unduly expands the federal courts' power into a sphere properly reserved to the Executive and Legislative Branches. Brief for Respondents 22-25. In making this argument, respondents misconceive the difference between a cause of action and a remedy. Unlike the finding of a cause of action, which authorizes a court to hear a case or controversy, the discretion to award appropriate relief involves no such increase in judicial power. See generally Note, Federal Jurisdiction in Suits for damages Under Statutes Not Affording Such Remedy, 48 Colum L Rev 1090, 1094-1095 (1948). Federal courts cannot reach out to award remedies when the Constitution or laws of the United States do not support a cause of action. Indeed, properly understood, respondents' position invites us to *abdicate* our historic judicial authority to award appropriate relief in cases brought in our court system. It is well to recall that such authority historically has been thought necessary to provide an important safeguard against abuses of legislative and executive power, see Kendall v United States, 12 Pet 524, 9 L Ed 1181 (1838), as well as to insure an independent judiciary. See generally Katz, The Jurisprudence of Remedies: Constitutional Legality and the Law of Torts in Bell v Hood, 117 U Pa L Rev 1, 16-17 (1968). Moreover, selective abdication of the sort advocated here would harm separation of powers principles in another way, by giving judges the power to render inutile causes of action authorized by Congress through a decision that no remedy is available.

B

Next, consistent with the Court of Appeals's reasoning, respondents and

the United States contend that the normal presumption in favor of all appropriate remedies should not apply because Title IX was enacted pursuant to Congress's Spending Clause power. In Pennhurst State School and Hospital v Halderman, 451 US 1, 28-29, 67 L Ed 2d 694, 101 S Ct 1531 (1981), the Court observed that remedies were limited under such Spending Clause statutes when the alleged violation was *unintentional*. Respondents and the United States maintain that this presumption should apply equally to *intentional* violations. We disagree. The point of not permitting monetary damages for an unintentional violation is that the receiving entity of federal funds lacks notice that it will be liable for a monetary award. See id. at 17, 67 L Ed 2d 694, 101 S Ct 1531. This notice problem does not arise in a case such as this, in which intentional discrimination is alleged. Unquestionably, Title IX placed on the Gwinnett County Schools the duty not to discriminate on the basis of sex, and "when a supervisor sexually harasses a subordinate because of the subordinate's sex, that supervisor 'discriminate[s]' on the basis of sex." Meritor Savings Bank, FSB v Vinson, 477 US 57, 64, 91 L Ed 2d 49, 106 S Ct 2399 (1986). We believe the same rule should apply when a teacher sexually harasses and abuses a student. Congress surely did not intend for federal monies to be expended to support the intentional actions it sought by statute to proscribe. Moreover, the notion that Spending Clause statutes do not authorize monetary awards for intentional violations is belied by our unanimous holding in Darrone. See 465 US, at 628, 79 L Ed 2d 568, 104 S Ct 1248. Respondents and the United States characterize the backpay remedy in Darrone as equitable relief, but this description is irrelevant to their underlying objection: that application of the traditional rule in this case will require state entities to pay monetary awards out of their treasuries for intentional violations of federal statutes.[7]

C

Finally, the United States asserts that the remedies permissible under Title IX should nevertheless be limited to backpay and prospective relief. In addition to diverging from our traditional approach to deciding what remedies are available for violation of a federal right, this position conflicts with sound logic. First, both remedies are equitable in nature, and it is axiomatic that a court should determine the adequacy of a remedy in law before resorting to equitable relief. Under the ordinary convention, the proper inquiry would be whether monetary damages provided an adequate remedy, and if not, whether equitable relief would be appropriate. Whitehead v Shattuck, 138 US 146, 150, 34 L Ed 873, 11 S Ct 276 (1891). See generally C. McCormick, Law of Damages 1 (1935). Moreover, in this case the equitable remedies suggested by respondent and the Federal Government are clearly

7. Franklin argues that, in any event, Title IX should not be viewed solely as having been enacted under Congress' Spending Clause powers and that it also rests on powers derived from § 5 of the Fourteenth Amendment. See Brief for Petitioner 19, n 10. Because we conclude that a money damages remedy is available under Title IX for an intentional violation irrespective of the constitutional source of Congress' power to enact the statute, we need not decide which power Congress utilized in enacting Title IX.

inadequate. Backpay does nothing for petitioner, because she was a student when the alleged discrimination occurred. Similarly, because Hill—the person she claims subjected her to sexual harassment—no longer teaches at the school and she herself no longer attends a school in the Gwinnett system, prospective relief accords her no remedy at all. The government's answer that administrative action helps other similarly-situated students in effect acknowledges that its approach would leave petitioner remediless.

V

In sum, we conclude that a damages remedy is available for an action brought to enforce Title IX. The judgment of the Court of Appeals, therefore, is reversed and the case is remanded for further proceedings consistent with this opinion.

So ordered.

Questions and Comments

1. What were the facts in this case?
2. What was the primary question that the court was seeking to answer?
3. What efforts had been made by Congress to strengthen Title IX prior to this case?
4. What judicial decisions preceded and occasioned the amendatory legislation?
5. What rationale did the court use for permitting damages as a remedy for Title IX violations?
6. Why would it be impossible to cite this case as the basis for a remedy for harassment suffered by an employee who works for a private recreational facility?
7. The Dupont Company is spending thousands of dollars to educate their employees about sexual harassment. Why are they doing this?
8. Does *Gwinnett* justify monetary damages for an employee who is harassed while working at a private recreational facility? Discuss your answer.

Suggested Recommendations for a Sexual Harassment Policy,
adapted from Tom Miller's 1990 discussion of *Stoneking v. Bradford Area School Dist.* 882 F.2d 720 (3rd Cir. 1989).

1. The policy should at least:
   a. state that sexual harassment will not be tolerated.
   b. emphasize that supervisory personnel are responsible for eliminating sexual harassment.
   c. encourage reporting of sexual harassment.
   d. prohibit retaliation for complaints or participation in investigations of alleged harassment.
   e. spell out disciplinary measures or sanctions for anyone who violates the policy.
   f. apply to all situations, including patron to patron to the extent possible [Statement added by O'Brien.]

g. include avenues for appeal where appropriate. [Statement added by O'Brien.]

2. The policy should include procedures for investigation of any and all complaints with provisions for confidentiality as allowable.
3. The policy should include standards for determining appropriate corrective or disciplinary action.
4. The policy should require staff training which addresses sexual harassment. [Statement added by O'Brien.]

SUMMARY

Federal legislation available for the victim of sexual harassment includes Title VII of the Civil Rights Act of 1964 and Title IX of the Education Amendments of 1972.

Sexual harassment falls into two categories: first, *quid pro quo*, which is the more blatant form of sexual harassment (You give me something, I give you something); and second, hostile environment, which includes such things as sexual jokes, pictures, and suggestions that are sufficiently pervasive to render the possibility of continuing employment impossible or at a price that a victim should not be called upon to pay.

Isolated instances of harassment probably will not be sufficient to trigger the enforcement of penalties. This is especially true if the victim has made known his or her displeasure with the conduct in question and, as a consequence, the offensive conduct has ceased.

Currently damages are available to the victim of sexual harassment under Title VII, as strengthened by the Civil Rights Act of 1991, and through Title IX, as strengthened by judicial interpretation.

Title IX was strengthened by the Civil Rights Restoration Act, which permitted the imposition of penalties if any portion of the employment entity received federal funds.

Common law remedies would include tort actions for assault and battery together with the tort of causing grave emotional distress.

Constitutional violations, especially in the equal protection field, may be successfully contested along the same lines as those developed in the pregnancy cases.

A sexual harassment policy should avoid the charge of vagueness and overbreadth. Such a policy should define sexual harassment and should make certain that the policy is explained and distributed throughout the employment unit.

It is possible for a male employee to be harassed. Sexual harassment is also possible in same sex situations. Other charges are also available.

For example, a charge of insubordination, incompetency, or neglect of duty may be available. Finally, it may be possible to simply nonrenew a contract following its expiration.

It is possible to successfully terminate employment on alternative grounds. This is especially true where the perpetrator has declined to give accurate information.

This could be you - check your response

Two questions are presented: First, do the Joneses have liability based on the allegation of Clark's harassment; and second, how could an employer reduce the probability of such a charge being filed?

In answer to the first question, one should remember that Title VII places a limitation on the employer; consequently, the Joneses would be liable under the theory of *respondeat superior* if their employee had in fact harassed Ms. Doe. The case postulates the most obvious form of harassment *quid pro quo*. Assuming that the violation occurred after the Civil Rights Act of 1991, the Joneses would be liable for both compensatory and punitive damages. The Civil Rights Act of 1991, however, is not retroactive. If Clark's act occurred prior to the Civil Rights Act of 1991, the employer would be responsible for equitable remedies as opposed to common-law remedies.

With respect to the second question, an employer should articulate and disseminate a clear and concise policy on sexual harassment. All employees should be instructed to report violations, and supervisors should be instructed to pay careful attention to complaints. It is important to keep records. It is also important to act in a timely fashion to remediate specific situations when necessary. Effective prevention is a prime consideration.

REFERENCES

Authors

Miller, T. (1990). *Comments on Stoneking v. Bradford* (1989). Law Firm of Miller, Tracy, Brown & Wilson, LTD. Monticello, IL: [Mimeographed monograph].

Cases

Adams v. Baker, 919 F.Supp. 1496 (D. Kan. 1996).

Benekritis v. Johnson, 882 F.Supp. 521 (D.S.C. 1995).

Clay v. Board of Trustees of Neosho, 905 F.Supp. 148 (D.Kan. 1995).

Cohen v. Brown University, 879 F.Supp. 185 (D.R.I. 1995).

Franklin v. Gwinnett County Public Schools, 503 U.S. 60, 117 L. Ed. 2d 208, 112 S. Ct. 1028 (1992).

Gonyo v. Drake University, 879 F.Supp. 1000 (D. Iowa, 1995).

Karibian v. Columbia University, 14 F.3rd 773 (2nd Cir. 1994), 812 F. Supp. 413 (S.D. N.Y. 1993).

Landgraf v. USI Film Products, 511 U.S.____, 128 L. Ed. 2d 229, 114 S. Ct. ___ (1994).

Leija v. Canutillo Ind. Sch. Dist., 887 F.Supp. 947 (W.D.Tex. 1995).

Meritor Saving Bank, F.S.B. v. Vinson, 477 U.S. 57, 106 S.Ct. 2399, 91 L.Ed.2d 49 (1986).

Pederson v. Louisiana State University, 912 F.Supp. 892 (M.D. La. 1996).

Rivers v. Roadway Express, Inc., 511 U.S. ___, 128 L. Ed. 2d 274, 114 S. Ct. ____ (1994).

Stoneking v. Bradford Area School Dist., 882 F.2d 720 (3rd Cir. 1989).

Model Codes, Restatements and Standards

Civil Rights Act of 1991, Pub. L. 102-166, Nov. 21, 1991, 105 Stat. 1071.

Equal Employment Opportunity Act of 1972, Pub. L. 92-261, Mar. 24, 1972, 86 Stat. 103. See 42 U.S.C.A. §2000e-1.

Title VII of the Civil Rights Act of 1964, 42 U.S.C.A. §§ 2000e-2(a)(1) and 2000e-2(a)(2).

Title IX of the Educational Amendments of 1972, Pub. L. 92-318, June 23, 1972, 86 Stat. 235.

CHAPTER 19

SEX DISCRIMINATION: EQUAL PAY ACT

INTRODUCTION

One of the first bits of federal legislation to receive approval in the field of labor management relations was the Fair Labor Standards Act (1938). This legislation provided for minimum wages and maximum hours. The legislation was upheld as a valid exercise of national power under the interstate commerce clause.

Subsequently, in 1963 the Act was amended to include the Equal Pay Act. This amendment is shown under Title 29 of the United States Code Annotated, Section 206(d)(1). The purpose of this amendment was to provide equal pay for equal work regardless of the gender of the employee. This chapter explores applications of the 1963 amendment.

IN THIS CHAPTER YOU WILL LEARN:

The purpose of the Equal Pay Act
The terms of the Equal Pay Act
Exemptions from the operation of the Equal Pay Act
The remedies available to one who feels aggrieved under the Equal Pay Act
Possible strategies for the defense of the lawsuit filed pursuant to the Act

---

KEY WORDS: *equal pay, equal work, temporary restraining order, equity, market conditions, "factors other than sex"*

This could be you!

Maria Jones is attending a national conference for aerobic instructors. During the course of the conference, Maria has the opportunity to meet and speak with Vladimer Murphy, a Russian emigrant, who is currently employed as an aerobics instructor in the recreation department at a prestigious Ivy League university.

Vladimir explains that Murphy is not his birth name but that he has changed his name officially so that American students can pronounce it.

Ms Jones is enthralled with what she considers to be the opportunity to hire an individual with great talent and potential in various aspects of the ever-growing business that Ms Jones is currently promoting.

... BUT MR. X HAS A FAMILY AND HE NEEDS MORE MONEY

Salary requirements, as set forth by Mr. Murphy, exceed those paid for various female employees currently teaching aerobics for Ms Jones, but this salary scale is comparable to what Murphy is currently receiving.

Can Ms Jones pay substantially higher wages to Murphy, assuming that he is performing basically the same function as the female employees who teach at Ms Jones's place of business? Why or why not?

TESTS TO DETERMINE VIOLATIONS

Provisions of the Act

29 United States Code Annotated, Section 206(d)(1) provides:

No employer having employees subject to any provisions of this section shall discriminate, within any establishment in which such employees are employed, between employees on the basis of sex by paying wages to employees in such establishment at a rate less than the rate at which he pays wages to employees of the opposite sex in such establishment for equal work on jobs the performance of which requires equal skill, effort, and responsibility, and which are performed under similar working conditions, except where such payment is made pursuant to (i) a seniority system; (ii) a merit system; (iii) a system which measures earnings by quantity or quality of production; or (iv) a differential based on any other factor other than sex: *provided*, That an employer who is paying a wage rate differential in violation of this subsection shall not, in order to comply with the provisions of this subsection, reduce the wage rate of any employee.

A Judicial Decision

The case that follows involves the women's basketball coach at the University of Southern California. This individual requested pay that was the equivalent of her male counterpart who coached the men's basketball team. The pay differential was several thousand dollars despite the fact that the women's team had won four national championships and, in general, had an excellent record. This case is an appeal of a denial of a preliminary injunction. This is noted in the way the appeals court reviews the case.

. . . . .

STANLEY v. UNIVERSITY OF SOUTHERN CALIFORNIA
13 F.3d 1313 (9th Cir. 1994)

ALARCON, Circuit Judge:

Marianne Stanley, former head coach of the women's basketball team at the University of Southern California (USC), appeals from an order denying her motion for a preliminary injunction against USC and Michael Garrett, the athletic director for USC (collectively USC).

Coach Stanley contends that the district court abused its discretion in denying a preliminary injunction on the ground that she failed to present sufficient evidence of sex discrimination or retaliation to carry her burden of establishing a clear likelihood of success on the merits. Coach Stanley also claims that the court misapprehended the nature of the preliminary injunction relief she sought. In addition, she argues that the district court clearly erred in finding that USC would suffer significant hardship if the preliminary injunction issued. Coach Stanley further asserts that she was denied a full and fair opportunity to present testimonial evidence at the preliminary injunction hearing and to demonstrate that USC's purported justification for paying a higher salary to George Raveling, head coach of the men's basketball team at USC, was a pretext for sex discrimination and retaliation. We affirm because we conclude that the district court did not abuse its discretion in denying the motion for a preliminary injunction. We also hold that the district court did not deny Coach Stanley a full and fair opportunity to present evidence of sex discrimination, retaliation, and pretext.

I. PERTINENT FACTS

Coach Stanley signed a four-year contract with USC on July 30, 1989, to serve as the head coach of the women's basketball team. The expiration date of Coach Stanley's employment contract was June 30, 1993. Coach Stanley's employment contract provided for an annual base salary of $60,000 with a $6,000 housing allowance.

Sometime in April of 1993, Coach Stanley and Michael Garrett began negotiations on a new contract. The evidence is in dispute as to the statement made by the parties. Coach Stanley alleges in her declarations that she told Garrett that she "was entitled to be paid equally with the Head Men's Basketball Coach, George Raveling[,] and that [she] was seeking a contract equal to the one that USC had paid the Head Men's Basketball coach" based on her outstanding record and the success of the women's basketball program at USC. She also requested a higher salary for the assistant coaches of the women's basketball team. According to Coach Stanley, Garrett verbally agreed that she should be paid what Coach Raveling was earning, but he asserted that USC did not have the money at that time. He indicated that "he would get back [to her] with an offer of a multi-year contract . . . that would be satisfactory." Garrett alleges in his affidavit, filed in opposition to the issuance of the preliminary injunction, that Coach Stanley told him that "she wanted a contract that was identical to that between USC and Coach Raveling."

On April 27, 1993, Garrett sent a memorandum which set forth an offer of a three-year contract with the following terms:

1993-94 Raising your salary to $80,000 with a $6,000 housing allowance.

1994-95 Salary of $90,000 with a $6,000 housing allowance.

1995-96 Salary of 100,000 with a $6,000 housing allowance.

Presently, Barbara Thaxton's base salary is $37,000 which I intend to increase to $50,000. It is not my policy to pay associate or assistant coaches housing allowances. Therefore that consideration is not addressed in this offer.

The memorandum concluded with the following words: "I believe this offer is fair, and I need you to respond within the next couple of days so we can conclude this matter. Thank you." According to Garrett, Coach Stanley said the offer was "an insult."

Coach Stanley alleged that, after receiving this offer, she informed Garrett that she "wanted a multi-year contract but his salary figures were too low." Coach Stanley also alleged that she told Garrett she "was to make the same salary as was paid to the Head Men's Basketball Coach at USC." Garrett asserted that Coach Stanley demanded a "three-year contract which would pay her a total compensation at the annual rate of $96,000 for the first 18 months and then increase her total compensation to the same level as Raveling for the last 18 months." He rejected her counter offer.

Coach Stanley alleged that Garrett stated to her that he thought his proposal was fair and he would "not spend a lot of time negotiating a contract." According to Coach Stanley, Garrett's attitude toward her changed and he became "hostile." Garrett told her that she would not be paid the same as Coach Raveling and that she should be satisfied with being the second highest paid women's basketball coach in the PAC-10 Conference.

After this discussion, Coach Stanley retained attorney Timothy Stoner to negotiate the terms of the new contract. Coach Stanley alleged that Garrett rejected her offer "to negotiate a contract that would allow me to gradually work my way to the contract salary and benefits level that USC had provided to George Raveling." Coach Stanley alleged further that Garrett refused to "negotiate in good faith." He withdrew the multi-year contract offer he had previously made to her. Coach Stanley also alleged that Garrett told her attorney that he would offer a one-year contract at a $90,000 salary, plus a $6,000 housing allowance.

Garrett alleges that Stoner proposed a three-year contract with compensation starting at $88,000 in the first year, $97,000 in the second year, and $112,000 in the third year. According to Garrett's affidavit, Coach Stanley also made certain "unprecedented demands, such as: free room and board for her daughter who is anticipated to attend USC as an undergraduate student;

radio and television shows where Stanley and the women's team would be spotlighted; and monetary payments tied to conference championships, wins in NCAA play-off games, and coach of the year honors." Garrett indicated that these "incentives" were unacceptable to USC.

On June 21, 1993, Garrett transmitted a written offer of a one-year contract to Mr. Stoner. The offer contains the following terms with reference to salary:

> In consideration of the performance of her duties and responsibilities as Head Women's Basketball Coach, USC shall pay to Stanley an annual salary of $96,000, commencing as of the effective date of this Agreement and payable in equal monthly installments. Stanley shall also be eligible to participate in all of the USC employee benefits as set forth from time to time in the USC Staff Handbook.

Coach Stanley alleges that she contacted Garrett sometime thereafter, "to remind him of the promise he and the University made to me for a multi-year contract that would fairly compensate me for my services and efforts . . . ." Garrett told her that she had until the end of that business day to accept the one-year contract at $96,000 or USC would begin to look at other candidates for her position.

Garrett alleged that he received a telephone call from Coach Stanley on July 13, 1993, in which she "renewed her demand for the three-year contract on the economic terms previously proposed by her counsel." Garrett reiterated that a one-year contract at $96,000 was USC's final offer. Garrett told Coach Stanley that her final decision to reject or accept the offer had to be communicated to him by the end of the day.

Garrett alleged that Coach Stanley did not accept the offer. The following day, Coach Stanley sent a memorandum requesting additional time to consider the offer because she was too distressed to make a decision. Garrett sent a memorandum to Coach Stanley on July 15, 1993, in which he stated, *inter alia:*

> My job as athletic director is to look out for the best interests of our women's basketball program as a whole, and that is what I have been trying to do all along. The best interests of the program are not served by indefinitely extending the discussions between you and the University, which have already dragged on for weeks. That is why I told you on Tuesday that I needed a final answer that day.
>
> Since I did not hear from you, as it now stands the University has no offers on the table. If you want to make any proposals, I am willing to listen. Meanwhile, for the protection of the program, I must, and am, actively looking at other candidates. I am sorry that you feel distressed by this situation. As I have said, I have to do what is best for our women's basketball program.
>
> Finally, I was not aware that you were in Phoenix on official University business. Your contract with the University expired at the end of June, and I must ask you not to perform any services for the University unless and until we enter a new contract. I will arrange for you to be compensated on a daily basis for the time you have expended thus far in July on University business....

Coach Stanley did not reply to Garrett's July 15, 1993, memorandum. Instead, on August 3, 1993, her present attorney, Robert L. Bell, sent a letter via facsimile to USC's Acting General Counsel in which he indicated that he had been retained to represent Coach Stanley. Bell stated he desired "to discuss an amicable resolution of the legal dispute between [his] client and the University of Southern California." Bell stated that if he did not receive a reply by August 4, 1993, he would "seek recourse in court." On August 4, 1993, USC's Acting General Counsel sent a letter to Bell via facsimile in which he stated that "[w]e are not adverse to considering carefully a proposal from you for an `informal resolution.'"

II. PROCEDURAL BACKGROUND

On August 5, 1993, Coach Stanley filed this action in the Superior Court for the County of Los Angeles. She also applied *ex parte* for a temporary restraining order (TRO) to require USC to install her as head coach of the women's basketball team.

The complaint sets forth various federal and state sex discrimination claims, including violations of the Equal Pay Act (EPA), 29 U.S.C. 206(d)(1) (1988), Title IX, 20 U.S.C. § 1681(a) (1988), the California Fair Employment and Housing Act (FEHA), Cal. Gov't Code § 12921 (West Supp.1993), and the California Constitution, Cal. Const. art. 1, § 8 (West 1983). The complaint also alleges common law causes of action including wrongful discharge in violation of California's public policy, breach of an implied-in-fact employment contract, intentional infliction of emotional distress, and conspiracy. As relief for this alleged conduct, Coach Stanley seeks a declaratory judgment that USC's conduct constituted sex discrimination, a permanent injunction restraining the defendants from discrimination and retaliation, an order "requiring immediate installation of [p]laintiff to the position of Head Coach of Women's Basketball at the USC," three million dollars in compensatory damages, and five million dollars in punitive damages.

On August 6, 1993, the Los Angeles Superior Court issued an oral order granting Coach Stanley's *ex parte* application for a TRO, pending a hearing on her motion for a preliminary injunction. The TRO ordered USC to pay Coach Stanley an annual salary of $96,000 for her services as head basketball coach of the women's team, and all benefits under the 1989 contract were to remain in effect. The record shows that, on June 30, 1993, the date that her four-year employment contract expired, Coach Stanley's salary was $62,000 per year with a $6,000 housing allowance.

On the same day that the TRO was issued, USC removed the action to the District Court for the Central District of California. On August 11, 1993, the district court ordered that the hearing on Coach Stanley's motion for a preliminary injunction be held on August 26, 1993, and that the TRO issued by the state court be extended and remain in effect until that date.

Coach Stanley and Garrett submitted their declarations prior to the August 26, 1993, hearing. At the hearing, Coach Stanley submitted the declaration of her physician, Dr. Elizabeth Monterio, regarding Coach Stanley's emotional state. Coach Stanley also made offers of proof as to the testimony of various witnesses. The court accepted the proffered testimony as true for purposes of ruling on the motion for preliminary injunction. These witnesses included one of the captains of the women's basketball team, two assistant coaches, and Timothy Stoner, Coach Stanley's former counsel.

Pursuant to Coach Stanley's request, the district court reviewed Coach Raveling's employment contract *in camera*. Later that day, the district court denied the motion for a preliminary injunction.

III. DISCUSSION

The gravamen of Coach Stanley's multiple claims against USC is her contention that she is entitled to pay equal to that provided to Coach Raveling for his services as head coach of the men's basketball team because the position of head coach of the women's team "require[s] equal skill, effort, and responsibility, and [is performed] under similar working conditions." Appellant's Opening Brief at 34. She asserts that USC discriminated against her because of her sex by rejecting her request. She also maintains that USC retaliated against her because of her request for equal pay for herself and her assistant coaches. According to Coach Stanley, USC retaliated by withdrawing the offer of a three-year contract and instead presenting her with a new offer of a one-year contract at less pay than that received by Coach Raveling.

We begin our analysis mindful of the fact that we are reviewing the denial of a *preliminary* injunction. There has been no trial in this matter. Because the hearing on the preliminary injunction occurred 21 days after the action was filed in state court, discovery had not been completed. Our prediction of the probability of success on the merits is based on the limited offer of proof that was possible under the circumstances. We obviously cannot now evaluate the persuasive impact of the evidence that the parties may bring forth at trial.

A. *Standard of Review.*

We review the denial of a motion for preliminary injunction for abuse of discretion. *Chalk v. United States Dist. Court*, 840 F.2d 701, 704 (9th Cir. 1988).

> An order is reversible for legal error if the court did not apply the correct preliminary injunction standard, or if the court misapprehended the law with respect to the underlying issues in litigation. An abuse of discretion may also occur if the district court rests its conclusions on clearly erroneous findings of fact.

Id. (citations omitted).

In *Martin v. International Olympic Committee*, 740 F.2d 670 (9th Cir. 1984), we described the legal standard a district court must apply in exercising its discretion:

> In this circuit, a party seeking preliminary injunctive relief must meet one of two tests. Under the first, a court may issue a preliminary injunction if it finds that:
>
> > (1) the [moving party] will suffer irreparable injury if injunctive relief is not granted, (2) the [moving party] will probably prevail on the merits, (3) in balancing the equities, the [non-moving party] will not be harmed more than [the moving party] is helped by the injunction, and

(4) granting the injunction is in the public interest.

Alternatively, a court may issue a preliminary injunction if the moving party demonstrates *either* a combination of probable success on the merits and the possibility of irreparable injury *or* that serious questions are raised and the balance of hardships tips sharply in his favor. Under this last part of the alternative test, even if the balance of hardships tips decidedly in favor of the moving party, it must be shown as an irreducible minimum that there is a fair chance of success on the merits. There is one additional factor we must weigh. In cases such as the one before us in which a party seeks mandatory preliminary relief that goes well beyond maintaining the status quo *pendente lite*, courts should be extremely cautious about issuing a preliminary injunction.

Id. at 674-75 (internal quotations and citations omitted) (emphasis in original).

Coach Stanley argues that she did not seek a mandatory preliminary injunction. She asserts that she was "not seeking to be instated by USC, she was seeking to continue her employment with USC." Appellant's Opening Brief at 28. Coach Stanley maintains that she requested a prohibitory preliminary injunction and that the district court erred in applying the test for a mandatory preliminary injunction.

A prohibitory injunction preserves the status quo. *Johnson v. Kay*, 860 F.2d 529, 541 (2d Cir. 1988). A mandatory injunction "'goes well beyond simply maintaining the status quo *pendente lite* [and] is particularly disfavored.'" *Anderson v. United States*, 612 F.2d 1112, 1114 (9th Cir. 1979) (quoting *Martinez v. Mathews*, 544 F.2d 1233, 1243 (5th Cir. 1976)). When a mandatory preliminary injunction is requested, the district court should deny such relief "'unless the facts and law clearly favor the moving party.'" *Id.* Our first task is to determine whether Coach Stanley requested a prohibitory injunction or a mandatory injunction.

Coach Stanley's four-year contract terminated on June 30, 1993. She was informed by Garrett on July 15, 1993, that her employment contract had expired and that she should not perform any services for the university until both parties entered into a new contract. On August 6, 1993, the date this action was filed in state court, Coach Stanley was no longer a USC employee.

Accordingly, an injunction compelling USC to install Coach Stanley as the head coach of the women's basketball team and to pay her $28,000 a year more than she received when her employment contract expired would not have maintained the status quo. Instead, it would have forced USC to hire a person at a substantially higher rate of pay than she had received prior to the expiration of her employment contract on June 30, 1993. The district court did not err in concluding that Coach Stanley was seeking a mandatory injunction, and that her request was subject to a higher degree of scrutiny because such relief is particularly disfavored under the law of this circuit. *Anderson*, 612 F.2d at 1114.

B. *There Has Been No Clear Showing of a Probability of Success on the Merits of Coach Stanley's Claim for Injunctive Relief.*

In light of our determination that Coach Stanley requested a mandatory preliminary injunction, we must consider whether the law and the facts clearly favor granting such relief. To obtain a preliminary injunction, Coach Stanley was required to demonstrate that her remedy at law was inadequate. *Beacon Theatres, Inc. v. Westover,* 359 U.S. 500, 506-07 & n.8, 79 S.Ct. 948, 954-55 & n. 8, 3 L.Ed.2d 988 (1959) ("The basis of injunctive relief in the federal courts has always been irreparable harm and inadequacy of legal remedies.") (footnote omitted).

In her motion for a preliminary injunction filed in the state court, Coach Stanley requested an order "enjoining the defendants from forcing plaintiff to enter into an unfair and sex discriminatory contract and interfering with plaintiff (sic) continued performance as head coach of women's basketball until such time as the Court may enter a final determination on the merits of this action." As described above, the state court granted a temporary restraining order installing Coach Stanley to the position of head coach of the women's basketball team, at a higher annual salary, 37 days after her four-year contract had expired. On August 6, 1993, this matter was removed to the district court, before the state court could rule on the motion for a preliminary injunction.

The district court ordered USC and Garrett to file their opposition to Coach Stanley's motion for a preliminary injunction on August 18, 1993. On August 24, 1993, Coach Stanley filed her reply. In her reply, Coach Stanley states:

> Thus, *Plaintiff,* in her motion for TRO, and in this hearing for a preliminary injunction, *is simply seeking to maintain the status quo between the parties at the firm and final salary offered by Defendants* and to restrain Defendants from wrongfully locking out Plaintiff from the performance of her duties as Head Women's Basketball Coach simply because she is engaged in protected activities, i.e., seeking equal pay and benefits as are provided to the Head Men's Basketball Coach at U.S.C.

(emphasis added).

Plaintiff's Reply to Defendants' Opposition to Plaintiff's Motion For Preliminary Injunction at 11 (emphasis added).

To the extent that Coach Stanley is seeking money damages and back pay for the loss of her job, her remedy at law is adequate. *Cf. Anderson v. United States,* 612 F.2d at 1115 (mandatory injunction is inappropriate where retroactive promotion and back pay are available if the employee succeeds on the merits). The district court, however, construed the motion for a preliminary injunction as including a request that future discrimination or retaliation based on the fact that she is a woman be enjoined. We do so as well for purposes of resolving the present appeal.

1. *Merits of Coach Stanley's Claim of Denial of Equal Pay for Equal Work.*

The district court concluded that Coach Stanley had failed to demonstrate that there is a likelihood that she would prevail on the merits of her claim of a denial of equal pay for equal work because she failed to present facts clearly showing that USC was guilty of sex discrimination in its negotiations for a new employment contract. The thrust of Coach Stanley's argument in this appeal is that she is entitled, as a matter of law, "to make the same salary as was paid to the Head Men's Basketball Coach at USC." Appellant's Opening Brief at 9. None of the authorities she has cited supports this theory.

In her reply brief, Coach Stanley asserts that she has "never said or argued in any of her submissions that the compensation of the men's and women's basketball coaches at USC or elsewhere must be identical." Appellant's Reply Brief at 2. Coach Stanley accuses USC of mischaracterizing her position. This argument ignores her insistence to Garrett that she was entitled to the "same salary" received by Coach Raveling. The denotation of the word "same" is "identical." Webster's Third New International Dictionary 2007.

In her reply brief, Coach Stanley asserts that she merely seeks equal pay for equal work. In *Hein v. Oregon College of Education*, 718 F.2d 910 (9th Cir. 1983), we stated that to recover under the Equal Pay Act of 1963, 29 U.S.C. §206(d)(1)(1988), "a plaintiff must prove that an employer is paying different wages to employees of the opposite sex for equal work." *Hein*, 718 F.2d at 913. We concluded that the jobs need not be identical, but they must be "substantially equal." *Id.* (internal quotation and citation omitted).

The EPA prohibits discrimination in wages "between employees on the basis of sex ... for equal work, on jobs the performance of which requires equal skill, effort, and responsibility, and which are performed under similar working conditions." 29 U.S.C. § 206(d)(1) (1988). Each of these components must be substantially equal to state a claim. *Forsberg v. Pacific Northwest Bell Tel.*, 840 F.2d 1409, 1414 (9th Cir. 1988).

Coach Stanley has not offered proof to contradict the evidence proffered by USC that demonstrates the differences in the responsibilities of the persons who serve as head coaches of the women's and men's basketball teams. Coach Raveling's responsibilities as head coach of the men's basketball team require substantial public relations and promotional activities to generate revenue for USC. These efforts resulted in revenue that is 90 times greater than the revenue generated by the women's basketball team. Coach Raveling was required to conduct twelve outside speaking engagements per year, to be accessible to the media for interviews, and to participate in certain activities designed to produce donations and endorsements for the USC Athletic Department in general. Coach Stanley's position as head coach did not require her to engage in the same intense level of promotional and revenue-raising activities. This quantitative dissimilarity in responsibilities justifies a different level of pay for the head coach of the women's basketball team. *See Horner v. Mary Inst.*, 613 F.2d 706, 713-14 (8th Cir. 1980) (evidence that male physical education teacher had a different job from a female physical education teacher because he was responsible for curriculum precluded finding that jobs were substantially similar; court may consider whether job requires more experience, training, and ability to determine whether jobs require substantially equal skill under EPA).

The evidence presented by USC also showed that Coach Raveling had substantially different qualifications and experience related to his public rela-tions and revenue-generation skills than Coach Stanley. Coach Raveling received educational training in marketing, and worked in that field for nine years. Coach Raveling has been employed by USC three years longer than Coach Stanley. He has been a college basketball coach for 31 years, while Coach Stanley has had 17 years experience as a basketball coach. Coach Raveling had served as a member of the NCAA Subcommittee on Recruiting. Coach Raveling also is the respected author of two bestselling novels. He has performed as an actor in a feature movie, and has appeared on national tele-vision to discuss recruiting of student athletes. Coach Stanley does not have the same degree of experience in these varied activities. Employers may reward professional experience and education without violating the EPA. *Soto v. Adams Elevator Equip. Co.*, 941 F.2d 543, 548 & n. 7 (7th Cir. 1991).

Coach Raveling's national television appearances and motion picture presence, as well as his reputation as an author, make him a desirable public relations representative for USC. An employer may consider the marketplace value of the skills of a particular individual when determining his or her salary. *Horner*, 613 F.2d at 714. Unequal wages that reflect market condi-tions of supply and demand are not prohibited by the EPA. *EEOC v. Madison Community Unit Sch. Dist. No. 12*, 818 F.2d 577, 580 (7th Cir. 1987).

The record also demonstrates that the USC men's basketball team gener-ated greater attendance, more media interest, larger donations, and produced substantially more revenue than the women's basketball team.[1] As a result, USC placed greater pressure on Coach Raveling to promote his team and to win. The responsibility to produce a large amount of revenue is evidence of a substantial difference in responsibility. *See Jacobs v. College of William and Mary*, 517 F.Supp. 791, 797 (E.D. Va. 1980) (duty to produce revenue demon-strates that coaching jobs are not substantially equal), *aff'd without opinion*, 661 F.2d 922 (4th Cir.), *cert. denied*, 454 U.S. 1033, 102 S.Ct. 572, 70 L.Ed. 2d 477 (1981).

---

1. The total average attendance per women's team game during Coach Stanley's tenure was 751 as compared to 4,035 for the men's team during the same period. The average sales of season ticket passes to faculty and staff for women's games were 13, while the average sales for men's games were 130. Alumni and other fans, on average, purchased 71 passes for women's home games as compared to over 1,200 season passes for men's home games during the same period. A season pass to the men's home games was more than double the price of a season pass to women's home games. The same disparity exists with respect to media interest in the men's and women's basketball teams. Television and radio stations paid USC to broad-cast the men's basketball games; all of the home games and many games off campus were broadcast on network or cable stations. All of the games were broadcast on commercial radio. Approximately three of the women's basketball games were broadcast on cable stations as part of a contract package that also covered several other sports. Donations and endowments were likewise greater for the men's basketball team, totalling $66,916 during the time period of Coach Stanley's contract, as compared to $4,288 for the women's basketball team. The same was true for revenue production. While the women's basketball team produced a total rev-enue of $50,262 during Coach Stanley's four years, the men's team generated $4,725,784 dur-ing the same time period.

Coach Stanley did not offer evidence to rebut USC's justification for paying Coach Raveling a higher salary. Instead, she alleged that the women's team generates revenue, and that she is under a great deal of pressure to win.[2] Coach Stanley argues that *Jacobs* is distinguishable because, in that matter, the head basketball coach of the women's team was not required to produce any revenue. *Jacobs*, 517 F.Supp. at 798. Coach Stanley appears to suggest that a difference in the amount of revenue generated by the men's and women's teams should be ignored by the court in comparing the respective coaching positions. We disagree.

We agree with the district court in *Jacobs* that revenue generation is an important factor that may be considered in justifying greater pay. We are also of the view that the relative amount of revenue generated should be considered in determining whether responsibilities and working conditions are substantially equal. The fact that the men's basketball team at USC generates 90 times the revenue than that produced by the women's team adequately demonstrates that Coach Raveling was under greater pressure to win and to promote his team than Coach Stanley was subject to as head coach of the women's team.

Coach Stanley's reliance on *Burkey v. Marshall County Board of Education*, 513 F.Supp. 1084 (N.D.W.Va. 1981), and *EEOC v. Madison Community Unit School District No. 12*, 818 F.2d 577 (7th Cir. 1987) to support her claim of sex discrimination is misplaced. In *Burkey*, the women coaches were "uniformly paid one-half (1/2) of the salary which male coaches of *comparable or identical boys' junior high school sports were paid." Burkey*, 513 F.Supp. at 1088 (emphasis added). Here, however, Coach Stanley has not shown that her responsibilities were identical.

In *Madison*, the Seventh Circuit held that the plaintiff established a prima facie EPA claim because "male and female coaches alike testified that the skill, effort, and responsibility required were the same and the working conditions [were] also the same—*not merely similar*, which is all the Act requires." *Madison*, 818 F.2d at 583 (emphasis added). In the instant matter, the uncontradicted evidence shows that Coach Raveling's responsibilities, as head coach of the men's basketball team, differed substantially from the duties imposed upon Coach Stanley.

Coach Stanley contends that the failure to allocate funds in the promotion of women's basketball team demonstrated gender discrimination. She appears to argue that USC's failure to pay her a salary equal to that of Coach Raveling was the result of USC's "failure to market and promote the women's basketball team." The only evidence Coach Stanley presented in support of this argument is that USC failed to provide the women's team with a poster

---

2. Coach Stanley also alleged that, as head coach, she had won four national women's basketball championships, but that Coach Raveling had won none. In addition, while head coach at USC, Coach Stanley was named PAC-10 Coach-of-the-Year in 1993 and the women's basketball team played in the last three NCAA Tournaments and advanced to the NCAA Sweet Sixteen in 1993 and the NCAA Elite in 1992. She also described numerous speaking engagements in which she had participated.

containing the schedule of games, but had done so for the men's team. This single bit of evidence does not demonstrate that Coach Stanley was denied equal pay for equal work. Instead, it demonstrates, at best, a business decision to allocate USC resources to the team that generates the most revenue.[3]

The district court also was "unconvinced" by Coach Stanley's claim that USC's disparate promotion of men's and women's basketball teams had "caused the enormous differences in spectator interest and revenue production." The court rejected Coach Stanley's assertion that the differences were due to societal discrimination and that this was evidence of a prima facie case under the EPA. The court reasoned that societal discrimination in preferring to witness men's sports in greater numbers cannot be attributed to USC. We agree. *Cf. Madison*, 818 F.2d at 580-82 (EPA does not prohibit wages that reflect market conditions of supply and demand, which may depress wages in jobs held mainly by women).

At this preliminary stage of these proceedings, the record does not support a finding that gender was the reason that USC paid a higher salary to Coach Raveling as head coach of the men's basketball team than it offered Coach Stanley as head coach of the women's basketball team. Garrett's affidavit supports the district court's conclusion that the head coach position of the men's team was not substantially equal to the head coach position of the women's team. The record shows that there were significant differences between Coach Stanley's and Coach Raveling's public relations skills, credentials, experience, and qualifications; there also were substantial differences between their responsibilities and working conditions. The district court's finding that the head coach positions were not substantially equal is not a "clear error of judgment." *Martin v. International Olympic Comm.*, 740 F.2d 670, 679 (9th Cir. 1984).

2.Merits of Coach Stanley's Claim of Retaliation.

The district court also rejected Coach Stanley's claim that USC terminated her contract or failed to renew her contract in retaliation for her involvement in protected activities. Rather, the court found that her contract had expired and she refused to accept any of the renewal options that USC offered. This finding is not clearly erroneous. Although Coach Stanley contends that she accepted the multi-year contract and continued only to negotiate the terms of the compensation, the district court found this assertion to be "contrary to the weight of the evidence which clearly suggests that Ms. Stanley failed to accept USC's three-year contract because she was dissatisfied with the proposed compensation." The record supports this finding. Coach Stanley rejected the three-year contract offered by USC. She made a counter offer which USC did not accept. The disagreement on the amount of pay precipitated an impasse in the negotiations.

Coach Stanley's argument that Garrett retaliated against her because she demanded equal pay does not square with the evidence she has produced.

---

3. Coach Stanley has not contended either in the district court or before this court that this evidence would support an inference that USC violated Title IX, 20 U.S.C. § 1681(a) (1988).

After she demanded the same pay that Coach Raveling receives, she was offered a multi-year contract at a substantially higher salary than she had received under her original employment agreement. This offer remained open until June 7, 1993. The offer was rejected by Coach Stanley.

Contrary to Coach Stanley's contention, the offer of a one-year contract at an increase of $28,000 in total compensation does not clearly demonstrate retaliation. Rather, it tends to show that USC wanted to retain her services, at a substantial increase in salary. The fact that she was offered a one-year contract after her four-year contract expired does not demonstrate discrimination or retaliation. The record shows Coach Raveling was offered a one-year renewal contract after his initial five year contract expired.[4]

We express no opinion as to whether Coach Stanley ultimately will establish a prima facie case of sex discrimination or retaliation at trial. We hold only that Coach Stanley has failed to demonstrate that the law and the facts clearly favor her position. *See Anderson v. United States*, 612 F.2d 1112, 1114 (9th Cir. 1979).

C. *There Has Been No Showing of a Nexus Between Hardship and the Conduct of USC.*

The district court found that Coach Stanley presented sufficient facts from which it could be inferred that she suffered emotional distress, loss of business opportunity, and injury to her reputation following the expiration of her four-year employment contract and the failure of negotiations for a new contract. The court was "persuaded that Coach Stanley [had] sustained her burden to demonstrate a threat of imminent irreparable harm if preliminary injunctive relief [was] denied."[5] Neither party challenges this finding.

The district court also concluded, however, that Coach Stanley failed to demonstrate that the facts clearly show that USC discriminated or retaliated against her on the basis of her gender. As discussed above, Coach Stanley failed to demonstrate that the facts developed in the record and the law clearly favored the issuance of a mandatory preliminary injunction. She has failed

---

4. *Miller v. Fairchild Industries, Inc.*, 797 F.2d 727 (9th Cir.1986) is therefore distinguishable. Coach Stanley did not produce evidence that a causal connection existed between her demand for equal pay and the failure to renew her contract as did the plaintiffs in *Miller*. There, we reversed a summary judgment in favor of the employer who advanced economic layoff as a justification for the discharge of two African American females who had previously filed EEOC discrimination claims against the employer and settled. The layoffs occurred less than two months after they negotiated the EEOC settlement agreement and the management personnel who participated in the EEOC settlement negotiations were also responsible for their layoffs. Plaintiff's [sic] declarations established that they were the only employees laid off; the employer disputed this fact. We held that summary judgment under these circumstances was not appropriate. *Miller*, 797 F.2d at 732-33.

5. The allegations of intentional sex discrimination, prospective loss of reputation, business opportunity, and serious emotional distress, the court reasoned, could not be remedied by money damages. There is legal support for the court's conclusion. *See, e.g., Chalk v. United States Dist. Court*, 840 F.2d 701, 709 (9th Cir. 1988) (emotional distress, depression, and anxiety may constitute irreparable injury); *Garcia v. Lawn*, 805 F.2d 1400, 1405 (9th Cir. 1986)(chilling effect of retaliation may be irreparable harm).

to show that the injury she suffered was caused by the alleged wrongful conduct of USC.

D. *The District Court's Finding that the Balance of Hardships Do Not Tip Sharply in Coach Stanley's Favor is Not Clearly Erroneous.*

Coach Stanley challenges the district court's finding that the balance of hardships did not tip sharply in her favor. She argues that USC presented no evidence to demonstrate any hardship.

Although the district court found that the balance of hardships was "tipped to some degree in [Coach] Stanley's favor[,]" it found that USC would suffer some prejudice if the injunction was granted. Garrett's affidavit and supporting exhibits demonstrate that a preliminary injunction would cause USC hardship. This evidence establishes that Garrett wanted to conclude contract negotiations before the June 30, 1993, expiration of Coach Stanley's contract because

> [t]he summer months are critical for recruiting of student athletes. In addition, it is essential that the head coach be in place by the time the students arrive for the Fall term, which at USC generally is the Monday before Labor Day. This is because the coach is responsible for providing general supervision of and counselling to the student athletes in their academic and personal lives. In addition, practices commence soon after the Fall term begins in preparation for pre-season games.

The district court drew a logical inference of hardship from this evidence. The district court reasoned that issuing the injunction would force USC into a unilateral contract which would provide Coach Stanley with a significant pay increase, but would not require any commitment by Coach Stanley to remain at USC as the head coach of women's basketball. If Coach Stanley were reinstated to the position pursuant to a preliminary injunction, her compensation would be $96,000, a sum she rejected when it was offered to her previously. Accordingly, USC would have a head coach who was dissatisfied with the terms of her employment. Her state of mind, and the impermanence of her position, would likely affect the ability of the school to recruit athletes concerned about the quality and identity of the coaching staff for the next four years. The court concluded that if USC was not permitted to seek out "a replacement of Coach Stanley prior to commencement of the Fall semester, USC will suffer a serious hardship."

The record supports the district court's finding that USC would suffer some hardship if the preliminary injunction issued. In light of the evidence of the impact on the women's basketball program if USC were forced to hire an employee, *pendente lite*, who claims the school discriminates on the basis of sex, we conclude that the district court did not clearly err in finding that the balance of hardships did not tip sharply in Coach Stanley's favor.

E. *The District Court's Finding that the Public's Interest Was Not Served by Granting the Preliminary Injunction Is Not Clearly Erroneous.*

Coach Stanley argues that the strong public interest in preventing intentional sex discrimination and discriminatory employment practices weighs in favor of granting the preliminary injunction. We agree with the district court that "[t]his argument would be quite persuasive had [Coach] Stanley come forward with some evidence that her termination was the result of sex discrimination and that she was reasonably likely to prevail on the merits of her discrimination claim."

Coach Stanley failed to present evidence that she would probably prevail on her claims of sex discrimination and retaliation. The evidence also does not establish that the balance of hardships tipped sharply in her favor. Consequently, the district court did not err in concluding that the public's interest in preventing sex discrimination and discriminatory employment practices did not clearly favor granting a mandatory preliminary injunction.

F. *Procedural Challenges to the Preliminary Injunction Hearing.*

Coach Stanley claims that the district court violated her right to due process by requiring her to make offers of proof rather than permitting her witnesses to testify. This contention is without merit. In this circuit, the refusal to hear oral testimony at a preliminary injunction hearing is not an abuse of discretion if the parties have a full opportunity to submit written testimony and to argue the matter. *Kenneally v. Lungren*, 967 F.2d 329, 335 (9th Cir. 1992), *cert. denied*, — U.S. —, 113 S.Ct. 979, 122 L.Ed.2d 133 (1993); *International Molders' & Allied Workers' Local Union v. Nelson*, 799 F.2d 547, 555 (9th Cir. 1986); *San Francisco-Oakland Newspaper Guild v. Kennedy*, 412 F.2d 541, 546 & n. 6 (9th Cir. 1969).

Coach Stanley had an opportunity to present additional affidavits. In addition, the district court accepted her offers of proof as conclusive proof of the matter represented.

Coach Stanley also asserts that the district court erred in resolving the preliminary injunction without providing her an opportunity to conduct discovery. We disagree. Coach Stanley requested a preliminary injunction on August 5, 1993. She did not file a request for a continuance in order to complete discovery prior to the August 26, 1993 hearing on the motion for a preliminary injunction. Thus, the opportunity to conduct discovery was not denied; Coach Stanley simply did not avail herself of it prior to the hearing. Nothing precluded her from conducting discovery prior to the hearing on the preliminary injunction. She could have moved, *ex parte*, for an order shortening time within which to conduct depositions. *See* Fed.R.Civ.P. 30(a); *see also* W. Scwarzer, A.W. Tashima, J. Wagstaffe, Federal Civil Procedure Before Trial § 11:157 (1993) (Federal Rules of Civil Procedure require a court order if plaintiff desires to take a deposition during the first 30 days after service of the summons and complaint, and "good cause [for such an order] may exist because of the urgent need for discovery in connection with an application for TRO or preliminary injunction") [internal quotations omitted].

IV. CONCLUSION

The district court did not abuse its discretion in denying a mandatory preliminary injunction. Coach Stanley did not meet her burden of demonstrating the irreducible minimum for obtaining a preliminary injunction: "that there is a fair chance of success on the merits." Martin v. International Olympic Comm., 740 F.2d at 675. Because mandatory preliminary injunctions are disfavored in this circuit, we are compelled to review the record to determine whether the facts and the law clearly favor Coach Stanley. Anderson, 612 F.2d at 1114. The evidence offered at the hearing on the motion for a preliminary injunction demonstrated that Coach Stanley sought pay from USC equal to Coach Raveling's income from that university, notwithstanding significant differences in job pressure, the level of responsibility, and in marketing and revenue-producing qualifications and performance. A difference in pay that takes such factors into consideration does not prove gender bias or violate the Equal Pay Act. The unfortunate impasse that occurred during the negotiations for the renewal of the employment contract of an outstanding basketball coach followed the offer of a very substantial increase in salary — not sex discrimination or retaliation. Because Coach Stanley failed to demonstrate that the law and the facts clearly favor her position, the judgment is AFFIRMED.

Questions and Comments

1. What remedy did the plaintiff seek?
2. What are the tests to determine if a temporary restraining order will be issued?
3. What is the primary distinction between a temporary restraining order and an injunction?
4. What are the essential prerequisites for obtaining an equitable remedy?
5. What tests would the court use to determine equal work and/or equal pay?
6. What factors were listed by the court to justify the temporary pay for the men's basketball coach?

Authors' Notes

Statute of Limitations

The statute of limitations is set forth under 29 U.S. Code Annotated, Section 255. Specifically, an action must be brought within two years after the cause of action has accrued unless the causation factor can be described as willful in which case the statute of limitations is three years.

Exhaustion of Administrative Remedies

The general principle of exhaustion of administrative remedies is applicable to an action brought under the Equal Pay Act. Notice should be directed to the fact that the administrative remedy now applicable is before the Equal Employment Opportunity Commission.

Factors Other Than Sex

Market conditions. One factor other than sex that serves as a justification for disparity in salary is market conditions. Case law in this connection includes *Horner v. Mary Institute* (1980). The court in this case stated:

> Although an employer's perception that women would generally work for less than will men is not a justification for paying women less, *see Corning Glass Works v. Brennan, supra*, 417 U.S. at 205 94 S.Ct. 2223, it is our view that an employer may consider the market place value of the skills of a particular individual when determining his or her salary. *See generally Christensen v. Iowa*, 563 F.2d 353, 356 (8th Cir. 1977). (p. 714)

Horner v. Mary Institute was cited with approval in *Stanley v. University of Southern California* (1994). The court in *Stanley* stated:

> An employer may consider the marketplace value of the skills of a particular individual when determining his or her salary. *Horner*, 613 F.2d at 714. Unequal wages that reflect market conditions of supply and demand are not prohibited by the EPA. *EEOC v. Madison Community Unit Sch. Dist. No. 12*, 818 F.2d 577, 580 (7th Cir. 1987). (p. 1322)

Offers from other schools. A university does not violate the Equal Pay Act when it raises the salary of one instructor so as to meet the offer from another institution. The desire to retain the employee is legitimate as a "factor other than sex." See *Winkes v. Brown University* (1984).

Wage settlement. A wage settlement that purports to equalize salaries will be used as a starting point in determining salary disparities. This principle was pronounced in *Anderson v. University of Northern Iowa* (1985). *Anderson* involved a class action suit in which the plaintiff participated in the settlement.

Change in assignment. A university policy that approves the retention of a higher salary when one is reassigned to what normally might be a lower paying job is well established. This principle of salary retention was reaffirmed in *Covington v. Southern Illinois University* (1987). *Covington* also emphasized employee morale and financial conditions at the time of hire as being legitimate if untainted by consideration of gender discrimination.

Subjective judgment. It is elementary that the decision-making process, when dealing with personnel in higher education, tends to be somewhat subjective in nature. The absence of specific quantitative measurements when hiring faculty and supervisory personnel does not eliminate value judgments if unaffected by discriminatory action. See *Schwartz v. Florida Bd. of Regents* (1991). A broad-brush postulate for such a conclusion has been alluded to by the United States Supreme Court when it cautions against judicial involvement in personnel matters in *Bishop v. Wood* (1976):

> The federal court is not the appropriate forum in which to review the multitude of personnel decisions that are made daily by public agencies. (Footnote omitted) We must accept the harsh fact that numerous individual mistakes are inevitable in the day-to-day administration of our affairs. The United States Constitution cannot feasibly be construed to require federal judicial review for every such error. In the absence of any claim that the public employer was motivated by a desire to curtail or to penalize the exercise of an employee's consti-

tutionally protected rights, we must presume that official action was regular and, if erroneous, can best be corrected in other ways. The Due Process Clause of the Fourteenth Amendment is not a guarantee against incorrect or ill-advised personnel decisions. (pp. 349-350)

Equal Work

The statute describes equal work in terms of skill, effort, and responsibility. Decisional law provides some flexibility in that reference is made to substantial equality as opposed to absolute exactitude. One case that asserts this principle is *Odomes v. Nucare, Inc.* (1981):

> To establish a claim of unequal pay for equal work a plaintiff has the burden to prove that the employer "pays different wages to employees of opposite sexes 'for equal work on jobs the performance of which require equal skill, effort and responsibility, and which are performed under similar working conditions.'" *Corning Glass Works v. Brennan, supra,* 417 U.S. at 195, 94 S.Ct. at 2228. Congress did not intend through use of the phrase "equal work" to require that the jobs be identical. *Schultz v. Wheaton Glass Company, supra,* 421 F.2d at 265. Instead, to effectuate the remedial purposes of the Equal Pay Act, only substantial equality of skill, effort, responsibility and working conditions is required. *Id.* at 265. Whether the work of nurse's aides and orderlies is substantially equal must be determined on a case-by-case basis, *Brennan v. South Davis Community Hospital,* 538 F.2d 859, 861 (10th Cir. 1976). This issue must be resolved by an overall comparison of the work, not its individual segments. *Gunther v. County of Washington, supra,* 623 F.2d at 1309. (p. 250)

The significance of this principle was reiterated in *EEOC v. Madison Comm. Unit Sch. Dist. No. 12* (1987):

> The first question we must decide is whether the pairs of jobs that the district judge compared in finding unequal pay are sufficiently similar to be "equal work" within the meaning of the Equal Pay Act. . . .

> Thus the jobs that are compared must be in some sense the same to count as "equal work" under the Equal Pay Act; and here we come to the main difficulty in applying the Act: whether two jobs are the same depends on how fine a system of job classifications the courts will accept. If coaching an athletic team in the Madison, Illinois school system is considered a single job rather than a congeries of jobs, the school district violated the Equal Pay Act prima facie by paying female holders of this job less than male holders, and the only question is whether the district carried its burden of proving that the lower wages which the four female coaches received were lower than the wages of their male counterparts because of a factor other than sex. If on the other hand coaching the girls' tennis team is considered a different job from coaching the boys' tennis team, and *a fortiori* if coaching the girls' volleyball or basketball team is considered a different job (or jobs) from coaching the boys' soccer team, there is no

prima facie violation. So the question is how narrow a definition of job the courts should be using in deciding whether the Equal Pay Act is applicable. (p. 580)

Compared With Title VII

A comparison of the Equal Pay Act and Title VII is to be found in *Odomes v. Nucare, Inc.*:

> The analysis of a claim of unequal pay for equal work is essentially the same under both the Equal Pay Act and Title VII. *Strecker v. Grand Forks Cty. Soc. Serv. Bd.*, 640 F.2d 96, 99 (8th Cir. 1980). But *see Gunther v. County of Washington*, 623 F.2d 1303, 1309 (9th Cir. 1979), aff'd — U.S. —, 101 S.Ct. 2242, 68 L.Ed.2d 751 (1981). The standard of review applicable to such a claim of unequal pay for equal work is the clearly erroneous rule of Fed.R.Civ.P., 52(a). *Brennan v. Owensboro-Daviess Cty. Hosp., etc.*, 523 F.2d 1013, 1015 (6th Cir. 1975), *cert. denied*, 425 U.S. 973, 96 S.Ct. 2170, 48 L.Ed.2d 796 (1976). (p. 250)
>
> The four exemptions enunciated by the Equal Pay Act are applicable to Title VII claims of unequal pay for equal work. 42 U.S.C. § 2000e-2(b). (p. 251)

SUMMARY

The purpose, terms, and exemptions of the Equal Pay Act have been set forth in the statute, together with the case law cited herein.

The applicable statute of limitations has also been set forth by statutory provision. Remedies are available both in equity and under the common law.

Defenses should hinge around a determination of equal work—equal pay—or a failure to comply with the statute of limitations or to exhaust administrative remedies.

This could be you - check your response

The primary test of the Equal Pay Act is whether or not equal wages are paid for equal work. Case law has developed some exceptions. For example, an employer who wishes to hire a particular man who is being paid at a higher rate than women already working for the employer is permitted such a differential. Market conditions and previous administrative experience are recognized as exceptions. Under the conditions noted above, Ms Jones could possibly pay Mr. Murphy more money than she pays her female employees.

The general rule postulates equal pay for equal work. Exceptions should be approached with caution.

REFERENCES

Cases

Anderson v. University of Northern Iowa, 779 F.2d 441 (8th Cir. 1985).

Bartges v. The University of North Carolina at Charlotte, 908 F.Supp. 1312 (W.D. NC 1995).

Bishop v. Wood, 426 U.S. 341, 48 L. Ed 684, 96 S.Ct. 2074 (1976).

Covington v. Southern Illinois University, 816 F.2d 317 (7th Cir. 1987).

EEOC v. Madison Comm. Unit Sch. Dist. No. 12, 818 F.2d 577 (7th Cir. 1987).

Horner v. Mary Institute, 613 F.2d 706 (8th Cir. 1980).

Odomes v. Nucare, Inc., 653 F.2d 246 (6th Cir. 1981).

Schwartz v. Florida Bd. of Regents, 954 F.2d 620 (11th Cir. 1991).

Stanley v. University of Southern California, 13 F.3d 1313 (9th Cir. 1994).

Winkes v. Brown Univ., 747 F.2d 792 (1st Cir. 1984).

Model Codes, Restatements, and Standards

Fair Labor Standards Act (1938), 29 U.S.C.A. Section 201 et seq.

Equal Pay Act (1963)

29 U.S.C.A., Section 206(d)(1)

29 U.S.C.A. Section 255

CIVIL RIGHTS:
SEX DISCRIMINATION

PERSPECTIVE

Legal developments are often explained in terms of what has happened in the past. In the case of women, specific legal consequences resulted from an overall attitude toward the place of women in society. This attitude is reflected in many documents. Two will suffice for our purposes. In 1872, Mr. Justice Bradley of the United States Supreme Court, in a concurring opinion, summarized thusly:

[T]he civil law, as well as nature herself, has always recognized a wide difference in the respective spheres and destinies of man and woman. Man is, or should be, woman's protector and defender. The natural and proper timidity and delicacy which belongs to the female sex evidently unfits it for many of the occupations of civil life. The constitution of the family organization, which is founded in the divine ordinance, as well as in the nature of things, indicates the domestic sphere as that which properly belongs to the domain and functions of womanhood. The harmony, not to say identity, of interests and views which belong, or should belong, to the family institution is repugnant to the idea of a woman adopting a distinct and independent career from that of her husband. So firmly fixed was this sentiment in the founders of the common law that it became a maxim of that system of jurisprudence that a woman had no legal existence separate from her husband, who was regarded as her head and representative in the social state; and, notwithstanding some recent modifications of this civil status, many of the special rules of law flowing from and dependent upon this cardinal principle still exist in full force in most States. One of these is, that a married woman is incapable, without her husband's consent, of making contracts which shall be binding on her or him. This very incapacity was one circumstance which the Supreme Court of Illinois deemed important in rendering a married woman incompetent fully to perform the duties and trusts that belong to the office of an attorney and counsellor.

.   .   .   .   .

[I]n my opinion, in view of the peculiar characteristics, destiny, and mission of woman, it is within the province of the legislature to ordain what offices, positions, and callings shall be filled and discharged by men, and shall receive the benefit of those energies and responsibilities, and that decision and firmness which are presumed to predominate in the sterner sex. (*Bradwell v. Illinois*, 1873, pp. 141-142)

The above statement should be read in connection with the Declaration of Sentiments—Adopted by the First Women's Rights Convention, Seneca Falls, N.Y., July 19, 1848, a document that tracked the style of the Declaration of Independence in setting forth the grievances suffered by women in American political society. Also of interest is the withering indictment of second-class citizenship as set forth in the colloquy between Susan B. Anthony and Judge Hunt following her conviction for voting. These documents can be readily found in *Sex Discrimination and the Law: Causes and Remedies* (Babcock, Freedman, Norton, & Ross, 1975).

The attitude expressed by Mr. Justice Bradley has undergone a profound change. Women's suffrage (the right to vote) was addressed in the Nineteenth Amendment to the United States Constitution. Property rights were also ensured by state legislation that extended the right to contract and to hold property to women separate and apart from their husbands. Belatedly, national legislation followed that addressed the issue of the civil rights for women as witness such legislation as the Equal Pay Act and Title IX legislation. Owners and managers working in the sport industry have both an opportunity and an obligation. The opportunity extends to ensuring working conditions that will not only conform to the law as currently expressed but will also take full advantage of the capabilities that women bring to the industry. This country suffered the loss of over 50% of its brain power for a prolonged period of time. This will no longer be the case. If owners and managers cannot see the advantages posed by such a change in attitude, they at least can understand the obligations that the law imposes in this direction. Right conduct has its own rewards. An abuse of that which is considered to be right conduct suffers a corresponding penalty. Legal developments in this area cannot be dismissed under the heading of technicalities or legal mumbo jumbo. The developments must be recognized and addressed in good faith.

Hypothetical Case - Part VI - Check Your Response

Please reread the summary at the end of the chapter on sexual harassment.

REFERENCES

Authors

Babcock, B.A., Freedman, A. E., Norton, E.H. Ross, S.C. (1975). *Sex discrimination and the law: Causes and remedies.* Boston: Little, Brown and Company.

Cases

Bradwell v. Illinois, 83 U.S. (16 Wall.) 130, 21 L. Ed. 442 (1873).

Civil Rights: Race Discrimination, Americans with Disabilities Act of 1990, Civil Rights Act of 1991

FOCUS

Overview

Prior to the Civil War, a large segment of the population was effectively deprived of those rights generally recognized as belonging to individuals under the natural law. The existence of slavery throughout much of the country obviously negated these rights. Following the Civil War, the Thirteenth, Fourteenth, and Fifteenth Amendments to the United States Constitution were adopted. These amendments read, in part, as follows:

AMENDMENT XIII

Section 1. Slavery prohibited (1865)

Neither slavery nor involuntary servitude, except as a punishment for crime whereof the party shall have been duly convicted, shall exist within the United States, or any place subject to their jurisdiction.

AMENDMENT XIV

Section 1. Citizenship; Due process; Equal Protection (1868)

All persons born or naturalized in the United States and subject to the jurisdiction thereof, are citizens of the United States and of the State wherein they reside. No State shall make or enforce any law which shall abridge the privileges or immunities of citizens of the United States; nor shall any State deprive any person of life, liberty, or property, without due process of law; nor deny to any person within its jurisdiction the equal protection of the laws.

AMENDMENT XV

Section 1. Right of citizens to vote; Race or color not to disqualify (1870)

The right of citizens of the United States to vote shall not be denied or abridged by the United States or by any State on account of race, color, or previous condition of servitude.

Each of the amendments contained a section that gave to Congress the power to enforce the amendment by appropriate legislation. Congress did enact legislation designed to enforce the Civil Rights Amendments. However, it was many years later before these rights were to receive the attention that the framers of the constitutional amendments had intended.

The purpose of this particular part is to highlight the struggle against race discrimination insofar as it impacts a sport enterprise. Problems that the sport enterprise owner and manager can be expected to confront will be stated, and solutions are suggested.

This part also discusses the Americans With Disabilities Act of 1990 and the Civil Rights Act of 1991. Practical applications of these statutes are noted. Case law for the disabled often references earlier race discrimination cases or statutes.

Practical Application - Hypothetical Case

Lawrence Washington, an African-American, is 52 years of age and has recently lost his job as bookkeeper in a local night club. Mr. Washington was a star athlete and is a college graduate. Rumor has it that Washington has been involved in substance abuse and has on one occasion been charged with selling illegal drugs. Looking around for a new position, he decides to put in an application with the Jones family.

Washington is advised that each of the Joneses has recently developed a test designed to indicate the intelligence of an applicant. Upon receipt of this information, Washington files suit in the appropriate federal court alleging that the test does not take into consideration cultural differences and consequently acts in a discriminatory fashion against him because of his race. The suit also alleges that Washington has been free from the use of mind-altering substances for some 60 days as evidenced by an evaluation conducted by one of the two treatment centers that Washington has attended. What issues are raised? What statutes and constitutional provisions are involved? What are the probabilities of success for Washington in this litigation?

CHAPTER 20

RACE DISCRIMINATION: EARLY LEGISLATION

INTRODUCTION

This chapter deals primarily with legislation enacted shortly after the Civil War, namely, 42 U.S.C.A. §§ 1981, 1982, and 1983. Decisional law interpreting these statutory provisions may on occasion discuss subsequent legislation. In pleading a case of discrimination, often more than one source of law is utilized. The Civil Rights Act of 1964 is often used in pleading a case of race discrimination. This Act, as amended, has expanded the post-Civil War legislation. It is interesting to note that although the primary purpose of the various Civil Rights acts that followed the Civil War was to promote equality regardless of race, on occasion the courts have extended that coverage to other groups.

A sport enterprise can be subjected to questions of race discrimination; specifically, these questions might relate to contracts, property, and a denial of constitutional or statutory rights. A 1992 lower court decision awarded damages in excess of $235,000 for racially motivated harassment at a skating rink (*Johnson v. Hugo's Skateway*). The case is discussed in this chapter. This chapter will aid the sport manager in promoting equality of opportunity and in preventing litigation related to race discrimination.

IN THIS CHAPTER YOU WILL LEARN:

The assurances of equal treatment regardless of race as articulated in 42 USCA §§ 1981, 1982, and 1983

The scope of protection set forth in each of the above-numbered sections of Title 42 USCA

The extent of protection accorded—private or public action

The types of relief accorded—equity or common law

KEY WORDS: *42 USCA 1982, 42 USCA 1983, Title VII Civil Rights Act 1964, 42 USCA 1981, punitive damages, compensatory damages, private club, real property, prima facie case, presumption, preponderance of evidence, Burdine/McDonell Douglas Standard.*

This could be you!

The fitness club organized and developed by the Joneses has proved to be an enormous success. Customers are no longer accepted on a contract basis. Instead, the clientele is restricted to membership in the club for which a fee is charged. This private membership carries with it the right to use any of the various sport, recreational, or fitness facilities available at the site.

The fitness club has 25 employees. Maria Jones announces that she is planning on promoting one of her employees to the position of general manager. Toshonda Harper, a young dance instructor of African-American descent, applies for the position but is not hired. Harper contends that she is more qualified than the person who was hired. Harper files suit alleging a violation of 42 U.S.C.A. §1981. Discuss the validity of this cause of action. Suppose that Harper had filed under Title VII of the Civil Rights Act of 1964. Would this have been preferable? Why or why not?

SPECIFIC PROTECTIONS DESIGNED TO PREVENT RACIAL DISCRIMINATION

Equal Rights Under the Law (Contracts—The Making and Enforcing)

Statutory law. Section 1981 of Title 42 U.S.C.A. reads as follows:

(a) Statement of equal rights

All persons within the jurisdiction of the United States shall have the same right in every State and Territory to make and enforce contracts, to sue, be parties, give evidence, and to the full and equal benefit of all laws and proceedings for the security of persons and property as is enjoyed by white citizens, and shall be subject to like punishment, pains, penalties, taxes, licenses, and exactions of every kind, and to no other.

(b) "Make and enforce contracts" defined

For purposes of this section, the term "make and enforce contracts" includes the making, performance, modification, and termination of contracts, and the enjoyment of all benefits, privileges, terms, and conditions of the contractual relationship.

(c) Protection against impairment

The rights protected by this section are protected against impairment by nongovernmental discrimination and impairment under color of State law.

Decisional law. The following case contains an application of 42 U.S.C. §1981. Read the case for applications of purposeful discrimination.

••

WALKER v. COUTURE
804 F.Supp. 1408 (D.Kan. 1992)

MEMORANDUM AND ORDER

THEIS, District Judge.

Plaintiffs brought this action against Don Couture alleging violation of civil rights under 42 U.S.C. § 1981. Plaintiffs also bring a state law claim for libel. This matter was tried to the court on August 17 and 18, 1992. The court heard the testimony of a number of witnesses and had the opportunity to evaluate their demeanor and credibility. The parties have now filed their post-trial briefs. After considering the evidence presented and the arguments of the parties, the court now issues the following findings of fact and conclusions of law.

FINDINGS OF FACT

Plaintiff Clarence Walker is an African-American. Plaintiff Esther Walker is Caucasian. Clarence and Esther Walker are husband and wife. Plaintiffs Travis Walker and Bettina Walker Okoro are the natural children of Clarence and Esther Walker. Travis was fifteen and Bettina was seventeen at the time of the events giving rise to this lawsuit. Plaintiff Marthina Ravon Walker was living with Clarence and Esther Walker at the time of the relevant events. She has since been adopted by Clarence and Esther Walker. Marthina is African-American and was eleven years old at the relevant time.

Plaintiffs reside in El Dorado, Kansas. Plaintiffs belong to a camping resort in Oklahoma known as the Pine Island Resort. Plaintiffs are also members of a nationwide camping organization known as Camp Coast to Coast. Membership in Camp Coast to Coast authorizes them to camp at other Camp Coast to Coast resorts for a nominal fee.

The plaintiffs made reservations to camp at the Crescent Lake camping facility near Abilene in Dickson County, Kansas from May 24, 1989, through May 28, 1989. This was Memorial Day weekend.

The defendant Don Couture was the manager of the Crescent Lake facility at the relevant times. Couture is Caucasian.

The plaintiffs invited two friends of Travis Walker's along on the camping trip. Ray Bennett and Wes Stewart are both Caucasian. They were both fifteen years old at the relevant time.

The plaintiffs reserved an RV campsite prior to their arrival at the campground. *See* Plaintiffs' Exhs. 1-5; Defendant's Exh. D. Plaintiffs arrived on May 24, 1989, stayed five nights, and left the campground on Memorial Day, May 29, 1989.

Since plaintiffs were members of Camp Coast to Coast, the charge for camping at Crescent Lake was one dollar ($1) per night.

Plaintiffs arrived at Crescent Lake on May 24, 1989, in two vehicles, a camper and a van.

Since there were so many in their party, the plaintiffs inquired at the camp entrance about renting a small cabin (called a "hobo") for the three teenage boys.

The guard on duty at the camp entrance agreed to rent a hobo to the Walker party. Clarence Walker paid the fee for the hobo ($25.32) and was given a receipt. Plaintiffs' Exh. 6.

At about this time, the defendant Don Couture arrived at the guard shack at the camp entrance. Couture inquired as to whether there was a problem. When Couture was informed that the plaintiffs had rented a hobo, Couture ordered the guard to refund the Walkers' money. Couture did not explain why, but merely told the guard that the Walkers could not have the hobo.

The plaintiffs camped at the RV campsite during the course of their stay. The three teenage boys slept in the van, while the rest of the family slept in the camper.

On May 30, 1989, the day after the Walker party left Crescent Lake, the defendant wrote the following letter to Clarence Walker:

> As a Coast to Coast camper from 5-24-89 through 5-28-89 at Crescent Lake, you are responsible for leaving a clean campsite at the end of your stay. Your campsite #78 was left in an appalling manner, of which I am sure you are aware (ie. sewer drainage on campsite, broken sewer drop, used condoms thrown on campsite and trees, etc.). Accordingly, a charge of $50.00 is due for the clean-up and repairs needed of your campsite. This charge is due upon receipt of this letter.
>
> Because of numerous complaints throughout your stay at Crescent Lake (ie. children skateboarding in the pool, using ping pong table as a skateboard ramp in the rec hall, unauthorized use of boat on the lake by the children, unsupervised use of the hot tub by the children, mess in pool restroom, children roaming the park in the middle of the night — 2:00 am, watermelon rinds scattered on the campsite, etc.), and the manner in which you left your campsite, I have informed the Security Office to refuse admittance to our park in the future.

Plaintiffs' Exh. 7. Copies of this letter were sent to Camp Coast to Coast and to the plaintiffs' home resort, Pine Island.

Also on May 30, 1989, defendant wrote the following letter to Camp Coast to Coast:

> Please find the enclosed letter to Coast to Coast member Mr. Clarence Walker, #549164. Mr. Walker and his family stayed at our park from 5-24-89 through 5-28-89. We received a number of complaints concerning Mr. Walker and his family throughout their stay. An example of the complaints follow:
>
> 1. Children skateboarding in the pool (before it was filled).

2. Children were using the ping pong table in the rec hall as a skateboard ramp.
3. Unauthorized use of boat on the lake by the children—no oars or life vests were checked out.
4. Unsupervised use of the hot tub by children.
5. Mess made in the pool restroom during the night.
6. Children roaming the park in the middle of the night—approx. 2:00 a.m.
7. Use of foul language by the children.
8. Watermelon rinds scattered on the campsite.
9. Campsite was left in an appalling manner upon departure — sewer drainage on campsite, broken sewer drop, used condoms thrown on campsite and trees.

I spoke with Mr. Walker a number of times throughout his stay concerning these complaints, but the complaints kept coming in. Accordingly, I have suspended them from further use of our park as a Coast to Coast member. I would urge some kind of corrective measure on your part to ensure that this type of disregard for Coast to Coast policies does not take place at other campgrounds.

Plaintiffs' Exh. 8. Copies of this letter were sent to Clarence Walker and to Pine Island Resort.

At trial, Ray Bennett denied that the boys skated in the empty swimming pool. Maintenance worker Larry Irvine testified, however, that he saw the three boys skating in the empty swimming pool. Security guard Mary Reaka observed three young men with skateboards in the pool area and overheard them swearing. Defendant testified that his personnel reported to him that the children were skateboarding in the pool. Defendant did not, however, observe this himself.

Marthina Walker saw the boys skateboarding on the concrete rec hall floor. Ray Bennett admitted that they were skateboarding in the rec room and that Travis Walker used a ping pong table as a skating ramp. Travis Walker admitted to skateboarding inside the rec room and using the table as a ramp. Security guard Robert Rutz testified that he told two or three young men not to skateboard in the rec hall. The defendant was informed by his security people that the boys were using the table as a skateboard ramp.

Ray Bennett and Travis Walker admitted that they had taken the boat out onto the lake without checking it out. Security guard Mary Reaka observed the three boys take the boat without checking it out. The defendant had personal knowledge of this event, since Reaka asked the defendant's assistance in bringing the boys back to shore with the boat.

The children admitted to using the hot tub without adult supervision. Bettina Walker testified that all five children used the hot tub without the supervision of Mr. or Mrs. Walker, most likely on the night of their arrival at Crescent Lake. Marthina, Travis and Ray also admitted to using the hot tub. The defendant was informed of this matter by his security guards.

A security guard reported to the defendant that the children had left a mess in the pool restroom.

The three boys did wander the park in the middle of the night. Travis Walker testified that one night around 2:00 a.m., the three boys went to get a soda and to use the telephone to call their girlfriends back in El Dorado. Travis testified that they were away from the campsite approximately 30 minutes. A security guard informed the defendant of this event.

Ray Bennett and Travis Walker admitted that the three boys used foul language among themselves. Marthina Walker heard the three teenage boys using foul language on one occasion. The defendant received complaints from campers and personally heard the boys using foul language at the lake.

Plaintiffs deny leaving any watermelon rinds on the campsite. Plaintiffs did admit that Wes Stewart (the only one of the campers who did not testify) had a watermelon and that some of them ate watermelon during their stay. Ray Bennett testified that Wes purchased a watermelon during the trip and that everyone in the party ate watermelon. Ray further testified that after eating watermelon, some of the party threw the rinds into the trees behind the campsite. Ray testified, however, that Clarence Walker found the rinds and made the boys pick them up. The defendant testified, however, that he personally saw the rinds which were left at the site. Other disinterested witnesses corroborated that watermelon rinds were left at the campsite.

Ray Bennett and Travis Walker admitted that someone had condoms on the trip. Ray Bennett testified that someone, probably Wes Stewart, had taken some condoms on the trip. Ray denied that he possessed any condoms or that he used any condoms himself. Ray further denied seeing any condoms scattered at the campsite. Travis Walker likewise testified that Wes Stewart brought some condoms. Travis denied throwing the condoms around the campsite. Travis further testified that Wes was "playing" with the condoms, opening the packages and looking at them. Clarence Walker testified that one morning he found condoms on the campsite, hanging in a tree, laying on the ground, and in the barbecue pit. Clarence Walker pointed the last one out to his wife before he picked them up and threw them away. Esther Walker testified that she found some condoms on the campsite, but that she did not know who put them there.

Plaintiffs generally deny leaving any mess behind. Plaintiffs testified that they cleaned up the site before they left and that Clarence Walker made Travis get out of the vehicle and pick up a can as they were leaving the campsite. Bettina testified that the campsite was clean when they left it. However, the defendant personally saw the condition of the campsite after the plaintiffs left. Several disinterested witnesses also testified that the campsite was left in poor condition.

Defendant never spoke to Esther Walker about the behavior of the children. Defendant spoke to Clarence Walker once, on Saturday morning, May 27, 1989. Clarence Walker had walked over to speak to the defendant. Defendant then told Clarence Walker that there had been complaints about profanity and to advise the children to watch their language. Clarence Walker stated that he would talk to the children. This was the only conversation the defendant had with Clarence Walker regarding complaints. The other complaints were never brought to the Walkers' attention. The defendant admitted that he only spoke with Clarence Walker once.

Marylin McCoy was camping at the campsite next to the Walkers over Memorial Day weekend. She testified that every morning she found several condoms strewn about near the campsite. She testified that she carefully picked them up and disposed of them, except for one morning when she put the condoms on the Walkers' campsite.

McCoy was present at the campsite when the Walkers left. She testified that she saw condoms left on the bushes, watermelon rinds at the back of the campsite, and raw sewage near the sewer pipe at the Walkers' campsite. McCoy testified that the sewer drainage may have been an accident, if someone flushed the camper toilet after the sewer line was disconnected. McCoy's husband complained to the defendant about the mess.

Robert McCall was camping at the campsite next to the McCoys over the Memorial Day weekend. McCall testified that he saw condoms out behind the Walker's [sic] camper in the hedgerow. McCall further testified that he say (sic) Marylin McCoy pick up one condom and place it on the Walker's [sic] grill.

Larry Irvine was a maintenance worker at Crescent Lake in 1989. He was called to clean up the Walker's [sic] campsite after they had left it. He testified that he found debris, including condoms, on the campsite and that the sewer drain pipe was plugged. Irvine testified that the sewer pipe was in good shape the morning the Walkers arrived at the campground. After the Walkers left, Irvine had to dig up the sewer line. The cap from the end of the pipe had been shoved inside the sewer pipe, plugging the sewer line and holding back the raw sewage.

Security guard Mary Reaka testified that she accompanied Irvine to the Walkers' campsite. Reaka testified that the campsite was a mess, with trash, toilet paper, food, and used condoms on the site.

Reaka testified that she had received several complaints about the family from other members camping nearby.

The defendant received complaints about the plaintiffs from local members, Camp Coast to Coast members, and the staff. After defendant spoke with Clarence Walker about the profanity, the complaints about profanity ceased.

After the Walkers checked out on Monday, May 29, defendant was called to the campsite by security. The defendant personally observed raw sewage, watermelon rinds and condoms on the site. The defendant observed that the sewage dump pipe was split and appeared to have been run over. The defendant assisted Larry Irvine with digging up and replacing the sewer pipe.

At trial, the Walker children and Ray Bennett admitted virtually all of the matters about which defendant complained in his May 30, 1989, letter to Camp Coast to Coast.

The court finds that it is more likely true than not true that the three teenage boys were responsible for throwing the condoms around the campsite.

The court further finds as a fact that the Walkers left trash behind at the campsite. Additionally, the Walkers most likely hooked up the camper's sewer line without removing the cap from the sewer drain pipe, thereby accidentally plugging the sewer drain and allowing sewage to drain on the campsite.

Camp Coast to Coast publishes a directory for its members which lists all affiliated campgrounds and various rules and regulations. Defendant's Exh. A. The plaintiffs received a copy of the directory in 1989. The Coast to Coast directory specifies that on major holiday weekends, accommodations at Coast to Coast resorts are usually reserved for home resort members. Memorial Day weekend is one of the listed holiday weekends. Defendant's Exh. A, p. 5, ¶ 4.

As a part of the courtesy code for Coast to Coast members, the directory advises campers to follow all host resort rules, even if they differ from the rules of the home resort. Defendant's Exh. A, p. 6, ¶ 3.

The rules of the Crescent Lake resort, as posted in the guard shack at the entrance to the facility, provide in relevant part: "NO RENTAL UNITS WILL BE RENTED TO GUESTS OR CCC [Camp Coast to Coast members] ON HOLIDAY WEEKENDS IN ORDER TO KEEP THEM FOR OUR LOCAL MEMBERS *[sic]* USAGE." Defendant's Exh. B. These rules were posted at the guard shack at the time of the plaintiffs' arrival at Crescent Lake.

Security guard Robert Rutz testified that Crescent Lake's rules and regulations, including the limitation on rental units for local members only, were posted on the wall of the security guard shack, where campers checked in. Security guard Mary Reaka also testified that the rules and regulations were posted at the guard shack.

Defendant testified that Crescent Lake's rules and regulations restricted the availability of rental units to local members on Memorial Day, Fourth of July and Labor Day holidays. The written rules and regulations, Defendant's Exh. B, were posted at the guard shack since 1985. Defendant testified that the rental units were restricted on those holidays because those were the busiest times of year.

From April 1988, when he became manager of Crescent Lake, the defendant never allowed the rental units (which previously included trailers as well as cabins) to be rented by guests of local members or by non-local Camp Coast to Coast members on the three major holidays (Memorial Day, Fourth of July, and Labor Day).

The plaintiffs telephoned Crescent Lake to reserve the campsite for Memorial Day weekend. Defendant personally took the call from Clarence Walker. Walker did not discuss renting a hobo cabin at that time.

Defendant observed the plaintiffs arrive at the campground. Defendant observed that Mr. Walker was in the guard shack for a long time. The defendant thought the check-in process was taking too long, so he went down to the guard shack to check it out.

When defendant arrived at the guard shack, the security guard was writing out a receipt for rental of one of the hobo cabins. The defendant informed the guard that the Walkers could not rent a cabin. Defendant asserts that he explained that the reason was because the Walkers were not local members. The plaintiffs deny that any reason was ever given to them.

Defendant testified that he was not angry at the plaintiffs, but he was angry at the security guard for renting the hobo cabin to nonmembers in violation of the rules.

Esther Walker testified that she got angry when the defendant came over and asked what the problem was when the plaintiffs were paying for their campsite and the hobo unit. Clarence Walker testified that he immediately thought that the defendant was a racist since no problem existed when the defendant came up to the guard shack to inquire about the nature of the problem.

Defendant failed to inform plaintiffs of the reason for his refusal to rent them a hobo unit. However, after considering the defendant's testimony and his credibility, the court finds that defendant was merely enforcing the rules of the resort. There was no objective evidence offered to show that the defendant acted out of racial animus. The undisputed testimony was that rental units were never rented to Camp Coast to Coast members on holiday weekends, even if there was no demand for the rental units on the part of the local members.

CONCLUSIONS OF LAW

Plaintiffs bring a claim for violation of their civil rights, pursuant to 42 U.S.C. §1981. Jurisdiction is conferred by 28 U.S.C. §§ 1343 and 1331. The court has personal jurisdiction of the parties. Venue is proper in this district. 28 U.S.C. § 1391(b). The plaintiffs' state law claim for libel is within this court's pendent jurisdiction.

. . . . .

For their federal claim, plaintiffs claim that the defendant interfered with their right to make a contract to rent the hobo cabin because of the racial makeup of the family, in violation of 42 U.S.C. § 1981.

Section 1981 prohibits, when based on race, the refusal to enter into a contract with someone, as well as an offer to make a contract only on discriminatory terms. *Patterson v. McLean Credit Union*, 491 U.S. 164, 176, 109 S.Ct. 2363, 2372, 105 L.Ed. 2d 132 (1989). To prevail under section 1981, a plaintiff must prove purposeful discrimination. *Id.* at 185, 109 S.Ct. at 2377. The *Burdine/McDonnell Douglas* scheme of proof developed in the Title VII context applies to claims of racial discrimination under section 1981. *Id.* at 185-87, 109 S.Ct. at 2377-78. The defendant concedes that this scheme of proof applies to the present case. *See* Doc. 45, Defendant's Proposed Findings of Fact and Conclusions of Law.

The plaintiff bears the initial burden of proving, by a preponderance of the evidence, a prima facie case of discrimination. Once the plaintiff establishes a prima facie case, an inference of discrimination arises. To rebut the inference, the defendant must present evidence that the plaintiff was rejected for a legitimate nondiscriminatory reason. Once the presumption of discrimination is rebutted, the plaintiff then has the opportunity to demonstrate that the defendant's proffered reasons for its decision were not its true reasons. The plaintiff retains the ultimate burden of persuasion on the issue of intentional discrimination. *Patterson*, at 187, 109 S. Ct. at 2378.

The plaintiffs established a prima facie case of discrimination. An inference of discrimination arises from the defendant's conduct in refusing to rent the plaintiffs the hobo cabin after the defendant's security guard had previously accepted the plaintiffs' money. It was natural and understandable for the plaintiffs to assume that they were being discriminated against on the basis of race in that situation.

The defendant came forth with evidence sufficient to rebut any inference that his actions were racially motivated. The defendant's testimony, which the court found credible, indicated that the plaintiffs were denied the use of the hobo cabin because Crescent Lake's rules required that the rental facilities be reserved for local members on that holiday weekend. The resort rules were posted at the entrance to the resort. Further, the 1989 Camp Coast to Coast directory contains a warning that campgrounds may not be available to Coast to Coast members during specified holiday weekends. Plaintiffs were aware of this rule. Couture was merely enforcing the rules.

Plaintiffs failed to demonstrate that defendant's proffered reason was not his true reason, i.e., that the proffered reason was pretextual. Couture uniformly enforced the rules restricting rental units to local members on holiday weekends. Plaintiffs presented no proof to the contrary, only their subjective belief that defendant's action was racially motivated. Plaintiffs failed in their ultimate burden of persuasion on the issue of intentional racial discrimination. Plaintiffs have failed to prove that the defendant's conduct was racially motivated.

IT IS BY THE COURT THEREFORE ORDERED that judgment be entered in favor of the defendant on all claims. Costs shall be assessed against plaintiffs.

Questions and Comments

1. What rule of law does this case articulate with respect to a case bottomed upon 42 U.S.C.A. §1981?
2. What is the Burdine/McDonnell Douglas standard referred to in the Court's opinion?
3. How could a sport manager avoid a claim of race discrimination in a similar situation?

Deprivation of Constitutional Rights

Statutory law. Section 42 U.S.C.A.§ 1983 reads as follows:

Every person who, under color of any statute, ordinance, regulation, custom, or usage, of any State or Territory or the District of Columbia, subjects, or causes to be subjected, any citizen of the United States or other person within the jurisdiction thereof to the deprivation of any rights, privileges, or immunities secured by the Constitution and laws, shall be liable to the party injured in an action at law, suit in equity, or other proper proceeding for redress. For the purposes of this section, any Act of Congress applicable exclusively to the District of Columbia shall be considered to be a statute of the District of Columbia.

Decisional law. This case contains an application of Title VII of the Civil Rights Act of 1964 and 42 U.S.C. §1981. In reading the case, also see if 42 U.S.C. 1983 was applied in this situation.

••

BAPTISTE v. CAVENDISH CLUB, INC.
670 F.Supp. 108 (S.D.N.Y. 1987)

MEMORANDUM OPINION AND ORDER
KRAM, District Judge.

Plaintiff Nathaniel Baptiste filed a complaint alleging that his former employer, The Cavendish Club, Inc. ("the Club"), violated Title VII of the Civil Rights Act of 1964, 42 U.S.C. § 2000e *et seq.,* 29 U.S.C. §§ 215(a)(3) and 216, 42 U.S.C. § 1981, and committed various torts. The claims under Title 29 have apparently been dropped.

The defendants move to dismiss the complaint on various grounds. They allege that the summons and complaint were not served upon them within the 120 day period required by Fed. R. Civ. P. 4(j) and lack of subject matter jurisdiction. On January 30, 1987, this Court rejected plaintiff's explanation for failure to serve within 120 days, but granted him an additional ten days to show good cause for failure to serve.

RULE 4(j) DISMISSAL

. . . . [Discussion of summons complaint omitted.]

SUBJECT MATTER JURISDICTION

1. *Title VII*

Title VII of the Civil Rights Act of 1964 prohibits employers from discriminating against employees on the basis of race. 42 U.S.C. § 2000e-2(a). Bona fide private membership clubs which are also exempt from tax under 26 U.S.C. § 501(c) are exempt from Title VII. Defendants claim that the Club is tax exempt and a private membership club, and thus exempt from Title VII, and therefore, this Court does not have subject matter jurisdiction over the case because it does not arise under federal law.

The Court finds that the Club is exempt from tax under 26 U.S.C. § 501(c). According to the affidavit of Jeffrey Rothstein, who has been the Club's accountant since 1982, the Club is exempt from federal tax under 26 U.S.C. §501(c)(7). He further states that during his time as accountant, the Internal Revenue Service has conducted an audit of the Club and found that its exemption under section 501(c)(7) is proper. Plaintiff offers no evidence in opposition to this, and apparently concedes that the Club is exempt from tax. See Affirmation in Opposition of Paulette Owens, affirmed May 22, 1984, at ¶ 4.

Tax exempt status alone is not sufficient to bring an organization within the Title VII exception. A court must next determine whether the club is a bona fide private membership club. In *Quijano v. University Federal Credit Union*, 617 F.2d 129, 131 (5th Cir. 1980), the court delineated four factors to consider in determining whether an employer is a private club under Title

VII. The club must be 1) an association of persons for social or recreational purposes; 2) legitimate; 3) private; and 4) require some meaningful conditions of limited membership.

Turning to the first factor, Thomas Smith, the Club's director of activities, filed an affidavit indicating the the Club is dedicated to the promotion of bridge and other games of skill. The Club, as an association of people joined together for common recreation, thus meets the first factor. The Club is also organized for a legitimate reason—promotion of the game of bridge. Smith also states that Club facilities are open only to members and their guests, thus satisfying the third factor. Finally, Smith's affidavit indicates that the Club requires meaningful conditions of limited membership. Prospective members must be sponsored by a current member and seconded by another member. They are subject to evaluation of their ethical reputation at the bridge table, their skill and knowledge of the game, their standards of dress and deportment, and their ability to meet their financial commitment to the Club. Members are admitted only if they are approved by the Board of Directors. According to the Club's by-laws, which defendants have also submitted, five members can block a candidate's application. Based on these factors, the Court finds that the Club is a bona fide membership club, and thus exempt from Title VII.

2. *Section 1981*

The plaintiff also claims he brought this action under 42 U.S.C. §§ 1981, 1983 and 1985. Although the plaintiff cites these statutes as providing jurisdiction, he does not cite them as grounds for relief. Nevertheless, if plaintiff could state a claim under these statutes, he should be permitted to amend his complaint.

Sections 1983 and 1985 do not create independent rights, but rather create causes of action for violation of federal rights under color of state law. Since plaintiff makes no showing in his complaint that the alleged violation was under color of state law, plaintiff's request as to Sections 1983 and 1985 is denied.

Defendant argues that plaintiff cannot recover because the private club exception of Title VII applies to Section 1981. The Supreme Court has ruled that "Congress clearly has retained § 1981 as a remedy against private employment discrimination separate from and independent of Title VII." *Johnson v. Railway Express Agency*, 421 U.S. 454, 466, 95 S.Ct. 1716, 1723, 44 L.Ed.2d 295 (1975). The Court in *Johnson*, in enumerating the ways in which Title VII and Section 1981 differed, stated that "[t]he latter is made inapplicable to certain employers. 42 U.S.C. § 2000e(b)...." *Id.* at 460, 95 S.Ct. at 1720. (Section 2000e(b) is the provision of Title VII which exempts private employers.) There are other substantive differences between the two statutes as well. Under Section 1981, a person can recover punitive damages and can recover backpay for more than two years. *Id.* at 460, 95 S.Ct. at 1720. The procedural provisions of Title VII, including the statute of limitations and the exhaustion requirement, do not apply to Section 1981. Thus, the scope of protection of Title VII and Section 1981, differ both in terms of relief and the ability to bring the claim.

While at least two courts have held that Title VII's exemption for private clubs does apply to section 1981, *see Hudson v. Charlotte Country Club, Inc.*, 535 F. Supp. 313, 317 (W.D. N.C. 1982); *Kemerer v. Davis*, 520 F.Supp. 256 (E.D. Mich. 1981), these rulings contradict the Supreme Court's statement in *Johnson*. Moreover, the language of Section 1981 does not support exempting private clubs from its coverage, and the argument expressed in these cases that Congress implicitly amended section 1981 when it passed Title VII is speculative and unpersuasive.

In conclusion, plaintiff may proceed with this action under 42 U.S.C. § 1981. To do so, however, plaintiff must amend his complaint. He must do this within ten days of this opinion.

SO ORDERED.

Questions and Comments

1. What principle of law does this case articulate with respect to 42 U.S.C.A. §1981?
2. How does a cause of action under Title VII of the Civil Rights Act of 1964 differ from a cause of action based upon 42 U.S.C.A. §1981?
3. What are the tests for a "private club" as stated in this opinion?
4. Under 1983 action, a person may not be deprived of any rights, privileges, or immunities secured by the Constitution and laws. Liability may result in action at law or in equity or other proper proceedings for redress.
5. 1983 action cannot be brought against the state. However, state officials are not immune. State officials cannot hide behind state office. Therefore, they cannot claim sovereign immunity. They might be able to claim qualified immunity.
6. A sport manager of a public or private sport business should be careful not to deprive any person of his or her constitutional rights.

Property Rights of Citizens

Statutory law. Section 1982 of Title 42 U.S.C.A. reads as follows:

> All citizens of the United States shall have the same right, in every State and Territory, as is enjoyed by white citizens thereof to inherit, purchase, lease, sell, hold, and convey real and personal property.

Decisional law. Read the following case for applications of Section 1982 to recreation facilities. Note in this case the court refers to other cases where recreational club memberships are in a playground and park, and in a swimming pool. There are two major points that are litigated, Section 1981 and 1982.

In the following case, the appellate court reversed the district court and ruled in favor of the Wrights. The case has been edited for major points.

•••

WRIGHT v. SALISBURY CLUB, LTD.
632 F. 2d 309 (4th Cir. 1980)

WINTER, Circuit Judge:

The plaintiffs, Thomas Wright and Barbara Wright,[1] sued the Salisbury Club[2] under 42 U.S.C. §§ 1981 and 1982 for denying them club membership because they are black. Although it found that the Wrights had been denied club membership because they were black, the district court denied them relief under § 1981, because it concluded that the Salisbury Club was a truly private club, and under § 1982, because it concluded that membership in the club was not "property" for the purposes of that statute. On both issues, we conclude to the contrary and we therefore reverse.

I.

The Salisbury Club, located near Richmond, Virginia, was established in 1963 by the developer of the adjacent Salisbury subdivision.[3] It is a privately-owned club which provides tennis, swimming, golf, and dining facilities for the use of its members. At first, residents of the Salisbury subdivision were formally given preference for membership in the club. In recent years the preference has been abolished to permit the club to attract new members without limitation. Currently, somewhat over half the members reside in the Salisbury subdivision, and until 1977, no resident of the Salisbury subdivision had been denied membership.

In May, 1977, the plaintiffs moved into a house that they had purchased in the Salisbury subdivision. Soon after moving, the plaintiffs twice applied for membership in the Salisbury Club. Their applications were sponsored by two club members, as required by club bylaws. On both occasions, the plaintiffs' applications were rejected. It is conceded that the plaintiffs were denied membership because they are black.

The plaintiffs then brought suit in district court, seeking injunctive relief and damages for denial of civil rights guaranteed by 42 U.S.C. §§ 1981 and 1982. Subsequently, the district court granted summary judgment for the defendants. After examining the club's formation, membership policies, and membership recruitment activities, the district court found that the Salisbury Club was a "truly private" club.[4] The district court ruled that § 1981 does not apply to truly private clubs and therefore rejected the plaintiffs' § 1981 claim.

In addition, the district court rejected the plaintiffs' § 1982 argument. It examined the connection between the subdivision and the club, and discovered

1. The plaintiffs are husband and wife.

2. The directors of the Salisbury Club were also included as parties defendant. Defendants collectively are referred to herein as the "club" or the "Salisbury Club."

3. The developer of the subdivision is the Salisbury Corporation. The two principal owners of the developer are J. Kenneth Timmons and C. Porter Vaughan.

4. The phrase "truly private" is derived from the Supreme Court's opinion in *Tillman v. Wheaton-Haven Recreation Ass'n*, 410 U.S. 431, 438 39, [sic] 93 S.Ct. 1090, 1094, 35 L.Ed.2d 403 (1973).

no formal link between club membership and ownership of a home in the sub-division.   Consequently, it concluded that membership in the club did not amount to "property" within the ambit of § 1982.

The critical facts of this case are undisputed, and we do not disagree with the factual findings made by the district court. We do disagree, however, with the court's application of §§ 1981 and 1982 to those facts. In our view, the characteristics of the Salisbury Club demonstrate that it is not a truly private club and the close connection between club membership and ownership of subdivision property establishes that club membership is "property" within the meaning of § 1982. Because we reverse the district court's §§1981 and 1982 rulings, we do not consider its decision that §§ 1981 and 1982 are sub-ject to a "private club" defense. [Footnote omitted.] . . . .

II.

. . . . . We, like the Supreme Court, find it unnecessary to determine whether § 1981 is subject to a "private club" defense, because in this case, we are per-suaded that, for three reasons, the Salisbury Club is not a truly private club.

First, the Salisbury Club does not follow a selective membership policy. Only three white persons have ever been denied membership in the Salisbury Club, and they all resided outside the Salisbury subdivision. Conversely and most critically for this case, no white resident of the Salisbury subdivision has been denied club membership throughout the entire history of the Salisbury Club. The only residents of the subdivision who have been denied member-ship are the plaintiffs and another black family who applied for membership at about the same time. They were admittedly refused membership because of their race. Thus, it is apparent that the club follows "no plan or purpose of exclusiveness." Rather, membership "is open to every white person within the geographic area, there being no selective element other than race." . . . . [Citation omitted.]

The district court was persuaded of the club's supposed selectivity by the formal requirements for membership. [Footnote omitted.] All applicants must have two members sponsor their applications. Then, the applicant must be approved by the membership committee. Finally, seventy-five percent of the board of directors must vote to admit the applicant to membership.

These formal membership requirements, however, do not prove that the Salisbury Club is a truly private club because in practice the club admits all white subdivision residents and practically all white applicants from outside the subdivision. The formalities have little meaning when in fact the club does not follow a selective membership policy. . . . .

Second, the Salisbury Club has actively solicited members through public advertising. The club has made extensive efforts to draw residents of the Salisbury subdivision into its membership. In November, 1975, the club insert-ed an announcement in the Salisbury *Village Crier*, a newsletter distributed by the subdivision developer to Salisbury residents. The ad was entitled "Notice to All Salisbury Residents". It invited the readers to "take advantage of a great opportunity" in the form of reduced initiation fees during a membership drive, and it concluded by asking, "Why not join us at the Salisbury Club?" . . . .

. . . . Particularly relevant to this case, the club represents itself as open to all residents of the Salisbury subdivision and has diligently tried to lure all subdivision residents onto its membership rolls. This extensive advertising belies the club's attempt to characterize itself as a truly private club. [Citation omitted.]

Third, from its inception, the club has served the commercial interests of the developer of the Salisbury subdivision. . . . . In order to insure that the club aided its efforts to promote the subdivision, the developer provided that ample memberships would be reserved for Salisbury residents by requiring in the deed that no more than 200 family memberships would be granted to families residing outside the subdivision. [Footnote omitted.] . . . .

This intimate, longstanding, and continuing relationship between the subdivision developer and the Salisbury Club completely undercuts the club's contention that it is truly private. . . . .

In sum, the club has no selective membership policy; it advertised extensively within the subdivision for new members and permits the subdivision developer to advertise the club's existence throughout the Richmond area; and it has since its inception been an important part of the subdivision developer's marketing efforts. Singly, any one of these characteristics belies the club's claim that it is a genuinely private organization. In combination, they demolish the club's "truly private" defense. As a result, the club has no response to the plaintiffs' claim that it violated § 1981 when it denied the plaintiffs membership because they are black.

III.

Next we consider plaintiffs' claim under § 1982. That statute insures that all citizens will have the same right "as is enjoyed by white citizens" to purchase and hold "real and personal property." *See generally Jones v. Alfred H. Mayer Co.*, 392 U.S. 409, 88 S.Ct. 2186, 20 L.Ed.2d 1189 (1968). We repeat that it is conceded that the club refused to sell the plaintiffs a club membership because they are black, so that the only issue is whether a club membership is "property." The district court ruled that club membership does not amount to "property." [Footnote omitted.] We disagree and conclude that membership in the Salisbury Club is part of the bundle of rights bought by a purchaser of a home in the Salisbury subdivision. [Footnote omitted.]

The Supreme Court has decided two cases which present facts similar to the facts of this case. *Tillman v. Wheaton-Haven Recreation Ass'n; Sullivan v. Little Hunting Park, Inc.* In both cases, the Supreme Court decided that racial discrimination in club membership policies violated § 1982 because club membership was closely associated with property ownership in a particular geographic area. . . . .

In *Sullivan*, Little Hunting Park operated a playground and a park for residents of a portion of Fairfax County, Virginia. The park bylaws provided that a member who rented his home could assign his membership to a tenant, subject to the approval of the board of directors. An area homeowner rented his home to a black tenant and attempted to assign the tenant his membership. The park board refused to approve the assignment.

The Supreme Court found that the right to assign a tenant park membership fell within the terms of § 1982. The Court identified the property interest conveyed as a leasehold of realty coupled with a membership share in a park organized for the benefit of owners and lessees of rental property in a designated residential area. 396 U.S. at 236, 90 S.Ct. at 404. . . . .

Four years later in *Tillman*, the Court confronted a club closely analogous to the Salisbury Club. The Wheaton-Haven Recreation Association operated a privately-owned community swimming pool. The association's bylaws provided that membership was open to residents within a three-quarter mile radius of the pool and to others who were recommended by a member. . . . .

The association denied membership to a black resident of the designated area, and he brought suit under § 1982. . . . .

The Court observed that the preference given area residents may have affected the price of homes and that by denying the plaintiff membership the association had diluted the plaintiff's [property] right to purchase a home in the area. 410 U.S. at 437, 93 S.Ct. at 1094. . . . .

.   .   .   .   .

Consequently, we reverse the decision of the district court. Through its membership practices and advertising, the Salisbury Club has inserted club membership into the bundle of rights a purchaser receives when he buys a home in the Salisbury subdivision. When the club refused the plaintiffs membership, it deprived them of part of the value of their home, solely because they are black. Thereby, the club interfered with the plaintiffs' right to purchase and hold "property." This action was in violation of § 1982.

IV.

The decision of the district court is reversed, and the case is remanded to the district court for a determination of appropriate relief.

REVERSED AND REMANDED.

Questions and Comments

1. How does this court determine the existence of a truly private club? What is the significance of such a characterization?
2. How does this Court treat the 1981 action insofar as a private club is concerned?
3. What was the relationship of the Salisbury Club membership to the plaintiffs' right to hold property?

Compensatory and Punitive Damages - Federal and State Statutes

In addition to national statutes, there may also be a state statute involved in a civil rights case. In the case of *Johnson v. Hugo's Skateway* (1992), compensatory damages were awarded to compensate a person for racial harassment or intimidation. Punitive damages were awarded as punishment for violating the due process rights of the Fifth Amendment of the United States Constitution. The initial awards by the lower court in this case totaled in excess of $215,000.

A jury awarded James H. Johnson, a black male, $25,000 compensatory damages and $175,000 punitive damages for racially motivated harassment and intimidation by Hugo's Skateway, a roller skating rink in Warrenton, Virginia, in violation of § 8.01-42.1 of the Virginia Code. In addition, the district court awarded $15,654 for attorney fees and expenses, although Johnson had filed requests for almost $138,000. . . . . (p. 1408)

In this case, federal and state civil rights claims were made after Johnson was ejected from the skating rink and arrested.

The sport manager is reminded that civil rights considerations are important from humanitarian and legal standpoints. Sport managers should train employees on how to handle sensitive situations between patrons and between employees and patrons. Knowledge of civil rights legislation will be an asset.

SUMMARY

Figure 4 summarizes early civil rights legislation.

42 USCA §	Exhaustion of adm'n remedies	Remedies: equitable & common law	Private/ Public	Intent	Scope
1981	Not required	Both	Both	Required	All persons
1982	Not required	Both	Both	Left open	All persons
1983	No strict requirement	Both	Both	No specific requirement	All persons

FIGURE 4
EARLY CIVIL RIGHTS LEGISLATION

This could be you - check your response

Ms Harper was not hired as a manager. Harper filed suit alleging violations of 42 USCA §1981. This is a valid cause of action as the Civil Rights Restoration Act of 1991 amended 42 U.S.C. §1981 to cover all employment practices including opportunities, conditions, and benefits. (This will be explained further in chapter 22.) Civil rights in this section are protected against nongovernmental discrimination. Harper would need to bring evidence of discrimination to win the suit. Under the Burdine/McDonnell Douglas standard, the discrimination against Harper would need to be purposeful discrimination.

Title VII of the Civil Rights Act of 1964 prohibits discrimination against employees on the basis of race or sex. Bona fide private membership clubs are exempt. The Joneses' fitness club might be a private club if it were for members only; therefore, a claim of discrimination would be exempt from the Title VII. Again, if the club meets the requirements of private membership,

Title VII would not apply. Remember, a club does not qualify as a private club if it is a subterfuge to limit membership in order to keep out minorities. Harper might file under Title VII but might not win.

REFERENCES *

Cases

Baptiste v. Cavendish Club, Inc., 670 F.Supp. 108 (S.D. N.Y. 1987).
Johnson v. Hugo's Skateway, 974 F.2d 1408 (4th Cir. 1992).
Sisk v. Texas Parks and Wildlife Dep't., 644 F.2d 1056 (5th Cir. 1981).
Sullivan v. Little Hunting Park, 396 U.S. 229, 24 L.Ed.2d 386, 90 S.Ct. 400 (1969).
Walker v. Couture, 804 F.Supp. 1408 (D. Kan. 1992).
Wright v. Salisbury Club, Ltd., 632 F.2d 309 (4th Cir. 1980).

Model Codes, Restatements and Standards

42 U.S.C.A., §§ 1981, 1982, 1983.
Civil Rights Act 1964, 42 U.S.C.A. §§2000e et seq.,
29 U.S.C. §§215(a)(3) and 216.

*For further references, see Appendix.

CHAPTER 21

RACE DISCRIMINATION: PUBLIC ACCOMMODATIONS, PUBLIC FACILITIES, AND TITLE VII

INTRODUCTION

Historically, race has been a subject for blatant discrimination. Certain aspects of race discrimination have been treated in the preceding chapter. This chapter will discuss the efforts that have been made to correct discrimination. Topics include public accommodations, public facilities, and employment generally. The picture is not a nice one. Progress has been made, and efforts made to correct have been substantial, although further efforts are needed.

IN THIS CHAPTER YOU WILL LEARN:

Relevant questions to determine compliance with the Public Accommodation (Title II) portion of the Civil Rights Act of 1964

Relevant questions to determine compliance with the Public Facilities (Title III) portion of the Civil Rights Act of 1964

Relevant questions to determine compliance with the Unlawful Employment Practices (Title VII) portion of the Civil Rights Act of 1964

The remedies currently available for one who feels aggrieved by a violation of Sections II, III, or VII of the Civil Rights Act of 1964

KEY WORDS: *private club, public accommodation, commerce, legislative history*

This could be you!

Sam Knight is employed as an instructor for young students who wish to be

taught the finer points of tennis. Mr. Knight has a master's degree from the state university and has demonstrated the ability to teach public school students, and more specifically, the ability to teach skills in tennis. Mr. Knight, a Caucasian, becomes engaged to marry an African-American student who is currently majoring in drama at the university. Certain of the parents voice an objection to permitting their children to take instruction in tennis from Knight because of his impending marriage to someone of a different race. The Joneses are pleased with the job performance of Knight at the recreation center and have no personal objection to Knight's choice for a future spouse. Cancellations of membership in the recreation center begin to mount considerably and classes that formerly "made up" without any trouble can no longer be offered because of declining enrollment. Faced with the impending economic boycott, the Joneses reluctantly advise Knight that his services will no longer be needed at the recreation center. Does Knight have a remedy? Can you give any advice to the Joneses? Be specific.

THE CIVIL RIGHTS ACT OF 1964: SELECTIVE PORTIONS

Public Accommodations

Title II of the Civil Rights Act of 1964 purports to deal with discrimination in places of public accommodation. The Act directs attention to recreation and places of entertainment generally. The following code provision explains equal access.

The Code Provisions

Equal Access

(a) All persons shall be entitled to the full and equal enjoyment of the goods, services, facilities, privileges, advantages, and accommodations of any place of public accommodation, as defined in this section, without discrimination or segregation on the ground of race, color, religion, or national origin.

Establishments affecting interstate commerce or supported in their activities by State action as places of public accommodation; lodgings; facilities principally engaged in selling food for consumption on the premises; gasoline stations; places of exhibition or entertainment; other covered establishments

(b) Each of the following establishments which serves the public is a place of public accommodation within the meaning of this subchapter if its operations affect commerce, or if discrimination or segregation by it is supported by State action:

(1) any inn, hotel, motel, or other establishment which provides lodging to transient guests, other than an establishment located within a building which contains not more than five rooms for rent or hire and which is actually occupied by the proprietor of such establishment as his residence;

(2) any restaurant, cafeteria, lunchroom, lunch counter, soda fountain, or other facility principally engaged in selling food for consumption on the premises, including, but not limited to, any such facility located on the premises of any retail establishment; or any gasoline station;

(3) any motion picture house, theater, concert hall, sports arena, stadium or other place of exhibition or entertainment; and

(4) any establishment (A)(i) which is physically located within the premises of any establishment otherwise covered by this subsection, or (ii) within the premises of which is physically located any such covered establishment, and (B) which holds itself out as serving patrons of such covered establishment.

Operations affecting commerce; criteria; "commerce" defined

(c) The operations of an establishment affect commerce within the meaning of this subchapter if (1) it is one of the establishments described in paragraph (1) of subsection (b) of this section; (2) in the case of an establishment described in paragraph (2) of subsection (b) of this section, it serves or offers to serve interstate travelers or a substantial portion of the food which it serves, or gasoline or other products which it sells, has moved in commerce; (3) in the case of an establishment described in paragraph (3) of subsection (b) of this section, it customarily presents films, performances, athletic teams, exhibitions, or other sources of entertainment which move in commerce; and (4) in the case of an establishment described in paragraph (4) of subsection (b) of this section, it is physically located within the premises of, or there is physically located within its premises, an establishment the operations of which affect commerce within the meaning of this subsection. For purposes of this section, "commerce" means travel, trade, traffic, commerce, transportation, or communication among the several States, or between the District of Columbia and any State, or between any foreign country or any territory or possession and any State or the District of Columbia, or between points in the same State but through any other State or the District of Columbia or a foreign country.

Support by State actions

(d) Discrimination or segregation by an establishment is supported by State action within the meaning of this subchapter if such discrimination or segregation (1) is carried on under color of any law, statute, ordinance, or regulation; or (2) is carried on under color of any custom or usage required or enforced by officials of the State or political subdivision thereof; or (3) is required by action of the State or political subdivision thereof.

Private establishments

(e) The provisions of this subchapter shall not apply to a private club or other establishment not in fact open to the public, except to the extent that the facilities of such establishment are made available to the customers or patrons of an establishment within the scope of subsection (b) of this section. (42 U.S.C.A. § 2000a)

Constitutionality. A similar statute was declared unconstitutional in a United States Supreme Court decision known as *the Civil Rights Cases* (1883). This case struck down the federal Civil Rights Act of March 1, 1875, as encroaching on the residual powers of the state (*Civil Rights Cases*, 1883). Title II of the Civil Rights Act of 1964 was bottomed upon the Commerce Clause of the United States Constitution and has uniformly been upheld (*Heart of Atlanta Motel, Inc. v. U. S.*, 1964).

Purpose. The purpose of the public accommodation provision of the 1964 Civil Rights Act has been variously described. A federal court in Louisiana described the purpose as "securing for all citizens the full enjoyment of facilities described in this section which are open to the general public" (*Miller v. Amusement Enterprises, Inc.*, 1968, p. 349). Another Louisiana decision described the purpose as being "to eliminate unfairness, humiliation, and insult of racial discrimination in facilities which purport to serve the general public (*Rousseve v. Shape Spa for Health and Beauty, Inc.*, 1975, p. 67). A federal court in South Carolina referenced the burden on interstate commerce (*Newman v. Piggie Park Enterprises, Inc.*, 1967).

Public accommodations: Defined and explained. The case that follows was an action to enjoin owners of a recreational area from denying admission to African-Americans solely on racial grounds. The recreational area had a snack bar and facilities for swimming, boating, sunbathing, miniature golf, and dancing. The United States Supreme Court held that this was not a private club, despite a token membership fee, and that this facility came under the definition of public accommodation, place, and entertainment.

Judicial decision. The following case involved a denial of admission to a recreation facility.

•••

DANIEL v. PAUL
395 U. S. 298, 23 L. Ed. 2d 318, 89 S. Ct. 1697 (1969)

Mr. Justice Brennan delivered the opinion of the Court.

Petitioners, Negro residents of Little Rock, Arkansas, brought this class action in the District Court for the Eastern District of Arkansas to enjoin respondent from denying them admission to a recreational facility called Lake

Nixon Club owned and operated by respondent, Euell Paul, and his wife. The complaint alleged that Lake Nixon Club was a "public accommodation" subject to the provisions of Title II of the Civil Rights Act of 1964, 78 Stat 243, 42 USC § 2000a et seq., and that respondent violated the Act in refusing petitioners admission solely on racial grounds.[1] After trial, the District Court, although finding that respondent had refused petitioners admission solely because they were Negroes,[2] dismissed the complaint on the ground that Lake Nixon Club was not within any of the categories of "public accommodations" covered by the 1964 Act. 263 F Supp 412 (1967). The Court of Appeals for the Eighth Circuit affirmed, one judge dissenting. 395 F2d 118 (1968). We granted certiorari. 393 US 975, 21 L Ed 2d 437, 89 S Ct 444 (1968). We reverse.

Lake Nixon Club, located 12 miles west of Little Rock, is a 232-acre amusement area with swimming, boating, sun bathing, picnicking, miniature golf, dancing facilities, and a snack bar. The Pauls purchased the Lake Nixon site in 1962 and subsequently operated this amusement business there in a racially segregated manner.

Title II of the Civil Rights Act of 1964 enacted a sweeping prohibition of discrimination or segregation on the ground of face, color, religion, or national origin at places of public accommodation whose operations affect commerce.[3] This prohibition does not extend to discrimination or segregation at private clubs.[4] But, as both courts below properly found, Lake Nixon is not a private club. It is simply a business operated for a profit with none of the attributes of self-government and member-ownership traditionally associated with private clubs. It is true that following enactment of the Civil Rights Act of 1964, the Pauls began to refer to the establishment as a private club. They even began to require patrons to pay a 25-cent "membership" fee, which gains a purchaser a "membership" card entitling him to enter the Club's premises for an entire season and, on payment of specified additional fees, to use the swimming, boating, and miniature golf facilities. But this "membership" device seems no more than a subterfuge designed to avoid coverage of the

1. Petitioners alleged that the denial of admission also constitutes a violation of the Civil Rights Act of 1866, as amended, 14 Stat 27, now 42 USC § 1981. Neither the District Court nor the Court of Appeals passed on this contention. Our conclusion makes it unnecessary to consider the question.

2. Respondent at trial answered affirmatively a question of the trial judge whether Negroes were denied admission "simply . . . because they were Negroes." Respondent's answer to an interrogatory why Negroes were refused admission was: "[w]e refused admission to them because white people in our community would not patronize us if we admitted Negroes to the swimming pool. Our business would be ruined and we have our entire life savings in it."

3. Section 201 (a) of the Act provides: "All persons shall be entitled to the full and equal enjoyment of the goods, services, facilities, privileges, advantages, and accommodations of any place of public accommodation, as defined in this section, without discrimination or segregation on the ground of race, color, religion, or national origin."

4. Section 201(e) of the Act provides: "The provisions of this title shall not apply to a private club or other establishment not in fact open to the public, except to the extent that the facilities of such establishment are made available to the customers or patrons of an establishment within the scope of subsection (b)."

1964 Act. White persons are routinely provided "membership" cards, and some 100,000 whites visit the establishment each season. As the District Court found, Lake Nixon is "open in general to all of the public who are members of the white race." 263 F Supp, at 418. Negroes, on the other hand, are uniformly denied "membership" cards, and thus admission, because of the Pauls' fear that integration would "ruin" the "business." The conclusion of the courts below that Lake Nixon is not a private club is plainly correct—indeed, respondent does not challenge that conclusion here.

We therefore turn to the question whether Lake Nixon Club is "a place of public accommodation" as defined by § 201(b) of the 1964 Act, and, if so, whether its operations "affect commerce" within the meaning of § 201(c) of that Act.

Section 201(b) defines four categories of establishments as covered public accommodations. Three of these categories are relevant here:

"Each of the following establishments which serves the public is a place of public accommodation within the meaning of this title if its operations affect commerce . . . .

. . . . . .

"(2) any restaurant, cafeteria, lunchroom, lunch counter, soda fountain, or other facility principally engaged in selling food for consumption on the premises, including, but not limited to, any such facility located on the premises of any retail establishment; or any gasoline station;

"(3) any motion picture house, theater, concert hall, sports arena, stadium, or other place of exhibition or entertainment; and

"(4) any establishment (A) . . . (ii) within the premises of which is physically located any such covered establishment, and (B) which holds itself out as serving patrons of such covered establishment."

Section 201(c) sets forth standards for determining whether the operations of an establishment in any of these categories affect commerce within the meaning of Title II:

"The operations of an establishment affect commerce within the meaning of this title if . . .

(2) in the case of an establishment described in paragraph (2) [set out supra] . . . , it serves or offers to serve interstate travelers or a substantial portion of the food which it serves, or gasoline or other products which it sells, has moved in commerce; (3) in the case of an establishment described in paragraph (3) [set out supra] . . . , it customarily presents films, performances, athletic teams, exhibitions, or other sources of entertainment which move in commerce; and (4) in the case of an establishment described in paragraph (4) [set out supra] . . . , there is physically located within its premises, an establishment the operations of which affect commerce within the meaning of this subsection. For purposes of this section, 'commerce' means travel, trade, traffic, commerce, transportation, or communication among the several States . . . ."

Petitioners argue first that Lake Nixon's snack bar is a covered public accommodation under §§ 201 (b) (2) and 201 (c) (2), and that as such it brings the entire establishment within the coverage of Title II under §§ 201 (b) (4) and 201 (c) (4). Clearly, the snack bar is "principally engaged in selling food for consumption on the premises." Thus, it is a covered public accommodation if "it serves or offers to serve interstate travelers or a substantial portion of the food which it serves . . . has moved in commerce." We find that the snack bar is a covered public accommodation under either of these standards.

The Pauls advertise the Lake Nixon Club in a monthly magazine called "Little Rock Today," which is distributed to guests at Little Rock hotels, motels, and restaurants, to acquaint them with available tourist attractions in the area. Regular advertisements for Lake Nixon were also broadcast over two area radio stations. In addition, Lake Nixon has advertised in the "Little Rock Air Force Base," a monthly newspaper published at the Little Rock Air Force Base, in Jacksonville, Arkansas. This choice of advertising media leaves no doubt that the Pauls were seeking broad-based patronage from an audience which they knew to include interstate travelers. Thus, the Lake Nixon Club unquestionably offered to serve out-of-state visitors to the Little Rock area. And it would be unrealistic to assume that none of the 100,000 patrons actually served by the Club each season was an interstate traveler.[5] Since the Lake Nixon Club offered to serve and served out-of-state persons, and since the Club's snack bar was established to serve all patrons of the entire facility, we must conclude that the snack bar offered to serve and served out-of-state persons. See Hamm v Rock Hill, 379 US 306, 309, 13 L Ed 2d 300, 303, 84 S Ct 384 (1964); see also Wooten v Moore, 400 F2d 239 (CA4th Cir 1968).

The record, although not as complete on this point as might be desired, also demonstrates that a "substantial portion of the food" served by the Lake Nixon Club snack bar has moved in interstate commerce. The snack bar serves a limited fare—hot dogs and hamburgers on buns, soft drinks, and milk. The District Court took judicial notice of the fact that the "principal ingredients going into the bread were produced and processed in other States" and that "certain ingredients [of the soft drinks] were probably obtained . . . from out-of-State sources." 263 F Supp, at 418. Thus, at the very least, three of the four food items sold at the snack bar contain ingredients originating outside of the State. There can be no serious doubt that a "substantial portion of the food" served at the snack bar has moved in interstate commerce. See Katzenbach v McClung, 379 US 294, 296-297, 13 L Ed 2d 290, 293, 294, 85 S Ct 377 (1964); Gregory v Meyer, 376 F2d 509, 511, n 1 (CA 5th Cir 1967).

The snack bar's status as a covered establishment automatically brings the entire Lake Nixon facility within the ambit of Title II. Civil Rights Act of 1964, §§ 201 (b) (4) and 201(c) (4), set out supra: see H. R. Rep. No. 914, 88th Cong., 1st Sess., 20; Fazzio Real Estate Co. v Adams, 396 F2d 146 (CA5th Cir 1968).[6]

---

5. The District Court, which did not find it necessary to decide whether the snack bar served or offered to serve interstate travelers, conceded that: "It is probably true that some out-of-State people spending time in or around Little Rock have utilized [Lake Nixon's] facilities." 263 F Supp, at 418.

6. Accord: Evans v Laurel Links, Inc., 261 F Supp 474 (DC ED Va 1966); United States v Fraley, 282 F Supp 948 (DC MD NC 1968); United States v All Star Triangle Bowl, Inc. 283 F Supp 300 (DC SC 1968).

Petitioners also argue that the Lake Nixon Club is a covered public accommodation under §§ 201 (b) (3) and 201 (c) (3) of the 1964 Act. These sections proscribe discrimination by "any motion picture house, theater, concert hall, sports arena, stadium or other place of exhibition or entertainment" which "customarily presents films, performances, athletic teams, exhibitions, or other sources of entertainment which move in commerce." Under any accepted definition of "entertainment," the Lake Nixon Club would surely qualify as a "place of entertainment."[7] And indeed it advertises itself as such.[8] Respondent argues, however, that in the context of § 201 (b) (3) "place of entertainment" refers only to establishments where patrons are entertained as spectators or listeners rather than those where entertainment takes the form of direct participation in some sport or activity. We find no support in the legislative history for respondent's reading of the statute. The few indications of legislative intent are to the contrary.

President Kennedy, in submitting to Congress the public accommodations provisions of the proposed Civil Rights Act, emphasized that "no action is more contrary to the spirit of our democracy and Constitution—or more rightfully resented by a Negro citizen who seeks only equal treatment—than the barring of that citizen from restaurants, hotels, theatres, *recreational areas* and other public accommodations and facilities."[9] (Emphasis added.) While Title II was being considered by the Senate, a civil rights demonstration occurred at a Maryland amusement park. The then Assistant Majority Leader of the Senate, Hubert Humphrey, took note of the demonstration and opined that such an amusement park would be covered by the provisions which were eventually enacted as Title II:

"In this particular instance, I am confident that merchandise and facilities used in the park were transported across State lines.

.   .   .   .   .   .

"The spectacle of national church leaders being hauled off to jail in a paddy wagon demonstrates the absurdity of the present situation regarding equal access to public facilities in Maryland and the absurdity of the arguments of those who oppose Title II of the President's omnibus civil rights bill." 109 Cong Rec 12276 (1963).

Senator Magnuson, floor manager of Title II, spoke in a similar vein.[10]

7. Webster's Third New International Dictionary, at 757, defines "entertainment" as "the act of diverting, amusing, or causing someone's time to pass agreeably: [synonymous with] amusement."

8. Respondent advertised over a local radio station that "Lake Nixon continues their policy of offering you year-round entertainment."

9. Special Message to the Congress on Civil Rights and Job Opportunities, June 19, 1963, in Public Papers of the Presidents, John F. Kennedy, 1963, at 485. This statement was originally made in a Special Message to the Congress on Civil Rights, Feb. 28, 1963, in Public Papers, supra, at 228.

10. "Motion picture theaters which refuse to admit Negroes will obviously draw patrons from a narrower segment of the market than if they were open to patrons of all races. . . .Thus, the demand for films from out of State, and the royalties from such films, will be less.

.   .   .   .   .   .

(continued on next page)

Admittedly, most of the discussion in Congress regarding the coverage of Title II focused on places of spectator entertainment rather than recreational areas. But it does not follow that the scope of § 201 (b) (3) should be restricted to the primary objects of Congress' concern when a natural reading of its language would call for broader coverage. In light of the overriding purpose of Title II "to remove the daily affront and humiliation involved in discriminatory denials of access to facilities ostensibly open to the general public," H. R. Rep. No. 914, 88th Cong., 1st Sess., 18, we agree with the en banc decision of the Court of Appeals for the Fifth Circuit in Miller v Amusement Enterprises, Inc. 394 F2d 342 (1968), that the statutory language "place of entertainment" should be given full effect according to its generally accepted meaning and applied to recreational areas.

The remaining question is whether the operations of the Lake Nixon Club "affect commerce" within the meaning of § 201 (c) (3). We conclude that they do. Lake Nixon's customary "sources of entertainment . . . move in commerce." The Club leases 15 paddle boats on a royalty basis from an Oklahoma company. Another boat was purchased from the same company. The Club's juke box was manufactured outside Arkansas and plays records manufactured outside the State. The legislative history indicates that mechanical sources of entertainment such as these were considered by Congress to be "sources of entertainment" within the meaning of § 201 (c) (3).[11]

Reversed.

Questions and Comments

1. What was the basis for the lower court's opinion?
2. What was the basis for the Supreme Court opinion?
3. What did the Supreme Court say with reference to the "private club" status?
4. What was the Supreme Court's opinion with reference to the "public accommodation" status.
5. What was the Supreme Court's opinion with respect to characterizing this establishment as a "source of entertainment"?

Place of Entertainment: Defined or Explained

One court has indicated that the term *places of entertainment* must be accorded its generally accepted meaning (*U.S. v. De Rosier*, 1973). Another court has elaborated by indicating that a "place of entertainment" includes

---

"These principles are applicable not merely to motion picture theaters but to *other establishments which receive supplies, equipment, or goods through the channels of interstate commerce.* If these establishments narrow their potential markets by artificially restricting their patrons to non-Negroes, the volume of sales and, therefore, the volume of interstate purchases will be less." (Emphasis added.) 110 Cong Rec 7402 (1964).

11. The Senate rejected an amendment which would have ruled out most mechanical sources by requiring that the source of entertainment be one which has "not come to rest within a State." 110 Cong Rec 13915-13921 (1964). See also the remarks of Senator Magnuson, supra, n. 10.

establishments where people watch other people and establishments that are provided for the amusement or enjoyment of the customers (*U.S. v. Williams*, 1974). Consequently, the patron may be the actor or may merely watch the actor. Bars and package stores were described as a place of entertainment in *U.S. v. Deyorio* (1973) and in *Westray v. Porthole, Inc.* (1984). Cabarets or nightclubs are similarly classified (*Robertson v. Johnston*, 1966). Women's health spas were determined to be "places of entertainment" (*Rousseve v. Shape Spa for Health and Beauty, Inc.*, 1975). A facility owned by an association that operated a youth football program constituted a "place of entertainment" (*U.S. v. Slidell Youth Football Ass'n*, 1974). A corporate recreational or sport complex comes within the definition of a "place of entertainment" because many people pay for admission to the swimming and dining facilities (*U.S. v. Johnson Lake Inc.*, 1970). Golf courses, pool rooms, and skating rinks all fall within the definition *(Evans v. Laurel Links, Inc.*, 1966); *Evans v. Seaman*, (1971); *U.S. v. Williams*, 1974.

Public Facilities

This section of the Civil Rights Act of 1964 is relevant to this book in an indirect way. Owners and managers of private sport facilities may find themselves engaged in working for a public agency. Such work can be carried on simultaneously with running a private business. In some instances, a student of sport management will work exclusively with the public agency. The following code explains complaints and jurisdiction.

The Code Provisions

Complaint; certifications; institution of civil action; relief requested; jurisdiction; impleading additional parties as defendants

(a) Whenever the Attorney General receives a complaint in writing signed by an individual to the effect that he is being deprived of or threatened with the loss of his right to the equal protection of the laws, on account of his race, color, religion, or national origin, by being denied equal utilization of any public facility which is owned, operated, or managed by or on behalf of any State or subdivision thereof, other than a public school or public college as defined in section 2000c of this title, and the Attorney General believes the complaint is meritorious and certifies that the signer or signers of such complaint are unable, in his judgment, to initiate and maintain appropriate legal proceedings for relief and that the institution of an action will materially further the orderly progress of desegregation in public facilities, the Attorney General is authorized to institute for or in the name of the United States a civil action in any appropriate district court of the United States against such parties and for such relief as may be appropriate, and such court shall have and shall exercise jurisdiction of proceedings instituted pursuant to this section. The Attorney General may implead as defendants such additional parties as are or become necessary to the grant of effective relief hereunder.

Persons unable to initiate and maintain legal proceedings
   (b) The Attorney General may deem a person or persons unable to initi-
        ate and maintain appropriate legal proceedings within the meaning of
        subsection (a) of this section when such person or persons are unable,
        either directly or through other interested persons or organizations, to
        bear the expense of the litigation or to obtain effective legal represen-
        tation; or whenever he is satisfied that the institution of such litigation
        would jeopardize the personal safety, employment, or economic
        standing of such person or persons, their families, or their property.
        (42 U.S.C.A. §2000b)

   Judicial decision. The following case illustrates some of the problems
which existed in 1963.

••

JOHNSON v. VIRGINIA
373 U.S. 61, 10 L.Ed.2d 195, 83 S.Ct. 1053 (1963)

Per Curiam.
   The petition for a writ of certiorari is granted, the judgment of the
Supreme Court of Appeals of Virginia is reversed, and the case is remanded
for proceedings not inconsistent with this opinion.
   The petitioner, Ford T. Johnson, Jr., was convicted of contempt of the
Traffic Court of the City of Richmond, Virginia, and appealed his conviction
to the Hustings Court, where he was tried without a jury and again convict-
ed. The Supreme Court of Appeals of Virginia refused to grant a writ of error
on the ground that the judgment appealed from was "plainly right," but the
Chief Justice of that court stayed execution of the judgment pending disposition of this petition for certiorari.
   The evidence at petitioner's trial in the Hustings Court is summarized in an
approved statement of facts. According to this statement, the witnesses for the
State testified as follows: The petitioner, a Negro, was seated in the Traffic
Court in a section reserved for whites, and when requested to move by the
bailiff, refused to do so. The judge then summoned the petitioner to the bench
and instructed him to be seated in the right-hand section of the courtroom, the
section reserved for Negroes. The petitioner moved back in front of the counsel table and remained standing with his arms folded, stating that he preferred
standing and indicating that he would not comply with the judge's order. Upon
refusal to obey the judge's further direction to be seated, the petitioner was
arrested for contempt. At no time did he behave in a boisterous or abusive
manner, and there was no disorder in the courtroom. The State, in its Brief in
Opposition filed in this Court, concedes that in the section of the Richmond
Traffic Court reserved for spectators, seating space "is assigned on the basis of
racial designation, the seats on one side of the aisle being for use of Negro citizens and the seats on the other side being for the use of white citizens."
   It is clear from the totality of circumstances, and particularly the fact that
the petitioner was peaceably seated in the section reserved for whites before

being summoned to the bench, that the arrest and conviction rested entirely on the refusal to comply with the segregated seating requirements imposed in this particular courtroom. Such a conviction cannot stand, for it is no longer open to question that a State may not constitutionally require segregation of public facilities. See, e. g., Brown v Board of Education, 347 US 483, 98 L ed 873, 74 S Ct 686, 38 ALR2d 1180; Baltimore City v Dawson, 350 US 877, 100 L ed 774, 76 S Ct 133; Turner v Memphis, 369 US 350, 7 L ed 2d 762, 82 S Ct 805. State-compelled segregation in a court of justice is a manifest violation of the State's duty to deny no one the equal protection of its laws.

Reversed and remanded.

Questions and Comments

None

Authors' Note

The objective sought under Title III has been supplemented by actions brought under the Fourteenth Amendment challenging segregation. One legal encyclopedia states the matter succinctly:

Aside from the remedies provided by Title III of the Civil Rights Act of 1964, a number of suits have been brought under the Fourteenth Amendment challenging segregation in state or municipally owned or operated public facilities, and the courts have uniformly decreed that segregation in such public facilities is unconstitutional. These suits include successful challenges to segregation in jails, restrooms in public buildings, recreational facilities, golf courses, parks, swimming pools, school auditoriums used by private groups, nursing homes, municipal auditoriums, fire stations, hospitals, and courtrooms. The "separate but equal" doctrine is dead, and continued segregation of public facilities cannot be justified on the ground that it is necessary to preserve the public peace. [Footnotes omitted.] (15 Am. Jur. 2d *Civil Rights* §60, p. 408 (1976))

Unlawful Employment Practices (Title VII)

Although initially restricted to race, color, religion, and national origin, the law was amended to include sex as a subject of discrimination. Further, the law has been amended to include educational bodies.

The Code Provision

Employer practices

(a) It shall be an unlawful employment practice for an employer—

    (1) to fail or refuse to hire or to discharge any individual, or otherwise to discriminate against any individual with respect to his compensation, terms, conditions, or privileges of employment, because of such individual's race, color, religion, sex, or national origin; or

    (2) to limit, segregate, or classify his employees or applicants for

employment in any way which would deprive or tend to deprive any individual of employment opportunities or otherwise adversely affect his status as an employee, because of such individual's race, color, religion, sex, or national origin. (42 U.S.C.A. §2000e-2)(a))

Authors' Note

The statute provides certain exceptions. For example, bona fide occupational qualifications that are reasonably necessary to the normal operation of that particular business or enterprise provide an exception. Additionally, educational institutions supported, controlled, managed, and owned by a particular religious group are also exempt. See 42 U.S.C.A. §2000e-2(e). National security and bona fide seniority or merit systems are excepted from the requirements of the Act. See 42 U.S.C.A. § 20003-2(g)(h). Finally, quotas are proscribed. See 42 U.S.C.A. 2000e-2(j).

STUDENT ASSIGNMENT: FURTHER INVESTIGATION

Earlier sections of this book introduced materials on how to read and analyze judicial decisions.Such an analysis, when supplemented by the expertise of scholars who write for law journals and publish treatises, should provide the basis for an ongoing investigation of particular subjects. This section presents questions that could serve as a class assignment for sport law students.

The student who has access to a law library within the institution of higher education should have little difficulty in tracking down the answers to specific questions. Students who do not have access to a law library should have access to smaller collections to be found in the offices of local attorneys. Some of these collections are quite thorough; all should be adequate for assisting the student to answer the questions in the section which follows. Title VII of the Civil Rights Act of 1964, as amended by the Civil Rights Act of 1991, will be the focal point of this search for specific points of law. Investigating the following questions will assist a sport law student in understanding these statutes. As individuals, or in small groups, students will be asked to ascertain from primary, or acceptable secondary, sources the answer to one of the following questions:

1. To what extent was the Civil Rights Act of 1964 changed by the Education Amendments of 1972?
2. To what extent was the Civil Rights Act of 1964 changed by the Civil Rights Act of 1991?
3. Is a claimant under the Civil Rights Act of 1964 obligated to exhaust administrative remedies?
4. To what extent should a claimant who claims to have been discriminated against on the basis of race plead statutes other than Title VII of the Civil Rights Act of 1964?
5. To what extent is affirmative action a viable component of remedies for one who claims to be aggrieved by an employment decision contrary to the Civil Rights Act of 1964?
6. What is meant by reverse discrimination?

7. How does the concept of reverse discrimination relate to statutory provisions concerning quotas?
8. Is it possible for protections against discrimination to have greater magnitude pursuant to state law as compared to federal law?
9. How does one determine the appropriate statute of limitations in effect for an action filed under Title VII of the Civil Rights Act of 1964?
10. To what extent can one sue directly under the 13th or 14th Amendment without eliciting the support of congressional action designed to implement a particular amendment?
11. Describe the relationship between the protections accorded by Title VII of the Civil Rights Act of 1964 and the democratic process.
12. How does the Civil Rights Act of 1964 affect the advertising of a position that has become vacant?
13. How does the Civil Rights Act of 1964 affect the interview process for one applying for a vacant position?
14. What is the relationship, if any, between the practice of nepotism and the protections accorded by Title VII of the Civil Rights Act of 1964?
15. What constitutional provisions are usually cited by one who seeks to challenge the constitutionality of the Civil Rights Act of 1964?
16. To what extent is the Eleventh Amendment a defense to an action filed pursuant to Title VII of the Civil Rights Act of 1964?
17. What remedies are available to a claimant who seeks to recover pursuant to Title VII of the Civil Rights Act of 1964?
18. Is it possible for a plaintiff to sue in federal and state court simultaneously for claimed discrimination as to employment?

Authors' Note

The classroom instructor may wish to assign these topics sometime around the middle of the semester, but to be reported on at the end of the semester.

This could be you - check your response

Knight could take his case to court if he had evidence of discrimination. The Joneses should carefully avoid discriminatory language or practices.

REFERENCES

Authors

Chester J. Antieau, *Federal civil rights acts,* §§ 1-369 (2d ed. 1980). New York, N.Y.: The Lawyers Co-Operative Publishing Co.

Chester J. Antieau, *Federal civil rights acts,* §§ 370-6107 (2d ed. 1980). New York, N.Y.: The Lawyers Co-Operative Publishing Co.

Cases

Civil Rights Cases, 109 U.S. 3, 27 L. Ed. 835, 3 S. Ct. 18 (1883).

Daniel v. Paul, 395 U.S. 298, 23 L. Ed. 2d 318, 89 S. Ct. 1697 (1969).

Evans v. Laurel Links, Inc., 261 F. Supp. 474 (E.D. Va. 1966).

Evans v. Seaman, 452 F.2d 749 (5th Cir. 1971).

Heart of Atlanta Motel, Inc. v. U. S., 379 U.S. 241, 13 L. Ed. 2d 258, 85 S. Ct. 348 (1964).

Johnson v. Virginia, 373 U.S. 61, 10 L. Ed. 2d 195, 83 S. Ct. 1053 (1963).

Miller v. Amusement Enterprises, Inc., 394 F.2d 342 (5th Cir. 1968).

Newman v. Piggie Park Enterprises, Inc., 377 F.2d 433 (4th Cir. 1967).

Robertson v. Johnston, 249 F. Supp. 618 (E.D. La. 1966). *Rousseve v. Shape Spa for Health and Beauty, Inc.*, 516 F.2d 64 (5th Cir. 1975).

U.S. v. De Rosier, 473 F.2d 749 (5th Cir. 1973).

U.S. v. Deyorio, 473 F.2d 1041 (5th Cir. 1973).

U.S. v. Johnson Lake Inc., 312 F. Supp. 1376 (S.D. Ala. 1970).

U.S. v. Slidell Youth Football Ass'n, 387 F. Supp. 474 (E.D. La. 1974).

U.S. v. Williams, 376 F. Supp. 750 (M. D. Fla. 1974).

Westray v. Porthole, Inc., 586 F. Supp. 834 (D. Md. 1984).

Legal Encyclopedias

15 Am. Jur. 2d *Civil Rights* § 60 (1976) with current updates.

14 C.J.S. *Civil Rights* §§1-142 (1991) with current updates.

14A C.J.S. *Civil Rights* §§ 143-483 (1991) with current updates.

Model Codes, Restatements, and Standards

Civil Rights Act 1964,

42 U.S.C.A. §§ 2000a and 2000b.

42 U.S.C.A. §2000e-2.

42 U.S.C.A. §2003-2(g)(h).

CHAPTER 22

AMERICANS WITH DISABILITIES ACT OF 1990 AND THE CIVIL RIGHTS ACT OF 1991

INTRODUCTION

The beauty of the democratic process rests in part upon its ability to correct itself. Legislation is passed; judicial decisions interpret that legislation; strengths and weaknesses of the legislation then become apparent. One result of this experience is corrective legislation designed to strengthen the overall process whereby rights are ensured and protected. Two examples of corrective legislation in the field of civil rights are readily apparent, namely, the Americans With Disabilities Act of 1990 and the Civil Rights Act of 1991. This chapter will touch on the highlights of each of these pieces of legislation.

IN THIS CHAPTER YOU WILL LEARN:

The more salient provisions of the Americans With Disabilities Act of 1990

The more salient provisions of the Civil Rights Act of 1991

KEY WORDS: *accommodation, undue hardship, major life activity, qualified individual with disability, punitive damages, medical examination, glass ceiling.*

This could be you!

Sue Stathis, an employee of the Joneses, has believed for some time that she has been subjected to unlawful discrimination based on a certain physical disability. To complicate matters, Stathis has started drinking excessively and frequently misses work because of hangovers. Her various demands for

alterations of the premises so as to make access more readily available were rejected by management during the past 2 years. The passage of the Civil Rights Act of 1991 was viewed by Stathis as a godsend because of its provisions for compensatory and punitive damages. Stathis immediately filed suit requesting not only injunctive and declaratory relief, but also damages and attorney's fees. Does the Civil Rights Act of 1991 or the Americans With Disabilities Act of 1990 afford relief for Stathis?

RECENT STATUTORY DEVELOPMENTS

The Americans With Disabilities Act of 1990 (ADA) (42 U.S.C.A §12.101, et seq.)

According to the ADA, a disability is "a physical or mental impairment that substantially limits one or more of the major life activities of such individual" (Sec. 12102). The ADA prohibits discrimination against individuals with disabilities in four areas: employment, public services and transportation, public accommodations, and telecommunications. (O'Brien & Overby, 1994, p. 29).

Title I covers employment. Title II covers public services; Section A includes discrimination, and Section B includes public transportation. Title III includes public accommodations and services operated by private entities. Title IV includes telecommunications, for example, relay services for hearing-impaired and speech-impaired individuals. Title V covers miscellaneous provisions, such as construction, attorneys' fees, and technical assistance.

Conditions noted in the ADA. Prior to the ADA, according to the statutes, there were serious social problems in dealing with individuals with disabilities. Historically, these individuals were isolated, segregated, and discriminated against.

Discrimination against individuals with disabilities was perceived in such critical areas as employment, housing, communication, recreation, institutionalization, health services, voting, and access to public services (Sec. 12101, a, 3). Prior to the ADA, there was often no effective legal recourse to redress discrimination against Americans with disabilities (Sec. 12101,a,4).

Discrimination grew out of overprotective rules, failure to make modification to facilities, exclusionary standards, segregation, and relegation to lesser programs and other opportunities (Sec. 12101, a, 5). Further, there was strong evidence that Americans with disabilities occupied an inferior status and were seriously disadvantaged socially, vocationally, economically, and educationally (Sec. 12101, a, 6).

Individuals with disabilities were relegated to positions which did not measure their true abilities (Sec. 12101,a,7). Equality of opportunity was needed in order to bring about economic self-sufficiency (Sec. 12101, a, 8). A tremendous expense resulted from lack of employment and the denial of opportunities to handicapped individuals (Sec. 12101, a, 9).

The Americans With Disabilities Act of 1990 may benefit as many as 43,000,000 Americans (Sec. 12101, a 1). (Summary by O'Brien & Overby, 1994, page 31).

A portion of the Americans with Disabilities Act of 1990 is quoted below:

Purposes of the ADA. It is the purpose of this chapter—
(1) to provide a clear and comprehensive national mandate for the elimination of discrimination against individuals with disabilities;
(2) to provide clear, strong, consistent, enforceable standards addressing discrimination against individuals with disabilities;
(3) to ensure that the Federal Government plays a central role in enforcing the standards established in this Act on behalf of individuals with disabilities; and
(4) to invoke the sweep of congressional authority, including the power to enforce the fourteenth amendment and to regulate commerce, in order to address the major areas of discrimination faced day-to-day by people with disabilities (Sec. 12101,a,1).

Basic concepts.
1. The Americans With Disabilities Act of July 26, 1990, *does not:*
   a. provide for quotas.
   b. provide for affirmative action.
   c. provide for preferential treatment in employment matters.
   d. have retroactive application.
   e. authorize punitive damages against a state.
   f. provide compensatory damages absent intentional discrimination.
2. The Americans With Disabilities Act *does* require the ability to perform the essential functions of a job.

Other helpful statutory provisions (summarized).
1. In determining a "qualified individual with a disability," two considerations are relevant: first, the employer's judgment as to what is essential; and second, the job description.
2. When an accommodation is necessary because of a disability, the accommodation must be reasonable. It may be permissible to restructure the job, modify work schedules, change policies, or reassign to a vacant position. Other aspects of the ADA are as follows:

Drugs and alcohol. According to O'Brien & Overby (1994), under the ADA:

It is permissible to test for illegal drugs and alcohol use (Sec. 12114, c, 1-4). This is not interdicted by limitations as to medical examinations

(Sec. 12114, d, 1, 2). Pre-employment drug screenings may be allowed if they are required of all employees and are given after an offer to hire. Drug addiction is not a disability (Sec. 12114,a). The use of alcoholic beverages and illegal drugs may be prohibited on the job (Sec. 12114, c, 1-4).

Persons who have received treatment for past alcohol and drug abuse are protected under the law (Sec. 12114, b, 1, 2, 3).

Other aspects of the ADA are as follows:

Safety and insurance. Legitimate safety requirements that are necessary for safe operation may be imposed. These requirements must be based on actual risks, not on speculation. Refusal of service may not occur because insurance company coverage does not cover persons with disabilities.

Removal of barriers. Under the law, public accommodations shall remove architectural barriers in facilities when this removal is easily accomplished. This includes installing ramps, widening doors, repositioning telephones, providing access to restroom facilities, etc. (See Uniform Federal Accessibility Standards 1984 for further information). A priority list for barrier removal is included in the ADA. Alternatives to barrier removal are listed for public accommodations in which barrier removal is not readily achievable. These include relocation of activities and providing home delivery.

Examinations and courses. Any private entity that offers examinations or courses relating to credentialing or licensing, etc. shall make examinations and courses accessible. This includes designing and administering examinations in a manner which would measure the skill and knowledge of the person effectively. This may mean offering the test in braille or providing courses through videotapes, cassettes, or notes.

Personal devices and services. Auxiliary aids and services must be provided to individuals with vision or hearing handicaps unless it causes an undue burden on the entity. Public accommodations are not required to provide personal devices such as wheelchairs or hearing aids. Furthermore, personal services such as aid in eating, toileting, or dressing are not required.

Transportation. Even though transportation is not the main function of the public accommodation, some transportation services are covered by the ADA. These include student transportation systems, shuttle busses and transportation within recreational facilities such as stadiums and zoos. Barriers shall be removed where such removal is readily achievable. Specific requirements for transportation are included in section 306 of the ADA (Sec. 12186).

New construction and alterations. Public structures occupied since January 26, 1993 must be designed and constructed in compliance with the ADA. Alterations to structures after January 26, 1993 must comply to the "maximum extent feasible." Elevators in facilities less than three stories are not required in most cases. However, if physics is offered on the second floor of a school, there should be some way to make that course accessible to a disabled student. Alterations to paths of travel should include the path of travel to the altered area and the restrooms, telephones, and drinking fountains, unless the cost of such alterations is disproportionate to the overall cost of alteration construction.

Considerations. There are particular considerations for recreational and fitness facilities, goods, and services. The law provides for separate but equal classes to accommodate the needs of individuals with disabilities. The individual must be able to participate in regular classes.

The law takes into consideration the size of buildings, the nature of the facility, and the undue hardship alterations would make. Accessibility paths are a concern.

Safety may be a legitimate concern. Such a concern should be documented with statistics concerning risks, not opinions. Safety to others can be a consideration.

New construction must be designed and implemented for individuals with disabilities. As noted earlier, this portion of the law took effect January 26, 1993. All government facilities, services, and communications must be accessible and meet the requirements of Section 504 of the Rehabilitation Act of 1973. (O'Brien and Overby, 1994, pp. 34-35.)

Violation. Persons with disabilities who feel their rights have been violated can file a complaint with an appropriate federal agency. Following an investigation of the complaint, the agency can file a lawsuit against the offending employer or business.

Employers in the fields of health, physical education, recreation, and sport may have distinctly different jobs and employment needs. A little forethought and knowledge of the Americans With Disabilities Act should help employers who want to aid the disabled persons and their business. (O'Brien and Overby, 1994, pp. 34-35.)

Conclusions concerning the ADA. The materials presented thus far have been confined to basic observations as opposed to detail. No useful purpose would be served by burdening the sports manager with technical information at this point. A conscious effort has been made to present those aspects of the law that make it livable. This is good legislation. It was needed, and it deserves thoughtful attention. The average owner or sport manager wishes to obey the law. To this end, the owner and manager are willing to expend time and effort to understand the law. Finally, it is believed that the average owner and sport manager have a deep-seated feeling that the interest of individuals with disabilities should be protected.

A democratic form of government postulates equality before the law. Such a postulate stresses the inherent dignity of the individual. The Americans With Disabilities Act conforms to these basic ideas.

ADA judicial application. In *Concerned Parents v. City of West Palm Beach* (1994), over 50 parents and volunteers brought suit against the City for elimination of certain recreational programs for persons with disabilities. The City had offered a variety of programs for persons with disabilities which were cut from the program when the budget was cut.

In 1992-93, the budget for Leisure Services was $6,573.550, with $384,560 allocated for special populations. In 1993-94, the entire budget was reduced to $5,919.731. The special populations budget was reduced from $384,560 to $82,827. The $82,827 was for salary and benefits for one staff member, a

Special Populations Supervisor.

Remember, Title II of the ADA prohibits discrimination in public services. In order to show a violation of Title II of the ADA, plaintiff must show:

1. he or she is, or represents the interests of, a qualified individual.
2. the individual was excluded from participation, or was denied the benefits of some public entity's services, programs, or activities or was otherwise discriminated against.
3. that discrimination was by reason of the plaintiff's disability. (p. 990)

The Court in this case ruled that the City was unable to account for the extreme disparity between the extent of budget cuts for the disabled and nondisabled . . . . (p. 992)

The Court ordered the City to "afford the benefits of the City's recreational program to persons with disabilities in full compliance with Title II of the ADA." (p. 993) What can the sport manager learn from this case?

The Civil Rights Act of 1991 (Pub.L. 102-166, Nov. 21, 1991)

Prefatory to the adoption of this legislation were the findings of Congress. These findings envisaged three things, as indicated by Section 2 quoted below:

The Congress finds that—

(1) additional remedies under Federal law are needed to deter unlawful harassment and intentional discrimination in the workplace;
(2) the decision of the Supreme Court in Wards Cove Packing Co. v. Atonio, 490 U.S. 642 (1989) has weakened the scope and effectiveness of Federal civil rights protections; and
(3) legislation is necessary to provide additional protections against unlawful discrimination in employment.

With these findings in mind, Congress felt that the Act should acknowledge the following purposes as indicated by the following quotation from Section 3:

(1) to provide appropriate remedies for intentional discrimination and unlawful harassment in the workplace;
(2) to codify the concepts of "business necessity" and "job related" enunciated by the Supreme Court in Griggs v. Duke Power Co., 401 U.S. 424 (1971), and in the other Supreme Court decisions prior to Wards Cove Packing Co. v. Atonio, 490 U.S. 642 (1989);
(3) to confirm statutory authority and provide statutory guidelines for the adjudication of disparate impact suits under title VII of the Civil Rights Act of 1964 (42 U.S.C. 2000e et seq.); and
(4) to respond to recent decisions of the Supreme Court by expanding the scope of relevant civil rights statutes in order to provide adequate protection to victims of discrimination. (Sect. 3)

After the statement of findings and purposes, the Civil Rights Act of 1991 made various innovative changes in civil rights legislation generally. Some of the more salient changes are enumerated below. In each case where a change has been noted, the language of the statute will be quoted or cited.

1. Compensatory or punitive damages may be recovered in case of intentional discrimination. However, the law places a cap on the amount of damages that can be recovered. This provision is to be found in Title I, Section 102 of the Civil Rights Act of 1991.

2. Jury trials are permitted when a party seeks compensatory or punitive damages, as indicated by the following statutory language taken from Title I, Section 102 of the Act:

   ...If a complaining party seeks compensatory or punitive damages under this section—

   (1) any party may demand a trial by jury; and

   (2) the court shall not inform the jury of the limitations described in subsection (b)(3).

3. For information on expert witness and attorney's fees, see Title I, Sec. 113 of the Civil Rights Act of 1991.

4. Alternative dispute resolution is encouraged by Title I, Section 118 of the Civil Rights Act of 1991:

   Where appropriate and to the extent authorized by law, the use of alternative means of dispute resolution, including settlement negotiations, conciliation, facilitation, mediation, factfinding, minitrials, and arbitration, is encouraged to resolve disputes arising under the Acts or provisions of Federal law amended by this title (Sec. 118).

5. 42 U.S.C.A. Section 1981 is clarified and strengthened by the following provision taken from Title I, Section 101 of the Civil Rights Act of 1991:

   (b) For purposes of this section, the term "make and enforce contracts" includes the making, performance, modification, and termination of contracts, and the enjoyment of all benefits, privileges, terms, and conditions of the contractual relationship (Sec. 101).

   (c) The rights protected by this section are protected against impairment by nongovernmental discrimination and impairment under color of State law (Sec. 101).

6. Test scores may not be adjusted; thus, protection is accorded against reverse discrimination as shown in Title I, Section 106 of the Civil Rights Act of 1991:

   (1) It shall be an unlawful employment practice for a respondent, in connection with the selection or referral of applicants or candidates for employment or promotion, to adjust the scores of, use different cutoff scores for, or otherwise alter the results of, employment related tests on the basis of race, color, religion, sex, or national origin (Sec. 106).

7. Discrimination need not be the sole motivating factor. A discharge or other unlawful employment practice is actionable even though factors other than unlawful employment practices based on race, color, religion, sex, or national origin motivated the practice. Specifically, Title I, Section 107 of the Civil Rights Act of 1991 states in part:

   (m) Except as otherwise provided in this title, an unlawful employment practice is established when the complaining party demonstrates that race, color, religion, sex, or national origin was a motivating factor for any employment practice, even though other factors also motivated the practice (Sec. 107).

8. The burden of proof is clarified in disparate impact cases. This provision is to be found in Title I, Section 105 of the Civil Rights Act of 1991.

9. The Act recognizes the difficulty that women face in breaking into managerial positions. To this end, a Glass Ceiling Commission is established with detailed instructions for research on advancement of women and minorities to management and decision-making positions in business. This provision is to be found in Title II, Sections 203-204, of the Civil Rights Act of 1991.

10. Although the statute does not speak directly to the issue of retroactive versus prospective application, the United States Supreme Court has held the Act to be prospective only. See *Landgraf v. USI Film Products* (1994) and *Rivers v. Roadway Express* (1994). In so holding, the Supreme Court affirmed a great majority of the United States Circuit Court opinions.

Conclusions. The Civil Rights Act of 1991 expanded remedies by providing for both compensatory and punitive damages in the case of intentional discrimination. The damages provision was strengthened by specifically providing for jury trials. Additionally, a court may, in its discretion, award the recovery of expert witness fees, along with attorney's fees. Previous acts have been strengthened and judicial decisions clarified.

SUMMARY

The Americans With Disabilities Act of 1990 and the Civil Rights Act of 1991 purport to put finishing touches on civil rights legislation. To this end, these two Acts solidify the notion that individuals are to be treated equally, regardless of race, sex, national origin, religion, age, or disability. Stated differently, the law purports to protect the status of each individual from the standpoint of opportunity to participate in the benefits derived from organized society. There is no second-class citizenship. The chart that follows at the end of the Perspective summarizes some of the federal antidiscrimination laws.

This could be you - check your response

There are several issues to be addressed in this situation. Stathis is disabled. Under the ADA, the Joneses are obligated to make reasonable accommodations for her if it would not be an undue hardship on the business. Under the ADA, alcoholism is not a disability. Yet, if Stathis decides to enter treatment for alcoholism, then that fact cannot be used to terminate her employment.

The Civil Rights Act of 1991 does extend the remedies of the ADA to include compensatory and punitive damages for intentional discrimination. In this situation, it is not clear if there has been intentional discrimination.

REFERENCES

Authors

O'Brien, D.B., & Overby, J. (1994). The Americans With Disabilities Act: Historical background and implications for physical education and recreation. *Journal of Legal Aspects of Sport, 4* (1), 29-36.

Cases

Concerned Parents v. City of West Palm Beach, 846 F.Supp. 986 (S.D.Fla. 1994).
Dennin v. Connecticut Inter. Athletic Conf., 913 F.Supp. 663 (D.Conn. 1996).
Johnson v. Florida HSAA, Inc., 899 F.Supp. 579 (M.D. Fla. 1995).
Landgraf v. USI Film Products, 511 U.S. ___, 128 L. Ed. 2d 229, 114 S. Ct. ___ (1994).
Maddox v. University of Tennessee, 62 F.3d 843 (6 Cir. 1995).
McPherson v. Mich. HSAA, 77 F.3d 883 (6 Cir. 1996).
Pahulu v. University of Kansas, 897 F.Supp. 1387 (D.Kan. 1995).
Rivers v. Roadway Express, 511 U.S. ___, 128 L. Ed. 2d 274, 114 S. Ct. ___ (1994).
Sandison v. Michigan HSAA, Inc., 64 F.3d 1026 (6 Cir. 1995).

Model Codes, Restatements and Standards

Americans With Disabilities Act of 1990, Pub. L. 101-336, 104 Stat. 324, July 26, 1990, and amendments, codified as 42 U.S.C. §12101, et seq.

Civil Rights Act of 1991, Pub. L. 102-166, 105 Stat. 1071, Nov. 21, 1991, and amendments.

Family and Medical Leave Act of 1993, PL 103-3, 107 +A +6 (1993).

Civil Rights:
Race Discrimination, Americans
with Disabilities Act of 1990,
Civil Rights Act of 1991

PERSPECTIVE

A test to determine the usefulness of law generally involves the law's capacity for change. This principle has been noted in connection with *stare decisis*[1] generally. Precedent does not embalm a bad decision. Courts seek to ensure predictability but retain the option to correct what is later perceived to be bad law. The change in perception may arise from rethinking the problem. It may arise from changing economic and social conditions. It may arise from new perceptions brought to the attention of the court by legal scholars, attorneys, or by a judge who gleans bits and pieces from factual situations before the court. The reader will recall that the principle of *certiorari*[2] leans upon the multiplicity of lower court opinions. In like fashion, the doctrine of constitutional restraint inhibits the courts from consideration of constitutional issues if a case can be decided on other grounds. Under the doctrine of constitutional restraint, the courts will not consider ruling on constitutional issues unless there is an actual case before the court. Most courts are not empowered to render advisory opinions. The point to remember is this: The law strives for stability as well as a positive reaction to the need for change.

Seldom does one find an area of the law that illustrates these principles

1. Precedent—"Let the decision stand."

2. A higher court will take a case decided by a lower court as a matter of grace, not as a matter of law. If there are a large number of similar cases in the lower courts, the higher court is more likely to hear the case.

more significantly than does the area of civil rights. The American Revolution provided a fresh start in broadening the base of the ruling class. A frontier society emphasized character, work, and the acquisition of property. These traits aided and abetted the evolution of the democratic process.

Despite the revolutionary nature of this new government, it should be remembered that, although noble in its sentiment, it was, nevertheless, limited in practice. Not all "men" could participate in the governmental process. Voting was restricted, and government of the masses was looked upon with disfavor.

The chapters that have dealt with race discrimination are useful to the owner or manager of a sports management business. The owner or manager should be sensitive to the feelings of others. A sizeable portion of the United States' population was enslaved for a prolonged period of time. There may be a temptation to say, "This does not affect me—I was not involved—I cannot be held accountable." On the face of it, this view may appear to be understandable. However, such an attitude precludes progressive action that should be taken to redress past oppression. Furthermore, it fails to appreciate the depth of emotion with which historically disadvantaged individuals view their situations. This intensity of emotions is not only undesirable from a humanistic perspective, but it also enhances the probability of litigation when racial discrimination is suspected. The backlog of racial oppression cannot be wiped out by judicial decisions or by legislation, however progressive. Upon reflection, one can see the slow and rather tortuous development in decisional law commencing with the dissenting opinion in *Plessy v. Ferguson* (1896) and culminating in *Brown v. Board of Education* (1954). One can also reflect on the ineffectual results from legislation enacted immediately after the Civil War as compared with the civil rights legislation in the 1960s and the years that followed.

In early America, the disadvantaged position of women was clearly reflected in their disfranchisement and exclusion from the learned professions. Women could not vote and could not enter some professions such as law. The inherent dignity of women, which is a basic and fundamental assumption of the democratic process, was ignored and largely disallowed. The position of the African-American[3] was far below the position of the white female in the United States, even though the white female was not accorded economic and political rights equal to men. Slavery was paternalistic at best, and brutal at its worst. Nevertheless, slavery was defended by intellectuals in many walks of life. Government officials and other influential citizens, including members of the clergy, held and expressed strong opinions on the subject.

This says something to the owner or manager of the sports industry; specifically, a decision affecting race can be expected to be challenged. This challenge may emerge in the form of what are considered to be unreasonable demands and expectations. Litigation is expensive and inconvenient. These problems of litigation are not softened appreciably because the owner or manager feels mistreated.

---

3. In 1994 Carnegie Foundation data indicated that 40% of this group prefer to be called Black, and 20% would like to be called African-American.

Law	Areas of Discrimination
14th Amendment to U.S. Constitution (1868)	Rights of citizens
Equal Pay Act (1963)	Sex (in pay)
Title VII, Civil Rights Act of 1964	Race, religion, sex, color, and national origin
E.O. 11246 (as amended by E.O. 11375) (1968)	Race, sex, color, and national origin
Title IX, Education Amendments of 1972	Sex
Rehabilitation Act, 1973 (Section 504)	Disabled
Individuals with Disabilities Education Act 1990, formerly Education for all Handicapped Children Act (P.L. 94-142) (1976)	Disabled students age 3-21
Pregnancy Discrimination Act (1978)	Sex (pregnancy)
Age Discrimination in Employment Act (1967)	Age
O.C.R.* Guidelines for Discrimination and Denial of Services on the Basis of Race, Color, National Origin, Sex and Handicap	Race, color, national origin, sex, and disability
Carl D. Perkins Vocational Education Act, 1984	Sex (also national origin and handicap)
42 U.S.C.A. §1983	Constitutional and federal law
Civil Rights Act of 1991	Race, sex, and national origin
Americans With Disabilities Act of 1990	Disabled
Civil Rights Act of 1964--Title II (public accommodation); Title VI (students); Title VII (employment)	Race, color, national origin, and sex
Family and Medical Leave Act, 1993	Medical problems in family

* Abbreviation: O.C.R., Office for Civil Rights
This chart is adapted from one from the Office for Civil Rights and is a partial summary of federal anti-discrimination laws. Readers are encouraged to check the status of the law and the enforcement for that law. The law is subject to being amended or repealed. Enforcement agencies may be changed or renamed. Often there are also internal or administrative remedies which should be exhausted in some discrimination situations.

FIGURE 5
FEDERAL ANTI-DISCRIMINATION LAWS:
A BRIEF SELECTED SUMMARY

Stated tersely, the question of access to public accommodations, the right to enter into contracts, the right to hold property, the right to the protection of all of the laws, when demanded, must be responded to in a court of law. The owner or manager of a sport enterprise needs to be able to respond adequately and effectively to questions involving race relations. Good information and good advice are essential. Preventive measures are always important. Attitudinal adjustments may be necessary. Celebration of diversity coupled with patience will assist in the prevention and resolution of disputes.

This section has discussed civil rights legislation that impacts the sport manager. The sport manager is encouraged to treat all minorities with dignity and respect. Knowledge of the law is important, but so is attitude. Figure 5 summarizes some of the federal antidiscrimination laws.

Hypothetical Case - Part VII - Check Your Response

The first question this situation raises is the validity of the intelligence test. Is he required to take the test? Is the test valid? Is there cultural bias? Tests which are not significantly related to job performance violate the Civil Rights Act of 1964.

The second question involves substance abuse. Does the fact that Washington has been drug free for 60 days ensure that he is cured? If he has a disability, what provision of the Americans With Disabilities Act (ADA) governs this disability?

The constitutional provision is the Equal Protection clause. The statutes are the Civil Rights Act of 1991 and Title VII and the ADA of 1990.

The situation is complex. Washington might be covered by the ADA if he is under treatment for drug abuse. However, Washington has not been denied the position; he has only considered the application. There has been no discrimination because he has not been denied the position at this point.

REFERENCES

Cases
Brown v. Board of Education, 347 U.S. 483, 98 L. Ed. 873, 74 S. Ct. 686 (1954).
Plessy v. Ferguson, 163 U.S. 537, 41 L. Ed. 256, 16 S. Ct. 1138 (1896).

Codes, Restatements, and Standards
Civil Rights Act 1964.
42 U.S.C.A. §§ 200a and 200b.
42 U.S.C.A. §200e-2.
42 U.S.C.A. §2003-2(g)(h).

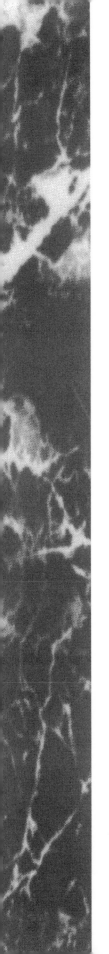

RISK MANAGEMENT: YOUR BEST INVESTMENT

CHAPTER 23

Risk Management

John and Maria Jones have enjoyed successful business ventures. The various business enterprises have become an established part of the community. The Joneses decide to retire and pursue other interests.

Pursuant to the plans to retire, the business is sold to Lee and Jan Tong. The contract to sell calls for the transfer of the businesses to be effective on a day in which the Chamber of Commerce gives John and Maria a citation commemorating their contribution to the business community. In accepting the award, the Joneses offer their hopes and expectations for the success of the new owners of the businesses. Their remarks are a summary of the sport management practices that have helped them to start the business, and manage legal issues. Avoiding and winning lawsuits have been important.

IN THIS CHAPTER YOU WILL LEARN:
Risk management strategies, a review of legal issues

KEY WORDS: *Contracts, partnership, corporation, negligence, product liability, workers' compensation, waiver, sexual harassment, First Amendment, Civil Rights Act of 1991, Americans With Disabilities Act of 1990, Age Discrimination Act of 1967, negligent hiring*

This could be you!

Can you predict what Jones will say about risk management? List several risk-management strategies available to the sport manager. Describe how you could use the information in your career 5 years from now.

OVERALL REVIEW BY THE JONESES

In accepting their award, the Joneses began their suggestions for risk management of a sport business by   stating that some strategies are efficient business practices, others are designed to prevent lawsuits, whereas others are designed to help in winning a lawsuit if one were to occur. They briefly reviewed the statutory and case law that gave them a basis for the strategies they discussed. They began with a discussion of the start of the business and proceeded through the developmental and concluding phases of their sport business entrepreneurship. Highlights of their advice are included in the following topics.

Getting The Business Started

The Joneses recommended that a sport manager elicit help from whatever knowledgeable source is available. Some advice will be free; other advice will be paid for. They advised the selection of educated advisors. Ms Jones said, "An attorney, an accountant, a real estate agent, a government official, and a banker will each be in a position to help on specialized issues."

"If land is purchased, buyers should make certain that there is a clear title to the property. One must be careful of zoning restrictions or lease agreements that might inhibit certain uses of a facility. Legal help with contracts should be sought."

"There are many forms of business organization. These include sole proprietorship, partnerships, and corporate forms. One should recall that partners are liable for the debts and negligent acts of the partner, whereas in a corporation there is limited liability of the shareholders," Ms Jones said.

Managing Risk

"Negligence refers to a duty to care, a breach of that duty, and an injury that results from that breach. Several strategies are available for avoiding and winning lawsuits related to negligence," Mr. Jones remarked.

Mr. Jones outlined some risk-management techniques related to the necessity of the employer to adequately train employees and to keep records of the training of participants and employees. Ms Jones also noted the importance of keeping records related to safety or maintenance checks of equipment and facilities.

Ms Jones stated, "Adequate warnings and waivers may also be factors that protect owners of businesses against litigation of negligence suits. A waiver signed by an adult may serve as defense against negligence claims. Adults cannot sign away the rights of minors. However, children can sign statements of consent to participate that give warnings. The present trend is toward comparative negligence. Adequate knowledge of the risks of an action is important in assumption of risk. Adequate insurance for the sport business and the participant is also important."

According to Mr. Jones, "Crowd control may be assisted by properly trained personnel and sport event planning." Mr. Jones recommended posted warnings and signs regulating conduct as measures to put clients on notice. Documentation of preventive measures is important in winning lawsuits.

Crowd control is also influenced by substance abuse. Drugs and alcohol use increase the risk of injury. The Joneses recommended adequate drug policies and enforcement of the policies for both employees and patrons.

Product liability and strict liability involve the concepts of contracts, warranty, and negligence. The manufacturer might warrant that the product will perform as specified and that the materials are adequate. The Joneses stated that all businesses should carefully follow the manufacturer's recommendations regarding installation and use of equipment and other products. Ms Jones cautioned that modifications of products may result in negligence liability for the sport manager.

Workers' compensation insurance was designed as a remedy without fault for an on-the-job accident. In her talk, Ms Jones noted the importance of employers providing for the safety of employees. OSHA regulations and EPA regulations are also standards that need to be met by the employer.

Work Place Rights

The Joneses enthusiastically talked about First Amendment rights that are so important in the United States. Freedom of religion, freedom of expression, freedom of the press, the right of association, and the right to a fair hearing are important. The concept of procedural due process involves notice and a fair hearing. According to Mr. and Ms Jones, the employer who allows for the rights of others may be effective in avoiding lawsuits.

Both Mr. and Ms Jones have sincerely supported civil rights of individuals in their business endeavors. Mr. Jones reminded future business owners that equal pay for equal work is a standard that relates to gender equity. He also reminded future sport managers that marital status, pregnancy, or gender should not influence employment questions.

In the work place, a requirement of employees to wear revealing clothing might be considered sexual harassment. However, when employees wear inappropriate clothing, it may also detract from the business atmosphere. Standards of dress might be upheld by the courts if the dress code reflects the businesslike standard, Mr. Jones said.

In regard to sexual harassment, he reminded employers that a clear message should be sent to employees that sexual harassment will not be tolerated among workers or with clients. Procedures for reporting sexual harassment should be a part of the business policy manual.

Ms Jones reminded the audience that strides in civil rights have been made by the enactment of the Civil Rights Act of 1991 and the Americans With Disabilities Act of 1990. When persons have been deliberately discriminated against, they may be compensated, and attorney fees and expert witness fees may be paid. She noted that quotas are not mandated by civil rights legislation. However, persons should not be discriminated against because of race, creed, color, or sex. She stated that it is very important to have clear job descriptions and to have written qualifications for jobs.

Under the ADA, public and private businesses must make accommodations for people with disabilities unless businesses can show undue hardship. Ms Jones noted with pride that the best reason for the programmatic and physical modifications she and her husband made for individuals with disabilities was not to avoid lawsuits under ADA but to better serve all disabled sport participants.

In conclusion, the Joneses noted their appreciation of the law in providing stability in a democratic society.

ENDING RISK-MANAGEMENT STRATEGIES

At the end of their talk, the Joneses made available two handouts to those individuals who wanted further information on risk management. The first handout was by O'Brien and Overby (1997) and the second by Janes (1997). The handouts contained suggestions that would be helpful to the sport manager.

* * * * * * * * * * * * * *

(Handout 1)

OTHER TOPICS RELEVANT TO RISK MANAGEMENT AND EMPLOYMENT LIABILITY[1]

by Dianne B. O'Brien, Ph.D. and James O. Overby, J.D. (1997)

Legal risk management in the scope of this discussion is presented in the broadest sense of the term. Risk management for the sport entrepreneur includes the many strategies for establishing a business and maintaining that business. The following topics and strategies not covered previously in the discussion are designed to supplement those materials that reduce the risk of employment liability. The topics addressed are selected for currency. The handout is not designed as a complete discussion on the topic.

Age Discrimination

Sport managers should be aware that the Age Discrimination In Employment Act (ADEA) of 1967 affects employment situations in which there is intentional discrimination or willful and wanton disregard for the ADEA. Under the ADEA, for a *prima facie* case, a person must show that (a) he or she is within a protected age group; (b) his or her performance was satisfactory; (c) his or her contract was not renewed; and (d) his or her duties were given to a younger person whose credentials were no better. The employee is entitled to liquidated damages or double damages if the employer willfully violated or showed reckless disregard for conduct prohibited by the ADEA.

In the case *Ryther v. KARE 11* (1994), Ryther, a television sportscaster, filed suit against KARE, an NBC affiliate in the Twin Cities. After winning the age discrimination suit, Ryther was awarded back pay of $272,444.00 and front pay of $433,330.30. The television station failed to produce sufficient evidence of its nondiscriminatory reasons for failure to renew Ryther's contract. It is important for sport managers not to discriminate against employees because of their age.

---

1. This material was specifically designed for the present text. It contains topics not discussed in-depth in the text.

Manager's Liability - Special Aspects

Under the doctrine of *vicarious liability* (also known as *respondeat superior*), the sport manager may be held liable for the acts of employees. The employer may be liable when the employee is acting in the scope and in the authority of his or her employment. Recent developments the sport manager should consider in a risk-management plan include the following cases.

In the case of *Matthews v. Rollins Hudig Hall Co.* (1995), the Court ruled that managers may be held personally liable for the intentional violations of the ADEA by their employees. Managers may also be held liable for employees who fail to take action when employees are guilty of sexual harassment (*Meritor Savings Bank, FS3 v. Vinson*, 1986). Managers may be liable for the actions of their employees for sexual harassment if the employee uses his or her authority as a position to aid in his or her harassment (*Karibian v. Columbia University*, 1994). Managers may be held liable for claims of retaliation under Title VII (*Carter Coal Co. v. Human Rights Commission*, 1994).

Employers cannot use short-term contracts (at-will employment agreements) for failure to provide due process in sexual harassment procedures (*Starishevsky v. Hofstra University*, 1994).

Disabilities - New Considerations

In some cases, the ADA may provide protection for females seeking infertility treatment (*Pacourek v. Inland Steel Co.*, 1994).

AIDS is covered under the ADA and under the Rehabilitation Act of 1973. Section 504 of the Rehabilitation Act of 1973 includes governmental agencies and those entities receiving federal assistance. In *Chalk v. U.S. District Court* (1988), the court ruled that a school board could not bar a teacher with AIDS from teaching in the classroom. There was not a significant risk of transmitting AIDS in that setting.

It is illegal to ask a prospective employee, "Do you have AIDS or cancer?" It is not illegal to ask if the applicant can perform the job as written on the job description or if he or she can meet a job attendance policy the sport business may have.

Negligent Hiring, Negligent Retention, and Negligent Supervision

In *Hernandez v. Rapid Bus Company* (1994), the Rapid Bus Company was held liable when one special education student raped another special education student. The rape occurred between the drop-off and the school. The court noted the duty to care by the bus driver who volunteered to supervise; not, the student's violent propensities, which could have been foreseen by the bus driver; and the failure of the driver to fulfill the duty to care.

In *Dismuke v. Quaynor* (1994), a university was held vicariously liable when a female attending a summer camp for 12-to 16-year-olds was raped by a male student university employee. The rape occurred during the day on campus immediately after classes had been dismissed because of bad weather.

Several states recognize the torts of negligent hiring, negligent supervision, or negligent retention. A sport manager/employer could be found liable if (a) after an investigation, it was found that the employee was unfit for the job; (b) the employer owed a duty to care to the injured person; (c) there was a causal connection between the employee and the injured party.

Risk-management suggestions to avoid claims of negligent hiring include

1. Carefully check references of future employees, and document that those checks have been made.
2. Ask applicants for complete work histories, reasons for leaving jobs, employers' names, and histories of criminal convictions.
3. Get applicants to sign releases for their previous employers to provide information from their work files.
4. Get applicants to sign documents that they know that they will be dismissed for providing false information on their job applications.
5. Be aware of gaps in employment histories.

Risk management suggestions for negligent retention include

1. Train personnel to be aware of signs of violence, threatening behavior, child abuse, or civil rights violations.
2. Respond in an expedient manner. This may be essential in preventing or winning a lawsuit.
3. Conduct an investigation. Be aware of confidentiality issues, the right to privacy, due process, defamation, and false arrest.
4. Notify appropriate employees and authorities as needed.
5. Document complaints, investigations, and remediations. Counseling, suspension, voluntary resignations, reassignment, and firing might be solutions to the problem. Where violence is a consideration, a court restraining order is a possibility.
6. Seek professional assistance in determining if a mental illness is a disability and in providing reasonable accommodations. Some mental disabilities are covered under the ADA.

The sport manager needs to know what constitutes good policy and how to carefully formulate employment policies. They need to know how to educate employees about the policy and how to read appropriate literature to update policies and procedures.

* * * * * * * * * * * * * * *

(Handout 2)

RISK MANAGEMENT IN SPORTS BUSINESSES AND RELATED ACTIVITIES

by Larry Janes, Ed.D. (1997)[2]

Any risk-management program that is successful is based upon a comprehensive, preventive approach that emphasizes the safety of the participants. Consequently, risk management begins with what the insurance

2. Larry Janes, professor at Eastern Illinois University, Charleston, developed this item specificaly for *Legal Issues of Sport Entrepreneurship.*

industry terms "risk-avoidance." Most experts agree that a sound risk management program has three key elements: (a) identification of risks, (b) evaluation of risks, and (c) control of risks. It is assumed that all practices will conform to facility, equipment, safety, and supervision standards that are provided by appropriate sport management organizations as well as public safety codes and regulations. The list that follows could serve as a checklist for sport managers.

I. Identification of environmental risks
    A. Facilities and equipment
        1. Appropriate design of facilities and adjoining areas such as parking lots and walkways.
        2. Appropriate selection and installation of equipment.
        3. Appropriate posting of safety directions/warning signs for given areas and equipment sites.
        4. A periodic dated inspection schedule.
        5. A formalized check list for facilities/equipment inspection.
        6. Procedures for conducting repairs, including time, date, and follow-up repair and maintenance activities.
        7. Procedures for securing unsafe areas and equipment so that they cannot be used until repaired.
        8. Records of inspection, maintenance, and repair of the facility and/or equipment.
        9. Identification and appropriate training of responsible parties for the above procedures.
    B. Conduct of sports activities
        1. Competent, credentialed instructors and on-going training.
        2. Safety instruction for all participants. *Tests* as needed for documentation and safety.
        3. Training cycles/sequences for activities.
        4. Appropriate training plans and documentation of all instructional activities.
        5. Written waivers identifying risk factors within the activity, noting those risks that are inherent in the specific activity or equipment utilization. A statement should be contained in any waiver: "whether negligent or not."
        6. Avoidance of any assumptions of a participant's competence until that competence has been demonstrated to appropriate supervisory personnel.
    C. Supervision
        1. Provision of appropriate codes of behavior for both participants and employees.
        2. Determination of physical limitations of participants.
        3. Sufficient numbers of supervisors so that constant supervision is available for instruction and safety purposes.
        4. Training in accident prevention as well as treatment for medical emergencies and follow-up.

5. Accident reporting forms that have been approved through the insurance agent.
6. Maintenance of records regarding accidents and follow-up.
7. Periodic staff meetings to discuss developing problems and potential solutions.

II. Evaluation of risk
   A. Assessment procedures to evaluate equipment, activities, and participants for potential risk.
   B. Determination of the potential severity of the risk for items that have been identified as having a high probability of causing injury.
   C. Identification of the potential magnitude as to the number of individuals that could face harm should equipment, activities, or individuals not be provided adequate safety assurances.

III. Risk control: When the high probability of risk exists, consider the need to minimize or eliminate the potential loss. The alternatives that follow should be considered.
   A. Elimination of the particular activity.
   B. Not allowing the client to participate.
   C. Appropriate insurance and legally sound waivers.
   D. Acceptance of the risk and the responsibility.
   E. Implementation of changes necessary to reduce the potential for injury. Includes programs/activity objectives if no other methodology is available.

Any sport manager recognizes that risks and the potential for injury are present in sport and recreational activities. This inherent risk concept, however, does not abrogate the need to be vigilant in addressing the above recommendations. Should an injury occur and a lawsuit commence, courts will rely heavily on the documentation a person has which demonstrates that he or she has practiced preventative measures in the interest of eliminating or minimizing injuries. Courts will not expect sport managers to be omnipotent or clairvoyant or to have eyes in the backs of their heads. However, the court's standard is one of reasonable care that prudent sport managers should have provided in the interest of user safety.

This could be you - check your response

With a friend, discuss answers to the questions on the second page of this chapter as they relate to you.

REFERENCES

Authors

Janes, L. (1996). *Risk management in sports businesses and related activities.* Mimeographed monograph. Dr. Janes is professor at Eastern Illinois University, Charleston, IL.

Cases

Carter Coal Co. v. Human Rights Commission, 633 N.E.2d 202 (Ill.App. 5 Dist. 1994).
Chalk v. U.S. District Court, 840 F.2d 701 (9th Cir. 1988).
Dismuke v. Quaynor, 637 So.2d 555 (La.App. 2 Cir. 1994).

Hernandez v. Rapid Bus Co., 641 N.E. 2d 886 (Ill.App. 1 Dist. 1994).

Karibian v. Columbia University, 14 F.3d 773 (2nd Cir. 1994).

Matthews v. Rollins Hudig Hall Co., 874 F.Supp. 192 (N.D.Ill. 1995).

Meritor Savings Bank, FS3 v. Vinson, 477 U.S. 57, 106 S.Ct. 2399, 91 L.Ed.2d 49 (1986)

Pacourek v. Inland Steel Co., 858 F.Supp. 1393 (N.D. Ill. 1994).

Ryther v. KARE 11, 864 F.Supp. 1510 (D.Minn. 1994).

Ryther v. KARE 11, 864 F.Supp. 1525 (D.Minn. 1994).

Starishevsky v. Hofstra University, 612 N.Y.S. 2d 794 (N.Y.Sup.Ct., 1994).

Other References

Age Discrimination in Employment Act of 1967, 2 et seq. 29 U.S.C.A. § 621 et seq.

Rehabilitation Act of 1973, Pub. L. 93-112, 87 Stat. 355. (Reg 42:22676-22702, 1977).

Uniform Federal Accessibility Standards 1984, *as amended,* Washington, D.C., General Services Administration published originally in the *Federal Register,* (August 7, 1984) (49 FR 31528).

United States Office of Civil Rights, Washington, D.C.

Americans With Disabilities Act of 1990 (42 U.S.C.A. §12.101 et seq.

Glossary

The definitions that follow are working definitions and are not designed to cover each and every nuance or variance in the meaning of the terms.

-A-

abstract. A title examination that summarizes relevant instruments.

additur. The power of a trial court to give damages or increase damages when necessary in denying a motion for a new trial.

ad hoc. Unique to a particular fact situation

administrative body. One individual, or a group of individuals, entrusted with carrying out broad policy. The action of the administrative body may be judicial or legislative in nature. Sometimes referred to as "quasi-judicial" or "quasi-legislative."

administrative rule. A regulation in the nature of legislation but emanated from the administrative branch.

administrator. One who is involved in the carrying out of a policy statement. It is sometimes said that government is composed of four branches rather than three, the fourth branch being the administrative branch. A noted proponent of this line of thinking was W. F. Willoughby. Some scholars have felt that government should be divided into two branches: the political and the administrative.

A term also used to refer to one who is appointed to handle the estate of an individual who dies without a will, namely, one who dies intestate.

adversary system. The common law judicial system provides for decisions to be made on a case-by-case basis. Each side is represented by counsel who argues that position. This clash of competing interests offers an in-depth look at a particular fact situation and provides insight into what the law ought to be. Such a system involves contests that not only resolve controversies but that enable law itself to be developed and refined.

advisory opinion. A judicial decision based upon a hypothetical situation. An advisory opinion is not sharpened by a direct contest as between parties having an interest in the outcome. Stated differently, the parties would not have standing to bring the litigation. There is no case or controversy as the terms are used in the national Constitution. Federal courts do not hand down advisory opinions, nor do a majority of the state courts.

affidavit. A statement under oath. An affidavit can be submitted in support of a motion for summary judgment. However, an affidavit cannot otherwise be introduced as testimony without the consent of the opposing counsel, because there is no right to cross-examination.

affirmative defenses. An affirmation that something exists that precludes liability outside of and independent of the general denial. NOTE: Should be pleaded prior to the general denial. Frequently pleaded separately in a motion to dismiss.

Age Discrimination in Employment Act of 1967. Prohibits age discrimination in employment on the basis of age.

agency. A relationship between two individuals or legal entities whereby one acts for and on behalf of another. The relationship is characterized as fiduciary. The two parties are known as principal and agent. The principal exercises a high degree of confidence in the agent. The obligations imposed on each of the parties are determined by the nature of the relationship.

A term used to characterize a governmental body that carries out policy initially articulated by a legislative body.

agency interpretation. Statutes may be interpreted by the administrative agency set up to carry out the details of the statute. Courts will look with respect to the interpretation placed on a statute by an administrative agency although it will not consider itself to be bound thereby.

A.L.R. 4th. *American Law Reports*, 4th edition.

ambivalent. A nonlegal term that connotes mixed feelings for or against.

Am. Jur. 2d. Refers to the second series of a standard encyclopedia known as *American Jurisprudence*. This set of books is published by Lawyers Cooperative and currently is composed of some 117 volumes, together with 9 miscellaneous volumes and the April 1994, cumulative supplement.

answer. The response of a party to a complaint.

appellant. The party who disagrees with the decision at the trial level and seeks to have that decision corrected.

appellate court. That court that reviews the action of a trial court or a lower appellate court.

appellee. The party who has won on some point of law at the trial level and against whom an appeal is taken.

articles of incorporation. The basic document that establishes the corporation. Sometimes referred to as analogous to a constitution in its scope.

assault. An encroachment upon the dignity and integrity of an individual short of physical contact with the individual. Postulates an element of danger, although not necessarily fear, on the part of the victim.

assumption of risk. A defense at common law whereby a plaintiff who had knowledge of dangerous conditions was said to enter into the sphere of danger voluntarily and thus was unable to recover if injured, that is, participant in a contact sport. NOTE: Such a defense was said to have aided the growth of industry in the 19th century.

-B-

bilateral contract. This contract involves an exchange of promises. One promise is in exchange for and in consideration of the other promise. Hence, the language "for and in consideration of the mutual promises contained herein...."

bill of attainder. A legislative act declaring someone guilty of a crime.

Bill of Rights. Generally used to refer to the first 10 amendments to the United States Constitution. The various state constitutions will also have a bill of rights.

Black, Hugo. (1886-1971) Associate Justice of the U. S. Supreme Court from 1937 until 1971. Black was a native of Alabama and held various public offices before being appointed to the U.S. Supreme Court. Black argued that the due process clause of the Fourteenth Amendment incorporated the protections accorded in the first 10 amendments. Initially viewed as a conservative, Black became known as a liberal who vigorously protected individual liberties.

blue laws. Laws that have been influenced by religious considerations, that is, Sunday closing laws.

Brandeis, Louis Dembitz. Associate Justice of the U.S. Supreme Court. He was the first Justice of Jewish descent. Justice Brandeis was famous for his dissenting opinions, which many times stated the law as it would later be interpreted. Louis Brandeis completed his course at Harvard Law School in 2 years, with honors. This was accomplished without benefit of undergraduate training. He served on the Supreme Court from 1916 to 1939. Justice Brandeis was born in 1856 and died in 1941 at 84 years of age.

brief. The term is usually used by law students in one of two ways: first, a statement of argument with authorities in support of a particular proposition; second, the word is often used when describing the process whereby a particular case is analyzed, namely, facts, issues, argument, holding.

bylaws. Administrative details involved in the operation of a corporation, for example, election of officers.

-C-

Cardozo, Benjamin. A member of the United States Supreme Court from 1932 to 1938. Justice Cardozo was born in 1870 and died in 1938. This Justice was known for his clarity of thinking and the beauty of his prose.

case of first impression. This is a case in which there is no precedent in the jurisdiction in which the case arises.

cause of action. A statement of the theory upon which a suit is filed, that is, in tort or contract.

certiorari. A procedural device for obtaining access to a higher court. The matter proceeds upward as a matter of grace rather than as a matter of right. The United States Supreme Court grants *certiorari* when there are conflicting opinions in the lower courts or when the matter is of great public interest.

checks and balances. A system whereby one branch of government checks on another branch. The check normally involves a part to be played by two of the branches in accomplishing an objective.

circuit court. In most state courts the circuit court acts primarily as a trial court; however, the court may on occasion have appellate jurisdiction from even lower courts. A federal circuit court is primarily an appellate court.

citation. The name of a case plus a reference to where the case is found.

close corporation. One in which the shareholders are exceedingly limited. Can be one individual. Frequently limited to members of a family.

common law. The common law is judge-made law as distinct from statutory law. This is law that is common to the King's realm and gives uniformity throughout the whole of the kingdom. Such judge-made law was received into the law of the colonies and later into the law of independent states to the extent that it was not incompatible with local conditions.

comparative negligence. A principle of law whereby the risk of loss is spread in proportion to the degree of fault influenced by certain aspects of federal law and by the harshness of the doctrine of contributory negligence.

compensatory damages. Those damages that make a party whole, that is, the difference between the market value and contract price.

complaint. A pleading that commences a legal action.

concurring opinion. An opinion that agrees with the majority in the final analysis but usually for different reasons.

consideration. The price given for a promise. The consideration may be a promise.

constitution. A basic, fundamental document that establishes broad principles of government. The United States has both a national Constitution and state constitutions.

constitutional limitations. A principle that denies power to a governmental body for the purpose of protecting individual liberty.

constructive notice. Differs from actual notice. Some event, such as recording, puts the actor in a position where he or she could have known.

contract. A contract is a binding obligation. A contract is a property right. A contract is an agreement enforceable by law.

contract of adhesion. Such a document smacks of overreaching in that its terms are such as to operate to the pronounced disadvantage of one of the parties. The term is usually used in retail contracts.

contributory negligence. An absolute defense at common law. If a plaintiff was negligent to any degree, each party took their losses and went on their way.

corporation. An artificial being, invisible, intangible, and existing in contemplation of the law.

counteroffer. When the offeree rejects the offer but submits a different offer. A counteroffer terminates the original offer.

creditor beneficiary. One who receives payment of a debt from an individual other than the original obligor, the payment being occasioned by an agreement as between the original obligor and someone else, for example, the assumption of a mortgage indebtedness.

crime. An act or omission punishable by law in the form of a fine or imprisonment.

cross-appeal. An appeal by a party against whom an appeal has already been taken. NOTE: The word "appeal" connotes an effort to go from one level of the judiciary to another.

curtesy. That portion of a woman's estate that passes to her husband on her death if she dies without a will.

-D-

declaratory judgment. A statement of the court, following litigation, that sets out the law on a particular point. A case or controversy is required, thus distinguishing this proceeding from that of an advisory opinion.

deed. An instrument that transfers title to real estate.

defendant. The party against whom legal relief is sought.

de novo review. This term reflects an appellate review that permits the retrial of an issue. Such a procedure has generally received the approval of attorneys but has been frowned upon by students of administrative law. Generally speaking, statutes have provided for a much more limited form of review, for example, the substantial evidence test, which upholds the administrative body in the event there is substantial evidence to support that holding.

dictum. That portion of a decision that is not necessary to the resolution of a case. Language by way of dictum may later become a rule of law in an appropriate case. Theoretically, dictum is not a part of the scheme of precedent as represented by *stare decisis* because the judge has not had benefit of argument of counsel on this particular point. The language will be listened to with respect but does not become a part of law under the theory of precedent because it has not been sharpened by a specific application to a definite fact situation under the adversary system.

directed verdict. The court terminates proceedings and issues an order instructing the jury to find in a particular way.

dissenting opinion. An opinion that disagrees with the majority opinion.

division of powers. The allocation of power as between the central unit of government and the various state governments.

donee beneficiary. A third party who benefits from a contract entered into by other individuals, for example, beneficiary of a life insurance policy.

Douglas, William Orville. (1898-1980) After graduating from Columbia Law School, Douglas taught at Columbia and Yale University. Later, he was appointed and served as a member and chairman of the Securities and Exchange Commission. An authority on business law, Douglas was also known for his powerful statement of individual rights. Douglas wrote extensively on matters outside the law.

-E-

ejusdem generis. The principle of statutory interpretation which says in general that a listing of particulars following a statement of a general principle will exhaust the category as enunciated in the general principle. The result is a technique of draftsmanship whereby framers of legislation or other documents may use language such as "including but not limited to," which is designed to take the case outside the application of the principle of *ejusdem generis*.

en banc. From all the judges.

equity. Equity developed to give a remedy where the common law would not. Equity acts *in personam* rather than *in rem*. Equity customarily acts without a jury. Equity is designed to alleviate the harshness and technicalities of the common law. Equity courts today tend to be merged with common-law courts both as to jurisdiction and as to pleading. This development is not without exceptions but is generally true.

exception. A procedural device whereby an attorney objects to a ruling of the court, usually on points of evidence.

executor. One appointed by the court to settle the estate of an individual who dies with a will (testate). An executor acts in a fiduciary capacity.

ex post facto law. A retroactive criminal law that operates to the detriment of the accused.

express contract. An express contract is one in which the terms are distinct and explicit, either orally or in writing.

extrahazardous activity. A form of strict liability imposed at common law in which the activity was sufficiently hazardous to put one on notice as to the dangers in the activity, for example, keeping of vicious animals, the blasting of materials with explosives.

-F-

fact. A fact is or is not, and is whatever it is. Usually associated with something relating to the senses. A fact may be simple or conclusionary in nature.

false imprisonment. The confinement of an individual against the will of that individual and without just cause. The confinement need not be within a physical structure.

federal court system. The United States has two levels of government, the national government and the state government. The national government is composed of legislative, executive, and judicial branches. The judicial branch for the national government is referred to as the federal court system.

fiduciary. This term connotes trust and confidence. A fiduciary relationship exists as between general partners, a principal and agent, guardian and ward, and a trustee in relationship to the beneficiary of a trust. The parties are not dealing at arms' length.

Fifth Amendment. Assures due process as against the national government.

firm offer. This is an offer in the law of sales that must be held open for a certain period of time and for which consideration is not granted. The offer is good as between merchants only. The reader should check the Uniform Commercial Code section of sales for more exact information.

First Amendment. The First Amendment to the national Constitution provides for freedom of speech, press, assembly, and religion. Certain freedoms such as freedom of association and privacy, even academic freedom, are said to emanate from the outer boundaries of these enumerated freedoms. The rights enumerated hereinabove are said to be basic and fundamental to our conception of ordered liberty.

fixtures. Personal property that has been attached to real estate so as to become an integral part of the real estate and pass by way of deed as opposed to a bill of sale.

Fourteenth Amendment. Assures due process of law as against the state government.

Fourth Amendment. Provides protection as against unreasonable search and seizure.

fraud. Fraud involves a misrepresentation of a material fact designed to cause someone to act in a way he or she would not normally act. The statement is generally made that fraud vitiates. The existence of fraud enables parties to undo actions that have been taken.

-G-

general damages. The loss of earning power.

general denial. Affirms the absence of negligence or any element thereof.

general rule. A broad statement as to principles governing a particular fact situation. The rule serves as guidance under the theory of precedence. Most general rules are said to have exceptions; hence, a knowledge of both the general rule and exceptions becomes important as one explores the complete fabric of the law.

general warranty deed. A deed whereby the seller guarantees the title to the buyers. This guarantee extends to any action taken by parties having a claim to the real estate. One who gives a general warranty deed guarantees the title as against the claims of all individuals.

grantee. The buyer in a real estate transaction.

grantor. The seller of real estate. A spouse may be listed as a grantor by virtue of the marriage relationship or by virtue of the spouse's name being on the deed.

gravamen. The gist of the complaint, or the material portion of a cause of action.

guardian ad litem. One who represents a minor, or someone incompetent to act for himself or herself, during the course of particular litigation.

-H-

headnote. States a principle of law asserted in a case. The property of West Publishing Company.

Holmes, Oliver Wendell, Jr. A noted American jurist. Author of *The Common Law* and a member of the United States Supreme Court from 1902 to 1932. Mr. Holmes died in 1894 at the age of 93.

-I-

implied contract. An implied contract is not stated explicitly but is inferred as a matter of reason and just from the acts or conduct of the parties. Implied contracts are sometimes divided into those that are implied in law whereas others are implied in fact.

injunction. This is an equitable remedy that directs a party to do or not to do some particular thing. An injunction can be permanent, or it can be temporary pending the outcome of the litigation. The law also recognizes what is known as a restraining order in some jurisdictions. A restraining order need not be predicated upon notice to the other party. However, certain restrictions on such a remedy are designed to prevent an abuse of the process. One who seeks an injunction should check the "Rules of Court" in that jurisdiction to be certain that procedural requirements are followed.

incidental beneficiary. One who receives benefits from a contractual obligation but who is not privy to the original contract. Such a beneficiary normally does not have standing to sue on the contract.

indemnification. This principle obligates someone to make the other contracting party whole in the event that a third party recovers damages. To this extent the principle of indemnification is like a suretyship arrangement. NOTE: In many states, a state agency cannot promise to indemnify. Such a promise runs contrary to the doctrine of sovereign immunity.

infant. An individual under the age of 18.

in personam. A theory under which the law acts directly on the person rather than on the thing. This is an equity action. An action *in personam* is in contrast to an action *in rem*. The issuance of an injunction is an example of an *in personam* action. When equity decrees specific performance of a contract, it is an action *in personam*.

instructions to jury. Juries determine facts. The judge gives the jury a statement of the law. Attorneys can make suggestions to the court.

integrated bar. A bar is said to be integrated when attorneys are required to have a membership therein in order to practice law.

intentional tort. A civil wrong predicated upon a conscious act of an individual outside the scope of negligent misconduct, for example, assault and battery.

interlocutory. Interim; not final; something that is intervening between the beginning and the end of a lawsuit which decides some points. *(Black's Law Dictionary,* 1990, p. 815)

interlocutory appeal. An appeal of a matter which is not determinable of the controversy, but which is necessary for a suitable adjudication of the merits. (*Black's Law Dictionary,* 1990, p. 815)

inter alia. Among other things.

issue. A question. Something to be decided. It may deal with fact; it may deal with law.

-J-

judicial review. This term has two meanings. First, it means the power of the courts to declare an act of the legislative branch unconstitutional. This doctrine was first espoused in the case of *Marbury v. Madison,* 1 Cranch 137 (1803). The term also is used to connote an appeal from an administrative body to the court system. The latter use of the term has been refined and perfected as administrative law develops. Another permissible use of the term involves the movement of a case from an inferior court to a higher court.

jurisdiction. The power to hear a case. This power may be conditioned as to the amount of money involved, the subject matter, or both.

-K-

-L-

law. A system of norms for the breach of which a penalty is prescribed. NOTE: One can refer to law generally as opposed to *a law,* which deals with a particular.

lease. An interest in real estate having a certain number of years. The term "lease" is sometimes referred to in connection with an interest in personal property.

legislation. Acts of a legislative body. A primary source of law.

liberal construction. An interpretation of a statute designed to effectuate the intent of the framers as measured by the objective to be accomplished.

limitation of action. Sometimes referred to as the statute of limitations. The fixing of a period of time in which suit must be commenced.

liquidated damages. Damages that are fixed in advance by agreement.

-M-

Magna Carta. A famous document whereby the powers of the King were limited as against the nobility and free men.

mailbox rule. A rule that is designed to reconcile competing rules as to the termination of contracts arising out of the offer and the acceptance. The rule normally involves a situation whereby a communication of the offer-or and the offeree crosses in the mail.

majority opinion. The rule of an appellate court. The opinion may be unanimous; it may be one over half.

majority rule. As used in the common law or in the application of the principle of *stare decisis*, this language refers to the holdings of other jurisdictions, the number of which predominates as against a contrary holding.

minor. One under the age of majority.

motion. A method whereby some relief is sought. An application for a rule or an order.

-N-

necessaries. A principle whereby an infant can be held liable for the value of his or her promise if the infant purchases something that is necessary to his or her continued existence, such as food or shelter. NOTE: An infant normally does not have the capacity to contract. The doctrine of necessaries does not permit an individual to sue an infant on his or her contract but does hold the infant responsible for the reasonable value of the goods which he or she has obtained.

negligence. The failure to use that degree of care that a reasonably sane or prudent person would use under similar or like circumstances.

negligence per se. The standard of care is defined by statute, a violation of which speaks for itself.

nominal damages. This is a remedy in name only, for example, $1.00. Thus, a principle of law is vindicated, and court costs may be awarded to the successful party.

notary public. An official who has been authorized to authenticate signatures. Legal instruments are customarily signed before a notary public. Such an official affixes his name and signature along with the seal showing that a signature is in fact authentic. Some state statutes require such authentication as a condition precedent to filing in a local clerk's office.

-O-

offeree. That party to a contract who has received an offer. The general law of contracts has developed rules and regulations concerning the acceptance of an offer. The offeree is especially concerned with such rules.

offer or proof. Assuming that a judge refuses to admit testimony, the attorney presenting the evidence may make an "offer of proof" that sets out what the evidence would have been had the court admitted it. This procedure enables a reviewing court to evaluate the significance of the evidence.

offeror. One party to a contract. The law of contracts generally places certain tests to determine if an offer is valid and enforceable. The offeror is that individual or legal entity which initially proposes.

-P-

parol evidence rule. Permits oral testimony to vary the terms of a written instrument.

partnership. A form of business organization whose primary characteristic is the unlimited liability of each general partner. A limited partnership does not carry unlimited liability.

penumbra. On the outskirts of—emanating from—usually used in connection with First Amendment law, that is, privacy, academic freedom, and association.

per curiam opinion. An opinion of the court as a whole in contradistinction to an opinion that reflects the thinking of one individual. Such an opinion expresses precedent rather than establishing precedent. A *per curiam* opinion is supposed to represent settled law. Occasionally, however, a dissenting opinion will be written. Such an opinion is a summary statement of the law.

peremptory. Normally used in connection with selection of a jury. A challenge to a juror may be peremptory, namely, without cause. These challenges are limited in number.

personal property. Items such as contracts, automobiles, fixtures—may be tangible or intangible.

piercing the corporate veil. Breaching the wall of limited liability for stockholders.

plain meaning. A canon of construction that mandates that the text of a statute or other document be taken as written. If the meaning is plain and unambiguous, a court need not search for canons of construction. The statute or contract will be taken as it is written unless the meaning becomes absurd or contrary to common sense.

plaintiff. The party who files a legal action.

police power. The power of a state to restrict the liberty or property of an individual for the purpose of protecting the public health, safety, welfare, or morals. The police power is the greatest power possible by a state and emanates from the Tenth Amendment to the national Constitution.

popular sovereignty. Generally defined as government by the people.

precedent. A case that has been decided based on a similar set of facts and that enunciates a rule or principle of law.

preparation statement. This statement is designed to prevent the unauthorized practice of law. In general, an individual can prepare a document to which that individual is a party. An individual cannot prepare a legal document for other parties unless the individual is appropriately licensed to practice. The abuse of this principle sometimes occurs in banks and real estate offices. Intentions are normally good, and the finished product may be well crafted. The law, however, has developed more stringent tests and prohibits such practices.

prescription. A right based on the passage of time. Used in connection with adverse possession.

prima facie. Meaning is self-evident.

proximate cause. An act or omission that results in an injury. Sometimes said to be "immediate" in relationship to the resulting injury.

punitive damages. This remedy is predicated upon willful or grossly negligent action. The remedy goes over and beyond actual damages and is said to serve as a deterrent effect upon others who would be prone to act in a highly unreasonable fashion. Legislative enactments sometimes provide for treble damages. Such a remedy is in the nature of punishment.

-Q-

quid pro quo. A consideration. Something given in exchange.

quitclaim deed. A deed that purports to transfer all of the right, title, and interest that a grantor may possess in real property. Such a deed does not guarantee anything; it merely purports to divest the grantor of any title which that party might happen to have. A quitclaim deed is frequently used to correct a defect in title.

-R-

real estate. Land as opposed to personal property.

real property. Land together with permanent attachments thereto including any undivided interest therein.

reckless misconduct. A statutory concept that approaches intentional misconduct, but one in which a state of mind is evidenced by the degree of carelessness involved.

recreational users' statute. A statute whereby one who permitted the use of land for recreational purposes without charge would not be liable for someone injured on the land absent willful or gross negligence.

reformation. Reformation is an equitable remedy that is predicated upon the need to state the true contractual intent of the parties. The principles that undergird the doctrine of reformation are similar to the principles that undergird the equitable remedy of rescission.

release. A document whereby a party is said to give up his or her right to sue for damages in the event of injury. Sometimes the release is expressed on the back of a ticket, by posted signs, or by individual contract.

relinquishment clause. That portion of a deed whereby a spouse relinquishes any right to homestead, dower, or curtesy in and to the land therein conveyed. (Dower is the right that a woman possesses in the estate of her husband when the husband dies. Curtesy is the right that a husband has in the estate of his wife when the wife dies. Prior to death this is referred to as an inchoate right. A homestead is that right in land free of the claims of creditors.)

rescission. This is an equitable doctrine that undoes a document that purports to have contractual significance. To rescind a document one would need to show such things as fraud or undue influence. A contract that can be rescinded does not reflect the true intent of the parties but is tainted in some fashion, that is, contrary to public policy.

rescript. Directions given either by the court to the clerk or by an appellate court to a trial court.

respondeat superior. A principle of law that holds the principal responsible for the act of the agent—the master for the act of the servant.

-S-

separation of powers. A division of power as between the executive, legislative, and judicial branches of government.

sexual harassment. A matter of civil rights generally discussed under two headings, either *quid pro quo* (in consideration of) or hostile environment—the totality of circumstances that causes an individual to be injured because of gender.

shareholder. One of the owners of a corporation. The ownership is evidenced by shares of stock.

source of title. A statement as to where the grantors obtained the title to the land conveyed. Such a statement enables one to trace a title and determine if the grantor has good and sufficient title to the property in question.

sovereign immunity. A doctrine whereby a state agency is free from tort liability arising out of injury occasioned by negligence. The theory is that the state's exchequer is determined by a budget that operates for a given period of time; thus, the state agency lacks the flexibility of private industry, which can pass the loss on to the consumer.

special damages. Such things as hospital bills and perhaps pain and suffering.

special warranty deed. The seller guarantees to the buyer that neither the seller nor his or her heirs will disturb the buyer in possession or ownership of the premises. Consequently, the guarantee in such a case is more limited than a general warranty deed, which guarantees as against the claims of all parties.

specific performance. A remedy in equity that acts directly on the person. Such a remedy requires something to be done. The remedy is usually predicated on the theory that damages would not suffice. The object of the contract, if it has sentimental value or if the object is unique, does not lend itself to a remedy at law for damages; hence, equity decrees that the contract be performed. Such a remedy is decided by the judge and not by a jury.

standing. Generally speaking, standing requires that a party either gains or loses. The rationale is that this gives a definite interest in the outcome and assures argument within the adversary context.

stare decisis. Let the decision stand. Precedent.

statute. The acts of a legislative body that sets forth policy, rules and regulations as to a particular subject matter. A statute may be federal or state and is considered to be a primary source of law.

statute of frauds. The statute of frauds identifies those contractual situations under which a contract must be in writing in order to be enforceable. One provision of a statute of frauds requires that a contract for the sale of land must be in writing in order to be enforceable. Every oral contract should be checked against the provisions of the statute of frauds.

statute of limitations. Sometimes referred to as limitation of action. A statement of the period of time within which suit can be filed for a particular action.

Stone, Harlan Fiske. Appointed Associate Justice of the United Chief Justice of the United States Supreme Court in 1924. In 1941 Justice Stone became Chief Justice and served in that capacity until 1946. Justice Stone was born in 1872 and died in 1946. He was Dean of Columbia Law School prior to being appointed to the United States Supreme Court. His opinions were noted for their organizational structure and for the power of persuasiveness exemplified.

strict liability. Liability without fault. The nature of the activity is such that the actor is on notice of the consequences of the action.

sub judice. Under judicial consideration.

subsidiary corporation. A corporation in which the majority of the stock is held by a parent corporation.

substantial evidence. Substantial evidence does not require a majority or a preponderance of the evidence. The evidence must be more than a scintilla but need not be persuasive of the truth or falsity of a conclusion. Substantial evidence proscribes arbitrary action but pays deference to the findings of administrative bodies.

summary judgment. A judgment based on the pleadings, depositions, affidavits, and in some cases oral testimony, which holds that there is no genuine issue of material fact to be tried and that one party is entitled to relief as a matter of law.

Sunday laws. Sometimes known as "Blue laws." These are laws that prohibit certain types of activity—usually commercial in nature—on the Sabbath. A large number of such laws have been repealed.

-T-

tangible personal property. Property that is not real but that one can touch, feel, and see, that is, a book as opposed to a right predicated upon a document such as a contract.

tenure of Supreme Court justices. The United States Constitution provides that Supreme Court justices in the federal court system shall hold office for life or good behavior. These justices are subject to removal by way of impeachment. State supreme court justices usually hold office for a fixed period of time.

The Law of Workmen's Compensation. The standard work dealing with the law of workers' compensation is a multivolume set whose primary author is Arthur Larson. The set is published by Matthew Bender & Company, Incorporated.

title examination. Lending institutions generally refuse to make loans on real estate unless an appropriate check has been made of the title to the property. Such an examination involves going back for a period of time, which will vary with the lending institution, to determine if the seller (grantor) does have good title. Such an examination involves a check of mortgages, encumbrances, leases, off-conveyances, and other court records.

tort. A civil wrong.

treble damages. Three times the actual damages. Sometimes classified as punitive damages.

trial court. A court of inferior jurisdiction that hears evidence and makes the initial determination.

-U-

unconscionable contract. A contract that is tainted by an element such as fraud which mitigates against its enforcement and validity. An unconscionable contract will shock the conscience of the court. Such a contract signals overreaching and unfairness. Courts will not lend themselves to the enforcement of such a document.

undue influence. A principle of law that permits a successful attack on the validity of a contract. The principle normally occurs under conditions whereby one of the parties has a pronounced advantage over the other because of age, emotional status, or relationship as between the parties; hence, a party takes action contrary to their interest because someone is taking advantage of a condition or relationship.

Uniform Commercial Code. A systematic expression of several areas of the law, which was originally formulated in 1952 by the National Conference of Commissioners on Uniform State Laws and which currently has widespread adoption with some alterations by jurisdictions.

unilateral contract. A promise for an act.

usury. An impermissible rate of interest. Penalties can vary from state to state.

-V-

vicarious liability. The liability of one individual for the act of another. Theory best enables the shifting of the burden of loss.

-W-

workers' compensation. A form of strict liability imposed by law that establishes a fixed rate of recovery for injury. No requirement of fault is imposed, but the statute does require that the injury arise out of and in the course of employment.

workers' compensation carrier. The insurance company that insures as against injury under the workers' compensation law.

APPENDIX

Civil Rights Cases (Chapter 20)

42 U.S.C.A. § 1981

Arnold v. Ballard, 448 F. Supp. 1025 (N.D. Ohio 1978).

Calhoun v. Lang, 694 S.W.2d 740 (Mo. Ct. App. 1985).

Cheyney State College Faculty v. Hufstedler, 703 F.2d 732 (3rd Cir. 1983).

Craig v. County of Los Angeles, 626 F.2d 659 (9th Cir. 1980).

Daniel v. Paul, 395 U.S. 298, 89 S. Ct. 1697, 23 L. Ed. 2d 318 (1969).

Durham v. Red Lake Fishing and Hunting Club, 666 F. Supp. 954 (W.D. Tex. 1987).

Flagg v. Control Data, 806 F. Supp. 1218 (E.D. Pa. 1992).

Frazier v. First Union Nat'l Bank, 747 F.Supp. 1540 (W.D. N.C. 1990).

Freeman v. Michigan Dep't of State, 808 F.2d 1174 (6th Cir. 1987).

General Building Contractors Ass'n v. Pennsylvania, 458 U.S. 375, 102 S. Ct. 3141, 73 L. Ed. 2d 835 (1982).

Guesby v. Kennedy, 580 F. Supp. 1280 (D. Kan. 1984).

Hornick v. Noyes, 708 F.2d 321 (7th Cir. 1983).

Hudson v. Charlotte Country Club, Inc., 535 F.Supp. 313 (W.D. N.C. 1982).

Ingram v. Madison Square Garden Ctr., Inc., 482 F. Supp. 414 (S.D. N.Y. 1979).

Jackson v. Drake University, 778 F. Supp. 1490 (S.D. Iowa 1991).

Johnson v. Brace, 472 F. Supp. 1056 (E.D. Ark. 1979).

Johnson v. Railway Express Agency, 421 U.S. 454, 95 S. Ct. 1716, 44 L. Ed. 2d 295 (1975).

Keller v. Braniff Int'l Airlines, Inc., 390 F. Supp. 537 (N.D. Tex. 1975).

Milner v. National Sch. of Health Technology, 409 F. Supp. 1389 (E.D. Pa. 1976)

Mister v. Illinois Cent. Gulf R.R. Co., 790 F. Supp. 1411 (S.D. Ill. 1992).

Murray v. Thistledown Racing Club, Inc., 770 F.2d 63 (6th Cir. 1985).

Olzman v. Lake Hills Swim Club, Inc., 495 F.2d 1333 (2nd Cir. 1974).

Perry v. City of Country Club Hills, 607 F. Supp. 776 (E.D. Mo. 1985).

Saunders v. George Washington Univ., 768 F. Supp. 854 (D. D.C. 1991).

Seidenberg v. McSorleys' Old Ale House, Inc., 308 F. Supp. 1253 (S.D. N.Y. 1969).

Stearnes v. Baur's Opera House, Inc., 3 F.3d 1142 (7th Cir. 1993).

Taylor v. Gillis, 405 F.Supp. 542 (E.D. Pa. 1975).

Thomas v. Resort Health Related Facility, 539 F. Supp. 630 (E.D. N.Y. 1982).

U.S. v. Lansdowne Swim Club, 894 F.2d 83 (3rd Cir. 1990).

Watson v. Fraternal Order of Eagles, 915 F.2d 235 (6th Cir. 1990).

Welsh v. Boy Scouts of America, 993 F.2d 1267 (7th Cir. 1993).

42 U.S.C.A. § 1982

Cato v. Jilek, 779 F. Supp. 937 (N.D. Ill. 1991).

Durham v. Red Lake Fishing and Hunting Club, 666 F. Supp. 954 (W.D. Tex. 1987).

Jones v. Alfred H. Mayer Co., 392 U.S. 409, 20 L. Ed. 2d 1189, 88 S. Ct. 2186 (1968).

Olzman v. Lake Hills Swim Club, Inc., 495 F. 2d 1333 (2d Cir. 1974).

Phillips v. Hunter Trails Community Ass'n, 685 F.2d 184 (7th Cir. 1982).

Taliaferro v. Voth, 774 F. Supp. 1326 (D. Kan. 1991).

42 U.S.C.A. § 1983

Brewer v. Chauvin, 938 F.2d 860 (8th Cir. 1991).

City of Newport v. Fact Concerts, Inc., 453 U.S. 247, 69 L. Ed. 2d 616, 101 S. Ct. 2748 (1981).

Fortin v. Darlington Little League, Inc., 514 F.2d 344 (1st Cir. 1975).

Gilmore v. City of Montgomery, 417 U.S. 556, 41 L. Ed. 2d 304, 94 S. Ct. 2416 (1974).

Goodloe v. Davis, 514 F.2d 1274 (5th Cir. 1975).

Hampton v. City of Jacksonville, Fla., 304 F. 2d 320 (5th Cir. 1962).

Hardin v. Straub, 954 F.2d 1193 (6th Cir. 1992).

Local No. 1903 Etc. v. Bear Archery, 617 F.2d 157 (6th Cir. 1980).

Magill v. Avonworth Baseball Conference, 516 F.2d 1328 (3rd Cir. 1975).

Memphis Community Sch. Dist. v. Stachura, 477 U.S. 299, 91 L.Ed 2d 249, 106 S.Ct. 2537 (1986).

Miltier v. Beorn, 896 F.2d 848 (4th Cir. 1990).

Monell v. Department of Social Services of N.Y., 436 U.S. 658, 56 L. Ed. 2d 611, 98 S. Ct. 2018 (1978).

Pacelli v. deVito, 972 F.2d 871 (7th Cir. 1992).

Patrum v. Martin, 292 F. Supp. 370 (W.D. Ky. 1968).

Rojas v. Alexander's Dep't Store, Inc., 924 F.2d 406 (2d Cir. 1990).

Smith v. Updegraff, 744 F.2d 1354 (8th Cir. 1984).

Smith v. Y.M.C.A. of Montgomery, 316 F. Supp. 899 (M.D. Ala. 1970).

Smith v. Y.M.C.A. of Montgomery, 462 F.2d 634 (5th Cir. 1972).

Williams v. Luna, 909 F.2d 121 (5th Cir. 1990).

Williams v. Rescue Fire Co., 254 F. Supp. 556 (D. Md. 1966).

Wilson v. City of North Little Rock, 801 F.2d 316 (8th Cir. 1986).

Wimbish v. Pinellas County, Fla., 342 F.2d 804 (5th Cir. 1965).

Wolfel v. Morris, 972 F.2d 712 (6th Cir. 1992).

INDEX OF TERMS

A

Acceptance - 17
Act of God - 51
Administrative tribunal - 260
Affirmative defenses - 95
Agent - 50, 101, 111
Agreement not to compete - 16
Alcohol - see drugs
Answer - 80
Applications - 9
Assault - 97, 98, 102, 112
Assumption of risk - see risk

B

Battery - 97, 98, 112
Beneficiary[ies]
    creditor - 23
    donee - 22, 34
    third-party - 22
Bona fide occupational
    qualification (BFOQ) - 296, 303,
        310, 397
Blue laws - 19
Business necessity - 308, 312

C

Canons of construction - 22
Checks and balances - 13
Child labor - 125
Citations, reading - 8
Civil Rights Acts
    ADA (1990) - 313, 364, 402, 408,
        421
    ADEA (1967) - 420
    CR Restoration Act - 382
    CR Act of 1991 - 364, 401, 406,
        408
    FMLA - 313

42 USCA 1981 - 365, 366, 373,
    376, 382
42 USCA 1982 - 307, 365, 377,
    380, 392
42 USCA 1983 - 250, 365, 374,
    382
42 USCA 1988 - 250
Title II - 385, 386, 388, 389
Title III - 385, 396
Title VII - 177, 316, 320, 325,
    336, 342. 356, 375, 382,
    396
Title IX - 315, 326, 342, 397
Common law - 20, 34, 155, 248
Complaint - 80
Consideration - 17
Consortium, loss of - 30, 33, 206
Constitution, U.S.
    Article I - 13
    Article VI - 13
    Bill of Rights - 14, 286
    1st Amendment - 11, 165, 229,
        265, 269, 272, 274, 278,
        284
    4th Amendment - 282, 285
    5th Amendment - 229, 249, 263,
        285, 297, 381
    10th Amendment - 135, 263
    13th Amendment - 363
    14th Amendment - 229, 249,
        263, 297, 298, 363
    15th Amendment - 363
Constitutional restraints - 231
Contracts - 15, 16, 34
    acceptance - 17
    assignment - 22, 34
    bilateral - 18
    breach - 34
    capacity of parties - 20

circumstantial evidence - 82
classifications - 18
competency - 17
consideration - 17, 18
    executory - 18
    failure to read - 29, 32, 91
    form - 17, 23, 34
    interpretation - 22, 34
    legality - 19, 23
    listing - 38
    minors - 20
    offer - 17, 18
    oral - 201
    privity - 140
    purchase - 39
    third parties - 22
    unilateral - 18
    written - 19, 34
Corporate veil - 50, 152
Corporation - 47, 54, 55
Course of employment - 128, 139,
    134, 136
Crowd control - 171, 187, 195, 418,
    419
Curfew - 270

D

Damages - 21
    causation - 76
    compensatory -21, 99, 104, 325,
        381, 407
    liquidated - 21
    nominal - 21, 98
    punitive - 21, 98, 325, 381, 407
Declaration of sentiments - 360
Deeds
    cloud - 45
    commissioner's - 40
    general warranty - 38, 40, 44
    parties to - 40
    provisions - 40, 41
    quit claim - 38
    special warranty - 38, 40, 44

    title examinations - 41, 44
    title insurance - 42
Deep pocket theory - 141
Defamation - 54, 276, 278
Defenses - 112, 148, 151, 353
Dictum - 97, 105
Directed verdict - 101, 103, 191
Disability - 421
Discrimination - 307
    age - 420
    race - 306
    sex - 295, 298
    sexual orientation - 301
Dramshop - 210, 222
Dress/grooming
    code - 174, 183, 185, 268
    religious - 173, 183
    sexually provocative - 173, 177,
        180
    sexually discriminatory - 175, 185
Due process - 247, 248, 250, 255, 303
    fair hearing - 256, 259, 261
    Impartial administrative tri-
        bunal - 260
    procedural - 256
    right to counsel - 260
    substantive - 262, 263
Drugs/alcohol/substance abuse
    policy - 205, 219
    searches - 220
    testing - 205, 220, 221, 282, 283,
        403
Duty
    to care - 30, 77, 78, 201, 213,
        219, 421
    to police premises - 190
    to protect - 199, 204, 206
    to warn - 199

E

Ejusdem generis - 242
Emotional distress - 281
Employer liability - 323

Employment policies - 422
Equal access - 386, 392
Equal Pay Act - 337, 339, 342, 348, 356
Equal work - 355
Equity - 20
    gender - 419

F

Facts - 9
Fair hearing - 256, 259, 261
False imprisonment - 97, 98,   112
Farmer's Home Administration - 42
Federal Land Bank - 42
Foreseeability - 145, 192, 200, 208, 213
Freedom of
    association - 274, 287
    expression - 267
    press - 275, 285
    religion - 271, 273
    speech - 267, 285
Funding - 271

H

Harassment, sexual - 175, 179, 182, 316, 317, 334,   335, 419, 421
    hostile environment - 317, 322, 324
    quid pro quo - 317, 321
Hazing - 281
Headnotes - 9
Hearing - 259
Holding - 9
Hostile environment - 317, 322, 324

I

Inherent danger - 67, 68, 238
Injunction - 21- 165
    mandatory - 343
    prohibitory - 344
Insurance
    liability - 95

Workers' Comp - 122, 123
Interlocutory appeal - 156
Intentional [mis]conduct - 63, 106
Intentional tort - 123, 217
Intoxication - 214, 216
Invasion of privacy - 281
Invitee - 189, 190, 193, 195, 209

J

Judicial
    opinions - 9
    restraints - 232, 236
    review - 14
Jurisdiction - 95

L

Landmark cases - 295
Leases - 42, 43, 44
    contingencies - 43
    intended use - 43
    subleasing - 43
Liability - 57, 101, 107, 202
    limited - 48, 52, 54
    of coaches, players - 111
    of landowner - 143
    product - 119, 139, 144, 167, 419
    strict - 121, 140, 141, 144, 145, 147, 167, 419
    unlimited - 57
    vicarious - 77, 110, 421
Libel - 276, 367
License, business - 39
Liens
    mechanics - 42
    mortgages - 41
    tax - 42
Lis pendens - 28, 42

M

Magna Carta - 248
Market conditions - 353
Merit system - 397
Minor - 123, 418

employing - 125
Minorities, rights of - 265
Mootness - 233, 243

N

Negligence - 63, 65, 66, 77, 107, 141,
    151, 418
    comparative - 63, 92, 93, 111
    contributory - 63, 92, 146, 151
    gross - 66
    inherently dangerous - 67
    per se - 66
    reckless disregard - 69, 70
    respondeat superior - 66, 106
    statutory - 66
Negligent hiring/retention/ supervi-
    sion - 421
Notary public - 41
Notice - 206, 256, 258, 250
Nuisance - 119, 155, 158
    private - 165
    public - 156, 158, 162, 165, 166

O

Offer - 17, 18
Opinion - 9
Ordinary care - 72

P

Parol evidence rule - 19
Partnership - 48, 418
    general - 56, 57
    limited - 57
    liability - 57
    property - 56
    Unified P. Act - 56
Per curiam - 71
Permits
    business - 39
    zoning - 39
Personal property - 34
Place of entertainment - 393
Plain meaning - 244

Powers of Fed. Govt
    division of - 12
    separation of - 12, 332
Precedent - 136, 411
Pregnancy - 295, 296
Preponderance of evidence - 129
Presumption of constitutionality -
    232, 235, 236
Prima facie - 52
Priority of occupation - 159, 163
Private club - 266, 378, 379, 388
Probable cause -192
Property interest - 254
Promissory estoppel - 18
Proximate cause - 83, 115, 193, 195
Public —
    accommodations - 383, 388
    concern - 271, 279
    facilities - 394
    forum - 272, 273
    funding - 271
    policy - 81

Q

Quid pro quo - 317, 321

R

Real estate - 34
    agent - 38
    listing contract - 38
    purchase contract -39
Reasonable cause - 222
Reckless disregard - 69, 108
Reckless misconduct - 105, 107, 108
Recreational user statutes - 94, 243
Release/waiver (liability) - 88 (See
    Huber v. Hovey, p. 30)
Remedy - 20, 22, 26, 350, 353, 419
Res ipsa loquitur - 71, 77
Rescission - 21
Respondeat superior - 66, 77, 96,
    110, 111, 336
Restatement of Torts - 141

Restraining order - 21
Rights
    to counsel - 261
    to privacy - 282, 284, 285
Risk
    assumption - 63, 70, 91, 93, 94,
        140, 151, 240
    control - 424
    evaluation - 424
    management - 115, 418, 420, 422
Role model - 299, 303, 304, 310

S

Salary retention - 354
Seniority system - 397
Separation of powers - 12
Shareholder - 54, 55
Sole proprietorship - 58, 418
Sovereign immunity - 63, 95
Specific performance - 21, 26
Speech -
    defamation - 276
    free- 267, 275
    libel - 276, 367
    limitations on - 267
    restricted - 267, 286
    slander - 276
    symbolic - 267, 286
Standard of care - 71
Standing - 244
Statute of frauds - 17, 19, 56
Statute of limitations - 18, 63, 84,
        96, 151, 353
Statute of repose - 152
Statutory interpretation - 232, 238
Subjective judgment - 354
Summary judgment - 10, 31, 82,
        134, 142, 143, 198

T

Title examination - 41
Tort - 19, 97, 107, 122, 139, 198

U

Usury - 19

V

Veterans Administration - 42

W

Waiver - 88, 418 (see Release)
Warranty - 146, 152
    express - 148
    implied - 148, 150, 151
Willful and wanton misconduct -
    144
Women's rights - 294, 360
Workers' Compensation - 121, 126,
    167
    exclusive remedy - 123, 124

Index of Cases

Andrews v. Drew Municipal Separate Sch. Dist., 507 F.2d 611
(5th Cir. 1975)   296

Ashwander v. Tennessee Valley Auth., 297 U.S. 288, 345-348,
56 S.Ct. 466, 80 L.Ed. 688 (1936)   237

Bangert v. Shaffner, 848 S.W.2d 353 (Tex. Ct. App. (1993)   67

Baptiste v. Cavendish Club, Inc., 670 F.Supp. 108(S.D. N.Y. 1987)   375

Bartlett v. Chebuhar, 479 N.W.2d 321 (Iowa 1992)   71

Bearfield v. City of Houston, 846 S.W.2d 399 (Tx. Ct. App. 1992)   196

Bearman v. University of Notre Dame, 453 N.E.2d1196
(Ind. Ct. App. 1983)   189

Benoit v. Louisiana State Racing Comm'n, 576 So.2d 578
(La. Ct. App. 1991)   256

Bishop v. Fair Lanes Georgia Bowling, Inc., 803 F.2d 1548
(11th Cir. 1986)   206

Cahill v. Hawaiian Paradise Park Corp., 543 P.2d 1356 (Haw, 1975)   54

Carpenteri-Waddlington v. Com'r of Rev., 650 A.2d 147 (Conn. 1994)   241

Chambers v. Omaha Girls Club, Inc., 834 F.2d 697 (8th Cir. 1987)   304

City of Boston v. Black Bay Cultural Ass'n, 635 N.E.2d 1175
(Mass. 1994)   268

*Concord Rod and Gun Club v. Massachusetts Comm. Against
Discrimination*, 524 N.W.2d 1364, 1376 (Mass. 1988)   274

Cozzi v. North Palos Elementary Sch. Dist. No. 117,
597 N.E.2d 683 (Ill. App. Ct. 1992)   142

D'Agostino v. Bank of Ravenswood, 563 N.E.2d 886 (Ill. App.
Ct. 1990)   26

Daniel v. Paul, 395 U.S. 298, 23 L.Ed.2d 318, 89 S.Ct. 1697 (1969)   388

Davenport v. Casteen, 878 F.Supp. 871 (W.D.Va. 1995)   251

EEOC Decision No. 85-9, 37 FEP Cases 1983, May 7, 1985   177

El Chico Corp. v. Poole, 732 S.W.2d 306 (Tex. 1987)   210

Filler v. Rayex Corp., 435 F.2d 336 (7th Cir. 1970)   148

Franklin v. Gwinnett County Public Schools, 503 U.S. 60, 117
    L.Ed.2d 208, 112 S. Ct. 1028 (1992)   326

Graven v. Vail Associates, Inc., 888 P.2d 310 (Colo. App. 1994)   241

Greenville Memorial Auditorium v. Martin, 391 S.E.2d 546
    (S.C. 1990)   191

Griswold v. Connecticut, 381 U.S. 479, 14 L.Ed.2d 510, 85 S.Ct.
    1678 (1965)   284

Hadges v. Corbisiero, 760 F.Supp. 388 (S.D. N.Y. 1991)   260

Halpern v. Wheeldon, 890 P.2d 562 (Wyo. 1995)   241

Hartland Sportsman's Club v. Town of Delafield, 827 F.Supp.
    562 (E.D.Wisc. 1993)   258

Havird v. Columbia YMCA, 418 S.E.2d 329 (S.C. Ct. App. 1992)   132

Huber v. Hovey, 501 N.W.2d 53 (Iowa, 1993)   30

*International Society of Krishna Consciousness v. N.J. Sports and
    Exposition Authority*, 532 F.Supp.1088 (D.N.J., 1981)   272

Jensen v. Sport Bowl, Inc., 469 N.W.2d 370 (S.D. 1991)   123

Johnson v. Mid-South Sports, Inc., 806 P.2d 1107 (Okl. 1991)   194

Johnson v. Virginia, 373 U.S. 61, 10 L.Ed.2d 195, 83 S.Ct. 1053
    (1963)   395

Karibian v. Columbia University, 14 F.3rd 773 (2d Cir. 1994)   317

Keesee v. Freeman, 772 S.W.2d 663 (Mo. Ct. App. 1989)   215

Kim v. Sportswear, 393 S.E.2d 418 (Va. Ct. App. 1990)   127

Las Vegas Hacienda, Inc., v. Gibson, 359 P.2d 85 (Nev. 1961)   24

Lockhart v. Louisiana-Pacific Corp., 796 P.2d 602
    (Or. Ct. App. 1990)   175

McCracken County Health Spa v. Henson, 568 S.W.2d 240
    (Ky. Ct. App. 1977)   134

Milton v. Cavaney, 364 P.2d 473 (Cal. 1961)   54

Morris v. New Orleans City Park Improvement Ass'n,
    586 So.2d 629 (La. Ct. App. 1991)   76

Orange Park Kennel Club v. State, 644 So.2d 547 (Fla. App. 1
    Dist. 1994)   242

Orlando Sports Stadium, Inc. v. State, 262 So.2d 881 (Fla. 1972)   156

Paulsen v. Gotbaum, 982 F.2d 825, 828-29 (2nd Cir., 1992)   273

Radwaner v. Usta National Tennis Center, 592 N.Y.S.2d 307
    (N.Y. App. Div. 1993)   93

Rappaport v. Little League Baseball, Inc., 65 F.R.D.545
    (U.S.D.C., D.Del. 1975)   233

Salem Tent & Awning v. Schmidt, 719 P.2d 899 (Or. Ct. App. 1986)   48

Sanchez v. Sunday River Skiway Corp., 802 F. Supp. 539
    (D. Me. 1992)   84

Skene v. Fileccia, 539 N.W.2d 531 (Mich. App. 1995)   238

Stanley v. University of Southern California, 13 F.3d 1313
    (9th Cir. 1994)   339

State v. Waterloo Stock Car Raceway, Inc., 409 N.Y.S.2d 40
    (Sup.Ct., Seneca Cty. N.Y. 1978)   160

Stamper v. Kanawha County Bd. of Educ. 445 S.E.2d 238
(W.Va. 1994)   243

Thompson v. McNeil, 559 N.E.2d 705 (Ohio 1990)   105

Toth v. Toledo Speedway, 583 N.E.2d 357 (Ohio Ct. App. 1989)   88

University of Nevada v. Tarkanian, 879 P.2d (Nev. 1994)   250

Walker v. Couture, 804 F. Supp. 1408 (D.Kan. 1992)   367

Washington V. Smith, 893 F.Supp. 60 (D.D.C. 1995)   276

Webbier v. Thoroughbred Racing Protective Bureau, Inc.,
254 A.2d 285 (R.I. 1969)   99

Wilderness World v. Dept. of Revenue, 882 P.2d 1281
(Ariz. App. Div. 1 1993)   242

Wilson v. Bell Fuels, Inc., 574 N.E.2d 200 (Ill. App. Ct. 1991)   80

Wright v. Salisbury Club, Ltd., 632 F.2d 309 (4th Cir. 1980)   378